The Firefly Dictionary of Plant Names: Common & Botanical

Compiled by
HAROLD BAGUST

FIREFLY BOOKS

A FIREFLY BOOK

Published by Firefly Books Ltd., 2003

Copyright © 2003 Helicon Publishing Ltd.

First Printing

National Library of Canada Cataloguing in Publication Data

Bagust, Harold
  The Firefly dictionary of plant names : common and botanical
  ISBN 1-55297-602-5
  1. Plant names, Popular-Dictionaries. 2. Botany-Nomenclature. I. Title.
  QK13.B33 2002   580'.3   C2001-904199-3

Publisher. Cataloging-in-Publication Data (U.S.)

The Firefly dictionary of plant names: common and botanical / compiled by Harold Bagust. - 1st ed.
[440] p. ; ill. : cm.
Summary: A dictionary of over 30,000 terms with listings of common names and their botanical equivalents. Also includes Latin epithets to identify whole groups of plants at a glance
ISBN 1-55297-602-5
1. Plant names, Popular-Dictionaries. 2. Botany-Nomenclature.
I. Bagust, Harold. II. Title.
580/.1/4 21   CIP   QK13.F574 2002

Published in Canada in 2003 by
Firefly Books Ltd.
3680 Victoria Park Avenue
Toronto, Ontario M2H 3K1

Published in the United States in 2003 by
Firefly Books (U.S.) Inc.
P.O. Box 1338, Ellicott Station
Buffalo, New York 14205

Cover Photograph: Red berried elder (Sambucus racemosa) © Jo Brewer
Picture Credits: All photographs © Corbis except p.145 © Photodisk

Typeset by Florence Production Ltd., Stoodleigh, Devon
Printed and bound in Italy by
Officine Grafiche De Agostini, Novara

Editorial Director
Hilary McGlynn

Managing Editor
Elena Softley

Project Editor
Heather Slade

Design Manager
Lenn Darroux

Illustrations
Julie Williams

Picture research
Sophie Evans

Page design
Helen Weller

Production Manager
John Normansell

Production Assistant
Stacey Penny

CONTENTS

PREFACE

This publication covers over 30,000 plants grown in the English-speaking areas of the world together with much of Europe. It is intended as a working tool for both amateur and professional gardeners as well as for plant lovers wishing to find the botanical name when only the common name is known, or vice versa.

For easy reference the book is divided into fourteen different plant sections, with lists of common names in the first half of the book and the botanical equivalents in the second half. In order to keep the number of pages within manageable proportions, the categories and individual plants included are those most frequently purchased from nurseries and garden centres in the UK and North America. Vegetables have been excluded because very few customers use botanical terms when buying them or their seeds. A certain amount of duplication is inevitable if an unacceptable amount of cross-referencing is to be avoided. Some herbs, for instance, may appear also under 'Wild Flowers' or 'Popular Garden Plants', and 'House Plants' includes species from several categories.

Since the use of common or vernacular plant names is often restricted to a limited region or to special groups, botanical names have become more widely employed as a method of positively identifying plants. Continual revision has however, resulted in the frequent occurence of synonyms of the botanical name. These have been included in many instances to reduce confusion caused by consulting old reference books still to be found on the bookshelves of many gardeners of my generation and earlier.

The standard binomial system has been used throughout – the genus, or family name followed by the specific epithet or species name, identifying the characteristics or growing areas of that plant; for sub-species a third name can be applied and also a varietal name, for example *Pinus sibirica pumila glauca* (Dwarf blue Siberian pine). In some publications the varietal name appears in italics, in a different typeface, within quotation marks, or preceded by the abbreviation *var*. Here, where varieties are included, we have used the system widespread in the USA and elsewhere of adding the varietal name after the epithet using the same typeface and without quotation marks.

Some symbols used in the book are:

× before or within a name indicates a sexually pollinated hybrid.
+ indicates a graft hybrid.

The Scottish and Irish prefixes "Mac", "Mc", and "M" are united with the rest of the name thus, *macintyre*, *macaulay*, *maginty*.

The Irish prefix "O" is united with the rest of the name thus, *oleary*.

To avoid confusion, the abbreviation St is listed alphabetically as Saint.

ACKNOWLEDGEMENTS

This volume is the product of many years in the horticultural business both as amateur and professional, during which time I have been fortunate in being befriended by many eminent gardeners and botanists from whom I have learned and am still learning. To list them all would cover a dozen pages or more, but the following call for special mention for they probably influenced my life more than they ever realized.

Percy Thrower, with whom I swapped rare plants for several years whilst he was Parks Superintendent at Shrewsbury. A knowledgable yet modest man, always willing to share his knowledge with other gardeners.

Bill Sowerbutts, a very down-to-earth character with a vast knowledge of general horticulture and, towards the end of his life, a popular radio personality.

Anthony Huxley, from whom I learned a great deal during the time I was a regular contributor to *Amateur Gardening* during his editorship.

Gervas Huxley, a lovely member of that great family who spent many hours at my nursery in the Cotswolds discussing his favourite plants and explaining their epithets. He was a cousin of Sir Julian Huxley and Aldous Huxley.

Christina Foyle, who persuaded me that I could write and actually published my first two books under her John Gifford imprint.

Joe Elliott, whose friendship and expertise I admired during the 23 years his nursery was situated near to mine and whose knowledge of botanical Latin and Greek was of immeasurable assistance.

Pierre Barandou of Agen, France, who, together with Professor Max Henry, has helped enormously in extending my knowledge of European varieties.

And finally to Professor William T Stearn, one of the leading horticulturists in the world today, who has kindly allowed me to quote from his books *Botanical Latin,* 4th ed. (David & Charles), and *Stearn's Dictionary of Plant Names* (Cassell).

I also gratefully acknowledge the help I have received from the staff of Cannington College, Bridgwater; Oxford University (Forestry), Southampton and Exeter Universities, and in the USA from Penn State and Cornell Universities.

The support of my family and friends has been invaluable during the long years of research and I thank them all for their tolerance.

Harold Bagurst
Southampton, 2000

EPITHETS

A selection of epithets frequently encountered

abruptus, -a, -um
ending suddenly

abscissus, -a, -um cut off

acaulis stemless or nearly so

acinaceus, -a, -um
sword or scimitar-shaped

acu- in compound words
signifying prickly or
sharply pointed

aduncus, -a, -um hooked

aesculifolius, -a, -um
with leaves like
horse-chestnut

aestivus, -a, -um
developing or
maturing in summer

africanus, -a, -um African

aggregatus, -a, -um clustered in
a dense mass

alatus, -a, -um winged;
having wings

alb, albi, albo in compound
words signifying white

albus, -a, -um white

alpinus, -a, -um alpine

alternans alternating

alternus, -a, -um alternate,
not opposite

altus, -a, -um tall

amarus, -a, -um bitter

americanus, -a, -um American,
north or south

ammophilus, -a, -um
sand-loving

amplexicaulis, -is, -e
stem-clasping

amplexifolius, -a, -um
leaf-clasping

anacantus, -a, -um
without thorns or prickles

androgynus, -a, -um
hermaphrodite; having
male and female flowers
separate but on the
same inflorescence

anglicus, -a, -um English

anguinus, -a, -um serpentine;
wavy

angustifolius, -a, -um
having narrow leaves

annulatus, -a, -um having rings

annuus, -a, -um annual

apiatus, -a, -um spotted

apiculatus, -a, -um terminating
in a point or spike

apricus, -a, -um sun-loving

areneosus, -a, -um cobwebby

arcticus, -a, -um from arctic
regions

arcuatus, -a, -um arched; curved;
bent like a bow

argentatus, -a, -um silver;
silvered

argutus, -a, -um sharply notched
or toothed

aridus, -a, -um growing in dry,
arid places

aristatus, -a, -um bearded

armatus, -a, -um having thorns
or spines

articulatus, -a, -um jointed

ascendens sloping upwards

asper, -a, -um rough

attenuatus, -a, -um attenuated;
pointed

aurantiacus, -a, -um
orange-coloured

aureus, -a, -um golden

auriculatus, -a, -um ear-shaped

autumnalis, -is, -e
pertaining to autumn or fall

azureus, a, -um sky blue

bathyphyllus, -a, -um
thickly leaved

betaceus, -a, -um beetlelike

bi- two

biennis, -is, -e biennial

bifidus, -a, -um
divided into two parts,
not necessarily equal

biflorus, -a, -um twin-flowered

EPITHETS

bifolius, -a, -um — twin-leaved

bifurcatus, -a, -um — bifurcate; divided into two almost equal parts

bisectus, -a, -um — divided into two equal parts

bombycinus, -a, -um — silky

brachiatus, -a, -um — branched at right angles

bracteatus, -a, -um — having bracts

brunneus, -a, -um — brown

bryoides — resembling moss

bufonius, -a, -um — found in damp conditions

bulbosus, -a, -um — bulbous; having a swollen underground stem

buxifolius, -a, -um — box-leaved

caeruleus, -a, -um — dark blue

caesius, -a, -um — light blue

calcareus, -a, -um — Lime-loving; pertaining to lime

californicus, -a, -um — Of California

cambricus, -a, -um — Welsh; of Wales

campaniflorus, -a, -um — having bell-shaped flowers

canadensis, -is, -e — Canadian; of Canada

canariensis, -is, -e — of the Canary islands

candicans — shining white

canescens — with off-white hairs

capensis, -is, -e — of the Cape of Good Hope

caperatus, -a,-um — wrinkled

capilliformis, -is, -e — hair-like

capsularis, -is, -e — having a capsule or capsules

cardinalis, -is, -e — cardinal red; scarlet

carinatus, -a, -um — keeled; having a keel

carneus, -a, -um — flesh pink

carnosus, -a, -um — fleshy

castus, -a, -um — clean; pure; chaste

cataria — pertaining to cats

caulescens — having a stem

cavus, -a, -um — hollow

centifolius, -a, -um — multi-leaved or -petalled

ceraceus, -a, -um — waxy

cereus, -a, -um — waxy

cernuus, -a, -um — drooping; nodding

chamae- — prefix indicating low growth or dwarf habit

chinensis, -is, -e — Chinese

chrysanthus, -a, -um — having golden flowers

chryseus, -a, -um — golden yellow

ciliaris, -is, -e — fringed with hairs

citrinus, -a, -um — lemon-yellow

citriodorus, -a, -um — lemon-scented

clavatus, -a, -um — club-shaped

cochlearis, -is, e — spoon-shaped

cochleatus, -a, -um — spiral

collinus, -a, -um — pertaining to hills

columnaris, -is, -e — column-shaped

comatus, -a, -um — tufted; having a tuft

communis, -is, -e — common; general

compactus, -a, -um — dense

concavus, -a, -um — concave

conifer — cone-bearing

consolidus, -a, -um — stable; firm; solid

contortus, -a, -um — twisted

cordatus, -a, -um — heart-shaped

corneus, -a, -um — horny

cornutus, -a, -um — horn-shaped or having horns

corticosus, -a, -um — having thick bark

costatus, -a, -um — ribbed or veined

crassicaulis, -is, -e — having thick stems

crassifolius, -a, -um — having thick leaves

crassus, -a, -um — thick; fleshy

crenatus, -a, -um — crenate; scalloped

crinitus, -a, -um — having long thin hairs

crispatus, -a, -um — wavy; curled

cristatus, -a, -um — crested

cruciatus, -a, -um — in the form of a cross

crustatus, -a, -um — encrusted

ctenoides — comb-like

cucculatus, -a, -um — resembling a hood; hooded

cuneatus, -a, -um — wedge-shaped

curtus, -a, -um — shortened

curvatus, -a, -um — curved

cuspidatus, -a, -um
cuspidate; having a sharp point

cyaneus, -a, -um blue

cymbiformis, -is, -e boat-shaped

dactyloides fingerlike

dealbatus, -a, -um
coated with white dust or powder

debilis, -is, -e weak; frail

declinatus, -a, -um
bent or curved downward

deformis, -is, -e
deformed; distorted

deltoides, -a, -um triangular

dentatus, -a, -um toothed

diaphanus, -a, -um transparent

diffusus, -a, -um spreading

dipterus, -a, -um two-winged

discolor of two colours

diurnus, -a, -um day-flowering

drupacius, -a, -um
producing drupes or fleshy fruits

dulcis, -is, -e sweet

durus, -a, -um hard

echinatus, -a, -um
covered in spines or prickles

edulis, -is, -e edible

effusus, -a, -um spreading

elatior taller

elatus, -a, -um tall

elegans; elegantulus, -a, -um
elegant

elongatus, -a, -um
elongated; stretched

ensiformis, -is, -e
sword-shaped with a sharp point

erosus, -a, -um
irregular; jagged

esculentus, -a, -um edible

falcatus, -a, -um
falcate; sickle-shaped

fallax false

farinosus, -a, -um
mealy; powdery; floury

fasciatus, -a, -um
linked or bound together

fenestralis, -is, -e
pierced or perforated

ferox
vicious, having sharp thorns

flaccidus, -a, -um weak; limp

flavens yellow

flexilis, -is, -e
pliant; flexible; easily bent

flexuosus, -a, -um
twisted; zigzag

floccosus, -a, -um woolly

floribundus, -a, -um
free-flowering

fluvialis, -is, -e
growing in running water

foetidus, -a, -um
foul-smelling; stinking

fragilis, -is, -e
brittle; fragile; delicate

fragrans fragrant

frigidus, -a, -um
growing in cold regions

fumosus, -a, -um smoky

galactinus, -a, -um
growing in cold regions

galanthus, -a, -um
having milky-white flowers

galeatus, -a, -um helmet-shaped

gallicus, -a, -um
French; appertaining to France

geniculatus, -a, -um
bent abruptly like an elbow

germanicus, -a, -um
German; appertaining to Germany

gibbosus, -a, -um
swollen on one side

gladiatus, -a, -um swordlike

glaucus, -a, -um
covered in bloom, the fine white or grey coating seen on grapes, plums, etc.

globosus, -a, -um spherical

glutinosus, -a, -um gluey; sticky

gracilis, -is, -e graceful; slender

grammopetalus, -a, -um
having striped petals

grandis, -is, -e showy; large

graveolens strongly scented

griseus, -a, -um grey

guttatus, -a, -um
speckled; spotted

halophilus, -a, -um salt-loving

hamatus, -a, -um hooked

hastatus, -a, -um spear-shaped

helix spiral or twisted

helveticus, -a, -um
Swiss; of Switzerland

hians open; gaping

hirsutus, -a, -um
hairy; covered in hairs

hispanicus, -a, -um
Spanish; of Spain

hispidus, -a, -um bristly

horizontalis, -is, -e
prostrate; horizontal; flat

horridus, -a, -um
very thorny or prickly

EPITHETS

hortensis, -is, -e
pertaining to gardens

humilis, -is, -e very dwarf

hybridus, -a, -um
of mixed parentage; hybrid

hypnoides mosslike

hystrix bristly or having
many spines or prickles

imbricatus, -a, -um
overlapping in a
regular pattern

immaculatus, -a, -um
spotless; immaculate

immersus, -a, -um
growing under water

implexus, -a, -um tangled

incurvatus, -a, -um
incurved; bent inward

inermis, -is, -e
without thorns or prickles

inquinans
marked; stained; flecked

integrifolius, -a, -um
having entire or
uncut foliage

italicus, -a, -um italian

jubatus, -a, -um crested

junceus, -a, -um rushlike

kewensis, -is, -e
of the Royal Botanic
Gardens, Kew

labiatus, -a, -um lipped

laciniatus, -a, -um
ripped or slashed into strips

lacrimans weeping

lanatus, -a, -um woolly

lanceolatus, -a, -um
spear-shaped

lateritius, -a, -um brick-red

laxus, -a, -um
relaxed; loose; open

lenticularis, -is, -e lens-shaped

lentiginosus, -a, -um freckled

lepidus, -a, -um
elegant; graceful; slender

lignosus, -a, -um woody

limbatus, -a, -um
bordered; edged

lineatus, -a, -um
having stripes

lingua tongue or tongue-like

lithophilus, -a, -um
rock-loving; growing
among or on rocks

longus, -a, -um long

lunatus, -a, -um shaped like a
crescent moon

luteolus, -a, -um yellowish

luteus, -a, -um yellow

maculatus, -a, -um spotted

magnificus, -a, -um
magnificent; splended

magnus, -a, -um large

majalis, -is, -e May-flowering

maliformis, -is, -e apple-shaped

malvinus, -a, -um mauve

marginalis, -is, -e
margined; bordered

maritimus, -a, -um
coastal; pertaining to the
sea or seashore

marmoratus, -a, -um
mottled; marbled

maxillaris, -is, -e of the jaws

maximus, -a, -um largest

medicus, -a, -um medicinal

medullaris, -is, -e pithy

melancholicus, -a, -um
limp; sad-looking; wilted

meleagris, -is, -e spotted

meridianus, -a, -um
blooming at noontime

militaris, -is, -e
upright; rigid; stiff

mirabilis, -is, -e
miraculous; wonderful

mollis, -is, -e
soft; having soft hairs;
velvety

moniliformis, -is, -e
like a necklace

monstrosus, -a, -um
abnormal; distorted

montanus, -a, -um
pertaining to mountains

monticola mountain-lover,
or a plant indigenous
to mountain areas

moschatus, -a, -um musky

mucosus, -a, -um slimy

mucronatus, -a, -um pointed

mucronulatus, -a, -um
terminating in a sharp point

mundulus, -a, -um neat; tidy

muralis, -is, -e growing on walls

muscarius, -a, -um
pertaining to flies
or flying insects

muscivorus, -a, -um fly-eating

muscosus, -a, -um
mossy; moss-like

nanus, -a, -um dwarf

natans floating; reclining
on the water surface

navicularis, -is, -e boat-shaped

nervosus, -a, -um
having conspicuous
veins or ribs

nidus a nest

niger; nigra, -um black

nipponicus, -a, -um Japanese

nitidifolius, -a, -um
having glossy leaves

nocturnus, -a, -um
night-flowering

non-scriptus unmarked

notatus, -a, -um spotted

nucifera, -um nut-bearing

nutans nodding

nyctagineus, -a, -um
night-blooming

obconicus, -a, -um
formed like an
inverted cone

obesus, -a, -um
succulent; bloated

obscurus, -a, -um
uncertain; indistinct

obtusus, -a, -um blunt

occidentalis, -is, -e western

odoratus, -a, -um
fragrant; scented

officinalis, -is, -e
used in medicine

oleraceus, -a, -um
vegetables, potherbs, etc.

oporinus, -a, -um
pertaining to the
autumn or fall

orientalis, -is, -e eastern; oriental

osmanthus, -a, -um
having fragrant flowers

oxyphilus, -a, -um
acid-loving (soil)

palliatus, -a, -um
cloaked; wrapped

palmatus, -a, -um
palmate, shaped like
an open hand

palustris, -is, -e
marsh-loving, found
in boggy areas

pannosus, -a, -um
torn; tattered; scruffy

papyraceus, -a, -um papery

pendulus, -a, -um
hanging; drooping

peregrinus, -a, -um
wandering; extending
laterally

perennial living more than
two years

perfoliatus, -a, -um
having leaves which
enclose or wrap round
the stem

persicus, -a, -um Persian

pes foot

petiole leaf-stalk

picturatus, -a, -um variegated

pileatus, -a, -um having a cap

pilosus, -a, -um
having a covering
of long soft hairs

pinnatus, -a, -um feathery

plebeius, -a, -um
common, not rare

plicatus, -a, -um pleated

plumatus, -a, -um plumed

pogonanthus, -a, -um
having bearded flowers

polifolius, -a, -um
having grey leaves

praecox very early

pratensis, -is, -e
of the fields or
meadows

procumbens prostrate

procurrens spreading

profusus, -a, -um
plentiful; abundant

pruriens
causing itching or irritation

psittacinus, -a, -um
parrot-like, with
contrasting colours

psycodes butterfly-like

pubescens downy

pulvinatus, -a, -um cushion-like

punctatus, -a, -um spotted

pungens sharp-pointed

pusillus, -a, -um very small

pyriformis, -is, -e pear-shaped

pyxidatus, -a, -um
having a lid or pyxis

racemosus, -a, -um
having flowers in racemes

radians radiating outward

radicans
with roots growing
from stems

radula file; rasp

ramosus, -a, -um branched

reclinatus, -a, -um
curved or bent backward

rectus, -a, -um erect; upright

reniformis, -is, -e kidney-shaped

repens; reptans creeping

reticulatus, -a, -um
covered with net-like
markings

rivalis, -is, -e
growing in or near
rivers or streams

rosaceus, -a, -um like a rose

rosea rose-like

*rubens, ruber, rubra,
rubrum* red

rufus, -a, -um red

rugosus, -a, -um wrinkled

EPITHETS

rupestris, -is, -e
rock-loving; indigenous to rocky areas

saggitatus, -a, -um   arrow-shaped

salinus, -a, -um
growing in salty areas

sanguineus, -a, -um   blood-red

saponaceus, -a, um   soapy

sarmentosus, -a, -um
equipped with runners

sativus, -a, -um
cultivated, not wild or natural

saxatilis, -is, -e
a rock plant; one found among rocks

scaber, scabra. scabrum
rough; coarse

scandens   climbing

scoparius, -a, -um   broom-like

scutatus, -a, -um   shield-shaped

semperflorens   everblooming

sempervirens   evergreen

sericeus, -a, -um   silky

serpens   creeping

serratus, -a, -um   saw-toothed

sessilis, -is, -e
sessile; without a stalk

setaceus, -a, -um
bristly; having bristles

siliceus, -a, -um
sand-loving; growing in sand

silvaticus, -a, -um;
silvestris, -is, -e
growing in woods or wooded areas; growing wild (not cultivated)

sinensis, -is, -e   chinese

solidus, -a, -um   dense

spectabilis, -is, -e
showy; spectacular

spinosus, -a, -um   spiny

spiralis, -is, -e   spiral

stragulus, -a, -um   mat-forming

striatus, -a, -um   striped

strictus, -a, -um   erect

sulcatus, -a, -um   furrowed

sulfureus, -a, -um;
sulphureus, -a, -um
sulfur (sulphur)-yellow

superbus, -a, -um   superb

supinus, -a, -um   prostrate

sylvaticus, -a, -um;
sylvestris, -is, -e
growing on woods and forests; wild, not cultivated

tenuis, -is, -e   slender

ternatus, -a, -um
in groups of three

tinctus, -a, -um   coloured

tomentosus, -a, -um
very woolly or furry

tortilis, -is, -e; tortus,
-a, -um   twisted; contorted

toxicarius, -a, -um;
toxifera -um   poisonous

tremulus, -a, -um
trembling; gently shaking

trivialis, -is, -e
ordinary; common; trivial

tropicus, -a, -um   tropical

tuberosus, -a, -um   tuberous

tumidus, -a, -um
swollen; distended

uliginosus, -a, -um
of swamps and boggy places

umbrosus, -a, -um
shade-loving

urens   stinging

utilis, -is, -e   useful

vacillans   variable; not constant

vagans   wandering

variegatus, -a, -um   variegated

velaris, -is, -e   veiled

velox   fast-growing

velutinus, -a, -um   velvety

veris   spring-flowering

vernalis, -is, -e   spring-flowering

vespertinus, -a, -um
evening-blooming

villosus, -a, -um
covered with soft hairs

virens   green

virgatus, -a, -um
twiggy; multi-branched

viridis, -is, -e   green

viscidus, -a, -um;
viscosus, -a, -um
sticky; gummy

volubilis, -is, -e
twisting; twining

vulgaris, -is, -e;
vulgatus, -a -um   common; not rare

xanthinus, -a, -um   yellow

zebrinus, -a, -um   zebra-striped

zibethinus, -a, -um   evil-smelling

zonalis, -is, -e; zonatus,
-a, -um   zoned

PERSONAL EPITHETS

When the name of a person ends in a vowel, the letter *i* is added, except when the name ends in a, when e is added.

When the name ends in a consonant, the letters ii are added, except when the name ends in er, when *i* is added.

COMMON
NAMES

ALPINES AND ROCKERY PLANTS

Alpines are plants whose natural habitat is the mountainous area above the tree line, but in gardening circles the term includes rock-gardening plants. Very little true alpine gardening is attempted in the English-speaking parts of the world because alpine conditions are rarely encountered naturally and it is very difficult to reproduce them artificially.

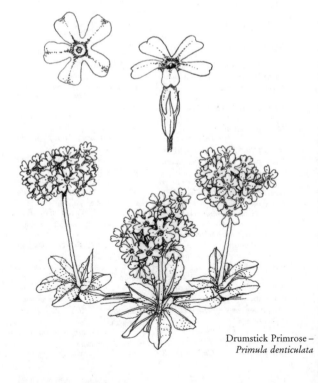

Drumstick Primrose –
Primula denticulata

Acanthus-leaved carline thistle
Carlina acanthifolia
Alaskan phlox *Phlox borealis*
Alaska violet *Viola langsdorfii*
Alpenrose
Rhododendron ferrugineum
Alpine aster *Aster alpinus*
Alpine avens *Geum montanum*
Alpine barrenwort
Epimedium alpinum
Alpine brook saxifrage
Saxifraga rivularis
Alpine buttercup
Ranunculus alpestris
Alpine calamint *Acinos alpinus*
Calamintha alpina
Alpine carline thistle
Carlina acaulis simplex
Alpine catchfly *Lychnis alpina*
Silene alpestris
Alpine cat's foot
Antennaria alpina
Alpine clematis *Clematis alpina*
Alpine columbine
Aquilegia alpina
Alpine forget-me-not
Myosotis alpestris
Alpine gentian *Gentiana alpina*
Gentiana newberryi
Alpine gypsophila
Gypsophila repens
Alpine lady's mantle
Alchemilla alpina
Alchemilla conjuncta
Alpine lychnis *Lychnis alpina*
Alpine marsh violet
Viola palustris
Alpine mouse-eared chickweed
Cerastium alpinum
Alpine pennycress
Thlaspi alpestre
Alpine phlox *Phlox douglasii*
Alpine pink *Dianthus alpinus*
Alpine poppy *Papaver alpinum*
Papaver burseri
Alpine rock cress *Arabis alpina*
Alpine rockrose
Helianthemum oelandicum
Alpine rose
Rhododendron ferrugineum
Alpine sandwort
Arenaria montana
Alpine sainfoin
Hedysarum obscurum
Alpine scullcap *Scutellaria alpina*
Alpine snowbell *Soldanella alpina*
Alpine speedwell *Veronica alpina*
Alpine spurge
Euphorbia capitulata
Alpine strawberry *Fragaria vesca*
Alpine thistle *Carlina acaulis*

Alpine veronica
Veronica alpina
Alpine violet
Cyclamen purpurascens
Alpine wallflower
Erysimum alpinum
American brooklime
Veronica americana
American dog violet
Viola conspersa
American dwarf iris *Iris lacustris*
Anemone *Anemone apennina*
Angel's eye *Veronica chamaedrys*
Apennine sandwort
Minuartia graminifolia
Appleblossom alpine anemone
Anemone narcissiflora
Arctic sandwort
Arenaria norvegica
Arrow-leaved violet
Viola sagittata
Asarabacca *Asarum europaeum*
Aubrietia *Aubrieta deltoidea*
Auricula *Primula auricula*
Primula × pubescens
Australian violet *Viola hederacea*
Autumn crocus
Colchicum bornmuelleri
Autumn-flowering gentian
Gentiana sino-ornata
Awl-leaved pearlwort
Sagina subulata
Baby joshua tree
Sedum multiceps
Baby primrose *Primula forbesii*
Primula malacoides
Baby's breath
Gypsophila repens
Bacon and eggs
Lotus corniculatus pleniforus
Baldmoney
Meum anthamanticum
Balloon flower
Platycodon grandiflorus
Barberry *Berberis candidula*
Barren strawberry
Waldsteinia geoides
Barrenwort *Epimedium alpinum*
Bastard balm
Melittis melissophyllum
Bastard jasmine
Androsace chamaejasme
Bearberry
Arctostaphylos uva-ursi
Bear's ear *Primula auricula*
Bear's foot *Alchemilla vulgaris*
Beaver's tail
Sedum morganianum
Beefsteak geranium
Saxifraga stolonifera

Bell flower
  Campanula cochleariifolia
Bethlehem sage
  Pulmonaria picta
  Pulmonaria saccharata
Bidgee-widgee
  Acaena anserinifolia
Bidi-bidi *Acaena anserinifolia*
Bididy-bid *Acaena anserinifolia*
Bird's eye *Veronica chamaedrys*
Bird's eye primrose
  Primula farinosa
  Primula laurentiana
  Primula mistassinica
Bird's foot trefoil
  Lotus corniculatus pleniforus
Bird's foot violet *Viola pedata*
Bistort *Polygonum bistorta superbum*
Biting stonecrop *Sedum acre*
Bitter cress *Cardamine pratensis*
Bitter root *Lewisia rediviva*
Bitterwort *Lewisia rediviva*
Black false helleborine
  Veratrum nigrum
Black snakeroot
  Cimicifuga racemosa
Bladder gentian
  Gentiana utriculosa
Bleeding heart
  Dicentra eximia
Blind gentian
  Gentiana clausa
Bloody cranesbill
  Geranium sanguineum
Blue alpine daisy
  Aster alpinus
Blue Chinese juniper
  Juniperus chinensis blaauw
Blue cowslip
  Pulmonaria angustifolia
Blue creeping juniper
  Juniperus horizontalis glauca
Blue dwarf spruce
  Picea abies pumila glauca
Blue-eyed grass
  Sisyrinchium angustifolium
Blue-eyed mary
  Omphalodes verna
Blue flaky juniper
  Juniperus squamata glauca
Blue monkshood
  Aconitum napellus
Blue Mountain bidi-bidi
  Acaena inermis
  Acaena microphylla
Blue phlox *Phlox divaricata*
Blue saxifrage *Saxifraga caesia*
Blue snakeroot *Liatris spicata*
Blue spruce *Picea glauca*
Blue spurge
  Euphorbia myrsinites

Bottle gentian
  Gentiana andrewsii
  Gentiana clausa
Bouncing bet *Saponaria officinalis*
Brass buttons
  Cotula coronopifolia
Breckland thyme
  Thymus serpyllum
Bridal wreath *Francoa sonchifolia*
Bristle-cone pine *Pinus aristata*
Broom *Cytisus decumbens*
  Genista lydia
Bugle *Ajuga reptans*
Bulbous buttercup
  Ranunculus bulbosus
Bulbous crowfoot
  Ranunculus bulbosus
Burmese dwarf rhododendron
  Rhododendron aperantum
Burnet saxifrage
  Pimpinella saxifraga
Burro's tail *Sedum morganianum*
Buttercup primrose
  Primula floribunda
Buttercup winter hazel
  Corylopsis pauciflora
Butter daisy *Ranunculus repens*
Butterwort *Pinguicula vulgaris*
Calathian violet
  Gentiana pneumonanthe
California golden violet
  Viola pedunculata
Californian fuchsia
  Zauschneria californica
Californian wild pansy
  Viola pendunculata
Canadian violet
  Viola canadensis
Candy mustard
  Acthionema saxatile
Candytuft
  Aethionema rotundifolium
  Iberis amara
  Iberis saxatilis
  Iberis sempervirens
Caraway thyme
  Thymus herba-barona
Carthusian pink
  Dianthus carthusianorum
Catesby's gentian
  Gentiana catesbaei
Catmint *Nepeta × faassenii*
Cat's foot *Antennaria dioica*
Chalk plant *Gypsophila repens*
Chamois cream
  Hutchinsia alpina
Cheddar pink *Dianthus caesius*
  Dianthus gratianopolitanus
Chinese primrose
  Primula sinensis
Christmas cheer
  Sedum × rubrotinctum

Christmas rose

Christmas rose *Helleborus niger*
Closed gentian
　　　　Gentiana andrewsii
　　　　Gentiana clausa
　　　　Gentiana linearis
Coast violet *Viola brittoniana*
Cobweb houseleek
　Sempervivum arachnoideum
Common broom
　　　　Cytisus scoparius
　　　　Sarothamnus scoparius
Common butterwort
　　　　Pinguicula vulgaris
Common foxglove
　　　　Digitalis purpurea
Common gromwell
　　Lithospermum officinale
Common houseleek
　Sempervivum tectorum
Common monkshood
　　　　Aconitum napellus
Common pasque flower
　　　　Anemone pulsatilla
　　　　Pulsatilla vulgaris
Common pearlwort
　　　　Sagina procumbens
Common periwinkle *Vinca minor*
Common pink
　　　　Dianthus plumarius
Common polypody
　　　Polypodium vulgare
Common primrose
　　　　Primula vulgaris
Common rockrose
　Helianthemum chamaecistus
　Helianthemum nummularium
Common speedwell
　　　Veronica officinalis
Common storksbill
　　　Erodium cicutarium
Common yew *Taxus baccata*
Confederate violet *Viola priceana*
Coral bells
　Heuchera sanguinea alba
Corsican sandwort
　　　　Arenaria balearica
Cowslip *Primula officinalis*
　　　　Primula veris
Cream violet *Viola striata*
Creeping buttercup
　　　Ranunculus repens
Creeping common juniper
　　Juniperus communis
　　　　hornibrookii
Creeping crowfoot
　　　Ranunculus repens
Creeping evening primrose
　Oenothera missouriensis
Creeping gypsophila
　　　Gypsophila repens
Creeping jenny
　Lysimachia nummularia

Creeping sailor
　　Saxifraga stolonifera
Creeping thyme
　　　Thymus serpyllum
Crested gentian
　　Gentiana septemfida
Cross gentian
　　　Gentiana cruciata
Crowfoot violet *Viola pedata*
Cuckoo flower
　　Cardamine pratensis
Cushion pink *Silene acaulis*
Dead men's bells
　　　Digitalis purpurea
Dog's tooth violet
　Erythronium dens-canis
Dog violet *Viola canina*
　　　　Viola riviniana
Dogwood *Cornus canadensis*
Donkey's tail
　　Sedum morganianum
Dovedale moss
　　Saxifraga hypnoides
Downy yellow violet
　　　　Viola pubescens
Dragon's mouth
　　Horminum pyrenaicum
Dropwort *Filipendula vulgaris*
Drumstick primrose
　　Primula denticulata
Dusty miller *Primula auricula*
Dwarf acanthus
　　Acanthus dioscoridis
Dwarf balsam fir
　　Abies balsamea nana
Dwarf birch *Betula nana*
Dwarf blue lawson's cypress
　Chamaecyparis lawsoni
　minima glauca
Dwarf blue Siberian pine
　Pinus sibirica pumila glauca
Dwarf Chinese juniper
　Juniperus chinensis blaauw
Dwarf common juniper
　Juniperus communis compressa
Dwarf eastern hemlock
　Tsuga canadensis jeddeloh
Dwarf golden sawara cypress
　Chamaecyparis pisifera filifera
　　　　aurea nana
Dwarf Grecian fir
　　Abies cephalonica nana
Dwarf hemlock
　　Tsuga canadensis nana
Dwarf hinoki cypress
　Chamaecyparis obtusa nana
Dwarf iris *Iris pumila*
Dwarf Japanese yew
　　Taxus cuspidata minima
Dwarf joshua tree
　　　Sedum multiceps

Dwarf lawson's cypress
　　Chamaecyparis lawsoniana
　　　　　minima

Dwarf Norway spruce
　　Picea abies compressa

Dwarf pencil cedar
　　Juniperus virginiana nana
　　　　　compacta

Dwarf pine　　*Pinus mugo pumila*

Dwarf pink thrift
　　Armeria juniperifolia

Dwarf Russian almond
　　Prunus tenella

Dwarf sawara cypress
　　Chamaecyparis pisifera
　　　　　filifera nana

Dwarf Scots pine
　　Pinus sylvestris beuvronensis
　　Pinus sylvestris nana

Dwarf Siberian pine
　　Pinus sibirica pumila

Dwarf solomon's seal
　　Polygonatum hookeri

Dwarf Spanish columbine
　　Aquilegia discolor

Dwarf spruce
　　Picea abies echiniformis

Dwarf Weymouth pine
　　Pinus strobus umbraculifera

Dwarf white pine
　　Pinus strobus nana

Dwarf willow
　　Salix hastata wehrhahnii

Dwarf yew
　　Taxus baccata compacta
　　Taxus baccata nana

Early blue violet
　　Viola palmata

Early yellow violet
　　Viola rotundifolia

Eastern water violet
　　Viola lanceolata

Edelweiss　*Leontopodium alpinum*

Edging candytuft
　　Iberis sempervirens

Einsel's columbine
　　Aquilegia einseleana

English primrose
　　Primula vulgaris

English stonecrop
　　Sedum anglicum

English violet　　*Viola odorata*

European brooklime
　　Veronica beccabunga

European spring adonis
　　Adonis vernalis

European wild pansy
　　Viola tricolor

Evergreen candytuft
　　Iberis sempervirens

Evergreen violet
　　Viola sempervirens

Fair maids of France
　　Saxifraga granulata

Fair maids of Kent
　　Ranunculus aconitifolius

Fairy cups　　　　*Primula veris*

Fairy primrose　*Primula malacoides*

Fairy's thimble
　　Campanula cochleariifolia
　　Campanula pusilla

Fairy thimbles　*Digitalis purpurea*

Fanweed　　　*Thlaspi arvense*

Feather grass　　*Stipa capillata*

Field anemone
　　Pulsatilla pratensis nigricans

Field forget-me-not
　　Myosotis arvensis

Field pansy　　*Viola rafinesquii*
　　　　　　Viola tricolor

Field pennycress
　　Thlaspi arvense

Fine-leaved sandwort
　　Minuartia hybrida

Fingered fumitory
　　Corydalis solida

Fleabane　　*Erigeron uniflorus*

Florist's violet　　*Viola odorata*

Flowering onion
　　Allium oreophilum

Foam flower　*Tiarella cordifolia*

French weed　　*Thlaspi arvense*

Fringed sandwort
　　Arenaria ciliata

Fumitory
　　Corydalis cheilanthifolia

Garden arabis　*Arabis caucasica*

Garden London pride
　　Saxifraga × urbium

Garden pansy
　　Viola × wittrockiana

Garden thyme　*Thymus vulgaris*

Garden violet　　*Viola odorata*

Gargano bellflower
　　Campanula garganica

Garland flower　*Daphne cneorum*

Garlic pennycress
　　Thlaspi alliaceum

German catchfly　*Lychnis viscaria*

Germander speedwell
　　Veronica chamaedrys

German primrose
　　Primula obconica

Giant bellflower
　　Campanula latifolia macrantha

Giant knapweed
　　Centaurea rhapontica
　　Leuzea rhapontica

Giant solomon's seal
　　Polygonatum commutatum

Gibralter candytuft
　　Iberis gibraltarica

Glabrous rupturewort
                    Herniaria glabra
Glacier crowfoot
                    Ranunculus glacialis
Globe candytuft   *Iberis umbellata*
Globe daisy
                    Globularia trichosantha
Globe flower   *Trollius pumilus*
Glory-of-the-snow
                    Chionodoxa luciliae
Gold alpine poppy
                    Papaver kerneri
Gold dust   *Alyssum saxatile*
Golden alyssum   *Alyssum saxatile*
Golden aster   *Aster linosyris*
Golden carpet   *Sedum acre*
Golden cinquefoil
                    Potentilla aurea
Golden-eye saxifrage
                    Saxifraga tennesseensis
Golden garlic   *Allium moly*
Golden Japanese maple
                    Acer japonicum aureum
Golden moss   *Sedum acre*
Golden rod   *Solidago virgaurea*
Golden sedum   *Sedum adolphi*
Golden star
                    Chrysogonum virginianum
Golden tuft   *Alyssum saxatile*
Gold plantain lily
                    Hosta fortunei aurea
Golden flax   *Linum flavum*
Goose grass   *Potentilla anserina*
Goose tansy   *Potentilla anserina*
Grape hyacinth
                    Muscari botryoides
Grass-leaved buttercup
                    Ranunculus gramineus
Grass-leaved day lily
                    Hemerocallis minor
Grass-leaved iris *Iris graminea*
Great basin violet
                    Viola beckwithii
Great butterwort
                    Pinguicula grandiflora
Great meadow rue
                    Thalictrum aquilegifolium
Great spurred violet
                    Viola selkirkii
Grey cinquefoil
                    Potentilla arenaria
                    Potentilla cinerea
Grey fescue   *Festuca cinerea*
Gromwell
                    Lithospermum officinale
Gypsyweed   *Veronica officinalis*
Hacquetia   *Hacquetia epipactis*
Hairy alpine rose
                    Rhododendron hirsutum
Hairy bitter cress
                    Cardamine hirsuta

Hairy rock cress   *Arabis hirsuta*
Hairy stonecrop   *Sedum villosum*
Hairy thyme   *Thymus praecox*
                    pseudolangiunosus
Halberd-leaved violet
                    Viola hastata
Hard fern   *Blechnum spicant*
Hart's tongue fern
                    Asplenium scolopendrium
                    Phyllitis scolopendrium
Heartsease   *Viola × wittrockiana*
Heath pearlwort   *Sagina subulata*
Hen-and-chickens houseleek
                    Jovibarba sobolifera
                    Sempervivum soboliferum
                    Sempervivum tectorum
Herb peter   *Primula veris*
Herringbone cotoneaster
                    Cotoneaster horizontalis
Himalayan may apple
                    Podophyllum hexandrum
Hinoki cypress
                    Chamaecyparis obtusa
Hoary alison   *Berteroa incana*
Hoary cinquefoil
                    Potentilla argentea
                    Potentilla argentea calabra
Hollow fumitory   *Corydalis cava*
Hookspur violet   *Viola adunca*
Hoop-petticoat daffodil
                    Narcissus bulbocodium
Horned pansy   *Viola cornuta*
Horned rampion
                    Phyteuma scheuchzeri
Horned violet   *Viola cornuta*
Horse's tail
                    Sedum morganianum
Host's saxifrage
                    Saxifraga altissima
                    Saxifraga hostii
Houseleek
                    Sempervivum tectorum
Hudson balsam fir
                    Abies balsamea hudsoniana
Humming-bird's trumpet
                    Zauschneria californica
Iceland poppy
                    Papaver nudicaule
Ice plant   *Sedum spectabile*
Indian paint
                    Lithospermum canescens
Indian physic   *Gillenia trifoliata*
Indian warpaint
                    Lithospermum canescens
Irish saxifrage   *Saxifraga rosacea*
Italian alyssum
                    Alyssum argenteum
Italian starwort   *Aster amellus*
Ivyleaf cyclamen
                    Cyclamen hederifolium
                    Cyclamen neapolitanum

Ivy-leaved violet
Viola hederacea

Japanese dwarf wormwood
Artemisia schmidtiana nana

Japanese gentian
Gentiana nipponica
Gentiana scabrae

Japanese maple
Acer japonicum aconitifolium
Acer palmatum

Japanese toadlily
Tricyrtis hirta

Jellybean plant
Sedum pachyphyllum

Jellybeans   *Sedum pachyphyllum*

Jersey thrift   *Armeria alliacea*

Johnny-jump-up
Viola pendunculata
Viola tricolor

Joshua tree   *Sedum multiceps*

Karst gentian   *Gentiana tergestina*

Kenilworth ivy
Cymbalaria muralis

Keyflower   *Primula veris*

Kidney-leaved violet
Viola renifolia

Kidney saxifrage
Saxifraga hirsuta

King cup   *Caltha palustris*

King's spear
Asphodeline lutea

Knotted pearlwort
Sagina nodosa

Labrador violet
Viola labradorica

Ladies' delight
Viola × wittrockiana

Lady's gloves   *Digitalis purpurea*

Lady's mantle
Alchemilla vulgaris

Lady's slipper orchid
Cypripedium calceolus

Lady's smock
Cardamine pratensis

Lamb's ears   *Stachys byzantina*

Lamb's tail
Chiastophyllum oppositifolium
Sedum morganianum

Lampshade poppy
Meconopsis integrifolia

Lance-leaved violet
Viola lanceolata

Large bellflower
Campanula tridentata

Large-flowered butterwort
Pinguicula grandiflora

Large-flowered sandwort
Arenaria grandiflora

Large self-heal
Prunella grandiflora

Large speedwell
Veronica austriaca teucrium

Large white plantain lily
Hosta plantaginea

Large yellow foxglove
Digitalis grandiflora

Large yellow loosestrife
Lysimachia punctata

Larkspur violet   *Viola pedatifida*

Lather root   *Saponaria officinalis*

Lavender cotton
Santolina chamaecyparissus

Lebanon candytuft
Aethionema warleyense

Lemon thyme
Thymus citriodorus
Thymus serpyllum

Lesser celandine
Ranunculus ficaria

Lesser periwinkle   *Vinca minor*

Lily-of-the-valley
Convallaria majalis

Limestone houseleek
Sempervivum calcareum
Sempervivum tectorum calcareum

Lion's foot   *Alchemilla vulgaris*
Leontopodium alpinum

Little joshua tree
Sedum multiceps

Livelong   *Sedum telephium*

Live-long saxifrage
Saxifraga aizoon major
Saxifraga paniculata major

Liverleaf   *Hepatica nobilis*

London pride   *Saxifraga umbrosa*

Long-leaved speedwell
Veronica longifolia

Long-spurred violet
Viola rostrata

Lungwort
Pulmonaria angustifolia
Pulmonaria rubra

Macedonian white pink
Dianthus pinifolius

Maidenhair spleenwort
Asplenium tricomanes

Maiden pink   *Dianthus deltoides*

Maiden's wreath
Francoa ramosa

Many fingers
Sedum pachyphyllum

Marsh cinquefoil
Potentilla palustris

Marsh five finger
Potentilla palustris

Marsh gentian
Gentiana pneumonanthe

Marsh marigold   *Caltha palustris*

Marsh spurge   *Euphorbia palustris*

Marsh violet   *Viola palustris*

Matted globularia
Globularia cordifolia

Mayflower   *Cardamine pratensis*

May lily

May lily *Maianthemum bifolium*
Meadow anemone
        Pulsatilla vulgaris
Meadow buttercup
        Ranunculus acris multiplex
Meadow cress
        Cardamine pratensis
Meadow saxifrage
        Saxifraga granulata
Mendocino gentian
        Gentiana setigera
Mexican butterwort
        Pinguicula caudata
Mexican puccoon
        Lithospermum distichum
Mezereon *Daphne mezereum*
Michaelmas daisy *Aster amellus*
Midsummer men
        Sedum telephium
Milfoil *Achillea serbica*
Milkwhite rock jasmine
        Androsace lactea
Milkwort
        Euphorbia myrsinites
Miniature joshua tree
        Sedum multiceps
Miniature pansy *Viola tricolor*
Missouri violet
        Viola missouriensis
Mithridate mustard
        Thlaspi arvense
Monkshood *Aconitum napellus*
Moss campion *Silene acaulis*
Moss phlox *Phlox subulata*
Moss pink *Phlox subulata*
Mossy rockfoil
        Saxifraga hypnoides
Mossy sandwort
        Moehringia muscosa
Mossy saxifrage
        Saxifraga × arendsii
        Saxifraga hypnoides
Mother-of-thousands
        Saxifraga stolonifera
Mountain alyson
        Alyssum montanum
Mountain alyssum
        Alyssum montanum
Mountain avens *Dryas octopetala*
Mountain buttercup
        Ranunculus alpestris
        Ranunculus montanus
Mountain butterwort
        Pinguicula montana
Mountain cat's ear
        Antennaria dioica
Mountian cornflower
        Centaurea montana
Mountain everlasting
        Antennaria dioica

Mountain houseleek
        Sempervivum montanum
Mountain kidney vetch
        Anthyllis montana
Mountain phlox *Phlox subulata*
Mountain pine *Pinus montana*
        Pinus mugo
Mountain rocket
        Bellendena montana
Mountain sandwort
        Arenaria montana
Mountain sedge *Carex montana*
Mountain soldanella
        Soldanella montana
Mountain tassel
        Soldanella montana
Mountain valerian
        Valeriana montana
Mountain willow *Salix alpina*
Mount Atlas daisy
        Anacyclus depressus
Anacyclus pyrethrum depressus
Mouse-eared chickweed
        Cerastium tomentosum
Mouse-ear hawkweed
        Hieracium pilosella
Musk mallow *Malva moschata*
Musk saxifrage
        Saxifraga moschata
Musky saxifrage
        Saxifraga muscoides
Myrtle *Vinca minor*
Nancy pretty *Saxifraga umbrosa*
Narcissus-flowered anemone
        Anemone narcissiflora
Narrow-leaved lungwort
        Pulmonaria angustifolia
                azurea
Narrow-leaved wormwood
        Artemisia nitida
New Zealand bur
        Acaena buchananii
New Zealand burr
        Acaena microphylla
Nodding catchfly *Silene pendula*
None-so-pretty
        Saxifraga × urbium
Northern blue violet
        Viola septentrionalis
Northern bog violet
        Viola nephrophylla
Northern downy violet
        Viola fimbriatula
Northern maidenhair fern
        Adiantum pedatum
Northern white violet
        Viola renifolia
October daphne *Sedum sieboldii*
October plant *Sedum sieboldii*
Oldfield cinquefoil
        Potentilla simplex

Redwood violet

Old-man-and-woman
    Sempervivum tectorum
Olympian violet   *Viola gracilis*
Olympic violet   *Viola flettii*
One-flowered cushion saxifrage
    Saxifraga burserana
Orange hawkweed
    Hieracium aurantiacum
Oregon sunshine
    Eriophyllum lanatum
Orpine   *Sedum telephium*
Oxlip   *Primula elatior*
Pale violet   *Viola striata*
Palm lily   *Yucca gloriosa*
Palsywort   *Primula veris*
Pansy   *Viola × wittrockiana*
Pansy violet   *Viola pedata*
Pasque flower
    Anemone pulsatilla
    Pulsatilla vulgaris
Patagonian slipper flower
    Calceolaria polyrrhiza
Peach-leaved bellflower
    Campanula persicifolia
Pearlwort   *Sagina pilifera*
Pellitory   *Anacyclus pyrethrum*
Pennycress   *Thlaspi arvense*
Perennial flax   *Linum perenne*
Perfoliate pennycress
    Thlaspi perfoliatum
Persian buttercup
    Ranunculus asiaticus
Persian ranunculus
    Ranunculus asiaticus
Persian stonecress
    Aethionema grandiflorum
Pilewort   *Ranunculus ficaria*
Pine-barren gentian
    Gentiana autumnalis
Pink lily-of-the-valley
    Convallaria majalis rosea
Pink rock jasmine
    Androsace carnea
Pink sandwort
    Arenaria purpurascens
Plains violet   *Viola viarum*
Poison primrose   *Primula obconica*
Polyanthus   *Primula × polyantha*
Pork and beans
    Sedum × rubrotinctum
Prairie tea   *Potentilla rupestris*
Prickly conesticks
    Petrophila sessilis
Prickly-pear cactus
    Opuntia engelmannii
Prickly thrift
    Acantholimon glumaceum
Primrose   *Primula vulgaris*
Primrose-leaved violet
    Viola primulifolia

Prince of Wales' feathers
    Tanacetum densum amani
Prophet flower   *Arnebia echioides*
    Arnebia pulchra
    Echioides longiflora
Prostrate juniper
    Juniperus communis depressa
Prostrate rhododendron
    Rhododendron chrysanthum
Puccoon
    Lithospermum canescens
    Lithospermum officinale
Purple bugle
    Ajuga reptans atropurpurea
Purple columbine   *Aquilegia atrata*
Purple loosestrife
    Lythrum salicaria
Purple mountain saxifrage
    Saxifraga oppositifolia
Purple prairie violet
    Viola pedatifida
Purple saxifrage
    Saxifraga oppositifolia
Pussy's toes   *Antennaria dioica*
Pygmy lewisia   *Lewisia pygmaea*
Pygmy spruce
    Picea abies pygmaea
Pyramidal saxifrage
    Saxifraga cotyledon
Pyrenean cinquefoil
    Potentilla pyrenaica
Pyrenean dragonmouth
    Horminum pyrenaicum
Pyrenean eryngo
    Eryngium bourgatii
Pyrenean primrose
    Ramonda myconi
    Ramonda pyrenaica
Pyrenean ramonda
    Ramonda myconi
Pyrenean saxifrage
    Saxifraga longifolia
Pyrenean woodruff
    Asperula hirta
Quaking grass   *Briza media*
Queen's slipper orchid
    Cypripedium reginae
Red baneberry   *Actaea rubra*
Red bidi-bidi
    Acaena novae-zealandiae
Red burning bush
    Dictamnus rubra
Reddish stonecrop
    Sedum anacampseros
Red-hot poker primrose
    Primula viallii
Red maids   *Calandrinia menziesii*
Red pasque flower
    Pulsatilla vulgaris rubra
Redwood violet
    Viola sempervirens

Reflexed stonecrop	*Sedum reflexum*
Reticulate willow	*Salix reticulata*
Rhaetian poppy	*Papaver rhaeticum*
Rock beauty	*Petrocallis pyrenaica*
Rock bells	*Aquilegia canadensis*
Rock buckthorn	*Rhamnus saxitilis*
Rock cinquefoil	*Potentilla rupestris*
Rock cranesbill	*Geranium macrorrhizum*
Rock cress	*Arabis albida*
	Arabis ferdinandi-coburgii
Rockery daisy	*Chrysanthemum arcticum*
Rocket candytuft	*Iberis amara*
Rock jasmine	*Androsace occidentalis*
Rock jessamine	*Androsace occidentalis*
Rock purslane	*Calandrinia menziesii*
Rock sandwort	*Arenaria stricta*
	Minuartia stricta
Rock soapwort	*Saponaria ocymoides*
Rock rose	*Helianthemum nummularium*
Rock stonecrop	*Sedum forsteranum*
	Sedum reflexum
Rock violet	*Viola flettii*
Rock windflower	*Anemone rupicola*
Rocky mountain columbine	*Aquilegia caerulea*
Roof iris	*Iris tectorum*
Roseroot sedum	*Sedum roseum*
Round-headed rampion	*Phyteuma orbiculare*
Round-leaved yellow violet	*Viola rotundifolia*
Royal fern	*Osmunda regalis*
Running myrtle	*Vinca minor*
Sagebrush violet	*Viola trinervata*
Saint Bruno's lily	*Paradisea liliastrum*
Saint Patrick's cabbage	*Saxifraga × urbium*
Saint Peter's wort	*Primula veris*
Sampson's snakeroot	*Gentiana catesbaei*
	Gentiana villosa
Sand phlox	*Phlox bifida*
Sandwort	*Arenaria tetraquetra*
Sargent's cedar	*Cedrus libani sargentii*
Satin flower	*Sisyrinchium angustifolium*
Scarlet bidi-bidi	*Acaena microphylla*
Sea alyssum	*Lobularia maritima*
Sea campion	*Silene maritima*
	Silene uniflora
Sea heath	*Frankenia laevis*
Sea pink	*Armeria maritima*
Sea storksbill	*Erodium maritimum*
Sedge	*Carex firma*
Sedum live-forever	*Sedum telephium*
Shaggy hawkweed	*Hieracium villosum*
Shooting star	*Dodecatheon meadia*
Short-leaved gentian	*Gentiana brachyphylla*
Showy lady's slipper orchid	*Cypripedium reginae*
Shrubby speedwell	*Veronica fruticulosa*
Shrubby-stalked speedwell	*Veronica fruticulosa*
Shrubby white flax	*Linum suffruticosum*
Siberian bugloss	*Brunnera macrophylla*
Siberian iris	*Iris sibirica*
Siberian phlox	*Phlox sibirica*
Siberian whitlow grass	*Draba sibirica*
Siebold's stonecrop	*Sedum sieboldii*
Sierra gentian	*Gentianopsis holopetala*
Silver sage	*Salvia argentea*
Silver speedwell	*Veronica spicata incana*
Silver-spiked speedwell	*Veronica spicata incana*
Silver stonecrop	*Sedum treleasii*
Silverweed	*Potentilla anserina*
Silvery cinquefoil	*Potentilla argentea*
Silvery milfoil	*Achillea clavennae*
Slender loosestrife	*Lythrum virgatum*
Slender sandwort	*Arenaria leptoclados*
Slipper flower	*Calceolaria biflora*
	Calceolaria plantaginea
Small celandine	*Ranunculus ficaria*
Snakeroot	*Liatris elegans*
	Polygonum bistorta superbum
Snake's head fritillary	*Fritillaria meleagris*
Snow-in-summer	*Cerastium tomentosum*

White stonecrop

Snow-on-the-mountain
Arabis albida

Solitary harebell *Campanula pulla*

Solomon's seal
Polygonatum × hybridum

Southern coast violet
Viola septemloba

Sowbread *Cyclamen purpurascens*

Spanish bluebell *Scilla hispanica*

Spanish dagger *Yucca gloriosa*

Spanish pellitory
Anacyclus pyrethrum

Spanish thrift *Armeria welwitschii*

Speedwell *Veronica filiformis*

Spider's web houseleek
Sempervivum arachnoideum

Spignel *Meum athamanticum*

Spotted gentian
Gentiana punctata

Spring adonis *Adonis vernalis*

Spring anemone
Pulsatilla vernalis

Spring cinquefoil *Potentilla verna*

Spring gentian *Gentiana verna*

Spring plantain lily
Hosta fortunei aurea

Spring sandwort *Minuartia verna*

Spring vetchling *Lathyrus vernus*

Spurge *Euphorbia myrsinites*

Starry bellflower
Campanula elatines

Starry saxifrage *Saxifraga stellata*

Stemless gentian *Gentiana acaulis*
Gentiana dinarica

Stemless thistle *Cirsium acaule*

Stepmother's flower
Viola × wittrockiana

Sticky sandwort *Minuartia viscosa*

Stinking hellebore
Helleborus foetidus

Stinkweed *Thlaspi arvense*

Store cress
Aethionema warleyense

Strapwort *Corrigiola litoralis*

Strawberry begonia
Saxifraga stolonifera

Strawberry geranium
Saxifraga stolonifera

Stream violet *Viola glabella*

Striped violet *Viola striata*

Sulphur cinquefoil
Potentilla recta warrenii

Summer gentian
Gentiana septemfida

Superb pink *Dianthus superbus*

Sweet alyssum
Lobularia maritima

Sweet coltsfoot *Petasites fragrans*

Sweet violet *Viola odorata*

Sweet white violet *Viola blanda*

Sweet woodruff
Galium odoratum

Swiss mountain pine
Pinus mugo mugo

Swiss rock jasmine
Androsace helvetica

Tall white violet *Viola canadensis*

Thick-leaved stonecrop
Sedum dasyphyllum suendermannii

Thread agave *Yucca filamentosa*

Three-toothed cinquefoil
Potentilla tridentata

Three-veined pink
Dianthus pavonius

Three-veined sandwort
Moehringia muscosa

Thrift *Armeria caespitosa*
Armeria maritima

Thyme-leaved sandwort
Arenaria serpyllifolia

Thyme-leaved speedwell
Veronica serpyllifolia

Tibetan cowslip
Primula florindae

Tibetan rhododendron
Rhododendron leucaspis

Trailing phlox *Phlox nivalis*

Trailing violet *Viola hederacea*

Triangle-leaved violet
Viola × emarginata

Triglav gentian
Gentiana terglouensis

Trumpet gentian *Gentiana acaulis*

Tufted saxifrage *Saxifraga cespitosa*

Tufted soapwort
Saponaria caespitosa

Tumbling ted
Saponaria ocymoides

Tunic flower
Petrorhagia saxifraga

Turtle head *Chelone obliqua*

Tussock bellflower
Campanula carpatica

Two-eyed violet *Viola ocellata*

Two-leaved scilla *Scilla bifolia*

Valerian *Valeriana supina*

Vernal gentian *Gentiana verna*

Vernal sandwort *Minuartia verna*

Virginian cowslip
Mertensia virginica

Variegated bugle
Ajuga reptans variegata

Vegetable sheep *Raoulia eximia*

Wall pellitory *Parietaria diffusa*
Parietaria judaica

Wallpepper *Sedum acre*
Sedum alba

Wall spleenwort
Asplenium ruta-muraria

White stonecrop *Sedum alba*

Water avens

Water avens	*Geum rivale*
Western cranesbill	*Geranium endressii*
Western dog violet	*Viola adunca*
Western round-leaved violet	*Viola orbiculata*
Western sweet white violet	*Viola macloskeyi*
White ball primrose	*Primula denticulata alba*
White baneberry	*Actea pachypoda*
White bells	*Platycodon grandiflorus*
White bloody cranesbill	*Geranium sanguineum album*
White burning bush	*Dictamnus albus*
White buttercup	*Ranunculus aconitifolius*
Whitecrop	*Sedum alba*
White false helleborine	*Veratrum album*
White musk mallow	*Malva moschata alba*
White pasque flower	*Pulsatilla alba*
	Pulsatilla vulgaris alba
White rock	*Arabis caucasica*
White sea lavender	*Armeria maritima alba*
White sea pink	*Armeria maritima alba*
White stonecrop	*Sedum album*
White storksbill	*Erodium chamaedryoides*
	Erodium reichardii
Wild candytuft	*Iberis amara*
Wild marjoram	*Origanum vulgare compactum*
Wild okra	*Viola palmata*
Wild pink	*Dianthus plumarius*
	Silene caroliniana
Wild strawberry	*Fragaria vesca*
Wild sweet william	*Phlox canadensis*
	Phlox divaricata
	Phlox maculata
Wild thyme	*Thymus articus coccineus*
	Thymus coccineus
	Thymus serpyllum

Willow gentian	*Gentiana asclepiadea*
Winter aconite	*Eranthis hyemalis*
Winter heliotrope	*Petasites fragrans*
Winter jasmine	*Jasminum nudiflorum*
Winter savory	*Satureja montana alba*
Witch's gloves	*Digitalis purpurea*
Wood anemone	*Anemone nemorosa*
Wood forget-me-not	*Myosotis sylvatica*
Woodruff	*Asperula nitida*
Wood sorrel	*Oxalis acetosella*
Wood violet	*Viola riviniana*
Woolly blue violet	*Viola sororia*
Yarrow	*Achillea serbica*
Yellow adonis	*Adonis vernalis*
Yellow asphodel	*Asphodeline lutea*
Yellow flag	*Iris pseudacorus*
Yellow flax	*Linum flavum compactum*
Yellow forget-me-not	*Myosotis discolor*
Yellow fumitory	*Corydalis lutea*
Yellow gentian	*Gentiana lutea*
Yellow gowan	*Ranunculus repens*
Yellow iris	*Iris orientalis*
Yellow milfoil	*Achillea tomentosa*
Yellow mountain cornflower	*Centaurea montana sulphurea*
Yellow mountain saxifrage	*Saxifraga aizoides*
Yellow prairie violet	*Viola nuttallii*
Yellow scullcap	*Scutellaria orientalis pinnatifida*
Yellow soapwort	*Saponaria lutea*
Yellow stonecrop	*Sedum acre*
Yellow whitlow grass	*Draba aizoides*
Yellow wood violet	*Viola biflora*
	Viola lobata
Yew	*Taxus baccata*

AQUATICS

This section applies to plants living usually in fresh water, either rooted in soil or free-floating, also to plants living in bogs, swamps, and around the edges of ponds and lakes.

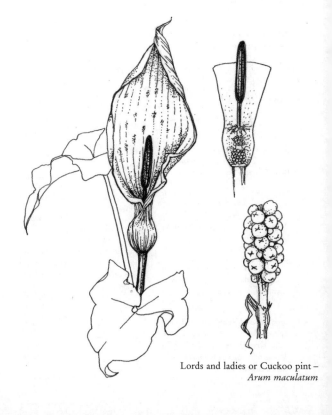

Lords and ladies or Cuckoo pint –
Arum maculatum

Amazon sword plant

Amazon sword plant
Echinodorus paniculatus
Echinodorus tenellus

Amazon water lily
Victoria amazonica
Victoria regia

Amazon water platter
Victoria amazonica
Victoria regia

American hornwort
Ceratophyllum demersum

American lotus *Nelumbo lutea*
Nelumbo pentapetala

American pondweed
Potamogeton epihydrus

American spatterdock
Nuphar advena

American swamp lily
Saururus cernuus

American water willow
Justicia americana

Australian water lily
Nymphaea gigantea

Autumnal water starwort
Callitriche hermaphroditum

Awl-leaf arrowhead
Sagittaria subulata

Awlwort *Subularia aquatica*

Baby tears *Bacopa monnieri*

Beaked tassel pondweed
Ruppia maritima

Biblical bulrush *Cyperus papyrus*

Blue Egyptian lotus
Nymphaea caerulea

Blue lotus
Nymphaea caerulea
Nymphaea stellata

Blue water lily
Nymphaea capensis

Blue water speedwell
Veronica anagallis-aquatica

Blunt-fruited water starwort
Callitriche obtusangula

Bog arum *Calla palustris*
Lysichiton americanum

Bog bean *Menyanthes trifoliata*

Bogmat *Wolffiella floridana*

Bog pondweed
Potamogeton polygonifolius

Branched bur-reed
Sparganium erectum

Brandy bottle *Nuphar luteum*

Brazilian waterweed
Anacharis densa
Elodea densa

Brook bean *Menyanthes trifoliata*

Bulrush *Cyperus papyrus*

Bulrush reedmace *Typha latifolia*

Bur-reed *Sparganium ramosum*

Canadian pondweed
Elodea canadensis

Canadian wild rice
Zizania aquatica

Cape asparagus
Aponogeton distachyus

Cape blue water lily
Nymphaea capensis

Cape pondweed
Aponogeton distachyus

Chinese water chestnut
Eleocharis dulcis

Common arrowhead
Sagittaria sagittifolia

Common boneset
Eupatorium perfoliatum

Common bur-reed
Sparganium ramosum

Common duckweed *Lemna minor*

Common eel grass
Zostera marina

Common grass wrack
Zostera marina

Common spatterdock
Nuphar advena

Common water crowfoot
Ranunculus aquatalis

Comman water dropwort
Oenanthe fistulosa

Common wolffia
Wolffia columbiana

Corkscrew rush
Juncus effusus spiralis

Creeping charlie
Lysimachia nummularia

Creeping jenny
Lysimachia nummularia

Crystalwort *Riccia fluitans*

Curled pondweed
Potamogeton crispus

Curly water thyme
Lagerosiphon major

Ditch moss
Anacharis canadensis
Elodea canadensis

Duck potato *Sagittaria latifolia*

Duckweed *Lemna minor*
Spirodela polyrhiza

Dwarf amazon sword plant
Echinodorus magdalenensis

Dwarf eel grass *Zostera noltii*

Dwarf grass wrack *Zostera noltii*

Dwarf papyrus *Cyperus isocladus*

East Indian lotus
Nelumbo nucifera
Nelumbo speciosa

Eel grass *Vallisneria spiralis*
Zostera angustifolia

Egyptian lotus
Nymphaea caerulea
Nymphaea lotus

Egyptian water lily
Nymphaea lotus

Marsh trefoil

Engelmann's quillwort	*Isoetes engelmannii*
European water clover	*Marsilea quadrifolia*
European white water lily	*Nymphaea alba*
	Nymphaea venusta
Fairy moss	*Azolla caroliniana*
Fanwort	*Cabomba caroliniana*
Fat duckweed	*Lemna gibba*
Fennel pondweed	*Potamogeton pectinatus*
Fen pondweed	*Potamogeton coloratus*
Fish grass	*Cabomba caroliniana*
Flag iris	*Iris pseudacorus*
Flat-stalked pondweed	*Potamogeton friesii*
Flexible naiad	*Najas flexilis*
Floating bur-reed	*Sparganium angustifolium*
Floating fern	*Ceratopteris pteridoides*
	Salvinia auriculata
Floating marsh-wort	*Apium inundatum*
Floating moss	*Salvinia rotundifolia*
Floating pondweed	*Potamogeton natans*
Floating water plantain	*Luronium natans*
Fool's watercress	*Apium nodiflorum*
Fountain moss	*Fontinalis antipyretica*
Fragrant water lily	*Castalia odorata*
	Nymphaea odorata
Frog-bit	*Hydrocharis morsus ranae*
Frog's lettuce	*Potamogeton densus*
Garden lysimachia	*Lysimachia punctata*
	Lysimachia vulgaris
Giant arrowhead	*Sagittaria montevidensis*
Golden water dock	*Rumex maritimus*
Gooseneck lysimachia	*Lysimachia clethroides*
Gorgon	*Euryale ferox*
Grass-wrack pondweed	*Potamogeton compressus*
Grassy pondweed	*Potamogeton obtusifolius*
Great(er) duckweed	*Spirodela polyrhiza*
Greater naiad	*Najas marina*
Greater water thyme	*Elodea callitrichoides*
Great water dock	*Rumex hydrolapathan*
Hair grass	*Eleocharis acicularis*
Hair-like pondweed	*Potamogeton trichoides*
Horned pondweed	*Zannichellia palustris*
Hornwort	*Ceratophyllum demersum*
Indian blue lotus	*Nymphaea stellata*
Indian red water lily	*Nymphaea rubra*
Italian-type eel grass	*Vallisneria spiralis*
Ivy duckweed	*Lemna trisulca*
Japanese arrowhead	*Sagittaria sagittifolia leucopetala*
Japanese mat rush	*Juncus effusus*
Jesuit's nut	*Trapa natans*
Joe-pye weed	*Eupatorium maculatum*
Kidney mud plantain	*Heteranthera reniformis*
Kingcup	*Caltha palustris*
Lace leaf	*Aponogeton fenestralis*
	Aponogeton madagascariensis
Latticeleaf	*Aponogeton fenestralis*
	Aponogeton madagascariensis
Least bulrush	*Typhe minima*
Least spike rush	*Eleocharis acicularis*
Lesser bulrush	*Typha angustifolia*
Lesser duckweed	*Lemna miniscula*
	Lemna minor
Lesser water plantain	*Baldellia ranunculoides*
Loddon pondweed	*Potamogeton nodosus*
Lotus	*Nymphaea lotus*
Madagascar lace plant	*Aponogeton fenestralis*
	Aponogeton madagascariensis
Mad-dog weed	*Alisma plantago-aquatica*
Magnolia water lily	*Nymphaea tuberosa*
Malayan sword	*Aglaonema simplex*
Marsh clover	*Menyanthes trifoliata*
Marsh dock	*Rumex palustris*
Marsh forget-me-not	*Myosotis secunda*
Marsh marigold	*Caltha palustris*
Marsh St John's wort	*Hypericum elodes*
Marsh trefoil	*Menyanthes trifoliata*

Ma-tai	*Eleocharis dulcis*
Miniature papyrus	
	Cyperus isocladus
Molly blobs	*Caltha palustris*
Moneywort	
	Lysimachia nummularia
Mosquito fern	*Azolla caroliniana*
Mosquito plant	*Azolla caroliniana*
Mud-midget	*Wolffiella floridana*
Myriad leaf	
	Myriophyllum verticillatum
Narrow-leaved eel grass	
	Zostera angustifolia
Narrow-leaved grass wrack	
	Zostera angustifolia
Nile blue lotus	
	Nymphaea stellata
Nodding avens	*Geum rivale*
Nodding bur-marigold	
	Bidens cernua
Nut grass	*Cyperus esculentus*
Nut sedge	*Cyperus esculentus*
Nuttall's water thyme	
	Elodea nuttallii
Old world arrowhead	
	Sagittaria sagittifolia
Opposite-leaved pondweed	
	Groenlandia densa
Paper plant	*Cyperus papyrus*
Papyrus	*Cyperus papyrus*
Parrot's feather	
	Myriophyllum aquaticum
Parsley water dropwort	
	Oenanthe lachenalis
Peacock hyacinth	
	Eichhornia azurea
Perfoliate pondweed	
	Potamogeton perfoliatus
Pickerel weed	*Pontederia cordata*
Pipewort	*Eriocaulon aquaticum*
Platterdock	*Nymphaea alba*
	Nymphaea venusta
Pond lily	*Castalia odorata*
	Nymphaea odorata
Pond nuts	*Nelumbo lutea*
	Nelumbo pentapetala
Prickly water lily	*Euryale ferox*
Purple loosestrife	
	Lythrum salicaria
Pygmy chainsword plant	
	Echinodorus intermedius
	Echinodorus martii
Pygmy water lily	
	Nymphaea pygmaea
	Nymphaea tetragona
Queen Victoria water lily	
	Victoria amazonica
	Victoria regia
Rattlebox	
	Ludwigia alternifolia

Red pondweed	
	Potamogeton alpinus
Red water milfoil	
	Myriophyllum hippuroides
Rigid hornwort	
	Ceratophyllum demersum
River crowfoot	
	Ranunculus fluitans
River water crowfoot	
	Ranunculus fluitans
River water dropwort	
	Oenanthe fluviatilis
Royal water lily	
	Victoria amazonica
	Victoria regia
Rushy pondweed	
	Potamogeton alpinus
Sacred lotus	*Nelumbo nucifera*
	Nelumbo speciosa
Salt rush	*Juncus lesuerii*
Santa Cruz water lily	
	Victoria cruziana
	Victoria trickeri
Santa Cruz water platter	
	Victoria cruziana
	Victoria trickeri
Seedbox	*Ludwigia alternifolia*
Shellflower	*Pistia stratiotes*
Shining pondweed	
	Potamogeton lucens
Skunk cabbage	
	Lysichiton americanum
Slender-leaved pondweed	
	Potamogeton filiformis
Slender spike rush	
	Eleocharis acicularis
Small bur-reed	
	Sparganium minimum
Small pondweed	
	Potamogeton pusillus
Smartweed	
	Polygonium hydropiper
Smokeweed	
	Eupatorium maculatum
Soft hornwort	
	Ceratophyllum submersum
Soft rush	*Juncus effusus*
Spatterdock	*Nuphar advena*
Spider tassel pondweed	
	Ruppia cirrhosa
Spiked lythrum	*Lythrum salicaria*
Spiked water milfoil	
	Myriophyllum spicatum
Spiny-spored quillwort	
	Isoetes echinospora
Spiral rush	*Juncus effusus spiralis*
Spring moss	
	Fontinalis antipyretica
Star duckweed	*Lemna trisulca*
Swamp lily	*Saururus cernuus*
Swamp potato	
	Sagittaria sagittifolia

Swan potato	
	Sagittaria sagittifolia
Sweet sedge	*Acorus calamus*
Sweet water lily	
	Nymphaea odorata
Tape grass	*Vallisneria spiralis*
	Zostera angustifolia
Texas mud-baby	
	Echinodorus cordifolius
	Echinodorus radicans
Thoroughwort	
	Eupatorium perfoliatum
Triangular water fern	
	Ceratopteris richardii
Tuberous water lily	
	Nymphaea tuberosa
Tufted lysimachia	
	Lysimachia thyrsiflora
Umbrella palm	
	Cyperus alternifolius
Umbrella plant	
	Cyperus alternifolius
Umbrella sedge	
	Cyperus alternifolius
Unbranched bur reed	
	Sparganium emerson
Various-leaved pondweed	
	Potamogeton gramineus
Victoria water lily	
	Victoria amazonica
	Victoria regia
Wapato	*Sagittaria cuneata*
	Sagittaria latifolia
Washington grass	
	Cabomba caroliniana
Water aloe	*Stratiotes aloides*
Water archer	
	Sagittaria sagittifolia
Water arum	*Calla palustris*
Water avens	*Geum rivale*
Water balsam	
	Hydrocera angustifolia
Water blinks	*Montia fontana*
Water blobs	*Caltha palustris*
Water buttercup	
	Ranunculus aquatalis
Water celery	
	Vallisneria americana
Water chestnut	*Trapa natans*
Water chickweed	
	Myosotis aquaticum
Water chinquapin	
	Nelumbo lutea
	Nelumbo pentapetala
Water convolvulus	
	Ipomoea aquatica
Water cowslip	*Caltha palustris*
Water crowfoot	
	Ranunculus aquatalis
Water dock	
	Rumex hydrolapathan
Water dragon	*Saururus cernuus*

Water dropwort	
	Oenanthe fistulosa
Water feather	
	Myriophyllum aquaticum
Water fern	*Azolla caroliniana*
	Ceratopteris thalictroides
Water flag	*Iris pseudacorus*
Water flaxseed	
	Spirodela polyrhiza
Water forget-me-not	
	Myosotis scorpioides
Water hawthorn	
	Aponogeton distachyus
Water hemlock	*Cicuta virosa*
Water hyacinth	
	Eichhornia crassipes
Water lettuce	*Pistia stratiotes*
Water lobelia	*Lobelia dortmanna*
Water lovage	*Oenanthe fistulosa*
Water maize	*Victoria amazonica*
	Victoria regia
Water mint	*Mentha aquatica*
Water moss	
	Fontinalis antipyretica
Water oats	*Zizania aquatica*
Water pepper	
	Polygonium hydropiper
Water plantain	
	Alisma plantago-aquatica
Water poppy	
	Hydrocleys nymphoides
Water purslane	*Isnardia palustris*
	Ludwigia palustris
Water shamrock	
	Menyanthes trifoliata
Water shield	*Brasenia schreberi*
Water soldier	*Stratiodes aloides*
Water speedwell	
	Veronica anagallis
	Veronica anagallis-aquatica
Water sprite	
	Ceratopteris thalictroides
Water star grass	
	Heteranthera dubia
Water starwort	
	Callitriche stagnalis
Water thyme	
	Anarchais canadensis
	Elodea canadensis
Water trumpet	
	Cryptocoryne affinis
Water violet	*Hottonia palustris*
Waterweed	
	Anarcharis canadensis
	Elodea canadensis
Water willow	*Justicia americana*
Water wistaria	
	Hygrophila difformis
Waterwort	*Elatine hexandra*
Water yam	
	Aponogeton fenestralis
	Aponogeton madagascariensis

Western milfoil

Western milfoil
Myriophyllum hippuroides
White Egyptian lotus
Nymphaea lotus
White water lily   *Castalia odorata*
Nymphaea alba
Nymphaea odorata
Whorled water milfoil
Myriophyllum verticillatum
Wild celery
Vallisneria americana
Wild jonquil   *Narcissus jonquilla*
Wild rice   *Zizania aquatica*
Willow moss
Fontinalis antipyretica
Wolffia   *Wolffia columbiana*

Wonkapin   *Nelumbo lutea*
Nelumbo pentapetala
Yanquapin   *Nelumbo lutea*
Nelumbo pentapetala
Yellow flag iris   *Iris pseudacorus*
Yellow nelumbo   *Nelumbo lutea*
Nelumbo pentapetala
Yellow nut grass
Cyperus esculentus
Yellow nut sedge
Cyperus esculentus
Yellow water lily   *Castalia flava*
Nuphar luteum
Nymphaea flava
Nymphaea mexicana

BULBS

Horticulturally the term 'bulb' includes bulbs, corms, tubers, and rhizomes, but here a few stoloniferous subjects have been included (some lilies, for instance) where confusion exists in the minds of some amateur gardeners. Orchids are listed separately elsewhere in the book.

Sieber's crocus –
Crocus sieberi

Achira

Achira	Canna edulis
Acidanthera	Gladiolus callianthus
Adam-and-Eve	Arum maculatum
Adder's tongue	
	Erythronium americanum
Adobe lily	Fritillaria pluriflora
African blood lily	
	Haemanthus multiflorus
African corn lily	Ixia maculata
	Ixia viridiflora
African lily	Agapanthus africanus
	Agapanthus umbellatus
African wonder flower	
	Ornithogalum thyrsoides
Alligator lily	
	Hymenocallis palmeri
Alpine lily	Lilium parvum
Alpine squill	Scilla bifolia
Alpine violet	
	Cyclamen hederifolium
Amazon lily	Eucharis amazonica
	Eucharis grandiflora
Amberbell	
	Erythronium americanum
American ornamental onion	
	Allium cernuum
American swamp lily	
	Saururus cernuus
American trout lily	
	Erythronium revolutum
American turk's cap lily	
	Lilium superbum
Angel's fishing-rod	
	Dierama pendulum
	Sparaxis pendula
Angel's tears	Narcissus triandrus
Arum lily	
	Zantedeschia aethiopica
	Zantedeschia africana
Asiatic poison bulb	
	Crinum asiaticum
Atamasco lily	
	Zephyranthes atamasco
Australian giant lily	
	Doryanthes excelsa
Autumn crocus	
	Colchicum autumnale
Autumn daffodil	
	Sternbergia lutea
Autumn snowdrop	
	Galanthus reginae-olgae
Autumn squill	Scilla autumnalis
Avalanche lily	
	Erythronium giganteum
	Erythronium grandiflorum
	Erythronium montanum
	Erythronium obtusatum
Aztec lily	Sprekelia formosissima
Baboon flower	
	Babiana rubrocyanea
Baby cyclamen	
	Cyclamen hederifolium

Bachelor's buttons	
	Ranunculus acris
Barbados lily	Hippeastrum edule
	Hippeastrum equestre
Basket flower	
	Hymenocallis × festalis
	Hymenocallis narcissiflora
Bath asparagus	
	Ornithogalum pyrenaicum
Bear's garlic	Allium ursinum
Beavertail grass	
	Calochortus coeruleus
Bedding dahlia	Dahlia merckii
Beefsteak begonia	
	Begonia × erythrophylla
Belladonna lily	
	Amaryllis belladonna
Bell-flowered squill	
	Endymion hispanicus
Bell lily	Lilium grayi
Bell tree dahlia	Dahlia imperialis
Berg lily	Galtonia candicans
Bermuda buttercup	Oxalis cernua
	Oxalis pes-caprae
Bermuda lily	Lilium longiflorum
Black arum	Dracunculus vulgaris
Blackberry lily	
	Belamcanda chinensis
Black calla	Arum palaestinum
	Arum pictum
Black fritillary	
	Fritillaria camschatensis
	Fritillaria camtschatensis
Black lily	
	Fritillaria camschatensis
	Fritillaria camtschatensis
Black sarana	
	Fritillaria camschatcensis
	Fritillaria camtschatcensis
Black-throated calla lily	
	Zantedeschia albomaculata
	Zantedeschia melanoleuca
Blazing star	Liatris aspera
Blonde lilian	
	Erythronium albidum
Blood lily	
	Haemanthus multiflorus
	Haemanthus natalensis
	Scadoxus multiflorus
Bloody butcher	
	Trillium recurvatum
Blotched panther lily	
	Nomocharis pardanthina
Blue agapanthus	
	Agapanthus africanus
	Agapanthus umbellatus
Blue-and-red baboon root	
	Babiana rubrocyanea
Blue anemone	Anemone appenina
Blue fall iris	Iris graeberiana
Blue flag	Iris versicolor
	Iris virginica

Common hyacinth

Blue lily   *Agapanthus africanus*
Blue onion   *Allium cyaneum*
Blue star   *Chamaescilla corymbosa*
Brazilian edelweiss
    Sinningia leucotricha
Brazilian gloxinia
    Sinningia speciosa
Brown beth   *Trillium erectum*
    Trillium flavum
Buckrams   *Allium ursinum*
Bulbous buttercup
    Ranunculus bulbosus
Bulbous crowfoot
    Ranunculus bulbosus
Bunch-flowered narcissus
    Narcissus tazetta
Bush lily   *Clivia mineata*
Butterfly ginger lily
    Hedychium coronarium
Butterfly iris   *Iris spuria*
    Iris ochroleuca
Butterfly lily
    Hedychium coronarium
Californian firecracker
    Brimeura ida-maia
    Dichelostemma ida-maia
Calla lily   *Zantedeschia aethiopica*
    Zantedeschia africana
Camass   *Camassia quamash*
Cambridge grape hyacinth
    Muscari tubergenianum
Camosh   *Camassia quamash*
Campernelle jonquil
    Narcissus calathinus
    Narcissus × odorus
Canada lily   *Lilium canadense*
Candelabra dahlia
    Dahlia imperialis
Candelabra flower
    Brunsvigia josephinae
Candlestick lily
    Lilium × hollandicum
    Lilium × umbellatum
Canterbury bells
    Gloxinia perennis
Cape belladonna
    Amaryllis belladonna
Cape cowslip   *Lachenalia aloides*
    Lachenalia bulbifera
    Lachenalia contaminata
    Lachenalia glaucina
    Lachenalia mutabilis
    Lachenalia ribida
    Lachenalia tricolor
Cape hyacinth
    Amphisiphon stylosa
Cape lily   *Crinum × powellii*
Cape pondweed
    Aponogeton distachyos
Cardinal flower
    Sinningia cardinalis
Carolina lily   *Lilium michauxii*

Catherine-wheel
    Haemanthus katharinae
Cat's ear   *Calochortus coeruleus*
Caucasian lily
    Lilium monadelphum
Celandine crocus
    Crocus korolkowii
Chamise lily   *Lilium rubescens*
Chaparral lily   *Lilium rubescens*
Checkered daffodil
    Fritillaria meleagris
Checkered lily
    Fritillaria meleagris
Checker lily   *Fritillaria lanceolata*
Chilean crocus
    Tecophilaea cyanocrocus
Chincherinchee
    Ornithogalum thyrsoides
Chinese chives   *Allium tuberosum*
Chinese lantern
    Narcissus poeticus physaloides
Chinese lantern lily
    Sandersonia aurantiaca
Chinese ornamental onion
    Allium amabile
Chinese sacred lily
    Narcissus canaliculatus
    Narcissus tazetta
Chinese squill   *Scilla chinensis*
    Scilla scilloides
Chinese white lily
    Lilium leucanthum
    Lilium formosum
Chive   *Allium schoenoprasum*
Christmas bells
    Sandersonia aurantiaca
Ciboule   *Allium fistulosum*
Cinderella slippers
    Sinningia regina
Cinnamon jasmine
    Hedychium coronarium
Cipollino   *Muscari comosum*
Cive   *Allium schoenoprasum*
Clanwilliam bluebell
    Ixia incarnata
Climbing lily   *Littonia modesta*
Cloth-of-gold   *Crocus angustifolius*
    Crocus susianus
Coastal lily   *Lilium maritimum*
Coast trillium   *Trillium ovatum*
Cobra lily   *Arisaema speciosum*
Columbia lily
    Lilium columbianum
Commom camass
    Camassia quamash
Common garden canna
    Canna × generalis
Common grape hyacinth
    Muscari botryoides
Common hyacinth
    Hyacinthus orientalis

Common snowdrop

Common snowdrop	*Galanthus nivalis*
Copper iris	*Iris fulva*
Coral lily	*Lilium pumilum*
	Lilium tenuifolium
Corn flag	*Gladiolus segetum*
Corn lily	*Ixia maculata*
	Ixia viridiflora
Crested iris	*Iris cristata*
Crimson flag	*Schizostylis coccinea*
Crowfoot	*Ranunculus asiaticus*
Crow garlic	*Allium vineale*
Crown imperial fritillary	*Fritillaria imperialis*
Crusaders' spears	*Urginea maritima*
Cuban lily	*Scilla peruviana*
Cuckoo pint	*Arum maculatum*
Culverkeys	*Hyacinthoides non-scriptus*
Daffodil	*Narcissus pseudonarcissus*
Daffodil garlic	*Allium neapolitanum*
Dasheen	*Colocasia esculenta*
Davis begonia	*Begonia davisii*
De caen anemone	*Anemone coronaria*
Desert candle	*Eremurus robustus*
Desert mariposa	*Calochortus kennedyi*
Dog's tooth violet	*Erythronium dens-canis*
Dove's dung	*Ornithogalum umbellatum*
Dragon arum	*Dracunculus vulgaris*
Dragonroot	*Arisaema dracontium*
	Arisaema triphyllum
Drakensberg star	*Rhodohypoxis baurii*
Drooping star-of-Bethlehem	*Ornithogalum nutans*
Dutch crocus	*Crocus vernus*
Dutch hyacinth	*Hyacinthus orientalis*
Dutch yellow crocus	*Crocus flavus*
Dwarf crested iris	*Iris cristata*
Dwarf iris	*Iris verna*
Dwarf jonquil	*Narcissus assoanus*
	Narcissus requienii
Dwarf squill	*Scilla monophyllos*
Dwarf white trillium	*Trillium nivale*
Easter lily	*Cardiocrinum giganteum*
	Lilium longiflorum
	Zephyranthes atamasco
Eastern camass	*Camassia scilloides*

Edible canna	*Canna edulis*
Elephant lily	*Crinum × powellii*
Elephant's ear begonia	*Begonia albo-coccinea*
English bluebell	*Endymion non-scriptus*
	Endymion nutans
	Hyacinthoides non-scriptus
	Hyacinthoides nutans
English iris	*Iris anglica*
	Iris latifolia
	Iris xiphioides
Eucharist lily	*Eucharis grandiflora*
Eureka lily	*Lilium occidentale*
European wood anemone	*Anemone nemorosa*
European wood sorrel	*Oxalis acetosella*
Ever-ready onion	*Allium cepa*
Eyelash begonia	*Begonia boweri*
Fair maids of February	*Galanthus nivalis*
Fairy-carpet begonia	*Begonia versicolor*
Fairy lantern	*Calochortus albus*
	Calochortus amoenus
Fairy lily	*Zephyranthes candida*
Falklands scurvy grass	*Oxalis enneaphylla*
Fall crocus	*Colchicum autumnale*
Falling stars	*Crocosmia × crocosmiiflora*
False sea onion	*Ornithogalum caudatum*
Fancy-leaved caladium	*Caladium × hortulanum*
Fawn lily	*Erythronium californicum*
Feather hyacinth	*Muscari comosum*
Few-flowered leek	*Allium paradoxum*
Field garlic	*Allium oleraceum*
	Allium vineale
Fireball lily	*Scadoxus multiflorus*
Fire-king begonia	*Begonia goegoensis*
Fire lily	*Clivia mineata*
	Cyrtanthus mackennii
	Lilium bulbiferum
Flag	*Iris × germanica*
Flame lily	*Gloriosa rothschildiana*
	Gloriosa superba
Flames	*Homoglossum merianella*
Fleur-de-lis	*Iris × germanica*
Florist's allium	*Allium neapolitanum*

Gray's lily

Florist's calla lily
Zantedeschia aethiopica
Zantedeschia africana

Florist's cyclamen
Cyclamen persicum

Florist's gloxinia
Sinningia speciosa

Flowering onion
Allium neapolitanum

Flower of the western wind
Zephyranthes candida

Flower of the wind
Zephyranthes candida

Forest lily Veltheimia brachteata
Veltheimia viridiflora

Fox's grape Fritillaria uva-vulpis

Foxtail lily Eremurus robustus

Fragrant-flowered garlic
Allium ramosum

French asparagus
Ornithogalum pyrenaicum

Fumewort Corydalis bulbosa

Galtonia Galtonia candicans

Garden calla lily
Zantedeschia aethiopica
Zantedeschia africana

Garden gladiolus
Gladiolus × hortulanus

Garden hyacinth
Hyacinthus orientalis

Garland flower
Hedychium coronarium

Garlic Allium sativum

Garlic chive Allium tuberosum

Gayfeather Liatris aspera

George lily Cyrtanthus purpureus
Vallota speciosa

German garlic Allium senescens

German onion
Ornithogalum caudatum

Giant bellflower
Ostrowskia magnifica

Giant bluebell
Hyacinthoides hispanica

Giant chincherinchee
Ornithogalum saundersiae

Giant garlic
Allium scorodoprasum

Giant Himalayan lily
Cardiocrinum giganteum

Giant lily
Cardiocrinum giganteum

Giant ornamental onion
Allium giganteum

Giant pineapple flower
Eucomis pallidiflora

Giant snowdrop
Galanthus elwesii

Giant snowflake
Leucojum aestivum

Giant spider plant Cleome spinosa

Giant stove brush
Haemanthus magnificus

Giant summer hyacinth
Galtonia candicans

Ginger lily
Hedychium coronarium

Gingerwort
Hedychium gardneranum

Gipsy onion Allium ursinum

Gladwin iris Iris foetidissima

Globe lily Calochortus albus

Gloriosa lily
Gloriosa rothschildiana
Gloriosa superba

Glory lily Gloriosa rothschildiana
Gloriosa superba

Glory-of-the-snow
Chionodoxa gigantea
Leucocoryne ixioides

Glory-of-the-sun
Leucocoryne ixioides
Leucocoryne odorata

Gloxinia Sinningia speciosa

Goddess mariposa
Calochortus vestae

Gold-banded lily Lilium auratum

Golden African lily
Amaryllis aurea
Lycoris africana

Golden-banded lily
Lilium auratum

Golden-bowl mariposa
Calochortus concolor

Golden calla lily
Zantedeschia elliottiana

Golden fairy lantern
Calochortus amabilis

Golden globe tulip
Calochortus amabilis

Golden hurricane lily
Amaryllis aurea
Lycoris africana

Golden garlic Allium moly

Golden lily Lycoris aurea

Golden-rayed lily Lilium auratum

Golden spider lily Amaryllis aurea
Lycoris africana
Lycoris aurea

Good-luck leaf Oxalis deppei

Good-luck plant Oxalis deppei

Grape hyacinth
Muscari moschatum
Muscari neglectum
Muscari racemosum

Grape-leaf begonia Begonia dregei
Begonia parvifolia
Begonia × speculata

Grapevine begonia
Begonia weltoniensis

Grassy bell Dierama pendulum
Sparaxis pendula

Gray's lily Lilium grayi

COMMON NAMES

Greek windflower
    Anemone blanda

Green-banded mariposa
    Calochortus macrocarpus

Green dragon
    Arisaema dracontium

Green ixia   *Ixia viridiflora*

Guernsey lily   *Nerine bowdenii*
    Nerine sarniensis

Guinea-hen tulip
    Fritillaria meleagris

Hardy begonia   *Begonia discolor*
    Begonia grandis

Harebell   *Endymion non-scriptus*

Harlequin flower   *Sparaxis elegans*
    Sparaxis grandiflora
    Sparaxis tricolor
    Streptanthera elegans

Hartshorn plant
    Anemone nuttalliana

Harvest brodiaea
    Brodiaea coronaria
    Brodiaea elegans

Heart-of-Jesus   *Caladium bicolor*

Helmet flower
    Sinningia cardinalis

Herb lily
    Alstroemeria haemantha

Hog's garlic   *Allium ursinum*

Hollyhock begonia
    Begonia gracilis
    Begonia martiana

Hoop-petticoat daffodil
    Narcissus bulbocodium

Horned tulip   *Tulipa acuminata*

Hot-water plant
    Achimenes longiflora

Humbold lily   *Lilium humboldtii*

Hurricane lily   *Rhodophiala bifida*

Hyacinth   *Hyacinthus orientalis*

Hyacinth-of-Peru   *Scilla peruviana*

Hyacinth squill
    Scilla hyacinthoides

Hybrid tuberous begonia
    Begonia × tuberhybrida

Ifafa lily   *Cyrtanthus mackennii*

Indian elephant flower
    Crinum × powellii

Indian pink   *Spigelia marilandica*

Indian shot   *Canna indica*

Indian turnip   *Arisaema triphyllum*

Indigo squill   *Camassia scilloides*

Iris-flowered crocus
    Crocus byzantinus
    Crocus iridiflorus

Irish shamrock   *Oxalis acetosella*

Iron-cross begonia
    Begonia masoniana

Italian arum   *Arum italicum*

Italian squill   *Endymion italicus*

Jack-in-the-pulpit
    Arisaema triphyllum

Jacobean lily
    Sprekelia formosissima

Japanese anemone
    Anemone hupehensis

Japanese bunching onion
    Allium fistulosum

Japanese iris   *Iris kaempferi*

Japanese jacinth   *Scilla chinensis*
    Scilla scilloides

Japanese lily
    Cardiocrinum cordatum
    Lilium japonicum
    Lilium krameri
    Lilium lancifolium
    Lilium makinoi
    Lilium speciosum

Japanese turk's cap lily
    Lilium hansonii

Jersey lily   *Amaryllis belladonna*

Jonquil   *Narcissus jonquilla*

Josephine's lily
    Brunsvigia josephinae

Kaffir lily   *Schizostylis coccinea*

Kahili ginger lily
    Hedychium gardneranum

Kahli ginger
    Hedychium gardneranum

Kamchatka lily
    Fritillaria camschatcensis
    Fritillaria camtschatcensis

Keeled garlic   *Allium carinatum*

Kerry lily   *Simethis planifolia*

Kidney begonia
    Begonia × erythrophylla

King begonia   *Begonia rex*

Kynassa lily   *Cyrtanthus obliquus*

Lacework lily
    Amaryllis reticulata
    Hippeastrum reticulatum

Lady tulip   *Tulipa clusiana*

Lady's leek   *Allium cernuum*

Lamance iris   *Iris brevicaulis*

Lavender globe lily
    Allium tanguticum

Lebanon squill
    Puschkinia libanotica
    Puschkinia scilloides

Lemon lily   *Lilium parryi*

Lent lily
    Narcissus pseudonarcissus

Leopard lily   *Lilium carolinianum*
    Lilium catesbaei
    Lilium pardalinum

Lesser celandine
    Ranunculus ficaria

Lesser turk's cap lily
    Lilium pomponium

Lettuce-leaf begonia
    Begonia × crestabruchii

Orange pearl

Lilac mariposa
    Calochortus splendens
Lily leek   *Allium moly*
Lily-of-the-Amazon
    Eucharis grandiflora
Lily-of-the-field *Sternbergia lutea*
Lily-of-the-Incas
    Alstroemeria aurantiaca
Lily-of-the-Nile
    Agapanthus africanus
    Agapanthus umbellatus
Lily-of-the-palace *Amaryllis aulica*
    Hippeastrum aulicum
    Hippeastrum robustum
Lily-of-the-valley
    Convallaria majalis
Lily-pad begonia
    Begonia nelumbiifolia
Lily-royal *Lilium superbum*
Lion's beard *Anemone nuttalliana*
Lion's paw
  Alstroemeria leontochir ovallei
Little turk's cap lily
    Lilium pomponium
Lizard flower
    Sauromatum guttatum
Loddon lily *Leucojum aestivum*
Long-headed anemone
    Anemone cylindrica
Lords and ladies
    Arum maculatum
Lucky clover *Oxalis deppei*
Madonna lily *Eucharis grandiflora*
    Lilium candidum
Magic lily *Amaryllis hallii*
    Lycoris squamigera
Maid of the mist
    Gladiolus primulinus
Maltese cross
    Sprekelia formosissima
Manipur lily *Lilium mackliniae*
Maple-leaf begonia *Begonia dregei*
    Begonia parvifolia
    Begonia weltoniensis
Marble martagon lily
    Lilium duchartrei
March lily *Amaryllis belladonna*
Mariposa lily
    Calochortus nuttallii
Martagon lily *Lilium martagon*
Maryland pink root
    Spigelia marilandica
Meadow hyacinth
    Camassia scilloides
Meadow leek *Allium canadense*
Meadow lily *Lilium canadense*
Meadow saffron
    Colchicum × agrippinum
    Colchicum autumnale
Mediterranean lily
    Pancratium maritimum

Meshed lily *Amaryllis reticulata*
    Hippeastrum reticulatum
Mexican lily *Hippeastrum reginae*
Mexican shell flower
    Tigridia pavonia
Mexican star *Milla biflora*
Michigan lily *Lilium michiganense*
Miniature begonia *Begonia boweri*
Miniature pond-lily begonia
    Begonia hydrocotylifolia
Minor turk's cap lily
    Lilium pomponium
Mission bells *Fritillaria biflora*
Montbretia
    Crocosmia × crocosmiiflora
Morocco iris *Iris tingitana*
Mountain lily *Lilium auratum*
Mountain spiderwort
    Lloydia serotina
Mourning iris *Iris basaltica*
    Iris susiana
Mouse garlic *Allium angulosum*
Mouse plant
    Arisarum proboscideum
Multiplier onion *Allium cepa*
Musk hyacinth *Muscari moschatum*
    Muscari muscarini
    Muscari racemosum
Mysteria *Colchicum autumnale*
Naked ladies
    Colchicum autumnale
Nap-at-noon
    Ornithogalum umbellatum
Nankeen lily *Lilium excelsum*
    Lilium × testaceum
Narrow-leaved fritillary
    Fritillaria lanceolata
Nasturtium-leaf begonia
    Begonia francisii
Natal iris *Curtonus paniculatus*
Natal paintbrush
    Haemanthus natalensis
Netted iris *Iris reticulata*
Nodding nerine *Nerine undulata*
Nodding onion *Allium cernuum*
Nodding squill *Scilla bifolia*
Nodding star-of-Bethlehem
    Ornithogalum nutans
Nodding trillium
    Trillium cernuum
North African narcissus
    Narcissus watieri
Nutmeg hyacinth
    Muscari moschatum
    Muscari racemosum
Orange-bell lily *Lilium grayi*
Orange-cup lily
    Lilium philadelphicum
Orange lily *Lilium bulbiferum*
Orange pearl
    Polianthes geminiflora

Orange tuberose
Polianthes geminiflora
Orange turk's cap lily
Lilium davidii
Orchid amaryllis
Sprekelia formosissima
Orchid-flowered canna
Canna × orchiodes
Orchid iris *Iris orchidoides*
Oregon lily *Lilium columbianum*
Oriental garlic *Allium tuberosum*
Orris *Iris odoratissima*
Iris pallida
Outdoor freesia *Freesia hybrida*
Oxford grape hyacinth
Muscari tubergenianum
Paint brush
Haemanthus multiflorus
Haemanthus natalensis
Painted-leaf begonia *Begonia rex*
Painted trillium
Trillium undulatum
Palestine iris *Iris basaltica*
Iris susiana
Panther lily *Lilium pardalinum*
Paperwhite narcissus
Narcissus papyraceus
Paradise lily *Paradisea liliastrum*
Pasque flower
Anemone nuttalliana
Anemone patens
Anemone pulsatilla
Pulsatilla patens
Peacock tiger flower
Tigridia pavonia
Pendant ornamental onion
Allium sikkimense
Pendulous begonia
Begonia × tuberhybrida
Pennywort begonia
Begonia hydrocotylifolia
Perfumed fairy lily
Chlidanthus fragrans
Persian buttercup
Ranunculus asiaticus
Persian iris *Iris persica*
Persian ranunculus
Ranunculus asiaticus
Persian sun's eye
Tulipa occulus-solis
Persian violet *Cyclamen persicum*
Peruvian daffodil
Chlidanthus fragrans
Hymenocallis amancaes
Hymenocallis narcissiflora
Peruvian jacinth *Scilla peruviana*
Peruvian lily
Alstroemeria aurantiaca
Peruvian mountain daffodil
Pyrolirion tubiflorum
Peruvian redbird
Gloxinia sylvatica

Petticoat daffodil
Narcissus bulbocodium
Pheasant's eye narcissus
Narcissus poeticus
Pig lily *Zantedeschia aethiopica*
Zantedeschia africana
Pilewort *Ranunculus ficaria*
Pineapple flower
Eucomis autumnalis
Eucomis bicolor
Eucomis comosa
Eucomis pallidiflora
Eucomis undulata
Eucomis zambesiaca
Pine lily *Lilium carolinianum*
Lilium catesbaei
Pink agapanthus
Tulbaghia simmleri
Pink arum lily
Zantedeschia rehmannii
Pink calla lily *Richardia rehmannii*
Zantedeschia rehmannii
Pink candelabra
Brunsvigia radulosa
Pink fritillary *Fritillaria pluriflora*
Pink star tulip
Calochortus uniflorus
Poetaz narcissus
Narcissus × medioluteus
Poet's narcissus *Narcissus poeticus*
Poison flag *Iris versicolor*
Polyanthus narcissus
Narcissus canaliculatus
Narcissus tazetta
Pond-lily begonia
Begonia nelumbiifolia
Poppy anemone
Anemone coronaria
Portuguese iris *Iris xiphium*
Portuguese paradise lily
Paradisea lusitanica
Potato onion *Allium cepa*
Pot-of-gold lily *Lilium iridollae*
Prairie onion *Allium stellatum*
Prairie smoke
Anemone nuttalliana
Prickly blazing star *Liatris aspera*
Primrose peerless narcissus
Narcissus × medioluteus
Prussian asparagus
Ornithogalum pyrenaicum
Purple globe tulip
Calochortus amoenus
Purple onion *Allium cyaneum*
Purple toadshade
Trillium recurvatum
Purple trillium *Trillium erectum*
Trillium flavum
Trillium recurvatum
Purple wake-robin
Trillium recurvatum

Pussy ears   Calochortus maweanus
            Calochortus tolmiei
Pyrenean fritillary
            Fritillaria pyrenaica
Quamash   Camassia quamash
Queen lily
            Amaryllis phaedranassa
Queensland arrowroot
            Canna edulis
Rain lily   Zephyranthes candida
Rakkyo   Allium bakeri
            Allium chinense
Ramp   Allium tricoccum
Ramsons   Allium ursinum
Ramsons wood garlic
            Allium ursinum
Rattlesnake plantain
            Goodyera pubescens
Red calla lily   Richardia rehmannii
            Zantedeschia rehmannii
Red ginger lily
            Hedychium coccineum
Red hot poker
            Kniphofia triangularis
Red iris   Iris fulva
Red-skinned onion
            Allium haematochiton
Red spider lily   Amaryllis radiata
            Lycoris radiata
Red squill   Urginea maritima
Redwood lily   Lilium rubescens
Redwood sorrel   Oxalis oregana
Regal lily   Lilium regale
Resurrection lily   Amaryllis hallii
            Lycoris squamigera
Rhodesian gladiolus
            Gladiolus dalenii
Ring-of-bells
            Hyacinthoides non-scriptus
River lily   Schizostylis coccinea
Roan lily   Lilium grayi
Rocambole   Allium sativum
            Allium scordoprasum
Rock harlequin
            Corydalis sempervirens
Roman hyacinth
            Bellevalia romana
            Hyacinthus orientalis
            Hyacinthus romanus
Roman wormwood
            Corydalis sempervirens
Roof iris   Iris tectorum
Rose leek   Allium canadense
Rosey garlic   Allium roseum
Round-headed garlic
            Allium sphaerocephalum
Round-headed leek
            Allium sphaerocephalum
Royal lily   Lilium regale

Royal paintbrush
            Haemanthus puniceus
            Scadoxus puniceus
Saffron crocus   Crocus sativus
Saint Brigid anemone
            Anemone coronaria
Saint Bruno's lily
            Paradisea liliastrum
Saint James's lily
            Sprekelia formosissima
Saint Joseph's lily
            Amaryllis × johnsonii
            Hippeastrum × johnsonii
Sand crocus   Romulea columnae
Sand leek   Allium scorodoprasum
Scarborough lily
            Cyrtanthus purpureus
            Vallota speciosa
Scarlet anemone   Anemone fulgens
Scarlet fritillary   Fritillaria recurva
Scarlet ginger lily
            Hedychium coccineum
Scarlet martagon lily
            Lilium chalcedonicum
Scarlet-seeded iris   Iris foetidissima
Scarlet turk's cap lily
            Lilium chalcedonicum
Scarlet windflower
            Anemone fulgens
Schnittlauch
            Allium schoenoprasum
Scotch crocus   Crocus biflorus
Scurvy grass   Oxalis enneaphylla
Sea daffodil
            Pancratium maritimum
Sea lily   Pancratium maritimum
Sea onion
            Ornithogalum caudatum
            Scilla verna
            Urginea maritima
Sea squill   Urginea maritima
Sego lily   Calochortus nuttallii
Serpent garlic   Allium sativum
Serpent's tongue
            Erythronium americanum
Shallot   Allium cepa
Showy Japanese lily
            Lilium lancifolium
            Lilium speciosum
Showy lily   Lilium lancifolium
            Lilium speciosum
Shrimp begonia
            Begonia limmingheiana
Siberian iris   Iris sibirica
Siberian squill   Scilla sibirica
Sierra iris   Iris hartwegii
Sierra lily   Lilium parvum
Sierra star tulip
            Calochortus nudus
Slender blue flag   Iris prismatica

Small celandine

Small celandine	*Ranunculus ficaria*
Small grape hyacinth	*Muscari botryoides*
Small tiger lily	*Lilium parvum*
Snake's head fritillary	*Fritillaria meleagris*
Snowdrop windflower	*Anemone sylvestris*
Snow trillium	*Trillium nivale*
Solomon's lily	*Arum palaestinum*
South African squill	*Scilla natalensis*
Southern blue flag	*Iris virginica*
Southern red lily	*Lilium carolinianum*
	Lilium catesbaei
Southern swamp crinum	*Crinum americanum*
Spanish bluebell	*Endymion campanulata*
	Endymion hispanica
	Hyacinthoides campanulata
	Hyacinthoides hispanicus
Spanish daffodil	*Narcissus hispanicus*
Spanish garlic	*Allium scorodoprasum*
Spanish iris	*Iris xiphium*
Spanish jacinth	*Endymion hispanicus*
Spanish onion	*Allium fistulosum*
Spider lily	*Amaryllis radiata*
	Hymenocallis × festalis
	Hymenocallis narcissiflora
	Ismene calathina
	Lycoris africana
	Lycoris radiata
Spiky gayfeather	*Liatris spicata*
Spire lily	*Galtonia candicans*
Spotted calla lily	*Zantedeschia albomaculata*
	Zantedeschia melanoleuca
Spotted Chinese lily	*Cardiocrinum cathayanum*
Spring fumitory	*Corydalis aurea*
Spring snowflake	*Leucojum vernum*
Spring squill	*Scilla verna*
Spring starflower	*Brodiaea uniflora*
	Ipheion uniflorum
	Leucocoryne uniflora
	Milla uniflora
Spuria iris	*Iris spuria*
Squawroot	*Trillium erectum*
	Trillium flavum
Stag's garlic	*Allium vineale*
Star begonia	*Begonia heracleifolia*
Star hyacinth	*Scilla amoena*

Star-leaf begonia	*Begonia heracleifolia*
Star lily	*Lilium concolor*
Star-of-Bethlehem	*Ornithogalum arabicum*
	Ornithogalum narbonense
	Ornithogalum pyrenaicum
	Ornithogalum umbellatum
Starry hyacinth	*Scilla autumnalis*
Stars-of-Persia	*Allium christophii*
Stinking benjamin	*Trillium erectum*
	Trillium flavum
Stinking gladwin iris	*Iris foetidissima*
Stinking iris	*Iris foetidissima*
Storm lily	*Zephyranthes candida*
Striped garlic	*Allium cuthbertii*
Striped squill	*Puschkinia scilloides*
Summer hyacinth	*Galtonia candicans*
	Hyacinthus candicans
Summer snowflake	*Leucojum aestivum*
	Ornithogalum umbellatum
Sunset lily	*Lilium pardalinum*
Swamp lily	*Crinum americanum*
	Lilium superbum
	Saururus cernuus
Swamp onion	*Allium validum*
Sweet beth	*Trillium vaseyi*
Sweet garlic	*Tulbaghia simmleri*
Sword-leaved iris	*Iris ensata*
Sword lily	*Gladiolus × hortulanus*
Taro	*Colocasia esculenta*
Tassel hyacinth	*Muscari comosum*
Tenby daffodil	*Narcissus obvallaris*
The pearl	*Polianthes tuberosa*
Thimble lily	*Lilium bolanderi*
Thimbleweed	*Anemone cylindrica*
	Anemone riparia
	Anemone virginiana
Tiger flower	*Tigridia pavona*
Tiger lily	*Lilium lancifolium*
	Lilium tigrinum
	Tigrida pavonia
Toadshade	*Trillium sessile*
Torch lily	*Kniphofia triangularis*
Tous-les-mois	*Canna edulis*
Tree dahlia	*Dahlia imperialis*
Triangular-stemmed garlic	*Allium triquetrum*
Triquetros leek	*Allium triquetrum*
Trout lily	*Erythronium americanum*
Trumpet lily	*Lilium longiflorum*
	Zantedeschia aethiopica
	Zantedeschia africana
Trumpet narcissus	*Narcissus pseudonarcissus*

Tuberose — *Polianthes tuberosa*
Turban buttercup — *Ranunculus asiaticus*
Turban lily — *Lilium martagon* / *Lilium pomponium*
Turkish grape hyacinth — *Muscari azureum*
Turkish snowdrop — *Galanthus elwesii*
Turkish tulip — *Tulipa acuminata* / *Tulipa cornuta* / *Tulipa turkistanica*
Turk's cap lily — *Lilium martagon* / *Lilium michauxii* / *Lilium superbum*
Twelve apostles — *Neomarica caerulea*
Two-bladed onion — *Allium fistulosum*
Veldt lily — *Crinum lugardiae*
Violet iris — *Iris verna*
Violet slipper gloxinia — *Sinningia regina* / *Sinningia speciosa*
Violet wood sorrel — *Ionoxalis violacea* / *Oxalis violacea*
Voodoo lily — *Sauromatum venosum*
Wake robin — *Trillium grandiflorum* / *Trillium sessile*
Walking iris — *Neomarica northiana*
Wall iris — *Iris tectorum*
Wand flower — *Dierama pulcherrimum* / *Ixia maculata* / *Ixia viridiflora*
Washington lily — *Lilium washingtonianum*
Water dragon — *Saururus cernuus*
Water flag — *Iris pseudacorus*
Water hawthorn — *Aponogeton distachyos*
Waterlily tulip — *Tulipa kaufmanniana*
Wax trillium — *Trillium erectum album*
Weed's mariposa — *Calochortus weedii*
Welsh onion — *Allium fistulosum*
Western blue flag — *Iris missouriensis*
Western lily — *Lilium occidentale*
West wind lily — *Zephyranthes candida*
Wheel lily — *Lilium medeoloides*
Whippoorwill flower — *Trillium cuneatum*
White dog's tooth violet — *Erythronium albidum*
White fritillary — *Fritillaria liliacea*

White ginger lily — *Hedychium coronarium*
White mariposa — *Calochortus venustus*
White squill — *Urginea maritima*
White trumpet lily — *Lilium longiflorum*
White wake-robin — *Trillium grandiflorum*
Widow iris — *Hermodactylus tuberosus* / *Iris tuberosa*
Wild crocus — *Anemone nuttalliana*
Wild daffodil — *Narcissus pseudonarcissus*
Wild garlic — *Allium canadense* / *Allium ursinum* / *Tulbaghia simmleri*
Wild hyacinth — *Camassia scilloides* / *Hyacinthoides non-scriptus* / *Lachenalia contaminata*
Wild iris — *Iris versicolor*
Wild leek — *Allium ampeloprasum* / *Allium tricoccum*
Wild onion — *Allium canadense* / *Allium cernuum*
Wild orange-red lily — *Lilium philadelphicum*
Wild tulip — *Tulipa sylvestris*
Wild yellow lily — *Lilium canadense*
Windflower — *Anemone appennina* / *Anemone blanda* / *Anemone coronaria* / *Anemone pavonina* / *Zephyranthes candida* / *Zephyranthes grandiflora* / *Zephyranthes rosea*
Winecups — *Babiana rubrocyanea*
Winter aconite — *Eranthis hyemalis*
Winter daffodil — *Sternbergia lutea*
Wonder bulb — *Colchicum autumnale*
Wonder flower — *Ornithogalum thyrsoides*
Wood anemone — *Anemone nemorosa*
Wood bells — *Hyacinthoides non-scriptus*
Wood hyacinth — *Hyacinthoides non-scriptus*
Wood lily — *Lilium philadelphicum*
Wood trillium — *Trillium viride*
Yellow adder'stongue — *Erythronium americanum*
Yellow-bell lily — *Lilium canadense*
Yellow calla lily — *Zantedeschia elliottiana*
Yellow fairy lantern — *Calochortus pulchellus*
Yellow fall iris — *Iris graeberiana*
Yellow flag — *Iris pseudacorus*
Yellow fritillary — *Fritillaria pudica*

Yellow ginger lily

Yellow ginger lily
Hedychium flavescens

Yellow grape hyacinth
Muscari macrocarpum

Yellow iris   *Iris pseudacorus*

Yellow lily   *Lilium canadense*

Yellow mariposa
Calochortus luteus

Yellow marsh afrikander
Gladiolus tristis

Yellow onion   *Allium flavum*

Yellow snowdrop
Erythronium americanum

Yellow star flower
Sternbergia lutea

Yellow star ornamental
onion   *Allium moly*

Yellow turk's cap lily
Lilium pyrenaicum

Zephyr lily   *Zephyranthes candida*

CACTI AND SUCCULENTS

The majority of cacti are succulent, arid- or desert-area plants with thickened stems that serve the plant both for water-storage and as photosynthetic organs, replacing the leaves which are usually miniscule or totally absent. Most are armed with vicious spines and should be handled with care. They should be kept well away from children and domestic pets.

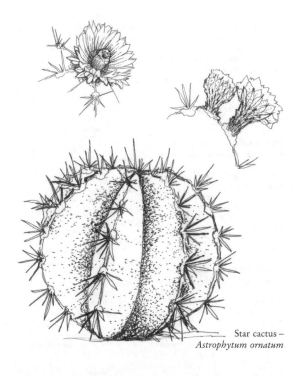

Star cactus –
Astrophytum ornatum

COMMON NAMES

Aaron's beard

Aaron's beard   *Opuntia leucotricha*

African living rock
    Pleiospilos bolusii

Agave cactus
    Leuchtenbergia principis

Agave salmiana   *Pulque agave*

American aloe   *Agave americana*

Annual mesembryanthemum
    Dorotheanthus bellidiformis

Apple cactus   *Cereus peruvianus*

Aristocrat plant
    Haworthia chalwinii

Arizona giant   *Carnegiea gigantea*

Artichoke cactus
    Obregonia denegrii

Bald old man
    Cephalocereus palmeri

Barbados aloe   *Aloe barbadensis*

Barbados gooseberry
    Pereskia aculeata

Barbary fig   *Opuntia vulgaris*

Barrel cactus
    Echinocactus grusonii
    Echinopsis multiplex

Bead vine   *Crassula rupestris*

Beavertail cactus   *Opuntia basilaris*

Beehive cactus
    Coryphantha vivipara
    arizonica

Big nipple cactus
    Coryphantha runyonii

Bird's nest cactus
    Mammillaria camptotricha

Bird's nest sansevieria
    Sansevieria hahnii

Bishop's cap cactus
    Astrophytum myriostigma
    Astrophytum ornatum

Bishop's hood cactus
    Astrophytum myriostigma

Black echeveria   *Echeveria affinis*

Black fingers   *Opuntia clavarioides*

Blind pear
    Opuntia microdasys rufida

Blue barrel cactus
    Echinocactus ingens
    Echinocereus horizonthalonius
    Ferocactus glaucescens

Blue blade
    Opuntia violacea santa-rita

Blue candle
    Myrtillocactus geometrizans

Blue century plant   *Agave palmeri*

Blue echeveria   *Echeveria glauca*
    Echeveria secunda glauca

Blue flame
    Myrtillocactus geometrizans

Blue myrtle cactus
    Myrtillocactus geometrizans

Bottle plant   *Hatiora salicornioides*

Bowstring hemp
    Sansevieria trifasciata laurentii

Boxing glove
    Opuntia fulgida mamillata

Brain cactus
    Echinofossulocactus
    zacatecasensis

Bunny ears   *Opuntia microdasys*

Burbank's spineless cactus
    Opuntia ficus-indica

Button cactus   *Epithelantha bokei*
    Epithelantha micromeris

Cactus spurge
    Euphorbia pseudocactus

Candelabra cactus
    Lemaireocereus weberi

Candelilla
    Euphorbia antisyphilitica

Candle plant   *Senecio articulatus*

Cane cactus   *Opuntia cylindrica*

Cantala   *Agave cantala*

Cape aloe   *Aloe ferox*

Caricature plant
    Graptophyllum pictum

Cat claw cactus
    Hamatocactus uncinatus

Cat's whiskers
    Schlumbergera gaertneri
    makoyana

Century plant   *Agave americana*

Chain cactus   *Rhipsalis paradoxa*

Chainlink cactus
    Opuntia imbricata
    Rhipsalis paradoxa

Chenille plant
    Echeveria leucotricha

Chin cactus
    Gymnocalycium gibbosum

Christmas cactus
    Epiphyllum truncatum
    Schlumbergera bridgesii
    Schlumbergera truncata
    Zygocactus truncatus

Cinnamon cactus
    Opuntia microdasys rufida
    Opuntia rufida

Claw cactus
    Schlumbergera truncata

Cleftstone   *Pleiospilos nelii*

Cloud grass
    Aichryson × domesticum

Club cactus
    Opuntia fulgida mamillata

Cob cactus   *Escobaria tuberculosa*
    Lobivia hertrichiana

Cobweb houseleek
    Sempervivum arachnoides
    Sempervivum arachnoideum

Cochineal plant
    Nopalea cochenillifera

Colombian ball cactus
    Wigginsia vorwerkiana

Gingham golf ball

Column-of-pearls
    Haworthia chalwinii

Comb cactus   *Pachycereus pecten-aboriginum*

Copper roses
    Echeveria multicaulis

Coral cactus
    Mammillaria heyderi
    Rhipsalis cereuscula

Corncob cactus
    Euphorbia mammillaris

Cotton-ball cactus   *Espostoa lanata*

Cotton-pole cactus
    Opuntia vestita

Crab cactus
    Schlumbergera truncata

Crab's claw cactus
    Epiphyllum truncatum
    Schlumbergera bridgesii
    Zygocactus truncatus

Cream cactus
    Mammillaria heyderi

Creeping devil cactus
    Lemaireocereus eruca
    Machaerocereus eruca

Crested opuntia
    Opuntia clavarioides

Crocodile jaws   *Aloe humilis*

Crown of thorns   *Euphorbia milii*
    Euphorbia milii splendens

Cuban hemp   *Furcraea hexapetala*

Cushion cactus   *Opuntia floccosa*

Dagger cactus
    Lemaireocereus gummosus

Dahlia cactus   *Wilcoxia poselgeri*

Dancing bones
    Hariota salicornioides
    Hatiora salicornioides
    Rhipsalis salicornioides

Desert candle
    Dasylirion leiophyllum

Desert christmas cactus
    Opuntia leptocaulis

Desert rose   *Adenium obesum*
    Echeveria rosea
    Trichodiadema densum

Devil cactus   *Opuntia schottii*

Devil's backbone
    Pedilanthus tithymaloides

Devil's root cactus
    Lophophora williamsii
    Lothophora williamsii

Devil's tongue   *Ferocactus corniger*
    Ferocactus latispinus

Dog cholla   *Opuntia schottii*

Dollar cactus
    Opuntia violacea santa-rita

Dominoes   *Opuntia erectoclada*

Dragon tree   *Dracaena draco*

Dragon's head   *Euphorbia gorgonis*

Drunkard's dream
    Hariota salicornioides
    Hatiora salicornioides
    Rhipsalis salicornioides

Dry whisky
    Lophophora williamsii
    Lothophora williamsii

Dumpling cactus
    Coryphantha runyonii
    Lophophora williamsii
    Lothophora williamsii

Eagle-claws cactus
    Echinocactus horizonthalonius

Easter cactus
    Rhipsalidopsis gaertneri

Easter-lily cactus
    Echinopsis multiplex

Electrode cactus   *Ferocactus histrix*

Emerald-idol   *Opuntia cylindrica*

Empress of Germany
    Nopalxochia phyllanthoides

English stonecrop   *Sedum anglicum*

Eve's pin cactus   *Opuntia subulata*

Fairy agave   *Hechtia scariosa*

Fairy castles   *Opuntia clavarioides*

Fairy-elephant's feet
    Fritha pulchra

Fairy needles   *Opuntia soehrensii*

Fairy washboard
    Haworthia limifolia

Falcon feather   *Aloe variegata*

Feather cactus
    Mammillaria plumosa

Finger tree   *Euphorbia tirucalli*

Firecracker cactus
    Cleistocactus smaragdifolius

Firecracker plant   *Echeveria setosa*

Fire crown cactus   *Rebutia senilis*

Fishbone cactus
    Epiphyllum anguliger

Fish-hook cactus
    Ancistrocactus scheeri
    Ferocactus latispinus
    Ferocactus wislizenii
    Mammillaria bocasana

Fish-hook pincushion cactus
    Mammillaria wildii

Flapjack cactus   *Opuntia chlorotica*

Fleshy-stalked pelargonium
    Pelargonium carnosum

Frangipani tree
    Plumiera acuminata

Ghost plant
    Graptopetalum paraguayense

Giant barrel cactus
    Echinocactus ingens

Giant cactus   *Carnegiea gigantea*

Giant Mexican cereus
    Pachycereus pringlei

Giant saguaro   *Carnegiea gigantea*

Gingham golf ball   *Euphorbia obesa*

Globe spear-lily

Globe spear-lily
Doryanthes excelsa

Glory of Texas
Thelocactus bicolor

Gnome's throne
Opuntia clavarioides

Goat's horn cactus
Astrophytum capricorne

Golden ball   *Echinocactus grusonii*
Notocactus leninghausii

Golden barrel cactus
Echinocactus grusonii

Golden bird's nest cactus
Mammillaria camptotricha

Golden column
Trichocereus spachianus

Golden lily cactus
Echinopsis aurea
Lobivia aurea

Golden old man
Cephalocereus chrysacanthus

Golden opuntia
Opuntia microdasys

Golden spines
Cephalocereus chrysacanthus

Golden star
Mammillaria elongata

Golden tom thumb
Parodia aureispina

Gold lace   *Mammillaria elongata*

Goldplush   *Opuntia microdasys*

Gorgon's head
Euphorbia gorgonis

Gouty pelargonium
Pelargonium gibbosum

Green aloe   *Furcraea foetida*

Green-flowered pitaya
Echinocereus viridiflorus

Green-flowered torch cactus
Echinocereus viridiflorus

Grizzly bear cactus
Opuntia erinacea ursina

Hairbrush cactus
Pachycereus pecten-aboriginum

Hatpin cactus
Ferocactus rectispinus

Hedge cactus   *Cereus peruvianus*

Hedgehog aloe   *Aloe humilis*

Hedgehog cactus
Echinocereus pectinatus

Hedgehog-cory cactus
Coryphantha echinus

Hen-and-chickens
Sempervivum tectorum

Henequen   *Agave fourcroydes*

Hollyhock-leaved pelargonium
Pelargonium cotyledonis

Honey-bunny
Opuntia microdasys albispina

Honolulu queen
Hylocereus undatus

Horned-leaf pelargonium
Pelargonium ceratophyllum

Hyacinth-scented rochea
Rochea coccinea

Ice plant   *Sedum spectabile*

Indian comb   *Pachycereus pecten aboriginum*

Indian fig   *Opuntia ficus-indica*

Irish mittens   *Opuntia vulgaris*

Jade plant   *Crassula arborescens*
Crassula argentea
Crassula portulacea

Jade tree   *Crassula ovata*

Japanese poinsettia
Pedilanthus tithymaloides

Jellybean plant
Sedum pachyphyllum

Jewbush
Pedilanthus tithymaloides

Jewel plant   *Titanopsis calcarea*

Joseph's coat cactus
Opuntia vulgaris

Joshua tree   *Yucca brevifolia*

Jumping cactus   *Opuntia fulgida*

Jumping cholla   *Opuntia prolifera*

Kanniedood   *Aloe variegata*

Lace cactus
Echinocereus reichenbachii
Mammillaria elongata

Lace haworthia   *Haworthia setata*

Lady finger   *Mammillaria elongata*

Lamb's tail
Chiastophyllum oppositifolium
Cotyledon simplicifolia

Lamb'stail cactus
Wilcoxia schmollii

Large barrel cactus
Echinocactus ingens

Leafy cactus   *Pereskia aculeata*

Lechuguilla   *Agave lophantha*

Lemon-ball cactus
Mammillaria pringlei
Notocactus submammulosus

Lemon vine   *Pereskia aculeata*

Lesser old man cactus
Echinocereus delaetii

Link plant   *Rhipsalis paradoxa*

Lion's tongue
Opuntia schickendantzii

Little candles
Mammillaria prolifera

Little tree opuntia   *Opuntia vilis*

Living rock cactus
Ariocarpus fissuratus
Pleiospilos bolusii

Living stones   *Lithops julii*

Madagascan palm
Pachypodium lamerei

Mauritius hemp   *Furcraea foetida*

Medicinal aloe   *Aloe barbadensis*

Plush plant

Medusa's head spurge
Euphorbia caput-medusae
Melon cactus
Melocactus communis
Mescal button
Lophophora williamsii
Lothophora williamsii
Mexican dwarf tree cactus
Opuntia vilis
Mexican giant
Cephalocereus fulviceps
Mexican giant barrel cactus
Echinocactus ingens
Mexican giant cactus
Pachycereus pringlei
Mexican sunball   *Rebutia miniscula*
Milk bush   *Euphorbia tirucalli*
Mimicry plant   *Pleiospilos bolusii*
Pleiospilos nelii
Missouri pincushion cactus
Coryphantha missouriensis
Mistletoe cactus
Rhipsalis baccifera
Rhipsalis cassutha
Money tree   *Crassula arborescens*
Monkshood cactus
Astrophytum myriostigma
Moon cactus   *Harrisia jusbertii*
Harrisia martinii
Moonstones
Pachyphytum oviferum
Mother-in-law's armchair
Echinocactus grusonii
Mother-in-law's tongue
Sansevieria trifasciata laurentii
Mother-of-pearl plant
Graptopetalum paraguayense
Mountain cereus
Borzicactus fossulatus
Mule-crippler cactus
Echinocactus horizonthalonius
Mule's ears
Opuntia schickendantzii
Native's comb
Pachycereus pecten-aboriginum
Night-blooming cereus
Epiphyllum oxypetalum
Hylocereus undatus
Nyctocereus serpentinus
Peniocereus greggii
Selenicereus grandiflorus
Nipple cactus   *Neobessya similis*
Nopal   *Opuntia megacantha*
Old-father-live-forever
Pelargonium cotyledonis
Old lady cactus
Mammillaria hahniana
Mammillaria lanata
Old lady of Mexico
Mammillaria hahniana
Old man cactus
Cephalocereus senilis

Old man of the Andes
Borzicactus trollii
Oreocereus trollii
Old man of the mountains
Borzicactus celsianus
Pilocereus celsianus
Old man opuntia   *Opuntia vestita*
Old man's head
Cephalocereus senilis
Old woman cactus
Mammillaria hahniana
Orange tuna   *Opuntia elata*
Orchid cactus
Epiphyllum ackermannii
Epiphyllum × hybridum
Nopalxochia ackermannii
Organ pipe cactus
Lemaireocereus marginatus
Lemaireocereus thurberi
Stenocereus thurberi
Ornamental monkshood
Astrophytum ornatum
Painted lady
Echeveria derenbergii
Palmer spear-lily
Doryanthes palmeri
Panda plant   *Kalanchoe tomentosa*
Panda-bear plant
Kalanchoe tomentosa
Paper cactus   *Opuntia articulata*
Partridge-breasted aloe
Aloe variegata
Peanut cactus
Chamaecereus silvestrii
Pearl plant
Haworthia margaritifera
Haworthia pumila
Pearly dots   *Haworthia papillosa*
Pebble cactus   *Lithops lesliei*
Pencil cactus   *Opuntia ramosissima*
Pencil cholla   *Opuntia arbuscula*
Peruvian apple   *Cereus peruvianus*
Peruvian apple cactus
Cereus peruvianus
Peyote cactus
Lophophora williamsii
Lothophora williamsii
Pheasant's wing   *Aloe variegata*
Pickle plant
Trichodiadema barbatum
Pincushion cactus
Coryphantha vivipara
Pink easter-lily cactus
Echinopsis multiplex
Pitahaya   *Carnegiea gigantea*
Plaid cactus
Gymnocalycium mihanovichii
Plain cactus
Gymnocalycium mihanovichii
Plush plant   *Echeveria pulvinata*
Kalanchoe tomentosa

COMMON NAMES

Polka dots

Polka dots
  Opuntia microdasys albispina
Pond-lily cactus
  Nopalxochia phyllanthoides
Popcorn cactus
  Rhipsalis cereuscula
  Rhipsalis warmingiana
Porcupine pelargonium
  Pelargonium hystrix
Powder-blue cereus
  Lemaireocereus pruinosus
Powder puff
  Mammillaria bocasana
  Mammillaria gracilis
Prickly pear   *Opuntia ficus-indica*
  Opuntia microdasys albispina
  Opuntia vulgaris
Princess of the night
  Selenicereus pteranthus
Prism cactus
  Leuchtenbergia principis
Purple hedgehog cereus
  Echinocereus sarissophorus
Purple pitaya   *Echinocereus dubius*
Purple prickly pear
  Opuntia santa-rita
Pussy ears   *Kalanchoe tomentosa*
Queen of the night
  Epiphyllum oxypetalum
  Hylocereus undatus
  Nyctocereus serpentinus
  Selenicereus grandiflorus
  Selenicereus macdonaldiae
Queen Victoria's aloe
  Aloe victoriae reginae
Rabbit ears   *Opuntia microdasys*
Rainbow cactus
  Echinocereus pectinatus rigidissimus
Rat's tail cactus
  Aporocactus flagelliformis
Rat-tail plant
  Crassula lycopodioides
Rattlesnake tail   *Crassula barklyi*
Red aloe   *Aloe ferox*
Redbird cactus
  Pedilanthus tithymaloides
Redbird flower
  Pedilanthus tithymaloides
Red bunny ears
  Opuntia microdasys rufida
  Opuntia rufida
Red crown cactus
  Rebutia kupperana
  Rebutia minuscula
Red orchid cactus
  Nopalxochia ackermannii
Red spike
  Cephalophyllum alstonii
Reina-de-la-noche
  Peniocereus greggii
Ribbon cactus
  Pedilanthus tithymaloides

Rice cactus   *Rhipsalis cereuscula*
Roof houseleek
  Sempervivum tectorum
Rosary vine   *Crassula rupestris*
Rose cactus   *Pereskia grandifolia*
Rose pincushion
  Mammillaria zeilmanniana
Rose-plaid cactus
  Gymnocalycium quehlianum
Rose tuna   *Opuntia basilaris*
Royal-cross cactus
  Mammillaria karwinskiana
Rubber spurge   *Euphorbia tirucalli*
Ruby dumpling
  Mammillaria tetracantha
Saguaro   *Carnegiea gigantea*
Sahuaro   *Carnegiea gigantea*
Samphire-leaved pelargonium
  Pelargonium crithmifolium
Sand dollar cactus
  Astrophytum asterias
Scarlet ball cactus
  Notocactus haselbergii
Scarlet bugler   *Cereus baumannii*
  Cleistocactus baumannii
Scarlet crown cactus
  Rebutia grandiflora
Scented cactus   *Wilcoxia poselgeri*
Sea coral   *Opuntia clavarioides*
Sea urchin cactus
  Astrophytum asterias
  Echinopsis eyriesii
Senita   *Lophocereus schottii*
Serpent cactus
  Nyctocereus serpentinus
Seven stars   *Ariocarpus retusus*
Silver ball cactus   *Notocactus scopa*
Silver beads   *Crassula deltoides*
  Crassula rhomboidea
Silver cluster cactus
  Mammillaria prolifera
Silver dollar cactus
  Astrophytum asterias
Silver torch   *Cleistocactus strausii*
Slipper flower
  Pedilanthus tithymaloides
Small barrel cactus
  Ferocactus viridescens
Snake cactus
  Nyctocereus serpentinus
Snowball cactus   *Espostoa lanata*
  Mammillaria bocasana
  Pediocactus simpsonii
Snowball pincushion
  Mammillaria candida
Snowdrop cactus
  Rhipsalis houlletiana
Socotrine aloe   *Aloe perryi*
South American golden-barrel
  Lobivia aurea

South American old man
  Borzicactus celsianus
Spice cactus
  Hariota salicornioides
  Hatiora salicornioides
  Rhipsalis salicornioides
Spider aloe *Aloe humilis*
Spider cactus
  Gymnocalycium denudatum
Spider houseleek
  Sempervivum arachnoides
  Sempervivum arachnoideum
Spineless cactus *Opuntia ficus-indica*
Spiny aloe *Aloe africana*
Split rock *Pleiospilos nelii*
Spoon plant
  Dasylirion leiophyllum
Sprawling cactus
  Morangaya pensilis
Square-stemmed pelargonium
  Pelargonium tetragonum
Staghorn cholla
  Opuntia versicolor
Star cactus *Ariocarpus fissuratus*
  Astrophytum ornatum
Star window plant
  Haworthia tessellata
Stick cactus *Euphorbia tirucalli*
Sticky moonstones
  Pachyphytum glutinicaule
Stonecrop *Sedum anglicum*
Stone plant *Lithops dorotheae*
  Lithops julii
Strawberry cactus
  Echinocereus enneacanthus
  Echinocereus salm-dyckianus
  Ferocactus setispinus
  Thelocactus setispinus
String of beads
  Senecio rowleyanus
String of hearts *Caralluma woodii*
String of pearls
  Senecio rowleyanus
Sugar-almond plant
  Pachyphytum oviferum
Sun cactus *Heliocereus speciosus*
Sun plant *Portulaca grandiflora*
Tasajillo *Opuntia leptocaulis*
Teddy-bear cactus
  Opuntia bigelovii
Teddy-bear cholla
  Opuntia bigelovii
Texas pride *Thelocactus bicolor*
Texas rainbow cactus
  Echinocereus dasyacanthus
Thanksgiving cactus
  Schlumbergera truncata
Thimble cactus
  Mammillaria fragilis
Thimble mammillaria
  Mammillaria fragilis

Thimble tuna *Opuntia sphaerica*
Tiger aloe *Aloe variegata*
Tiger jaws *Faucaria tigrina*
Tom thumb cactus
  Parodia aureispina
Toothpick cactus *Stetsonia coryne*
Tortoise cactus *Deamia testudo*
Totem-pole cactus
  Lophocereus schottii
Turk's cap cactus
  Melocactus communis
  Melocactus intortus
Turk's head
  Ferocactus hamatacanthus
Turk's head cactus
  Melocactus communis
  Melocactus maxonii
Unguentine cactus
  Aloe barbadensis
Velvet opuntia *Opuntia velutina*
Wallflower crown
  Rebutia pseudodeminuta
Wandering cactus
  Morangaya pensilis
Wax plant
  Euphorbia antisyphilitica
Wax rose *Pereskia bleo*
Whisker cactus
  Lophocereus schottii
White chin cactus
  Gymnocalycium schickendantzii
White jewel
  Titanopsis schwantesii
White torch cactus
  Trichocereus spachianus
Whitsun cactus
  Schlumbergera gaertneri
Window aloe
  Haworthia cymbiformis
Window cushion
  Haworthia cymbiformis
Window plant
  Fenestraria rhopalophylla
  Haworthia cymbiformis
Woolly sheep *Opuntia floccosa*
Woolly torch cactus
  Cephalocereus palmeri
Yellow bunny ears
  Opuntia microdasys
Yellow old man
  Cephalocereus palmeri
Yellow rabbit ears
  Opuntia microdasys
Youth-and-old-age
  Aichryson × domesticum
Zanzibar aloe *Aloe perryi*
Zebra haworthia
  Haworthia fasciata
Zygocactus
  Schlumbergera truncata

CARNIVOROUS PLANTS

Otherwise known as insectivorous plants, these are plants that have developed special mechanisms for trapping and digesting mainly, but not exclusively, small insects. There are several types of carnivorous plants including the pitcher plants, the sticky-leaved sundews and butterworts, and the spring-trap leaves of Venus's flytrap. The strange nature of these plants makes them popular subjects for exhibiting at horticultural shows and school study groups. They are also extensively grown indoors and in greenhouses as a nature control for flying insects.

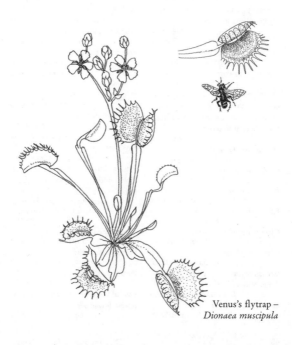

Venus's flytrap –
Dionaea muscipula

Alabama canebrake
pitcher plant

Alabama canebrake pitcher plant
  Sarracenia alabamensis
Alpine butterwort
  Pinguicula alpina
Amethyst bladderwort
  Utricularia amethystina
Australian pitcher plant
  Cephalotus follicularis
Blue butterwort
  Pinguicula caerulea
Branched butterwort
  Pinguicula ramosa
Bristly flytrap   *Genlisea hispidula*
Butterwort   *Pinguicula vulgaris*
California pitcher plant
  Chrysamphora californica
  Darlingtonia californica
Cobra lily
  Chrysamphora californica
  Darlingtonia californica
Cobra orchid
  Chrysamphora californica
  Darlingtonia californica
Cobra plant
  Chrysamphora californica
  Darlingtonia californica
Common butterwort
  Pinguicula vulgaris
Common pitcher plant
  Sarracenia purpurea
Common sundew
  Drosera rotundifolia
Creeping genlisea   *Genlisea repens*
Deep red pitcher plant
  Nepenthes sanguinea
Dew thread   *Drosera filiformis*
Downy bladderwort
  Utricularia pubescens
Dwarf butterwort
  Pinguicula pumila
Dwarf genlisea   *Genlisea pygmaea*
Dwarf sundew   *Drosera brevifolia*
Eared sundew   *Drosera auriculata*
Erect Australian sundew
  Byblis gigantea
Floated bladderwort
  Utricularia inflata
Floating pondtrap
  Aldrovanda vesiculosa
Flytrap sensitive
  Dionaea muscipula
Funnelform pitcher plant
  Nepenthes hookerana
Giant marsh pitcher plant
  Heliamphora tatei
Giant sun pitcher plant
  Heliamphora tatei
Golden flytrap   *Genlisea aurea*
Great bladderwort
  Utricularia macrorhiza
Greater butterwort
  Pinguicula grandiflora

Great sundew   *Drosera anglica*
Green pitcher plant
  Sarracenia oreophila
Guayan sun pitcher plant
  Heliamphora nutans
Hooded pitcher plant
  Sarracenia minor
Horned bladderwort
  Utricularia cornuta
Humped bladderwort
  Utricularia gibba
Huntsman's cup
  Sarracenia purpurea
Huntsman's horn   *Sarracenia flava*
Indian cup   *Sarracenia purpurea*
Inverted bladderwort
  Utricularia resupinata
Lesser bladderwort
  Utricularia minor
Marsh pitcher plant
  Heliamphora nutans
Mottled purple pitcher plant
  Nepenthes × atrosanguinea
Monkey pitcher
  Nepenthes merrilliana
Monkey's larder
  Nepenthes merrilliana
Monkey's rice pot
  Nepenthes merrilliana
Mouse pitcher
  Nepenthes merrilliana
New Zealand bladderwort
  Utricularia nova-zealandiae
Northern pitcher plant
  Sarracenia purpurea
Pale green pitcher plant
  Nepenthes ventricosa
Pale pitcher   *Sarracenia alata*
  Sarracenia sledgei
Pale violet butterwort
  Pinguicula lilacina
Parrot pitcher plant
  Sarracenia psittacina
Pink fans   *Polypompholyx tenella*
Pink petticoat
  Polypompholyx multifida
Pink rainbow   *Drosera menziesii*
Pink sundew   *Drosera capillaris*
Pitcher plant
  Chrysamphora californica
  Darlingtonia californica
  Sarracenia purpurea
Portuguese butterwort
  Pinguicula lusitanica
Portuguese sundew
  Drosophyllum lusitanicum
Purple pitcher plant
  Sarracenia purpurea
Rainhat trumpet   *Sarracenia minor*
Round-leaved sundew
  Drosera rotundifolia

Yellow trumpets

Sensitive flytrap
Dionaea muscipula

Side-saddle flower
Sarracenia purpurea

Small marsh pitcher
Heliamphora minor

Small sun pitcher
Heliamphora minor

Southern pitcher plant
Sarracenia purpurea

Spikey pondtrap
Aldrovanda vesiculosa

Spiral-leaved flytrap
Genlisea filiformis

Sprawling Australian sundew
Byblis liniflora

Sundew *Drosera capensis*

Swamp pitcher plant
Cephalotus follicularis

Sweet pitcher plant
Sarracenia purpurea
Sarracenia rubra

Sweet trumpet *Sarracenia rubra*

Thread-leaved sundew
Drosera filiformis

Tipitiwitchet *Dionaea muscipula*

Toothed butterwort
Pinguicula crenatiloba

Trumpet leaf *Sarracenia flava*

Trumpets *Sarracenia flava*

Twining bladderwort
Utricularia spiralis

Umbrella trumpets
Sarracenia flava

Variegated butterwort
Pinguicula variegata

Venus's flytrap *Dionaea muscipula*

Violet butterwort
Pinguicula ionantha
Pinguicula lilacina

Watches *Sarracenia flava*

Waterbug trap
Aldrovanda vesiculosa

Waterwheel plant
Aldrovanda vesiculosa

White trumpet pitcher plant
Sarracenia drummondii
Sarracenia leucophylla

Winged trumpets *Sarracenia alata*

Yellow butterwort *Pinguicula lutea*

Yellow pitcher plant
Sarracenia flava

Yellow trumpets *Sarracenia alata*

FERNS AND FERN ALLIES

These are flowerless plants bearing leaves (fronds) and reproducing by spores on the lower surface of the mature foliage. Ferns and fern allies share a similar life-cycle and are treated horticulturally in a similar manner. For example, the so-called asparagus fern *Asparagus setaceus* is not a fern but one of the *liliaceae*.

Toothed Davallia –
Davallia denticulata

Adder's fern

Adder's fern   *Polypodium vulgare*
Adder's tongue
        Ophioglossum vulgatum
Alpine bladder fern
        Cystopteris regia
Alpine polypody
        Polypodium alpestre
Alpine woodsia   *Woodsia alpina*
Alternate spleenwort
        Asplenium germanicum
American maidenhair
        Adiantum pedatum
American oak fern
        Onoclea sensibilis
American tree fern   *Ctenitis sloanei*
American wall fern
        Polypodium virginianum
Annual maidenhair
        Gymnogramma leptophylla
Ash-leaf polypody
        Polypodium fraxinifolium
Australian bracken
        Pteridium esculentum
Australian brake   *Pteris tremula*
Australian cliff brake
        Pellaea falcata
Australian lady fern
        Athyrium australe
Australian maidenhair
        Adiantum formosum
Australian slender brake
        Pteris ensiformis
Australian tree fern
        Cyathea cooperi
Australian water fern
        Blechnum cartilagineum
Autumn fern
        Dryopteris erythrosora
Ball fern   *Davallia bullata*
                Davallia mariesii
Basket selaginella   *Selaginella apoda*
                Selaginella densa
Bat's wing fern   *Histiopteris incisa*
Bead fern   *Onoclea sensibilis*
Bear's foot fern
        Humata tyermannii
Beautiful hard-shield fern
        *Polystichum aculeatum
        pulchrum*
Beech fern   *Phegopteris connectilis*
        Polypodium phegopteris
        Thelypteris phegopteris
Berry bladder fern
        Cystopteris bulbifera
Bird's nest fern   *Asplenium nidus*
Black maidenhair spleenwort
        Asplenium adiantum-nigrum
Black spleenwort
        Asplenium adiantum-nigrum
Blackstem maidenhair
        Adiantum formosum
Black tree fern   *Cyathea medullaris*

Blue selaginella
        Selaginella uncinata
Blunt-lobed woodsia
        Woodsia obtusa
Boston fern   *Nephrolepis exaltata*
Boulder fern
        Dennstaedia punctilobula
        Dicksonia punctilobula
Bracken   *Pteridium aquilinum*
                Pteris aquilinum
Bramble fern   *Hyolepis punctata*
Branch-crested hartstongue
        *Scolopendrium vulgare
        ramo-cristatum*
Branch-crested shield fern
        *Polystichum angulare
        ramulosum*
Branched black maidenhair
  spleenwort
        *Asplenium adiantum-
        nigrum ramosum*
Branched hard fern
        Blechnum spicant ramosum
Branched maidenhair fern
        *Asplenium trichomanes
        ramosum*
Branched maidenhair spleenwort
        *Asplenium trichomanes
        ramosum*
Branched male fern
        Lastrea filix-mas ramosa
Branched sea spleenwort
        Asplenium marinum ramosum
Braun's holly fern
        Polystichum braunii
Bristle fern
        Blechnum cartilagineum
Bristly shield fern
        Lastreopsis hispida
Bristly tree fern
        Dicksonia youngiae
Brittle bladder fern
        Cystopteris fragilis
Brittle maidenhair
        Adiantum tenerum
Broad beech fern
        Thelypteris hexagonoptera
        Thelypteris phegopteris
Broad buckler fern
        Dryopteris austriaca
        Dryopteris dilatata
        Lastrea dilatata
Broad curly hartstongue
        *Scolopendrium vulgare
        crispum-latum*
Buckhorn   *Osmunda cinnamomea*
Bulbil bladder fern
        Cystopteris bulbifera
Button fern   *Pellaea rotundifolia*
                Tectaria cicutaria
                Tectaria gemmifera
Californian adder's tongue
        Ophioglossum californicum

FERNS

Double-fronded hartstongue

California polypody
  Polypodium californicum
Chinese brake   *Pteris longifolia*
    Pteris vittata
Chinese fern   *Pteris multifida*
    Pteris serrulata
Christmas fern
  Polystichum acrostichoides
Cinnamon fern
  Osmunda cinnamomea
Cleft maidenhair
  *Adiantum capillus-
veneris incisum*
Cleft moonwort
  Botrychium lunaria incisum
Cleft true maidenhair
  *Adiantum capillus-
veneris incisum*
Climbing bird's nest fern
  Polypodium integrifolium
  Polypodium irioides
  Polypodium punctatum
Climbing fern
  Lygodium palmatum
Climbing swamp fern
  Stenochlaena palustris
Cloven green spleenwort
  Asplenium viride multifidum
Cloven lady fern   *Athyrium filix-
femina multifidum*
Cloven maidenhair fern
  *Asplenium trichomanes
multifidum*
Cloven maidenhair
 spleenwort
  *Asplenium trichomanes
multifidum*
Cloven mountain polypody
  *Polypodium phegopteris
multifidum*
Cloven rock spleenwort
  *Asplenium fontanum
multifidum*
Common bracken
  Pteridium aquilinum
  Pteris aquilinum
Common buckler fern
  Dryopteris filix-mas
  Lastrea filix-mas
Common fishbone fern
  Nephrolepis cordifolia
Common ground fern
  Culcita dubia
Common horsetail
  Equisetum hyemale
Common maidenhair
  Adiantum aethiopicum
Common oak fern
  Gymnocarpium dryopteris
  Polypodium dryopteris
Common polypody
  Polypodium vulgare
Common rasp fern   *Doodia media*

Common scouring brush
  Equisetum hymale
Common woodsia
  Woodsia obtusa
Confluent maidenhair fern
  *Asplenium trichomanes
confluens*
Confluent maidenhair spleenwort
  *Asplenium trichomanes
confluens*
Creeping shield fern
  Lastreopsis microsora
Crested bracken
  Pteris aquilina cristata
Crested broad buckler fern
  Lastrea dilatata cristata
Crested buckler fern
  Dryopteris cristata
  Lastrea cristata
Crested climbing bird's nest fern
  *Polypodium integrifolium
cristatum*
Crested hartstongue
  *Scolopendrium vulgare
cristatum*
Crested male fern
  Lastrea filix-mas cristata
Crested mountain buckler fern
  Lastrea montana cristata
Crested polypody
  Polypodium vulgare cristatum
Crested royal fern
  Osmunda regalis cristata
Crested soft prickly shield fern
  Polystichum angulare cristatum
Crested wood fern
  Dryopteris cristata
Cretan brake   *Pteris cretica*
Cretan fern   *Pteris cretica*
Crown fern   *Blechnum discolor*
Crow's nest fern   *Asplenium nidus*
Curly-grass fern   *Schizaea pusilla*
Dagger fern
  Polystichum acrostichoides
Deer fern   *Blechnum spicant*
Deer's foot fern
  Davallia canariensis
Delta maidenhair
  Adiantum cuneatum
  Adiantum decorum
  Adiantum raddianum
Dense holly fern
  *Polystichum lonchitis
confertum*
Diamond maidenhair
  Adiantum trapeziforme
Divided soft prickly shield fern
  *Polystichum angulare sem
tripinnatum*
Double-fronded hard fern
  Blechnum spicant duplex
Double-fronded hartstongue
  Scolopendrium vulgare duplex

Double-pinnuled polypody

Double-pinnuled polypody
Polypodium vulgare bifidum

Douglas's spike-moss
Selaginella douglasii

Drooping adder's-tongue
Ophioglossum pendulum

Dwarf cloven lady fern
Athyrium filix-femina multifidum nanum

Dwarf horsetail
Equisetum scirpoides

Dwarf leather fern
Polystichum tsus-simense

Dwarf lycopod
Selaginella rupestris

Dwarf scouring brush
Equisetum scirpoides

Ear-lobed polypody
Polypodium vulgare auritum

Eastern bracken
Pteridium latiusculum

Ebony spleenwort
Asplenium platyneuron

Elkhorn *Platycerium bifurcatum*
Platycerium superbum

Engelmann's adder's tongue
Ophioglossum engelmannii

Engelmann's quillwort
Isoetes engelmannii

Erect sword fern
Nephrolepis cordifolia

European bristle fern
Trichomanes radicans

European chain fern
Woodwardia radicans

European polypody
Polypodium vulgare

European water clover
Marsilea quadrifolia

Fairy moss *Azolla caroliniana*

False bracken *Culcita dubia*

Fan-like hard fern
Blechnum spicant flabellata

Fiddleheads
Osmunda cinnamomea

Filmy maidenhair
Adiantum diaphanum

Fine-toothed brake *Pteris dentata*
Pteris flabellata
Pteris flaccida

Finger fern *Grammitis australis*
Grammitis billardieri

Fishbone fern
Nephrolepis cordifolia
Nephrolepis exaltata

Fishbone rib fern
Blechnum nudum

Fishbone water fern
Blechnum nudum

Five-fingered jack
Adiantum hispidulum

Flexible alpine polypody
Polypodium alpestre flexile

Floating fern
Ceratopteris pteridoides

Floating moss
Salvinia rotundifolia

Floating pepperwort
Marsilea crenata

Florida tree fern *Ctenitis sloanei*

Florist's fern *Dryopteris dilatata*

Flowering fern *Osmunda regalis*

Forked bristle fern
Trichomanes radicans furcans

Forked brittle bladder fern
Cystopteris fragilis furcans

Forked hard fern
Blechnum spicant furcans

Forked hard shield fern
Polystichum aculeatum furcatum

Forked male fern
Lastrea filix-mas furcans

Forked mountain buckler fern
Lastrea montana furcans

Forked spleenwort
Asplenium septentrionale

Fragile bladder fern
Cystopteris fragilis

Fragrant fern
Microsorium pustulatum
Microsorium scandens
Polypodium pustulatum
Polypodium scandens

Fringed alpine polypody
Polypodium alpestre laciniatum

Giant brake *Pteris tripartita*

Giant chain fern
Woodwardia chamissoi
Woodwardia fimbriata

Giant fern *Angiopteris evecta*

Giant holly fern
Polystichum munitum

Giant maidenhair
Adiantum formosum

Giant wood fern
Dryopteris goldiana

Glade fern
Aglaomorpha pycnocarpon

Golden polypody
Phlebodium aureum
Polypodium aureum

Golden-scaled male fern
Dryopteris borreri

Golden tree fern
Dicksonia fibrosa

Gold fern
Pityrogramma austroamericana
Pityrogramma chrysophylla

Goldie's fern *Dryopteris goldiana*

Grand-tasselled shield fern
Polystichum angulare grandiceps

FERNS

Maidenhair fern

Green cliff brake   *Pellaea viridis*
Green spleenwort
                Asplenium viride
Ground cedar
                Lycopodium complanatum
                Lycopodium tristachyum
Ground pine
                Lycopodium clavatum
                Lycopodium complanatum
                Lycopodium obscurum
Hacksaw fern   *Doodia aspera*
                Doodia media
Hairy-lip fern   *Cheilanthes lamosa*
Hammock fern
                Blechnum occidentale
Hand fern   *Doryopteris pedata*
Hanging spleenwort
                Asplenium flaccidum
                Asplenium majus
                Asplenium mayi
Hapu tree fern   *Cibotium glaucum*
Hard fern   *Blechnum spicant*
Hard shield fern
                Polystichum aculeatum
Hard water fern   *Blechnum watsii*
Hare's foot fern   *Davallia fejeensis*
                Davallia mariesii
                Phlebodium aureum
                Polypodium aureum
Hartford fern
                Lygodium palmatum
Hart's tongue fern
                Phyllitis scolopendrium
Hawaiian tree fern
                Cibotium glaucum
Hay-scented buckler fern
                Dryopteris aemula
                Lastrea recurva
Hay-scented fern
                Dennstaedia punctilobula
                Dicksonia punctilobula
Hedge fern   *Polystichum setiferum*
Hen-and-chickens fern
                Asplenium bulbiferum
Herringbone fern
                Nephrolepis cordifolia
Holly fern   *Polystichum lonchitis*
House holly fern
                Cyrtomium falcatum
Huguenot fern   *Pteris multifida*
                Pteris serrulata
Interrupted fern
                Osmunda claytoniana
Irish holly fern
                Polystichum lonchitis
                confertum
Irish polypody
                Polypodium vulgare
                semilacerum
Jagged-edge hartstongue
                Scolopendrium vulgare
                laceratum

Japanese buckler fern
                Dryopteris erythrosora
Japanese climbing fern
                Lygodium japonicum
Japanese felt fern   *Pyrossia lingua*
Japanese holly fern
                Cyrtomium falcatum
                Polystichum falcatum
Japanese painted fern
                Aglaomorpha
                goeringianum pictum
Japanese shield fern
                Dryopteris erythrosora
Jersey fern
                Anogramma leptophylla
Jointed pine
                Polypodium subauriculatum
Kangaroo fern
                Microsorium diversifolium
Kidney maidenhair
                Adiantum reniforme
Kidney-shaped hartstongue
                Scolopendrium
                vulgare reniforme
King fern   *Angiopteris evecta*
                Marattia fraxinea
                Marattia salicina
Korau   *Cyathea medullaris*
Lacy ground fern
                Dennstaedia davallioides
Ladder brake   *Pteris longifolia*
                Pteris vittata
Ladder fern   *Blechnum spicant*
Lady fern   *Athyrium filix-femina*
Lanceolate spleenwort
                Asplenium billottii
                Asplenium lanceolatum
Leather fern   *Acrostichum aureum*
                Rumohra adiantiformis
Leatherwood fern
                Dryopteris marginalis
Leathery moonwort
                Botrychium multifidum
Leathery polypody
                Polypodium scouleri
Leathery shield fern
                Rumohra adiantiformis
Lemon-scented fern
                Oreopteris limbosperma
Licorice fern
                Polypodium glycyrrhiza
Limestone oak fern
                Gymnocarpium robertianum
Limestone polypody
                Polypodium calcareum
Little adder's tongue
                Ophioglossum lusitanicum
Maidenhair   *Adiantum capill*
                veneris
Maidenhair fern
                Adiantum pedatum
                Asplenium trichomanes

Maidenhair spleenwort

Maidenhair spleenwort
  Asplenium trichomanes

Malayan flowering fern
  Helminthostachys zeylanica

Malay climbing fern
  Lygodium circinatum

Male fern *Dryopteris filix-mas*
  Lastrea filix-mas

Mamaku *Cyathea medullaris*

Many-shaped hartstongue
  *Scolopendrium vulgare
  multiforme*

Marginal buckler fern
  Dryopteris marginalis

Marginal shield fern
  Dryopteris marginalis

Marsh buckler fern
  Lastrea thelypteris

Marsh fern *Dryopteris thelypteris*
  Thelypteris palustris

Mat spike moss
  Selaginella kraussiana

Mauritius spleenwort
  Asplenium daucifolium
  Asplenium viviparum

Mexican tree fern
  Cibotium schiedei

Moonwort *Botrychium lunaria*

Moosehorn *Platycerum superbum*

Mosquito fern *Azolla caroliniana*

Mosquito plant *Azolla caroliniana*

Moss fern *Selaginella cuspidata*
  Selaginella pallescens

Mother fern
  Asplenium bulbiferum

Mother shield fern
  Polystichum proliferum

Mother spleenwort
  Asplenium bulbiferum

Mountain bladder fern
  Cystopteris montana

Mountain buckler fern
  Lastrea montana
  Thelypteris oreopteris

Mountain holly fern
  Polystichum lonchitis

Mountain male fern
  Dryopteris oreades

Mountain polypody
  Polypodium phegopteris

Multi-crested male fern
  Lastrea filix-mas multi-cristata

Multi-forked lady fern
  *Athyrium filix-
  femina multifurcatum*

Narrow-branched hard fern
  *Blechnum spicant
  contractum-ramosum*

Narrow-leaved strap fern
  Polypodium angustifolium

Narrow-lined shield fern
  Polystichum angulare lineare

Necklace fern
  Asplenium flabellifolium

New York fern
  Thelypteris noveboracensis

New Zealand cliff brake
  Pellaea rotundifolia

New Zealand tree fern
  Dicksonia squarrosa

Northern beech fern
  Phegopteris connectilis
  Thelypteris phegopteris

Northern elkhorn
  Platycerium hillii

Northern maidenhair
  Adiantum pedatum

Northern oak fern
  Gymnocarpium robertianum

Notched polypody
  Polypodium vulgare crenatum

Oak fern
  Gymnocarpium dryopteris
  Histiopteris incisa
  Polypodium dryopteris

Oak-leaf fern *Drynaria quercifolia*
  Phymatodes quercifolia

Oblong woodsia *Woodsia ilvensis*

One-sided filmy fern
  Hymenophyllum unilaterale

One-sided rue-leaved
  spleenwort *Asplenium ru
  muraria unilaterale*

Ostrich-feather fern
  Matteuccia struthiopteris
  Struthiopteris germanica

Pala *Marattia douglasii*

Palm-leaf fern *Blechnum capense*

Para fern *Marattia fraxinea*
  Marattia salicina

Parasol fern *Gleichnia microphylla*

Parsley fern *Allosorus crispus*
  Cryptogramma crispa

Peacock fern
  Selaginella willldenovii

Peacock moss *Selaginella uncinata*

Pine fern *Aneimia adiantifolia*

Plums and custard fern
  Tricholomopsis rutilans

Ponga *Cyathea dealbata*

Potato fern *Marattia fraxinea*
  Marattia salicina

Pouched coral fern
  Gleichnia dicarpa

Princess pine
  Lycopodium obscurum

Prince of Wales' feather
  Leptopteris superba

Prickly buckler fern
  Lastrea spinulosa

Prickly rasp fern *Doodia aspera*

Prickly shield fern
  Arachniodes aristata
  Polystichum vestitum

Purple cliff brake
    Pellaea atropurpurea
Queen lady fern   *Athyrium filix-femina victoriae*
Rabbit's foot fern
    Davallia canariensis
    Davallia fejeensis
    Phlebodium aureum
    Polypodium aureum
Rainbow fern   *Culcita dubia*
    Selaginella uncinata
Rasp fern   *Doodia aspera*
Rattlesnake fern
    Botrychium virginianum
Refracted rock spleenwort
    Asplenium fontanum refractum
Resurrection fern
    Polypodium incanum
    Polypodium polypodioides
Resurrection plant
    Selaginella lepidophylla
Ribbon brake   *Pteris cretica*
Ribbon fern
    Polypodium phyllitidis
    Pteris cretica
Rigid buckler fern
    Dryopteris submontana
    Lastrea rigida
Rock felt fern   *Pyrossia rupestris*
Rock polypody
    Polypodium virginianum
Rock selaginella
    Selaginella rupestris
Rock spleenwort
    Asplenium fontanum
Rose-of-Jericho
    Selaginella lepidophylla
Rosy maidenhair
    Adiantum hispidulum
Rough dicksonia
    Dicksonia squarrosa
Rough maidenhair
    Adiantum hispidulum
Rough tree fern   *Cyathea australis*
Royal fern   *Osmunda regalis*
Rue-leaved spleenwort
    Asplenium ruta-muraria
Running pine
    Lycopodium clavatum
Rusty back fern
    Asplenium ceterach
    Ceterach officinarum
Rusty brake   *Pteris longifolia*
    Pteris vittata
Rusty woodsia   *Woodsia ilvensis*
Savannah fern
    Gleichnia dichotoma
    Gleichnia linearis
Scaly broad buckler fern
    Lastrea dilatata lepidota
Scaly male fern   *Dryopteris affinis*

Scaly spleenwort
    Asplenium ceterach
    Ceterach officinarum
Scrambling coral fern
    Gleichnia microphylla
Sea spleenwort
    Asplenium marinum
Sensitive fern   *Onoclea sensibilis*
Sharp-toothed alternate spleenwort
    Asplenium germanicum acutidentatum
Shield hare's foot
    Rumohra adiantiformis
Shining club moss
    Lycopodium lucidulum
Shining fan fern
    Sticherus flabellatus
Short-fronded hartstongue
    Scolopendrium vulgare truncatum
Shuttlecock fern
    Matteuccia struthiopteris
    Struthiopteris germanica
Sickle fern   *Pellaea falcata*
Silky fan fern   *Sticherus tener*
Silver dollar fern
    Adiantum peruvianum
Silver elkhorn   *Platycerium veitchii*
Silver fern
    Pityrogramma calomelanos
Silver glade fern
    Aglaomorpha thelypteroides
Silver king fern   *Cyathea dealbata*
Silvery glade fern
    Athyrium thelypteroides
    Diplazium acrostichoides
Silvery spleenwort
    Athyrium thelypteroides
    Diplazium acrostichoides
Skeleton soft prickly shield fern   *Polystichum angulare depauperatum*
Slender brake   *Pteris ensiformis*
Small rasp fern   *Doodia caudata*
Snail fern   *Tectaria cicutaria*
    Tectaria gemmifera
Snow brake   *Pteris ensiformis*
Soft-prickly shield fern
    Polystichum angulare
Soft shield fern
    Polystichum angulare
    Polystichum setiferum
Soft tree fern   *Dicksonia antarctica*
Southern beech fern
    Thelypteris hexagonoptera
Southern maidenhair
    Adiantum capillus-veneris
Spider fern   *Pteris multifida*
    Pteris serrulata
Spiny-spored quillwort
    Isoetes echinospora

COMMON NAMES

Split-fronded bracken

Common name	Scientific name
Split-fronded bracken	*Pteris aquilina bisulca*
Squirrel's foot fern	*Davallia bullata*
	Davallia mariesii
	Davallia trichomanoides
Staghorn	*Platycerium bifurcatum*
	Platycerium superbum
Stemless pepperwort	*Marsilea pubescens*
	Marsilea strigosa
Strap fern	*Polypodium phyllitidis*
Strap rib fern	*Blechnum patersonii*
Strap water fern	*Blechnum patersonii*
Sweat plant	*Selaginella cuspidata*
	Selaginella pallescens
Sword brake	*Pteris ensiformis*
Sword fern	*Nephrolepis cordifolia*
	Nephrolepis exaltata
	Polystichum munitum
Tangle fern	*Gleichnia dicarpa*
Tapering polypody	*Polypodium vulgare acutum*
Tasmanian tree fern	*Dicksonia antarctica*
Tasselled lady fern	*Athyrium filix-femina corymbiferum*
Thousand-leaved fern	*Hypolepis millefolia*
Tongue fern	*Pyrossia lingua*
Toothed brake	*Pteris tremula*
Toothed davallia	*Davallia denticulata*
Toothed wood fern	*Dryopteris austriaca spinulosa*
	Dryopteris carthusiana
	Dryopteris spinulosa
Trailing selaginella	*Selaginella kraussiana*
	Selaginella uncinata
Trailing spike moss	*Selaginella kraussiana*
Tree fern	*Cyathea arborea*
Treelet spike-moss	*Selaginella braunii*
Trembling brake	*Pteris tremula*
Trembling fern	*Pteris tremula*
Triangular water fern	*Ceratopteris richardii*
Tri-pinnate soft prickly shield fern	*Polystichum angulare tripinnatum*
Triple-branched polypody	*Polypodium dryopteris*
Trisect brake	*Pteris tripartita*
True maidenhair	*Adiantum capillus-veneris*
Truncate shield fern	*Polystichum angulare truncatum*
Tsusima holly fern	*Polystichum tsus-simense*
Tunbridge filmy fern	*Hymenophyllum tunbridgense*
Twin-fronded hartstongue	*Scolopendrium vulgare ramo-palmatum*
Twin-fronded lanceolate spleenwort	*Asplenium lanceolatum kalon*
Umbrella fern	*Gleichnia microphylla*
	Sticherus flabellatus
Variegated black maidenhair spleenwort	*Asplenium adiantum-nigrum variegatum*
Variegated black spleenwort	*Asplenium adiantum-nigrum variegatum*
Variegated horsetail	*Equisetum variegatum*
Variegated scouring brush	*Equisetum variegatum*
Venus' hair	*Adiantum capill veneris*
Virginia chain fern	*Woodwardia virginica*
Virginian moonwort	*Botrychium virginianum*
Walking fern	*Camptosorus rhizophyllus*
Wall fern	*Polypodium vulgare*
Wall polypody	*Polypodium vulgare*
Wall rue	*Asplenium ruta-muraria*
Wart fern	*Phymatodes scolopendrium*
	Polypodium phymatodes
	Polypodium scolopendria
	Polypodium vulgare
Water fern	*Azolla caroliniana*
	Ceratopteris thalictroides
Wavy hartstongue	*Scolopendrium vulgare undulato-ramosum*
Weeping spleenwort	*Asplenium flaccidum*
	Asplenium majus
	Asplenium mayi
Welsh polypody	*Polypodium vulgare cambricum*
Western bracken	*Pteridium pubescens*
Western polypody	*Polypodium hesperium*
	Polypodium interjectum
West Indian tree fern	*Cyathea arborea*
Wheki	*Dicksonia squarrosa*
Wheki-ponga	*Dicksonia fibrosa*
Whisk fern	*Psilotum nudum*
Wide-fronded scaly spleenwort	*Asplenium ceterach kalon*

FERNS

Woolly tree fern

Wig tree fern   *Cyathea baileyana*
Willdenow's selaginella
          Selaginella willdenovii
Woolly tree fern
          Dicksonia antarctica
          Dicksonia fibrosa

FUNGI

A large group of simple plants lacking chlorophyll is covered by the word fungi. This section is concerned only with the larger edible, inedible, and poisonous fungi which are visible to the naked eye. Many edible fungi are matched in appearance with inedible, or even poisonous types so it is reckless to gather wild fungi unless you are experienced and familiar with the subtle differences. In the following list entries have been classified by the use of bracketed initials thus:

(E) – Edible, but some may be allergic to them.
(I) – Inedible for a variety of reasons.
(P) – Poisonous, but not usually fatal.
(F) – Can be fatal if eaten, sometimes within minutes.

Field mushroom –
Agaricus campestris

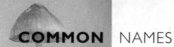

Amethyst deceiver

Amethyst deceiver
Laccaria amethystea (E)
Aniseed toadstool
Clytocybe odora (E)
Bachelor's buttons
Bulgaria inquinans (E)
Bare-tooth russala
Russala vesca (E)
Basket fungus
Clathrus cancellatus (E)
Clathrus ruber (E)
Bay boletus   *Boletus badius* (E)
Xerocomus badius (E)
Beech tuft
Oudemansiella mucida (I)
Beechwood sickener
Russula mairei (I)
Beefsteak fungus
Fistulina hepatica (E)
Bigelow's blewit   *Lepista irina* (E)
Birch bracket fungus
Piptoporus betulinus (E)
Polyporus betulinus (E)
Birch polypore
Piptoporus betulinus (E)
Bird's nest fungus
Crucibulum crucibuliforme (I)
Crucibulum laeve (I)
Bitter bolete   *Tylopilus felleus* (I)
Bitter boletus
Gyroporus castaneus (E)
Bitter cep   *Tylopilus felleus* (I)
Bitter hydnum
Hydnum scabrosum (I)
Bitter-sweet fungus
Hebeloma sacchariolens (P)
Black birch boletus
Leccinum melaneum (E)
Black bulgar
Bulgaria inquinans (E)
Blackening russula
Russula nigricans (I)
Black helvella
Helvella lacunosa (P)
Black saddle helvella
Helvella fusca (P)
Blewits   *Lepista saeva* (E)
Tricholoma personatum (E)
Blue and yellow russula
Russula cyanoxantha (E)
Blushing bracket fungus
Daedaleopsis confragosa (I)
Bonnet mycena
Mycena galericulata (I)
Bootlace fungus
Armillaria mellea (E)
Clitocybe mellea (E)
Brain fungus   *Sparassis crispa* (E)
Branched oyster fungus
Pleurotus cornucopiae (E)
Brick-red agaric
Hypholoma sublateritium (I)

Bronze boletus   *Boletus aereus* (E)
Brown birch boletus
Boletus leucophareus (E)
Leccinum scabrum (E)
Brown roll-rim
Paxillus involutus (P)
Brown star fungus
Peziza ammophila (P)
Brown wood mushroom
Agaricus sylvaticus (E)
Psalliota sylvatica (E)
Buckler agaric
Entoloma clypeatum (I)
Butter cap   *Collybia butyracea* (E)
Buttery collybia
Collybia butyracea (E)
Caesar's mushroom
Amanita caesarea (I)
Candlesnuff fungus
Xylaria hypoxylon (I)
Carpet fungus
Thelephora terrestris (I)
Cauliflower fungus
Masseola crispa (E)
Sparassis crispa (E)
Sparassis ramosa (E)
Cep   *Boletus edulis* (E)
Changeable agaric
Kuehneromyces mutabilis (E)
Changeable mutabilis
Kuehneromyces mutabilis (E)
Chanterelle
Cantharellus cibarius (E)
Chestnut boletus
Gyroporus castaneus (E)
Cinnabar polypore
Pycnoporus cinnabarinus (I)
Clouded agaric
Clitocybe nebularis (E)
Lepista nebularis (E)
Clouded clitocybe
Clitocybe nebularis (E)
Lepista nebularis (E)
Clover windling
Marasmius oreades (E)
Club foot   *Clitocybe clavipes* (I)
Clustered tough shank
Collybia confluens (I)
Coconut-scented milk cap
Lactarius glyciosmus (I)
Coffin filler   *Amanita virosa* (F)
Common earthball
Scleroderma citrinum (P)
Common grisette
Amanita vaginata (E)
Common morel
Morchella esculenta (E)
Common puffball
Lycoperdon gemmatum (E)
Lycoperdon perlatum (E)
Common white helvella
Helvella crispa (P)

Goat's lip mushroom

Common white inocybe
Inocybe geophylla (P)

Conical inocybe
Inocybe fastigiata (P)

Conical morel
Morchella conica (E)

Conical wax cap
Hygrocybe conica (I)

Copper trumpet
Clitocybe illudens (P)
Clitocybe olearia (P)
Omphalotus olearius (P)

Coral spot fungus
Nectria cinnabarina (I)

Corn smut *Ustilago maydis* (P)

Cow boletus *Suillus bovinus* (E)

Cow fungus
Boletus leucophareus (E)
Leccinum scabrum (E)

Crazed boletus
Boletus chrysenteron (I)

Crested coral fungus
Clavulina coralloides (P)
Clavulina cristata (P)

Cultivated mushroom
Agaricus bisporus (E)

Cupped vellosa
Helvella vellosa (P)

Dark red russula
Russula xerampelina (E)

Dead man's fingers
Xylaria polymorpha (I)

Death cap *Amanita phalloides* (F)

Deceiver *Laccaria laccata* (E)

Deer mushroom
Pluteus atricapillus (E)
Pluteus cervinus (E)

Destroying angel
Amanita virosa (F)

Devil's boletus *Boletus satanas* (P)

Devil's egg fungus
Phallus hadriani (I)

Dingy agaric
Tricholoma portentosum (E)

Distorted helvella
Helvella elastica (P)

Dog stinkhorn *Mutinus caninus* (I)

Donkey's ear fungus
Otidea onotica (I)

Downy boletus
Boletus subtomentosus (E)
Xerocomus subtomentosus (E)

Dryad's saddle
Polyporus squamosus (E)

Ear-pick fungus
Auriscalpium vulgare (I)

Earthfan *Thelephora terrestris* (I)

Earthstar *Geastrum fimbriatum* (I)
Geastrum fornicatum (I)
Geastrum pectinatum (I)
Geastrum sessile (I)
Geastrum triplex (I)

Elf cup *Sarcoscypha coccinea* (E)

Emetic russula *Russula emetica* (P)

Ergot *Claviceps purpurea* (P)

Eyelash cup fungus
Scutellinia scutellata (I)

Eyelash fungus
Scutellinia scutellata (I)

Faded russala
Russala decolorans (E)

Fairy bonnets
Coprinus disseminatus (P)

Fairy cake fungus
Hebeloma crustuliniforme (F)

Fairy ring mushroom
Marasmius oreades (E)

Fairy sunshade *Lepiota procera* (E)
Macrolepiota procera (E)

False blusher
Amanita pantherina (P)

False chanterelle
Hygrophoropsis aurantiaca (I)

False death cap *Amanita citrina* (I)
Amanita mappa (I)

False morel
Gyromitra esculenta (P)

Fawn agaric *Pluteus atricapillus* (E)
Pluteus cervinus (E)

Field mushroom
Agaricus campestris (E)
Psalliota campestris (E)

Firwood agaric
Tricholoma equestre (E)
Tricholoma flavovirens (E)

Fleecy milk cap
Lactarius vellereus (I)

Fly agaric *Amanita muscaria* (P)

Fool's mushroom
Amanita verna (F)

Foxy spot *Collybia maculata* (I)

Fragile russula *Russula fragilis* (P)

French truffle
Tuber melanosporum (E)

Gas tar fungus
Trichloma sulphureum (P)

Giant club
Clavariadelphus pistillaris (E)

Giant giromitra
Neogyromitra gigas (E)

Giant polypore
Meripilus giganteus (I)

Giant puffball *Calvatia gigantea* (E)
Langermannia gigantea (E)
Lycoperdon maximum (E)

Gipsy mushroom
Pholiota caperata (E)
Rozites caperata (E)

Glistening inkcap
Coprinus micaceus (I)

Goat's lip mushroom
Boletus subtomentosus (E)
Xerocomus subtomentosus (E)

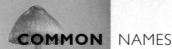

Goaty-smell cortinarius

Goaty-smell cortinarius
Cortinarius traganus (I)
Golden russula   *Russula aurata* (E)
Grass-green russula
Russula aeruginea (E)
Green agaric
Russula cyanoxantha (E)
Russula virescens (E)
Green cracking russula
Russula virescens (E)
Green earth tongue
Microglossum viride (I)
Greenstain fungus
Chlorociboria aeruginacens (I)
Chlorosplenium aeruginosum (I)
Green wood-cup
Chlorociboria aeruginacens (I)
Chlorospenium aeruginacens (I)
Grey agaric
Tricholoma terreum (E)
Grey coral fungus
Clavulina cinerea (P)
Grey inkcap
Coprinus atramentarius (E)
Hairy stereum   *Sterum hirsutum* (I)
Hare's ear fungus *Otidea onotica* (I)
Hedgehog fungus
Hericium erinaceum (E)
Hydnum repandum (E)
Lycoperdon echinatum (E)
Hen-of-the-woods
Grifola frondosa (E)
Polyporus frondosus (E)
Honey fungus *Armillaria mellea* (E)
Clitocybe mellea (E)
Hoof fungus *Fomes fomentarius* (I)
Hornbeam boletus
Leccinum carpini (E)
Leccinum griseum (E)
Horn of plenty
Cantharellus cornucopioides (E)
Craterellus cornucopioides (E)
Horse agaric   *Agaricus arvensis* (E)
Psalliota arvensis (E)
Horse-dung fungus
Coprinus niveus (I)
Horsehair fungus
Marasmius androsaceus (I)
Horse mushroom
Agaricus arvensis (E)
Psalliota arvensis (E)
Indian paint fungus
Echinodontium tinctorium (I)
Indigo boletus
Boletus cyanescens (E)
Gyroporus cyanescens (E)
Inkcap *Coprinus atramentarius* (E)
Coprinus comatus (E)
Ivory wax-cap
Hygrophorus eburneus (I)
Japanese sunshade
Coprinus plicatilis (P)
Jellybaby fungus *Leotia lubrica* (E)

Jellybean fungus   *Leotia lubrica* (E)
Jellybrain fungus
Tremella mesenterica (I)
Jello tongue
Pseudohydnum gelatinosum (P)
Jelly tongue
Pseudohydnum gelatinosum (P)
Jersey cow boletus
Suillus bovinus (E)
Jew's ear
Hirneola auricula-judae (P)
Judas's ear
Auricularia auricula-judae (E)
King Alfred's balls
Daldinia concentrica (I)
King Alfred's cakes
Daldinia concentrica (I)
King Alfred's cramp balls
Daldinia concentrica (I)
Knotted fungus
*Gymnosporangium
clavariaeforme* (I)
Larch boletus   *Suillus grevillei* (E)
Lawyer's wig *Coprinus comatus* (E)
Leathery russula
Russula alutacea (E)
Liberty cap
Psilocybe semilanceata (P)
Little Japanese umbrella
Coprinus plicatilis (P)
Little nail fungus *Mycena ribula* (P)
Livid entoloma
Entoloma lividum (P)
Entoloma sinuatum (P)
Long root mushroom
Oudemansiella radicata (E)
Lurid boletus   *Boletus luridus* (E)
Magpie fungus
Coprinus picaceus (P)
Man-on-horseback
Tricholoma equestre (E)
Tricholoma flavovirens (E)
March mushroom
Hygrophorus marzuolus (E)
Maze gill *Daedalea quercina* (P)
Meadow wax cap
Hygrocybe pratensis (I)
Mica inkcap *Coprinus micaceus* (E)
Milk agaric *Lactarius deliciosus* (E)
Milk cap *Lactarius deliciosus* (E)
Milky conocybe *Conocybe lactea* (I)
Miller mushroom
Clitopilus prunulus (E)
Moor club *Clavaria argillacea* (I)
Morel *Morchella elata* (E)
Mortician cap
Amanita phalloides (F)
Multi-branched fungus
Ramaria formosa (P)

Shaggy pholiota

Multi-zoned bracket fungus
    Coriolus versicolor (P)
    Polyporus versicolor (P)
    Trametes versicolor (P)

Multi-zoned polypore
    Coriolus versicolor (P)
    Polyporus versicolor (P)
    Trametes versicolor (P)

Oak milk cap   *Lactarius quietus* (I)

Oaktree boletus
    Leccinum quercinum (E)

Oaktree collybia
    Collybia dryophila (E)

Olive boletus   *Boletus calopus* (I)

Olive-green russula
    Russula olivacea (E)

Orange birch boletus
    Leccinum testaceoscabrum (E)
    Leccinum versipelle (E)

Orange cap boletus
    Leccinum aurantiacum (E)

Orange-peel fungus
    Aleuria aurantia (E)
    Peziza aurantia (E)

Oyster mushroom
    Pleurotus ostreatus (E)

Padi-straw fungus
    Volvaria volvacea (E)
    Volvariella volvacea (E)

Panther   *Amanita pantherina* (P)

Panther cap
    Amanita pantherina (P)

Parasol mushroom
    Lepiota procera (E)
    Macrolepiota procera (E)

Parrot fungus
    Hygrocybe psittacina (E)
    Hygrophorus psittacinus (E)

Parrot wax cap
    Hygrocybe psittacina (E)

Pavement mushroom
    Agaricus bitorquis (E)

Penny bun fungus   *Boletus edulis* (E)

Perigord truffle
    Tuber melanosporum (E)

Piedmont truffle
    Tuber magnatum (E)

Pine fire fungus
    Rhyzina undulata (P)

Pine forest mushroom
    Gomphidius rutilis (E)

Pink bottom mushroom
    Agaricus campestris (E)
    Psalliota campestris (E)

Pixie cup   *Sarcoscypha coccinea* (E)

Pixie's cap fungus   *Mycena vitilis* (I)

Plum agaric   *Clitopilus prunulus* (E)

Plums and custard
    Tricholomopsis rutilans (E)

Poached egg fungus
    Oudemansiella mucida (I)

Poison pie
    Hebeloma crustuliniforme (F)

Poor man's sweetbread
    Lycoperdon gemmatum (E)
    Lycoperdon perlatum (E)

Purple-black russula
    Russula undulata (P)

Purple boletus
    Boletus rhodoxanthus (P)

Rainfall boletus   *Suillus bovinus* (E)

Razor-strop fungus
    Piptoporus betulinus (E)
    Polyporus betulinus (E)

Red cracked boletus
    Boletus chrysenteron (I)

Red-leg boletus
    Boletus erythropus (E)

Red-staining inocybe
    Inocybe patouillardii (F)

Ringed boletus   *Suillus luteus* (E)

Roll-rim fungus
    Paxillus involutus (P)

Root fomes
    Heterobasidion annosum (I)

Rose-gilled grisette
    Volvaria speciosa (E)
    Volvariella speciosa (E)

Rose mildew
    Sphaerotheca pannosa (I)

Royal amanita   *Amanita regalis* (P)

Royal boletus   *Boletus regius* (E)

Rusty agaric
    Kuehneromyces mutabilis (E)

Rusty milk cap   *Lactarius rufus* (I)

Rusty oak fungus
    Fistulina hepatica (E)

Saffron milk cap
    Lactarius deliciosus (E)

Saint George's mushroom
    Calocybe gambosa (E)
    Tricholoma gambosa (E)
    Tricholoma georgii (E)

Satan's mushroom
    Boletus satanas (P)

Scaly hydnum
    Hydnum imbricatum (E)
    Sarcodon imbricatum (E)

Scaly polypore
    Polyporus squamosus (E)

Scarlet caterpillar fungus
    Cordyceps militaris (P)

Scarlet cup
    Sarcoscypha coccinea (E)

Scarlet elf cap
    Sarcoscypha coccinea (E)

Shaggy cap   *Coprinus comatus* (E)

Shaggy inkcap
    Coprinus comatus (E)

Shaggy milk cap
    Lactarius torminosus (I)

Shaggy parasol   *Lepiota rhacodes* (E)
    Macrolepiota rhacodes (E)

Shaggy pholiota
    Pholiota squarrosa (I)

COMMON NAMES

Sheathed agaric

Sheathed agaric   *Amanita fulva* (E)
Shiitake fungus
          Lentinula edodes (E)
Shining inkcap
          Coprinus micaceus (I)
Showy mushroom
          Boleta speciosus (E)
Sickener mushroom
          Russula emetica (P)
Silverleaf fungus
   Chondrostereum purpureum (I)
Skullcap inocybe
          Inocybe napipes (P)
Slippery jack   *Suillus luteus* (E)
Smokey-gilled woodlover
   Hypholoma capnoides (I)
Snowy wax cap
          Hygrocybe virginea (I)
Spindle shank   *Collybia fusipes* (E)
Splash cup   *Cyathus striatus* (I)
Split gill fungus
   Schizophyllum commune (P)
Spotted tough-shank
          Collybia maculata (I)
Spring amanita   *Amanita verna* (F)
Spurred rye
          Claviceps purpurea (P)
Stinging-nettle fungus
          Calyptella capula (I)
Stinkhorn   *Phallus impudicus* (E)
Sulfur polypore
          Laetiporus sulphureus (E)
Sulfur tuft
   Hypholoma fasciculare (P)
   Namatoloma fasciculare (P)
Sulphur polypore
          Laetiporus sulphureus (E)
Sulphur tuft
   Hypholoma fasciculare (P)
   Namatoloma fasciculare (P)
Summer boletus
          Boletus aestivalis (E)
          Boletus reticulatus (E)
Summer truffle   *Tuber aestivum* (E)
Sweetbread mushroom
          Clitopilus prunulus (E)
Sycamore tarspot
          Rhytisma acerinum (I)
Tasselated toadstool
          Lepiota castanea (P)
Tawny grisette   *Amanita fulva* (E)
The blusher
          Amanita rubescens (E)
The deceiver   *Laccaria laccata* (E)
Tiger tricholoma
   Tricholoma pardalotum (P)
   Tricholoma pardinum (P)
Tinder fungus
          Fomes fomentarius (I)
Tripe fungus
          Auricularia mesenterica (I)

Trooping crumble cap
          Coprinus disseminatus (P)
   Pseudocoprinus disseminatus (P)
Truffle   *Tuber aestivum* (E)
Trumpet agaric
          Clitocybe geotropa (E)
Trumpet of death
   Craterellus cornucopioides (E)
Turban fungus
          Gyromitra infula (E)
          Hevella infula (E)
Ugly mushroom
          Lactarius necator (I)
          Lactarius plumbeus (I)
          Lactarius turpis (I)
Urban mushroom
          Agaricus bitorquis (E)
Variegated boletus
          Suillus variegatus (E)
Velvet cap   *Lacrymaria velutina* (I)
Velvet shank
          Collybia velutipes (E)
          Flammulina velutipes (E)
Verdigris fungus
          Stropharia aeruginosa (E)
Weeping widow
   Lacrymaria lacrymabunda (I)
          Lacrymaria velutina (I)
White birch boletus
          Leccinum holopus (E)
White poplar mushroom
          Leccinum duriusculum (E)
White truffle
          Tuber magnatum (E)
Winter mushroom
          Collybia velutipes (E)
          Flammulina velutipes (E)
Witch's broom
          Taphrina betulina (P)
Witch's butter
          Exidia glandulosa (I)
Wood agaric
          Collybia dryophila (E)
Wood blewits
          Lapista nuda (E)
          Tricholoma nudum (E)
Wood hedgehog
          Dentinum repandum (E)
          Hydnum repandum (E)
Woodland black spot
          Gomphidius glutinosus (E)
Woodland pink mushroom
          Amanita rubescens (E)
Wood mushroom
          Agaricus silvicola (E)
          Psalliota silvicola (E)
Wood woollyfoot
          Collybia peronata (I)
Woolly milk cap
          Lactarius torminosus (I)
Wrinkled club
          Clavulina rugosa (P)

FUNGI

Yellow swamp russula

Yellow agaric
    Tricholoma sulphureum (P)
Yellow brain fungus
    Tremella mesenterica (I)
Yellow russula
    Russula ochroleuca (I)
Yellow stainer
    Agaricus xanthodermus (P)
Yellow swamp russula
    Russula claroflava (E)
    Russula flava (E)

GRASSES, REEDS, SEDGES, BAMBOOS, VETCHES, ETC.

True grasses are members of the family *Gramineae* and are found in almost every corner of the planet in one form or another, but in this section we are concerned with the ornamentals, meadow grasses, timber grasses (bamboos), soil-holding or sandbinding grasses, as well as wetland subjects such as sedges and reeds. Some grasses may also be listed under 'Aquatics'.

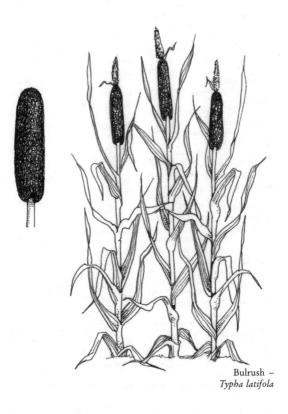

Bulrush –
Typha latifola

Abyssinian feathertop

Abyssinian feathertop	
	Pennisetum villosum
Adrue	*Cyperus articulatus*
African Bermuda grass	
	Cynodon transvaalensis
African fountain grass	
	Pennisetum setaceum
African millet	*Eleusine coracana*
	Pennisetum americanum
Alaska wheat	*Triticum turgidum*
Aleppo grass	*Sorghum halepense*
Alfalfa	*Medicago sativa*
Alpine cat's tail	*Phleum alpinum*
	Phleum commutatum
Alpine clover	*Trifolium alpinum*
Alpine foxtail	*Alopecurus alpinus*
Alpine hair grass	
	Deschampsia alpina
Alpine meadow grass	*Poa alpina*
Alpine rush	
	Juncus alpinoarticulatus
Alpine sedge	*Carex norvegica*
Alpine timothy	*Phleum alpinum*
	Phleum commutatum
Alsike clover	*Trifolium hybridum*
Alta fescue	*Festuca elatior*
Altai wild rye	*Elymus angustus*
American beach grass	
	Ammophila breviligulata
American cord grass	
	Spartina alterniflora
American wild oats	
	Chasmanthium latifolium
Amur silver grass	
	Miscanthus sacchariflorus
Angleton bluestem	
	Dichanthium aristatum
Angleton grass	
	Dichantium aristatum
Animated oat grass	*Avena sterilis*
Animated oats	*Avena sterilis*
Annual beard grass	
	Polypogon monspeliensis
Annual bluegrass	*Poa annua*
Annual meadow-grass	*Poa annua*
Annual vernal grass	
	Anthroxanthum puelii
Annual wild rice	*Zizania aquatica*
Aral wild rye	*Elymus aralensis*
Arrow bamboo	
	Arundinaria japonica
	Pseudosasa japonica
Arrow cane	*Gynerium sagittatum*
Australian bluestem	
	Bothriochloa intermedia
Australian danthonia	
	Danthonia semiannularis
Australian feather grass	
	Stipa elegantissima
Australian oat grass	
	Danthonia semiannularis

Australian rye grass	
	Lolium multiflorum
Australian windmill grass	
	Chloris ventricosa
Autumn bent	*Agrostis perennans*
Awnless brome	*Bromus inermis*
Awnless sheep's fescue	
	Festuca tenuifolia
Bahia grass	*Paspalum notatum*
Balfour's meadowgrass	
	Poa balfouri
Balkan bluegrass	
	Sesleria heufleriana
Baltic rush	*Juncus ballicus*
Bambusa	*Bambusa beecheyana*
Barley	*Hordeum vulgare*
Barn grass	*Echinochloa crus-galli*
Barnyard grass	*Echinochloa*
	crus-galli
Barnyard millet	*Echinochloa*
	crus-galli
Barren brome	*Bromus sterilis*
Basket grass	*Oplismenus hirtellus*
Beach pea	*Lathyrus japonicus*
	Lathyrus littoralis
Beaked sedge	*Carex rostrata*
Bearded couch	
	Agropyron caninum
	Elymus caninus
Bearded fescue	*Vulpia ambigua*
Bearded twitch	
	Agropyron caninum
Bear grass	*Xerophyllum tenax*
Beechey bamboo	
	Bambusa beecheyana
Bengal grass	*Setaria italica*
Bermuda grass	*Cynodon dactylon*
Big bluegrass	*Poa ampla*
Big bluestem grass	
	Andropogon gerardii
Big galleta	*Hilaria rigida*
Birdseed grass	
	Phalaris canariensis
Bird's foot sedge	
	Carex ornithopoda
Bird's foot trefoil	
	Lotus corniculatus
Bird vetch	*Vicia cracca*
Bitter vetch	*Vicia ervilia*
Black bamboo	*Phyllostachys nigra*
Black bent	*Agrostis gigantea*
Black bog rush	*Schoenus nigricans*
Black grama	*Bouteloua eriopoda*
Black grass	
	Alopecurus myosuroides
Black medick	*Medicago lupulina*
Black sedge	*Carex atrata*
Black twitch	
	Alopecurus myosuroides
Bladder sedge	*Carex vesicaria*

Blue bent — *Molinia caerulea*

Bluebunch wheatgrass — *Agropyron spicatum*

Blue couch grass — *Digitaria didactyla*

Blue fescue — *Festuca ovina glauca* / *Festuca glauca*

Blue finger grass — *Digitaria didactyla*

Blue grama — *Bouteloua gracilis*

Blue love grass — *Eragrostis chloromelas*

Blue moor grass — *Sesleria caerulea* / *Sesleria albicans*

Blue panic grass — *Panicum antidotale*

Blue stem — *Schizachyrium scoparium*

Blue wild rye — *Elymus glaucous*

Blunt-flowered rush — *Juncus subnodulosus*

Boer love grass — *Eragrostis chloromelas*

Bog hair grass — *Deschampsia setacea*

Bog sedge — *Carex limosa*

Borrer's saltmarsh grass — *Puccinellia fasciculata*

Bottle sedge — *Carex rostrata*

Bowles' golden grass — *Milium effusum aureum*

Brahman grass — *Dichanthium annulatum*

Branched bur reed — *Sparganium erectum*

Branched cup grass — *Eriochloa aristata*

Bread wheat — *Triticum aestivum*

Bristle bent — *Agrostis curtisii*

Bristle club rush — *Scirpus setaceus*

Bristle grass — *Setaria viridis*

Bristle oat — *Avena strigosa*

Bristle scirpus — *Scirpus setaceus*

Bristly bent — *Agrostis setacea*

Broad bean — *Vicia faba*

Broad-leaved cotton grass — *Eriophorum latifolium*

Broad-leaved meadow grass — *Poa chaixii*

Broad-leaved mud sedge — *Carex paupercula*

Broad red clover — *Trifolium pratense praecox*

Broom — *Schizachyrium scoparium*

Broom beard grass — *Schizachyrium scoparium*

Broomcorn — *Panicum miliaceum* / *Sorghum vulgare*

Broomcorn millet — *Panicum miliaceum*

Brown beak sedge — *Rhynchospora fusca*

Brown bent — *Agrostis canina*

Brown bent grass — *Agrostis perennans*

Brown bog rush — *Schoenus ferrugineus*

Brown cyperus — *Cyperus fuscus*

Brown durra — *Sorghum vulgare durra*

Brown sedge — *Carex disticha*

Brown top — *Agrostis tenuis*

Browntop millet — *Panicum ramosum*

Buddham bamboo — *Bambusa ventricosa*

Buddha's belly bamboo — *Bambusa ventricosa*

Buffalo grass — *Buchloe dactyloides* / *Stenotaphrum secundatum*

Buffel grass — *Pennisetum ciliare*

Bulbous barley — *Hordeum bulbosum*

Bulbous bluegrass — *Poa bulbosa*

Bulbous foxtail — *Alopecurus bulbosus*

Bulbous meadow grass — *Poa bulbosa*

Bulbous panic grass — *Panicum bulbosum*

Bulbous rush — *Juncus bulbosus*

Bulrush — *Typha latifolia*

Bulrush (biblical) — *Cyperus papyrus*

Bunch grass — *Schizachyrium scoparium*

Bur clover — *Medicago hispida*

Burma reed — *Neyraudia reynaudiana*

Bush grass — *Calamagrostis epigejos*

Caithness sedge — *Carex recta*

Calcutta bamboo — *Dendrocalamus strictus*

Caley pea — *Lathyrus hirsutus*

Californian brome — *Bromus carinatus*

Cana brava — *Arundo donax*

Canada pea — *Vicia cracca*

Canadian bluegrass — *Poa compressa*

Canadian wild rye — *Elymus canadensis*

Canary grass — *Phalaris canariensis*

Canebrake bamboo — *Arundinaria gigantea*

Cane reed — *Arundinaria gigantea*

Capitate rush — *Juncus capitatus*

Carib grass — *Eriochloa polystachya*

Carnation grass — *Carex panicea*

Carnation sedge — *Carex panicea*

Carpet grass — *Axonopus affinis*

Carrizo — *Arundo donax* / *Phragmites australis*

Cat grass

Cat grass	*Leersia oryzoides*
Cat's tail grass	*Phleum pratense*
Caucasian bluestem	*Bothriochloa caucasica*
Centipede grass	*Eremochloa ophiuroides*
Chalk false brome	*Brachypodium pinnatum*
Chalk sedge	*Carex polyphylla*
Chamois grass	*Hutchinsia alpina*
Chee grass	*Stipa splendens*
Chestnut rush	*Juncus castaneus*
Chewing's fescue	*Festuca rubra*
China grass	*Boehmeria nivea*
Chinese fountain grass	*Pennisetum alopecuroides*
Chinese mat grass	*Cyperus tagetiformis*
Chinese pennisetum	*Pennisetum alopecuroides*
Chinese silver grass	*Miscanthus sinensis*
Chinese sugar maple	*Sorghum saccharatum*
Chinese sweet cane	*Saccarum sinense*
Chinese water chestnut	*Eleocharis dulcis*
	Eleocharis tuberosa
Chinese wild rye	*Elymus chinensis*
Citronella grass	*Cymbopogon nardus*
Chufa	*Cyperus esculentus*
Cloud bent	*Agrostis nebulosa*
Cloud grass	*Agrostis nebulosa*
Club rush	*Scirpus lacustris*
Club sedge	*Carex buxbaumii*
Club wheat	*Triticum compactum*
Cocksfoot	*Dactylis glomerata*
Cockspur grass	*Echinochloa crus-galli*
Colonial bent	*Agrostis tenuis*
Colorado grass	*Panicum texanum*
Common bamboo	*Bambusa vulgaris*
Common barley	*Hordeum vulgare*
Common bent	*Agrostis tenuis*
Common bird's foot	*Ornithopus perpusillus*
Common bulrush	*Scirpus lacustris*
Common carpet grass	*Axonopus affinis*
Common cat-tail	*Typha latifolia*
Common cord grass	*Spartina anglica*
Common cotton grass	*Eriophorum angustifolium*
Common couch	*Elymus repens*

Common feather grass	*Stipa pennata*
Common foxtail	*Alopecurus pratensis*
Common horsetail	*Equisetum hyemale*
Common meadow grass	*Poa pratensis*
Common millet	*Panicum miliaceum*
Common quaking grass	*Briza media*
Common reed	*Phragmites australis*
	Phragmites communis
Common rush	*Juncus subuliflorus*
	Juncus communis
Common rye	*Secale cereale*
Common saltmarsh grass	*Puccinellia maritima*
Common scouring brush	*Equisetum hyemale*
Common sedge	*Carex nigra*
Common spike rush	*Eleocharis palustris*
Common timothy	*Phleum pratense*
Common vetch	*Vicia angustifolia*
	Vicia sativa
Common wheat	*Triticum aestivum*
Common wild oat	*Avena fatua*
Common wood rush	*Luzula campestris*
Compact brome	*Bromus madritensis*
Cordgrass	*Spartina pectinata*
Corn	*Zea mays*
Corn silk	*Zea mays*
Cossack asparagus	*Typha latifolia*
Couch grass	*Agropyron repens*
	Elymus repens
Cow hop clover	*Trifolium procumbens*
Cow vetch	*Vicia cracca*
Crab grass	*Digitaria sanguinalis*
Creeping bent	*Agrostis stolonifera*
Creeping brown sedge	*Carex disticha*
Creeping dog's tooth grass	*Cynodon dactylon*
Creeping fescue	*Festuca rubra*
Creeping finger grass	*Cynodon dactylon*
	Digitaria serotina
Creeping foxtail	*Alopecurus arundinaceus*
Creeping signal grass	*Brachiaria subquadripara*
Creeping soft grass	*Holcus mollis*

GRASSES

European feather grass

Creeping twitch grass	*Agropyron repens*
	Elymus repens
Creeping windmill grass	*Chloris truncata*
Crested dogstail	*Cynosurus cristatus*
Crested hair grass	*Koeleria cristata*
	Koeleria gracilis
	Koeleria macrantha
Crested wheatgrass	*Agropyron cristatum*
Crimson clover	*Trifolium incarnatum*
Crinkled hair grass	*Deschampsia flexuosa*
Culeu	*Chusquea culeou*
Curly mesquite	*Hilaria belangeri*
Curved sea hard grass	*Parapholis incurva*
Curved sedge	*Carex maritima*
Curved wood rush	*Luzula arcuata*
Cuscus	*Pennisetum glaucum*
Cut grass	*Leersia oryzoides*
Cyperus sedge	*Carex pseudocyperus*
Dallis grass	*Paspalum dilatatum*
Dark sedge	*Carex buxbaumii*
Darnel	*Lolium temulentum*
Darnel sedge	*Carex loliacea*
Deer grass	*Scirpus cespitosus*
Dense silky bent	*Apera interrupta*
Desert wheatgrass	*Agropyron sibiricum*
Diaz bluestem	*Dichanthium annulatum*
Dioecious sedge	*Carex dioica*
Distant-flowered sedge	*Carex remota*
Distant sedge	*Carex distans*
Doddering dillies	*Briza media*
Dog grass	*Agropyron caninum*
Dog hair grass	*Deschampsia setacea*
Dogstooth grass	*Dichanthium ischaenum*
Don's twitch	*Agropyron donianum*
Doob grass	*Cynodon dactylon*
Dotted sedge	*Carex punctata*
Double-grain spelt	*Triticum dicoccon*
Double-grain wheat	*Triticum dicoccon*
Double-stemmed sedge	*Carex diandra*
Downy-fruited sedge	*Carex filiformis*
	Carex lasiocarpa
Downy oat grass	*Helictotrichon pubescens*
Drake	*Avena fatua*

Drooping brome	*Bromus tectorum*
Drooping love grass	*Eragrostis curvula*
Drooping sedge	*Carex pendula*
Dune fescue	*Vulpia membranacea*
	Vulpia fasciculata
Dune grass	*Elymus arenarius*
Durra	*Sorghum vulgare durra*
Durum wheat	*Triticum durum*
Dutch mice	*Lathyrus tuberosus*
Dutch rush	*Equisetum hyemale*
Dutch white clover	*Trifolium repens*
Dwarf bamboo	*Arundinaria pumila*
Dwarf fern leaf bamboo	*Arundinaria disticha*
Dwarf meadow grass	*Poa annua*
Dwarf papyrus	*Cyperus isocladus*
Dwarf rush	*Juncus capitatus*
Dwarf sedge	*Carex humilis*
Dwarf spike-rush	*Eleocharis parvula*
Dwarf wheat	*Triticum compactum*
Dwarf white-stripe bamboo	*Arundinaria variegata*
Early hair grass	*Aira praecox*
Early meadow grass	*Poa infirma*
Early sand grass	*Mibora minima*
Earth nut pea	*Lathyrus tuberosus*
Earth almond	*Cyperus esculentus*
Eel grass	*Vallisneria spiralis*
Egyptian millet	*Sorghum halepense*
Egyptian paper rush	*Cyperus papyrus*
Einkorn	*Triticum monococcum*
Elephant grass	*Pennisetum purpureum*
	Typha elephanta
Elk grass	*Xerophyllum tenax*
Elongated sedge	*Carex elongata*
Emmer	*Triticum dicoccon*
English bean	*Vicia faba*
English bluegrass	*Festuca pratensis*
English rye grass	*Lolium perenne*
English wheat	*Triticum turgidum*
Esparcet	*Onobrychis viciifolia*
Erect brome	*Bromus erectus*
Ervil	*Vicia ervilia*
Esparto grass	*Stipa tenacissima*
Eulalia	*Miscanthus sinensis*
European beach grass	*Ammophila arenaria*
European bean	*Vicia faba*
European dune grass	*Elymus arenarius*
European feather grass	*Stipa pennata*

Everlasting pea

Everlasting pea
Lathyrus grandiflorus
Lathyrus latifolius
Lathyrus sylvestris
Eyelash pearl grass   Melica ciliata
Fairy crested wheatgrass
Agropyron cristatum
False brome
Brachypodium sylvaticum
False fox sedge   Carex otrubae
False oat grass
Arrhenatherum elatius
False sedge   Kobresia simpliciuscula
False wheatgrass   Elymus chinensis
Fanwort   Cabomba caroliniana
Feather bunchgrass   Stipa viridula
Feather grass   Stipa pennata
Feather love grass
Eragrostis amabilis
Feathertop   Pennisetum villosum
Fenland sedge   Cladium mariscus
Fenland wood rush
Luzula pallescens
Fern grass   Catapodium rigidum
Desmazeria rigida
Feterita
Sorghum vulgare caudatum
Fevergrass   Cymbopogon citratus
Few-flowered sedge
Carex pauciflora
Carex rariflora
Field bean   Vicia faba
Field brome   Bromus arvensis
Field wood rush   Luzula campestris
Fine bent   Agrostis tenuis
Fine-leaved sheep's fescue
Festuca tenuifolia
Fingered sedge   Carex digitata
Finger millet   Eleusine coracana
Fire lily   Xerophyllum tenax
Fish grass   Cabomba caroliniana
Fishpole bamboo
Phyllostachys aurea
Flat pea   Lathyrus sylvestris
Flat sedge   Blysmus compressus
Flat-stalked meadow grass
Poa compressa
Flaver   Avena fatua
Flawn   Zoysia matrella
Flea sedge   Carex puticaris
Floating bur reed
Sparganium angustifolium
Floating foxtail
Alopecurus geniculatus
Floating mud rush   Scirpus fluitans
Floating sweet grass
Glyceria fluitans
Flowering rush
Butomus umbellatus
Flying bent   Molinia caerulea

Forage bamboo
Phyllostachys aureosulcata
Forster's wood rush
Luzula forsteri
Fountain grass
Pennisetum setaceum
Fox sedge   Carex vulpina
Foxtail barley   Hordeum jubatum
Foxtail bristle grass   Setaria italica
Foxtail chess   Bromus rubens
Foxtail grass   Setaria italica
Foxtail millet   Setaria italica
Freshwater cordgrass
Spartina pectinata
Fringed brome   Bromus canadensis
Galingale   Cyperus longus
Galleta   Hilaria jamesii
Gardener's garters
Phalaris arundinacea picta
German wheat   Triticum dicoccon
Giant bamboo
Dendrocalamus gigantea
Giant cane   Arundinaria gigantea
Giant fescue   Festuca gigantea
Giant finger grass   Chloris berroi
Giant panic grass
Panicum antidotale
Giant reed   Arundo donax
Giant rye   Triticum polonicum
Giant thorny bamboo
Bambusa arundinacea
Giant timber bamboo
Phyllostachys bambusoides
Giant wild rye   Elymus condensatus
Glaucous bristle grass
Setaria glauca
Glaucous club rush
Scirpus tabernaemontani
Glaucous meadow grass   Poa glauca
Glaucous sedge   Carex flacca
Glaucous sweet grass
Glyceria declinata
Golden bamboo
Phyllostachys aurea
Golden feathergrass
Stipa pulcherrima
Golden foxtail
Alopecurus pratensis 'aureus'
Golden-groove bamboo
Phyllostachys aureosulcata
Golden oat grass
Trisetum flavescens
Golden oats   Stipa gigantea
Goldentop   Lamarckia aurea
Goose grass   Eleusine indica
Grass sorghum   Sorghum halepense
Grassy rush   Butomus umbellatus
Great brome   Bromus diandrus
Greater tussock sedge
Carex paniculata

Japanese millet

Great fenland sedge
Cladium mariscus
Great millet   *Sorghum halepense*
Great pond sedge   *Carex riparia*
Great tussock sedge
Carex paniculata
Great wood rush   *Luzula sylvatica*
Green bristle grass   *Setaria viridis*
Green needlegrass   *Stipa viridula*
Green-ribbed sedge   *Carex binervis*
Grey fescue   *Festuca glauca*
Grey hair grass
Corynephorus canescens
Grey sedge   *Carex divulsa*
Guinea grass   *Panicum maximum*
Guinea rush   *Cyperus articulatus*
Hair fescue   *Festuca tenuifolia*
Hair grass   *Eleocharis acicularis*
Hair sedge   *Carex capillaris*
Hairy brome   *Bromus ramosus*
Hairy crab grass
Digitaria sanguinalis
Hairy cup grass   *Eriochloa villosa*
Hairy finger grass
Digitaria sanguinalis
Hairy grama   *Bouteloua hirsuta*
Hairy oat grass
Helictotrichon pubescens
Hairy sedge   *Carex hirta*
Hairy vetch   *Vicia villosa*
Hairy wood rush   *Luzula pilosa*
Hard fescue   *Festuca longifolia*
Hard grass   *Parapholis strigosa*
Hard rush   *Juncus inflexus*
Hard wheat   *Triticum durum*
Hardy bamboo
Pseudosasa japonica
Hardy timber bamboo
Phyllostachys bambusoides
Hare's foot sedge   *Carex lachenalii*
Hare's tail   *Lagurus ovatus*
Hare's tail cotton grass
Eriophorum vaginatum
Hare's tail grass
Eriophorum vaginatum
Lagurus ovatus
Heath false brome grass
Brachypodium pinnatum
Heath grass
Danthonia decumbens
Sieglingia decumbens
Heath pea   *Lathyrus japonicus*
Heath rush   *Juncus squarrosus*
Heath sedge   *Carex ericetorum*
Heath wood rush
Luzula multiflora
Hedge bamboo
Bambusa glaucesens
Bambusa multiplex

Hedgehog wheat
Triticum compactum
Hegari
Sorghum vulgare caffrorum
Henon bamboo
Phyllostachys nigra henon
Herd's grass   *Phleum pratense*
Himalaya fairy grass
Miscanthus nepalensis
Himalayan bamboo
Arundinaria anceps
Hog millet   *Panicum miliaceum*
Holy clover   *Onobrychis viciifolia*
Holy grass   *Hierochloe odorata*
Hop clover   *Medicago lupulina*
Trifolium agrarium
Horse bean   *Vicia faba*
Horsetail   *Equisetum hymale*
Hunangemoho
Chionochloa conspicua
Hungarian brome   *Bromus inermis*
Hungarian clover
Trifolium pannonicum
Hungarian grass   *Setaria italica*
Hybrid fescue
Festulolium loliaceum
Hybrid marram grass
Ammocalamagrostis baltica
Hybrid sweet grass
Glyceria pedicellata
Indian basket grass
Xerophyllum tenax
Indian corn   *Zea mays*
Indian grass   *Molinia caerulea*
Sorghastrum avenaceum
Indian millet
Oryzopsis hymenoides
Pennisetum americanum
Indian rice   *Oryzopsis hymenoides*
Zizania aquatica
Intermediate wheatgrass
Agropyron intermedium
Interrupted brome
Bromus interruptus
Irish shamrock
Trifolium procumbens
Italian clover   *Trifolium incarnatum*
Italian millet   *Setaria italica*
Italian rye grass
Lolium multiflorum
Japanese brome   *Bromus japonicus*
Japanese carpet grass
Zoysia matrella
Japanese chess   *Bromus japonicus*
Japanese lawn grass   *Zoysia japonica*
Japanese love grass
Eragrostis amabilis
Japanese mat rush   *Juncus effusus*
Japanese millet
Echinochloa crus-galli
Setaria italica

Japanese timber bamboo

Japanese timber bamboo	
	Phyllostachys bambusoides
Jersey club rush	*Scirpus americanus*
Job's tears	*Coix lacryma-jobi*
Johnson grass	*Sorghum album*
	Sorghum halepense
Jointed rush	*Juncus articulatus*
June grass	*Poa pratensis*
Kaffir corn	
	Sorghum vulgare caffrorum
Kentucky bluegrass	*Poa pratensis*
Khas-khas	*Vetiveria zizanioides*
Khus-khus	*Vetiveria zizanioides*
Kidney vetch	*Anthyllis vulneraria*
Kleberg grass	
	Dichanthium annulatum
Korakan	*Eleusine coracana*
Korean grass	*Zoysia japonica*
	Zoysia tenuifolia
Korean lawn grass	*Zoysia japonica*
	Zoysia tenuifolia
Korean velvet grass	*Zoysia japonica*
	Zoysia tenuifolia
Kuma bamboo grass	*Sasa veitchii*
Kura clover	*Trifolium ambiguum*
Kweek grass	*Cynodon dactylon*
Lace grass	*Eragrostis capillaris*
Lady's fingers	*Anthyllis vulneraria*
Large hop clover	
	Trifolium campestre
Large quaking grass	*Briza maxima*
Large Russian vetch	*Vicia villosa*
Late-flowering red clover	
	Trifolium pratense serotinum
Late-flowering sedge	
	Carex serotina
Lazy-man's grass	
	Eremochloa ophiuroides
Least spike rush	
	Eleocharis acicularis
Lehmann's love grass	
	Eragrostis lehmanniana
Lemongrass	*Cymbopogon citratus*
Lesser burnet	
	Poterium sanguisorba
Lesser cat's tail	*Phleum bertolonii*
Lesser pond sedge	
	Carex acutiformis
Lesser quaking grass	*Briza minor*
Lesser tussock sedge	
	Carex appropinquata
	Carex diandra
Little bluestem	
	Schizachyrium scoparium
Little quaking grass	*Briza minor*
Long-bracted sedge	*Carex extensa*
Loose silky bent	
	Apera spica-venti
Loose-spiked wood sedge	
	Carex strigosa

Love grass	*Eragrostis elegans*
Low clover	*Trifolium campestre*
Low sedge	*Carex demissa*
Low spear grass	*Poa annua*
Lucerne	*Medicago sativa*
Lyme grass	*Elymus arenarius*
	Lolium perenne
Mace sedge	*Carex grayi*
Madake	
	Phyllostachys bambusoides
Madrid brome	*Bromus madritensis*
Maize	*Zea mays*
Malacca cane	*Calamus scipionum*
Male bamboo	
	Dendrocalamus strictus
Malogilla	*Eriochloa polystachya*
Malojilla	*Eriochloa polystachya*
Malojillo	*Eriochloa polystachya*
Manila grass	*Zoysia matrella*
Many-flowered wood rush	
	Luzula multiflora
Many-stemmed spike rush	
	Eleocharis multicaulis
Marram grass	
	Ammophila arenaria
Marsh foxtail	
	Alopecurus geniculatus
Marsh grass	*Spartina maritima*
Marsh meadow grass	*Poa palustris*
Mascarene grass	*Zoysia tenuifolia*
Ma-tai	*Eleocharis dulcis*
Mat grass	*Nardus stricta*
Mat-grass fescue	
	Vulpia unilateralis
Mauritania vine reed	
	Ampelodesmos mauritanicus
Meadow barley	
	Hordeum secalinum
Meadow brome	
	Bromus commutatus
Meadow cat's tail	*Phleum pratense*
Meadow fescue	*Festuca pratensis*
Meadow foxtail	
	Alopecurus pratensis
Meadow grass	*Poa pratensis*
Meadow oat grass	
	Arenula pratensis
	Helictotrichon pratense
Meadow soft grass	*Holcus lanatus*
Meadow vetchling	
	Lathyrus pratensis
Means grass	*Sorghum halepense*
Mediterranean brome	
	Bromus lanceolatus
Mediterranean wheat	
	Triticum turgidum
Metake	*Arundinaria japonica*
	Pseudosasa japonica
Mexican everlasting grass	
	Eriochloa aristata

Prairie cordgrass

Meyer's bamboo	*Phyllostachys meyeri*
Millet	*panicum miliaceum*
Miniature papyrus	*Cyperus isocladus*
Moa grass	*Gynerium sagittatum*
Molasses grass	*Melinis minutiflora*
Moor grass	*Molinia caerulea*
Moor mat grass	*Nardus stricta*
Moso bamboo	*Phyllostachys pubescens*
Mosquito grass	*Bouteloua gracilis*
Mountain brome	*Bromus marginatus*
Mountain heath grass	*Sieglingia decumbens*
Mountain melick	*Melica nutans*
Mountain sedge	*Carex montana*
Mountain timothy	*Phleum pratense*
Mountain vetch	*Anthyllis montana*
Mountain water sedge	*Carex aquatilis*
Mud sedge	*Carex limosa*
Multi-spiked cord grass	*Spartina alterniflora*
Muriel bamboo	*Thamnocalamus spathaceus*
Napier grass	*Pennisetum purpurea*
Nail-rod	*Typha latifolia*
Nard grass	*Cymbopogon nardus*
Narihira bamboo	*Semiarundinaria fastuosa*
Narrow-leaved cat-tail	*Typha angustifolia*
Narrow-leaved meadow grass	*Poa angustifolia*
Narrow-leaved reedmace	*Typha angustifolia*
Narrow small-reed	*Calamagrostis stricta*
Narrow-spiked sedge	*Carex acuta*
Natal grass	*Tricholaena rosea*
	Rhynchelytrum repens
Needle-and-thread	*Stipa comata*
Needle spike rush	*Eleocharis acicularis*
Nepal barley	*Hordeum vulgare*
Nepal silver grass	*Miscanthus nepalensis*
New Zealand bent	*Agrostis tenuis*
Nit grass	*Gastridium ventricosum*
Nodding melick	*Melica nutans*
Nonesuch	*Medicago lupulina*
Nut grass	*Cyperus esculentus*
Nut sedge	*Cyperus esculentus*
Oat grass	*Arrhenatherum elatius*
	Helictotrichon sempervirens
Oats	*Avena sativa*
Oldham bamboo	*Bambusa oldhamii*

Old-witch grass	*Panicum capillare*
One-grain wheat	*Triticum monococcum*
Orange foxtail	*Alopecurus aequalis*
Orchard grass	*Dactylis glomerata*
Oriental hedge bamboo	*Bambusa glaucesens*
Oval sedge	*Carex ovalis*
Pale sedge	*Carex curta*
	Carex pallescens
Palm grass	*Setaria palmifolia*
Pampas grass	*Cortaderia argentea*
	Cortaderia selloana
Pangola grass	*Digitaria decumbens*
Paper plant	*Cyperus papyrus*
Paper reed	*Cyperus papyrus*
Papyrus	*Cyperus papyrus*
Para grass	*Panicum purpurascens*
Pearl barley	*Hordeum distichon*
Pearl grass	*Briza maxima*
Pearl millet	*Pennisetum americanum*
	Pennisetum glaucum
Pendulous sedge	*Carex pendula*
Pentz finger grass	*Digitaria pentzii*
Perennial beard grass	*Agropogon littoralis*
Perennial oat grass	*Avena pratensis*
Perennial pea	*Lathyrus latifolius*
	Lathyrus sylvestris
Perennial rye grass	*Lolium perenne*
Perennial veldt grass	*Ehrharta calycina*
Persian clover	*Trifolium resupinatum*
Peruvian paspalum	*Paspalum racemosum*
Pheasant grass	*Stipa arundinacea*
Pheasant-tail grass	*Stipa arundinacea*
Pigmy bamboo	*Arundinaria pygmaea*
Pigmy rush	*Juncus mutabilis*
Pill sedge	*Carex pilulifera*
Plains bristle grass	*Setaria macrostachya*
Plicate sweet grass	*Glyceria plicata*
Plume grass	*Erianthus ravennae*
Poiret's bristle grass	*Setaria poiretiana*
Polish wheat	*Triticum polonicum*
Pond sedge	*Carex riparia*
Potato oat	*Avena fatua*
Poulard wheat	*Triticum turgidum*
Prairie beard grass	*Schizachyrium scoparium*
Prairie brome	*Bromus unioloides*
Prairie cordgrass	*Spartina pectinata*

Prickly sedge	*Carex muricata*
Pride of California	
	Lathyrus splendens
Proso	*Panicum miliaceum*
Pubescent wheatgrass	
	Agropyron trichophorum
Punting-pole bamboo	
	Bambusa tuldoides
Purple moor grass	
	Molinia caerulea
Purple small reed	
	Calamagrostis canescens
Purple-stemmed cat's tail	
	Phleum phleoides
Purple vetch	*Vicia benghalensis*
Quack grass	*Agropyron repens*
Quaking grass	*Briza media*
Quick grass	*Agropyron repens*
Quitch grass	*Agropyron repens*
Rabbit's foot	
	Polypogon monspeliensis
Rabbit-foot grass	
	Polypogon monspeliensis
Rabbit's tail grass	*Lagurus ovatus*
Ragi	*Eleusine coracana*
Ramie fibre	*Boehmeria nivea*
Rancheria grass	
	Elymus arenarius
Rat's tail fescue	*Vulpia myuros*
Rattan	*Calamus rotang*
Rattan cane	*Calamus rotang*
Rattlesnake brome	
	Bromus briziformis
Rattlesnake chess	
	Bromus briziformis
Ravenna grass	*Erianthus ravennae*
Red blysmuss	*Blysmus rufus*
Red clover	*Trifolium pratense*
Red fescue	*Festuca rubra*
Red millet	*Digitaria ischaemum*
Red top	*Agrostis gigantea*
Reed canary grass	
	Phalaris arundinacea
Reed fescue	*Festuca altissima*
	Festuca elatior
Reed foxtail	
	Alopecurus arundinaceus
Reedmace	*Typha latifolia*
Reed sweet grass	*Glyceria maxima*
Reflexed salt-marsh grass	
	Puccinellia distans
Rescue brome	*Bromus unioloides*
	Bromus wildenowii
Rescue grass	*Bromus unioloides*
Reversed clover	
	Trifolium resupinatum
Rhode Island bent	*Agrostis tenuis*
Rhodes grass	*Chloris gayana*
Ribbed paspalum	
	Paspalum malacophyllum
Ribbon grass	
	Phalaris arundinacea picta
Rice	*Leersia oryzoides*
	Oryza sativa
Rice grass	*Spartina townsendii*
Rice wheat	*Triticum dicoccon*
Ringal	*Arundinaria anceps*
Ringed beard grass	
	Dichanthium annulatum
River wheat	*Triticum turgidum*
Rock sedge	*Carex rupestris*
Rough bluegrass	*Poa trivialis*
Rough dog's tail	
	Cynosurus echinatus
Rough meadow-grass	*Poa trivialis*
Rough pea	*Lathyrus hirsutus*
Rough-stalked bluegrass	
	Poa trivialis
Rough-stalked meadow grass	
	Poa trivialis
Round-fruited rush	
	Juncus compressus
Round-headed club rush	
	Scirpus holoschoenus
Ruby grass	*Rhynchelytrum repens*
	Tricholaena rosea
Rush-leaved fescue	
	Festuca juncifolia
Rush nut	*Cyperus esculentus*
Russet sedge	*Carex saxatilis*
Russian wild rye	*Elymus junceus*
Rye brome	*Bromus secalinus*
Rye grass	*Lolium perenne*
Sainfoin	*Onobrychis sativa*
Saint Augustine's grass	
	Stenotaphrum secundatum
Salt meadow sedge	*Carex divisa*
Salt mud rush	*Juncus gerardii*
Salt rush	*Juncus lesueurii*
Sand bent	*Mibora minima*
Sandberg's bluegrass	
	Poa sandbergii
Sand bluestem grass	
	Andropogon hallii
Sand cat's tail	*Phleum arenarium*
Sand couch	
	Agropyron junceiforme
	Elymus farctus
Sand dropseed	
	Sporobolus cryptandrus
Sand love grass	*Eragrostis trichodes*
Sand sedge	*Carex arenaria*
Sand twitch	
	Agropyron junceiforme
Sainfoin	*Onobrychis viciifolia*
Saw grass	*Eleocharis effusum*
Scented vernal grass	
	Anthoxanthum odoratum
Scilly Isles meadow grass	
	Poa infirma

Southern cane

Scottish small reed	*Calamagrostis scotica*
Scouring brush	*Equisetum hyemale*
Scutch grass	*Agropyron repens*
Sea arrow grass	*Triglochia palustris*
Sea barley	*Hordeum marinum*
Sea club rush	*Scirpus maritimus*
Sea couch	*Agropyron pungens*
	Elymus pycnanthus
Sea hard grass	*Parapholis strigosa*
Sea lyme grass	*Elymus arenarius*
Sea oats	*Uniola paniculata*
Sea rush	*Juncus maritimus*
Seaside pea	*Lathyrus japonicus*
Sea twitch	*Agropyron pungens*
Sedge grass	*Carex pendula*
Sedge-like club rush	*Blysmus compressus*
Shade fescue	*Festuca rubra*
Shallu	*Sorghum vulgare roxburghii*
Shamrock	*Trifolium procumbens*
	Trifolium repens
Sharp-flowered rush	*Juncus acutiflorus*
Sharp rush	*Juncus acutus*
Sharp sea rush	*Juncus acutus*
Sheep's fescue	*Festuca ovina*
Shore grass	*Stenotaphrum secundatum*
Shoreline cordgrass	*Spartina maritima*
Short-awned barley	*Hordeum brevisubulatum*
Short-awned foxtail	*Alopecurus aequalis*
Siberian melic grass	*Melica altissima*
Siberian wheatgrass	*Agropyron sibiricum*
Siberian wild rye	*Elymus sibiricus*
Sickle bamboo	*Chimonobambusa falcata*
Sickle grass	*Parapholis incurva*
Sideoats grama	*Bouteloua curtipendula*
Silk grass	*Oryzopsis hymenoides*
Silky melic grass	*Melica ciliata*
Silky-spike melica	*Melica ciliata*
Silver beard grass	*Bothriochloa saccharoides*
Silvery hair grass	*Aira caryophyllea*
Simon bamboo	*Arundinaria simonii*
Single-cut cow grass	*Trifolium pratense serotinum*
Single-glumed spike rush	*Eleocharis uniglumis*

Single-grain wheat	*Triticum monococcum*
Singletary pea	*Lathyrus hirsutus*
Sitka vetch	*Vicia gigantea*
Six-rowed barley	*Hordeum vulgare*
Six-weeks grass	*Poa annua*
Slender brome	*Bromus lepidus*
Slender cotton grass	*Eriophorum gracile*
Slender foxtail	*Alopecurus myosuroides*
Slender grama	*Bouteloua repens*
Slender rush	*Juncus tenuis*
Slender-spiked sedge	*Carex acuta*
Slender spike rush	*Eleocharis acicularis*
	Eleocharis uniglumis
Slender wheatgrass	*Agropyron trachycaulum*
Slender wild oat	*Avena barbata*
Slough grass	*Spartina pectinata*
Small bulrush	*Typha angustifolia*
Small bur reed	*Sparganium minimum*
Small cane	*Arundinaria tecta*
Small cat's tail	*Phleum nodosum*
Small hop clover	*Trifolium procumbens*
Small oat	*Avena strigosa*
Small quaking grass	*Briza minor*
Small reed	*Calamagrostis nana*
Smilo grass	*Oryzopsis miliacea*
Smooth brome	*Bromus inermis*
	Bromus racemosus
Smooth cord grass	*Spartina alterniflora*
Smooth finger grass	*Digitaria ischaemum*
Smooth meadow grass	*Poa pratensis*
Smooth sedge	*Carex laevigata*
Smooth-stalked meadow grass	*Poa pratensis*
Snowy woodrush	*Luzula nivea*
Soft brome grass	*Bromus hordeaceus*
	Bromus mollis
Soft chess	*Bromus mollis*
Soft flag	*Typha angustifolia*
Soft grass	*Holcus mollis*
Soft rush	*Juncus effusus*
Somerset grass	*Koeleria vallesiana*
Sorghum	*Holcus sorghum*
	Sorghum bicolor
	Sorghum vulgare
Sorgo	*Sorghum vulgare saccharatum*
Southern cane	*Arundinaria gigantea*

Spanish vetch

Spanish vetch	*Anthyllis montana*
Spear grass	*Poa pratensis*
Spike grass	*Dezmazeria sicula*
	Uniola paniculata
Spiked sedge	*Carex spicata*
Spiked wood rush	*Luzula spicata*
Spreading meadow grass	
	Poa subcaerulea
Spring sedge	*Carex caryophyllea*
Spring vetch	*Lathyrus vernus*
	Vicia sativa
Spring wild oat	*Avena fatua*
Square bamboo	
	Chimonobambusa quadrangularis
Square-stem bamboo	
	Chimonobambusa quadrangularis
Square-stemmed bamboo	
	Arundinaria quadrangularis
Squaw grass	*Xerophyllum tenax*
Squirrel tail barley	
	Hordeum jubatum
Squirrel tail fescue	
	Vulpia bromoides
Squirrel tail grass	
	Hordeum jubatum
	Hordeum marinum
Stake bamboo	
	Phyllostachys aureosulcata
Standard crested wheatgrass	
	Agropyron sibiricum
Starch wheat	*Triticum dicoccon*
Star grass	*Chloris truncata*
Star sedge	*Carex echinata*
Starved wood sedge	
	Carex depauperata
Stiff brome	*Bromus rigidus*
Stiff-hair wheatgrass	
	Agropyron trichophorum
Stiff salt-marsh grass	
	Puccinellia rupestris
Stiff sand grass	
	Catapodium marimum
Stiff sedge	*Carex bigelowii*
Strand wheat	*Lolium perenne*
Strawberry clover	
	Trifolium fragiferum
Strawberry-headed clover	
	Trifolium fragiferum
Subclover	*Trifolium subterraneum*
Subterranean clover	
	Trifolium subterraneum
Sudan grass	*Sorghum sudanese*
Sugarcane	*Saccharum officinarum*
Sugar sorghum	
	Sorghum vulgare saccharatum
Swamp grass	*Scolochloa festucacea*
Swamp meadow grass	
	Poa palustris
Sweet galingale	*Cyperus longus*
Sweetshoot bamboo	
	Phyllostachys dulcis
Sweet sorghum	
	Sorghum vulgare saccharatum
Sweet vernal grass	
	Anthoxanthum odoratum
Switch cane	*Arundinaria tecta*
Switch grass	*Panicum virgatum*
Tall fescue	*Festuca arundinacea*
	Festuca elatior
Tall festuca	*Festuca arundinacea*
Tall oat grass	
	Arrhenantherum elatius
Tall wheatgrass	
	Agropyron elongatum
Tare	*Vicia sativa*
Tartarian oat	*Avena fatua*
Tawny sedge	*Carex hostiana*
Teosinte	*Zea mexicana*
Terrell grass	*Lolium perenne*
Texas bluegrass	*Poa arachnifera*
Texas needlegrass	*Stipa leucotricha*
Texas winter grass	*Stipa leucotricha*
Thin-glumed sedge	
	Carex stenolepis
Thin-spiked wood sedge	
	Carex strigosa
Thread rush	*Juncus filiformis*
Three-flowered rush	
	Juncus triglumis
Three-leaved rush	*Juncus trifidus*
Tick bean	*Vicia flaba*
Tiger grass	
	Miscanthus sinensis zebrinus
Tiger nut	*Cyperus esculentus*
Timber bamboo	
	Phyllostachys bambusoides
Timothy grass	*Phleum pratense*
Toad rush	*Juncus bufonius*
Tobosa grass	*Hilaria mutica*
Toe-toe	*Cortaderia richardii*
Tonkin bamboo	
	Arundinaria amabilis
Tonkin cane	*Arundinaria amabilis*
Toothed bur clover	
	Medicago hispida
Tor grass	
	Brachypodium pinnatum
	Brachypodium sylvaticum
Tortoiseshell bamboo	
	Phyllostachys heterocycla
Totter grass	*Briza media*
Townsend's cord grass	
	Spartina townsendii
Transvaal dogtooth grass	
	Cynodon transvaalensis
Trefoil	*Medicago lupulina*

Winter wild oat

Triangular club rush	*Scirpus triquetrus*
Trifolium	*Trifolium incarnatum*
Tsingli cane	*Arundinaria amabilis*
Tuberous foxtail	*Alopecurus bulbosus*
Tuberous vetch	*Lathyrus tuberosus*
Tufted fescue	*Festuca amethystina*
Tufted hair grass	*Deschampsia caespitosa*
Tufted salt-marsh grass	*Puccinellia fasciculata*
Tufted sedge	*Carex elata*
Tufted soft grass	*Holcus lanatus*
Tufted vetch	*Vicia cracca*
Tunis grass	*Holcus virgatus*
Turkestan bluestem	*Bothriochloa ischaemum*
Twitch grass	*Agropyron repens*
	Elymus repens
Two-flowered pea	*Lathyrus grandifloris*
Two-flowered rush	*Juncus biglumis*
Umbrella grass	*Cyperus alternifolius*
Umbrella palm	*Cyperus alternifolius*
Umbrella plant	*Cyperus alternifolius*
Umbrella sedge	*Cyperus alternifolius*
Unbranched bur reed	*Sparganium emerson*
Upland bent	*Agrostis perennans*
Upland bent grass	*Agrostis perennans*
Upright brome	*Bromus erectus*
Uruguay finger grass	*Chloris berroi*
Uruguay pennisetum	*Pennisetum latifolium*
Uva grass	*Gynerium sagittatum*
Vanilla grass	*Hierochloe odorata*
Variegated cord grass	*Spartina pectinata aureo-marginata*
Variegated creeping soft grass	*Holcus mollis variegatus*
Variegated oat grass	*Arrhenatherum bulbosum*
	Arrhenatherum elatius
Various-leaved fescue	*Festuca heterophylla*
Vasey grass	*Paspalum urvillei*
Velvet bent	*Agrostis canina*
Velvet grass	*Holcus lanatus*
Vetiver	*Vetiveria zizanioides*
Vine mesquite	*Panicum obtusum*
Virginian wild rye	*Elymus virginicus*
Volga wild rye	*Elymus racemosus*
Wallaby grass	*Danthonia setacea*

Wall barley	*Hordeum murinum*
Washington grass	*Cabomba caroliniana*
Water bent	*Agrostis semiverticillata*
	Polypogon viridis
Water celery	*Vallisneria americana*
Water chestnut	*Eleocharis dulcis*
Water gladiolus	*Butomus umbellatus*
Water oats	*Zizania aquatica*
Water sedge	*Carex aquatilis*
Water star grass	*Heteranthera dubia*
	Heteranthera graminea
Water whorl grass	*Catabrosa aquatica*
Wavy hair grass	*Deschampsia flexuosa*
Wavy meadow grass	*Poa flexuosa*
Weeping love grass	*Eragrostis curvula*
Weeping widow	*Lacrymaria velutina*
Western wheatgrass	*Agropyron smithii*
West Indian lemongrass	*Cymbopogon citratus*
White beak sedge	*Rhynchospora alba*
White clover	*Trifolium repens*
White durra	*Sorghum vulgare cernuum*
White dutch clover	*Trifolium repens*
White sedge	*Carex curta*
Whitlow grass	*Erophila versa*
Whorl grass	*Catabrosa aquatica*
Wide-sheathed sedge	*Carex vaginata*
Wild barley	*Hordeum murinum*
Wild cane	*Gynerium sagittatum*
Wild celery	*Vallisneria americana*
Wild fescue	*Festuca altissima*
Wild oat	*Avena fatua*
Wild oats	*Chasmanthium latifolium*
Wild red clover	*Trifolium pratense spontaneum*
Wild winter pea	*Lathyrus hirsutus*
Wind grass	*Apera spica-venti*
Windsor bean	*Vicia faba*
Winter pea	*Lathyrus hirsutus*
Winter vetch	*Vicia villosa*
Winter wild oat grass	*Avena ludoviciana*
Winter wild oat	*Avena ludoviciana*
	Avena sterilis

Wire grass	*Eleusine indica*
	Poa compressa
	Schizachyrium scoparium
Witch grass	*Agropyron repens*
	Elymus repens
	Panicum capillare
Wood barley	
	Hordelymus europaeus
Wood bluegrass	*Poa nemoralis*
Wood club rush	*Scirpus sylvaticus*
Wood false brome	
	Brachypodium sylvaticum
Wood fescue	*Festuca altissima*
Wood grass	
	Sorghastrum avenaceum
Woodland brome	
	Bromus ramosus
Woodland meadow grass	
	Poa nemoralis
Wood meadow grass	
	Poa nemoralis
Wood melick	*Melica uniflora*
Wood millet	*Milium effusum*
Wood rush	*Luzula campestris*
Wood sedge	*Carex sylvatica*
Wood small reed	
	Calamagrostis epigejos
Woolly beard grass	
	Erianthus ravennae
Woolly-pod vetch	*Vicia dasycarpa*

Woolly vetch	*Vicia dasycarpa*
Woundwort	*Anthyllis vulneraria*
Yellow bluestem	
	Bothriochloa ischaemum
Yellow bristle grass	*Setaria glauca*
Yellow clover	*Trifolium agrarian*
	Trifolium procumbens
Yellow-groove bamboo	
	Phyllostachys aureosulcata
Yellow oat grass	
	Trisetum flavescens
Yellow nut grass	
	Cyperus esculentus
Yellow nut sedge	
	Cyperus esculentus
Yellow sedge	*Carex flava*
Yellow suckling	
	Trifolium procumbens
Yellow suckling clover	
	Trifolium dubium
	Trifolium procumbens
Yellow trefoil	*Medicago lupulina*
Yellow vetchling	*Lathyrus pratensis*
Yorkshire fog	*Holcus lanatus*
Zebra grass	
	Miscanthus sinensis zebrinus
Zigzag bamboo	
	Phyllostachys flexuosa
Zoysia grass	*Zoysia matrella*
Zulu nut	*Cyperus esculentus*

HERBS

Horticulturally, not botanically, the word 'herb' covers a range of plants used in cooking for flavouring and seasoning, as garnishes, and as domestic remedies. They are also widely used in orthodox and homeopathic medicines. The following list includes many subjects that are extremely poisonous, and drastic reactions, even occasional deaths are not unknown from the ignorant use of them. Experimentation by the general public cannot be too strongly condemned. In addition to the common culinary and medicinal herbs, a few herbal trees have been included.

English lavender –
Lavandula angustifolia

Aaron's rod

Aaron's rod	*Verbascum thapsus*
Absinthe	*Artemisia absinthium*
Aconite	*Aconitum napellus*
Adam's flannel	*Verbascum thapsus*
Adonis	*Adonis vernalis*
Agrimony	*Agrimonia eupatoria*
Alecost	*Balsamita major*
	Chrysanthemum balsamita
	Chrysanthemum vulgare
	Tanacetum balsamita
	Tanacetum vulgare
Alehoof	*Glechoma hederacea*
	Nepeta hederacea
Alder buckthorn	*Frangula alnus*
Alespice	
	Chrysanthemum balsamita
	Tanacetum balsamita
Alexanders	*Smyrnium olusatrum*
Alkanet	*Anchusa officinalis*
All-heal	*Valeriana officinalis*
Allspice	*Calycanthus floridus*
Almond	*Prunus dulcis*
Aloe	*Aloe barbadensis*
	Aloe vera
	Aloe vulgaris
Alpine strawberry	*Fragaria vesca*
Alpine wormwood	*Artemisia laxa*
Althea	*Althaea officinalis*
Alum root	*Heuchera richardsonii*
Ambrosia	*Chenopodium botrys*
American centaury	
	Sabatia angularis
Anchusa	*Anchusa sempervirens*
	Pentaglottis sempervirens
Angelica	*Angelica archangelica*
Anise	*Anisum vulgare*
	Foeniculum vulgare azoricum
	Myrrhis odorata
	Pimpinella anisum
Aniseed	*Anisum vulgare*
	Pimpinella anisum
Anise fern	*Myrrhis odorata*
Anise hyssop	
	Agastache anethiodora
	Agastache foeniculum
Annual marjoram	
	Origanum majorana
Apothecary's rose	
	Rosa gallica officinalis
Apple mint	*Mentha rotundifolia*
	Mentha suaveolens
Arnica	*Arnica montana*
Artemisia	*Artemisia abrotanum*
	Artemisia absinthium
	Artemisia dracunculus
Arugula	*Eruca vesicaria*
Asafetida	*Ferula foetida*
Ass's ear	*Symphytum officinale*
Autumn crocus	
	Colchicum autumnale

Bachelor's buttons	
	Ranunculus acris
	Tanacetum parthenium
Balm	*Melissa officinalis*
	Monarda didyma
Balm of Gilead	
	Cedronella canariensis
	Cedronella triphylla
	Commiphora opobalsamum
Balsam herb	
	Chrysanthemum balsamita
Balsamita	
	Chrysanthemum balsamita
Balsam poplar	*Populus balsamifera*
Baneberry	*Actaea spicata*
Barbados aloe	*Aloe barbadensis*
	Aloe vera
	Aloe vulgaris
Basil	*Ocimum basilicum*
Basil thyme	*Acinos arvensis*
	Calamintha acinos
Basin sagebrush	
	Artemisia tridentata
Bastard balm	
	Melittis melissophyllum
Bastard saffron	
	Carthamus tinctorus
Bay	*Laurus nobilis*
Bay leaf	*Laurus nobilis*
	Do not confuse with
	Kalmia latifolia (poisonous)
Bay laurel	*Laurus nobilis*
Beach morning glory	
	Ipomoea pes-caprae
Beach wormwood	
	Artemisia stellerana
Bean herb	
	Satureia (Satureja) hortensis
	Satureia montana
Bear's foot	*Alchemilla vulgaris*
	Alchemilla xanthochlora
Beaver poison	*Conium maculatum*
Bee balm	*Melissa officinalis*
	Monarda didyma
Bee bread	*Borago officinalis*
Beefsteak plant	
	Perilla frutescens crispa
Beggar's buttons	*Arctium lappa*
Belladonna	*Atropa belladonna*
Bengal root	*Zingiber cassumunar*
Bergamot	*Monarda didyma*
Bergamot mint	*Mentha citrata*
Betony	*Stachys officinalis*
Bhang	*Cannabis sativa*
Bible leaf	
	Chrysanthemum balsamita
Bilberry	*Vaccinium myrtillus*
Birdlime mistletoe	*Viscum alba*
Bird's foot	
	Trigonella foenum-graecum
Bishopswort	*Stachys officinalis*

Cheese rennet

Bistort	*Polygonum bistorta*
Bitter aloe	*Aloe barbadensis*
Bitter broom	*Sabatia angularis*
Bitter buttons	
	Chrysanthemum vulgare
	Tanacetum vulgare
Bitter clover	*Sabatia angularis*
Bitter cress	*Cardamine pratensis*
Bittersweet	*Solanum dulcamara*
Bittersweet nightshack	
	Solanum dulcamara
Black American willow	*Salix nigra*
Black bryony	*Tamus communis*
Black dogwood	*Frangula alnus*
Blackeye root	*Tamus communis*
Black hellebore	*Helleborus niger*
Black horehound	*Ballota nigra*
Black mulberry	*Morus nigra*
Black mustard	*Brassica nigra*
	Sinapis nigra
Black sugar	*Glycyrrhiza glabra*
Black wort	*Symphytum officinale*
Blanket leaf	*Verbascum thapsus*
Blessed thistle	*Cnicus benedictus*
Blood flower	
	Asclepias curassavica
Bloody fingers	*Digitalis purpurea*
Blowball	*Leontodon taraxacum*
	Taraxacum officinale
Blue gum	*Eucalyptus globulus*
Blue rocket	*Aconitum napellus*
Blue sage	*Salvia azurea*
Boneset	*Symphytum officinale*
Borage	*Borago officinalis*
Border catmint	*Nepeta mussini*
Bore tree	*Sambucus nigra*
Bouncing bet	*Saponaria officinalis*
Bowman	*Anthemis nobilis*
Bramble	*Rubus fruticosus*
Brandy mint	*Mentha × piperita*
Bread-and-cheese tree	
	Crataegus oxyacantha
British myrrh	*Myrrhis odorata*
Broad-leaved dock	
	Rumex obtusifolius
Broad-leaved thyme	
	Thymus pulegioides
Broom	*Cytisus scoparius*
	Sarothamnus scoparius
Brown mustard	*Brassica juncea*
	Sinapis juncea
Bruisewort	*Bellis perennis*
	Saponaria officinalis
Buckeye	*Aesculus hippocastanum*
Buckler-leaf sorrel	*Rumex scutatus*
Buckthorn	*Rhamnus catharticus*
Buffalo herb	*Medicago sativa*
Bugbane	*Actaea spicata*
Bugle	*Ajuga reptans*

Bugleweed	*Ajuga reptans*
Bugloss	*Anchusa officinalis*
Bullsfoot	*Tussilago farfara*
Burdock	*Arctium lappa*
Burnet	*Poterium sanguisorba*
	Sanguisorba minor
Burnet saxifrage	
	Pimpinella saxifraga
Burning bush	*Dictamnus albus*
	Dictamnus fraxinella
	Eonymus europaeus
Burrage	*Borago officinalis*
Bush basil	*Ocinum minimum*
Bush lawyer	*Rubus australis*
Bushy mint	*Mentha × gentilis*
Buttercup	*Ranunculus acris*
Butter dock	*Rumex obtusifolius*
Buttered haycocks	
	Linaria vulgaris
Buttons	*Tanacetum vulgare*
Calamint	*Calamintha acinos*
	Calamintha grandiflora
Calamus	*Acorus calamus*
Calendula	*Calendula officinalis*
California sagebrush	
	Artemisia californica
Call-me-to-you	*Viola tricolor*
Camphor plant	*Balsamita major*
	tomentosum
Camphor tree	
	Cinnamomum camphora
Cape ginger	*Costus speciosus*
Caraway	*Carum carvi*
Caraway thyme	
	Thymus herba-barona
Cardoon	*Cynara cardunculus*
Carob	*Ceratonia siliqua*
Carolina allspice	
	Calycanthus floridus
Carpenter's square	
	Scrophularia marilandica
Cassilata	*Hyoscyamus niger*
Catmint	*Nepeta cataria*
Catnep	*Nepeta cataria*
Catnip	*Nepeta cataria*
Cat's peas	*Cytisus scoparius*
	Sarothamnus scoparius
Cat's valerian	*Valeriana officinalis*
Centaury	*Centaurium minus*
	Centaurium umbellatum
	Erythraea centaurium
Chamomile	*Anthemis nobilis*
	Chamaemelum nobile
Charity	*Polemoneum coeruleum*
Checkerberry	
	Gaultheria procumbens
Cheese rennet	*Galium verum*

Cherry pie

Cherry pie
Heliotropium arborescens
Heliotropium corymbosum
Heliotropium peruvianum
Chervil *Anthriscus cerefolium*
Chaerophyllum temulentum
Chickweed *Stellaria media*
Chicory *Cichorium intybus*
Chinese parsley
Coriandrum sativum
Chiretta *Swertia chirata*
Chive *Allium schoenoprasum*
Christmas rose *Helleborus niger*
Christ's ladder *Centaurium minus*
Church steeples
Agrimonia eupatoria
Churnstaff *Linaria vulgaris*
Cinnamon
Cinnamomum zeylanicum
Clary *Salvia sclarea*
Clary sage *Salvia sclarea*
Clear eye *Salvia sclarea*
Clot-bur *Arctium lappa*
Cloves *Eugenia aromatica*
Cobbler's bench
Lamuim maculatum
Cockle-bur *Arctium lappa*
Cockleburr *Agrimonia eupatoria*
Coltsfoot *Tussilago farfara*
Columbine *Aquilegia vulgaris*
Comfrey *Symphytum officinale*
Common balm *Melissa officinalis*
Common buckthorn
Rhamnus catharticus
Common chamomile
Anthemis nobilis
Common comfrey
Symphytum officinale
Common dandelion
Leontodon taraxacum
Taraxacum officinale
Common heliotrope
Heliotropium arborescens
Heliotropium corymbosum
Heliotropium peruvianum
Common horehound
Marrubium vulgare
Common jasmine
Jasminum officinale
Common mallow *Malva sylvestris*
Common mint *Mentha spicata*
Common oak *Quercus robur*
Common sagebrush
Artemisia tridentata
Common thyme *Thymus vulgaris*
Common tormentil
Potentilla erecta
Potentilla tormentilla
Common wormwood
Artemisia absinthium

Compass weed
Rosmarinus lavandulaceus
Rosmarinus officinalis
Cone flower
Echinacea angustifolia
Consound *Symphytum officinale*
Cool tankard *Borago officinalis*
Coral bells *Heuchera richardsonii*
Coriander *Coriandrum sativum*
Corn salad *Valerianella locusta*
Valerianella olitoria
Corsican mint *Mentha requienii*
Costmary
Chrysanthemum balsamita
Tanacetum balsamita
Cotton lavender
Santolina chamaecyparissus
Santolina incana
Santolina tomentosa
Cotton thistle
Onopordon acanthium
Coughwort *Tussilago farfara*
Cowslip
Primula officinalis
Primula veris
Crape ginger *Costus speciosus*
Creeping charlie *Nepeta hederacea*
Creeping comfrey
Symphytum grandiflorum
Creeping savory
Satureia (Satureja) repanda
Creeping thyme
Thymus serphyllum
Crème de menthe plant
Mentha requienii
Crete dittany *Amaracus dictamnus*
Origanum dictamnus
Crimson clover
Trifolium incarnatum
Cuckoo flower
Cardamine pratensis
Cuckoo's meat *Rumex acetosa*
Cuckoo sorrow *Rumex acetosa*
Cudweed *Artemisia ludoviciana*
Cumin *Cuminum cyminum*
Cuminum odorum
Culverwort *Aquilegia vulgaris*
Curdwort *Galium verum*
Curled dock *Rumex crispus*
Curly mint *Mentha crispa*
Curly parsley
Petroselinum crispum
Curry plant
Helichrysum angustifolium
Helichrysum italicum
Daisy *Bellis perennis*
Dame's violet *Hesperis matronalis*
Dandelion *Leontodon taraxacum*
Taraxacum officinale
Dark opal basil
Ocimum basilicum purpurescens

Deadly nightshade *Atropa belladonna*

Dead man's bells *Digitalis purpurea*

Dead nettle *Lamium maculatum*

Devil's apple *Mandragora officinarum*

Devil's bit scabious *Succisa pratensis*

Devil's cherries *Atropa belladonna*

Devil's nettle *Achillea millefolium*

Didi *Thymus mastichina didi*

Dill *Anethum graveolens* *Peucedanum graveolens*

Dock *Rumex obtusifolius*

Dog poison *Aethusa cynapium*

Dog violet *Viola riviana*

Donkey's ears *Stachys lanata* *Stachys olympica*

Double mint *Mentha × piperita*

Dropwort *Filipendula hexapetala* *Filipendula vulgaris* *Spiraea filipendula* *Ulmaria filipendula*

Durmast oak *Quercus petraea* *Quercus sessilis*

Dusty miller *Artemisia stellerana*

Dwarf purple foxglove *Digitalis thrapsi*

Dyer's weed *Isatis tinctoria*

Eau-de-cologne mint *Mentha citrata* *Mentha × piperita citrata*

Echinacea *Echinacea angustifolia*

Eggs and bacon *Linaria vulgaris*

Egyptian mint *Mentha rotundifolia*

Egyptian onion *Allium cepa aggregatum* *Allium cepa viviparum*

Elder *Sambucus nigra*

Elecampane *Inula helenium*

Elephant garlic *Allium ampeloprasum*

English daisy *Bellis perennis*

English lavender *Lavandula angustifolia* *Lavandula officinalis* *Lavandula spica* *Lavandula vera*

English mace *Achillea decolorans*

English mandrake *Bryonia dioica*

English pennyroyal *Mentha pulegium*

English thyme *Thymus vulgaris*

English yew *Taxus baccata*

Estragon *Artemisia dracunculus*

European crowfoot *Aquilegia vulgaris*

European vervain *Verbena officinalis*

European white hellebore *Veratrum album*

European willow *Salix alba*

Evening primrose *Oenothera biennis*

Eyebright *Euphrasia officinalis*

Everlasting onion *Allium perutile*

Fairy thimbles *Digitalis purpurea*

False dittany *Dictamnus albus* *Dictamnus fraxinella*

False hellebore *Veratrum viride*

False mistletoe *Loranthus europaeus*

False saffron *Carthamus tinctorius*

False tarragon *Artemisia dracunculoides* *Artemisia dranunculus*

Fat hen *Chenopodium album*

Featherfew *Chrysanthemum parthenium* *Matricaria eximia* *Primula parthenium*

Featherfoil *Chrysanthemum parthenium* *Matricaria eximia* *Primula parthenium*

Felon herb *Artemisia vulgaris*

Felonwood *Solanum dulcamara*

Fenkel *Foeniculum officinale* *Foeniculum vulgare*

Fennel *Foeniculum officinale* *Foeniculum vulgare*

Fennel hyssop *Agastache anethiodora* *Agastache foeniculum*

Fenugreek *Trigonella foenu graecum*

Feverfew *Chrysanthemum parthenium* *Matricaria eximia* *Primula parthenium* *Tanacetum parthenium*

Field balm *Nepeta hederacea*

Field horsetail *Equisetum arvense*

Field mint *Mentha arvensis piperascens*

Fine-leaved basil *Ocimum minimum*

Finocchio *Foeniculum dulce* *Foeniculum vulgare azoricum*

Flag iris *Iris germanica florentina*

Flax *Linum usitatissimum*

Flaxweed *Linaria vulgaris*

Flirtwort *Chrysanthemum parthenium* *Matricaria eximia* *Primula parthenium*

Florence fennel *Foeniculum dulce* *Foeniculum vulgare azoricum*

Florentine iris *Iris germanica florentina*

Florist's violet

Florist's violet	*Viola odorata*
Fluellin	*Linaria vulgaris*
Foalfoot	*Tussilago farfara*
Fool's parsley	*Aethusa cynapium*
Forget-me-not	*Myosotis arvensis*
	Myosotis sylvatica
Foxglove	*Digitalis purpurea*
Fox's clote	*Arctium lappa*
Fraxinella	*Dictamnus albus*
	Dictamnus fraxinella
French lavender	
	Lavandula dentata
	Lavandula stoechas
	Santolina chamaecyparissus
	Santolina incana
	Santolina tomentosa
French parsley	
	Petroselinum neapolitanum
French sorrel	*Rumex scutatus*
French spinach	*Atriplex hortensis*
French tarragon	
	Artemisia dracunculus
French thyme	*Thymus vulgaris*
Friar's cap	*Aconitum napellus*
Fringed lavender	
	Lavandula dentata
Fuller's herb	*Saponaria officinalis*
Fusoria	*Eonymus europaeus*
Galbanum	*Ferula gabaniflua*
Garden angelica	
	Angelica archangelica
Garden columbine	
	Aquilegia vulgaris
Garden cress	*Lepidium sativum*
Garden heliotrope	
	Valeriana officinalis
Garden mint	*Mentha spicata*
	Mentha viridis
Garden rhubarb	
	Rheum rhabarbarum
Garden sage	*Salvia officinalis*
Garden sorrel	*Rumex acetosa*
Garden thyme	*Thymus vulgaris*
Garlic	*Allium sativum*
Garlic chive	*Allium tuberosum*
Garlic mustard	*Alliaria petiolata*
Gas plant	*Dictamnus albus*
	Dictamnus fraxinella
Gentian	*Gentiana lutea*
German chamomile	
	Chamomilla recutira
	Matricaria chamomilla
	Matricaria recutira
Germander	*Teucrium chamaedrys*
Giant chive	
	Allium schoenoprasum sibiricum
Giant fennel	*Ferula communis*
Gill-go-over-the-ground	
	Nepeta hederacea
Gillyflower	*Dianthus caryophyllus*

Ginger	*Zingiber officinale*
Ginger mint	*Mentha × gentilis*
Ginseng	*Panax ginseng*
Glabrous rupture-wort	
	Herniaria glabra
Goat's leaf	*Lonicera periclymenum*
Goat's rue	*Galega officinalis*
Golden balm	
	Melissa officinalis aurea
Golden buttons	
	Tanacetum vulgare
Golden chain	
	Laburnum anagyroides
Golden chair	*Cytisus scoparius*
	Sarothamnus scoparius
Golden-edged thyme	
	Thymus × citriodorus aureus
Golden hop	
	Humulus lupulus aureus
Golden sage	*Salvia aurea*
	Salvia officinalis icterina
Golden seal	*Hydrastis canadensis*
Golden thyme	
	Thymus × citriodorus aureus
	Thymus vulgaris aureus
Gold knots	*Ranunculus acris*
Golds	*Calendula officinalis*
Good King Henry	
	Chenopodium bonus-henricus
Goose tansy	*Potentilla anserina*
Gran's bonnet	*Aquilegia vulgaris*
Grape ginger	*Costus speciosus*
Grape hyacinth	*Muscari botryoides*
Gravelroot	
	Eupatorium purpureum
Greasewood	*Salvia apiana*
Great chervil	*Myrrhis odorata*
Greater burnet saxifrage	
	Pimpinella major
Greater periwinkle	*Vinca major*
Great-headed garlic	
	Allium ampeloprasum
Great mullein	*Verbascum thapsus*
Great spurred violet	*Viola selkirkii*
Greek basil	*Ocimum minimum*
Greek hayseed	*Trigonella foenum-graecum*
Greek valerian	
	Polemoneum coeruleum
Green ginger	
	Artemisia absinthium
Green hellebore	*Veratrum viride*
Green sauce	*Rumex acetosa*
Grey santolina	
	Santolina chamaecyparissus
	Santolina incana
	Santolina tomentosa
Ground ivy	*Glechoma hederacea*
	Nepeta hederacea
Gum tree	*Eucalyptus gunnii*

Lamb's ears

Gypsy's rhubarb	*Arctium lappa*
Hack matack	*Juniperus communis*
Hag taper	*Verbascum thapsus*
Hamburg parsley	
	Carum petroselinum tuberosum
	Petroselinum crispum fusiformis
	Petroselinum tuberosum
Hartshorn	*Rhamnus catharticus*
Hawthorn	*Crataegus oxyacantha*
Haymaids	*Nepeta hederacea*
Heal-all	*Valeriana officinalis*
Healing herb	*Symphytum officinale*
Heartsease	*Viola tricolor*
Heather	*Calluna vulgaris*
Hedge hyssop	*Gratiola officinalis*
Helmet flower	*Aconitum napellus*
	Scutellaria galericulata
	Scutellaria lateriflora
Hemlock	*Conium maculatum*
Hemp agrimony	
	Eupatorium cannabinum
Hen-and-chickens	
	Sempervivum tectorum
Henbane	*Hyoscyamus niger*
Herb christopher	*Actaea spicata*
Herb constancy	*Viola tricolor*
Herb louisa	*Aloysia triphylla*
	Lippia citriodora
	Lippia triphylla
	Verbena triphylla
Herb masticke	*Thymus mastichina*
Herb of gladness	*Borago officinalis*
Herb of grace	*Ruta graveolens*
	Verbena officinalis
Herb of the cross	
	Verbena officinalis
Highway thorn	
	Rhamnus catharticus
Himalayan parsley	
	Selinum tenuifolium
Hoarhound	*Marrubium vulgare*
Hog's bean	*Hyoscyamus niger*
Holly	*Ilex aquifolium*
Holy basil	*Ocimum sanctum*
Honeysuckle	
	Lonicera periclymenum
Hop	*Humulus lupulus*
Hop marjoram	
	Amaracus dictamnus
	Origanum dictamnus
Horehound	*Marrubium vulgare*
Horse chestnut	
	Aesculus hippocastanum
Horseheal	*Inula helenium*
Horsehoof	*Tussilago farfara*
Horse mint	*Mentha longifolia*
	Monarda punctata
Horseradish	*Armoracia rusticana*
	Cochlearia armoracia
Horse savin	*Juniperus communis*

Houseleek	*Sempervivum tectorum*
Hyssop	*Hyssopus officinalis*
Iceland moss	*Cetraria islandica*
Indian arrowroot	
	Eonymus europaeus
Indian cress	*Tropaeolum majus*
Indian elm	*Ulmus fulva*
Indian plume	*Monarda didyma*
Italian fitch	*Galega officinalis*
Italian lovage	*Levisticum officinale*
	Ligusticum paludapifolium
Italian parsley	
	Petroselinum neapolitanum
Jack-by-the-hedge	*Alliaria petiolata*
Jacob's ladder	
	Polemoneum coeruleum
Jacob's staff	*Verbascum thapsus*
Jamaica pepper	
	Calycanthus floridus
Japanese mint	
	Mentha arvensis piperascens
Jasmine	*Jasminum officinale*
Jerusalem cowslip	
	Pulmonaria officinalis
Jimson weed	*Datura stramonium*
July flower	*Dianthus caryophyllus*
Juniper	*Juniperus communis*
Kangaroo apple	
	Solanum laciniatum
Kecksies	*Conium maculatum*
Kex	*Conium maculatum*
Kingcup	*Caltha palustris*
King's cure-all	*Oenothera biennis*
Kiss-her-in-the-buttery	
	Viola tricolor
Kit runabout	*Viola tricolor*
Knight's spur	*Delphinium ajacis*
Knitbone	*Symphytum officinale*
Knotted marjoram	
	Majorana hortensis
	Origanum majorana
Korean mint	*Agastache rugosa*
Laburnum	*Laburnum anagyroides*
Ladder to heaven	
	Convallaria majalis
Ladies' meat	
	Crataegus oxyacantha
Ladies' seal	*Bryonia dioica*
Lad's love	*Artemisia abrotanum*
Lady's bedstraw	*Galium verum*
Lady's mantle	*Alchemilla vulgaris*
	Alchemilla xanthochlora
Lady's slipper	*Cytisus scoparius*
	Sarothamnus scoparius
Lady's smock	*Cardamine pratensis*
Lamb mint	*Mentha spicata*
	Mentha viridis
Lamb's ears	*Stachys lanata*
	Stachys olympica

Lamb's lettuce

Lamb's lettuce	*Valerianella locusta*
	Valerianella olitoria
Lark's heel	*Delphinium ajacis*
Larkspur	*Delphinium ajacis*
Lavender cotton	
	Santolina chamaecyparissus
	Santolina incana
	Santolina tomentosa
Leek	*Allium porrum*
Lemon basil	*Ocimum americanum*
Lemon balm	*Melissa officinalis*
	Ocimum americanum
Lemon basil	*Ocimum citriodorum*
Lemon bergamot	
	Monarda citriodora
Lemon catmint	
	Nepeta cataria citriodorum
Lemon thyme	*Thymus serphyllum*
	Thymus × citriodorus
Lemon verbena	*Aloysia citriodora*
	Aloysia triphylla
	Lippia citriodora
	Lippia triphylla
	Verbena triphylla
Leopard's bane	*Arnica montana*
Lesser hemlock	*Aethusa cynapium*
Lettuce-leaved basil	
	Ocimum basilicum lactucafolium
Licorice	*Glycyrrhiza glabra*
Lignum crucis	*Viscum alba*
Lily-of-the-valley	
	Convallaria majalis
Lion's foot	*Alchemilla vulgaris*
	Alchemilla xanthochlora
Little dragon	
	Artemisia dracunculus
Liverwort	*Agrimonia eupatoria*
Lizzy-run-up-the-hedge	
	Nepeta hederacea
London lily	*Allium ursinum*
Lovage	*Levisticum officinale*
	Ligusticum paludapifolium
Love-in-idleness	*Viola tricolor*
Love leaves	*Arctium lappa*
Love-lies-bleeding	*Viola tricolor*
Low sagebrush	
	Artemisia arbuscula
Lungwort	*Pulmonaria officinalis*
Lupin	*Lupinus polyphyllus*
Lurk-in-the-ditch	
	Mentha pulegium
Mace	*Myristica fragrans*
Mackerel mint	*Mentha spicata*
	Mentha viridis
Madder root	*Rubia tinctoria*
Madonna lily	*Lilium candidum*
Madweed	*Scutellaria galericulata*
	Scutellaria lateriflora
Maid's hair	*Galium verum*
Mandrake	
	Mandragora officinarum

Manzanilla	*Anthemis nobilis*
Marigold	*Calendula officinalis*
Marihuana	*Cannabis sativa*
Marjoram	*Origanum vulgare*
Marshmallow	*Althaea officinalis*
Marsh marigold	*Caltha palustris*
Marsh samphire	
	Arthrocnemum perenne
Marygold	*Calendula officinalis*
Mary gowles	*Calendula officinalis*
May	*Crataegus oxyacantha*
May lily	*Convalleria majalis*
Maythen	*Anthemis nobilis*
Meadowsweet	
	Filipendula hexapetala
	Filipendula ulmaria
	Filipendula vulgaris
	Spiraea filipendula
	Ulmaria filipendula
Melilot	*Melilotus officinalis*
Menthella	*Mentha requienii*
Mignonette	*Reseda odorata*
Milfoil	*Achillea millefolium*
Miner's lettuce	
	Claytonia perfoliata
Mint geranium	*Balsamita major*
	Chrysanthemum balsamita
Mistletoe	*Viscum album*
Mock orange	
	Philadelphus coronarius
Monkshood	*Aconitum napellus*
Monk's pepper	*Vitex agnus-castus*
Monster-leaved basil	
	Ocimum basilicum lactucafolium
Moonflower	*Oenothera biennis*
Moose elm	*Ulmus fulva*
Moss rose	*Rosa centifolia muscosa*
Mother of thyme	
	Calamintha acinos
Motherwort	*Leonurus cardiaca*
Mountain balm	*Calamintha acinos*
Mountain radish	
	Armoracia rusticana
	Cochlearia armoracia
Mountain tea	
	Gaultheria procumbens
Mountain tobacco	*Arnica montana*
Mugwort	*Artemisia vulgaris*
Mullein	*Verbascum thapsus*
Myrtle	*Myrtus communis*
	Myrtus communis tarentina
Nasturtium	*Tropaeolum majus*
Nettle	*Urtica diorica*
Nine hooks	*Alchemilla vulgaris*
	Alchemilla xanthochlora
Nosebleed	*Achillea millefolium*
Nutmeg	*Myristica fragrans*
Nutmeg-scented geranium	
	Pelargonium × fragrans
Oak	*Quercus rober*

Russian comfrey

Old man	*Artemisia abrotanum*
Old man's pepper	
	Achillea millefolium
Old warrior	*Artemisia pontica*
Old woman	*Artemisia absinthium*
	Artemisia stellerana
Opium poppy	*Papaver somniferum*
Orach	*Atriplex hortensis*
Orache	*Atriplex hortensis*
Orange mint	*Mentha citrata*
Orange root	*Hydrastis canadensis*
Origano	*Origanum vulgare*
Organy	*Origanum vulgare*
Oriental chive	*Allium tuberosum*
Orris	*Iris florentina*
	Iris germanica
	Iris germanica florentina
Orris root	*Iris florentina*
	Iris germanica
	Iris germanica florentina
Oswega tea	*Monarda didyma*
Our Lady's bedstraw	
	Galium verum
Our Lady's candle	
	Verbascum thapsus
Our Lady's tears	
	Convallaria majalis
Parma violet	*Viola pallida plena*
Parsley	*Petroselinum crispum*
Pattens and clogs	*Linaria vulgaris*
Peasant's clock	
	Leontodon taraxacum
	Taraxacum officinale
Peasant's mattress	*Galium verum*
Pennyroyal	*Mentha pulegium*
Pepper	*Capsicum annuum*
Pepper cress	*Lepidium sativum*
Peppermint	*Mentha × piperita*
Peppermint-scented geranium	
	Pelargonium tomentosum
Perfoliate honeysuckle	
	Lonicera caprifolium
Periwinkle	*Vinca major*
Petersylinge	*Petroselinum crispum*
Phew plant	*Valeriana officinalis*
Phu	*Valeriana officinalis*
Pigeon's grass	*Verbena officinalis*
Pimento	*Capsicum frutescens*
Pineapple mint	
	Mentha suaveolens variegata
Pineapple sage	*Salvia elegans*
	Salvia rutilans
Pineapple shrub	
	Calycanthus floridus
Pink	*Dianthus caryophyllus*
Pink-of-my-john	*Viola tricolor*
Pipe tree	*Sambucus nigra*
Pixie's slipper	*Cytisus scoparius*
	Sarothamnus scoparius

Poison hemlock	
	Conium maculatum
Poison parsley	*Conium maculatum*
Pokeweed	*Phytolacca americana*
Polar plant	
	Rosmarinus lavandulaceus
	Rosmarinus officinalis
Poor man's treacle	*Allium sativum*
Pot marigold	*Calendula officinalis*
Pot marjoram	
	Origanum heracleoticum
	Origanum onites
	Origanum vulgare
Priest's crown	
	Leontodon taraxacum
	Taraxacum officinale
Primrose	*Primula vulgaris*
Pudding grass	*Mentha pulegium*
Purple basil	
	Ocimum basilicum aurauascens
Purple perilla	
	Perilla frutescens crispa
Purple sage	*Salvia purpurescens*
Purslane	*Portulaca oleracea*
Pussy willow	*Salix nigra*
Quickthorn	*Crataegus oxycantha*
Ram's horn	*Rhamnus catharticus*
Ramsons	*Allium ursinum*
Ram's thorn	*Rhamnus catharticus*
Red centaury	*Centaurium minus*
Red clover	*Trifolium incarnatum*
Red cole	*Armoracia rusticana*
	Cochlearia armoracia
Red elm	*Ulmus fulva*
Red mint	*Mentha × gentilis*
Red orache	
	Atriplex hortensis rubra
Red sage	
	Salvia officinalis purpurescens
Restharrow	*Ononis spinosa*
Rhubarb	*Rheum palmatum*
Rocket	*Hesperis matronalis*
Rock hyssop	*Hyssopus aristatus*
Roman chamomile	
	Anthemis nobilis
Roman laurel	*Laurus nobilis*
Roquette	*Hesperis matronalis*
Rosemary	
	Rosmarinus lavandulaceus
	Rosmarinus officinalis
Round-leaved mint	
	Mentha rotundifolia
Ruddes	*Calendula officinalis*
Rue	*Ruta graveolens*
Run-by-the-ground	
	Mentha pulegium
Russian comfrey	
	Symphytum perigrinum
	Symphytum uplandicum

Russian tarragon

Russian tarragon
Artemisia dracunculoides
Artemisia dranunculus
Safflower *Carthamus tinctorius*
Saffron *Crocus sativus*
Saffron thistle *Carthamus tinctorus*
Sage *Salvia officinalis*
Sagebrush *Artemisia tridentata*
Sage of Bethlehem *Mentha spicata*
Mentha viridis
Sainfoin *Onobrychis viciifolia*
Saint John's plant
Artemisia vulgaris
Saint John's wort
Hypericum perforatum
Saint Patrick's cabbage
Sempervivum tectorum
Salad burnet *Poterium sanguisorba*
Sanguisorba minor
Salad rocket *Eruca vesicaria*
Sambal *Ferula suaveolens*
Samphire *Crithmum maritimum*
Sand sage *Artemisia filifolia*
Santolina
Santolina chamaecyparissus
Santolina incana
Santolina tomentosa
Satan's apple
Mandragora officinarum
Savory
Satureia (Satureja) hortensis
Satureia montana
Scabwort *Inula helenium*
Scarlet monarda *Monarda didyma*
Scented geranium
Pelargonium graveolens
Scented mayweed
Chamomilla recutita
Matricaria chamomilla
Scotch mint *Mentha × gentilis*
Scots lovage *Levisticum scoticum*
Scullcap *Scutellaria galericulata*
Scutellaria laterifolia
Sea fennel *Crithmum maritimum*
Sea holly *Eryngium maritimum*
Sea purslane *Atriplex hortensis*
Semsem *Sesamum indicum*
Sesamum orientale
Sesame *Sesamum indicum*
Sesamum orientale
Setwall *Valeriana officinalis*
Shallot *Allium ascalonicum*
Shepherd's club *Verbascum thapsus*
Shepherd's needle *Myrrhis odorata*
Silver birch *Betula pendula*
Betula verrucosa
Silver posy *Thymus vulgaris*
Silver queen *Thymus citriodorus*
Silver sage *Salvia argentea*
Silver weed *Potentilla anserina*

Simpler's joy *Verbena officinalis*
Skewerwood *Eonymus europaeus*
Skirret *Sium sisarum*
Skullcap *Scutellaria galericulata*
Scutellaria lateriflora
Slippery elm *Ulmus fulva*
Smallage *Apium graveolens*
Small-leaved lime *Tilia cordata*
Smearwort *Chenopodium bonus-henricus*
Smooth cicely *Myrrhis odorata*
Sneezewort *Achillea millefolium*
Soapwort *Saponaria officinalis*
Sorrel *Rumex acetosa*
Sour sabs *Rumex acetosa*
South African wood sage
Buddleia salviifolia
Southernwood
Artemisia abrotanum
Spanish juice *Glycyrrhiza glabra*
Spanish sage
Salvia barrelieri
Spanish lavender
Lavandula stoechas
Spearmint *Mentha crispa*
Mentha spicata
Mentha viridis
Speedwell *Veronica officinalis*
Spindle tree *Eonymus europaeus*
Spire mint *Mentha spicata*
Mentha viridis
Spotted alder
Hamamelis virginiana
Spotted dead nettle
Lamium maculatum
Spotted hemlock
Conium maculatum
Squirting cucumber
Echallium elaterium
Star flower *Borago officinalis*
Starch hyacinth *Muscari botryoides*
Staunchweed *Achillea millefolium*
Sticklewort *Agrimonia eupatoria*
Stinging nettle *Urtica dioica*
Stink bomb *Allium ursinum*
Stinking goosefoot
Chenopodium vulvaria
Stinking lily *Allium ursinum*
Stinking motherwort
Chenopodium vulvaria
Stinking nanny *Allium ursinum*
Stinking nightshade
Hyoscyamus niger
Strawberry shrub
Calycanthus floridus
Straw foxglove *Digitalis lutea*
Succory *Cichorium intybus*
Sumbul *Ferula sumbul*
Summer coleus
Perilla frutescens crispa

White mustard

Summer purslane	*Portulaca oleracea*
Summer savory	*Satureia (Satureja) hortensis*
Sundew	*Drosera rotundifolia*
Sunflower	*Helianthus annuus*
Sweet balm	*Melissa officinalis*
Sweet basil	*Ocimum basilicum*
Sweet bay	*Laurus nobilis*
	Melissa officinalis
Sweet bracken	*Myrrhis odorata*
Sweetbriar	*Rosa eglanteria*
Sweet chervil	*Myrrhis odorata*
Sweet cicely	*Myrrhis odorata*
Sweet elder	*Sambucus nigra*
Sweet flag	*Acorus calamus*
Sweet marjoram	*Majorana hortensis*
	Origanum majorana
Sweet olive	*Osmanthus fragrans*
Sweet rocket	*Hesperis matronalis*
Sweet violet	*Viola odorata*
Sweet woodruff	*Asperula odorata*
	Galium odoratum
Sweet wormwood	*Artemisia annua*
Swine's snout	*Leontodon taraxacum*
	Taraxacum officinale
Tailwort	*Borago officinalis*
Tall agrimony	*Agrimonia eupatoria*
Tansy	*Chrysanthemum vulgare*
	Tanacetum vulgare
Tarentum myrtle	*Myrtus communis tarentina*
Tarragon	*Artemisia dracunculus*
Tasmanian blue gum	*Eucalyptus globulus*
Teaberry	*Gaultheria procumbens*
Tea jasmine	*Jasminum officinale*
Teasel	*Dipsacus fullonum*
	Dipsacus sylvestris
Tetterbury	*Bryonia dioica*
Thornapple	*Datura stramonium*
Thunder plant	*Sempervivum tectorum*
Thyme	*Thymus vulgaris*
Toadflax	*Linaria vulgaris*
Toadroot	*Actaea spicata*
Tonka bean	*Dipterix odorata*
Tonquin bean	*Dipterix odorata*
Toothache weed	*Achillea millefolium*
Torches	*Verbascum thapsus*
Tree onion	*Allium cepa proliferum*
Treefoil	*Trifolium incarnatum*
Tricolor sage	*Salvia officinalis tricolor*

True aloe	*Aloe barbadensis*
	Aloe vera
	Aloe vulgaris
True laurel	*Laurus nobilis*
True lavender	*Lavandula angustifolia*
	Lavandula officinalis
	Lavandula spica
	Lavandula vera
Trumpet weed	*Eupatorium purpureum*
Turmeric	*Curcuma longa*
Turnip-rooted parsley	*Petroselinum crispum fusiformis*
Valerian	*Valeriana officinalis*
Vanilla	*Vanilla fragrans*
Variegated applemint	*Mentha suaveolens variegata*
Variegated lemon balm	*Melissa officinalis variegata*
Variegated sage	*Salvia officinalis tricolor*
Velvet dock	*Inula helenium*
Vervain	*Verbena officinalis*
Vesper flower	*Hesperis matronalis*
Violet	*Viola odorata*
Violet bloom	*Solanum dulcamara*
Viper's bugloss	*Echium vulgare*
Virginian scullcap	*Scutellaria galericulata*
	Scutellaria lateriflora
Wahoo	*Eonymus europaeus*
Wall germander	*Teucrium chamaedrys*
Watercress	*Nasturtium officinale*
	Rorippa nasturtium-aquaticum
Water mint	*Mentha aquatica*
Water pepper	*Polygonum hydropiper*
Welsh onion	*Allium fistulosum*
Western mugwort	*Artemisia ludoviciana*
Western yew	*Taxus brevifolia*
White bryony	*Bryonia dioica*
White dittany	*Dictamnus albus*
	Dictamnus fraxinella
White hellebore	*Veratrum album*
	Veratrum viride
White horehound	*Marrubium incanum*
	Marrubium vulgare
White jasmine	*Jasminum officinale*
White lavender	*Lavandula alba*
White mignonette	*Reseda alba*
White mugwort	*Artemisia lactiflora*
White mulberry	*Morus alba*
White mustard	*Brassica alba*
	Brassica hirta
	Sinapis alba

White periwinkle

White periwinkle	*Vinca major alba*
White sage	*Artemisia ludoviciana*
	Salvia apiana
White thyme	*Thymus alba*
White violet	*Viola odorata alba*
White willow	*Salix alba*
Wild arrach	
	Chenopodium vulvaria
Wild artichoke	
	Cynara cardunculus
Wild bergamot	*Monarda fistulosa*
Wild celery	*Apium graveolens*
Wild chamomile	
	Matricaria chamomilla
Wild dagga	*Leonotus leonurus*
Wild garlic	*Allium ursinum*
Wild marjoram	*Origanum vulgare*
Wild mignonette	*Reseda lutea*
Wild pansy	*Viola tricolor*
Wild parsnip	*Pastinaca sativa*
Wild strawberry	*Fragaria vesca*
Wild succory	*Sabatia angularis*
Wild sweet william	
	Saponaria officinalis
Wild thyme	*Thymus serpyllum*
Wild vine	*Bryonia dioica*
Willow	*Salix nigra*
Winterbloom	
	Hamamelis virginiana
Wintergreen	
	Gaultheria procumbens
Winter marjoram	
	Origanum heracleoticum
Winter purslane	
	Claytonia perfoliata

Winter savory	*Satureia montana*
Wintersweet marjoram	
	Origanum heracleoticum
Witches' gloves	*Digitalis purpurea*
Witch-hazel	
	Hamamelis virginiana
Woad	*Isatis tinctoria*
Wood betony	*Stachys officinalis*
Woodbine	*Lonicera periclymenum*
Wood garlic	*Allium ursinum*
Woodrova	*Asperula odorata*
	Galium odoratum
Woodruff	*Asperula odorata*
	Galium odoratum
Wood sage	*Teucrium scorodonia*
Woody nightshade	
	Solanum dulcamara
Woolly betony	*Stachys lanata*
	Stachys olympica
Woolly mint	*Mentha rotundifolia*
Wormseed	*Artemisia maritima*
Wormwood	*Artemisia absinthium*
Woundwort	*Stachys officinalis*
Wuderove	*Asperula odorata*
	Galium odoratum
Yarrow	*Achillea millefolium*
Yellow bedstraw	*Galium verum*
Yellow gentian	*Gentiana lutea*
Yellow mustard	*Brassica alba*
	Sinapis alba
Yellow puccoon	
	Hydrastis canadensis
Yellow root	*Hydrastis canadensis*
Yellow starwort	*Inula helenium*
Yew	*Taxus baccata*
	Taxus brevifolia

HOUSE PLANTS

This section deals with those plants normally associated with hotel foyers, civic halls, restaurants, and public functions in addition to those found in private houses, sun rooms, and conservatories. Many subjects have been duplicated elsewhere in this book which, in their natural environment, would grow too large for indoor use but by regular pruning and root restriction can be controlled within acceptable limits. With a few exceptions bulbs and cacti are listed elsewhere under those headings.

Flaming katy –
Kalanchoe blossfeldiana

Aerial yam

Aerial yam   *Dioscorea bulbifera*
African hemp   *Sparmannia africana*
African marigold   *Tagetes erecta*
Air potato   *Dioscorea bulbifera*
Akeake   *Dodonaea viscosa*
Albany catspaw
   Anigozanthos preissii
Alexander palm
   Ptychosperma elegans
   Seaforthia elegans
Alexandra palm
   Archontophoenix alexandrae
Algaroba   *Ceratonia siliqua*
Aluminium plant   *Pilea cadierei*
Amaryllis
   Hippeastrum × ackermannii
   Hippeastrum × acramanii
Amazon lily   *Eucharis amazonica*
   Eucharis grandiflora
American aloe   *Agave americana*
American lotus   *Nelumbium lutea*
   Nelumbo lutea
   Nelumbo pentapetala
American marigold   *Tagetes erecta*
Angel's trumpet   *Datura × candida*
Angel's wing begonia
   Begonia coccinea
Angel's wings
   Caladium × hortulanum
Apple-scented geranium
   Pelargonium odoratissimum
Apple-scented pelargonium
   Pelargonium odoratissimum
Arabian coffee   *Coffea arabica*
Arabian jasmine   *Jasminum sambac*
Areca palm
   Chrysalidocarpus lutescens
Arrowhead vine
   Syngonium podophyllum
Arrowroot   *Maranta arundinacea*
Artillery plant   *Pilea microphylla*
   Pilea muscosa
Asparagus fern
   Asparagus plumosus
   Asparagus setaceus
Ass's tail   *Sedum morganianum*
Aubergine   *Solanum melongena*
Australian banyan
   Ficus macrophylla
Australian bluebell
   Sollya fusiformis
   Sollya heterophylla
Australian bluebell creeper
   Sollya fusiformis
   Sollya heterophylla
Australian fountain palm
   Livistona australis
Australian maidenhair fern
   Adiantum formosum

Australian pea
   Dolichos lablab lignosus
   Dolichos lignosus
Australian rosemary
   Westringia fruticosa
   Westringia rosmariniformis
Autograph tree   *Clusia rosea*
Autumn cattleya   *Cattleya labiata*
Autumn crocus
   Colchicum autumnale
Avocado   *Persea americana*
   Persea gratissima
Aztec lily   *Amaryllis formosissima*
   Sprekelia formosissima
Baboon flower   *Babiana stricta*
Baby blue eyes
   Nemophila menziesii
Baby rubber plant
   Peperomia clusiifolia
Baby smilax
   Asparagus asparagoides
   myrtifolius
Baby's tears   *Helxine soleirolii*
   Soleirolia soleirolii
Ball fern   *Davallia mariesii*
Balloon vine
   Cardiospermum halicacabum
Balm mint bush
   Prostanthera melissifolia
Balsam apple   *Clusia rosea*
   Momordica balsamina
Balsam pear   *Momordica charantia*
Bamboo palm
   Chamaedorea erumpens
   Rhapis excelsa
Banana passion fruit
   Passiflora mollissima
   Tacsonia mollissima
Banyan   *Ficus benghalensis*
Barbados cherry   *Malpighia glabra*
Barbados gooseberry
   Pereskia aculeata
Barbados pride
   Caesalpinia pulcherrima
   Poinciana pulcherrima
Barberton daisy   *Gerbera jamesonii*
Basket flower
   Hymenocallis calathina
   Hymenocallis narcissiflora
Basket grass   *Oplismenus hirtellus*
Bat flower   *Tacca chantrieri*
Bay   *Laurus nobilis*
Bead plant   *Nertera granadensis*
Bead tree   *Melia azederach*
Bead vine   *Crassula rupestris*
Beefsteak begonia
   Begonia × erythrophylla
   Begonia × feastii
Beefsteak plant   *Iresine herbstii*
Belladonna lily
   Amaryllis belladonna
Bell pepper   *Capsicum annuum*

Cactus geranium

Bermuda buttercup   *Oxalis cernua*
     Oxalis pes-caprae
Bilimbi   *Averrhoa bilimbi*
Bird-catching tree
     Pisonia umbellifera
Bird of paradise flower
     Caesalpinia gilliesii
     Strelitzia reginae
Bird's eyes   *Gilia tricolor*
Bird's nest bromeliad
     Nidularium innocentii
Bird's nest fern   *Asplenium nidus*
     Asplenium nidus-avis
Birth wort   *Aristolochia elegans*
Black bean   *Kennedia nigricans*
Blackboy   *Xanthorrhoea preissii*
Black echeveria   *Echeveria affinis*
Black-eyed susan   *Thunbergia alata*
Black-gold philodendron
     Philodendron andreanum
     Philodendron melanochrysum
Black leaf panamiga   *Pilea repens*
Black pepper   *Piper nigrum*
Black sarana
     Fritillaria camtschatcensis
Black tree fern   *Cyathea medullaris*
Blackwood acacia
     Acacia melanoxylon
Bleeding heart   *Dicentra spectabilis*
Bleeding heart vine
     Clerodendrum thomsonae
Blood flower   *Asclepias curassavica*
     Haemanthus katherinae
     Haemanthus multiflorus
Blood leaf   *Iresine lindenii*
Blue amaryllis
     Hippeastrum procerum
     Worsleya rayneri
Blue cape leadwort
     Plumbago auriculata
     Plumbago capensis
Blue cape plumbago
     Plumbago auriculata
     Plumbago capensis
Blue echeveria   *Echeveria glauca*
     Echeveria secunda glauca
Blue glory bower
     Clerodendrum ugandense
Blue gum   *Eucalyptus globulus*
Blue-leaved wattle
     Acacia cyanophylla
Blue lotus   *Nymphaea stellata*
Blue marguerite   *Agathaea coelestis*
     Felicia amelloides
Blue passion flower
     Passiflora caerulea
Blue potato bush
     Solanum rantonnetii
Blue sage
     Daedalacanthus nervosum
     Eranthemum nervosum
     Eranthemum pulchellum

Blue screw pine   *Pandanus baptisii*
Blue shamrock pea
     Parochetus communis
Blue taro   *Xanthosma violaceum*
Blue thimble flower   *Gilia capitata*
Blue tiger lily   *Cypella plumbea*
Blue trumpet vine
     Thunbergia grandiflora
Blue water lily   *Nymphaea capensis*
Blushing bromeliad
     Guzmania picta
     Nidularium fulgens
     Nidularium pictum
Blushing philodendron
     Philodendron erubescens
Boat lily   *Rhoeo discolor*
     Rhoeo spathacea
Botany bay gum
     Xanthorrhoea arborea
Bo tree   *Ficus religiosa*
Bottlebrush   *Callistemon speciosus*
Bottle gourd   *Lagenaria siceraria*
     Lagenaria vulgaris
Bower plant   *Pandorea jasminoides*
Brazilian coleus
     Plectranthus oertendahlii
Brazilian potato tree
     Solanum macranthum
Bread tree cycad
     Encephalartos altensteinii
Bridal flower
     Stephanotis floribunda
Bridal wreath
     Francoa appendiculata
Bronze inch plant   *Zebrina purpusii*
Brush cherry   *Eugenia australis*
     Eugenia myrtifolia
     Eugenia paniculata
     Syzygium paniculatum
Bullock's heart   *Annona reticulata*
Burning bush   *Kochia scoparia*
Burn plant   *Aloe barbadensis*
Burro's tail   *Sedum morganianum*
Bush violet   *Browallia speciosa*
Busy lizzie   *Impatiens holstii*
     Impatiens sultanii
     Impatiens walleriana
Butcher's broom
     Ruscus hypoglossum
Butterfly ginger lily
     Hedychium coronarium
Butterfly orchid   *Oncidium papilio*
Butterfly vine
     Stigmaphyllon ciliatum
Butterwort   *Pinguicula vulgaris*
Button fern   *Pellaea rotundifolia*
Cabbage palm   *Cordyline australis*
Cabbage tree   *Cordyline australis*
Cactus geranium
     Pelargonium echinatum

Cactus pelargonium
Pelargonium echinatum

Cactus spurge
Euphorbia pseudocactus

Cajeput   *Melaleuca leucodendron*

Calabash gourd   *Lagenaria siceraria*
Lagenaria vulgaris

Calamondin   × *Citrofortunella mitis*
Citrus mitis
Citrus reticulata × fortunella

Calico flower   *Aristolochia elegans*

Calico hearts
Adromischus maculatus
Cotyledon maculata
Crassula maculata

Calico plant
Alternanthera bettzickiana

Californian pitcher plant
Darlingtonia californica

Californian poppy
Eschscholzia californica

Canary bird bush
Crotalaria agatiflora

Canary creeper
Tropaeolum canariensis
Tropaeolum peregrinum

Canary Islands ivy
Hedera canariensis

Canary Islands date palm
Phoenix canariensis

Candelabra tree
Araucaria angustifolia

Candle plant   *Kleinia articulatus*
Plectranthus coleoides
Senecio articulatus

Cape cowslip   *Lachenalia aloides*
Lachenalia tricolor

Cape grape   *Cissus capensis*
Rhoicissus capensis
Vitis capensis

Cape honeysuckle
Bignonia capensis
Tecoma capensis
Tecomaria capensis

Cape ivy   *Senecio macroglossus*

Cape jasmine   *Ervatamia coronaria*
Gardenia florida
Gardenia grandiflora
Gardenia jasminoides
Tabernaemontana coronaria
Tabernaemontana divaricata

Cape myrtle   *Lagerstroemia indica*

Cape primrose   *Streptocarpus rexii*

Cape tulip   *Homeria breyniana*
Homeria collina

Carambola tree
Averrhoa carambola

Cardinal flower   *Gesneria cardinalis*
Sinningia cardinalis

Cardinal's guard   *Justicia coccinea*
Pachystachys cardinalis
Pachystachys coccinea

Caricature plant
Graptophyllum pictum

Carnation   *Dianthus caryophyllus*

Carob   *Ceratonia siliqua*

Carolina yellow jasmine
Gelsemium sempervirens

Cassava   *Manihot esculenta*
Manihot utilissima

Cast iron plant   *Aspidistra elatior*
Aspidistra lurida

Castor oil plant   *Ricinus communis*

Cathedral bells   *Cobaea scandens*

Cat's claw vine
Doxantha unguis-cati

Cat's jaws   *Faucaria felina*

Catspaw   *Anigozanthos humilis*

Cat's whiskers   *Tacca chantrieri*

Century plant   *Agave americana*

Ceriman   *Monstera deliciosa*
Monstera pertusa
Philodendron pertusum

Chandelier plant
Kalanchoe tubiflora

Chenille plant   *Acalypha hispida*
Echeveria leucotricha

Cherimoya   *Annona cherimolia*

Cherry tomato
*Lycopersicon lycopersicum cerasif
orme*

Chestnut dioon   *Dioon edule*

Chestnut vine
Cissus voinierianum
Tetrastigma voinierianum
Vitis voinierianum

Chilean bellflower   *Lapageria rosea*

Chilean glory flower
Eccremocarpus scaber

Chilean jasmine   *Mandevilla laxa*
Mandevilla suaveolens

Chilean potato tree
Solanum crispum

Chilean wine palm   *Jubaea chilensis*
Jubaea spectabilis

Chillies   *Capsicum annuum*

Chimney bellflower
Campanula pyramidalis

China grass   *Boehmeria nivea*

Chincherinchee
Ornithogalum thyrsoides

Chinese evergreen
Aglaonema modestum

Chinese fountain palm
Livistona chinensis

Chinese jasmine
Jasminum polyanthum

Chinese lantern plant
Ceropegia woodii

Chinese primrose   *Primula sinensis*

Chinese yam   *Dioscorea batatus*
Dioscorea opposita

Chives   *Allium schoenoprasum*

Christmas begonia
Begonia × cheimantha

Christmas fern
Polystichum acrostichoides

Christmas orchid
Cattleya labiata trianaei
Cattleya trianaei

Christmas palm *Veitchia merrillii*

Chufa nut *Cyperus esculentus*

Chusan palm
Trachycarpus fortunei

Cigar flower *Cuphea ignea*
Cuphea platycentra

Cinnamon yam *Dioscorea batatus*
Dioscorea opposita

Citron *Citrus medica*

Climbing aloe *Aloe ciliaris*

Climbing fig *Ficus pumila*
Ficus repens

Climbing onion *Bowiea volubilis*

Cluster cattleya
Cattleya bowringiana

Cobra plant
Darlingtonia californica

Cockle-shell orchid
Epidendrum cochleatum

Cockscomb
Celosia argentea cristata
Celosia cristata

Cockspur coral tree
Erythrina crista-galli

Cocktail orchid
Cattleya intermedia

Coconut palm *Cocos nucifera*

Cocoyam *Colocasia esculenta*

Coin leaf *Peperomia polybotrya*

Common banana
Musa × paradisiaca
Musa × sapientum

Common blackboy
Xanthorrhoea preissii

Common dumb cane
Dieffenbachia maculata

Common gardenia
Gardenia florida
Gardenia grandiflora
Gardenia jasminoides

Common ginger
Zingiber officinale

Common green kangaroo paw
Anigozanthos manglesii

Common heliotrope
Heliotropium arborescens
Heliotropium peruvianum

Common hop *Humulus lupulus*

Common hydrangea
Hydrangea hortensis
Hydrangea macrophylla

Common ivy *hedera helix*

Common lavender
Lavandula angustifolia

Common maidenhair fern
Adiantum capillus-veneris

Common marigold
Calendula officinalis

Common morning glory
Ipomoea purpurea
Pharbitis purpurea

Common myrtle
Myrtus communis

Common passion flower
Passiflora caerulea

Common pitcher plant
Sarracenia purpurea

Common polypody
Polypodium vulgare

Common sage *Salvia officinalis*

Common screw pine
Pandanus utilis

Common snowdrop
Galanthus nivalis

Common stag's horn fern
Platycerium alcicorne
Platycerium bifurcatum

Common sundew
Drosera rotundifolia

Common throatwort
Trachelium caeruleum

Common trigger plant
Stylidium graminifolium

Common wallflower
Cheiranthus cheiri

Common white jasmine
Jasminum officinale

Coontie *Zamia floridana*

Cootamunda wattle
Acacia baileyana

Copperleaf *Acalypha wilkesiana*

Copper roses
Echeveria multicaulis

Coquito *Jubaea chilensis*
Jubaea spectabilis

Coral aloe *Aloe striata*

Coralberry *Aechmea fulgens*
Ardisia crispa

Coral drops *Bessera elegans*

Coral gem *Lotus berthelotii*

Corallita *Antigonon leptopus*

Coral moss *Nertera depressa*

Coral plant *Berberidopsis corallina*
Jatropha multifida
Russelia equisetiformis
Russelia juncea

Coral vine *Antigonon leptopus*

Cornflower *Centaurea cyanus*

Corn plant *Dracaena fragrans*

Cow's horn
Euphorbia grandicornis

Creeping charlie
Pilea nummulariifolia

Creeping fig *Ficus pumila*
Ficus repens

Creeping peperomia

Creeping peperomia
Peperomia prostrata
Peperomia rotundifolia pilosior

Crepe ginger   *Costus speciosus*

Cretan brake   *Pteris cretica*

Croton
Codiaeum variegatum pictum

Crown imperial
Fritillaria imperialis

Crown of thorns   *Euphorbia milii*

Crown stag's horn
Platycerium biforme
Platycerium coronarium

Cruel plant   *Araujia sericofera*

Crystal anthurium
Anthurium crystallinum

Cuban royal palm   *Roystonea regia*

Cup-and-saucer creeper
Cobaea scandens

Cupid peperomia
Peperomia scandens

Cup of gold   *Solandra guttata*
Solandra hartwegii
Solandra maxima
Solandra nitida

Curly palm   *Howeia belmoreana*
Kentia belmoreana

Currant tomato
Lycopersicon pimpinellifolium

Curry leaf   *Murraya koenigii*

Curry plant
Helichrysum angustifolium
Helichrysum italicum
Helichrysum serotinum

Curuba   *Passiflora mollissima*
Tacsonia mollissima

Custard apple   *Annona reticulata*

Cypress vine   *Ipomoea quamoclit*

Damper's pea   *Clianthus formosus*
Clianthus dampieri

Dancing doll orchid
Oncidium flexuosum

Darling River pea
Swainsona greyana

Dasheen   *Colocasia esculenta*

Date palm   *Phoenix dactylifera*

Day flower   *Commelina coelestis*

Desert fan palm   *Pritchardia filifera*
Washingtonia filifera

Desert privet
Peperomia magnoliifolia

Desert rose   *Adenium obesum*
Echeveria rosea

Devil's backbone
Kalanchoe diagremontiana

Devil's ivy   *Epipremnum aureum*
Pothos aureus
Raphidophora aurea
Scindapsus aureus

Devil's tail
Amorphophallus bulbifer

Devil's tongue
Amorphophallus rivieri
Sansevieria zeylanica

Dewflower
Drosanthemum speciosum

Dinner-plate aralia
Polyscias balfouriana

Donkey's tail   *Sedum morganianum*

Dove orchid
Oncidium ornithorhynchum
Peristeria elata

Dragon plant   *Arum dracunculus*
Dracunculus vulgaris

Dragon's tree   *Dracaena draco*

Drooping star of Bethlehem
Ornithogalum nutans

Dusky coral pea
Kennedia rubicunda

Dusty miller   *Centaurea cineraria*
Centaurea gymnocarpa
Cineraria maritima
Senecio bicolor cineraria
Senecio cineraria
Senecio maritimus

Dutchman's breeches
Dicentra spectabilis

Dwarf fan palm
Chamaerops humilis

Dwarf ginger lily
Kaempferia roscoana

Dwarf mountain palm
Chamaedorea elegans
Neanthe elegans

Easter orchid
Cattleya labiata mossiae
Cattleya mossiae

East Indian arrowroot
Tacca leontopetaloides
Tacca pinnatifida

East Indian holly fern
Arachnoides aristata
Polystichum aristata

East Indian rosebay
Ervatamia coronaria
Tabernaemontana coronaria
Tabernaemontana divaricata

Ebony spleenwort
Asplenium platyneuron

Egg-plant   *Solanum melongena*

Egyptian blue lotus
Nymphaea caerula

Egyptian paper reed
Cyperus papyrus

Egyptian star cluster   *Pentas carnea*
Pentas lanceolata

Elephant foot
Beaucarnea recurvata
Nolina recurvata
Nolina tuberculata

Elephant's ear   *Colocasia esculenta*
Philodendron domesticum
Philodendron hastatum

German ivy

Elephant's ear begonia	
	Begonia haageana
	Begonia scharffii
Elephant's ear fern	
	Acrostichum crinitum
	Elaphoglossum crinitum
	Platycerium angolense
Elkhorn fern	*Platycerium hillii*
Emerald ripple	*Peperomia caperata*
English ivy	*Hedera helix*
English lavender	
	Lavandula angustifolia
Fairy lachenalia	
	Lachenalia mutabilis
Fairy primrose	*Primula malacoides*
False African violet	
	Streptocarpus saxorum
False castor-oil plant	
	Aralia japonica
	Aralia sieboldii
	Fatsia japonica
False heather	*Cuphea hyssopifolia*
False yellow jasmine	
	Gelsemium sempervirens
Fan begonia	*Begonia rex*
Fancy geraniums	
	Pelargonium × domesticum
Fancy pelargoniums	
	Pelargonium × domesticum
Fat pork tree	*Clusia rosea*
Fern-leaf aralia	*Polyscias filicifolia*
Fernleaf begonia	*Begonia foliosa*
Fern palm	*Cycas circinalis*
Fiddle-leaf fig	*Ficus lyrata*
	Ficus pandurata
Fingernail plant	
	Neoregelia spectabilis
Finger tree	*Euphorbia tirucalli*
Fire cracker	*Brodiaea coccinea*
	Brodiaea ida-maia
Firecracker plant	
	Crossandra infundibuliformis
	Crossandra undulifolia
	Echeveria setosa
Firecracker vine	*Manettia bicolor*
	Manettia inflata
	Manettia luteo-rubra
Fishpole bamboo	
	Phyllostachys aurea
Five fingers	*Philodendron auritum*
	Syngonium auritum
Five spot	*Nemophila maculata*
Flame flower	*Bignonia venusta*
	Pyrostegia ignea
	Pyrostegia venusta
Flame ivy	*Hemigraphis alternata*
	Hemigraphis colorata
Flame nettle	*Coleus blumei*
Flame-of-the-woods	*Ixora coccinea*
Flame vine	*Bignonia venusta*
	Pyrostegia ignea
	Pyrostegia venusta

Flame violet	*Episcia cupreata*
Flaming katy	
	Kalanchoe blossfeldiana
Flamingo flower	
	Anthurium scherzerianum
Flaming sword	*Vriesea splendens*
Flaming torch	
	Guzmania berteroana
Flaming trumpets	*Bignonia venusta*
	Pyrostegia ignea
	Pyrostegia venusta
Floating fern	
	Ceratopteris pteridoides
Floating moss	*Salvinia auriculata*
Florida arrowroot	
	Zamia furfuracea
	Zamia pumila
Florida ribbon fern	*Vittaria lineata*
Florist's genista	*Cytisus canariensis*
	Genista canariensis
	Teline canariensis
Florist's mimosa	*Acacia dealbata*
Flowering banana	*Musa coccinea*
Flowering mignonette	
	Peperomia fraseri
Flower of the west wind	
	Zephyranthes candida
Fountain bush	
	Russelia equisetiformis
	Russelia juncea
Fountain flower	
	Ceropegia sandersonii
Fox brush orchid	*Aerides fieldingii*
Frangipani	*Plumeria acuminata*
	Plumeria rubra
Freckle face	
	Hypoestes phyllostachya
French hydrangea	
	Hydrangea hortensis
	Hydrangea macrophylla
French lavender	
	Lavandula stoechas
French marigold	*Tagetes patula*
Friendship plant	*Billbergia nutans*
	Pilea involucrata
Fuchsia begonia	
	Begonia fuchsioides
Gardenia	*Gardenia florida*
	Gardenia grandiflora
	Gardenia jasminoides
Garden pansy	*Viola × hortensis*
	Viola × wittrockiana
Garland flower	
	Hedychium coronarium
Gebang	*Corypha elata*
	Corypha gembanga
Geraldton wax flower	
	Chamaelaucium uncinatum
German ivy	*Senecio mikanioides*

Ghost plant
  Echeveria paraguayense
  Graptopetalum paraguayense
  Sedum weinbergii

Giant chincherinchee
  Ornithogalum saundersiae

Giant dumb cane
  Dieffenbachia amoena

Giant elephant's ear
  Alocasia macrorrhiza

Giant granadilla
  Passiflora quadrangularis

Giant holly fern
  Polystichum munitum

Giant pineapple flower
  Eucomis pole-evansii

Giant potato vine
  Solanum wendlandii

Giant reed   *Arundo donax*

Giant snowdrop   *Galanthus elwesii*

Ginger   *Zingiber officinale*

Gippsland fountain palm
  Livistona australis

Globe amaranth
  Gomphrena globosa

Glory bower
  Clerodendrum thomsonae

Glory bush
  Tibouchina semidecandra
  Tibouchina urvilleana

Glory lily   *Gloriosa rothschildiana*

Glory-of-the-sun
  Leucocoryne ixioides

Glory pea   *Clianthus dampieri*
  Clianthus formosus

Gloxinia   *Gloxinia speciosa*
  Sinningia speciosa

Golden bamboo
  Phyllostachys aurea

Golden butterfly orchid
  Oncidium varicosum

Golden creeper
  Stigmaphyllon ciliatum

Golden dewdrop   *Duranta plumieri*
  Duranta repens

Golden feather palm
  Chrysalidocarpus lutescens

Golden male fern
  Dryopteris borreri
  Dryopteris pseudomas

Golden pothos
  Epipremnum aureum
  Pothos aureus
  Raphidophora aurea
  Scindapsus aureus

Golden rain   *Acacia prominens*

Golden stars   *Bloomeria crocea*

Golden trumpet
  Allamanda cathartica

Golden vine
  Stigmaphyllon ciliatum

Gold dust dracaena
  Dracaena godseffiana
  Dracaena surculosa

Goldfish plant   *Columnea gloriosa*
  Columnea microphylla

Goosefoot plant
  Syngonium podophyllum

Gosford wattle   *Acacia prominens*

Gout plant   *Jatropha podagrica*

Grapefruit   *Citrus paradisi*

Grape ivy   *Cissus rhombifolia*

Grass nut   *Brodiaea laxa*
  Triteleia laxa

Grass trigger plant
  Stylidium graminifolium

Greater butterwort
  Pinguicula grandiflora

Great sundew   *Drosera anglica*

Green brake fern
  Pellaea adiantoides
  Pellaea hastata
  Pellaea viridis

Green earth star
  Cryptanthus acaulis

Green kangaroo paw
  Anigozanthos viridis

Green pepper   *Capsicum annuum*

Ground ivy   *Glechoma hederacea*

Groundnut   *Arachis hypogaea*

Ground rattan   *Rhapis excelsa*

Guernsey lily   *Nerine sarniensis*
  Vallota purpurea
  Vallota speciosa

Guinea flower   *Hibbertia scandens*
  Hibbertia volubilis

Hairy toad plant   *Stapelia hirsuta*

Hard shield fern
  Polystichum aculeatum

Hare's foot fern
  Davallia canariensis
  Phlebodium aureum
  Polypodium aureum

Harlequin flower   *Sparaxis tricolor*

Hart's tongue fern
  Asplenium scolopendrium
  Phyllitis scolopendrium

Heart leaf   *Philodendron cordatum*
  Philodendron scandens

Heart pea
  Cardiospermum halicacabum

Heart seed
  Cardiospermum halicacabum

Heavenly bamboo
  Nandina domestica

Holly fern   *Aspidium falcatum*
  Cyrtomium falcatum
  Polystichum falcatum

Holly-leaved begonia
  Begonia cubensis

Holy ghost plant   *Peristeria elata*

Honeybush   *Melianthus major*

Ladder fern

Honey flower	*Protea mellifera*
	Protea repens
Honey palm	*Jubaea chilensis*
	Jubaea spectabilis
Hong Kong kumquat	
	Fortunella hindsii
Hoop pine	
	Araucaria cunninghamii
Hop bush	*Dodonaea viscosa*
Horse-shoe geranium	
	Pelargonium zonale
Horse-shoe pelargonium	
	Pelargonium zonale
Hottentot fig	
	Carpobrotus acinaciformis
	Carpobrotus edulis
Humble plant	*Mimosa pudica*
Huntsman's horn	*Sarracenia flava*
Hyacinth bean	*Dolichos lablab*
Ifafa lily	*Cyrtanthus mackenii*
Illawarra palm	*Archontophoenix*
	cunninghamiana
Indian bean	*Dolichos lablab*
Indian day flower	
	Commelina benghalensis
Indian ginger	*Alpinia calcarata*
Indian kale	*Xanthosma lindenii*
Indian pink	*Dianthus chinensis*
Indian shot	*Canna × generalis*
Indoor fig	*Ficus diversifolia*
Iron cross begonia	
	Begonia masoniana
Italian bellflower	
	Campanula isophylla
Ithuriel's spear	*Brodiaea laxa*
	Triteleia laxa
Ivyleaf peperomia	
	Peperomia griseoargentea
	Peperomia hederifolia
Ivy-leaved geraniums	
	Pelargonium peltatum
Ivy-leaved pelargoniums	
	Pelargonium peltatum
Ivy-leaved toadflax	
	Cymbalaria muralis
	Linaria cymbalaria
Ivy-leaved violet	*Viola hederacea*
Jacobean lily	
	Amaryllis formosissima
	Sprekelia formosissima
Jacob's ladder	
	Pedilanthes tithymaloides smallii
Jade plant	*Crassula argentea*
	Crassula portulacea
Japanese azalea	*Azalea obtusa*
Japanese banana	*Musa basjoo*
Japanese buckler fern	
	Dryopteris erythrosora
Japanese hop	*Humulus japonicus*
Japanese lantern	
	Hibiscus schizopetalus

Japanese pittosporum	
	Pittosporum tobira
Japanese sago palm	*Cycas revoluta*
Japanese sedge	*Carex morrowii*
Japanese shield fern	
	Dryopteris erythrosora
Jasmine nightshade	
	Solanum jasminoides
Java glorybean	
	Clerodendrum speciosissimum
	Clerodendrum fallax
Jerusalem cherry	
	Solanum pseudocapsicum
Jewel plant	*Bertolonia hirsuta*
Josephine's lily	
	Brunsvigia josephinae
Joseph's coat	
	Codiaeum variegatum pictum
Joshua tree	*Yucca brevifolia*
Jungle geranium	*Ixora javanica*
Kahili ginger	
	Hedychium gardnerianum
Kaffir lily	*Clivia miniata*
	Imantophyllum miniatum
Kaka beak	*Clianthus puniceus*
Kangaroo apple	*Solanum aviculare*
Kangaroo thorn	*Acacia armata*
Kangaroo vine	*Cissus antarctica*
Karaka	*Corynocarpus laevigatus*
Karo	*Pittosporum crassifolium*
Kenilworth ivy	*Cymbalaria muralis*
	Linaria cymbalaria
Kentia palm	*Howeia forsterana*
	Kentia forsterana
Key palm	*Thrinax microcarpa*
	Thrinax morrisii
King anthurium	*Anthurium veitchii*
Kingfisher daisy	*Aster bergeriana*
	Felicia bergeriana
King of the bromeliads	
	Vriesea hieroglyphica
King plant	*Anoectochilus regalis*
King's crown	*Jacobinia carnea*
	Jacobinia velutina
	Justicia carnea
Knife acacia	*Acacia cultriformis*
Kohuhu	*Pittosporum tenuifolium*
Kris plant	*Alocasia sanderiana*
Lablab bean	*Dolichos lablab*
Lace flower	*Episcia dianthiflora*
Lace orchid	
	Odontoglossom crispum
Lacy ground fern	
	Dennstaedtia davallioides
Lacy pine fern	
	Polypodium subauriculatum
Lacy tree philodendron	
	Philodendron selloum
Ladder fern	*Nephrolepis cordifolia*
	Pteris vittata

Lady-in-the-bath

Lady-in-the-bath
Dicentra spectabilis

Lady of the night
Brunfelsia americana
Brunfelsia violacea

Lady Washington geranium
Pelargonium × domesticum

Lady Washington pelargonium
Pelargonium × domesticum

Lamp flower *Ceropegia caffrorum*

Lance copperleaf
Acalypha godseffiana

Laurel fig *Ficus macrocarpa*
Ficus nitida
Ficus retusa

Laurustinus *Viburnum tinus*

Leather fern *Acrostichum aureum*
Rumohra adiantiformis

Lehua *Metrosideros collina*

Lemon bottlebrush
Callistemon citrinus
Callistemon lanceolatus

Lemon geranium
Pelargonium crispum

Lemon pelargonium
Pelargonium crispum

Lemon-scented gum
Eucalyptus citriodora

Lemon verbena *Aloysia citriodora*
Lippia citriodora
Verbena triphylla

Leopard orchid *Ansellia africana*

Levant cotton
Gossypium herbaceum

Lily of the Incas
Alstroemeria pelegrina alba

Lily-of-the-valley
Convallaria majalis

Lily-of-the-valley orchid
Odontoglossum pulchellum

Lily-of-the-valley tree
Clethra arborea

Lime *Citrus aurantifolia*
Citrus limetta
Limonia aurantifolia

Lipstick vine
Aeschynanthus lobbianus

Liquorice plant
Helichrysum petiolatum

Little lady palm *Rhapis excelsa*

Livingstone daisy
Dorotheanthus bellidiformis
Mesembryanthemum criniflorum

Lobster claw *Clianthus puniceus*

Lobster claws *Vriesea carinata*

Locust *Ceratonia siliqua*

Lollipop plant *Pachystachys lutea*

London pride *Saxifraga × urbium*

Loofah *Luffa cylindrica*
Luffa aegyptica

Loquat *Eriobotrya japonica*

Lorraine begonia
Begonia × cheimantha

Love charm *Bignonia purpurea*
Clytostoma binatum
Clytostoma purpureum

Love-lies-bleeding
Amaranthus caudatus

Lucky clover *Oxalis deppei*

Madagascar dragon tree
Dracaena marginata

Madagascar jasmine
Stephanotis floribunda

Madagascar periwinkle
Catharanthus roseus
Vinca rosea

Magic plant *Aloe barbadensis*

Maguey *Agave americana*

Maidenhair fern
Adiantum capillus-veneris

Maidenhair vine
Muehlenbeckia complexa

Maid of the mist
Gladiolus primulinus

Malabar plum *Eugenia jambos*
Syzygium jambos

Malayan urn vine
Dischidia rafflesiana

Malay ginger *Costus speciosus*

Male fern *Dryopteris filix-mas*

Mandarin *Citrus nobilis*
Citrus reticulata

Mangle's kangaroo paw
Anigozanthos manglesii

Manioc *Manihot esculenta*
Manihot utilissima

Manuka *Leptospermum scoparium*

Marble plant *Aregelia marmorata*
Neoregelia marmorata

Marlberry *Ardisia crispa*

Marmalade bush
Streptosolen jamesonii

Martha Washington geranium
Pelargonium × domesticum

Martha Washington pelargonium
Pelargonium × domesticum

Mask flower *Alonsoa warscewiczii*

Mauritius hemp *Furcraea foetida*
Furcraea gigantea

Meadow saffron
Colchicum autumnale

Medicine plant *Aloe barbadensis*

Medusa's head
Euphorbia caput-medusae

Meiwa kumquat
Fortunella crassifolia

Metal leaf begonia
Begonia metallica

Mexican bread fruit
Monstera deliciosa
Monstera pertusa
Philodendron pertusum

Oak-leaved pelargonium

Mexican dwarf palm
    Chamaedorea elegans

Mexican fern palm   *Dioon edule*

Mexican flame vine
    Senecio confusus

Mexican foxglove
    Allophyton mexicanum
    Tetranema mexicanum
    Tetranema roseum

Mexican orangeblossom
    Choisya ternata

Mexican violet
    Allophyton mexicanum
    Tetranema mexicanum
    Tetranema roseum

Mickey mouse plant
    Ochna serrulata

Milk bush   *Euphorbia tirucalli*

Mind your own business
    Helxine soleirolii
    Soleirolia soleirolii

Miniature eyelash begonia
    Begonia bowerii

Miniature fan palm   *Rhapis excelsa*

Miniature fishtail palm
    Chamaedorea metallica

Miniature holly
    Malpighia coccigera

Miniature maple-leaf begonia
    Begonia dregei

Miniature wax plant   *Hoya bella*

Mistletoe fig   *Ficus deltoidea*
    Ficus diversifolia

Monarch of the east
    Sauromatum guttatum

Monkey flower   *Mimulus guttatus*
    Mimulus luteus

Monkey musk   *Mimulus guttatus*
    Mimulus luteus

Monkey plant   *Ruellia mackoyana*

Moonflower
    Calonyction bona-nox
    Ipomoea bona-nox
    Ipomoea noctiflora

Moreton Bay fig   *Ficus macrophylla*

Moreton Bay pine
    Araucaria cunninghamii

Morning glory   *Ipomoea purpurea*
    Pharbitis purpurea

Moses-in-a-boat   *Rhoeo discolor*
    Rhoeo spathacea

Mosquito plant   *Azolla caroliniana*

Mother fern
    Asplenium daucifolium
    Asplenium viviparum

Mother-in-law's tongue
    Sansevieria trifasciata

Mother-of-pearl plant
    Echeveria paraguayense
    Graptopetalum paraguayense
    Sedum weinbergii

Mother of thousands
    Saxifraga sarmentosa
    Saxifraga stolonifera

Mother spleenwort
    Asplenium bulbiferum

Mottlecah   *Eucalyptus macrocarpa*

Mountain flax   *Phormium colensoi*
    Phormium cookianum

Mountain pepper
    Drimys aromatica
    Drimys lanceolata
    Tasmannia latifolia
    Winterania latifolia

Mount Morgan wattle
    Acacia podalyriifolia

Mouse plant
    Arisarum proboscideum

Mulberry fig   *Ficus sycamorus*

Musk   *Mimulus moschatus*

Nagami kumquat
    Fortunella margarita

Narrow-leaved ribbon fern
    Polypodium angustifolium

Narrow-leaved strap fern
    Polypodium angustifolium

Nasturtium   *Tropaeolum majus*

Natal ivy   *Senecio macroglossus*

Natal plum   *Carissa grandiflora*

Nerve plant   *Fittonia verschaffeltii*

New Zealand christmas tree
    Metrosideros excelsa
    Metrosideros tomentosa

New Zealand flax   *Phormium tenax*

New Zealand laurel
    Corynocarpus laevigatus

New Zealand tea tree
    Leptospermum scoparium

Nodding pincushion
    Leucospermum cordifolium
    Leucospermum nutans

Norfolk Island pine
    Araucaria excelsa
    Araucaria heterophylla

Northern bungalow palm
    Archontophoenix alexandrae

Notch-leaf statice
    Limonium sinuatum

Nun's hood orchid   *Phaius bicolor*
    Phaius blumei
    Phaius grandiflorus
    Phaius gravesii
    Phaius tankervillae
    Phaius wallichii

Nutmeg geranium
    Pelargonium × fragrans

Nutmeg pelargonium
    Pelargonium × fragrans

Oak fern   *Drynaria quercifolia*

Oak-leaved geranium
    Pelargonium quercifolium

Oak-leaved pelargonium
    Pelargonium quercifolium

Octopus tree

Octopus tree	*Brassaia actinophylla*
	Schefflera actinophylla
Oleander	*Nerium oleander*
Olive	*Olea europaea*
Opal lachenalia	
	Lachenalia glaucina
Orange jasmine	*Murraya exotica*
	Murraya paniculata
Orange kaleidoscope flower	
	Streptanthera cuprea
Ornamental pepper	
	Piper crocatum
	Piper ornatum crocatum
Ornamental yam	
	Dioscorea discolor
Our Lord's candle	
	Hesperoyucca whipplei
	Yucca whipplei
Oval kumquat	
	Fortunella margarita
Oven's wattle	*Acacia pravissima*
Owl eyes	*Huernia zebrina*
Ox tongue	*Gasteria verrucosa*
Paco	*Athyrium esculentum*
	Diplazium esculentum
Pagoda flower	
	Clerodendrum paniculatum
Pagoda tree	*Plumeria acutifolia*
	Plumeria rubra acutifolia
Paintbrush	*Haemanthus albiflos*
Painted feathers	*Vriesea psittacina*
Painted lady	*Echeveria derenbergii*
	Gladiolus blandus
	Gladiolus carneus
Painted leaf begonia	*Begonia rex*
Painted net leaf	
	Fittonia verschaffeltii
Painted nettle	*Coleus blumei*
Painted tongue	*Salpiglossis sinuata*
Palmella	*Yucca elata*
Palmetto thatch palm	
	Thrinax parviflora
Palm grass	*Curculigo capitulata*
	Curculigo recurvata
Palm-leaf begonia	
	Begonia luxurians
Panamiga	*Pilea involucrata*
Panda plant	*Kalanchoe pilosa*
	Kalanchoe tomentosa
Pansy	*Viola × hortensis*
	Viola × wittrockiana
Papaya	*Carica papaya*
Paper flower	*Bougainvillea glabra*
Paprika	*Capsicum annuum*
Papyrus	*Cyperus papyrus*
Parachute plant	
	Ceropegia sandersonii
Paradise palm	*Howeia forsterana*
	Kentia forsterana
Parana pine	*Araucaria angustifolia*
Parapara	*Pisonia umbellifera*

Parlour palm	
	Chamaedorea elegans
	Neanthe elegans
Parrot leaf	*Alternanthera ficoidea*
Parrot's beak	*Lotus berthelotii*
Parrot's bill	*Clianthus puniceus*
Passion fruit	*Passiflora edulis*
Patient lucy	*Impatiens holstii*
	Impatiens sultanii
	Impatiens walleriana
Pawpaw	*Carica papaya*
Peace lily	*Spathiphyllum wallisii*
Peacock moss	*Selaginella uncinata*
Peacock plant	*Calathea makoyana*
	Kaempferia roscoana
Peanut	*Arachis hypogaea*
Pearl plant	
	Haworthia margaritifera
	Haworthia pumila
Peppermint-scented geranium	
	Pelargonium tomentosum
Peppermint-scented pelargonium	
	Pelargonium tomentosum
Pepper tree	*Drimys colorata*
	Pseudowintera colorata
Pepul	*Ficus religiosa*
Persian ivy	*Hedera colchica*
Persian lilac	*Melia azederach*
Persian shield	
	Strobilanthes dyerianus
Peruvian daffodil	
	Hymenocallis calathina
	Hymenocallis narcissiflora
Peruvian mastic tree	
	Schinus molle
Peruvian pepper tree	
	Schinus molle
Petticoat palm	*Pritchardia filifera*
	Washingtonia filifera
Philippines sugar plum	
	Corypha elata
	Corypha gembanga
Philippine wax flower	
	Alpinia magnifica
	Nicolaia elatior
	Phaeomeria magnifica
Physic nut	*Jatropha multifida*
Piccabeen bungalow palm	
	Archontophoenix
	cunninghamiana
Piccabeen palm	*Archontophoenix*
	cunninghamiana
Pigeon berry	*Duranta plumieri*
	Duranta repens
Piggyback plant	*Tolmiea menziesii*
Pineapple flower	*Eucomis comosa*
Pineapple guava	*Acca sellowiana*
	Feijoa sellowiana
Pineapple sage	*Salvia elegans*
	Salvia rutilans
Pine fern	*Anemia adiantifolia*

Redbird cactus

Pink jasmine
　　Jasminum polyanthum
Pink porcelain lily　*Alpinia nutans*
　　Alpinia speciosa
　　Alpinia zerumbet
Pink rainbow　*Drosera menziesii*
Pitanga　*Eugenia uniflora*
Plume albizia　*Acacia lophantha*
　　Albizia distachya
　　Albizia lophantha
Plush plant　*Echeveria pulvinata*
Pocket book plant
　　Calceolaria × herbeohybrida
Poet's jessamine
　　Jasminum officinale
Poinsettia　*Euphorbia pulcherrima*
Polka dot plant
　　Hypoestes phyllostachya
Polyanthus　*Primula × tommasinii*
Pomegranate　*Punica granatum*
Ponga　*Alsophila tricolor*
　　Cyathea dealbata
Pony tail　*Beaucarnea recurvata*
　　Nolina recurvata
　　Nolina tuberculata
Poor man's orchid
　　Schizanthus pinnatus
Poppy anemone
　　Anemone coronaria
Porcelain berry
　　Ampelopsis brevipedunculata
　　Ampelopsis heterophylla
Port Jackson fig　*Ficus rubiginosa*
Potato vine　*Solanum jasminoides*
Pot marigold　*Calendula officinalis*
Prairie gentian
　　Eustoma grandiflorum
　　Eustoma russellianum
　　Lisianthus russellianus
Prayer plant　*Maranta leuconeura*
Prickly moses　*Acacia verticillata*
Prickly shield fern
　　Polystichum aculeatum
Primrose　*Primula vulgaris*
Primrose jasmine
　　Jasminum mesneyi
　　Jasminum primulinum
Prince of Wales feathers
　　Celosia argentea pyramidalis
　　Celosia plumosa
　　Celosia pyramidalis
Prince Rupert geranium
　　Pelargonium crispum
Prince Rupert pelargonium
　　Pelargonium crispum
Prince's feather
　　Amaranthus hybridus
　　Amaranthus hypochondriacus
Princess vine　*Cissus sicyoides*
Prostrate rosemary
　　Rosmarinus lavandulaceum
　　Rosmarinus officinalis prostratus

Pummelo　*Citrus decumanus*
　　Citrus grandis
　　Citrus maxima
Purple bell vine
　　Rhodochiton atrosanguineum
　　Rhodochiton volubile
Purple granadilla　*Passiflora edulis*
Purple ragwort　*Senecio elegans*
Purple-stemmed cliff brake
　　Pellaea atropurpurea
Purple viper's bugloss
　　Echium lycopsis
　　Echium plantagineum
Purple wreath　*Petrea volubilis*
Pussy ears　*Cyanotis somaliensis*
　　Kalanchoe pilosa
　　Kalanchoe tomentosa
Pygmy date palm
　　Phoenix roebelenii
Pygmy water lily
　　Nymphaea pygmaea
　　Nymphaea tetragona
Queen anthurium
　　Anthurium warocqueanum
Queen cattleya
　　Cattleya labiata dowiana
Queen of the night
　　Hylocereus undatus
Queensland silver wattle
　　Acacia podalyriifolia
Queensland tassel fern
　　Lycopodium phlegmaria
Queensland umbrella tree
　　Brassaia actinophylla
　　Schefflera actinophylla
Queen's tears　*Billbergia nutans*
Queen's wreath　*Petrea volubilis*
Rabbit's foot　*Maranta leuconeura*
　　kerchoveana
Rabbit's foot fern　*Davallia fijiensis*
　　Davallia solida fijiensis
Rabbit tracks　*Maranta leuconeura*
　　kerchoveana
Radiator plant
　　Peperomia maculosa
Rainbow fern　*Selaginella uncinata*
Rainbow star
　　Cryptanthus bromelioides
Ramie　*Boehmeria nivea*
Rangoon creeper　*Quisqualis indica*
Rat's tail statice
　　Limonium suworowii
Rat tail plant
　　Crassula lycopodioides
Rattlesnake plant　*Calathea insignis*
　　Calathea lancifolia
Rattlesnake tail　*Crassula barklyi*
　　Crassula teres
Red alder　*Cunonia capensis*
Redbird cactus
　　Pedilanthes tithymaloides

Red-flowering gum
    Eucalyptus ficifolia
Red ginger   *Alpinia purpurata*
Red ginger lily
    Hedychium coccineum
Red granadilla   *Passiflora coccinea*
Red-hot cat's tail   *Acalypha hispida*
Red ivy   *Hemigraphis alternata*
    Hemigraphis colorata
Red kangaroo paw
    Anigozanthos rufus
Red latan palm   *Latania borbonica*
    Latania commersonii
    Latania lontaroides
Red-leaf philodendron
    Philodendron domesticum
    × *erubescens*
    Philodendron × *mandaianum*
Red morning glory
    Ipomoea coccinea
Red nodding bells
    Streptocarpus dunnii
Red passion flower
    Passiflora coccinea
    Passiflora racemosa
Red pepper   *Capsicum annuum*
Red pineapple   *Ananas bracteatus*
Reed palm   *Chamaedorea seifrizii*
Regal elkhorn fern
    Platycerium grande
Regal geraniums
    Pelargonium × *domesticum*
Regal pelargoniums
    Pelargonium × *domesticum*
Resurrection plant
    Anastatica hierochuntica
    Selaginella lepidophylla
Rex begonia vine   *Cissus discolor*
Ribbon fern
    Campyloneurum phyllitidis
    Polypodium phyllitidis
    Pteris cretica
Ribbon plant   *Dracaena sanderiana*
Rice-paper plant   *Aralia papyrifera*
    Fatsia papyrifera
    Tetrapanax papyriferus
River tea tree
    Melaleuca leucodendron
Rosary vine   *Ceropegia woodii*
    Crassula rupestris
Rose apple   *Eugenia jambos*
    Syzygium jambos
Rose balsam   *Impatiens balsamina*
Rose bay   *Nerium oleander*
Rose geranium
    Pelargonium graveolens
Rose grape   *Medinilla magnifica*
Rose maidenhair fern
    Adiantum hispidulum
    Adiantum pubescens
Rosemary   *Rosmarinus officinalis*

Rose of China
    Hibiscus rosasinensis
Rose of Jericho
    Anastatica hierochuntica
    Selaginella lepidophylla
Rose pelargonium
    Pelargonium graveolens
Rose-scented geranium
    Pelargonium capitatum
Rose-scented pelargonium
    Pelargonium capitatum
Rouge plant   *Rivina humilis*
    Rivina laevis
Royal red bugler
    Aeschynanthus pulcher
Rubber plant   *Ficus elastica*
Rubber spurge   *Euphorbia tirucalli*
Running postman
    Kennedia prostrata
Russian statice
    Limonium suworowii
Sacred bamboo
    Nandina domestica
Sacred fig tree   *Ficus religiosa*
Sage rose   *Turnera trioniflora*
    Turnera ulmifolia
Sago fern   *Cyathea medullaris*
Sago fern palm   *Cycas circinalis*
Sago palm   *Caryota urens*
Saint Augustine grass
    Stenotaphrum secundatum
Saint John's bread   *Ceratonia siliqua*
Salad tomato
    Lycopersicon lycopersicum
    cerasiforme
Satin leaf   *Philodendron gloriosum*
Satsuma   *Citrus nobilis*
    Citrus reticulata
Scarborough lily   *Vallota purpurea*
    Vallota speciosa
Scarlet banana   *Musa coccinea*
Scarlet ginger lily
    Hedychium coccineum
Scarlet leadwort   *Plumbago indica*
    Plumbago rosea
Scarlet plume   *Euphorbia fulgens*
Scarlet sage   *Salvia splendens*
Scarlet star   *Guzmania lingulata*
Scarlet trompetilla
    Bouvardia ternifolia
    Bouvardia triphylla
Scorpion senna   *Coronilla emerus*
Scotch attorney
    Clusia grandiflora
Sea daffodil
    Pancratium maritimum
Sea fig   *Carpobrotus chilensis*
Sea lily   *Pancratium maritimum*
Sealing wax palm
    Cyrtostachys lakka
Seaside grape   *Coccoloba uvifera*

Seersucker plant	Geogenanthus undatus
Seminole bread	Zamia floridana
Sensitive plant	
	Biophytum sensitivum
	Mimosa pudica
Sentry palm	Howeia belmoreana
	Howeia forsterana
	Kentia belmoreana
	Kentia forsterana
Seville orange	Citrus aurantium
	Citrus bigarardia
Shaddock	Citrus decumanus
	Citrus grandis
	Citrus maxima
Shell ginger	Alpinia nutans
	Alpinia speciosa
	Alpinia zerumbet
Shingle plant	
	Monstera latevaginata
	Rhaphidophora celatocaulis
	Rhaphidophora decursiva
Shining gum	Eucalyptus nitens
Shiny tea tree	
	Leptospermum nitidum
Show geranium	
	Pelargonium × domesticum
Show pelargonium	
	Pelargonium × domesticum
Shrimp plant	Beloperone guttata
Siberian squill	Scilla sibirica
Siberian wallflower	
	Cheiranthus × allionii
Sicklethorn	Asparagus falcatus
Signet marigold	Tagetes signata
	Tagetes tenuifolia
Silk tree	Albizia julibrissin
Silky oak	Grevillea robusta
Silver beads	Crassula deltoidea
	Crassula rhomboidea
Silver heart	Peperomia marmorata
Silver latan palm	Latania loddigesii
Silverleaf peperomia	
	Peperomia griseoargentea
	Peperomia hederifolia
Silver net leaf	Fittonia argyroneura
Silver tree	
	Leucadendron argenteum
Silver tree fern	Alsophila tricolor
	Cyathea dealbata
Silver vase	Aechmea fasciata
Silver wattle	Acacia dealbata
Silvery inch plant	Zebrina pendula
Skyflower	Duranta plumieri
	Duranta repens
Skyrocket	Gilia coronipifolia
	Gilia rubra
	Ipomopsis rubra
Slipper cactus	
	Pedilanthes tithymaloides
Slipper flower	
	Calceolaria × herbeohybrida

Smilax	Asparagus asparagoides
	Asparagus medeoloides
	Smilax asparagoides
Snake gourd	Trichosanthes anguina
Snake lily	Brodiaea volubilis
	Stropholirion californicum
Snake plant	Sansevieria trifasciata
Snake's head fritillary	
	Fritillaria meleagris
Snake vine	Hibbertia scandens
	Hibbertia volubilis
Snapdragon	Antirrhinum majus
Snow bush	Breynia nivosa
	Phyllanthus nivosa
Snowdrop	Galanthus nivalis
Snowflake aralia	Trevesia palmata
Snowy mint bush	
	Prostanthera nivea
Soap tree	Yucca elata
Soft shield fern	
	Polystichum setiferum
Soft tree fern	Alsophila smithii
	Cyathea smithii
	Dicksonia antarctica
	Hemitelia smithii
Solitaire palm	
	Ptychosperma elegans
	Seaforthia elegans
South sea arrowroot	
	Tacca leontopetaloides
	Tacca pinnatifida
Spade leaf	
	Philodendron domesticum
	Philodendron hastatum
Spanish dagger	Yucca gloriosa
Spanish moss	Tillandsia usneioides
Spiceberry	Ardisia crispa
Spider fern	Pteris multifida
	Pteris serrulata
Spider plant	Anthericum comosum
	Anthericum elatum
	Chlorophytum capense
	Chlorophytum comosum
	Chlorophytum elatum
Spineless yucca	Yucca elephantipes
	Yucca gigantea
	Yucca guatemalensis
Spiral ginger	Costus igneus
Sponge gourd	Luffa aegyptica
	Luffa cylindrica
Spotted dead nettle	
	Lamium maculatum
Spring cattleya	
	Cattleya labiata mossiae
	Cattleya mossiae
Spring star flower	
	Ipheion uniflorum
Squirrel's foot fern	
	Davallia dissecta
	Davallia mariesii
	Davallia pyxidata
	Davallia trichomanoides

Squirting cucumber

Squirting cucumber	
	Ecballium elaterium
Standing cypress	*Gilia coronipifolia*
	Gilia rubra
	Ipomopsis rubra
Star begonia	*Begonia heracleifolia*
Star cluster	*Pentas carnea*
	Pentas lanceolata
Star ipomoea	*Ipomoea coccinea*
Star jasmine	*Jasminum nitidum*
Star of Bethlehem	
	Ornithogalum arabicum
	Ornithogalum umbellatum
Star sansevieria	
	Sansevieria grandicuspis
Star window plant	
	Haworthia tessellata
Stock	*Matthiola incana*
Strap fern	
	Campyloneurum phyllitidis
	Polypodium phyllitidis
Strap water fern	
	Blechnum patersonii
Strawberry geranium	
	Saxifraga sarmentosa
	Saxifraga stolonifera
Strawberry tree	*Arbutus unedo*
String of beads	*Senecio rowleyanus*
String of hearts	*Ceropegia woodii*
String of pearls	*Senecio rowleyanus*
Sturt's desert rose	
	Gossypium sturtianum
	Gossypium sturtii
Sugar apple	*Annona squamosa*
Sugarbush	*Protea mellifera*
	Protea repens
Summer cypress	*Kochia scoparia*
Summer hyacinth	
	Galtonia candicans
Summer jasmine	
	Jasminum officinale
Sunn hemp	*Crotalaria juncea*
Sun plant	*Portulaca grandiflora*
Surinam cherry	*Eugenia uniflora*
Swamp lily	*Crinum × powellii*
Swan orchid	
	Cycnoches ventricosum
Swedish ivy	
	Plectranthus oertendahlii
Sweet bay	*Laurus nobilis*
Sweet flag	*Acorus gramineus*
Sweet garlic	*Tulbaghia fragrans*
Sweet granadilla	*Passiflora ligularis*
Sweetheart plant	
	Philodendron scandens
Sweet orange	
	Citrus aurantium sinense
	Citrus sinensis
Sweet pepper	*Capsicum annuum*
Sweet potato	*Ipomoea batatas*
Sweet sop	*Annona squamosa*

Sweet sultan	*Centaurea moschata*
Swiss cheese plant	
	Monstera deliciosa
	Monstera pertusa
	Philodendron pertusum
Sword brake	*Pteris ensiformis*
Sword fern	*Nephrolepis cordifolia*
	Nephrolepis exaltata
Sycamore fig	*Ficus sycamorus*
Sydney golden wattle	
	Acacia longifolia
Table fern	*Pteris cretica*
Tagetes	*Tagetes signata*
	Tagetes tenuifolia
Tailflower	*Anthurium andreanum*
Talipot palm	
	Corypha umbraculifera
Tall kangaroo paw	
	Anigozanthos flavidus
Tangerine	*Citrus nobilis*
	Citrus reticulata
Tapioca	*Manihot esculenta*
	Manihot utilissima
Taro	*Colocasia esculenta*
Taro vine	*Epipremnum aureum*
	Pothos aureus
	Raphidophora aurea
	Scindapsus aureus
Tartogo	*Jatropha podagrica*
Tasmanian blue gum	
	Eucalyptus globulus
Teddy bear vine	*Cyanotis kewensis*
Temple bells	
	Smithiana cinnabarina
Thatchleaf palm	*Howeia forsterana*
	Kentia forsterana
Thread agave	*Agave filifera*
Tiger jaws	*Faucaria tigrina*
Tiger nut	*Cyperus esculentus*
Tiger orchid	*Oncidium tigrinum*
Ti tree	*Cordyline terminalis*
Toadflax	*Linaria maroccana*
Tobira	*Pittosporum tobira*
Toddy palm	*Caryota urens*
Tomato	*Lycopersicon esculentum*
	Lycopersicon lycopersicum
Tonkin bamboo	
	Arundinaria amabilis
Torch ginger	*Alpinia magnifica*
	Nicolaia elatior
	Phaeomeria magnifica
Touch-me-not	
	Impatiens balsamina
Trailing water-melon begonia	
	Pellionia daveauana
Transvaal daisy	*Gerbera jamesonii*
Traveller's tree	
	Ravenala madagascariensis
Tree cotton	*Gossypium arboreum*

Wonga-wonga vine

Tree philodendron
    Philodendron bipinnatifidum
    Philodendron eichleri

Tree tomato
    Cyphomandra betacea

Trigger plant
    Stylidium graminifolium

Tropical crocus
    Kaempferia rotunda

Trumpet vine
    Bignonia callistegioides
    Bignonia speciosa
    Clytostoma callistegioides

Tsusina holly fern
    Polystichum tsus-simense

Tuberose   *Polianthes tuberosa*

Tulip cattleya   *Cattleya citrina*

Tulip orchid   *Anguloa clowesii*
    Anguloa uniflora

Turkish cotton
    Gossypium herbaceum

Turmeric   *Curcuma domestica*
    Curcuma longa

Umbrella grass
    Cyperus alternifolius

Umbrella plant
    Cyperus alternifolius
    Cyperus diffusus

Urn plant   *Aechmea fasciata*

Variegated ginger   *Alpinia sanderae*

Vegetable fern
    Athyrium esculentum
    Diplazium esculentum

Velour philodendron
    Philodendron andreanum
    Philodendron melanochrysum

Velvet leaf   *Kalanchoe beharensis*

Velvet plant   *Gynura aurantiaca*

Venus flytrap   *Dionaea muscipula*

Victorian box
    Pittosporum undulatum

Voodoo lily   *Sauromatum guttatum*

Wallflower   *Cheiranthus cheiri*

Wandering jew   *Callisia elegans*
    Setcreasea striata
    Tradescantia albiflora
    Tradescantia fluminensis
    Zebrina pendula

Wand flower   *Sparaxis tricolor*

Waratah   *Telopea speciosissima*

Water clover
    Marsilea drummondi
    Marsilea quadrifolia

Water feather
    Myriophyllum aquaticum
    Myriophyllum brasiliense
    Myriophyllum proserpinacoides

Water fern   *Azolla caroliniana*
    Ceratopteris cornuta
    Ceratopteris pteridoides
    Ceratopteris siliquosa
    Ceratopteris thalictroides

Water hyacinth
    Eichhornia crassipes
    Eichhornia speciosa

Water lettuce   *Pistia stratiotes*

Water-melon begonia
    Peperomia argyreia
    Peperomia sandersii

Wax begonia
    Begonia semperflorens

Wax plant   *Hoya carnosa*

Wax privet   *Peperomia glabella*

Wax torch   *Aechmea bromeliifolia*

Wax vine   *Senecio macroglossus*

Waxy jasmine
    Stephanotis floribunda

Weeping fig   *Ficus benjamina*

Western sword fern
    Polystichum munitum

West Indian tree fern
    Cyathea arborea

White kaleidoscope flower
    Streptanthera elegans

White lily turf   *Mondo jaburan*
    Ophiopogon jaburan

White rain tree
    Brunfelsia undulata

White sails   *Spathiphyllum wallisii*

Whorled peperomia
    Peperomia pulchella
    Peperomia verticillata

Wild coffee   *Gardenia citriodora*
    Mitriostigma axillare
    Polyscias guilfoylei

Wild pineapple   *Ananas bracteatus*

Wild sarsparilla
    Hardenbergia comptoniana

Windmill jasmine
    Jasminum nitidum

Windmill palm
    Trachycarpus fortunei

Wine palm   *Caryota urens*

Winged pea   *Lotus berthelotii*

Winged statice
    Limonium sinuatum

Winter cattleya
    Cattleya labiata trianaei
    Cattleya trianaei

Winter cherry
    Solanum capsicastrum

Winter heath   *Erica carnea*
    Erica herbacea

Winter's bark   *Drimys winteri*
    Wintera aromatica

Wintersweet
    Acokanthera spectabilis

Wire vine
    Muehlenbeckia complexa

Wirilda   *Acacia retinodes*

Wishbone flower   *Torenia fournieri*

Wonga-wonga vine
    Pandorea pandorana

Wood forget-me-not
Myosotis sylvatica
Woolly bear   *Begonia leptotricha*
Wormwood cassia
Cassia artemisioides
Yautia   *Xanthosma violaceum*
Yellow bells   *Bignonia stans*
Stenolobium stans
Tecoma stans
Yellow elder   *Bignonia stans*
Stenolobium stans
Tecoma stans
Yellow flax   *Reinwardtia indica*
Reinwardtia trigyna
Yellow latan palm   *Latania aurea*
Latania verschaffeltii
Yellow oleander
Thevetia peruviana

Yellow pagoda tree
Plumeria rubra lutea
Yellow pitcher plant
Sarracenia flava
Yellow sage   *Lantana camara*
Yesterday, today and tomorrow
Brunfelsia calycina
Brunfelsia paucifolia calycina
Zebra haworthia
Haworthia fasciata
Zebra plant   *Aphelandra squarrosa*
Calathea zebrina
Zonal geranium
Pelargonium × hortorum
Zonal pelargonium
Pelargonium × hortorum

ORCHIDS

Orchids are members of the very large family *Orchidaceae*. Various genera are grown by commercial specialists for the cut flower market, and by hobbyists as garden plants, in greenhouses or the home. Many artificial hybrids have been produced and are often to be found in private collections. The following list includes those most commonly offered for sale in nurseries and garden centres.

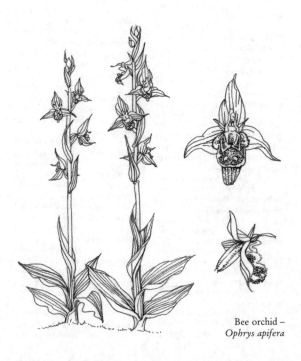

Bee orchid –
Ophrys apifera

Adam-and-Eve

Adam-and-Eve *Aplectrum hymale*
  Aplectrum spicatum
Adder's mouth
  Pogonia ophioglossoides
Adder's tongue-leaved pogonia
  Pogonia ophioglossoides
Adder's tongue *Malaxis unifolia*
Alaskan orchid
  Habenaria unalascensis
Alaska piperia
  Habenaria unalascensis
Autumn cattleya *Cattleya labiata*
Autumn coralroot
  Corallorhiza odontorhiza
Autumn lady's tresses
  Spiranthes spiralis
Baby orchid
  Epidendrum × obrienianum
Bamboo orchid
  Arundina bambusifolia
  Arundina graminifolia
Bastard helleborine
  Epipactis helleborine
  Epipactis latifolia
Bat orchid *Coryanthes speciosa*
Beardflower
  Pogonia ophioglossoides
Bee orchid *Ophrys apifera*
Bee-swarm orchid
  Cyrtopodium punctatum
Bird's nest orchid
  Neottia nidus-avis
Black orchid *Coelogyne pandurata*
Blue butcher *Orchis mascula*
Blue orchid *Vanda coerulea*
Blunt-leaf orchid
  Habenaria obusata
Bog candle *Habenaria dilatata*
Bog orchid *Arethusa bulbosa*
  Calypso bulbosa
  Habenaria dilatata
Bog rose orchid *Arethusa bulbosa*
Bog torch *Habenaria nivea*
Bog twayblade *Liparis loeselii*
Booth's epidendrum
  Epidendrum boothianum
  Epidendrum erythronioides
Bottle orchid *Physosiphon tubatus*
Broadleaved helleborine
  Epipactis helleborine
  Epipactis latifolia
Broad-leaved marsh orchid
  Dactylorhiza majalis
Broad-leaved twayblade
  Listera convallarioides
Broad-lipped twayblade
  Listera convallarioides
Bucket orchid
  Coryanthes macrantha
  Coryanthes speciosa
Bug orchid *Orchis coriophora*

Burnt orchid *Orchis ustulata*
Burnt-tip orchid *Orchis ustulata*
Butterfly orchid
  Epidendrum × obrienianum
  Epidendrum tampense
  Habenaria psycodes
  Oncidium krameranum
  Oncidium papilio
  Platanthera chlorantha
Calypso *Calypso borealis*
  Calypso bulbosa
Chatterbox *Amesia gigantea*
  Epipactis gigantea
Checkered rattlesnake plantain
  Goodyera tesselata
Chicken toes
  Corallorhiza odontorhiza
Chocolate orchid
  Epidendrum phoeniceum
Christmas cattleya *Cattleya labiata*
  Cattleya percivaliana
Christmas orchid *Cattleya trianaei*
Cigar orchid
  Cyrtopodium punctatum
Clam-shell orchid
  Epidendrum cochleatum
Cockle-shell orchid
  Epidendrum cochleatum
Colombia buttercup
  Oncidium cheirophorum
Common lady's tresses
  Spiranthes cernua
Common spotted orchid
  Dactylorhiza fuchsii
Common twayblade *Listera ovata*
Cooktown orchid
  Dendrobium bigibbum
Coral orchid *Rodriguezia secunda*
Coralroot orchid
  Corallorhiza trifida
Cow-horn orchid
  Cyrtopodium punctatum
Cradle orchid *Anguloa clowesii*
  Anguloa uniflora
Cranefly orchid *Tipularia discolor*
  Tipularia unifolia
Crawley root
  Corallorhiza odontorhiza
Creeping lady's tresses
  Goodyera repens
Crested ettercap
  Pogonia ophioglossoides
Crested fringed orchid
  Habenaria cristata
Crested rein orchid
  Habenaria cristata
Crested yellow orchid
  Habenaria cristata
Crippled cranefly *Tipularia discolor*
  Tipularia unifolia

Cypripedium
    Paphiopedilum concolor
    Paphiopedilum insigne

Cytherea   *Calypso borealis*
    Calypso bulbosa

Daffodil orchid   *Ipsea speciosa*

Dancing-doll orchid
    Oncidium flexuosum

Dancing-lady orchid
    Oncidium flexuosum

Dark red helleborine
    Epipactis atrorubans

Dead man's fingers   *Orchis mascula*

Dense-flowered orchid
    Neotinea maculata

Dollar orchid
    Epidendrum boothianum
    Epidendrum erythronioides

Dove flower   *Peristeria elata*

Dove orchid   *Peristeria elata*

Downy rattlesnake orchid
    Goodyera pubescens

Downy rattlesnake plantain
    Goodyera pubescens

Dragon's claw
    Corallorhiza odontorhiza

Dragon's mouth orchid
    Arethusa bulbosa

Dune helleborine
    Epipactis dunensis

Dwarf orchid   *Orchis ustulata*

Dwarf rattlesnake plantain
    Goodyera repens

Early marsh orchid
    Dactylorhiza incarnata

Early purple orchid   *Orchis mascula*

Early spider orchid
    Ophrys sphegodes

Easter cattleya   *Cattleya mossiae*

Elfin-spur   *Tipularia discolor*
    Tipularia unifolia

Esmaralda   *Arachnis clarkei*

Ettercap   *Pogonia ophioglossoides*

Fairy fringe   *Habenaria psycodes*

Fairy-slipper orchid
    Calypso borealis
    Calypso bulbosa

False musk orchid
    Chamorchis alpina

Fen orchid   *Liparis loeselii*

Florida butterfly orchid
    Epidendrum tampense

Fly orchid   *Ophrys insectifera*

Foxtail orchid   *Aerides odorata*

Fragrant orchid
    Gymnadenia conopsea

Fried-egg orchid
    Dendrobium chrysotoxum

Fringed orchis   *Habenaria ciliaris*

Frog orchid   *Coeloglossum viride*

Frog spear   *Habenaria nivea*

Frog spike   *Habenaria clavellata*

Funnel-crest orchid
    Cleistes divaricata
    Pogonia divaricata

Gandergoose   *Orchis morio*

Ghost orchid   *Epipogium aphyllum*

Giant helleborine   *Amesia gigantea*
    Epipactis gigantea

Giant lady's tresses
    Spiranthes praecox

Grass-leaved lady's tresses
    Spiranthes praecox

Giant orchid   *Amesia gigantea*
    Epipactis gigantea

Giant rattlesnake plantain
    Goodyera oblongifolia

Golden chain orchid
    Dendrochilum filiforme

Golden fringed orchid
    Habenaria cristata

Gold-lace orchid
    Haemaria discolor

Grass pink   *Calopogon tuberosus*

Greater butterfly orchid
    Platanthera chlorantha

Green adderling   *Isotria verticillata*
    Pogonia verticillata

Green adder's mouth
    Malaxis unifolia

Green-flowered helleborine
    Epipactis phyllanthes

Green-fly orchid
    Epidendrum conopseum

Green fringed orchid
    Habenaria lacera

Green malaxis   *Malaxis unifolia*

Green man orchid
    Aceras anthropothora

Green pearl-twist
    Spiranthes gracilis

Green rein orchid
    Habenaria clavellata

Green-winged orchid   *Orchis morio*

Green woodland orchid
    Habenaria clavellata

Ground coco   *Eulophia alta*

Hay-scented orchid
    Dendrochilum glumaceum

Heal-all   *Habenaria orbiculata*
    Lysias orbiculata

Heath spotted orchid
    Dactylorhiza maculata

Heart-leaf twayblade
    Listera cordata

Helmet orchid   *Galeandra lacustris*

Holy Ghost flower   *Peristeria elata*

Hooded lady's tresses
    Spiranthes romanzoffiana

Hooker's orchid
    Habenaria hookeri

Hyacincth orchid

Hyacinth orchid
  Arpophyllum giganteum
  Arpophyllum spicatum
Indian crocus *Pleione maculata*
Irish lady's tresses
  Spiranthes romanzoffiana
Jersey orchid *Orchis laxifolia*
Jewel orchid *Anoectochilus setaceus*
Jumping orchid
  Catasetum macrocarpum
  Catasetum tridentatum
King-of-the-forest
  Anoectochilus setaceus
Kirtle-pink orchid
  Orchis spectabilis
Lace orchid
  Odontoglossum crispum
Lady's slipper
  Paphiopedilum concolor
  Paphiopedilum insigne
Lady's tresses *Spiranthes cernua*
Lady-of-the-night
  Brassavola nodosa
Lady orchid *Orchis purpurea*
Lady's slipper orchid
  Cypridium calceolus
  Phragmipedium caricinum
Large coralroot
  Corallorhiza maculata
  Corallorhiza multiflora
Large twayblade *Liparis liliifolia*
Late coralroot
  Corallorhiza odontorhiza
Late spider orchid *Ophrys fuciflora*
  Ophrys holoserica
Leafy northern green orchid
  Habenaria hyperborea
  Limnorchis hyperborea
Leafy white orchid
  Habenaria dilatata
Lesser butterfly orchid
  Habenaria bifolia
  Platanthera bifolia
Lesser purple-fringed orchid
  Habenaria psycodes
Lesser rattlesnake plantain
  Goodyera repens
Lesser twayblade *Listera cordata*
Lily-leaved pogonia
  Cleistes divaricata
  Pogonia divaricata
Lily-of-the-valley orchid
  Odontoglossum pulchellum
Link vine *Vanilla articulata*
  Vanilla barbellata
Little bog orchid
  Hammarbya paludosa
Little club-spur orchid
  Habenaria clavellata
Little lady's tresses *Spiranthes grayi*
Little pearl-twist *Spiranthes grayi*

Lizard orchid
  Himantoglossum hircinum
Loesel's twayblade *Liparis loeselii*
Long tresses *Spiranthes gracilis*
Madeira orchid *Orchis maderensis*
Man orchid
  Aceras anthropophorum
Marsh helleborine
  Epipactis palustris
Marsh orchid
  Dactylorhiza latifolia
  Orchis latifolia
Mauve sleekwort *Liparis liliifolia*
Meadow orchid
  Dactylorhiza incarnata
Menzies' rattlesnake plantain
  Goodyera oblongifolia
Mirror-of-venus *Ophrys speculum*
Mirror orchid *Ophrys speculum*
Moccasin flower
  Cypripedium acaule
Moccasin orchid
  Cypripedium acaule
Monkey orchid
  Coryanthes macrantha
  Orchis simia
Moon-set *Habenaria orbiculata*
  Lysias orbiculata
Moth orchid *Phalaenopsis amabilis*
Mottled cranefly *Tipularia discolor*
  Tipularia unifolia
Musk orchid
  Herminium monorchis
Musk orchis
  Herminium monorchis
Narrow-lipped orchid
  Epipactis leptochila
Nerveroot *Cypripedium acaule*
Nodding lady's tresses
  Spiranthes cernua
Northern green orchid
  Habenaria hyperborea
  Limnorchis hyperborea
Northern marsh orchid
  Dactylorhiza purpurella
Northern rattlesnake plantain
  Goodyera repens
Northern small bog orchid
  Habenaria obusata
Nun orchid *Lycaste skinneri*
  Lycaste virginalis
Nun's hood orchid
  Phaius tankervilliae
Nun's orchid *Phaius tankervilliae*
Olive scutcheon *Liparis loeselii*
One-leaf rein orchid
  Habenaria obusata
Orange crest *Habenaria cristata*
Orange fringe *Habenaria ciliaris*
Orange plume *Habenaria ciliaris*

Palm-polly *Polyradicion lindenii*
            Polyrrhiza lindenii
Pansy orchid *Miltonia candida*
              Miltonia flavescens
              Miltonia spectabilis
              Miltonia vexillaria
Pigeon orchid
            Dendrobium crumenatum
Pine pink orchid *Bletia alta*
                  Bletia purpurea
Pink lady's slipper
            Cypripedium acaule
Pink scorpion orchid
            Arachnis × maingayi
Pink-slipper orchid
            Calypso borealis
            Calypso bulbosa
Pompona vanilla
            Vanilla grandiflora
            Vanilla pompona
Pride-of-the-peak
            Habenaria peramoena
Purple five-leaved orchid
            Isotria verticillata
            Pogonia verticillata
Purple fret-lip
            Habenaria peramoena
Purple fringeless orchid
            Habenaria peramoena
Purple-hooded orchid
            Orchis spectabilis
Purple scutcheon *Liparis liliifolia*
Purple spire orchid
            Habenaria peramoena
Puttyroot *Aplectrum hymale*
           Aplectrum spicatum
Pyramidal orchid
            Anacamptis pyramidalis
Queen cattleya *Cattleya dowiana*
                Cattleya labiata
Queen of orchids
    Grammatophyllum sanderanum
    Grammatophyllum speciosum
Ragged fringed orchid
            Habenaria lacera
Ragged orchid *Habenaria lacera*
Rainbow orchid
            Epidendrum prismatocarpum
Rattlesnake orchid
            Pholidota imbricata
Rattlesnake plantain
            Goodyera oblongifolia
Red helleborine
            Cephalanthera rubra
Rock lily *Dendrobium speciosum*
Romanzoff's lady's tresses
            Spiranthes romanzoffiana
Rosebud orchid *Cleistes divaricata*
                Pogonia divaricata
Rose crest-lip
            Pogonia ophioglossoides
Rose pogonia
            Pogonia ophioglossoides

Round-headed orchid
            Traunsteinera globosa
Round-leaved orchid
            Habenaria orbiculata
            Lysias orbiculata
Russet witch *Liparis loeselii*
Salep orchid *Orchis morio*
Savannah orchid *Habenaria nivea*
Sawfly orchid
            Ophrys tenthredinifera
Scarlet orchid
            Epidendrum × obrienianum
Scent bottle *Habenaria dilatata*
Scorpion orchid *Arachnis cathcartii*
Screw-augur *Spiranthes cernua*
Scrofula weed *Goodyera pubescens*
Showy orchid *Orchis spectabilis*
Silver chain
            Dendrochilum glumaceum
Single-leaf rein orchid
            Habenaria obusata
Slender bog orchid
            Habenaria gracilis
            Habenaria saccata
Slender lady's tresses
            Spiranthes gracilis
Slipper orchid
            Paphiopedilum concolor
            Paphiopedilum insigne
Small bog orchid
            Habenaria obusata
Small coralroot
            Corallorhiza odontorhiza
Small purple-fringed orchid
            Habenaria psycodes
Small round-leaved orchid
            Orchis rotundifolia
Small white orchid
            Leucorchis albida
Smooth rattlesnake plantain
            Goodyera tesselata
Snake's mouth orchid
            Pogonia ophioglossoides
Snowy orchid
            Habenaria blephariglottis
            Habenaria nivea
Soldier orchid *Orchis militaris*
Soldier's plume
            Habenaria psycodes
Southern lady's tresses
            Spiranthes gracilis
Southern marsh orchid
            Dactylorhiza praetermissa
Southern rein orchid
            Habenaria clavellata
Southern small white orchid
            Habenaria nivea
Spice orchid
            Epidendrum atropurpureum
            Epidendrum macrochilum

Spider orchid

Spider orchid   *Arachnis flos-aeris*
    Arachnis × maingayi
    Arachnis moschifera

Spotted coralroot
    Corallorhiza maculata
    Corallorhiza multiflora

Spotted kirtle-pink orchid
    Orchis rotundifolia

Spreading pogonia
    Cleistes divaricata
    Pogonia divaricata

Spring cattleya   *Cattleya mossiae*

Star-of-Bethlehem orchid
    Angraecum sesquipedale

Stream orchid   *Amesia gigantea*
    Epipactis gigantea

Summer cattleya
    Cattleya gaskelliana

Summer lady's tresses
    Spiranthes aestivalis

Swamp pink   *Calopogon tuberosus*

Swamp pink orchid
    Arethusa bulbosa

Swan orchid
    Cychnoches pentadactylon

Sweet-scented orchid
    Gymnadenia conopsea

Tall white bog orchid
    Habenaria dilatata

Tenderwort   *Malaxis unifolia*

Tiger orchid
    Odontoglossum grande

Toothed orchid   *Orchis tridentata*

Tulip cattleya   *Cattleya citrina*

Two-leaved lady's slipper
    Cypripedium acaule

Vanilla   *Vanilla planifolia*

Violet bird's nest orchid
    Limodorum abortiva

Violet helleborine
    Epipactis purpurata

Virgin Mary orchid
    Caularthron bicornutum
    Diacrium bicornutum

Virgin orchid
    Caularthron bicornutum
    Diacrium bicornutum

Water tresses   *Spiranthes praecox*

Western coralroot
    Corallorhiza mertensiana

West Indian vanilla
    Vanilla grandiflora
    Vanilla pompona

White butterfly orchid
    Polyradicion lindenii
    Polyrrhiza lindenii

White fringed orchid
    Habenaria blephariglottis

White frog-arrow   *Habenaria nivea*

White helleborine
    Cephalanthera damasonium

White nun orchid   *Lycaste skinneri*
    Lycaste virginalis

White rein orchid
    Habenaria nivea

Whorled pogonia
    Isotria verticillata
    Pogonia verticillata

Wide adder's mouth
    Malaxis unifolia

Widow orchid
    Pleurothallis macrophylla

Wild coco   *Eulophia alta*

Wild pink orchid   *Arethusa bulbosa*

Windmill orchid
    Bulbophyllum refractum

Winter cattleya   *Cattleya trianaei*

Woodland orchid   *Orchis spectabilis*

Worm vine   *Vanilla articulata*
    Vanilla barbellata

Wormwood   *Vanilla articulata*
    Vanilla barbellata

Yellow fringed orchid
    Habenaria ciliaris

Yellow lady's slipper
    Cypripedium pubescens

Yellow twayblade   *Liparis loeselii*

POPULAR GARDEN PLANTS

Annuals, biennials, and perennials that are not usually listed under specific sections elsewhere. Popular flowering plants grown in many gardens as bedding plants, container plants, or climbers are covered.

Marguerite –
Argyranthemum frutescens

Aaron's rod	*Verbascum thapsus*
Abcess root	*Polemonium reptans*
Absinthe	*Artemisia absinthium*
Aconite-leaved buttercup	
	Ranunculus aconitifolius
Adam's flannel	*Verbascum thapsus*
Adriatic bellflower	
	Campanula elatines garganica
	Campanula garganica
African daisy	*Arctotis breviscapa*
	Arctotis grandis
	Dimorphotheca osteospermum
African marigold	*Tagetes erecta*
African violet	*Saintpaulia ionantha*
Agrimony	*Agrimonia eupatoria*
Ague root	*Aletris farinosa*
Algerian statice	
	Limonium bonduellii
	Statice bonduellii
Alkanet	*Anchusa officinalis*
Allegheny monkey flower	
	Mimulus ringens
Allegheny spurge	
	Pachysandra procumbens
Alpine anemone	*Pulsatilla alpina*
Alpine auricula	*Primula auricula*
Alpine avens	*Geum montanum*
Alpine bistort	
	Polygonum viviporum
Alpine buttercup	
	Ranunculus alpestris
Alpine campanula	
	Campanula allionii
	Campanula alpestris
Alpine campion	*Lychnis alpina*
	Silene alpestris
	Silene quadrifida
	Viscaria alpina
Alpine cinquefoil	*Potentilla crantzii*
Alpine coltsfoot	*Homogyne alpina*
Alpine fleabane	*Erigeron borealis*
Alpine forget-me-not	
	Myosotis alpestris
Alpine gypsophila	
	Gypsophila repens
Alpine lady's mantle	
	Alchemilla alpina
Alpine meadow rue	
	Thalictrum alpinum
Alpine moon daisy	
	Leucanthemopsis alpina
Alpine pennycress	*Thlaspi alpestre*
Alpine penstemon	
	Penstemon alpinus
Alpine phlox	*Phlox douglasii*
Alpine pink	*Dianthus alpinus*
Alpine poppy	*Papaver alpinum*
	Papaver burseri
Alpine snowbell	*Soldanella alpina*
Alpine speedwell	*Veronica alpina*
Alpine toadflax	*Linaria alpina*

Alpine wallflower	
	Erysimum alpinum
Alpine yarrow	*Achillea tomentosa*
Amaranth	*Amaranthus retroflexus*
American barrenwort	
	Vancouveria hexandra
American bluebell	*Mertensia ciliata*
American brooklime	
	Veronica americana
American bugbane	
	Cimicifuga americanum
American burnet	
	Poterium canadensis
	Sanguisorba canadensis
American cranesbill	
	Geranium maculatum
American fumitory	*Fumaria indica*
American Greek valerian	
	Polemonium reptans
American marigold	*Tagetes erecta*
American monkey flower	
	Mimulus guttatus
American sea lavender	
	Limonium carolinianum
American speedwell	
	Veronica peregrina
American sundrops	
	Oenothera fruticosa
	Oenothera linearis
American trumpet creeper	
	Campsis radicans
American white hellebore	
	Veratrum viride
American wild columbine	
	Aquilegia canadensis
American willowherb	
	Epilobium ciliatum
Angel's eye	*Veronica chamaedrys*
Annual anchusa	*Anchusa capensis*
Annual aster	*Callistephus chinensis*
Annual blue flax	
	Linum usitatissimum
Annual candytuft	*Iberis umbellata*
Annual cape marigold	
	Dimorphotheca annua
Annual clary	*Salvia horminum*
Annual gaillardia	
	Gaillardia pulchella
Annual gypsophila	
	Gypsophila muralis
Annual mallow	*Lavatera trimestris*
Annual phlox	*Phlox drummondii*
Annual pink	*Dianthus chinensis*
Annual poinsettia	
	Euphorbia heterophylla
Annual rudbeckia	*Rudbeckia hirta*
Annual sunflower	
	Helianthus annuus
Annual wall rocket	
	Diplotaxis muralis

POPULAR GARDEN PLANTS

Black hellebore

Antarctic forget-me-not
Myosotidium hortensia
Myosotidium nobile
Antwerp hollyhock
Althaea ficifolia
Apache beads
Anemonopsis californica
Apple of Peru Nicandra physalodes
Apple of sodom
Solanum carolinense
Solanum sosomeum
Arabian thistle
Onopordum arabicum
Onopordum nervosum
Arabian violet Exacum affine
Archangel Lamium album
Arctic poppy Papaver nudicaule
Papaver radicatum
Arizona poppy
Kalistroemia grandiflora
Armstrong Polygonum ariculare
Ass's tail Sedum morganianum
Asthma weed Euphorbia hirta
Lobelia inflata
Auricula Primula auricula
Australian fleabane
Erigeron karkinskianus
Australian violet Viola hederacea
Austrian speedwell
Veronica austriaca
Auvergne pink
Dianthus × arvernensis
Avens Geum urbanum
Aztec marigold Tagetes erecta
Baby blue-eyes Nemophila insignis
Nemophila menziesii
Baby's breath Gypsophila elegans
Gypsophila paniculata
Bachelor's buttons
Ranunculus acris
Tanacetum parthenium
Bacon and eggs Lotus corniculatus
Balkan cranesbill
Geranium macrorrhizum
Balloon flower
Platycodon grandiflorum
Balsam Impatiens balsamina
Balsam weed Impatiens aurea
Banana passionfruit
Passiflora mollissima
Tacsonia mollissima
Band plant Vinca major
Barberton daisy Gerbera jamesonii
Barren strawberry
Potentilla sterilis
Basket flower
Centaurea americana
Bastard box
Polygala chamaebuxus
Bastard jasmine
Androsace chamaejasme

Bats-in-the-belfry
Campanula trachelium
Campanula urticifolia
Beach pea Lathyrus littoralis
Lathyrus maritimus
Beach wormwood
Artemisia stellerana
Beaked hawk's beard
Crepis vesicaria
Bearded bellflower
Campanula barbata
Bear's breeches Primula auricula
Bear's ear Primula auricula
Bear's foot Alchemilla vulgaris
Beaver tail Sedum morganianum
Bee balm Monarda didyma
Bee nettle Lamium album
Bedding begonia
Begonia semperflorens
Bedding dahlia Dahlia merckii
Bedding lobelia Lobelia erinus
Bellflower
Wahlenbergia albomarginata
Bells of Ireland Moluccella laevis
Bellwort Uvularia grandiflora
Belvedere
Kochia scoparia trichophylla
Bergamot Monarda didyma
Bethlehem sage
Pulmonaria saccharata
Betony Betonica grandiflora
Betonica macrantha
Stachys betonica
Stachys officinalis
Bidgee-widgee
Acaena anserinifolia
Big marigold Tagetes erecta
Bird's eye Veronica chamaedrys
Bird's-eye primrose
Primula farinosa
Bird's eyes Gilia tricolor
Bird's foot trefoil
Lotus corniculatus
Bird's tongue Polygonum aviculare
Bishop's flower Ammi majus
Bishop's wort Betonica officinalis
Stachys betonica
Stachys officinalis
Biting stonecrop Sedum acre
Bitter root Lewisia rediviva
Bittersweet Solanum dulcamara
Bitter vetch Lathyrus montanus
Black baneberry Actaea spicata
Black cosmos
Cosmos atrosanguineus
Black-eyed susan Rudbeckia hirta
Thunbergia alata
Black false hellebore
Veratrum nigrum
Black hellebore Helleborus niger

Black helleborine	
	Veratrum nigrum
Black knapweed	*Centaurea nigra*
Black medick	*Medicago lupulina*
Black nightshade	*Solanum nigrum*
Black rampion	*Phyteuma nigrum*
Black root	*Veronica virginica*
	Veronicastrum virginica
Black samson	*Echinacea purpurea*
Black snakeroot	
	Cimicifuga racemosa
Bladder campion	*Silene vulgaris*
Bladder cherry	*Physalis alkekengi*
Bladder fumitory	*Fumaria vesicaria*
Bladder gentian	
	Gentiana utriculosa
Blanket flower	*Gaillardia aristata*
	Gaillardia pulchella
Blazing star	*Aletris farinosa*
	Bartonia aurea
	Liatris spicata
	Mentzelia lindleyi
Bleeding heart	*Dicentra spectabilis*
Blessed thistle	*Cnicus benedictus*
	Silybum marianum
Blind nettle	*Lamium album*
Blood drop	
	Stylomecon heterophylla
Blood-red geranium	
	Geranium sanguineum
Bloodroot	*Potentilla erecta*
	Sanguinaria canadensis
Bloody cranesbill	
	Geranium sanguineum
Bluebeard	*Salvia horminum*
Bluebell	*Campanula rotundifolia*
Blue bells	*Polemonium reptans*
Blue boneset	
	Eupatorium coelestinum
Bluebottle	*Centaurea cyanus*
Blue bugle	*Ajuga genevensis*
Blue buttons	*Vinca major*
Blue cornflower	*Centaurea cyanus*
Blue cowslip	
	Pulmonaria angustifolia
Blue cupidone	
	Catananche coerulea
Blue daisy	*Agathaea coelestis*
	Felicia amelloides
Blue dawn flower	
	Ipomoea acuminata
Blue-eyed grass	
	Sisyrinchium angustifolium
Blue-eyed mary	
	Collinsia grandiflora
	Omphalodes verna
Blue fescue	*Festuca glauca*
	Festuca ovina glauca
Blue flax	*Linum perenne*
Blue fleabane	*Erigeron acre*

Blue lace flower	*Didiscus caerulea*
	Trachymene caerulea
Blue lips	*Collinsia grandiflora*
Blue lobelia	*Lobelia siphilitica*
	Lobelia urens
Blue marguerite	*Agathaea coelestis*
	Felicia amelloides
Blue mountains bidi-bidi	
	Acaena inermis
	Acaena microphylla
Blue passionflower	
	Passiflora caerulea
Blue phlox	*Phlox canadensis*
	Phlox divaricata
Blue pimpernel	*Anagallis foemina*
	Anagallis linifolia
	Anagallis monelli linifolia
Blue poppy	
	Meconopsis betonicifolia
Blue sage	*Salvia azurea*
	Salvia patens
Blue saxifrage	*Saxifraga caesia*
Blue spurge	*Euphorbia myrsinites*
Blue succory	*Catananche coerulea*
Blue thimble flower	*Gilia capitata*
Bluets	*Hedyotis caerulea*
Blue throatwort	
	Trachelium caeruleum
Blue vervain	*Verbena hastata*
Blueweed	*Echium vulgare*
Blue wings	*Torenia fournieri*
Bog pimpernel	*Anagallis tenella*
Bog sage	*Salvia uliginosa*
Bog spurge	*Euphorbia palustris*
Bokhara fleece flower	
	Bilderdykia baldschuanicum
	Polygonum baldschuanicum
Boneset	*Symphytum officinale*
Border carnation	
	Dianthus caryophyllus
Border pink	*Dianthus plumarius*
Border sea lavender	
	Limonium latifolium
	Statice latifolium
Border thrift	*Armeria plantaginea*
	Armeria pseudarmeria
Boule d'or	*Trollius europaeus*
Bouncing bess	*Centranthus ruber*
Bouncing bet	*Saponaria officinalis*
Box honeysuckle	*Lonicera nitida*
Branched larkspur	
	Consolida regalis
Brass buttons	*Cotula coronopifolia*
Breckland thyme	
	Thymus serpyllum
Bridal wreath	*Francoa sonchifolia*
Brideweed	*Linaria vulgaris*
Brilliant scabious	*Scabiosa lucida*
Broad-leaved ragwort	
	Senecio fluviatilis

Cathedral bells

Broad-leaved sea lavender
Limonium latifolium
Statice latifolium

Broad-leaved spurge
Euphorbia platyphyllos

Broad-leaved willowherb
Epilobium montanum

Brompton stock   *Matthiola incana*

Brooklime   *Veronica beccabunga*

Broom cypress
Kochia scoparia trichophylla

Brown-eyed susan
Rudbeckia triloba

Bruisewort   *Symphytum officinale*

Bugle   *Ajuga reptans*

Bugleweed   *Lycopus virginicus*

Bugloss   *Anchusa arvensis*

Bulbous buttercup
Ranunculus bulbosus

Bull nettle   *Solanum carolinense*

Bullock's eye
Sempervivum tectorum

Bunny rabbits   *Linaria maroccana*

Bupleurum   *Bupleurum fruticosum*

Bur medick   *Medicago minima*

Burning bush   *Dictamnus albus*
Dictamnus fraxinella
Kochia scoparia trichophylla
Kochia trichophylla

Burro's tail   *Sedum morganianum*

Bush monkey flower
Diplacus glutinosus
Mimulus aurantiacus
Mimulus glutinosus

Bush morning glory
Convolvulus cneorum

Busy lizzie   *Impatiens sultanii*
Impatiens wallerana

Butter and eggs   *Linaria vulgaris*

Butter daisy   *Verbesina encelioides*

Butterfly flag   *Diplarrhena moraea*

Butterwort   *Pinguicula vulgaris*

Button pink   *Dianthus × latifolius*

Buttons   *Tanacetum vulgare*

Button snakeroot   *Liatris spicata*

Buxbaum's speedwell
Veronica persica

Cactus dahlia   *Dahlia juarezii*

Calamint   *Calamintha grandiflora*
Calamintha nepeta nepeta

Calathian violet
Gentiana pneumonanthe

Calico plant   *Aristolochia elegans*

California bluebell
Nemophila phacelia
Phacelia campanularia
Phacelia whitlavia

California blue-eyed grass
Sisyrinchium bellum

Californian fuchsia
Zauschneria californica

Californian golden bells
Emmenanthe penduliflora

Californian pea   *Lathyrus splendens*

Californian poppy
Eschscholzia californica

Californian whispering bells
Emmenanthe penduliflora

Calvary clover   *Medicago echinus*

Calve's snout   *Linaria vulgaris*

Canadian burnet
Poterium canadensis
Sanguisorba canadensis

Canadian golden rod
Solidaga canadensis

Canary-bird flower
Tropaeolum peregrinum

Canary-bird vine
Tropaeolum peregrinum

Canary creeper
Tropaeolum canariensis
Tropaeolum peregrinum

Candlewick   *Verbascum thapsus*

Candytuft   *Iberis amara*
Iberis umbellata

Canterbury bell
Campanula grandiflora
Campanula medium

Cape daisy   *Venidium fastuosum*

Cape forget-me-not
Anchusa capensis

Cape marigold
Dimorphotheca annua

Cape primrose
Streptocarpus hybridus

Caper spurge   *Euphorbia lathyris*

Cape stock   *Heliophila longifolia*

Caraway thyme
Thymus herba-barona

Cardinal climber
Ipomoea cardinalis
Ipomoea × multifida

Cardinal flower   *Lobelia cardinalis*
Lobelia fulgens

Cardinal sage   *Salvia fulgens*

Cardinal salvia   *Salvia fulgens*

Carnation   *Dianthus caryophyllus*

Carolina lupin
Thermopsis caroliniana

Carpathian bellflower
Campanula carpatica

Carpathian harebell
Campanula carpatica

Carpenter's herb   *Ajuga reptans*

Carpet plant   *Ionopsidium acaule*

Castor bean   *Ricinus communis*

Castor-oil plant   *Ricinus communis*

Catchfly   *Lychnis silene*
Lychnis viscaria
Lychnis vulgaris
Viscaria vulgaris

Cathedral bells   *Cobaea scandens*

Catmint

Catmint	*Nepeta cataria*
	Nepeta × faassenii
	Nepeta mussinii
Catnep	*Nepeta cataria*
Catnip	*Nepeta cataria*
Cat's hair	*Euphorbia pilulifera*
Cat's valerian	*Valeriana officinalis*
Cat-tail gayfeather	
	Liatris pycnostachya
Celandine poppy	
	Stylophorum diphyllum
Celery-leaved crowfoot	
	Ranunculus sceleratus
Chaff weed	*Anagallis minima*
Chalk milkwort	*Polygala calcarea*
Chalk plant	*Gypsophila paniculata*
Chatham Island lily	
	Myosotidium hortensia
	Myosotidium nobile
Cheddar pink	*Dianthus caesius*
	Dianthus gratianopolitanus
Cherry pie	
	Heliotropium arborescens
	Heliotropium corymbosum
	Heliotropium hybridum
	Heliotropium peruvianum
Chickling pea	*Lathyrus sativus*
Chickweed willowherb	
	Epilobium alsinifolium
Chilean avens	*Geum chiloense*
	Geum coccineum
	Geum quellyon
Chilean bellflower	
	Nolana acuminata
	Nolana rupicola
Chilean potato tree	
	Solanum crispum
Chimney bellflower	
	Campanula pyramidalis
China aster	*Callistephus chinensis*
China fleece flower	
	Bilderdykia aubertii
	Polygonum aubertii
Chinaman's breeches	
	Dicentra spectabilis
Chinese artichoke	*Stachys affinis*
Chinese bellflower	
	Platycodon grandiflorum
Chinese forget-me-not	
	Cynoglossom amabile
Chinese foxglove	
	Rehmannia angulata
Chinese houses	*Collinsia bicolor*
	Collinsia heterophylla
Chinese jasmine	
	Jasminum polyanthum
Chinese lantern	*Physalis alkekengi*
Chinese loosestrife	
	Lysimachia clethroides
Chinese paeony	*Paeonia albiflora*
	Paeonia lactiflora

Chinese pink	*Dianthus chinensis*
	Dianthus sinensis
Chinese trumpet creeper	
	Campsis chinensis
	Campsis grandiflora
Chinese trumpet flower	
	Incarvillea delavayi
	Incarvillea grandiflora
Chinese wax flower	
	Dregea sinensis
	Wattakaka chinensis
	Wattakaka sinensis
Chinese woodbine	
	Lonicera tragophylla
Chocolate cosmos	
	Cosmos atrosanguineus
Chorogi	*Stachys affinis*
Christmas horns	
	Delphinium nudicaule
Christmas rose	*Helleborus niger*
Christmas star	
	Euphorbia pulcherrima
Church steeples	
	Agrimonia eupatoria
Cigar flower	*Cuphea ignea*
Circle flower	*Lysimachia punctata*
Clarkia	*Clarkia unguiculata*
Clary	*Salvia sclarea*
Clear eye	*Salvia sclarea*
Climbing gazania	*Mutisia decurrens*
Clock vine	*Thunbergia grandiflora*
Clove pink	*Dianthus caryophyllus*
Cloveroot	*Geum urbanum*
Clump verbena	
	Verbena canadensis
Clustered bellflower	
	Campanula glomerata
Cobweb houseleek	
	Sempervivum arachnoideum
Cockle	*Vaccaria pyramidata*
Cockscomb	
	Celosia argentea cristata
	Celosia cristata childsii
Codlins and cream	
	Epilobium hirsutum
Colic root	*Aletris farinosa*
Comfrey	*Symphytum officinale*
Common agrimony	
	Agrimonia eupatoria
Common amaranth	
	Amaranthus retroflexus
Common aubrieta	
	Aubrieta deltoides
Common bleeding heart	
	Dicentra spectabilis
Common blue flax	
	Linum usitatissimum
Common blue passionflower	
	Passiflora caerulea
Common bugle	*Ajuga reptans*

Common butterwort
    Pinguicula vulgaris

Common candytuft
    Iberis umbellata

Common chamomile
    Anthemis nobilis

Common comfrey
    Symphytum officinale

Common daisy   *Bellis perennis*

Common edelweiss
    Leontopodium alpinum

Common foxglove
    Digitalis purpurea

Common fumitory
    Fumaria officinalis

Common globe flower
    Trollius europaeus

Common hawkweed
    Hieracium vulgatum

Common honeysuckle
    Lonicera periclymenum

Common houseleek
    Sempervivum tectorum

Common immortelle
    Xeranthemum anuum

Common knotgrass
    Polygonum aviculare

Common ladybell
    Adenophora lilifolia

Common lady's mantle
    Alchemilla mollis
    Alchemilla vulgaris

Common mallow   *Malva sylvestris*

Common marjoram
    Origanum vulgare

Common meadow rue
    Thalictrum flavum

Common meadowsweet
    Filipendula ulmaria

Common millwort
    Polygala vulgaris

Common monkshood
    Aconitum napellus

Common morning glory
    Ipomoea purpurea

Common mullein
    Verbascum thapsus

Common orach   *Atriplex patula*

Common pearlwort
    Sagina procumbens

Common periwinkle   *Vinca minor*

Common persicaria
    Polygonum persicaria

Common pink
    Dianthus plumarius

Common ramping fumitory
    Fumaria muralis

Common red poppy
    Papaver rhoeas

Common sage   *Salvia officinalis*

Common shooting star
    Dodecatheon meadia

Common speedwell
    Veronica officinalis

Common sunflower
    Helianthus annuus

Common thrift   *Armeria maritima*

Common throatwort
    Trachelium caeruleum

Common thyme   *Thymus vulgaris*

Common toadflax   *Linaria vulgaris*

Common tobacco
    Nicotiana tabacum

Common valerian
    Valeriana officinalis

Common wallflower
    Cheiranthus cheiri

Common white jasmine
    Jasminum officinale

Common yarrow
    Achillea millefolium

Common yellow alyssum
    Alyssum saxatile
    Aurinia saxatilis

Common zinnia   *Zinnia elegans*

Cone flower   *Rudbeckia fulgida*

Coolwort   *Tiarella cordifolia*

Coral bells   *Heuchera sanguinea*

Coral flower   *Heuchera sanguinea*

Corn buttercup
    Ranunculus arvensis

Corn campion
    Agrostemma githago

Corn cockle   *Agrostemma githago*

Corn crowfoot
    Ranunculus arvensis

Cornflower   *Centaurea cyanus*

Cornflower aster   *Stokesia cyanea*
    Stokesia laevis

Corn lily   *Veratrum californicum*

Corn marigold
    Chrysanthemum segetum

Corn mignonette
    Reseda phyteuma

Corn pink   *Agrostemma githago*

Corn poppy   *Papaver rhoeas*

Corn woundwort   *Stachys arvensis*

Corsican hellebore
    Helleborus argutifolius
    Helleborus corsicus
    Helleborus lividus

Corsican speedwell
    Veronica repens

Cottage pink
    Dianthus caryophyllus
    Dianthus plumarius

Cotton thistle
    Onopordum acanthium

Coventry bells
    Campanula trachelium
    Campanula urticifolia

Cowbells   *Uvularia grandiflora*

Cow cress   *Veronica beccabunga*

Cow herb	*Saponaria vaccaria*
	Vaccaria pyramidata
Cowslip	*Primula officinalis*
	Primula veris
Cream cups	
	Platystemon californicus
Creeping avens	*Geum reptans*
Creeping buttercup	
	Ranunculus repens
Creeping cinquefoil	
	Potentilla reptans
Creeping forget-me-not	
	Omphalodes verna
Creeping jacob's ladder	
	Polemonium reptans
Creeping jenny	
	Lysimachia nummularia
Creeping phlox	*Phlox reptans*
	Phlox stolonifera
Creeping Saint John's wort	
	Hypericum humifusum
Creeping thyme	*Thymus serpyllum*
Creeping vervain	*Verbena aubletia*
	Verbena canadensis
Creeping zinnia	
	Sanvitalia procumbens
Crested gentian	
	Gentiana septemfida
Crested poppy	
	Argemone platyceras
Cretan bear's tail	*Celsia arcturus*
Cretan dittany	
	Amaracus dictamnus
	Origanum dictamnus
Cretan mullein	*Celsia arcturus*
Crimson star glory	*Ipomoea lobata*
	Mina lobata
	Quamoclit lobata
Cross gentian	*Gentiana cruciata*
Crow flower	
	Geranium sylvaticum
Crown daisy	
	Chrysanthemum coronarium
Cudweed	*Artemisia gnaphalodes*
	Artemisia ludoviciana
	Artemisia purshiana
Culver's root	
	Veronicastrum virginicum
	Veronica virginica
Cup-and-saucer canterbury	
bell	*Campanula medium*
	calycanthema
Cup-and-saucer vine	
	Cobaea scandens
Cupid's dart	*Catananche coerulea*
Curled mallow	*Malva crispa*
Curly mallow	*Malva crispa*
Curry plant	
	Helichrysum angustifolium
	Helichrysum seotinum
Curuba	*Passiflora mollissima*
	Tacsonia mollissima
Cushion pink	*Silene acaulis*
Cushion spurge	
	Euphorbia epithymoides
	Euphorbia polychroma
Cut-leaved cranesbill	
	Geranium dissectum
Cut-leaved mallow	*Malva alcea*
Cyphel	*Minuartia sedoides*
Cypress spurge	
	Euphorbia cyparissias
Cypress vine	*Ipomoea quamoclit*
Dairy pink	*Saponaria vaccaria*
	Vaccaria pyramidata
Dakota vervain	
	Verbena bipinnatifida
Dalmatian pellitory	
	Tanacetum cinerariifolium
Dalmatian pyrethrum	
	Tanacetum cinerariifolium
Damask violet	*Hesperis matronalis*
Dame's rocket	*Hesperis matronalis*
Dame's violet	*Hesperis matronalis*
Dandelion	*Taraxacum officinale*
Dark mullein	*Verbascum nigrum*
Dead men's bells	
	Digitalis purpurea
Dead nettle	*Lamium maculatum*
Deer's tongue	*Liatris odoratissima*
Deer weed	*Lotus scoparius*
Deptford pink	*Dianthus armeria*
Devil's fig	*Argemone mexicana*
Devil's paintbrush	
	Hieracium aurantiacum
Diamond flower	
	Ionopsidium acaule
Digger's speedwell	
	Veronica perfoliata
Dittany	*Dictamnus albus*
	Dictamnus fraxinella
Dog daisy	*Leucanthemum vulgare*
Dog poison	*Aethusa cynapium*
Donkey plant	*Onosma pyramidale*
Donkey's tail	
	Sedum morganianum
Dotted loosestrife	
	Lysimachia punctata
Double orange daisy	
	Erigeron aurantiacus
Dovedale moss	
	Saxifraga hypnoides
Dove's foot cranesbill	
	Geranium columbinum
Downy lupin	*Lupinus pubescens*
Downy Saint John's wort	
	Hypericum lanuginosum
Downy thistle	
	Onopordum acanthium
Downy woundwort	
	Stachys germanica
Dragon mouth	
	Horminum pyranaicum

POPULAR GARDEN PLANTS

Field forget-me-not

Dropwort   *Filipendula hexapetala*
            Filipendula vulgaris
Drumstick primula
            Primula denticulata
Drunken sailor   *Centranthus ruber*
Dun daisy   *Leucanthemum vulgare*
Dusky cranesbill
            Geranium phaeum
Dusty miller   *Artemisia stellerana*
            Centaurea candidissima
            Centaurea cineraria
            Centaurea gymnocarpa
            Centaurea ragusina
            Primula auricula
Dutch agrimony
            Eupatorium cannabinum
Dutchman's breeches
            Dicentra spectabilis
Dutchman's pipe
            Aristolochia durior
    Aristolochia macrophylla
            Aristolochia sipho
Dwarf cape marigold
            Dimorphotheca barberae
            Osteospermum barberae
Dwarf globe flower   *Trollius pumilis*
Dwarf jasmine   *Jasminum parkeri*
Dwarf mallow   *Malva neglecta*
Dwarf meadow rue
            Thalictrum coreanum
Dwarf morning glory
            Convolvulus minor
            Convolvulus tricolor
Dwarf nasturtium
            Tropaeolum minus
Dwarf snowbell   *Soldenella pusilla*
Dwarf spurge   *Euphorbia exigua*
Dwarf sundrops
            Oenothera perennis
            Oenothera pumila
Dwarf valerian   *Valeriana saxatilis*
Dyer's rocket   *Reseda luteola*
Early meadow rue
            Thalictrum dioicum
Earth smoke   *Fumaria officinalis*
Eastern rocket
            Sisymbrium orientale
Edelweiss   *Leontopodium alpinum*
Edging lobelia   *Lobelia erinus*
Eggs and bacon   *Linaria vulgaris*
Elecampane   *Inula helenium*
English daisy   *Bellis perennis*
English harebell
            Campanula rotundifolia
English primrose   *Primula acaulis*
            Primula vulgaris
English stonecrop   *Sedum anglicum*
English wallflower
            Cheiranthus cheiri
European brooklime
            Veronica beccabunga

European honeysuckle
            Lonicera periclymenum
European wild columbine
            Aquilegia vulgaris
European wild paeony
            Paeonia officinalis
European wild thyme
            Thymus drucei
            Thymus serpyllum
Evening primrose
            Oenothera biennis
Evening stock   *Matthiola bicornis*
Everlasting daisy
            Helichrysum bellidiodes
Everlasting pea   *Lathyrus latifolius*
Ewe daisy   *Potentilla erecta*
Fair maids of France
            Saxifraga granulata
Fair maids of Kent
            Ranunculus aconitifolius
Fairy clock   *Taraxacum officinale*
Fairy cups   *Primula veris*
Fairy flax   *Linum catharticum*
Fairy foxglove   *Erinus alpinus*
Fairy primrose   *Primula malacoides*
Fairy's thimbles
            Campanula cochleariifolia
            Campanula pusilla
Fairy thimbles   *Digitalis purpurea*
False African violet
            Streptocarpus saxorum
False anemone
            Anemonopsis macrophylla
False bishop's weed   *Ammi majus*
False clary   *Salvia viridis*
False dragonhead
            Physostegia virginiana
False London rocket
            Sisymbrium loeselii
Fanweed   *Thlaspi arvense*
Farewell-to-spring   *Clarkia amoena*
            Godetia amoena
Feathered bronze leaf
            Rodgersia pinnata
Fen spurge   *Euphorbia palustris*
Fernleaf yarrow
            Achillea eupatorium
            Achillea filipendulina
Fern-leaved paeony
            Paeonia tenuifolia
Feverfew
    Chrysanthemum parthenium
            Matricaria eximia
            Tanacetum coccineum
            Tanacetum parthenium
Fibrous-rooted begonia
            Begonia semperflorens
Field daisy   *Leucanthemum vulgare*
Field fleawort   *Senecio integrifolius*
Field forget-me-not
            Myosotis arvensis

COMMON NAMES

Field pennycress

Field pennycress	Thlaspi arvense
Field poppy	Papaver rhoeas
Field primrose	Oenothera biennis
Field scabious	Knautia arvensis
Field speedwell	Veronica agrestis
Field woundwort	Stachys arvensis
Figleaf hollyhock	Althaea ficifolia
Fire bush	
	Kochia scoparia trichophylla
Firecracker plant	Cuphea ignea
Fire on the mountain	
	Euphorbia heterophylla
Fire plant	Euphorbia pulcherrima
Fireweed Epilobium angustifolium	
	Erechtites hieracifolia
Five-faced bishop	
	Adoxa moschatellina
Five fingers	Potentilla reptans
Five-leaved grass	Potentilla reptans
Five-spot	Nemophila maculata
Five-spot nemophila	
	Nemophila maculata
Flame creeper	
	Tropaeolum speciosum
Flame nasturtium	
	Tropaeolum speciosum
Flame violet	Episcia cupreata
Flaming poppy	
	Stylomecon heterophylla
Flanders poppy	Papaver rhoeas
Flannel flower	Actinotus helianthi
Flannel mullein	Verbascum thapsus
Flax	Linum usitatissimum
Flax-leaved Saint John's wort	
	Hypericum linarifolium
Flaxweed	Linaria vulgaris
Flore pleno	Clarkia elegans
Florist's scabious	
	Scabiosa caucasica
Floss flower	
	Ageratum houstonianum
	Ageratum mexicanum
Flowering spurge	
	Euphorbia corollata
Flowering tobacco	
	Nicotiana sylvestris
Flower of Jove	
	Agrostemma flos-jovis
	Lychnis flos-jovis
Fly honeysuckle	
	Lonicera xylosteum
Foam flower	Tiarella cordifolia
	Tiarella polyphylla
Fool's parsley	Aethusa cynapium
Forget-me-not	Myosotis alpestris
	Myosotis oblongata
	Myosotis sylvatica
Forked catchfly	Silene dichotoma
Forking larkspur	Consolida regalis
Four o'clock plant	Mirabilis jalapa

Foxbane	
	Aconitum lycotonum vulparia
Foxglove	Digitalis purpurea
Fragrant evening primrose	
	Oenothera stricta
French cranesbill	
	Geranium endressii
French hawk's beard	
	Crepis nicaeensis
French lilac	Galega officinalis
French marigold	Tagetes patula
Frenchweed	Thlaspi arvense
Friar's cap	Aconitum napellus
Fringe-bell	
	Schizocodon soldanelliodes
	Shortia soldanelliodes
Fringed bleeding heart	
	Dicentra eximia
Fringed pink	Dianthus superbus
Frosted orache	Atriplex lociniata
Fumitory	Fumaria officinalis
Garden chamomile	
	Anthemis nobilis
Garden globe flowers	
	Trollius × cultorum
	Trollius × hybridus
Garden heliotrope	
	Valeriana officinalis
Garden hollyhock	
	Althaea chimensis
	Althaea rosea
Garden loosestrife	
	Lysimachia punctata
Garden lupin	Lupinus polyphyllus
Garden nasturtium	
	Tropaeolum majus
Garden phlox	Phlox decussata
	Phlox paniculata
Garden pinks Dianthus × allwoodii	
Garden thyme	Thymus vulgaris
Garden verbenas	
	Verbena × hortensis
	Verbena × hybrida
Garlic pennycress	
	Thlaspi alliaceum
Gas plant	Dictamnus albus
	Dictamnus fraxinella
Gayfeather	Liatris spicata
Gentian sage	Salvia patens
German catchfly	Lychnis viscaria
	Lychnis vulgaris
	Viscaria vulgaris
Germander speedwell	
	Veronica chamaedrys
German primrose	
	Primula obconica
German violet	Exacum affine
Ghost flower	Monotropa uniflora
Giant bellflower	
	Campanula latifolia
Giant cowslip	Primula florindae

Green chamomile

Giant daisy
    Chrysanthemum serotinum
    Chrysanthemum uliginosum
Giant deadnettle   *Lamium orvala*
Giant forget-me-not
    Myosotidium hortensia
    Myosotidium nobile
Giant honeysuckle
    Lonicera hildebrandiana
Giant inula   *Inula magnifica*
Giant kingcup   *Caltha polypetala*
Giant knapweed
    Centaurea rhaponticum
Giant marigold *Helianthus annuus*
Giant potato vine
    Solanum wendlandii
Giant ragwort *Ligularia japonica*
Giant scabious
    Cephalaria gigantea
    Cephalaria tatarica
Giant spaniard
    Aciphylla scott-thomsonii
Giant stapelia   *Stapelia gigantea*
Giant starfish   *Stapelia gigantea*
Giant toad plant *Stapelia gigantea*
Gilliflower *Dianthus caryophyllus*
    Matthiola incana
Gipsyweed *Lycopus virginicus*
Gipsywort *Lycopus europaeus*
Glacier crowfoot
    Ranunculus glacialis
Glacier pink   *Dianthus glacialis*
    Dianthus neglectus
    Dianthus pavonius
Globe amaranth
    Gomphrena globosa
Globe candytuft *Iberis umbellata*
Globe centaurea
    Centaurea macrocephala
Globe flower *Trollius europaeus*
Globe thistle   *Echinops ritro*
Glory-of-the-marsh
    Primula helodoxa
Glory pea   *Clianthus dampieri*
    Clianthus formosus
    Clianthus speciosus
Goat-leaf honeysuckle
    Lonicera caprifolium
Goat root   *Ononis natrix*
Goat's beard   *Aruncus dioicus*
    Aruncus sylvester
    Aruncus vulgaris
    Spiraea aruncus
Goat's rue *Galega officinalis*
Godetia *Godetia grandiflora*
Golden crown beard
    Verbesina encelioides
Gold cup   *Ranunculus acris*
Gold dust   *Alyssum saxatile*
    Aurinia saxatilis

Golden deadnettle
    Galeobdolon luteum
    Lamium galeobdolon
    Lamiastrum galeobdolon
Golden drop *Onosma tauricum*
Golden eardrops
    Dicentra chrysantha
Golden-eyed grass
    Sisyrinchium californicum
Golden flax   *Linum flavum*
Golden groundsel *Senecio aureus*
Golden marguerite
    Anthemis tinctoria
Golden moss   *Sedum acre*
Golden rod *Solidago canadensis*
    Solidago virgaurea
Golden samphire
    Inula crithmoides
Golden sedum   *Sedum adolphi*
Golden spaniard *Aciphylla aurea*
Goldilocks   *Aster linosyris*
    Helichrysum stoechas
    Lynosyris vulgaris
    Ranunculus auricumus
Golds   *Calendula officinalis*
Good-luck plant *Oxalis deppei*
Goosewort *Achillea ptarmica*
Grand bellflower
    Adenophora lilifolia
Granny's bonnet *Aquilegia vulgaris*
Grass pea   *Lathyrus sativus*
Grass pink *Dianthus plumarius*
Grass vetchling *Lathyrus nissolia*
Grass widow
    Sisyrinchium douglasii
Gravel root
    Eupatorium purpureum
Gravel weed
    Eupatorium purpureum
Greater butterwort
    Pinguicula grandiflora
Greater hawk's beard
    Crepis biennis
Greater periwinkle *Vinca major*
Great eyebright *Euphorbia arctica*
Great golden knapweed
    Centaurea macrocephala
Great knapweed
    Centaurea scabiosa
Great leopard's bane
    Doronicum pardalianches
Great lobelia *Lobelia siphililea*
Great spearwort
    Ranunculus lingua
Great willowherb
    Epilobium hirsutum
Greek valerian
    Polemonium caeruleum
Green amaranthus
    Amaranthus hybridus
Green chamomile *Anthemis nobilis*

Green hellebore

Green hellebore	*Helleborus viridus*
Grey cinquefoil	*Potentilla cinerea*
Grim collier	*Hieracium aurantiacum*
Ground box	*Polygala chamaebuxus*
Ground pine	*Ajuga chamaepitys*
Groundsel	*Senecio vulgaris*
Gypsyweed	*Veronica officinalis*
Hag's taper	*Verbascum thapsus*
Hairy Saint John's wort	*Hypericum hirsutum*
Hairy saxifrage	*Saxifraga hirsuta*
Hairy spurge	*Euphorbia villosa*
Hairy starfish flower	*Stapelia variegata*
Hairy stonecrop	*Sedum villosum*
Hairy thyme	*Thymus praecox*
Hairy toad plant	*Stapelia hirsuta*
Hairy vetchling	*Lathyrus hirsutus*
Hairy willowherb	*Epilobium parviflorum*
Hardheads	*Centaurea nigra*
Hardy age	*Eupatorium rugosum*
Hardy ageratum	*Eupatorium coelestinum*
Harebell	*Campanula rotundifolia*
Harebell bellflower	*Campanula rotundifolia*
Harebell poppy	*Meconopsis quintuplinerva*
Hawk's beard	*Crepis rubra*
Hawkweed saxifrage	*Saxifraga hieracifolia*
Haybells	*Uvularia grandiflora*
Heart-leaved valerian	*Valeriana pyrenaica*
Heartsease	*Viola tricolor*
Heath aster	*Aster ericoides*
Heather	*Calluna vulgaris*
	Erica vulgaris
Heath lobelia	*Lobelia urens*
Heath milkwort	*Polygala serpyllifolia*
Heath pearlwort	*Sagina subulata*
Heath speedwell	*Veronica officinalis*
Hedge mustard	*Sisymbrium officinale*
Hedgerow cranesbill	*Geranium pyrenaicum*
Hedge woundwort	*Stachys sylvatica*
Helenium	*Helenium autumnale*
Heliopsis	*Heliopsis helianthoides*
	Heliopsis scabra
Hemp agrimony	*Eupatorium cannabinum*

Hen-and-chickens houseleek	*Jovibarba soboliferum*
	Sempervivum soboliferum
Hen-and-chickens marigold	*Calendula officinalis prolifera*
Henbit	*Lamium amplexicaule*
Henbit deadnettle	*Lamium amplexicaule*
Heraldic thistle	*Onopordum arabicum*
	Onopordum nervosum
Herald of heaven	*Eritrichium nanum*
Herb bennet	*Geum urbanum*
Herb of grace	*Ruta graveolens*
Herb peter	*Primula veris*
Herb robert	*Geranium robertianum*
Himalayan balsam	*Impatiens glandulifera*
Himalayan blue poppy	*Meconopsis baileyi*
	Meconopsis betonicifolia
Himalayan comfrey	*Onosma pyramidale*
Himalayan cowslip	*Primula florindae*
	Primula sikkimensis
Himalayan elecampane	*Inula royleana*
Himalayan knotweed	*Polygonum campanulatum*
Himalayan mayflower	*Podophyllum emodii*
Himalayan touch-me-not	*Impatiens glandulifera*
	Impatiens roylei
Himalayan whorlflower	*Morina longifolia*
Hoary cinquefoil	*Potentilla argentea*
Hoary ragwort	*Senecio erucifolius*
Hoary mullein	*Verbascum pulverulentum*
Hoary vervain	*Verbena stricta*
Hoary willowherb	*Epilobium parviflorum*
Hollyhock	*Althaea chinensis*
	Althaea rosea
Hollyhock mallow	*Malva alcea*
Holy rope	*Eupatorium cannabinum*
Holy thistle	*Cnicus benedictus*
	Silybum marianum
Honesty	*Lunaria annua*
	Lunaria biennis
	Lunaria rediviva
Honeysuckle	*Lonicera periclymenum*
Horned poppy	*Glaucium flavum*
Horned rampion	*Phyteuma comosum*

Horned violet	*Viola cornuta*
Horse daisy	
	Leucanthemum vulgare
Horsefly	*Baptisia tinctoria*
Horse nettle	*Solanum carolinense*
Horse's tail	*Sedum morganianum*
Hound's tongue	
	Cynoglossum amabile
Humming bird's trumpet	
	Zauschneria californica
Hungarian daisy	
	Chrysanthemum serotinum
	Chrysanthemum uliginosum
	Leucanthemella serotina
Hyssop	*Hyssopus aristatus*
Iberian cranesbill	
	Geranium ibericum
Iceland poppy	*Papaver nudicaule*
Ice plant	
	Cryophytum crystallinum
	Mesembryanthemum crystallinum
	Sedum maximum
	Sedum spectabile
Immortelle	*Xeranthemum anuum*
Inch plant	*Tradescantia zebrina*
Indian balsam	
	Impatiens glandulifera
Indian chocolate	*Geum rivale*
	Geum urbanum
Indian cress	*Tropaeolum majus*
Indian pink	*Dianthus chinensis*
Indian pipe	*Monotropa uniflora*
Indian poke	*Veratrum viride*
Indian tobacco	*Lobelia inflata*
Indian valerian	*Valeriana walichii*
Innocence	*Collinsia bicolor*
	Hedyotis caerulea
Inside-out flower	
	Vancouveria planipetala
Irish lace	*Tagetes filifolia*
Irish saxifrage	*Saxifraga rosacea*
Irish spurge	*Euphorbia hyberna*
Italian aster	*Aster amellus*
Italian bellflower	
	Campanula isophylla
Italian bugloss	*Anchusa azurea*
	Anchusa italica
Italian catchfly	*Silene italica*
Italian verbena	*Verbena tenera*
Itchweed	*Veratrum viride*
Ivy-leaved bellflower	
	Wahlenbergia hederacea
Ivy-leaved crowfoot	
	Ranunculus hederaceus
Ivy-leaved geraniums	
	Pelargonium peltatum
Ivy-leaved harebell	
	Wahlenbergia hederacea
Ivy-leaved pelargoniums	
	Pelargonium peltatum

Ivy-leaved speedwell	
	Veronica hederifolia
Jack-by-the-hedge	*Alliaria petiolata*
Jacobea	*Senecio jacobaea*
Jacob's ladder	
	Polemonium caeruleum
Jacob's staff	*Verbascum thapsus*
Jamaica honeysuckle	
	Passiflora laurifolia
Jamaica vervain	
	Verbena jamaicensis
Japanese artichoke	*Stachys affinis*
Japanese gentian	*Gentiana scabrae*
Japanese honeysuckle	
	Lonicera japonica
Japanese jasmine	*Jasminum mesnyi*
	Jasminum primulinum
Japanese morning glory	
	Ipomoea nil
Japanese pink	
	Dianthus × heddewigii
Japanese primrose	
	Primula japonica
Japanese spurge	
	Pachysandra terminalis
Jasmine nightshade	
	Solanum jasminoides
Jelly-bean plant	
	Sedum pachyphyllum
Jerusalem cowslip	
	Pulmonaria officinalis
Jerusalem cross	
	Lychnis chalcedonica
Jerusalem sage	
	Pulmonaria officinalis
Jewel weed	*Impatiens aurea*
	Impatiens biflora
	Impatiens capensis
Joe-pye weed	
	Eupatorium maculatum
	Eupatorium purpureum
Joseph's coat	*Amaranthus tricolor*
Jumping jack	
	Impatiens glandulifera
Jupiter's beard	*Centranthus ruber*
Jupiter's distaff	*Salvia glutinosa*
Jupiter's staff	*Verbascum thapsus*
Kangaroo apple	
	Solanum laciniatum
Kangaroo vine	*Cissus antarctica*
Kansas gayfeather	*Liatris callilepis*
	Liatris pycnostachya
Kansas niggerhead	
	Echinacea angustifolia
Kerosene bush	
	Helichrysum ledifolium
	Ozothamnus ledifolium
Keyflower	*Primula veris*
Kidney saxifrage	*Saxifraga hirsuta*
Kidneywort	*Umbilicus rupestris*
Kingcup	*Caltha palustris*

Kingfisher daisy	*Felicia bergerana*
King of the alps	
	Eritrichium nanum
King-of-the-meadow	
	Thalictrum polygamum
Knapweed	*Centaurea nigra*
Knitbone	*Symphytum officinale*
Knotgrass	*Polygonum aviculare*
Knotroot	*Stachys affinis*
Knotted pearlwort	*Sagina nodosa*
Korean chrysanthemum	
	Chrysanthemum rubellum
Lace flower	*Episcia dianthiflora*
Lad's love	*Artemisia abrotanum*
Ladybell	*Adenophora lilifolia*
Ladybird poppy	
	Papaver commutatum
Lady rue	*Thalictrum clavatum*
Lady's foxglove	*Verbascum thapsus*
Lady's gloves	*Digitalis purpurea*
Lady's locket	*Dicentra spectabilis*
Lady's mantle	*Alchemilla mollis*
	Alchemilla vulgaris
Lady Washington geraniums	
	Pelargonium × domesticum
Lady Washington pelargoniums	
	Pelargonium × domesticum
Lamb's ear	*Stachys byzantina*
	Stachys lanata
	Stachys olympica
Lamb's lugs	*Stachys byzantina*
Lamb's tail	*Sedum morganianum*
Lamb's tongue	*Stachys byzantina*
	Stachys lanata
	Stachys olympica
Lampshade poppy	
	Meconopsis integrifolia
Large blue alkanet	*Anchusa azurea*
Large-flowered butterwort	
	Pinguicula grandiflora
Large-leaved evening primrose	
	Oenothera glazioviana
Large pink	*Dianthus superbus*
Larger periwinkle	*Vinca major*
Large speedwell	*Veronica austriaca*
Large thyme	*Thymus pulegioides*
Large yellow foxglove	
	Digitalis grandiflora
Large yellow ox-eye	
	Telekia speciosa
Larkspur	*Consolida ambigua*
	Delphinium consolida
Lavender cup	
	Nierembergia caerulea
	Nierembergia hippomanica
Leafy hawkweed	
	Hieracium umbellatum
Leafy spurge	*Euphorbia esula*
Lemon-scented geranium	
	Pelargonium citriodorum
	Pelargonium crispum

Lemon-scented pelargonium	
	Pelargonium citriodorum
	Pelargonium crispum
Lemon-scented thyme	
	Thymus × citriodorus
Lemon verbena	*Aloysia triphylla*
	Lippia citriodora
Lenten rose	*Helleborus orientalis*
Leopard's bane	
	Doronicum caucasicum
Lesser bugloss	*Lycopsis arvensis*
Lesser celandine	
	Ranunculus ficaria
Lesser dandelion	
	Taraxacum erythrospermum
	Taraxacum laevicatum
Lesser herb robert	
	Geranium purpurea
Lesser knapweed	*Centaurea nigra*
Lesser meadow rue	
	Thalictrum minus
Lesser periwinkle	*Vinca minor*
Lesser plume poppy	
	Bocconia microcarpa
	Macleaya microcarpa
Lesser spearwort	
	Ranunculus flammula
Lilac pink	*Diantus superbus*
Ling	*Calluna vulgaris*
	Erica vulgaris
Linseed	*Linum usitatissimum*
Lion's foot	*Alchemilla vulgaris*
	Leontopodium alpinum
Lion's heart	*Physostegia virginiana*
Lion's teeth	*Taraxacum officinale*
Liquorice plant	
	Helichrysum petiolatum
Live forever	*Sedum telephium*
Livelong	*Sedum telephium*
Livingstone daisy	
	Cleretum bellidiforme
	Dorotheanthus bellidiflorus
	Mesembryanthemum
	criniflorum
Lobster claw	*Clianthus puniceus*
Lobster plant	
	Euphorbia pulcherrima
London pride	*Saxifraga umbrosa*
	Saxifraga × urbium
London rocket	*Sisymbrium irio*
Long-headed poppy	
	Papaver dubium
Lord Anson's pea	
	Lathyrus nervosus
Lousewort	*Pedicularis sylvatica*
Love-in-a-mist	*Nigella damascena*
Love-lies-bleeding	
	Amaranthus caudatus
Lyre flower	*Dicentra spectabilis*

POPULAR GARDEN PLANTS

Moon daisy

Madagascar periwinkle
    Amsonia roseus
    Catharanthus roseus
    Vinca rosea
Maiden pink   *Dianthus deltoides*
Maiden's wreath   *Francoa ramosa*
Mallowwort   *Malope trifolia*
Maltese cross   *Lychnis chalcedonica*
Marguerite
    Argyranthemum frutescens
    Leucanthemum vulgare
Marigold of Peru
    Helianthus annuus
Marjoram   *Origanum vulgare*
Marsh cinquefoil
    Potentilla palustris
Marsh fleawort   *Senecio palustris*
Marsh flower
    Limnanthes douglasii
Marsh gentian
    Gentiana pneumonanthe
Marsh hawk's beard
    Crepis paludosa
Marsh marigold   *Caltha palustris*
Marsh pea   *Lathyrus palustris*
Marsh ragwort   *Senecio aquaticus*
Marsh speedwell
    Veronica scutellata
Marsh valerian   *Valeriana dioica*
Marsh violet   *Viola cucullata*
Marsh willowherb
    Epilobium palustra
Marsh woundwort
    Stachys palustris
Martha Washington geraniums
    Pelargonium × domesticum
Martha Washington pelargoniums
    Pelargonium × domesticum
Marvel of Peru   *Mirabilis jalapa*
Mask flower   *Alonsoa warscewiczii*
Matted sea lavender
    Limonium bellidifolium
May apple   *Podophyllum peltatum*
Meadow anemone
    Pulsatilla vulgaris
Meadow buttercup
    Ranunculus acris
Meadow bloom   *Ranunculus acris*
Meadow clary   *Salvia pratensis*
Meadow cranesbill
    Geranium pratense
Meadow daisy   *Bellis perennis*
Meadow foam
    Limnanthes douglasii
Meadow geranium
    Geranium pratense
Meadow rue
    Thalictrum aquilegiifolium
Meadow saxifrage
    Saxifraga granulata
Meadowsweet   *Filipendula ulmaria*

Mealy-cup sage   *Salvia farinacea*
Medusa's head
    Euphorbia caput-medusae
Merry bells   *Uvularia grandiflora*
Mexican aster   *Cosmos bipinnatus*
Mexican fire plant
    Euphorbia heterophylla
Mexican flame vine
    Senecio confusus
Mexican fleabane
    Erigeron karkinskianus
Mexican foxglove
    Tetranema mexicana
    Tetranema roseum
Mexican ivy   *Cobaea scandens*
Mexican poppy
    Argemone mexicana
Mexican red sage   *Salvia fulgens*
Mexican sunflower
    Tithonia rotundifolia
    Tithonia speciosa
Mexican violet   *Tetranema roseum*
Mexican zinnia   *Zinnia haageana*
Michaelmas daisy
    Aster novae-angliae
Midsummer men   *Sedum telephium*
Mignonette   *Reseda odorata*
Milfoil   *Achillea millefolium*
Milk purslane   *Euphorbia maculata*
Milk thistle   *Silybum marianum*
Milkwhite rock jasmine
    Androsace lactea
Milkwort   *Polygala calcarea*
Milky bellflower
    Campanula lactiflora
Milky rock jasmine
    Androsace lactea
Mistflower
    Eupatorium coelestinum
    Eupatorium rugosum
Mithridate mustard
    Thlaspi arvense
Mock cypress
    Kochia scoparia trichophylla
Mole plant   *Euphorbia lathyris*
Molucca balm   *Moluccella laevis*
Monarch of the veldt
    Venidium fastuosum
Monastery bells   *Cobaea scandens*
Money plant   *Lunaria annua*
    Lunaria biennis
Moneywort
    Lysimachia nummularia
Monkey flower   *Mimulus luteus*
Monkey musk   *Mimulus luteus*
Monkshood   *Aconitum napellus*
Moon daisy
    Chrysanthemum leucanthemum
    Leucanthemella serotina
    Leucanthemum vulgare

Moonflower

Moonflower	*Ipomoea alba*
	Ipomoea bona-nox
	Ipomoea noctiflora
	Ipomoea roxburghii
Moonlight primula	*Primula alpicola*
	Primula microdonta alpicola
Moonvine	*Ipomoea alba*
	Ipomoea bona-nox
	Ipomoea noctiflora
	Ipomoea roxburghii
Moonwort	*Lunaria annua*
	Lunaria biennis
Morning glory	*Ipomoea acuminata*
	Ipomoea purpurea
Moschatel	*Adoxa moschatellina*
Moss campion	*Silene acaulis*
Moss phlox	*Phlox setacea*
	Phlox subulata
Moss pink	*Phlox setacea*
	Phlox subulata
Moss verbena	*Verbena tenuisecta*
Mossy cyphel	*Minuartia sedoides*
Mossy rockfoil	*Saxifraga hypnoides*
Mossy saxifrage	*Saxifraga hypnoides*
Mother of thousands	*Saxifraga sarmentosa*
	Saxifraga stolonifera
Moth mullein	*Verbascum blattaria*
Mountain bluet	*Centaurea montana*
Mountain cranesbill	*Geranium pyrenaicum*
Mountain fleece	*Polygonum amplexicaule*
Mountain foxglove	*Ourisia macrophylla*
Mountain garland	*Clarkia unguiculata*
Mountain hollyhock	*Iliamna rivularis*
Mountain houseleek	*Sempervivum montanum*
Mountain knapweed	*Centaurea montana*
Mountain pansy	*Viola lutea*
Mountain phlox	*Linanthus grandiflorus*
Mountain sandwort	*Minuartia rubella*
Mountain snow	*Euphorbia marginata*
Mountain snowbell	*Soldanella montana*
Mountain sorrel	*Oxyria dignya*
Mountain speedwell	*Veronica montana*
Mountain tassel	*Soldanella montana*
Mountain valerian	*Valeriana montana*

Mount Atlas daisy	*Anacyclus depressus*
Mournful widow	*Scabiosa atropurpurea*
Mourning widow	*Geranium phaeum*
Moutan paeony	*Paeonia arborea*
	Paeonia moutan
	Paeonia suffruticosa
Mullein pink	*Agrostemma coronaria*
	Lychnis coronaria
Musk	*Mimulus moschatus*
Musk mallow	*Malva moschata*
Muskrat weed	*Thalictrum polygamum*
Musky saxifrage	*Saxifraga moschata*
Muster-john-henry	*Tagetes minuta*
Namaqualand daisy	*Dimorphotheca pluvialis*
	Dimorphotheca sinuata
	Venidium fastuosum
Nancy pretty	*Saxifraga × urbium*
Narrow-leaved inula	*Inula ensifolia*
Narrow-leaved zinnia	*Zinnia angustifolia*
	Zinnia haageana
Navelwort	*Omphalodes cappadocica*
	Omphalodes umbilicus
	Umbilicus rupestris
Nettle-leaved bellflower	*Campanula trachelium*
	Campanula urticifolia
New England aster	*Aster novae-angliae*
New York aster	*Aster novi-belgii*
New Zealand burr	*Acaena microphylla*
New Zealand flax	*Linum monogynum*
New Zealand lilac	*Hebe hulkeana*
	Veronica hulkeana
New Zealand willowherb	*Epilobium brunnescens*
Night-flowering catchfly	*Silene noctiflora*
Night-scented stock	*Matthiola bicornis*
Nine-joints	*Polygonum aviculare*
Nodding avens	*Geum rivale*
Nodding catchfly	*Silene pendula*
None-so-pretty	*Saxifraga × urbium*
Nonsuch	*Medicago lupulina*
Northern hawk's beard	*Crepis mollis*
Northern shore wort	*Mertensia maritima*
Northern wolfsbane	*Aconitum lycotonum lycotonum*

Pincushion flower

Nosebleed	*Achillea millefolium*
Notch-leaf statice	
	Limonium sinuatum
	Statice sinuatum
Nottingham catchfly	*Silene nutans*
Obedient plant	
	Physostegia virginiana
Old man	*Artemisia abrotanum*
Old woman	*Artemisia stellerana*
Opium poppy	*Papaver somniferum*
Orange balsam	*Impatiens capensis*
Orange daisy	*Erigeron aurantiacus*
Orange hawkweed	
	Hieracium aurantiacum
	Hieracium brunneocroceum
Orange mullein	
	Verbascum phlomoides
Oregano	*Origanum vulgare*
Oriental periwinkle	
	Rhazya orientalis
Oriental poppy	*Papaver orientale*
Oriental rocket	
	Sisymbrium orientale
Ornamental cabbage	
	Brassica oleracea acephala
Orpine	*Sedum telephium*
Oswega tea	*Monarda didyma*
Our Lady's milk thistle	
	Silybum marianum
Ox-eye chamomile	
	Anthemis tinctoria
Ox-eye daisy	
	Chrysanthemum leucanthemum
	Leucanthemum vulgare
Oxford ragwort	*Senecio squalidus*
Oxlip	*Primula elatior*
Oyster plant	*Mertensia maritima*
Ozark sundrops	
	Oenothera macrocarpa
	Oenothera missouriensis
Paigles	*Primula elatior*
Painted daisy	
	Chrysanthemum carinatum
	Chrysanthemum coccineum
	Pyrethrum hybridum
	Pyrethrum roseum
	Tanacetum coccineum
Painted spurge	
	Euphorbia heterophylla
Painted tongue	*Salpiglossis sinuata*
Pale flax	*Linum bienne*
Pale persicaria	
	Polygonum lapathifolium
Pale toadflax	*Linaria repens*
Pale willowherb	*Epilobium roseum*
Palm Springs daisy	
	Anthemis arabicus
Palsywort	*Primula veris*
Pampas grass	*Cortaderia argentea*
	Cortaderia selloana
Pansy	*Viola tricolor*

Paris daisy	
	Argyranthemum frutescens
Parrot's beak	*Lotus berthelotii*
Parrot's bill	*Clianthus puniceus*
Pasque flower	*Pulsatilla vulgaris*
Patience	*Impatiens sultanii*
	Impatiens wallerana
Patient lucy	*Impatiens sultanii*
	Impatiens wallerana
Peach-leaved bellflower	
	Campanula grandis
	Campanula latiloba
	Campanula persicifolia
Peacock poppy	*Papaver pavonium*
Pedlar's basket	*Linaria vulgaris*
Pee the bed	*Taraxacum officinale*
Pellitory	*Anacyclus pyrethrum*
Pellitory of Spain	
	Anacyclus pyrethrum
Pennycress	*Thlaspi arvense*
Pennywort	*Umbilicus rupestris*
Pepper saxifrage	*Silaum silaus*
Perennial cornflower	
	Centaurea dealbata
	Centaurea montana
Perennial honesty	*Lunaria rediviva*
Perennial morning glory	
	Ipomoea acuminata
Perennial pea	*Lathyrus latifolius*
Perennial sage	*Salvia superba*
Perennial sweet pea	
	Lathyrus latifolius
Perennial wall rocket	
	Diplotaxis tenuifolia
Perfoliate pennycress	
	Thlaspi perfoliatum
Perforate Saint John's wort	
	Hypericum perforatum
Persian buttercup	
	Ranunculus asiaticus
Persian everlasting pea	
	Lathyrus rotundifolius
Persian speedwell	*Veronica persica*
Persian violet	*Exacum affine*
Peruvian marigold	
	Helianthus annuus
Petty spurge	*Euphorbia peplis*
	Euphorbia peplus
Pheasant's eye	*Adonis annua*
Phu	*Valeriana officinalis*
Picotee	*Dianthus caryophyllus*
Pigmy hawk's beard	
	Crepis pygmaea
Pigmy sunflower	
	Actinea grandiflora
Pilewort	*Erechtites hieracifolia*
	Ranunculus ficaria
Pill-bearing spurge	*Euphorbia hirta*
Pincushion flower	
	Scabiosa atropurpurea
	Scabiosa caucasica

Pincushion plant	*Cenia barbata*
	Cotula barbata
	Cotula cenia
Pineapple sage	*Salvia rutilans*
Pink dandelion	*Crepis incana*
Pink evening primrose	
	Oenothera rosea
Pink-head knotweed	
	Polygonum capitatum
Pink oxalis	*Oxalis articulata*
Pink pokers	*Limonium suworowii*
Pink purslane	*Montia sibirica*
Pink rock-jasmine	
	Androsace carnea
Pink sand verbena	
	Abronia umbellata
Pink willowherb	*Epilobium roseum*
Piss the bed	*Taraxacum officinale*
Ploughman's spikenard	
	Inula conyza
Plume flower	*Celosia plumosa*
Plume poppy	*Bocconia cordata*
	Macleaya cordata
Poached egg flower	
	Limnanthes douglasii
Poached egg plant	
	Limnanthes douglasii
Poet's jessamine	
	Jasminum officinale
Poinsettia	*Euphorbia pulcherrima*
Poison potato	*Solanum carolinense*
Policeman's helmet	
	Impatiens glandulifera
Polyanthus	*Primula polyantha*
Poor man's weather glass	
	Anagallis arvensis
Pork and beans	
	Sedum × rubrotinctum
Poroporo	*Solanum laciniatum*
Potato bush	*Solanum rantonnetii*
Potato vine	*Solanum jasminoides*
Pot marigold	*Calendula officinalis*
Prairie blazing star	
	Liatris pycnostachya
Prairie evening primrose	
	Oenothera missouriensis
Prairie flax	*Linum lewisii*
Prairie lupin	*Lupinus lepidus*
Prayer plant	*Maranta leuconeura*
Pretty betsy	*Centranthus ruber*
Prickly phlox	*Gilia californica*
Prickly poppy	
	Argemone grandiflora
Pride of California	
	Lathyrus splendens
Primrose	*Primula acaulis*
	Primula vulgaris
Primrose jasmine	
	Jasminum mesnyi
	Jasminum primulinum

Prince of Wales' feathers	
	Celosia cristata plumosa
	Tanacetum densum amani
Prince's feather	
	Amaranthus hypochondriacus
Privet honeysuckle	*Lonicera pileata*
Procumbent cinquefoil	
	Potentilla anglica
Prophet flower	*Arnebia echioides*
Prostrate vervain	
	Verbena bracteata
Purple archangel	
	Lamium purpureum
Purple avens	*Geum rivale*
Purple boneset	
	Eupatorium purpureum
Purple bugloss	
	Echium plantagineum
Purple coneflower	
	Echinacea purpurea
Purple deadnettle	
	Lamium purpureum
Purple-eyed grass	
	Sisyrinchium douglasii
Purple granadilla	*Passiflora edulis*
Purple loosestrife	
	Lythrum salicaria
Purple mullein	
	verbascum phoeniceum
Purple sage	
	Salvia officinalis purpurascens
Purple saxifrage	
	Saxifraga oppositifolia
Purple spurge	*Euphorbia peplis*
	Euphorbia peplus
Purple toadflax	*Linaria purpurea*
Purple willowherb	
	Lythrum salicaria
Puya	*Puya alpestris*
	Puya berteroniana
Pyramidal bugle	*Ajuga pyramidalis*
Pyramidal saxifrage	
	Saxifraga cotyledon
Pyrenean valerian	
	Valeriana pyrenaica
Pyrethrum	
	Chrysanthemum coccineum
	Pyrethrum hybridum
	Pyrethrum roseum
	Tanacetum cinerariifolium
	Tanacetum coccineum
Queen Anne's thimbles	
	Gilia capitata
Queen of the meadow	
	Eupatorium purpureum
	Filipendula ulmaria
Queen of the night	
	Ipomoea noctiflora
Queen of the prairie	
	Filipendula rubra
	Spiraea lobata
Quicksilver weed	
	Thalictrum dioicum

POPULAR GARDEN PLANTS

Russian aconite

Ragged robin *Lychnis flos-cuculi*
Rag paper *Verbascum thapsus*
Ragwort *Senecio jacobaea*
Rainbow pink *Dianthus chinensis*
Rain daisy
Dimorphotheca pluvialis
Ramping fumitory
Fumaria capreolata
Rampion *Campanula rapunculus*
Rampion bellflower
Campanula rapunculus
Rat's tail statice
Limonium suworowii
Psylliostachys suworowii
Statice suworowii
Rattlesnake master
Liatris squarrosa
Rattlesnake root *Polygala senega*
Red baneberry *Actaea erythocarpa*
Actaea rubra
Actaea spicata rubra
Red campion *Lychnis dioica*
Melandrium diurnum
Silene dioica
Red catchfly *Lychnis viscaria*
Red deadnettle
Lamium purpureum
Red flax *Linum grandiflorum*
Linum rubrum
Red horned poppy
Glaucium corniculatum
Glaucium grandiflorum
Red legs *Polygonum persicaria*
Red maids *Calandrinia menziesii*
Red morning glory
Ipomoea coccinea
Red mountain spinach
Atriplex hortensis rubra
Red orach
Atriplex hortensis rubra
Red pepper *Capsicum annuum*
Red rattle *Pedicularis palustris*
Red ribbons *Clarkia concinna*
Euchardium concinna
Red root *Potentilla erecta*
Red shank *Polygonum persicaria*
Red star thistle
Centaurea calcitrapa
Red valerian *Centranthus ruber*
Kentranthus ruber
Redwood ivy
Vancouveria planipetala
Reflexed stonecrop
Sedum reflexum
Regal geraniums
Pelargonium × domesticum
Regal pelargoniums
Pelargonium × domesticum
Rest harrow *Ononis repens*
Robb's bonnet *Euphorbia robbiae*
Rock campion *Silene rupestris*

Rock cinquefoil *Potentilla rupestris*
Rock cranesbill
Geranium macrorrhizum
Rockery speedwell
Veronica prostrata
Rocket *Hesperis matronalis*
Rocket candytuft *Iberis amara*
Iberis coronaria
Rocket larkspur
Consolida ambigua
Delphinium ajacis
Rock fringe willowherb
Epilobium obcordatum
Rock purslane
Calandrinia umbellata
Rock sea lavender
Limonium binervosum
Rock soapwort
Saponaria ocymoides
Rock speedwell *Veronica fruticans*
Rock stonecrop
Sedum forsteranum
Rockwood lily *Ranunculus lyalli*
Roman chamomile
Anthemis nobilis
Roof houseleek
Sempervivum tectorum
Rose balsam *Impatiens balsamina*
Rosebay willowherb
Epilobium angustifolium
Rose campion
Agrostemma coronaria
Lychnis coronaria
Rose mallow *Lavatera trimestris*
Rose moss *Portulaca grandiflora*
Rose of heaven *Lychnis coeli-rosa*
Silene coeli-rosa
Silene oculata
Viscaria elegans
Rose periwinkle *Amsonia roseus*
Catharanthus roseus
Vinca rosea
Roseroot *Rhodiola rosea*
Sedum rhodiola
Sedum rosea
Rose root sedum *Sedum rosea*
Rose-scented geranium
Pelargonium capitatum
Rose-scented pelargonium
Pelargonium capitatum
Rose verbena *Verbena aubletia*
Verbena canadensis
Rough hawk's beard *Crepis biennis*
Round-leaved speedwell
Veronica filiformis
Rue *Ruta graveolens*
Rue-leaved saxifrage
Saxifraga tridactylotes
Running myrtle *Vinca minor*
Russian aconite
Aconitum orientale

Russian chamomile
Anthemis nobilis

Russian comfrey
Symphytum peregrinum
Symphytum × uplandicum

Russian knotgrass
Polygonum erectum

Russian statice
Limonium suworowii
Psylliostachys suworowii
Statice suworowii

Russian vine
Bilderdykia baldschuanicum
Polygonum baldschuanicum

Rusty foxglove Digitalis ferruginea

Sage Salvia officinalis

Sage brush Artemisia tridentata

Saint Barnaby's thistle
Centaurea solstitalis

Saint Benedict's thistle
Cnicus benedictus

Saint James' wort Senecio jacobaea

Saint John's chamomile
Anthemis sancti-johannis

Saint Mary's milk thistle
Silybum marianum

Saint Mary's thistle
Silybum marianum

Saint Patrick's cabbage
Saxifraga umbrosa
Saxifraga × urbium

Saint Peter's wort Primula veris

Salpiglossis Salpiglossis sinuata

Sand catchfly Silene conica

Sand flower Ammobium alatum

Sand phlox Phlox bifida

Sand pink Dianthus arenarius

Sand toadflax Linaria arenaria

Sand verbena Abronia latifolia

Saponaria Vaccaria pyramidata

Satin flower Clarkia amoena
Godetia grandiflora
Lunaria annua
Lunaria biennis
Sisyrinchium stratiatum

Satin leaf Heuchera hispida

Satin poppy
Meconopsis napaulensis

Savannah flower Echites andrewsii

Sawwort Serratula shawii

Scabwort Inula helenium

Scarlet bidi-bidi
Acaena microphylla

Scarlet flax Linum grandiflorum
Linum rubrum

Scarlet larkspur
Delphinium cardinale

Scarlet lobelia Lobelia cardinalis

Scarlet monkey flower
Mimulus cardinalis

Scarlet pimpernel
Anagallis arvensis

Scarlet plume Euphorbia fulgens

Scarlet sage Salvia splendens

Scarlet trumpet honeysuckle
Lonicera × brownii

Scarlet wisteria
Daubentonia tripetii
Sesbania tripetii

Scotch creeper
Tropaeolum speciosum

Scotch marigold
Calendula officinalis

Scotch thistle
Onopordum acanthium

Scottish bluebell
Campanula rotundifolia

Scottish flame flower
Tropaeolum speciosum

Sea alyssum Lobularia maritima

Sea campion Silene maritima
Silene vulgaris maritima

Sea fig Cryophytum crystallinum
Mesembryanthemum
crystallinum

Sea holly Eryngium maritimum

Sea pea Lathyrus japonicus
Lathyrus maritimus

Sea pearlwort Sagina maritima

Sea pink Armeria maritima

Sea poppy Glaucium corniculatum
Glaucium grandiflorum

Sea spurge Euphorbia paralias

Senega Polygala senega

Serbian bellflower
Campanula poscharskyana

Setterwort Helleborus foetidus

Shaggy hawkweed
Hieracium villosum

Shaggy starfish Stapelia hirsuta

Shamrock Medicago lupulina
Oxalis acetosella

Shasta daisy
Chrysanthemum maximum
Chrysanthemum × superbum
Leucanthemum × superbum

Sheep's fescue Festuca ovina

Shell flower Moluccella laevis

Shepherd's barometer
Anagallis arvensis

Shepherd's club Verbascum thapsus

Shepherd's crook
Lysimachia clethroides

Shepherd's knot
Potentilla tormentilla

Shield nasturtium
Tropaeolum lobbianum
Tropaeolum peltophorum

Shining cranesbill
Geranium lucidum

Shining scabious Scabiosa lucida

POPULAR GARDEN PLANTS

Shoo-fly *Nicandra physalodes*

Shooting star
Dodecatheon alpinum
Dodecatheon meadia

Short-leaved gentian
Gentiana brachyphylla

Show geraniums
Pelargonium × domesticum

Show pelargoniums
Pelargonium × domesticum

Shrubby musk
Mimulus aurantiacus

Shrubby penstemon
Penstemon cordifolius

Siberian bugloss
Brunnera macrophylla

Siberian wallflower
Cheiranthus × allionii
Erysimum asperum
Erysimum perofskianum

Sicily thyme *Thymus nitidus*
Thymus richardii nitidus

Sierra shooting star
Dodecatheon jeffreyi

Signet marigold *Tagetes signata*
Tagetes tenuifolia

Silver lace vine
Bilderdykia aubertii
Polygonum aubertii

Silver ragwort *Senecio bicolor*

Silver sage *Salvia argentea*

Silver thistle
Onopordum arabicum
Onopordum nervosum

Silver weed *Potentilla anserina*

Silvery cinquefoil
Potentilla anserina

Simpler's joy *Verbena hastata*

Skyrocket *Gilia coronopifolia*
Gilia rubra

Small balsam *Impatiens parviflora*

Small catchfly *Silene gallica*

Small mallow *Malva pusilla*

Small scabious *Scabiosa columbaria*

Small yellow foxglove
Digitalis lutea

Smooth hawk's beard
Crepis capillaris

Snakeroot *Polygala senega*

Snakeweed *Polygonum bistorta*

Snapdragon *Antirrhinum majus*

Sneezeweed *Achillea ptarmica*
Helenium autumnale

Sneezewort *Achillea ptarmica*

Snow-in-summer
Helichrysum thyrsoideum
Ozothamnus thyrsoideum

Snow-on-the-mountain
Euphorbia marginata

Snow poppy *Eomecon chionanthe*

Soapwort *Saponaria officinalis*

Soft cranesbill *Geranium molle*

Soldiers and sailors
Pulmonaria officinalis

Southernwood
Artemisia abrotanum

Sow's ear *Stachys byzantina*

Spaniard *Aciphylla colensoi*

Spanish catchfly *Silene otites*

Spanish pellitory
Anacyclus pyrethrum

Spanish poppy
Papaver rupifragum

Spear-leaved willowherb
Epilobium lanceolatum

Speedwell *Veronica officinalis*

Spider flower *Cleome spinosa*

Spider houseleek
Sempervivum arachnoideum

Spiderworts
Tradescantia × andersoniana
Tradescantia virginiana

Spike gayfeather *Liatris spicata*

Spiked loosestrife
Lythrum salicaria

Spiked rampion
Phyteuma spicatum

Spiked speedwell *Veronica spicata*

Spiny alyssum *Alyssum spinosum*

Spotted deadnettle
Lamium maculatum

Spotted dog *Pulmonaria officinalis*

Spotted gentian *Gentiana punctata*

Spotted hawkweed
Hieracium maculatum

Spotted loosestrife
Lysimachia punctata

Spotted medick *Medicago arabica*

Spotted touch-me-not
Impatiens biflora
Impatiens capensis

Spreading bellflower
Campanula patula

Spreading globe flower
Trollius laxus

Spring adonis *Adonis vernalis*

Spring anemone *Anemone vernalis*
Pulsatilla vernalis

Spring beauty *Montia perfoliata*

Spring bell *Sisyrinchium douglasii*

Spring cinquefoil
Potentilla tabernaemontani
Potentilla verna

Spring gentian *Gentiana verna*
Gentiana verna angulosa

Spring sandwort *Minuartia verna*

Spring speedwell *Veronica verna*

Spring vetch *Lathyrus vernuus*

Spurred bellflower
Campanula alliarifolia

Square-stalked willowherb
Epilobium tetragonum

Square-stemmed
Saint John's wort

Square-stemmed Saint John's
wort *Hypericum tetrapterum*

Squirrel corn *Dicentra canadensis*

Staggerweed *Dicentra canadensis*

Staggerwort *Senecio jacobaea*

Standing cypress
Gilia coronopifolia
Gilia rubra

Star daisy *Lindheimera texana*

Stardust *Gilia hybrida*
Gilia lutea
Leptosiphon hybridus

Starfish plant *Stapelia variegata*

Star ipomoea *Ipomoea coccinea*

Star of Bethlehem
Campanula isophylla

Star of the veldt
Dimorphotheca aurantiaca
Dimorphotheca sinuata

Starry saxifrage *Saxifraga stellaris*
Saxifraga stellata

Star thistle *Centaurea calcitrapa*

Starwort *Aletris farinosa*

Statice *Limonium latifolium*
Limonium sinuatum
Statice latifolium

Stavesacre
Delphinium staphisagria

Steeple bellflower
Campanula pyramidalis

Steeple bells *Cobaea scandens*

Stemless gentian *Gentiana acaulis*

Sticklewort *Agrimonia eupatoria*

Sticky catchfly *Lychnis viscaria*

Sticky groundsel *Senecio viscosus*

Sticky phacelia *Eutoca viscida*
Phacelia viscida

Sticky sage *Salvia glutinosa*

Sticky sandwort *Minuartia viscosa*

Stinking bob
Geranium robertianum

Stinking hawk's beard
Crepis foetida

Stinking hellebore
Helleborus foetidus

Stinkweed *Thlaspi arvense*

Stock *Matthiola incana*

Stokes's aster *Stokesia cyanea*
Stokesia laevis

Stone orpine *Sedum reflexum*

Strawbells *Uvularia perfoliata*

Strawberry geranium
Saxifraga sarmentosa
Saxifraga stolonifera

Strawflower
Helichrysum bracteatum

Striated catchfly *Silene conica*

String of beads *Senecio rowleyanus*

String of pearls *Senecio rowleyanus*

String of sovereigns
Lysimachia nummularia

Sturt's desert pea
Clianthus speciosus

Sugar scoop *Tiarella unifoliata*

Sulphur cinquefoil *Potentilla recta*

Summer adonis *Adonis aestivalis*

Summer cypress
Kochia scoparia trichophylla

Summer forget-me-not
Anchusa capensis

Summer jasmine
Jasminum officinale

Summer pheasant's eye
Adonis aestivalis

Summer starwort *Erinus alpinus*

Sundrops *Oenothera fruticosa*
Oenothera linearis

Sunflower *Helianthus annuus*

Sun plant *Portulaca grandiflora*

Sunray *Helipterum manglesii*
Rhodanthe manglesii

Sun spurge *Euphorbia helioscopia*

Swan river daisy
Brachycome iberidifolia

Swan river everlasting
Helipterum manglesii
Rhodanthe manglesii

Sweat root *Polemonium reptans*

Sweet alison *Lobularia maritima*

Sweet alyssum
Alyssum maritimum
Lobularia maritima

Sweet bergamot *Monarda didyma*

Sweet bugle *Lycopus virginicus*

Sweet four o'clock
Mirabilis longiflora

Sweet golden rod *Solidago odora*

Sweet mace *Tagetes lucida*

Sweet nancy *Achillea ageratum*

Sweet pea *Lathyrus odoratus*

Sweet rocket *Hesperis matronalis*

Sweet scabious *Erigeron annuus*
Scabiosa atropurpurea

Sweet-scented marigold
Tagetes lucida

Sweet spurge *Euphorbia dulcis*

Sweet sultan *Centaurea imperialis*
Centaurea moschata

Sweet violet *Viola odorata*

Sweet william *Dianthus barbatus*

Sweet william catchfly
Silene armeria

Swine's snout *Taraxacum officinale*

Tagetes *Tagetes signata*
Tagetes tenuifolia

Tahoka daisy *Aster tenacetifolius*

Tall gayfeather *Liatris scariosa*

Tall meadow rue
Thalictrum polygamum

Tall nasturtium *Tropaeolum majus*

Tall rocket *Sisymbrium altissimum*

POPULAR GARDEN PLANTS

Virginia bluebell

Tangier pea *Lathyrus tingitanus*
Tangier scarlet pea
    Lathyrus tingitanus
Tansy *Tanacetum vulgare*
Tansy phacelia
    Phacelia tanacetifolia
Tartarian honeysuckle
    Lonicera tatarica
Tassel flower
    Amaranthus caudatus
Telegraph plant *Desmodium gyrans*
Ten-week stock
    Matthiola incana annua
Thick-leaved stonecrop
    Sedum dasyphyllum
Thoroughwort
    Eupatorium perfoliatum
Thyme-leaved speedwell
    Veronica serpyllifolia
Texas blue-bonnet
    Lupinus subcarnosus
    Lupinus texensis
Thousand weed
    Achillea millefolium
Tickseed *Coreopsis grandiflora*
Tidy tips *Layia elegans*
    Layia platyglossa
Toad cactus *Stapelia variegata*
Toadflax *Linaria maroccana*
Toad plant *Stapelia variegata*
Tobacco *Nicotiana tabacum*
Tobacco plant *Nicotiana affinis*
    Nicotiana alata
Tormentil *Potentilla erecta*
Touch-me-not
    Impatiens balsamina
    Impatiens noli-tangere
Town hall clock
    Adoxa moschatellina
Trailing bellflower
    Cyananthus lobatus
Trailing gazania
    Gazania leucolaena
    Gazania rigens leucolaena
    Gazania uniflora
Trailing lobelia
    Lobelia erinus pendula
Trailing myrtle *Vinca minor*
Trailing violet *Viola hederacea*
Transvaal daisy *Gerbera jamesonii*
Treacle mustard
    Erysimum cheiranthoides
Treasure flowers
    Gazania × hybrids
Tree paeony *Paeonia arborea*
    Paeonia moutan
    Paeonia suffruticosa
Trinity flowers
    Tradescantia × andersoniana
    Tradescantia virginiana
Tropaeolum
    Tropaeolum polyphyllum

True clary *Salvia sclarea*
True columbine *Aquilegia vulgaris*
True michaelmas daisy
    Aster novi-belgii
Trumpet gentian *Gentiana acaulis*
    Gentiana kochiana
Trumpet honeysuckle
    Lonicera sempervirens
Trumpet vine *Campsis radicans*
Tuberous pea *Lathyrus tuberosus*
Tufted alkanet *Anchusa caespitosa*
Tufted harebell
    Wahlenbergia albomarginata
Tufted pansy *Viola cornuta*
Tufted saxifrage
    Saxifraga caespitosa
Tulip poppy *Papaver glaucum*
Tumbleweed
    Amaranthus graecizans
Tumbling ted *Saponaria ocymoides*
Turban buttercup
    Ranunculus asiaticus
Turkey corn *Dicentra canadensis*
Turkey pea *Dicentra canadensis*
Turkish tobacco *Nicotiana rustica*
Tussock bellflower
    Campanula carpatica
Twiggy mullein
    Verbascum virgatum
Twinberry *Lonicera involucrata*
Twinspur *Diascia barberae*
Umbrella plant
    Peltiphyllum peltatum
    Saxifraga peltata
Unicorn plant *Martynia louisiana*
    Proboscidea jussieui
Upright cinquefoil *Potentilla recta*
Upright spurge *Euphorbia stricta*
Valley lupin *Lupinus vallicola*
Vanilla leaf *Achlys triphylla*
    Liatris odoratissima
Velvet flower *Salpiglossis sinuata*
Velvet groundsel *Senecio petasites*
Velvet mullein *Verbascum thapsus*
Venus's looking glass
    Legousia speculum-veneris
    Specularia speculum
    Specularia speculum-veneris
Venus's navelwort
    Omphalodes linifolia
Vernal gentian *Gentiana verna*
Vernal sandwort *Minuartia verna*
Vervain *Verbena lasiostachys*
    Verbena officinalis
    Verbena rigida
Violet cress *Ionopsidium acaule*
Viper's bugloss *Echium lycopsis*
    Echium plantagineum
    Echium vulgare
Virginia bluebell
    Mertensia virginica

Virginia cowslip

Virginia cowslip
    Mertensia virginica
Virginian cowslip
    Mertensia pulmonarioides
Virginia(n) stock
    Cheiranthus maritimus
    Malcolmia maritima
Wall daisy   *Erigeron karkinskianus*
Wall fumitory   *Fumaria muralis*
Wall harebell
    Campanula portenschlagiana
Wall mustard   *Diplotaxis tenuifolia*
Wall pennywort
    Umbilicus rupestris
Wall-pepper   *Sedum acre*
Wall rocket   *Diplotaxis tenuifolia*
Wall speedwell   *Veronica arvensis*
Wandering jenny
    Lysimachia nummularia
Wandering jew
    Tradescantia albiflora
    Tradescantia fluminensis
Water avens   *Geum rivale*
Water bugle   *Lycopus virginicus*
Water cowslip   *Caltha palustris*
Water flower   *Geum urbanum*
Water forget-me-not
    Myosotis palustris
Water pimpernel
    Veronica beccabunga
Waxbells   *Kirengeshoma palmata*
Weasel's snout
    Antirrhunum majus
    Lamium album
    Lamium galeobdolon
Weld   *Reseda luteola*
Welsh poppy   *Meconopsis cambrica*
Western bleeding heart
    Dicentra formosa
Western mugwort
    Artemisia gnaphalodes
    Artemisia ludoviciana
    Artemisia purshiana
White amaranth   *Amaranthus albus*
White bachelor's buttons
    Ranunculus aconitifolius
White baneberry   *Actaea alba*
    Actaea pachypoda
    Actaea spicata alba
White buttercup
    Ranunculus amplexicaulis
White campion   *Silene alba*
    Silene latifolia
White cinquefoil   *Potentilla alba*
White cohosh   *Actaea alba*
White comfrey
    Symphytum orientale
White cup   *Nierembergia repens*
White deadnettle   *Lamium album*
White false hellebore
    Veratrum album

White flax   *Linum catharticum*
White fumitory
    Fumaria capreolata
White helleborine
    Veratrum album
    Veratrum viride
White jasmine   *Jasminum officinale*
White-leaved everlasting
    Helichrysum angustifolium
White lupin   *Lupinus albus*
White mignonette   *Reseda alba*
White mugwort
    Artemisia lactiflora
    Artemisia purshiana
White mullein   *Verbascum lychnitis*
    Verbascum thapsus
White pasque flower
    Pulsatilla alba
White poppy   *Papaver somniferum*
White purslane
    Euphorbia corollata
White rocket   *Diplotaxis erucoides*
White sage   *Artemisia gnaphalodes*
    Artemisia ludoviciana
    Artemisia purshiana
White sails   *Spathiphyllum wallisii*
White sanicle
    Eupatorium ageratoides
    Eupatorium rugosum
White snakeroot
    Eupatorium ageratoides
    Eupatorium rugosum
White stonecrop   *Sedum album*
White vervain   *Verbena urticifolia*
White weed
    Leucanthemum vulgare
Whorlflower   *Morina longifolia*
Wig knapweed   *Centaurea phrygia*
Wild balsam
    Impatiens noli-tangere
Wild candytuft   *Iberis amara*
Wild carnation
    Dianthus caryophyllus
Wild clary   *Salvia verbenacea*
Wild cranesbill
    Geranium maculatum
Wild geranium
    Geranium maculatum
Wild horehound
    Eupatorium teucrifolium
Wild horsehound
    Eupatorium teucrifolium
Wild indigo   *Baptisia tinctoria*
Wild marjoram   *Origanum vulgare*
Wild mignonette   *Reseda lutea*
Wild paeony   *Paeonia officinalis*
Wild pansy   *Viola tricolor*
Wild pea   *Lathyrus sylvestris*
Wild pink   *Dianthus plumarius*
Wild sage   *Salvia horminoides*
    Salvia nemorosa

POPULAR GARDEN PLANTS

Wild spaniard   *Aciphylla colensoi*

Wild sunflower   *Inula helenium*

Wild thyme   *Thymus drucei*
Thymus serpyllum

Wild vanilla   *Liatris odoratissima*

Wild woodbine
Lonicera periclymenum

Willow bellflower
Campanula grandis
Campanula latiloba
Campanula persicifolia

Willow gentian
Gentiana asclepiadea

Willow-leaf ox-eye
Buphthalum salicifolium

Wind poppy
Stylomecon heterophylla

Winged everlasting
Ammobium alatum

Winged pea   *Lotus berthelotii*

Winged statice
Limonium sinuatum
Statice sinuatum

Winter cherry
Solanum capsicastrum

Winter jasmine
Jasminum nudiflorum

Winter savory   *Satureia montana*

Wishbone flower   *Torenia fournieri*

Witch's gloves   *Digitalis purpurea*

Wolfsbane   *Aconitum lycotonum*
Aconitum lycotonum vulgaria
Aconitum vulparia

Wood avens   *Geum urbanum*

Wood betony   *Betonica officinalis*
Stachys betonica
Stachys officinalis

Woodbine   *Lonicera periclymenum*

Wood cranesbill
Geranium sylvaticum

Wood forget-me-not
Myosotis sylvatica

Wood groundsel   *Senecio sylvaticus*

Wood pimpernel
Lysimachia nemorum
Lysimachia vulgaris

Wood pink   *Dianthus inodorus*
Dianthus sylvestris

Wood poppy
Stylophorum diphyllum

Wood ragwort   *Senecio nemorensis*

Wood sorrel   *Oxalis acetosella*

Wood speedwell
Veronica montana

Wood spurge
Euphorbia angydaloides

Wood woundwort
Stachys sylvatica

Woody nightshade
Solanum dulcamara

Woolly betony   *Stachys byzantina*
Stachys lanata
Stachys olympica

Woolly foxglove   *Digitalis lanata*

Woolly hawkweed
Hieracium lanatum

Woolly mullein   *Verbascum thapsus*

Woolly speedwell
Veronica candida
Veronica incana

Woolly thistle
Onopordum acanthium

Woolly woundwort
Stachys byzantina

Wormwood   *Artemisia absinthium*

Woundwort   *Betonica grandiflora*
Betonica macrantha
Solidago virgaurea
Stachys grandiflora
Stachys macrantha

Yarrow   *Achillea millefolium*

Yellow aconite
Aconitum napellus lycotonum

Yellow archangel
Galeobdolon luteum
Lamiastrum galeobdolon
Lamium galeobdolon

Yellow bachelor's buttons
Ranunculus acris

Yellow bellflower
Campanula thyrsoides

Yellow bird's nest
Monotropa hypophega

Yellow bugle   *Ajuga chamaepitys*

Yellow bush tobacco
Nicotiana glauca

Yellow centaury   *Cicendia filiformis*

Yellow chinese poppy
Meconopsis integrifolia

Yellow daisy   *Rudbeckia hirta*

Yellow flax   *Linum flavum*

Yellow forget-me-not
Myosotis discolor

Yellow gentian   *Gentiana lutea*

Yellow horned poppy
Glaucium flavum
Glaucium luteum

Yellow loosestrife
Lysimachia punctata
Lysimachia vulgaris

Yellow lupin   *Lupinus luteus*

Yellow meadow rue
Thalictrum flavum

Yellow medick   *Medicago falcata*

Yellow monkshood
Aconitum anthora

Yellow mountain saxifrage
Saxifraga aizoides

Yellow ox-eye
Buphthalum salicifolium

Yellow pheasant's eye
Adonis vernalis

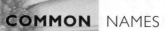

Yellow pimpernel

Yellow pimpernel
    Lysimachia nemorum
Yellow rest harrow   *Ononis natrix*
Yellow scabious
    Scabiosa columbaria ochraleuca
Yellow sorrel   *Oxalis corniculata*
Yellow star thistle
    Centaurea solstitalis
Yellow toadflax   *Linaria vulgaris*
Yellow tuft   *Alyssum argenteum*
    Alyssum murale
Yellow vetchling   *Lathyrus aphaca*

Yellow violet   *Viola saxatilis*
Yellow willowherb
    Lysimachia vulgaris
Yellow woundwort   *Stachys recta*
Yerba mansa
    Anemonopsis californica
Youth and old age   *Zinnia elegans*
Zonal geraniums
    Pelargonium × hortorum
Zonal pelargoniums
    Pelargonium × hortorum
Zulu giant   *Stapelia gigantea*

TREES, BUSHES, AND SHRUBS

It is often said that the difference between trees and shrubs is simple; trees have a single woody stem from which branches grow to form a crown whereas a shrub has several woody stems rising from ground level, forming a crown. But this is over-simplification. The exact shape of a tree can be completely altered by wind action, by a difference in spacing or even by artificial pruning.

A bush is generally defined as a woody plant that is between a shrub and a tree in size.

Silver maple –
Acer saccharinum

COMMON NAMES

Aaron's beard

Aaron's beard	
	Hypericum calycinum
Abaca	*Musa textilis*
Abata cola	*Cola acuminata*
Abele	*Populus alba*
Abelitzia	*Zelkova abelicea*
Abyssinian euphorbia	
	Euphorbia trigona
Abyssinian tea	*Catha edulis*
Aceituno	*Simarouba glauca*
Achiote	*Bixa orellana*
Achocha	*Cyclanthera pedata*
Adam's apple	
	Tabernaemontana coronaria
	Tabernaemontana divaricata
Adam's laburnum	
	+ *Laburnocytisus adami*
Adam's needle	*Yucca filamentosa*
	Yucca gloriosa
Adventure bay pine	
	Phyllocladus asplenifolius
Afara	*Terminalia superba*
Afghan ash	
	Fraxinus xanthoxyloides
Afghan cherry	
	Prunus jacquemontii
African boxwood	*Myrsine africana*
African bread tree	
	Treculia africana
African cypress	
	Widdringtonia cupressoides
African fern pine	
	Podocarpus gracilior
African hemp	*Sparmannia africana*
African juniper	*Juniperus procera*
African locust	*Parkia biglobosa*
African locust bean	
	Parkia filicoidea
African mahogany	*Khaya nysasica*
	Khaya senegalensis
African milk barrel	
	Euphorbia horrida
African milkbush	
	Synadenium grantii
African milk tree	
	Euphorbia trigona
African nutmeg	
	Monodora myristica
African oil palm	*Elaeis guineensis*
African peach	*Nauclea latifolia*
African red alder	*Cunonia capensis*
African tulip tree	
	Spathodea campanulata
African walnut	*Coula edulis*
African yellowwood	
	Podocarpus elongatus
Aguacate	*Persea americana*
Ague tree	*Sassafras albidum*
Ahuehuete	
	Taxodium mucronatum
Ailanto	*Ailanthus glandulosa*

Aino mulberry	*Morus australis*
Akee	*Blighia sapida*
Alabama snow wreath	
	Neviusia alabamensis
Alaska cedar	
	Chamaecyparis nootkatensis
Alaska yellow cedar	
	Chamaecyparis nootkatensis
Albany bottlebrush	
	Callistemon speciosus
Alberta white spruce	
	Picea glaucaalbertiana
Alcock's spruce	*Picea alcoquiana*
	Picea bicolor
Alder buckthorn	*Frangula alnus*
	Rhamnus frangula
Alder-leaved rowan	
	Sorbus alnifolia
Aleppo pine	*Pinus halepensis*
Alerce	*Fitzroya cupressoides*
	Tetraclinis articulata
Alexander palm	
	Ptychosperma elegans
Alexandra palm	
	Archontophoenix alexandrae
Alexandrian laurel	
	Calophyllum inophyllum
	Danae racemosa
Alexandrian senna	*Cassia acutifolia*
	Cassia senna
Algarroba bean	*Ceratonia siliqua*
Algarrobo	*Prosopis chilensis*
	Prosopis juliflora
Algerian ash	
	Fraxinus xanthoxyloides dimorpha
Algerian fir	*Abies numidica*
Algerian oak	*Quercus canariensis*
	Quercus mirbeckii
Allamanda	*Allamanda cathartica*
Alleghany plum	
	Prunus alleghaniensis
Alleghany service berry	
	Amelanchier laevis
Alleghany spurge	
	Pachysandra procumbens
Alligator apple	*Annona glabra*
	Annona palustris
Alligator juniper	
	Juniperus deppeana pachyphlaea
	Juniperus pachyphloea
Alligator pear	*Persea americana*
All saint's cherry	
	Prunus cerasus semperflorens
Allspice	*Pimenta dioica*
	Pimenta officinalis
Almond	*Prunus dulcis*
Almond-leaved pear	
	Pyrus amygdaliformis
Almond willow	*Salix amygdaloides*
	Salix triandra

TREES, BUSHES, AND SHRUBS

Alpen rose
    Rhododendron ferrugineum
Alpine ash   *Eucalyptus delegatensis*
    Eucalyptus gigantea
Alpine azalea   *Azalea procumbens*
    Chamaecistus procumbens
    Loiseleuria procumbens
Alpine buckthorn   *Rhamnus alpina*
Alpine celery-topped pine
    Phyllocladus alpinus
Alpine currant   *Ribes alpinum*
Alpine elder   *Sambucus racemosa*
Alpine fir   *Abies lasiocarpa*
    Abies amabilis
Alpine gum   *Eucalyptus archeri*
Alpine laburnum
    Laburnum alpinum
Alpine larch   *Larix lyalli*
Alpine laurel   *Kalmia microphylla*
Alpine rose   *Rosa alpina*
Alpine totara   *Podocarpus nivalis*
Alpine whitebeam
    Sorbus chamaemespilus
Altai mountain thorn
    Crataegus altaica
Althaea   *Althaea frutex*
    Hibiscus syriacus
Amatungulu   *Carissa grandiflora*
    Carissa macrocarpa
Ambarella   *Spondias cytherea*
Ambash   *Herminiera elaphroxylon*
Amboina pine   *Agathis dammara*
Amboina pitch tree   *Agathis alba*
American arbor-vitae
    Thuya occidentalis
American ash   *Fraxinus americana*
American aspen
    Populus tremuloides
American basswood
    Tilia americana
American beautybush
    Kolkwitzia amabilis
American beech   *Fagus americana*
    Fagus grandifolia
American black cherry
    Prunus serotina
American blackcurrant
    Ribes americanum
American bladdernut
    Staphylea trifolia
American boxwood   *Cornus florida*
American chestnut
    Castanea dentata
American colombo
    Frasera carolinensis
American crab apple
    Malus angustifolia
American cranberry
    Oxycoccus macrocarpus
    Vaccinium macrocarpon
American dogwood   *Cornus sericea*

American elder
    Sambucus canadensis
American elm   *Ulmus americana*
American filbert
    Corylus americana
American fringe tree
    Chionanthus virginicus
American green alder
    Alnus crispa mollis
American hazel   *Corylus americana*
American holly   *Ilex opaca*
American hop-hornbeam
    Ostrya virginiana
American hornbeam
    Carpinus caroliniana
American judas tree
    Cercis canadensis
American larch   *Larix laricina*
American laurel   *Kalmia latifolia*
American lime   *Tilia americana*
American mangrove
    Rhizophora mangle
American mastic tree   *Schinus molle*
American mock orange
    Prunus caroliniana
American mountain ash
    Sorbus americana
American mulberry   *Morus rubra*
American oil palm
    Elaeis melanococca
    Elaeis oleifera
American olive
    Osmanthus americanus
American persimmon
    Diospyros virginiana
American pistachio   *Pistacia texana*
American plane
    Platanus occidentalis
American red buckeye
    Aesculus pavia
American redbud   *Cercis canadensis*
American red elder
    Sambucus pubens
American red oak   *Quercus rubra*
American red pine   *Pinus resinosa*
American red plum
    Prunus americana
American red spruce   *Picea rubens*
American sarsaparilla
    Aralia niducaulis
American silverberry
    Elaeagnus argentea
    Elaeagnus commutata
American sloe
    Prunus alleghaniensis
American smoke tree
    Cotinus americanus
    Cotinus obovatus
American spikenard
    Aralia racemosa

American storax
Styrax americanus

American swamp laurel
Kalmia glauca

American sweet gum
Liquidambar styraciflua

American sycamore
Platanus occidentalis

American wayfaring tree
Viburnum lantanoides

American white ash *Fraxinus alba*
Fraxinus americana

American white oak
Quercus bicolor

American wild plum
Prunus americana

American yellowwood
Cladrastis lutea
Cladrastis tinctoria

American yew *Taxus brevifolia*
Taxus canadensis

Ammoniacum
Dorema ammoniacum

Amur cork tree
Phellodendron amurense

Amur lilac *Syringa amurensis*

Amur lime *Tilia amurensis*

Amur maple *Acer ginnala*
Acer tataricum ginnala

Amur privet *Ligustrum amurense*

Anacahuita *Cordia boissieri*

Anaconoa *Cordia sebestena*

Ana tree *Acacia albida*

Andaman marble *Diospyros kurzii*

Angelica tree *Aralia elata*
Aralia spinosa

Angel's trumpet *Datura suaveolens*

Angelwing jasmine
Jasminum nitidum

Aniseed tree *Illicium floridanum*

Anglo-Japanese yew *Taxus media*

Anime resin *Hymenaea courbaril*

Aniseed tree *Illicium anisatum*

Annatto *Bixa orellana*

Annual mallow *Lavatera trimestris*

Annual poinsettia
Euphorbia heterophylla

Anona blanca *Annona diversifolia*

Antarctic beech
Nothofagus antarctica

Anthony nut *Staphylea pinnata*

Ant tree *Triplaris americana*

Apache pine *Pinus engelmannii*

Apache plume *Fallugia paradoxa*

Apamata *Tabebuia serratifolia*

Apiesdoring *Acacia galpinii*

Apothecary's rose
Rosa gallica officinalis
Rosa officinalis

Appalachian tea *Ilex glabra*

Appleblossom cassia
Cassia javanica

Appleblosson senna
Cassia javanica

Apple box *Eucalyptus bridgesiana*

Apple guava *Psidium guajava*

Apple gum *Eucalyptus clavigera*

Apple-ring acacia *Acacia albida*

Apple rose *Rosa villosa*

Apricot *Prunus armeniaca*

Apricot plum *Prunus simonii*

Arabian coffee *Coffea arabica*

Arabian jasmine *Jasminum sambac*

Arabian tea *Catha edulis*

Araroba *Andira araroba*

Arar tree *Tetraclinis articulata*

Arbor-vitae *Thuya occidentalis*

Arching forsythia
Forsythia suspensa fortunei

Arctic willow *Salix arctica*

Areca-nut palm *Areca catechu*

Areca palm
Chrysalidocarpus lutescens

Areng palm *Arenga pinnata*

Argan tree *Argania spinosa*

Argyle apple *Eucalyptus cinerea*

Arizona ash *Fraxinus velutina*

Arizona cork fir
Abies lasiocarpa arizonica

Arizona cypress
Cupressus arizonica

Arizona pine
Pinus ponderosa arizonica

Arizona walnut *Juglans major*

Arkansas rose *Rosa arkansana*

Armand's pine *Pinus armandii*

Armenian oak *Quercus pontica*

Arolla pine *Pinus cembra*

Aronia prunifolia
Purple chokeberry

Arrow broom *Genista sagittalis*

Arrowwood
Viburnum acerifolium
Viburnum dentatum

Arroyo willow *Salix lasiolepis*

Asgara *Pterostyrax hispida*

Ashe juniper *Juniperus ashei*

Ashe magnolia *Magnolia ashei*

Ashleaf maple *Acer negundo*

Asian pear *Pyrus pyrifolia*

Asiatic sweetleaf
Symplocos paniculata

Asoka tree *Saraca indica*

Aspen *Populus tremula*

Assai palm *Euterpe edulis*
Euterpe oleracea

Assam rubber *Ficus belgica*
Ficus elastica

TREES, BUSHES, AND SHRUBS

Balsam willow

Assam tea
  Camellia sinensis assamensis
Assyrian plum   *Cordia myxa*
Athel   *Tamarix aphylla*
Atlantic white cedar
  Chamaecyparis thyoides
Atlas cedar   *Cedrus atlantica*
August plum   *Prunus americana*
Australian banyan *Ficus macrocarpa*
  Ficus macrophylla
Australian beech
  Eucalyptus polyanthemos
  Nothofagus moorei
Australian beefwood
  Casuarina equisetifolia
Australian blackwood
  Acacia melanoxylon
Australian bottle plant
  Jatropha podagrica
Australian bower plant
  Pandorea jasminoides
Australian brush cherry
  Eugenia myrtifolia
  Syzygium paniculatum
Australian cabbage palm
  Corypha australis
  Livistona australis
Australian cherry
  Exocarpus cupressiformis
Australian fan palm
  Corypha australis
  Livistona australis
Australian fever bush
  Alstonia scholaris
Australian finger lime
  Microcitrus australasica
Australian forest oak
  Casuarina torulosa
Australian heath   *Epacris impressa*
Australian honeysuckle
  Banksia grandis
Australian ivy palm
  Brassaia actinophylla
Australian laurel
  Pittosporum tobira
Australian lilac
  Hardenbergia monophylla
Australian mountain ash
  Eucalyptus regnans
Australian nut
  Macadamia integrifolia
Australian pepper tree
  Schinus molle
Australian pine
  Araucaria heterophylla
  Casuarina equisetifolia
Australian river oak
  Casuarina cunninghamiana
Australian rosemary
  Westringia fruticosa
Australian round lime
  Microcitrus australis

Australian sarsaparilla
  Hardenbergia violacea
Australian smokebush
  Conospermum stoechadis
Australian tea tree
  Leptospermum laevigatum
Australian umbrella tree
  Brassaia actinophylla
Australian willow myrtle
  Agonis flexuosa
Austrian briar   *Rosa foetida*
Austrian copper rose
  Rosa foetida bicolor
Austrian pear   *Pyrus austriaca*
Austrian pine   *Pinus nigra*
  Pinus nigra caramanica
  Pinus nigra nigra
Austrian whitebeam
  Sorbus austriaca
Austrian yellow rose   *Rosa foetida*
Autumn cherry
  Prunus subhirtella autumnalis
Autumn olive *Elaeagnus umbellata*
Avaram   *Cassia auriculata*
Avignon berry *Rhamnus infectoria*
Avocado pear   *Persea americana*
Awl tree   *Morinda citrifolia*
Ayrshire rose   *Rosa arvensis*
Azarole   *Crataegus azarolus*
Azediracta   *Melia azedarach*
Azorean holly   *Ilex perado*
Azure ceanothus
  Ceanothus caeruleus
Babassu   *Orbignya barbosiana*
Babassu palm   *Orbignya speciosa*
Babul   *Acacia nilotica*
Bachelor's buttons
  Kerria japonica plena
Bael tree   *Aegle marmelos*
Bag-flower
  Clerodendrum thomsoniae
Balata   *Manilkara bidentata*
Bald cypress *Taxodium distichum*
Baldhip rose   *Rosa gymnocarpa*
Balearic box   *Buxus balearica*
Balfour's aralia
  Polyscias balfouriana
Balkan gorse   *Genista lydia*
Balkan maple   *Acer heldreichii*
  Acer hyrcanum
Ball tree   *Aegle marmelos*
Balm of gilead   *Abies balsamea*
  Cedronella canariensis
  Populus candicans
  Populus gileadensis
Balsam fir   *Abies balsamea*
Balsam of Peru *Myroxylon pereirae*
Balsam poplar *Populus balsamifera*
  Populus tacamahaca
Balsam willow   *Salix pyrifolia*

Balsa wood   *Ochroma pyramidale*
Bamboo briar   *Acacia nudicaulis*
Bamboo-leaved oak
     Quercus myrsinaefolia
     Quercus prinus
Bamboo palm
     Chamaedorea erumpens
     Rhapis excelsa
Bamenda cola   *Cola anomala*
Banana   *Musa acuminata*
Banana shrub   *Michelia figo*
Banana yucca   *Yucca baccata*
Banksian rose   *Rosa banksiae*
Banyan   *Ficus benghalensis*
     Ficus indica
Baobab   *Adansonia digitata*
Barbados cedar   *Cedrela odorata*
Barbados cherry   *Eugenia michelii*
     Eugenia uniflora
     Malpighia glabra
Barbados nut   *Jatropha curcus*
Barbados pride
     Adenanthera pavonina
     Caesalpinia pulcherrima
Barbary gum   *Acacia gummifera*
Barbasco   *Jacquinia armillaris*
     Jacquinia barbasco
Barberry   *Berberis vulgaris*
Barrel palm   *Colpothrinax wrightii*
Barren's clawflower
     Calothamnus validus
Bartram oak
     Quercus × heterophylla
Barwood   *Baphia nitida*

     Pterocarpus erinaceus
Basford willow   *Salix basfordiana*
   Salix × rubens basfordiana
Basket oak   *Quercus prinus*
Basket willow   *Salix purpurea*
     Salix viminalis
Basswood   *Tilia americana*
Bastard bullet tree
     Houmiria floribunda
Bastard cedar   *Guazuma ulmifolia*
Bastard cherry   *Eretia tinifola*
Bastard gimlet   *Eucalyptus diptera*
Bastard indigo   *Amorpha fruticosa*
Bastard jute   *Hibiscus cannabinus*
Bastard logwood   *Acacia berteriana*
Bastard sandalwood
     Myoporum sandwicense
Bastard service tree
     Sorbus × thuringiaca
Bastard teak
     Pterocarpus marsupium
Batoko plum   *Flacourtia indica*
     Flacourtia ramontchi
Bat willow   *Salix alba coerulea*
Bayberry   *Myrica pennsylvanica*

Bay gall bush   *Ilex coriacea*
     Ilex lucida
Bay laurel   *Laurus nobilis*
Bay-rum tree   *Pimenta racemosa*
Bay tree   *Pimenta racemosa*
Bay willow   *Salix pentandra*
Beach plum   *Prunus maritima*
Beach pine   *Pinus contorta*
Bead tree   *Melia azedarach*
Beaked filbert   *Corylus cornuta*
Beaked hazel   *Corylus cornuta*
Beak willow   *Salix bebbiana*
Bearberry
     Arctostaphylos manzanita
     Rhamnus purshiana
Bearberry willow   *Salix uva-ursi*
Bear huckleberry
     Gaylussacia ursina
Bear oak   *Quercus ilicifolia*
Bear's grape
     Arctostaphylos uva-ursi
Beautiful fir   *Abies amabilis*
Beautyberry   *Callicarpa americana*
Beauty bush   *Kolkwitzia amabilis*
Bechtel crab apple
     Malus ioensis plena
Beechwood
     Casuarina equisetifolia
Beefsteak plant
     Acalypha wilkesiana
Beefwood   *Mimusops balata*
Bela tree   *Aegle marmelos*
Belgian evergreen
     Dracaena sanderana
Bell-flowered cherry
     Prunus campanulata
Bellflower heather   *Erica cinerea*
Bell-fruited mallee
     Eucalyptus preissiana
Bell-fruit tree
     Codonocarpus cotinifolius
Bell heather   *Erica cinerea*
Belmore sentry palm
     Howea belmoreana
     Kentia belmoreana
Bengal quince   *Aegle marmelos*
Benguet pine   *Pinus insularis*
Benjamin bush   *Lindera benzoin*
Benjamin tree   *Ficus benjamina*
Ben oil tree   *Moringa oleifera*
Bentham's cornel   *Cornus capitata*
Benzoin   *Lindera benzoin*
     Styrax benzoin
Bergamot
     Citrus aurantium bergamia
Bergamot orange
     Citrus aurantium bergamia
     Citrus bergamia
Berg cypress
     Widdringtonia cupressoides

TREES, BUSHES, AND SHRUBS

Black fibre palm

Berlin poplar	
	Populus × berolinensis
Bermuda cedar	
	Juniperus bermudiana
Bermuda olivewood bark	
	Cassine laneana
Bermuda palmetto	
	Sabal bermudana
Berry heath	*Erica baccans*
Besom heath	*Erica scoparia*
Be-still tree	*Thevetia peruviana*
Betel	*Piper betel*
	Piper betle
Betel-nut palm	*Areca aleracea*
	Areca catechu
Betel palm	*Areca catechu*
Betel pepper	*Piper betel*
	Piper betle
Bhendi tree	*Thespesia populnea*
Bhutan cypress	
	Cupressus duclouxiana
	Cupressus torulosa
Bhutan pine	*Pinus excelsa*
	Pinus wallichiana
Bible fig	*Ficus sycomorus*
Bible leaf	
	Hypericum androsaemum
Bigarade	*Citrus aurantium*
Big-berry manzanita	
	Arctostaphylos glauca
Bigbud hickory	*Carya tomentosa*
Big-cone pine	*Pinus coulteri*
Big-cone spruce	
	Pseudotsuga macrocarpa
Big-leaved maple	
	Acer macrophyllum
Big-leaved storax	*Styrax obassia*
Bignay	*Antidesma bunius*
Big-toothed aspen	
	Populus grandidentata
Big-tooth euphorbia	
	Euphorbia grandidens
Bilberry	*Vaccinium myrtillus*
Bilimbi	*Averrhoa bilimbi*
Bilsted gum	
	Liquidambar styraciflua
Bimble box	*Eucalyptus populifolia*
	Eucalyptus populnea
Bimli jute	*Hibiscus cannabinus*
Bimlipatum	*Hibiscus cannabinus*
Birch bark cherry	*Prunus serrula*
Birch leaf maple	*Acer tetramerum*
Bird-catcher tree	
	Pisonia umbellifera
Bird cherry	*Prunus avium*
	Prunus padus
	Prunus pennsylvanica
Bird of paradise	
	Caesalpinia gilliesii
	Poinciana gilliesii

Bird's eye bush	*Ochna japonica*
	Ochna serrulata
Bird's eye maple	*Acer saccharinum*
Biscochito	*Ruprechtia coriacea*
Bishop pine	*Pinus muricata*
Bitter almond	*Prunus dulcis amara*
Bitter apple	*Citrullus colocynthis*
Bitter ash	*Picraena excelsa*
Bitter bark	*Alstonia scholaris*
	Pinckneya pubens
Bitterbush	*Picramnia pentandra*
Bitter cassava	*Manihot esculenta*
	Manihot utilissima
Bitter cherry	*Prunus emarginata*
Bitter damson	*Simarouba amara*
Bitter gallberry	*Ilex glabra*
Bitternut	*Carya cordiformis*
Bitter oak	*Quercus cerris*
Bitter orange	*Citrus aurantium*
Bitter pecan	
	Carya aquatica
Bitterwood	*Quassia amara*
	Simarouba glauca
Black alder	*Alnus glutinosa*
	Ilex verticillata
	Viburnum molle
Black apricot	*Prunus × dasycarpa*
Black ash	*Fraxinus nigra*
Black bark	*Diospyros whyteana*
Blackbead	
	Pithecellobium guadalupense
	Pithecellobium unguis-cati
Black bean tree	
	Castanospermum australe
Black bearberry	*Arctous alpinus*
Black beech	*Nothofagus solandri*
Blackberry	*Robus fruticosus*
Black birch	*Betula lenta*
	Betula nigra
Black box	*Eucalyptus largiflorens*
	Eucalyptus × rariflora
Black boy	*Xanthorrhoea preissii*
Blackbutt	*Eucalyptus pilularis*
Blackbutt peppermint	
	Eucalyptus smithii
Black calabash	*Enallagma latifolia*
Black cherry	*Prunus serotina*
Black chokeberry	
	Aronia melanocarpa
Black cottonwood	
	Populus heterophylla
	Populus trichocarpa
Blackcurrant	*Ribes nigrum*
Black cutch tree	*Acacia catechu*
Black cypress pine	
	Callitris calcarata
	Callitris endlicheri
Black dogwood	*Rhamnus frangula*
Black elder	*Sambucus nigra*
Black fibre palm	*Arenga pinnata*

Black gum	*Eucalyptus aggregata*
	Nyssa sylvatica
Black haw	*Bumelia lanuginosa*
	Viburnum lentago
	Viburnum prunifolium
Black hawthorn	
	Crataegus douglasii
Black highbush blueberry	
	Vaccinium atrococcum
Black huckleberry	
	Gaylussacia baccata
	Gaylussacia resinosa
Blacking plant	*Hibiscus sinensis*
Black ironwood	*Olea laurifolia*
Black Italian poplar	
	Populus serotina
Blackjack oak	*Quercus marilandica*
Black juniper	*Juniperus wallichiana*
Black kauri pine	
	Agathis microstachys
Black larch	*Larix laricina*
Black laurel	*Gordonia lasianthus*
Black-leaved plum	
	Prunus cerasifera nigra
Black locust tree	
	Robinia pseudoacacia
Black mangrove	*Avicennia nitida*
Black maple	*Acer nigrum*
Black mountain ash	
	Eucalyptus sieberi
Black mulberry	*Morus nigra*
Black oak	*Quercus velutina*
Black olive	*Bucida buceras*
Black palm	*Normanbya normanbyi*
Black peppermint	
	Eucalyptus amygdalina
	Eucalyptus salicifolia
Black persimmon	*Diospyros nigra*
	Diospyros texana
Black pine	*Pinus thunbergii*
	Podocarpus amarus
Black plum	*Syzygium cumini*
Black poplar	*Populus nigra*
Black pussy willow	
	Salix melanostachys
Black sally	*Eucalyptus stellulata*
Black sapote	*Diospyros digyna*
	Diospyros nigra
Black sassafras	
	Atherosperma moschatum
Black spruce	*Picea mariana*
	Picea nigra
Black stinkwood	*Ocotea bullata*
Blackthorn	
	Crataegus calpodendron
	Prunus spinosa
Blackthorn oak	
	Quercus marilandica
Black titi	*Cliftonia monophylla*
	Cyrilla racemiflora
Black tupelo	*Nyssa sylvatica*

Black walnut	*Juglans nigra*
Black wattle	*Acacia mearnsii*
Black willow	*Salix nigra*
Blackwood	*Acacia melanoxylon*
	Acacia penninervis
Blackwood acacia	
	Acacia melanoxylon
Black wood	*Dalbergia latifolia*
Bladder ketmia	*Hibiscus trionum*
Bladdernut	*Diospyros whyteana*
	Staphylea holocarpa
Blaeberry	*Vaccinium myrtillus*
Blakely's red gum	
	Eucalyptus blakelyi
Blaxland's stringybark	
	Eucalyptus blaxlandii
Blaze	*Prunus cerasifera nigra*
Bleeding glory flower	
	Clerodendrum thomsoniae
Bleeding heart vine	
	Clerodendrum thomsoniae
Blood-leaf Japanese maple	
	Acer palmatum atropurpureum
Blood-twig dogwood	
	Cornus sanguinea
Bloodwood	
	Haematoxylum campeachianum
Blue ash	*Fraxinus quadrangulata*
Blue atlas cedar	
	Cedrus atlantica glauca
Blue barberry	*Mahonia aquifolium*
Blue beech	*Carpinus caroliniana*
Blueberry	*Vaccinium corymbosum*
Blueberry ash	
	Elaeocarpus reticulatus
Blue birch	*Betula coerulea-grandis*
Blueblossom	
	Ceanothus thyrsiflorus
Blue broom	*Erinacea anthyllis*
	Erinacea pungens
Bluebush	*Eucalyptus macrocarpa*
Blue cedar	*Cedrus atlantica glauca*
Blue Chinese juniper	
	Juniperus chinensis columnaris glauca
Blue douglas fir	
	Pseudotsuga menziesii glauca
Blue dracaena	*Cordyline indivisa*
	Dracaena indivisa
Blue elder	*Sambucus caerulea*
Blue fan palm	*Brahea armata*
	Erythea armata
Blue gum	*Eucalyptus globulus*
Blue haw	*Viburnum rufidulum*
Blue hesper palm	*Brahea armata*
	Erythea armata
Blue holly	*Ilex × meservae*
Bluejack oak	*Quercus incana*
Blue latan	*Latania loddigesii*
Blue-leaf wattle	*Acacia cyanophylla*

Blue-leaved stringybark
    Eucalyptus agglomerata
Blue lilly-pilly
    Syzygium coolminianum
Blue magnolia *Magnolia acuminata*
Blue mountain mallee
    Eucalyptus stricta
Blue oak   *Quercus douglasii*
Blue palm   *Erythea armata*
Blue palmetto
    Rhapidophyllum hystrix
    Sabal palmetto
Blue passion flower
    Passiflora caerulea
Blue pine   *Pinus wallichiana*
Blue Spanish fir
    Abies pinsapo glauca
Blue spruce   *Picea pungens*
    Picea pungens glauca
Blue tangle *Gaylussacia frondosa*
Blue wattle *Acacia cyanophylla*
Blue weeping gum
    Eucalyptus sepulcralis
Blue willow *Salix alba caerulea*
    Salix caesia
Blue yucca   *Yucca baccata*
Bog bilberry *Vaccinium uliginosum*
Bog heather   *Erica tetralix*
Bog kalmia   *Kalmia poliifolia*
Bog laurel   *Kalmia poliifolia*
Bog myrtle   *Myrica gale*
Bog rosemary
    Andromeda polifolia
Bog spruce   *Picea mariana*
    Picea nigra
Bog whortleberry
    Vaccinium uliginosum
Boldo   *Peumus boldus*
Bolinus ridge ceanothus
    Ceanothus masonii
Boobyalla *Myoporum insulare*
Boojum tree *Idria columnaris*
Bornmüller's fir
    Abies bornmuellerana
Bosisto's box
    Eucalyptus bosistoana
Bosnian pine *Pinus leucodermis*
Botany Bay gum
    Xanthorrhoea arborea
Botany Bay tea tree *Correa alba*
Bo tree   *Ficus religiosa*
Bottlebrush buckeye
    Aesculus parviflora
Bottle brush *Callistemon citrinus*
Bottle palm *Colpothrinax wrightii*
    Hyophorbe lagencaulis
Bottle tree *Adansonia gregori*
Bourbon palm *Latania borbonica*
Bourbon rose *Rosa × borboniana*
Bournemouth pine *Pinus pinaster*

Bourtree   *Sambucus nigra*
Bower plant *Pandorea jasminoides*
Bowstring hemp
    Calotropis gigantea
Bow-wood tree *Maclura pomifera*
Boxberry *Gaultheria procumbens*
Box blueberry *Vaccinium ovatum*
Box elder   *Acer negundo*
Box huckleberry
    Gaylussacia brachycera
Box-leaved holly *Ilex crenata*
Box sand myrtle
    Leiophyllum buxifolium
Box thorn   *Bursaria spinosa*
Boxwood *Buxus sempervirens*
Bracelet honey myrtle
    Melaleuca armillaris
Bracelet wood *Jacquinia armillaris*
Bracted fir   *Abies procera*
Bramble   *Rubus fruticosus*
Bramble acacia *Acacia victoriae*
Bramble wattle *Acacia victoriae*
Branch thorn *Erinacea anthyllis*
    Erinacea pungens
Brasiletto *Caesalpinia vesicaria*
Brazilian araucaria
    Araucaria angustifolium
Brazil cherry *Eugenia brasiliensis*
    Eugenia dombeyi
    Eugenia michelii
    Eugenia uniflora
Brazilian ironwood
    Caesalpinia ferrea
Brazilian passion flower
    Passiflora caerulea
Brazilian pepper tree
    Schinus terebinthifolia
Brazilian pine
    Araucaria angustifolia
Brazilian skyflower *Duranta ellisia*
    Duranta repens
Brazil nut *Bertholletia excelsa*
Brazilwood
    Caesalpinia braziliensis
    Caesalpinia echinata
    Caesalpinia sappan
Bread and cheese
    Crataegus monogyna
Breadfruit   *Artocarpus altilis*
    Artocarpus incisus
    Pandanus odoratissimus
Breadnut *Brosimum alicastrum*
Bread tree
    Encephalartos altensteinii
Brewer's weeping spruce
    Picea brewerana
Briançon apricot
    Prunus brigantina
Briar   *Erica arborea*
Briar rose   *Rosa canina*
Bridewort *Spiraea salicifolia*

Brisbane box	*Tristania conferta*
Bristle-cone fir	*Abies bracteata*
	Abies venusta
Bristle-cone pine	
	Pinus aristata engelm
Bristly locust	*Robinia hispida*
Bristly sarsaparilla	*Aralia hispida*
Brittle-leaf manzanita	
	Arctostaphylos crustacea
Brittle willow	*Salix fragilis*
Broadleaf cockspur thorn	
	Crataegus × prunifolia
Broadleaf podocarpus	
	Podocarpus nagi
Broad-leaved bottle tree	
	Brachychiton australis
Broad-leaved ironbark	
	Eucalyptus fibrosa
Broad-leaved kindling bark	
	Eucalyptus dalrympleana
Broad-leaved lime	
	Tilia platyphyllos
Broad-leaved mahogany	
	Swietenia macrophylla
Broad-leaved peppermint	
	Eucalyptus dives
Broad-leaved sally	
	Eucalyptus camphora
Broad-leaved spindle	
	Euonymus latifolius
Broad-leaved whitebeam	
	Sorbus latifolia
Bronvaux medlar	
	+ *Crataegomespilus dardarii*
Bronze shower	*Cassia moschata*
Broom hickory	*Carya glabra*
Broom palm	
	Coccothrinax argentea
	Thrinax argentea
Broom wattle	*Acacia calamifolia*
Brown barrel	*Eucalyptus fastigiata*
Brown cabbage tree	
	Pisonia grandis
Brown dogwood	*Cornus glabrata*
Brown mallee	
	Eucalyptus astringens
Brown pine	*Podocarpus elatus*
Brown stringybark	
	Eucalyptus baxteri
	Eucalyptus capitellata
Brush box	*Tristania conferta*
Brush cherry	
	Syzygium paniculatum
Buckberry	*Gaylussacia ursina*
Buckbrush	*Ceanothus cuneatus*
Buckthorn	*Bumelia lycioides*
Buckwheat brush	
	Cliftonia monophylla
Buckwheat tree	
	Cliftonia monophylla

Buddhist pine	
	Podocarpus macrophyllus
Buddleia	*Buddleia davidii*
Buffalo berry	*Shepherdia argentea*
	Shepherdia canadensis
Buffalo currant	*Ribes aureum*
	Ribes odoratum
Buffalo thorn	*Ziziphus mucronata*
Buffalo wattle	*Acacia kettlewelliae*
Buisson ardent	
	Pyracantha coccinea
Bulgarian fir	*Abies borisii-regis*
Bullace	*Prunus domestica institia*
	Prunus insititia
Bull banksia	*Banksia grandis*
Bull bay	*Magnolia grandiflora*
Bull-hoof tree	*Bauhinia purpurea*
Bull-horn acacia	*Acacia cornigera*
Bullick	*Eucalyptus megacarpa*
Bullock's heart	*Annona reticulata*
Bull's horn acacia	
	Acacia spadicigera
Bull thatch	*Sabal jamaicensis*
Bunchberry	*Cornus canadensis*
Bundy	*Eucalyptus elaeophora*
	Eucalyptus goniocalyx
Bungalay	*Eucalyptus botryoides*
Bunya-bunya	*Araucaria bidwillii*
Bunya pine	*Araucaria bidwillii*
Burdekin plum	
	Pleiogynium cerasiferum
Burmese fishtail palm	*Caryota mitis*
Burmese pride	*Amhertsia nobilis*
Burmese rosewood	
	Pterocarpus indicus
Burnet rose	*Rosa pimpinellifolia*
Burning bush	
	Combretum macrophyllum
	Cotinus coggygria purpureus
	Euonymus atropurpurea
Burracoppin mallee	
	Eucalyptus burracoppinensis
Burr oak	*Quercus macrocarpa*
Burr rose	*Rosa roxburghii*
Bursting heart	
	Euonymus americana
Bush chinquapin	*Castanea alnifolia*
	Castanea sempervirens
	Castanopsis sempervirens
	Chrysolepis sempervirens
Bush fig	*Ficus capensis*
Bush hollyhock	*Althaea frutex*
	Hibiscus syriacus
Bush honeysuckle	*Lonicera nitida*
Bush mallow	*Althaea frutex*
	Lavatera olbia
	Hibiscus syriacus
Bush palmetto	*Sabal adansonii*
	Sabal minor
Bush willow	
	Combretum erythrophyllum

TREES, BUSHES, AND SHRUBS

Californian sassafras

Bush yate *Eucalyptus lehmanii*

Butcher's broom *Ruscus aculeatus*

Buttercup bush *Cassia corymbosa*

Buttercup flower
Allamanda cathartica

Buttercup tree
Cochlospermum religiosum
Cochlospermum vitifolium

Buttercup winter hazel
Corylopsis paucifolia

Butterfly bush
Buddleia alternifolia
Buddleia davidii

Butterfly lavender
Lavandula stoechas

Butterfly palm *Areca lutescens*
Chrysalidocarpus lutescens

Butterfly pea *Clitoria ternatea*

Butterfly tree *Bauhinia purpurea*

Butter nut *Juglans cinerea*

Buttonball *Platanus occidentalis*

Button bush
Cephalanthus occidentalis

Buttonwood *Conocarpus erectus*
Platanus occidentalis

Cabbage gum
Eucalyptus amplifolia
Eucalyptus clavigera
Eucalyptus paucifolia

Cabbage palm *Areca aleracea*
Corypha australis
Livistonia australis
Roystonea oleracea

Cabbage palmetto *Sabal palmetto*

Cabbage rose *Rosa centifolia*

Cabbage tree *Andira araroba*
Cordyline australis
Cussonia paniculata
Cussonia spicata
Sabal palmetto

Cacao *Theobroma cacao*

Cade *Juniperus oxycedrus*

Cafta *Catha edulis*

Caimito *Chrysophyllum cainito*

Cajuput *Melaleuca leucadendron*

Calaba tree
Calophyllum brasiliense

Calabash nutmeg
Monodora myristica

Calabash tree *Crescenta cujete*

Calabrian pine *Pinus brutia*

Calabur *Muntingia calabura*

Calamondin × *Citrofortunella mitis*

Calappa palm
Actinorhytis calapparia

Calico bush *Kalmia latifolia*

Calif of Persia willow
Salix aegyptiaca

California big tree
Sequoiadendron giganteum

California huckleberry
Vaccinium ovatum

California incense cedar
Calocedrus decurrens

California juniper
Juniperus occidentalis

Californian allspice
Calycanthus occidentalis

Californian anemone bush
Carpenteria californica

Californian bay
Umbellularia californica

Californian bayberry
Myrica californica

Californian blackcurrant
Ribes bracteosum

Californian black oak
Quercus kelloggii

Californian black walnut
Juglans hindsii

Californian buckeye chestnut
Aesculus californica

Californian buckthorn
Rhamnus purshiana

Californian coast redwood
Sequoia sempervirens

Californian cypress
Cupressus goveniana
Cupressus stephensonii

Californian fan palm
Washingtonia filifera

Californian field oak
Quercus agrifolia

Californian fuchsia
Zauschneria californica

Californian horse chestnut
Aesculus californica

Californian juniper
Juniperus californica

Californian laurel
Umbellularia californica

Californian lilac
Ceanothus thyrsiflorus

Californian live oak
Quercus agrifolia
Quercus chrysolepis

Californian mock orange
Carpenteria californica

Californian mountain pine
Pinus monticola

Californian nutmeg
Torreya californica

Californian olive
Umbellularia californica

Californian pepper tree
Schinus molle

Californian privet
Ligustrum ovalifolium

Californian red fir *Abies magnifica*

Californian redwood
Sequoia sempervirens

Californian sassafras
Umbellularia californica

Californian scrub oak

Californian scrub oak
  Quercus dumosa
Californian tree mallow
  Lavatera assurgentiflora
California wax myrtle
  Myrica californica
Californian white oak
  Quercus lobata
Californian walnut
  Juglans californica
Californian yew *Taxus brevifolia*
Calisaya *Cinchona calisaya*
Calotropis *Calotropis procera*
Calumba *Jateorhiza calumba*
Cambridge oak *Quercus warburgii*
Camden woollybutt
  Eucalyptus macarthurii
Camel's foot *Bauhinia purpurea*
Camel thorn *Acacia giraffae*
  Alhagi camelorum
Campbell's magnolia
  Magnolia campbellii
Campeachy-wood
  Haematoxylum campeachianum
Camperdown elm
  Ulmus glabra camperdown
Camphor tree
  Cinnamomum camphora
Camwood *Baphia nitida*
Canada pitch *Tsuga canadensis*
Canada plum *Prunus nigra*
Canadian dwarf juniper
  Juniperus depressa
Canadian hemlock
  Tsuga canadensis
Canadian juniper
  Juniperus communis depressa
Canadian maple *Acer rubrum*
Canadian red pine *Pinus resinosa*
Canadian tea
  Gaultheria procumbens
Canadian yew *Taxus canadensis*
Canary balm
  Cedronella canariensis
Canary date palm
  Phoenix canariensis
Canary holly *Ilex perado*
Canary Island date palm
  Phoenix canariensis
Canary Island juniper
  Juniperus cedrus
Canary Island pine
  Pinus canariensis
Canary Island holly
  Ilex platyphylla
Canary Island laurel
  Laurus azorica
  Laurus canariensis
  Laurus maderensis
Canary palm *Phoenix canariensis*

Candelabra cactus
  Euphorbia lactea
Candelabra spruce
  Picea montigena
Candelabra tree
  Araucaria angustifolia
  Euphorbia candelabrum
  Euphorbia ingens
Candelilla
  Euphorbia antisyphilitica
Candle-bark gum
  Eucalyptus rubida
Candleberry
  Myrica pennsylvanica
Candleberry myrtle
  Myrica carolinensis
  Myrica cerifera
  Myrica faya
Candleberry tree
  Aleurites moluccana
Candle bush *Cassia didymobotrya*
Candlenut tree
  Aleurites moluccana
Candlestick senna *Cassia alata*
Candle tree *Parmentiera cereifera*
Cane apple *Arbutus unedo*
Canistel *Pouteria campechiana*
Cannonball tree
  Couroupita guianensis
Canoe birch *Betula papyrifera*
Canoe cedar
  Chamaecyparis nootkatensis
Canyon live oak
  Quercus chrysolepis
Canyon maple *Acer macrophyllum*
Caoutchouc *Hevea brasiliensis*
Cape box *Buxus macowani*
Cape chestnut
  Calodendrum capense
Cape fig *Ficus capensis*
Cape figwort *Phygelius capensis*
Cape gardenia
  Tabernaemontana divaricata
Cape gum *Acacia horrida*
  Acacia senegal
Cape heath *Erica hyemalis*
Cape hibiscus
  Hibiscus diversifolius
Cape jasmine *Acacia senegal*
  Gardenia florida
  Gardenia grandiflora
  Gardenia jasminoides
  Tabernaemontana coronaria
  Tabernaemontana divaricata
Cape myrtle *Lagerstroemia indica*
  Myrsine africana
Cape pittosporum
  Pittosporum viridiflorum
Caper bush *Capparis spinosa*
Caper spurge *Euphorbia lathyris*
Cappadocian maple
  Acer cappadocicum

Cedar pine

Capulin cherry   *Prunus salicifolia*
Cardinal spear   *Erythrina arborea*
                  Erythrina herbacea
Cardinal willow
                  Salix fragilis decipiens
Caribbean pine   *Pinus caribaea*
Caribbean royal palm
                  Roystonea oleracea
Carib wood   *Sabinea carinalis*
Caricature plant
                  Graptophyllum hortense
                  Graptophyllum pictum
Carmel ceanothus
                  Ceanothus griseus
Carmel creeper
        Ceanothus griseus horizontalis
Carnanba palm   *Copernica cerifera*
Carnauba palm   *Copernica cerifera*
Carnauba wax palm
                  Copernica prunifera
Carob   *Ceratonia siliqua*
Carob tree   *Jacaranda procera*
Carolina allspice
                  Calycanthus fertilis
                  Calycanthus floridus
Carolina ash   *Fraxinus caroliniana*
Carolina buckthorn
                  Rhamnus carolinian
Carolina hemlock
                  Tsuga caroliniana
Carolina ipecac
        Euphorbia ipecacuanhae
Carolina poplar   *Populus eugenei*
Carolina silverbell   *Halesia carolina*
Carolina spurge
        Euphorbia ipecacuanhae
Caroline poplar   *Populus angulata*
                  Populus × canadensis
Carpathian spruce
                  Picea abies carpathica
Carrion tree
                  Couroupita guianensis
Cartagena bark
                  Cinchona cordifolia
Cascade fir   *Abies amabilis*
Cascara   *Picramnia antidesma*
Cascara sagrada
                  Rhamnus purshiana
Cascarilla   *Croton cascarilla*
Cashew   *Anacardium occidentale*
Caspian locust   *Gleditsia caspica*
Caspian willow   *Salix acutifolia*
Cassa-banana   *Sicana odorifera*
Cassada wood
                  Turpinia occidentalis
Cassandra
        Chamaedaphne calyculata
Cassava   *Manihot esculenta*
Cassava wood
                  Turpinia occidentalis
Cassia   *Cinnamomum cassia*

Cassia bark tree
                  Cinnamomum cassia
Cassia flower tree
                  Cinnamomum loureirii
Cassie   *Acacia farnesiana*
Cassina   *Ilex cassine*
                  Ilex vomitoria
Castilla rubber tree
                  Castilla elastica
Castor aralia   *Kalopanax pictus*
Castor bean   *Ricinus communis*
Castor oil palm   *Aralia japonica*
                  Fatsia japonica
Castor oil plant   *Fatsia japonica*
                  Ricinus communis
Catalina ceanothus
                  Ceanothus arboreus
Catalina cherry   *Prunus lyonii*
Catalina ironwood
        Lyonothamnus floribundus
Catalina mountain lilac
                  Ceanothus arboreus
Catalonian jasmine
        Jasminum grandiflorum
Catalpa   *Catalpa bignonioides*
Catawba   *Catalpa speciosa*
Catberry
        Nemopanthus mucronatus
Catclaw acacia   *Acacia greggii*
Catechu   *Acacia catechu*
                  Areca catechu
Catesby oak   *Quercus laevis*
Cat's claw   *Pithecellobium unguis-
                  cati*
Cat spruce   *Picea glauca*
Cat thyme   *Teucrium marum*
Caucasian alder   *Alnus subcordata*
Caucasian ash   *Fraxinus oxycarpa*
Caucasian elm
                  Zelkova carpinifolia
                  Zelkova crenata
Caucasian fir   *Abies nordmanniana*
Caucasian lime   *Tilia × euchlora*
Caucasian maple
                  Acer cappadocicum
Caucasian nettle tree
                  Celtis caucasica
Caucasian oak
                  Quercus macranthera
Caucasian pear   *Pyrus caucasica*
Caucasian wing-nut
        Pterocarya fraxinifolia
Caucasian whortleberry
        Vaccinium arctostaphylos
Cayenne cherry   *Eugenia michelii*
                  Eugenia uniflora
Ceara rubber   *Manihot glaziovii*
Cedar elm   *Ulmus crassifolia*
Cedar of Goa   *Cupressus lusitanica*
Cedar of Lebanon   *Cedrus libani*
Cedar pine   *Pinus glabra*

Cedar wattle

Cedar wattle	*Acacia alata* *Acacia terminalis*
Cedrat lemon	*Citrus medica cedra*
Cedron	*Simaba cedron*
Celery pine	*PhylTocladus alpinus* *Phyllocladus asplenifolius* *Phyllocladus trichomanoides*
Celery-top pine	*Phyllocladus rhomboidalis*
Celery-topped pine	*Phyllocladus asplenifolius*
Century plant	*Yucca recurvifolia*
Cevennes pine	*Pinus nigra cebennensis*
Ceylon cinnamon	*Cinnamomum zeylanicum*
Ceylon date palm	*Phoenix zelanica*
Ceylon ebony	*Diospyros ebenaster* *Diospyros ebenum*
Ceylon gooseberry	*Aberia gardneri* *Dovyalis hebecarpa*
Ceylon mahogany	*Melia dubium*
Ceylon oak	*Schleichera oleosa*
Ceylon olive	*Elaeocarpus serratus*
Ceylon rosewood	*Albizzia odoratissima*
Ceylon tea	*Cassine glauca*
Chaconia	*Warszewiczia coccinea*
Chalk maple	*Acer leucoderme*
Champaca	*Michelia champaca*
Champion's oak	*Quercus velutina rubrifolia*
Champney rose	*Rosa × noisettiana*
Charcoal tree	*Byrsonima crassifolia*
Chaste tree	*Vitex agnus-castus*
Chat	*Catha edulis*
Chattamwood	*Bumelia lanuginosa*
Cheken	*Eugenia cheken* *Luma chequen*
Checkerberry	*Gaultheria procumbens* *Mitchella repens*
Cheddar whitebeam	*Sorbus anglica*
Chenille plant	*Acalypha hispida*
Chennar tree	*Platanus orientalis*
Chequered juniper	*Juniperus deppeana pachyphlaea*
Chequer tree	*Sorbus torminalis*
Cherimalla	*Annona cherimola*
Cherimoya	*Annona cherimola*
Cherokee bean	*Erythrina arborea* *Erythrina herbacea*
Cherokee rose	*Rosa laevigata*
Cherry birch	*Betula lenta*
Cherry elaeagnus	*Elaeagnus edulis* *Elaeagnus multiflora*

Cherry laurel	*Prunus caroliniana* *Prunus laurocerasus*
Cherry plum	*Prunus cerasifera*
Cherrystone juniper	*Juniperus monosperma*
Chess apple	*Sorbus aria*
Chestnut dioon	*Dioon edule*
Chestnut-leaved oak	*Quercus castaneifolia*
Chestnut oak	*Quercus acutissima* *Quercus muehlenbergii* *Quercus prinus*
Chestnut rose	*Rosa roxburghii*
Chichester elm	*Ulmus × vegeta*
Chickasaw plum	*Prunus angustifolia*
Chicle	*Achras sapota*
Chicot	*Gymnocladus dioica*
Chicozapote	*Manilkara zapota*
Chilean boldo tree	*Peumus boldus*
Chilean cedar	*Austrocedrus chilensis*
Chilean fire bush	*Embothrium coccineum*
Chilean fire tree	*Embothrium coccineum*
Chilean guava	*Eugenia ugni* *Myrtus ugni* *Ugni molinae*
Chilean hazel	*Gevuina avellana*
Chilean incense cedar	*Austrocedrus chilensis* *Calocedrus chilensis*
Chilean jasmine	*Mandevilla suaveolens*
Chilean myrtle	*Myrtus chequen*
Chilean nut	*Gevuina avellana*
Chilean tea tree	*Lycium chilense* *Lycium gracillianum*
Chilean totara	*Podocarpus nubigenus*
Chilean wine palm	*Jubaea chilensis* *Jubaea spectabilis*
Chilean yew	*Podocarpus andinus*
Chile pine	*Araucaria araucana*
Chilghoza pine	*Pinus gerardiana*
Chinaberry	*Melia azedarach*
China cane	*Rhapis excelsa*
China rose	*Hibiscus sinensis* *Rosa chinensis*
China tree	*Koelreuteria paniculata* *Melia azedarach*
China turpentine tree	*Pistacia terebinthus*
Chinese angelica tree	*Aralia chinensis*
Chinese anise	*Illicium anisatum*
Chinese arbor-vitae	*Thuya orientalis*
Chinese ash	*Fraxinus chinensis*
Chinese aspen	*Populus adenopoda*

TREES, BUSHES, AND SHRUBS

Chinese rubber tree

Chinese banyan   *Ficus retusa*

Chinese beech   *Fagus englerana*
                       Fagus longipetiolata

Chinese bottle tree
                       Firmiana simplex

Chinese box   *Murraya paniculata*

Chinese box orange
                       Severinia buxifolia

Chinese box thorn
                       Lycium barbarum
                       Lycium chinense

Chinese bramble
                       Rubus cockburnianus

Chinese bush cherry
                       Prunus glandulosa
                       Prunus tomentosa

Chinese butternut
                       Juglans cathayensis

Chinese catalpa   *Catalpa ovata*

Chinese cedar   *Cedrela sinensis*
                       Toona sinensis

Chinese cherry   *Prunus conradinae*

Chinese chestnut
                       Castanea mollissima

Chinese cinnamon
                       Cinnamomum cassia

Chinese coffee tree
                       Gymnocladus chinensis

Chinese cork oak
                       Quercus variabilis

Chinese cork tree
                       Phellodendron chinensis

Chinese cowtail pine
                       Cephalotaxus sinensis

Chinese crab apple
                       Malus hupehensis
                       Malus spectabilis

Chinese date   *Ziziphus jujuba*

Chinese dogwood
                       Cornus kousa chinensis

Chinese douglas fir
                       Pseudotsuga sinensis

Chinese elm   *Ulmus parvifolia*

Chinese evergreen magnolia
                       Magnolia delavayi

Chinese fan palm
                       Livistona chinensis

Chinese filbert   *Corylus chinensis*

Chinese fir
                       Cunninghamia lanceolata

Chinese flowering apple
                       Malus spectabilis

Chinese flowering ash
                       Fraxinus mariesii

Chinese fountain palm
                       Livistona chinensis

Chinese fringe tree
                       Chionanthus retusa

Chinese hackberry   *Celtis japonica*
                       Celtis sinensis

Chinese hawthorn
                       Crateagus pinnatifida
                       Photinia serrulata

Chinese hazel   *Corylus chinensis*

Chinese hemlock   *Tsuga chinensis*

Chinese hibiscus
                       Hibiscus rosa-sinensis
                       Hibiscus sinensis

Chinese hickory   *Carya cathayensis*

Chinese hill cherry
                       Prunus mutabilis stricta
                   Prunus serrulata hupehensis

Chinese holly   *Ilex cornuta*
                       Osmanthus heterophyllus

Chinese honey locust
                       Gleditsia chinensis
                       Gleditsia sinensis

Chinese incense cedar
                       Calocedrus macrolepis

Chinese ixora   *Ixora chinensis*

Chinese jujube tree
                       Ziziphus jujuba

Chinese juniper   *Juniperus chinensis*

Chinese kidney bean
                       Wisteria sinensis

Chinese larch   *Larix potaninii*

Chinese lilac   *Syringa × chinensis*

Chinese lime   *Tilia oliveri*

Chinese laurel   *Antidesma bunius*

Chinese magnolia
                       Magnolia sinensis

Chinese mint bush
                       Elsholtzia stauntonii

Chinese mountain ash
                       Sorbus hupehensis

Chinese necklace poplar
                       Populus lasiocarpa

Chinese parasol tree
                       Firmiana simplex

Chinese peach   *Prunus davidiana*

Chinese pear   *Pyrus ussuriensis*

Chinese persimmon
                       Diospyros chinensis
                       Diospyros kaki

Chinese pine   *Keteleeria davidiana*
                       Pinus tabuliformis

Chinese pistachio   *Pistacia chinensis*

Chinese plum-yew
                       Cephalotaxus fortuni

Chinese poplar   *Populus lasiocarpa*

Chinese privet   *Ligustrum lucidum*
                       Ligustrum sinense

Chinese quince
                       Pseudocydonia sinensis

Chinese red-barked birch
                       Betula albosinensis

Chinese redbud   *Cercis chinensis*
                       Cercis racemosa

Chinese rowan   *Sorbus hupehensis*

Chinese rubber tree
                       Eucommia ulmoides

Chinese sacred bamboo	Chittamwood *Cotinus americanus*
Nandina domestica	*Cotinus obovatus*
Chinese sand pear *Pyrus pyrifolia*	Chocolate tree *Theobroma cacao*
Chinese scarlet rowan	Chokeberry *Aronia arbutifolia*
Sorbus commixta embley	Choke cherry *Prunus virginiana*
Sorbus discolor	Christmas berry
Chinese scholar tree	*Heteromeles arbutifolia*
Sophora japonica	Christmas berry tree
Chinese silk thread tree	*Schinus terebinthifolia*
Eucommia ulmoides	Christmas box
Chinese silkworm thorn	*Sarcococca buxaceae*
Cudrania tricuspidata	Christmas candle *Cassia alata*
Chinese snakebark maple	Christmas heather
Acer davidii	*Erica canaliculata*
Chinese snowball	Christmas palm *Veitchia merrillii*
Viburnum macrocephalum	Christmas star
Chinese soapberry	*Euphorbia pulcherrima*
Sapindus mukorossi	Christmas tree *Nuytsia floribunda*
Chinese spruce *Picea asperata*	*Picea abies*
Chinese star anise *Illicium verum*	Christ's thorn *Paliurus aculeatus*
Chinese stewartia	*Paliurus australis*
Stewartia sinensis	*Paliurus spina-christi*
Chinese stuartia *Stewartia sinensis*	*Paliurus virgatus*
Chinese swamp cypress	Chusan palm
Glyptostrobus lineatus	*Trachycarpus fortunei*
Chinese tallow tree	Cider gum *Eucalyptus gunnii*
Sapium sebiferum	Cigar-box cedar *Cedrela odorata*
China tea plant *Lycium chinense*	Cigar tree *Catalpa speciosa*
Chinese thuya *Thuya orientalis*	Ciliate heath *Erica ciliaris*
Chinese sweet gum	Cilician fir *Abies cilicica*
Liquidambar formosana	Cinnamon
Chinese tulip tree	*Cinnamomum zeylanicum*
Liriodendron chinense	Cinnamon rose *Rosa majalis*
Chinese varnish tree	Cinnamon tree
Rhus potaninii	*Cinnamomum zeylanicum*
Chinese walnut *Juglans cathayensis*	Cinnamon wattle *Acacia leprosa*
Chinese water pine	Citrange × *Citroncirus webberi*
Glyptostrobus lineatus	Citron *Citrus medica*
Chinese weeping cypress	Clammy azalea
Cupressus funebris	*Rhododendron viscosum*
Chinese whitebeam *Sorbus folgneri*	Clammy locust *Robinia viscosa*
Chinese white cedar	Clanwilliam cedar
Thuya orientalis	*Widdringtonia juniperoides*
Chinese white pine *Pinus armandii*	Claret ash
Chinese wing-nut	*Fraxinus oxycarpa raywood*
Pteryocarya stenoptera	Clearing nut *Strychnos potatorum*
Chinese witch-hazel	Clementine *Citrus reticulata*
Hamamelis mollis	Cliff date palm *Phoenix rupicola*
Chinese wood-oil tree	Cliff whitebeam *Sorbus rupicola*
Aleurites fordii	Climbing fig *Ficus pumila*
Chinese yellow wood	*Ficus repens*
Cladrastis chinensis	*Ficus stipulata*
Cladrastris sinensis	Climbing hydrangea
Chinese yew *Taxus celebica*	*Pileostegia viburnoides*
Taxus chinensis	*Schizophragma viburnoides*
Chinese zelkova *Zelkova sinica*	Clove tree *Eugenia caryophyllus*
Chinquapin chestnut	*Syzygium aromaticum*
Castanea pumila	Clown fig *Ficus aspera*
Chinquapin oak *Quercus prinoides*	Clustered fishtail palm
Chinquapin rose *Rosa roxburghii*	*Caryota mitis*
Chios mastic tree *Pistacia lentiscus*	

TREES, BUSHES, AND SHRUBS

Common mulberry

Cluster fig	*Ficus glomerata*
	Ficus racemosa
Cluster pine	*Pinus pinaster*
Coach-whip	*Fouquieria splendens*
Coarse-leaved mallee	
	Eucalyptus grossa
Coastal myall	*Acacia binervia*
Coast banksia	*Banksia integrifolia*
Coast ceanothus	
	Ceanothus ramulosus
Coast redwood	
	Sequoia sempervirens
Cobana	*Stahlia monosperma*
Cobnut	*Corylus avellana*
Coca	*Erythroxylum coca*
Cocaine plant	*Erythroxylum coca*
Cock's comb	*Erythrina crista-galli*
Cockscomb beech	
	Fagus sylvatica cristata
Cockspur coral tree	
	Erythrina crista-galli
Cockspur thorn	
	Crataegus crus-galli
Cocoa	*Theobroma cacao*
Coco-de-mer	*Lodoicea maldavica*
Cocona	*Solanum topiro*
Coconut palm	*Cocos nucifera*
Coco palm	*Chrysobalanus icaco*
Coco plum	*Chrysobalanus icaco*
Coffee	*Coffea arabica*
Coffee berry	*Rhamnus californica*
Coffee senna	*Cassia occidentalis*
Coffee tree	*Polyscias guilfoylei*
Coffin juniper	
	Juniperus recurva coxii
Coffin tree	*Taiwania flousiana*
Cohune palm	*Orbignya cohune*
Coigue	*Nothofagus dombeyi*
Coigue de magellanes	
	Nothofagus betuloides
Cola	*Cola nitida*
Cola tree	*Cola acuminata*
Colorado blue spruce	
	Picea pungens glauca
Colorado red cedar	
	Juniperus scopulorum
Colorado white fir	*Abies concolor*
Colorado spruce	*Picea pungens*
Columnar spruce	
	Juniperus communis stricta
Commercial apple	*Malus pumila*
Common acacia	
	Robinia pseudoacacia
Common alder	*Alnus glutinosa*
Common almond	
	Prunus amygdalus
	Prunus communis
	Prunus dulcis
Common apricot	
	Prunus armeniaca

Common ash	*Fraxinus excelsior*
Common barberry	
	Berberis vulgaris
Common beech	*Fagus sylvatica*
Common bearberry	
	Arctostaphylos uva-ursi
Common briar	*Rosa canina*
Common broom	*Cytisus genista*
Common box	*Buxus sempervirens*
Common broom	*Cytisus scoparius*
Common buckthorn	
	Rhamnus catharticus
Common camellia	
	Camellia japonica
Common coral bean	
	Erythrina corallodendron
Common crab apple	
	Malus sylvestris
Common cypress pine	
	Callitris preissii
	Callitris robusta
Common dogwood	
	Cornus sanguinea
Common elder	*Sambucus nigra*
Common elm	*Ulmus procera*
Common fig	*Ficus carica*
Common gardenia	
	Gardenia florida
	Gardenia grandiflora
	Gardenia jasminoides
Common goosberry	
	Ribes uva-crispa
Common gorse	*Ulex europaeus*
Common guava	*Psidium guajava*
Common hawthorn	
	Crataegus monogyna
Common hazel	*Corylus avellana*
Common holly	*Ilex aquifolium*
Common hornbeam	
	Carpinus betulus
Common horse chestnut	
	Aesculus hippocastanum
Common jujube tree	
	Ziziphus jujuba
Common juniper	
	Juniperus communis
Common laburnum	
	Laburnum anagyroides
	Laburnum vulgare
Common larch	*Larix decidua*
Common laurel	
	Prunus laurocerasus
Common lavender	
	Lavandula angustifolium
Common lilac	*Syringa vulgaris*
Common lime	*Tilia × europaea*
	Tilia × vulgaris
Common maple	*Acer campestre*
Common mountain ash	
	Sorbus aucuparia
Common mulberry	*Morus nigra*

Common myrtle *Myrtus communis*
Common oak *Quercus robur*
Common oleander
Nerium oleander
Common olive *Olea europaea*
Common osier *Salix viminalis*
Common papaw *Carica papaya*
Common pawpaw *Carica papaya*
Common peach *Prunus persica*
Common pear *Pyrus communis*
Common persimmon
Diospyros virginiana
Common privet
Ligustrum vulgare
Common quince *Cydonia oblonga*
Common rose mallow
Hibiscus moscheutos
Common rowan *Sorbus aucuparia*
Common sage *Salvia officinalis*
Common sallow *Salix cinerea*
Salix cinerea oleifolia
Common screw pine
Pandanus utilis
Common silver birch
Betula pendula
Common silver fir *Abies alba*
Common spindle tree
Euonymus europaea
Common spruce *Picea abies*
Common walnut *Juglans regia*
Common white birch
Betula pubescens
Common white jasmine
Jasminum officinale
Common witch hazel
Hamamelis virginiana
Common yellow azalea
Rhododendron luteum
Common yellowwood
Podocarpus falcatus
Common yew *Taxus baccata*
Confederate jasmine
Jasminum nitidum
Confederate rose
Hibiscus mutabilis
Confetti bush
Coleonema pulchrum
Congo fig *Ficus dryepondtiana*
Congo mallee *Eucalyptus dumosa*
Connemara heath
Daboecia cantabrica
Contorted hazel
Corylus avellana contorta
Contorted pagoda tree
Sophora japonica + pendula
Contorted willow
Salix babylonica pekinensis tortuosa
Salix matsudana tortuosa
Cooba *Acacia salicina*
Coolibah *Eucalyptus microtheca*

Cootamundra wattle
Acacia baileyana
Acacia saileyana
Copal tree *Ailanthus altissima*
Copper beech
Fagus sylvatica purpurea
Copper-leaf *Acalypha wilkesiana*
Copper-pod tree
Peltophorum pterocarpum
Coquito palm *Jubaea chilensis*
Jubaea spectabilis
Coralbark maple
Acer japonicum aconitifolium
Acer palmatum senkaki
Coralbark willow
Salix alba britzensis
Salix alba chermesina
Salix caprea chermesina
Coral bean *Erythrina arborea*
Erythrina herbacea
Coralberry *Ardisia crenata*
Symphoricarpus orbiculatus
Symphoricarpus rubra vulgaris
Symphoricarpus vulgaris
Coral gum *Eucalyptus torquata*
Coral hibiscus
Hibiscus schizopetalus
Coral pea *Adenanthera pavonina*
Coral plant *Jatropha multifida*
Russelia equisetiformis
Russelia juncea
Coral tree
Erythrina corallodendron
Erythrina crista-galli
Macaranga grandifolia
Coralwood *Adenanthera pavonina*
Cordia *Cordia sebestena*
Cork elm *Ulmus thomasii*
Cork fir *Abies lasiocarpa arizonica*
Cork hopbush
Kallstroemia platyptera
Cork oak *Quercus suber*
Corkscrew hazel
Corylus avellana contorta
Corkscrew wattle *Acacia tortuosa*
Corkscrew willow
Salix babylonica pekinensis tortuosa
Salix matsudana tortuosa
Corkwood *Leitneria floridana*
Ochroma pyramidale
Corkwood tree
Duboisia myoporoides
Cornel *Cornus mas*
Cornelian cherry
Cornus capitata mas
Cornus mas
Cornish elm *Ulmus angustifolia*
Ulmus angustifolia cornubiensis
Ulmus carpinifolia cornubiensis
Ulmus minor stricta cornubiensis
Ulmus stricta

TREES, BUSHES, AND SHRUBS

Cuban belly palm

Cornish heath *Erica vagans*
Coromandel ebony
    Diospyros melanoxylon
Correosa *Rhus microphylla*
Corsican heath *Erica terminalis*
Corsican pine
    Pinus nigra maritima
Corylopsis *Corylopsis spicata*
Cosmetic bark tree
    Murraya paniculata
Costa Rican guava
    Psidium friedrichsthalianum
Costa Rican holly
    Olmediella betschlerana
Costorphine plane
    Acer pseudoplatanus
    costorphinense
Cotoneaster *Cotoneaster frigidus*
Cottage mezereon
    Daphne mezereum
Cottage tea tree *Lycium barbarum*
    Lycium chinense
Cotton gum *Nyssa aquatica*
Cotton rose *Hibiscus mutabilis*
Cotton tree
    Bombax malabaricum
Cottonwood *Populus deltoides*
Cottony jujube
    Ziziphus mauritania
Council tree *Ficus altissima*
Country walnut
    Aleurites moluccana
Cowberry *Viburnum lentago*
    Vaccinium vitisidaea
Cow-itch *Rhus radicans*
Cow-itch cherry *Malpighia urens*
Cow-itch tree
    Lagunaria patersonii
Cow's tail pine
    Cephalotaxus harringtonia
Cowtail pine *Cephalotaxus fortunii*
Cow tree *Brosimum alicastrum*
Coyoli palm *Acrocomia mexicana*
Coyote willow *Salix exigua*
Cox's juniper
    Juniperus recurva coxii
Crackerberry *Cornus canadensis*
Crack willow *Salix fragilis*
Crampbark *Viburnum trilobum*
    Viburnum opulus
Cranberry
    Vaccinium macrocarpon
    Vaccinium oxycoccus
    Vaccinium vitis-idaea
Cranberry bush *Viburnum opulus*
    Viburnum trilobum
Cranberry cotoneaster
    Cotoneaster apiculatus
Cranberry tree
    Viburnum trilobum

Cranesbill myrtle
    Lagerstroemia indica
Cream bush *Holodiscus ariifolius*
    Holodiscus discolor
Cream nut *Bertholleta excelsa*
Creeping barberry *Mahonia repens*
Creeping blue blossom
    Ceanothus thyrsiflorus repens
Creeping boobialla
    Mysporum parvifolium
Creeping cedar
    Juniperus horizontalis
Creeping dogwood
    Cornus canadensis
Creeping fig *Ficus pumila*
    Ficus repens
    Ficus stipulata
Creeping juniper
    Juniperus horizontalis
    Juniperus procumbens
Creeping mountain ash
    Sorbus reducta
Creeping rubber plant *Ficus pumila*
    Ficus repens
    Ficus stipulata
Creeping savin juniper
    Juniperus horizontalis
Creeping willow *Salix repens*
Creeping winterberry
    Gaultheria procumbens
Creosote bush *Larrea divaricata*
    Larrea tridentata
Crested moss rose
    Rosa centifolia cristata
Cretan maple *Acer sempervirens*
Cretan zelcova *Zelcova abelicea*
Cricket-bat willow
    Salix alba caerulea
Crimean lime *Tilia × euchlora*
Crimean pine
    Pinus nigra caramanica
Crimson bottle brush
    Callistemon citrinus
Crimson dwarf cherry
    Prunus × cistena
Crimson mallee box
    Eucalyptus lansdowneana
Cross-leaved heath *Erica tetralix*
Croton *Codiaeum variegatum*
Crowberry *Empetrum nigrum*
Crown of thorns
    Paliurus spina-christi
Crown plant *Calotropis gigantea*
Crucifixion thorn
    Holacantha emoryi
Cry-baby tree
    Erythrina crista-galli
Cuachilote *Parmentiera edulis*
Cuban bast *Hibiscus elatus*
Cuban belly palm
    Colpothrinax wrightii

Cuban manac *Calyptronoma dulcis*
Cuban pine *Pinus caribaea*
  Pinus occidentalis
Cuban pink trumpet tree
  Tabebuia pallida
Cuban royal palm *Roystonea regia*
Cucumber tree
  Magnolia acuminata
Cucurite palm
  Maximiliana caribaea
  Maximiliana maripa
  Maximiliana regia
Cuipo *Cavanillesia platanifolia*
Cultivated apple *Malus domestica*
Cup gum *Eucalyptus cosmophylla*
Curare
  Chondrodendron tomentosum
  Strychnos toxifera
Curly palm *Howea belmoreana*
  Kentia belmoreana
Curly sentry palm
  Howea belmoreana
Curry-leaf tree *Murraya koenigii*
  Murraya paniculata
Curry plant
  Helichrysum serotinum
Custard apple *Annona cherimola*
  Annona reticulata
  Annona squamosa
Cutch *Acacia catechu*
Cut-leaf birch
  Betula pendula dalecarlica
Cut-leaf lilac *Syringa laciniata*
Cut-leaf oak
  Quercus robur filicifolia
Cut-leaf purple beech
  Fagus sylvatica rohanii
Cut-leaf walnut
  Juglans regia laciniata
Cutleaf zelkova
  Zelkova sinica verschaffeltii
Cut-leaved alder
  Alnus glutinosa imperialis
Cut-leaved beech
  Fagus sylvatica heterophylla
Cut-leaved elder
  Sambucus nigra laciniata
Cut-leaved hazel
  Corylus avellana heterophylla
Cut-leaved mountain ash
  Sorbus aucuparia asplenifolia
Cut-tail *Eucalyptus fastigiata*
Cuyamaca cypress
  Cupressus stephensonii
Cypress golden oak
  Quercus alnifolia
Cypress hebe *Hebe cupressoides*
Cypress oak
  Quercus robur fastigiata
Cypress spurge
  Euborbia cyparissias
Cyprian cedar *Cedrus brevifolia*

Cyprian plane
  Platanus orientalis insularis
Cyprus cedar *Cedrus brevifolia*
Cyprus strawberry tree
  Arbutus andrachne
Cyprus turpentine tree
  Pistacia terebinthus
Dagger plant *Yucca aloifolia*
Dahoon holly *Ilex cassine*
Dahurian buckthorn
  Rhamnus davurica
Dahurian larch *Larix gmelinii*
Daimyo oak *Quercus dentata*
Daisy bush
  Olearia nummularifolia
  Olearia phlogopappa
Dalmatian broom
  Genista dalmatica
  Genista sylvestris pungens
Damask rose *Rosa damascena*
Dammar *Agathis dammara*
Damson *Prunus domestica*
  Prunus domestica institia
  Prunus insititia
Dane's elder *Sambucus ebulus*
Danewort *Sambucus ebulus*
Dangleberry *Gaylussacia frondosa*
Daniell's euodia *Euodia daniellii*
Daphne lilac
  Syringa microphylla superba
Dark-leaved willow
  Salix myrsinifolia
  Salix nigricans
Darlington oak *Quercus laurifolia*
Darwin stringybark
  Eucalyptus tetradonta
Darwin woollybutt
  Eucalyptus miniata
Date palm *Phoenix dactylifera*
Date plum *Diospyros chinensis*
  Diospyros kaki
  Diospyros lotus
  Diospyros virginiana
Datil *Yucca baccata*
Dattock tree
  Detarium senegalense
David's pine *Pinus armandii*
Dawick beech
  Fagus sylvatica dawyck
Dawn redwood
  Metasequoia glyptostroboides
Day cestrum *Cestrum diurnum*
Day jessamine *Cestrum diurnum*
Dead-rat tree *Adansonia digitata*
Deal pine *Pinus strobus*
Deane's gum *Eucalyptus deanei*
Deccan hemp *Hibiscus cannabinus*
Deciduous cypress
  Taxodium distichum
Deckaner hemp
  Hibiscus cannabinus

TREES, BUSHES, AND SHRUBS

Deciduous camellia
Stewartia pseudocamellia
Stuartia pseudocamellia
Deep-veined maple   *Acer argutum*
Deerberry   *Vaccinium stamineum*
Deerbrush
Ceanothus integerrimus
Deer bush   *Ceanothus integerrimus*
Deer oak   *Quercus sadlerana*
Degame
Calycophyllum candissimum
Delavay's silver fir   *Abies delavayi*
Del norte manzanita
Arctostaphylos cinerea
Deodar   *Cedrus deodara*
Derris   *Derris elliptica*
Desert almond   *Prunus fasciculata*
Desert apricot   *Prunus fremontii*
Desert cassia   *Cassia covesii*
Cassia eremophila
Desert fan palm
Washingtonia filifera
Desert gum   *Eucalyptus rudis*
Desert ironwood   *Olneya tesota*
Desert juniper   *Juniperus utahensis*
Desert kurrajong
Brachychiton gregorii
Desert olive
Forestiera neomexicana
Desert peach   *Prunus andersonii*
Desert rose   *Adenium obesum*
Desert rose mallow
Hibiscus farragei
Desert sumac   *Rhus microphylla*
Desert tea   *Ephedera vulgaris*
Desert willow   *Chilopsis linearis*
Desmond mallee
Eucalyptus desmondensis
Deutzia   *Deutzia gracilis*
Devil's bit   *Alstonia scholaris*
Devil's club   *Oplopanax horridus*
Devi's fig   *Argemone mexicana*
Devil's maple   *Acer diabolicum*
Devil's shoestrings
Viburnum alnifolium
Devil's walking stick   *Aralia spinosa*
Devil tree   *Alstonia scholaris*
Devil wood
Osmanthus americanus
Dhobi's nut
Semecarpus anacardium
Digger pine   *Pinus sabiniana*
Dita bark   *Alstonia scholaris*
Divi-divi   *Caesalpinia coriaria*
Dockmackie
Viburnum acerifolium
Dogberry   *Cornus sanguinea*
Sorbus americana
Viburnum alnifolium
Dog briar   *Rosa canina*

Dog hobble   *Viburnum alnifolium*
Dog rose   *Rosa canina*
Dogwood   *Cornus sanguinea*
Dombey's southern beech
Nothofagus dombeyi
Doom palm   *Hyphaene thebaica*
Dorset heath   *Erica ciliaris*
Doub pine   *Borassus flabellifer*
Double almond
Prunus dulcis roseoplena
Double cherry-plum
Prunus × blireana
Double coconut
Lodoicea maldavica
Doble crimson thorn
Crataegus laevigata
Double flowering gorse
Ulex europaeus plenus
Double gean   *Prunus avium plena*
Double pink thorn
Crataegus laevigata
Double spruce   *Picea mariana*
Picea nigra
Double white cherry
Prunus avium plena
Double white thorn
Crataegus laevigata
Douglas fir   *Pseudotsuga menziesii*
Douglas maple
Acer glabrum douglasii
Doum palm   *Hyphaene thebaica*
Palmae hyphaene
Dove tree   *Davidia involucrata*
Downton elm
Ulmus × hollandica smithii
Downy birch   *Betula pubescens*
Downy black poplar
Populus nigra betulifolia
Downy cherry   *Prunus tomentosa*
Downy chestnut   *Castanea alnifolia*
Downy clethra   *Clethra tomentosa*
Downy hawthorn   *Crataegus mollis*
Downy Japanese maple
Acer japonicum
Downy myrtle
Rhodomyrtus tomentosa
Downy oak   *Quercus pubescens*
Downy poplar
Populus heterophylla
Downy rose   *Rosa tomentosa*
Downy tree of heaven
Ailanthus vilmoriniana
Downy willow   *Salix lapponum*
Dracaena fig   *Ficus pseudopalma*
Dragon bones   *Euphorbia lactea*
Dragon-eye palm
Pinus densiflora oculus-draconis
Dragon's blood
Daemonorops draco

Dragon's claw willow
    Salix babylonica pekinensis
        tortuosa
    Salix matsudana tortuosa
Dragon spruce   *Picea asperata*
Dragon tree   *Dracaena draco*
Drooping cowtail pine
    Cephalotaxus harringtonia
        drupacea
Drooping juniper
    Juniperus recurva
Drooping she-oak
    Casuarina stricta
Duck's foot tree   *Ginkgo biloba*
Dudgeon   *Buxus sempervirens*
Duke cherry   *Prunus × effusus*
    Prunus × gondouinii
Duke of Argyll's tea tree
    Lycium barbarum
    Lycium chinense
Dunkeld larch   *Larix × eurolepis*
Durian   *Durio zibethinus*
Durmast oak   *Quercus petraea*
Dutch elm   *Ulmus × hollandica*
    Ulmus major
Dutch lavender
    Lavandula angustifolia vera
    Lavandula vera
Dwarf Alberta spruce
    Picea glauca albertiana nana
Dwarf American cherry
    Prunus pumila
Dwarf banana   *Musa nana*
Dwarf bilberry
    Vaccinium caespitosum
Dwarf birch   *Betula glandulosa*
    Betula nana
Dwarf broom   *Cytisus demissus*
Dwarf buckeye   *Aesculus parviflora*
Dwarf buckthorn   *Rhamnus pumila*
Dwarf cherry   *Prunus fruticosa*
    Prunus pumila
Dwarf chestnut oak
    Quercus prinoides
Dwarf cornel   *Cornus canadensis*
    Cornus suecica
Dwarf elder   *Sambucus ebulus*
Dwarf elm   *Ulmus pumila*
Dwarf fan palm
    Chamaerops humilis
Dwarf furze   *Ulex minor*
Dwarf gorse   *Ulex minor*
Dwarf hawthorn
    Crataegus monogyna compacta
Dwarf holly   *Malpighia coccigera*
Dwarf horse chestnut
    Aesculus parviflora
Dwarf huckleberry
    Gaylussacia dumosa
    Gaylussacia frondosa
Dwarf laurel   *Kalmia angustifolia*

Dwarf mountain pine   *Pinus mugo*
Dwarf nealie   *Acacia bynoeana*
Dwarf palmetto   *Sabal adansonii*
    Sabal minor
Dwarf pea tree   *Caragana pygmaea*
Dwarf poinciana
    Caesalpinia pulcherrima
Dwarf pomegranate
    Punica granatum nana
Dwarf quince
    Chaenomeles japonica
Dwarf russian almond
    Prunus tenella
Dwarf she-oak   *Casuarina nana*
Dwarf Siberian pine   *Pinus pumila*
Dwarf stone pine   *Pinus pumila*
Dwarf sumac   *Rhus copallina*
Dwarf willow   *Salix herbacea*
Dyer's broom   *Genista tinctoria*
Dyer's greenweed
    Genista tinctoria
Dysentery bark   *Simarouba amara*
Eagle's claw maple
    Acer platanoides laciniatum
Eared willow   *Salix aurita*
Ear-leaved umbrella tree
    Magnolia fraseri
East African juniper
    Juniperus procera
Eastern cottonwood
    Populus deltoides
Eastern hemlock   *Tsuga canadensis*
Eastern hop-hornbeam
    Ostrya virginiana
Eastern hornbeam
    Carpinus orientalis
Eastern larch   *Larix laricina*
Eastern red cedar
    Juniperus virginiana
Eastern strawberry tree
    Arbutus andrachne
Eastern sycamore
    Platanus occidentalis
Eastern white pine   *Pinus strobus*
East Himalayan fir   *Abies spectabilis*
    Abies webbiana
East Himalayan spruce
    Picea spinulosa
East Indian ebony
    Diospyros ebenaster
    Diospyros ebenum
East Indian fig tree
    Ficus benghalensis
    Ficus indica
East Indian satinwood
    Chloroxylon swietenia
East Indian walnut   *Albizzia lebbeck*
East Indian wine palm
    Phoenix rupicola
East Siberian fir   *Abies nephrolepis*

TREES, BUSHES, AND SHRUBS

Evergreen currant

Eastwood manzanita
　　　　Arctostaphylos glandulosa
Ebony　　　Diospyros ebenaster
　　　　　　Diospyros ebenum
Ebonywood　Bauhinia variegata
Ecuador laurel　Cordia alliodora
Edging box　Buxus suffruticosa
Edible banana　Musa acuminata
　　　　　　Musa × paradisiaca
Eggfruit　Pouteria campechiana
Egg-yolk willow　Salix alba vitellina
Eglantine rose　　Rosa eglanteria
　　　　　　　　Rosa rubiginosa
Egyptian doom palm
　　　　　　Hyphaene thebaica
Egyptian privet　Lawsonia inermis
Egyptian sycamore　Ficus sycomorus
Egyptian thorn　　Acacia senegal
Elephant apple　Feronia elephantum
　　　　　　　　Feronia limonia
Elephant apple tree　Dillenia indica
Elephant bush　Portulacaria afra
Elephant's ear
　　　　Enterolobium cyclocarpum
Elephant hedge bean tree
　　　　　　Schotia latifolia
Elephant's ear wattle　Acacia dunnii
Elephant's foot
　　　　Beaucarnea recurvata
Elephant tree　Bursera microphylla
Elliott's blueberry
　　　　　　Vaccinium elliottii
Elliott's pine　　Pinus elliottii
Elm-leaved sumac　Rhus coriaria
Emblic　　Phyllanthus emblica
Emmerson's thorn
　　　　　　Crataegus submollis
Emory oak　　Quercus emoryi
Empress candle plant　Cassia alata
Empress tree
　　　　Paulownia tomentosa
Emu bush　Eremophila maculata
Encina　　Quercus agrifolia
Engelmann's oak
　　　　Quercus engelmannii
Engelmann's spruce
　　　　　　Picea engelmannii
Engler's beech　Fagus englerana
English elm　　Ulmus procera
English hawthorn
　　　　Crataegus laevigata
English holly　Ilex aquifolium
English laurel　Prunus laurocerasus
English oak　　Quercus rober
English walnut　Juglans regia
English yew　　Taxus baccata
Epaulette tree　Pterostyrax hispida
Erect Japanese cherry
　　　　Prunus amanogawa
Erman's birch　Betula ermanii

Escabon　　Cytisus proliferus
Escallonia　Escallonia macrantha
Ethiopian acacia　Acacia abyssinica
Ethiopian date palm
　　　　　　Phoenix abyssinica
Eucryphia　Eucryphia glutinosa
　　　　　Eucryphia pinnatifolia
Euodia　　Euodia hupehensis
European alder　Alnus incana
European ash　Fraxinus excelsior
European aspen　Populus tremula
European bird cherry　Prunus padus
European bladdernut
　　　　　　Staphylea pinnata
European chestnut
　　　　　　Castanea sativa
European cranberry bush
　　　　　　Viburnum opulus
European elder　Sambucus nigra
European fan palm
　　　　　Chamaerops humilis
European field elm
　　　　　　Ulmus carpinifolia
European golden ball
　　　　　　Forsythia europaea
European green alder　Alnus viridis
European hop-hornbeam
　　　　　　Ostrya carpinifolia
European hornbeam
　　　　　　Carpinus betulus
European larch　　Larix decidua
European mountain ash
　　　　　　Sorbus aucuparia
European red elder
　　　　　　Sambucus racemosa
European scrub pine
　　　　　　Pinus mugo pumilo
European silver fir　Abies alba
European spindle tree
　　　　　　Euonymus europaea
European whitebeam
　　　　Sorbus aria wilfred fox
European white birch
　　　　　　Betula pendula
European white elm　Ulmus laevis
European wild cranberry
　　　　Oxycoccus oxycoccus
　　　　Oxycoccus palustris
　　　　Vaccinium oxycoccus
Everblooming French heather
　　　　　　Erica doliiformis
Everglades palm
　　　　Acoelorrhaphe wrightii
Evergreen ash　Fraxinus uhdei
Evergreen blueberry
　　　　Vaccinium myrsinites
Evergreen cherry　Prunus ilicifolia
Evergreen currant
　　　　Ribes viburnumifolium

Evergreen laburnum
    Piptanthus laburnifolius
    Piptanthus nepalensis
Evergreen magnolia
    Magnolia grandiflora
Evergreen oak   *Quercus ilex*
Evergreen pear   *Pyrus kawakamii*
Evergreen rose   *Rosa sempervirens*
Evergreen spindle tree
    Euonymus japonica
Evergreen sumac   *Rhus virens*
Ewart's mallee
    Eucalyptus ewartiana
Exeter oak   *Quercus × hispanica*
    lucombeana
Fairy rose   *Rosa chinensis minima*
False acacia   *Robinia pseudoacacia*
False buckeye   *Ungnadia speciosa*
False buckthorn
    Bumelia lanuginosa
False brazilwood
    Caesalpinia peltophoroides
False cactus   *Euphorbia lactea*
False castor oil plant
    Fatsia japonica
False dogwood   *Sapindus saponaria*
False heath   *Fabiana imbricata*
False holly
    Osmanthus heterophyllus
False indigo   *Amorpha fruticosa*
False ipecac   *Psychotria emetica*
False lombardy poplar
    Populus robusta
False medlar
    Sorbus chamaemespilus
False olive   *Cassine orientalis*
False winter's bark
    Cinnamodendron corticosum
Fancy annie   *Delonix regia*
Farges catalpa   *Catalpa fargesii*
Farges fir   *Abies fargesii*
    Abies sutchuenensis
Farkleberry   *Vaccinium arboreum*
Fastigiate beech
    Fagus sylvatica fastigiata
Fearn tree   *Jacaranda acutifolia*
Feather-cone fir   *Abies procera*
Feather-duster palm
    Rhopalostylis sapida
Feathery cassia
    Cassia artemisioides
February daphne
    Daphne mezereum
Fehi banana   *Musa fehi*
    Musa troglodytarum
Feijoa   *Feijoa sellowiana*
Felt-leaf ceanothus
    Ceanothus arboreus
Female lombardy poplar
    Populus nigra italica foemina
Fern-leaf aralia   *Polyscias filicifolia*

Fernleaf beech
    Fagus sylvatica asplenifolia
Fern-leaved beech
    Fagus sylvatica heterophylla
Fern-leaved bramble
    Rubus laciniatus
Fern-leaved elder
    Sambucus nigra laciniata
Fern-leaved oak
    Quercus robur asplenifolia
Fern palm   *Cycas circinalis*
Fern podocarpus
    Podocarpus elongatus
Fern rhapis   *Rhapis excelsa*
Fetterbush *Leucothoe fontanesiana*
    Lyonia lucida
Fever bush   *Garrya fremontii*
    Lindera benzoin
Fever tree   *Acacia xanthophloea*
    Pinckneya pubens
Fiddle-leaf fig   *Ficus lyrata*
    Ficus pandurata
Fiddler's spurge
    Euphorbia cyathophora
Fiddlewood
    Citharexylum fruticosum
    Citharexylum spinosum
Field briar   *Rosa agrestis*
Field maple   *Acer campestre*
Field rose   *Rosa arvensis*
Fig-leaf palm   *Aralia japonica*
    Aralia sieboldii
    Fatsia japonica
Fijian kauri pine   *Agathis vitiensis*
Fiji fan palm   *Pritchardia pacifica*
Filbert   *Corylus avellana*
    Corylus maxima
Finger tree   *Euphorbia tirucalli*
Finnish whitebeam *Sorbus fennica*
    Sorbus × hybrida
Fire birch   *Betula populifolia*
Firebush   *Hamelia patens*
Firecracker   *Russelia juncea*
Fire cherry   *Prunus pennsylvanica*
Fire-dragon   *Acalypha wilkesiana*
Fire-on-the-mountain
    Euphorbia cyathophora
    Euphorbia heterophylla
Firethorn   *Pyracantha coccinea*
Fire tree   *Nuytsia floribunda*
Firewheel   *Grevillea wilsonii*
Firewheel tree
    Stenocarpus sinuatus
Fish-poison tree   *Piscidia erythrina*
Fishtail camellia
    Camellia × williamsii c.f.coates
Five fingers tree
    Neopanax arboreus
Five-seeded hawthorn
    Crataegus pentagyna
Flaky fir   *Abies squamata*

Fragrant olive

Flamboyant tree *Delonix regia*

Flame bottle tree
Brachychiton acerifolius

Flame creeper
Combretum microphyllum

Flamegold *Koelreuteria elegans*

Flame of the forest *Delonix regia*
Spathodea campanulata

Flame-of-the-woods *Ixora coccinea*
Ixora incarnata

Flame tree
Brachychiton acerifolius
Brachychiton australis
Delonix regia
Sterculia acerfolia

Flat-topped yate
Eucalyptus occidentalis

Flooded box
Eucalyptus microtheca

Flooded gum *Eucalyptus grandis*

Florida corkwood
Leitneria floridana

Florida mahogany *Persea borbonia*

Florida maple *Acer barbatum*

Florida royal palm *Roystonea elata*

Florida silver palm
Coccothrinax argentata

Florida strangler fig *Ficus aurea*

Florida thatch palm
Thrinax parviflora

Florida yew *Taxus floridana*

Florist's genista *Genista canariensis*

Florist's willow *Salix caprea*

Floss silk tree *Chorisia speciosa*

Flower fence
Caesalpinia pulcherrima

Flowering almond
Prunus glandulosa
Prunus jacquemontii
Prunus japonica
Prunus triloba

Flowering ash *Fraxinus dipetala*
Fraxinus ornus

Flowering banana *Musa ornata*

Flowering currant
Ribes sanguineum

Flowering dogwood
Cornus capitata florida
Cornus florida

Flowering nutmeg
Leycesteria formosa

Flowering plum *Prunus cerasifera*

Flowering quince
Chaenomeles speciosa

Flowering spurge
Euphorbia corollata

Flowering willow *Chilopsis linearis*

Flower-of-an-hour
Hibiscus trionum

Flower-of-love
Tabernaemontana divaricata

Fly honeysuckle
Lonicera xylosteum

Foetid yew *Torreya taxifolia*

Folgner's whitebeam
Sorbus folgneri

Folhado *Clethra arborea*

Foliage flower *Breynia disticha*

Fontainebleau service tree
Sorbus × latifolia

Forest fever tree
Anthockistazam besiaca

Forest red gum
Eucalyptus tereticornis

Forest wild medlar
Vangueria esculenta

Formosa incense cedar
Calocedrus formosana

Formosan azalea *Azalea oldhamii*
Rhododendron oldhamii

Formosan cedar
Chamaecyparis formosensis

Formosan cherry
Prunus campanulata

Formosan cypress
Chamaecyparis formosensis

Formosan gum
Liquidambar formosana

Formosan hemlock
Tsuga formosana

Formosa rice tree *Aralia japonica*
Fatsia japonica

Forrest's fir *Abies delavayi forrestii*

Forrest's maple *Acer forrestii*

Forrest's marlock
Eucalyptus forrestiana

Forrest's silver fir
Abies delavayi forrestii

Forster's sentry palm
Howea forsterana
Kentia forsterana

Forsythia *Forsythia × intermedia*

Fountain buddleia
Buddleia alternifolia

Fountain bush
Russelia equisetiformis
Russelia juncea

Fountain dracaena
Cordyline australis

Fountain tree
Spathodea campanulata

Four-winged mallee
Eucalyptus tetraptera

Foxberry *Vaccinium vitis-idaea*

Foxglove tree
Paulownia tomentosa

Foxtail *Acalypha hispida*

Foxtail pine *Pinus balfouriana*

Fragrant champaca
Michelia champaca

Fragrant myall
Acacia homalophylla

Fragrant olive *Osmanthus fragrans*

Fragrant snowbell

Fragrant snowbell	Styrax obassia
Fragrant sumac	Rhus aromatica
Franceschi palm	Brahea elegans
Frangipani	Plumeria acuminata
Frangipani tree	Plumeria rubra
Frankincense	Boswellia thurifera
Frankincense pine	Pinus taeda
Franklin tree	Franklinia alatamaha
Fraser's balsam fir	Abies fraseri
Frazer river douglas fir	
	Pseudotsuga menziesii caesia
Fremont's box thorn	
	Lycium pallidum
Fremont poplar	Populus fremontii
French hales	Sorbus devoniensis
French heather	Erica hyemalis
French lavender	
	Lavandula stoechas
French mulberry	
	Callicarpa americana
French physic nut	Jatropha curcas
French rose	Rosa gallica
French tamarisk	Tamarix gallica
French willow	Salix triandra
Fringed heath	Erica ciliaris
Fringed hibiscus	
	Hibiscus schizopetalus
Fringed lavender	
	Lavandula dentata
Fringe tree	Chionanthus virginicus
Frosted thorn	
	Crataegus × prunifolia
Frosty wattle	Acacia pruinosa
Fuchsia-flowered gooseberry	
	Ribes speciosum
Fuchsia gum	
	Eucalyptus forrestiana
Fuji cherry	Prunus incisa
Full-moon maple	Acer japonicum
Furin holly	Ilex geniculata
Furry willow	Salix adenophylla
	Salix cordata
Furze	Ulex europaeus
Fustic	Chlorophora tinctoria
Gaboon	Aucomea klainiana
Galapee tree	
	Sciadophyllum brownii
Gale	Myrica gale
Gallberry	Ilex glabra
Gambel's oak	Quercus gambelii
Gander's oak	Quercus × ganderi
Garland crab apple	
	Malus coronaria
Garland flower bush	
	Daphne cneorum
Garlic pear	Crataera gynandra
Gbanja cola	Cola nitida
Gean	Prunus avium
	Prunus avium sylvestris

Gebang palm	Corypha elata
Geiger tree	Cordia sebestena
Genipap	Genipa americana
Genipe	Melicoccus bijugatus
Genista	Cytisus canariensis
Genoa broom	Genista januensis
Georgia bark tree	
	Pinckneya pubens
Georgia pine	Pinus palustris
Geraldton wax	
	Chamaelaucium uncinatum
Geranium-leaf aralia	
	Polyscias guilfoylei
Geranium tree	Cordia sebestena
Gerard's pine	Pinus gerardiana
German greenweed	
	Genista germanica
Ghost gum	Eucalyptus papuana
Ghost tree	Davidia involucrata
Ghostweed	Euphorbia marginata
Giant cedar	Thuya plicata
Giant chinquapin	
	Castanopsis chrysophylla
Giant dogwood	
	Cornus controversa
Giant dracaena	Cordyline australis
Giant filbert	Corylus maxima
Giant fir	Abies grandis
Giant gum	Eucalyptus regnans
Giant pine	Pinus lambertiana
Giant protea	Protea cynaroides
Giant sequoia	
	Sequoiadendron giganteum
Giant woolly protea	
	Protea barbigera
Gibb's firethorn	
	Pyracantha atalantoides
Gidgee myall	Acacia homalophylla
Giles' netbush	Calothamnus gilesii
Gimlet gum	Eucalyptus salubris
Gingerbread palm	
	Hyphaene thebaica
	Palmae hyphaene
Gingerbread plum	
	Parinari macrophylla
Gingerbread tree	
	Parinari macrophylla
Gippsland fountain palm	
	Livistona australis
Gippsland palm	Corypha australis
	Livistona australis
Gippsland waratah	Telopea oreades
Glastonbury thorn	
	Crataegus monogyna biflora
	Crataegus monogyna praecox
	Crataegus praecox
Glory bower	
	Clerodendrum fargesii
Glory pea	Clianthus formosus

TREES, BUSHES, AND SHRUBS

Glory tree *Clerodendrum fargesii*
Clerodendrum thomsoniae
Clerodendrum trichotomum

Glory wattle *Acacia spectabilis*

Glossy-leaf fig *Ficus retusa*

Glossy privet *Ligustrum lucidum*

Goat willow *Salix caprea*

Goddess magnolia
Magnolia sprengeri diva

Godsberry *Diospyros lotus*

Gold coast bombax
Bombax buonopozense

Gold dust *Acacia acinacea*

Gold-dust dracaena
Dracaena surculosa

Golden acacia
Robinia pseudoacacia frisia

Golden American elder
Sambucus canadensis aurea

Golden apple *Aegle marmelos*
Spondias lutea
Spondias cytherea

Golden ash
Fraxinus excelsior jaspidea

Golden ashleaf maple
Acer negundo auratum

Golden-bark ash
Fraxinus excelsior jaspidea

Golden bay *Laurus nobilis aureus*

Golden beech
Fagus sylvatica zlatia

Golden bell *Forsythia suspensa*

Golden bush *Cassinia fulvida*

Golden-blotched hedgehog holly
Ilex aquifolium ferox aurea

Golden cassia *Cassia fasciculata*

Golden chain
Laburnum anagyroides
Laburnum vulgare

Golden chain tree
Laburnum × watereri

Golden chestnut
Chrysolepis chrysophylla

Golden Chinese juniper
Juniperus chinensis aurea

Golden-cup oak
Quercus chrysolepis

Golden curls tree
Salix babylonica pekinensis
tortuosa aurea

Golden curls willow
Salix xerythroflexuosa

Golden currant *Ribes aureum*
Ribes odoratum

Golden deodar cedar
Cedrus deodara aurea

Golden dewdrop *Duranta ellisia*
Duranta repens

Golden dogwood
Cornus alba aurea

Golden elder
Sambucus nigra aurea

Golden-feather palm
Chrysalidocarpus lutescens

Golden fig *Ficus aurea*

Golden-flowered daphne
Daphne aurantiaca

Golden hazel
Corylus avellana aurea

Golden heather *Cassinia fulvida*

Golden hinoki cypress
Chamaecyparis obtusa crippsii

Golden holly
Ilex aquifolium aurea

Golden Irish yew
Taxus baccata aureovariegata
Taxus baccata fastigiata aurea

Golden larch *Pseudolarix amabilis*
Pseudolarix kaempferi

Golden lawson's cypress
Chamaecyparis lawsoniana
stewartii

Golden-leaved barberry
Berberis thunbergii aurea

Golden-leaved catalpa
Catalpa bignonioides aurea

Golden-leaved Japanese maple
Acer shirasawanum aureum

Golden-leaved laburnum
Laburnum anagyroides aureum

Golden locust
Robinia pseudoacacia frisia

Golden mimosa *Acacia baileyana*

Golden moon maple
Acer japonicum aureum

Golden oak *Quercus alnifolia*
Quercus robur concordia

Golden poplar
Populus serotina aurea

Golden privet
Ligustrum ovalifolium aureum

Golden rain *Cassia fistula*
Laburnum anagyroides
Laburnum vulgare

Golden rain tree
Koelreuteria paniculata

Golden rain wattle
Acacia prominens

Golden shower *Cassia fistula*

Golden sycamore
Acer pseudoilatanus worlei

Golden trumpet
Allamander cathartica

Golden trumpet tree
Tabebuia chrysantha

Golden variegated dogwood
Cornus alba spaethii

Golden wattle *Acacia pycnantha*

Golden weeping ash
Fraxinus excelsior aurea pendula

Golden weeping holly
Ilex aquifolium aurea pendula

Golden weeping willow
Salix sepulcralis chrysocoma

Golden willow	*Acacia cyanophylla*
	Salix alba vitellina
Golden wonder	
	Cassia didymobotrya
	Cassia splendida
Golden wreath	*Acacia saligna*
Golden yew	*Taxus baccata aurea*
Goldilocks	*Helichrysum stoechas*
Goldspire	*Azara integrifolia*
Gomuti palm	*Arenga pinnata*
Good-luck palm	
	Chamaedorea elegans
Good-luck plant	
	Cordyline fruticosa
	Cordyline terminalis
	Dracaena terminalis
Goodyer elm	*Ulmus angustifolia*
Goora nut	*Cola acuminata*
Gooseberry	*Ribes uva-crispa*
Goosegog	*Ribes uva-crispa*
Gooseberry tree	
	Phyllanthus acidus
Goose plum	*Prunus americana*
Gorse	*Ulex europaeus*
Governor's plum	*Flacourtia indica*
	Flacourtia ramontchi
Gowen's cypress	
	Cupressus goveniana
Graceful wattle	*Acacia decora*
Grampian stringybark	
	Eucalyptus alpina
Grand fir	*Abies grandis*
Granite bottlebrush	
	Melaleuca armillaris
Granjeno	*Celtis iguanaea*
Grapefruit	*Citrus × paradisi*
Grass palm	*Cordyline australis*
Grass tree	*Xanthorrhoea australis*
Greater malayan chestnut	
	Chrysolepis megacarpa
Great laurel	
	Rhododendron maximum
	Rhododendron ponticum
Great Malayan chestnut	
	Castanopsis megacarpa
Great plains cottonwood	
	Populus sargentii
Great rose mallow	
	Hibiscus grandiflorus
Great sallow	*Salix caprea*
Great white cherry	
	Prunus tai-haku
Grecian fir	*Abies cephalonica*
Grecian juniper	*Juniperus excelsa*
Grecian strawberry tree	
	Arbutus andrachne
Greek fir	*Abies cephalonica*
Greek myrtle	*Myrtus communis*
Greek whitebeam	*Sorbus graeca*

Green alder	*Alnus crispa mollis*
	Alnus viridis
Green almond	*Pistacia vera*
Green ash	*Fraxinus pennsylvanica*
Green-bark ceanothus	
	Ceanothus spinosus
Green briar	*Smilax rotundifolia*
Green ebony	*Tabebuia flavescens*
Greengage	
	Prunus domestica italica
Greenglow plum	*Prunus cerasifera*
Greenheart	*Nectandra rodiaei*
	Ocotea bullata
	Ocotea radiaei
Greenleaf manzanita	
	Arctostaphylos patula
Green manzanita	
	Arctostaphylos patula
Green mountain sallow	
	Salix andersoniana
Green oak	*Quercus pubescens*
Green osier	*Cornus alternifolia*
Green rose	
	Rosa chinensis viridiflora
Green wattle	*Acacia decurrens*
	Acacia farnesiana
Greenweed	*Genista tinctoria*
Gregg's pine	*Pinus greggii*
Grey alder	*Alnus incana*
Grey birch	*Betula alleghaniensis*
	Betula populifolia
Grey box	*Eucalyptus moluccana*
Grey-budded snakebark maple	
	Acer rufinerve
Grey corkwood	
	Erythrina vespertilio
Grey dogwood	*Cornus racemosa*
Grey douglas fir	
	Pseudotsuga menziesii caesia
Grey goddess	*Brahea armata*
Grey gum	*Eucalyptus punctata*
	Eucalyptus tereticornis
Grey heath	*Erica cinerea*
Grey ironbark	
	Eucalyptus paniculata
Greyleaf cherry	*Prunus canescens*
Grey mulga	*Acacia brachybotrya*
Grey peppermint	
	Eucalyptus radiata
Grey pine	*Pinus banksiana*
Grey poplar	*Populus canescens*
Grey sage brush	*Atriplex canescens*
Grey sallow	*Salix cinerea*
	Salix cinerea atrocinerea
Grey willow	*Salix cinerea*
	Salix humilis
Ground cherry	*Prunus fruticosa*
Ground rattan cane	*Rhapis excelsa*
Ground senna	*Cassia chamaecrista*
Grouseberry	*Viburnum trilobum*

Grumichama *Eugenia brasiliensis*
Eugenia dombeyi
Grumixameira *Eugenia brasiliensis*
Eugenia dombeyi
Guadalupe cypress
Cupressus guadalupensis
Guadalupe palm *Brahea edulis*
Guajilote *Parmentiera edulis*
Guanabana *Annona muricata*
Guatemalan rhubarb
Jatropha integerrima
Guava *Psidium guajava*
Psidium guineense
Guayabo hormiguero
Triplaris surinamensis
Guelder rose *Viburnum opulus*
Guernsey elm
Ulmus carpinifolia sarniensis
Ulmus minor stricta sarniensis
Guiana chestnut *Pachira aquatica*
Guindo *Nothofagus antartica*
Guinea pepper *Xylopia aethiopica*
Guinea plum *Parinari excelsa*
Gully ash *Eucalyptus smithii*
Gully gum *Eucalyptus smithii*
Gulmohur *Delonix regia*
Gum acacia *Acacia nilotica*
Acacia senegal
Gum ammoniac
Dorema ammoniacum
Gum-arabic tree *Acacia nilotica*
Acacia senegal
Acacia seyal
Gumbo-limbo *Bursera simaruba*
Gum cistus *Cistus ladanifer*
Gum elastic *Bumelia lanuginosa*
Gum elemi *Bursera simaruba*
Gumi *Elaeagnus edulis*
Elaeagnus multiflora
Gum-lac *Schleichera oleosa*
Gum-top stringybark
Eucalyptus delegatensis
Gum tragacanth
Astragalus gummiferi
Gungurru *Eucalyptus caesia*
Gutta percha *Palaquim gutta*
Gutta-percha tree
Eucommia ulmoides
Habbel *Juniperus drupacea*
Hackberry *Celtis occidentalis*
Hackmatack *Larix laricina*
Populus balsamifera
Hagberry *Prunus padus*
Hag briar *Smilax hispida*
Hairy alpen rose
Rhododendron hirsutum
Hairy birch *Betula pubescens*
Hairy greenweed *Genista pilosa*
Hairy greenwood *Genista pilosa*

Hairy huckleberry
Vaccinium hirsutum
Hairy manzanita
Arctostaphylos columbiana
Hairy wattle *Acacia pubescens*
Hai-tung crab apple
Malus spectabilis
Halberd-leaved willow *Salix hastata*
Hall's crab apple *Malus halliana*
Handflower tree
Chiranthodendron pentadactylon
Handkerchief tree
Davidia involucrata
Hansen's cherry *Prunus tomentosa*
Hard beech *Nothofagus truncata*
Hard maple *Acer saccharum*
Hardy fuchsia *Fuchsia conica*
Fuchsia magellanica
Hardy orange *Citrus trifoliata*
Poncirus trifoliata
Harrington plum yew
Cephalotaxus harringtonia
Harry Lauder's walking stick
Corylus avellana contorta
Hat-rack cactus *Euphorbia lactea*
Hat tree *Brachychiton discolor*
Havard oak *Quercus havardii*
Hawaiian good-luck plant
Cordyline terminalis
Dracaena terminalis
Hawaiian hibiscus *Hibiscus sinensis*
Hawthorn *Crataegus monogyna*
Hawthorn-leaf crab apple
Malus florentina
Hawthorn-leaved maple
Acer crataegifolium
Hazel alder *Alnus rugosa*
Heart-leaf manzanita
Arctostaphylos andersonii
Heart-leaved silver gum
Eucalyptus cordata
Heart-leaved willow *Salix cordata*
Heartnut *Juglans ailantifolia*
Heather *Calluna erica*
Heavenly bamboo
Nandina domestica
Hedge euphorbia
Euphorbia neriifolia
Hedgehog broom
Erinacea anthyllis
Erinacea pungens
Hedgehog fir *Abies pinsapo*
Hedgehog holly
Ilex aquifolium ferox
Hedgehog rose *Rosa rugosa*
Hedge maple *Acer campestre*
Hedge thorn *Carissa bispinosa*
Hedge wattle *Acacia armata*
Heldreich's maple *Acer heldreichii*
Hemlock *Conium maculatum*

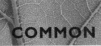

Hemp palm	*Trachycarpus fortunei*
Hemp tree	*Vitex agnus-castus*
Hemsley's storax	
	Styrax hemsleyana
Henna	*Lawsonia alba*
	Lawsonia inermis
Hercules' club	*Aralia spinosa*
	Zanthoxylum clava-herculis
Hers' maple	*Acer hersii*
Hiba	*Thujopsis dolabrata*
	Thuyopsis dolabrata
Hiba arbor-vitae	
	Thujopsis dolabrata
	Thuyopsis dolabrata
Hibiscus	*Althaea frutex*
	Hibiscus syriacus
Hickory pine	*Pinus aristata*
	Pinus pungens
Hicks' yew	*Taxus media hicksii*
Higan cherry	*Prunus subhirtella*
	Prunus subhirtella autumnalis
High-bush blueberry	
	Vaccinium corymbosum
Highbush cranberry	
	Viburnum trilobum
Highclere holly	
	Ilex × altaclarensis golden king
High-ground willow oak	
	Quercus incana
Highland pine	
	Pinus sylvestris rubra
Hill cherry	*Prunus serrulata*
	Prunus serrulata spontanea
Hill gooseberry	
	Rhodomyrtus tomentosa
Hill guava	*Rhodomyrtus tomentosa*
Himalayan alder	*Alnus nitida*
Himalayan birch	
	Betula jacquemontii
	Betula utilis
Himalayan bird cherry	
	Prunus cornuta
Himalayan cedar	*Cedrus deodara*
Himalayan cherry	*Prunus rufa*
Himalayan cotoneaster	
	Cotoneaster simonsii
Himalayan cypress	
	Cupressus torulosa
Himalayan fir	*Abies spectabilis*
	Abies webbiana
Himalayan hemlock	*Tsuga dumosa*
Himalayan holly	*Ilex dipyrena*
Himalayan honeysuckle	
	Leycesteria formosa
Himalayan jasmine	
	Jasminum humile
Himalayan juniper	
	Juniperus recurva
Himalayan larch	*Larix griffithii*
Himalayan lilac	*Syringa emodi*

Himalayan musk rose	
	Rosa brunonii
Himalayan pine	*Pinus wallichiana*
Himalayan spruce	*Picea smithiana*
Himalayan tree-cotoneaster	
	Cotoneaster frigidus
Himalayan whitebeam	
	Sorbus cuspidata
Himalayan white pine	
	Pinus wallichiana
Himalayan yew	*Taxus wallichiana*
Hinoki cypress	
	Chamaecyparis obtusa
Hoarwithy	*Viburnum lantana*
Hoaryleaf ceanothus	
	Ceanothus crassifolius
Hoary manzanita	
	Arctostaphylos canescens
Hoary willow	*Salix elaeagnus*
Hobblebush	*Viburnum alnifolium*
	Viburnum lantanoides
Hobble marsh	
	Viburnum alnifolium
Hog cranberry	
	Arctostaphylos uva-ursi
Hogg's double yellow rose	
	Rosa lutea hoggii
Hognut	*Carya glabra*
Hog plum	*Prunus americana*
	Prunus reverchonii
	Spondias mombin
	Ximenia americana
Holford pine	*Pinus × holfordiana*
Holly barberry	
	Mahonia aquifolium
Holly-leaf ceanothus	
	Ceanothus purpureus
Hollyleaf sweetspire	*Itea illicifolia*
Holly-leaved barberry	
	Berberis ilicifolia
Holly-leaved cherry	
	Prunus ilicifolia
Holly-leaved grevillea	
	Grevillea aquifolium
Holly-leaved olive	
	Osmanthus heterophyllus
Holly mahonia	
	Mahonia aquifolium
Holly oak	*Quercus ilex*
Hollywood juniper	
	Juniperus chinensis kaizuka
Holm oak	*Quercus ilex*
Holy flax	*Santolina rosmarinifolia*
Hondapara	*Dillenia indica*
Hondo spruce	
	Picea jezoensis hondoensis
Honduras mahogany	
	Swietenia macrophylla
Honeyberry	*Celtis australis*
	Melicoccus bijugatus
Honey bush	*Melianthus major*

Honey flower	*Protea mellifera*
Honey locust	*Gleditsia triacanthos*
	Gleditschia triacanthos
Honey myrtle	*Melaleuca huegelii*
Honey palm	*Jubaea chilensis*
	Jubaea spectabilis
Honey protea	*Protea mellifera*
Honeyshuck	*Gleditsia triacanthos*
Hoop pine	
	Araucaria cunninghamii
Hop hornbeam	*Ostrya carpinifolia*
Hop tree	*Ptelea trifoliata*
Horizontal box	*Buxus prostrata*
Hornbeam	*Carpinus betulus*
Hornbeam-leaved maple	
	Acer carpinifolium
Hornbeam maple	
	Acer carpinifolium
Horned holly	*Ilex cornuta*
Horned mallee	
	Eucalyptus eremophila
Horned maple	*Acer diabolicum*
Horse briar	*Smilax rotundifolia*
Horse cassia	*Cassia grandis*
Horse chestnut	
	Aesculus hippocastanum
Horseradish tree	*Moringa oleifera*
	Moringa pterygosperma
Horse sugar	*Symplocos tinctoria*
Horsetail she-oak	
	Casuarina equisetifolia
Horsetail tree	
	Casuarina equisetifolia
Hottentot's bean	*Schotia afra*
House lime	*Sparmannia africana*
House pine	
	Araucaria heterophylla
Hualo	*Nothofagus glauca*
Huamuchii	*Pithecellobium dulce*
Huanuco	*Cinchona micrantha*
Huckleberry	*Cyrilla racemiflora*
	Vaccinium myrtillus
Huckleberry oak	
	Quercus vaccinifolia
Huisache	*Acacia farnesiana*
Hulver bush	*Ilex aquifolium*
Hungarian hawthorn	
	Crataegus nigra
Hungarian lilac	*Syringa josikaea*
Hungarian oak	*Quercus conferta*
	Quercus frainetto
Hungarian thorn	*Crataegus nigra*
Huntingdon elm	
	Ulmus × hollandica vegeta
	Ulmus × vegeta
Huon pine	*Dacrydium franklinii*
	Lagarostrobus franklinii
Hupeh cherry	
	Prunus serrulata hupehensis
Hupeh crab apple	
	Malus hupehensis
Hupeh rowan	*Sorbus hupehensis*
Hurricane palm	
	Ptychosperma macarthurii
Hybrid black poplar	
	Populus × canadensis
Hybrid buckeye	*Aesculus × hybrida*
Hybrid catalpa	
	Catalpa × erubescens
	Catalpa × hybrida
Hybrid cockspur thorn	
	Crataegus × lavallei
Hybrid larch	*Larix × eurolepis*
Hybrid magnolia	
	Magnolia ×soulangeana
Hybrid rowan	*Sorbus × thuringiaca*
Hybrid strawberry tree	
	Arbutus × andrachnoides
Hybrid wing nut	
	Pterocarya × rehderana
Icaco	*Chrysobalanus icaco*
Ichang lemon	*Citrus ichangensis*
Idesia	*Idesia polycarpa*
Ignatius bean	*Strychnos ignatii*
ligiri tree	*Idesia polycarpa*
llama	*Annona diversifolia*
Ilang-ilang	*Cananga odorata*
Illawarra flame tree	
	Brachychiton acerifolius
Illyarie	*Eucalyptus erythrocorys*
Illyarri	*Eucalyptus erythrocorys*
Imou pine	*Dacrydium cupressinum*
Inaja palm	*Maximiliana caribaea*
	Maximiliana maripa
	Maximiliana regia
Incense cedar	
	Calocedrus decurrens
	Libocedrus decurrens
Incense juniper	*Juniperus thurifera*
Incense rose	*Rosa primula*
India date palm	*Phoenix rupicola*
	Phoenix sylvestris
Indian almond	*Sterculia foetida*
	Terminalia catappa
Indian azalea	*Rhododendron simsii*
Indian bael	*Aegle marmelos*
Indian banyan	*Ficus benghalensis*
	Ficus indica
Indian bean	*Catalpa speciosa*
Indian bean tree	
	Catalpa bignonioides
Indian cedar	*Cedrus deodara*
Indian cher pine	*Pinus roxburghii*
Indian cherry	*Rhamnus caroliniana*
Indian currant	
	Symphoricarpus orbiculatus
	Symphoricarpus rubra vulgaris
	Symphoricarpus vulgaris
Indian elm	*Ulmus rubra*

Indian gooseberry	
	Phyllanthus acidus
Indian gum	*Acacia arabica*
Indian hawthorn	*Raphiolepis indica*
	Raphiolepis umbellata
Indian hemp	*Hibiscus cannabinus*
Indian horse chestnut	
	Aesculus indica
Indian jalap	*Ipomoea turpethum*
Indian jujube	*Ziziphus mauritania*
Indian laburnum	*Cassia fistula*
Indian laurel	
	Calophyllum inophyllum
	Ficus retusa
	Persea indica
	Terminalia alata
Indian lilac	*Melia azedarach*
Indian mulberry	*Morinda citrifolia*
Indian neem tree	*Melia indica*
Indian night jasmine	
	Nyctanthes arbor-tristis
Indian oak	
	Barringtonia acutangula
Indian olive	*Olea ferruninea*
Indian plum	*Oemleria cerasiformis*
Indian rhododendron	
	Melastoma malabathricum
Indian sarsaparilla	
	Hemidesmus indica
Indian senna	*Cassia angustifolia*
Indian silk-cotton tree	
	Bombax malabaricum
Indian sorrell	*Hibiscus sabdariffa*
Indian spice tree	*Vitex agnus-castus*
Indian spruce	*Picea smithiana*
Indian tree spurge	
	Euphorbia tirucalli
Indian walnut	*Aleurites moluccana*
Indian rubber tree	*Ficus belgica*
	Ficus elastica
Indigbo	*Terminalia ivorensis*
Inkberry	*Ilex glabra*
Inland lodgepole pine	
	Pinus contorta latifolia
Interior live oak	*Quercus wislizenii*
Ipecac spurge	
	Euphorbia ipecacuanhae
Ipecacuanha	
	Cephaelis ipecacuanha
	Uragoga ipecacuanha
Irish gorse	*Ulex europaeus strictus*
Irish heath	*Daboecia cantabrica*
	Erica erigena
	Erica mediterranea
Irish juniper	
	Juniperus communis hibernica
	Juniperus communis stricta
Irish yew	*Taxus baccata fastigiata*
Iroko	*Chlorophora excelsa*
Iron tree	*Metrosideros robusta*
	Parrotia persica

Ironwood	*Bumelia lycioides*
	Cliftonia monophylla
	Cyrilla racemiflora
	Mesurea ferrea
	Ostrya virginiana
Ironwood tree	*Eugenia confusa*
	Eugenia garberi
Island manzanita	
	Arctostaphylos insularis
Island oak	*Quercus tomentella*
Islay plum	*Prunus ilicifolia*
Isu tree	*Distylium racemosum*
Italian alder	*Alnus cordata*
Italian buckthorn	
	Rhamnus alaternus
Italian cypress	
	Cupressus sempervirens
Italian jasmine	*Jasminum humile*
Italian maple	*Acer opalus*
Italian oak	*Quercus frainetto*
Italian poplar	*Populus nigra italica*
Italian stone pine	*Pinus pinea*
Ita palm	*Mauritia flexuosa*
	Mauritia setigera
Ivory nut palm	
	Phytelephas macrocarpa
Ivory palm	
	Phytelephas macrocarpa
Ivybush	*Kalmia latifolia*
Jaboncillo	*Sapindus saponaria*
Jaborand	*Pilocarpus jaborandi*
Jaborandi	*Pilocarpus jaborandi*
Jaboticaba	*Myrciaria cauliflora*
Jacaranda	*Jacaranda acutifolia*
	Jacaranda mimosifolia
Jacareuba	*Calophyllum brasiliense*
Jack fruit	*Artocarpus heterophyllus*
Jack oak	*Quercus ellipsoidalis*
	Quercus marilandica
Jack pine	*Pinus banksiana*
Jackwood	*Cordia dentata*
Jacobite rose	*Rosa × alba*
Jacob's coat	*Acalypha wilkesiana*
Jacob's staff	*Fouquieria splendens*
Jacquemont's birch	
	Betula jacquemontii
Jaggery palm	*Caryota urens*
Jalap	*Ipomoea purga*
Jamaica caper tree	
	Capparis cynophallophora
Jamaica dogwood	
	Piscidia erythrina
Jamaica mandarin orange	
	Glycosmis pentaphylla
Jamaican damson plum	
	Chrysophyllum oliviforme
Jamaican dogwood	
	Piscidia piscipula
Jamaican manac	
	Calyptronoma occidentalis

Jamaican trumpet tree
Tabebuia riparia

Jamaica nutmeg
Monodora myristica

Jamaica palmetto *Sabal jamaicensis*

Jamaica pepper *Pimenta officinalis*

Jamaica plum *Spondias lutea*

Jamaica quassia *Picraena excelsa*

Jamaica sarsaparilla *Smilax ornata*

Jamaica sorrel *Hibiscus sabdariffa*

Jambolan *Eugenia jambolana*

Jambolan plum *Syzygium cumini*

Jambool *Syzygium cumini*
Syzygium samarangense

Jambosa *Syzygium samarangense*

Jambu *Syzygium cumini*

Jambul *Eugenia jambolana*

Japanese alder *Alnus japonica*

Japanese alpine cherry
Prunus nipponica

Japanese angelica tree *Aralia elata*

Japanese anise *Illicium anisatum*

Japanese apricot *Prunus mume*

Japanese arbor-vitae
Thuya standishii

Japanese aspen *Populus sieboldii*

Japanese barberry
Berberis thunbergii

Japanese bead tree
Melia azedarach

Japanese beech *Fagus crenata*
Fagus japonica
Fagus sieboldii

Japanese bigleaf magnolia
Magnolia hypoleuca

Japanese bitter orange
Poncirus trifoliata

Japanese black pine
Pinus thunbergii

Japanese bush cherry
Prunus japonica

Japanese cedar
Cryptomeria japonica

Japanese cherry *Prunus serrulata*

Japanese cherry birch
Betula grossa

Japanese chestnut
Castanea crenata
Chrysolepis cuspidata

Japanese chestnut oak
Quercus acutissima

Japanese chinquapin
Castanopsis cuspidata

Japanese cork tree
Phellodendron japonicum

Japanese cornel *Cornus officinalis*

Japanese cornelian cherry
Cornus officinalis

Japanese cowtail pine
Cephalotaxus harringtonia

Japanese crab apple
Malus floribunda

Japanese cucumber tree
Magnolia hypoleuca

Japanese dogwood
Cornus controversa
Cornus kousa

Japanese double pink cherry
Prunus serrulata kanzan

Japanese douglas fir
Pseudotsuga japonica

Japanese elm
Ulmus davidiana japonica
Ulmus japonica

Japanese euonymus
Euonymus japonica

Japanese euptelea
Euptelea polyandra

Japanese evergreen oak
Quercus acuta

Japanese false cypress
Chamaecyparis obtusa

Japanese fatsia *Aralia japonica*
Fatsia japonica

Japanese fern palm *Cycas revoluta*

Japanese figleaf palm
Fatsia japonica

Japanese fir *Abies firma*

Japanese flowering cherry
Prunus yedoensis

Japanese hackberry *Celtis japonica*
Celtis sinensis

Japanese hairy alder *Alnus hirsuta*

Japanese hazel *Corylus sieboldiana*

Japanese hemlock *Tsuga sieboldii*

Japanese hill cherry
Prunus sargentii

Japanese hibiscus
Hibiscus schizopetalus

Japanese holly *Ilex crenata*
Ilex integra

Japanese honey locust
Gleditsia japonica

Japanese hop-hornbeam
Ostrya japonica

Japanese hornbeam
Carpinus japonica

Japanese horse chestnut
Aesculus turbinata

Japanese jasmine *Jasminum mesnyi*

Japanese lacquer tree
Rhus verniciflua

Japanese lantern
Hibiscus schizopetalus

Japanese larch *Larix kaempferi*

Japanese large-leaved birch
Betula maximowicziana

Japanese laurel *Aucuba japonica*

Japanese lime *Tilia japonica*

Japanese linden *Tilia japonica*

Japanese loquat
Eriobotrya japonica

Japanese magnolia
Magnolia obovata
Japanese mahonia
Mahonia japonica
Japanese maple *Acer japonicum*
Acer palmatum
Japanese medlar
Eriobotrya japonica
Japanese nutmeg *Torreya nucifera*
Japanese pagoda tree
Sophora japonica
Japanese pear *Pyrus pyrifolia*
Japanese persimmon
Diospyros chinensis
Diospyros kaki
Japanese photinia *Photinia glabra*
Japanese pittosporum
Pittosporum tobira
Japanese plum *Eriobotrya japonica*
Prunus japonica
Prunus salicina
Prunus triflora
Japanese plum-fruited yew
Cephalotaxus harringtonia
Japanese plum yew
Cephalotaxus harringtonia
drupacea
Japanese poplar
Populus maximowiczii
Japanese privet
Ligustrum japonicum
Ligustrum ovalifolium
Japanese pussy willow
Salix gracilistyla
Japanese quince
Chaenomeles speciosa
Japanese raisin tree *Hovenia dulcis*
Japanese red birch
Betula maximowicziana
Japanese red cedar
Cryptomeria japonica
Japanese red oak *Quercus acuta*
Japanese red pine *Pinus densiflora*
Japanese rose *Rosa rugosa*
Japanese rowan *Sorbus commixta*
Japanese sago palm *Cycas revoluta*
Japanese snakebark maple
Acer capillipes
Japanese snowball
Viburnum plicatum
Japanese snowbell *Styrax japonica*
Japanese snow flower
Deutzia gracilis
Japanese spindle tree
Euonymus hamiltonianus
yedoensis
Euonymus japonica
Japanese spruce
Picea maximowiczii
Picea polita
Japanese stewartia
Stewartia pseudocamellia

Japanese stone pine *Pinus pumila*
Japanese sweetspike *Itea japonica*
Japanese thuya *Thuya standishii*
Japanese torreya *Torreya nucifera*
Japanese tree lilac
Syringa reticulata
Japanese umbrella pine
Sciadopitys verticillata
Japanese varnish tree
Firmiana simplex
Rhus verniciflua
Japanese viburnum
Viburnum japonicum
Japanese walnut *Juglans ailantifolia*
Japanese white birch
Betula japonica
Betula mandschurica
Betula platyphylla japonica
Japanese white pine
Pinus parviflora
Japanese willow *Salix urbaniana*
Japanese wing nut
Pterocarya rhoifolia
Japanese winterberry *Ilex serrata*
Japanese witch hazel
Hamamelis japonica
Japanese woodoil tree
Aleurites cordata
Japanese yellowwood
Cladrastis platycarpa
Japanese yew
Podocarpus macrophyllus
Taxus cuspidata
Japanese zelkova *Zelkova serrata*
Japan pepper
Zanthoxylum piperitum
Jarrah *Eucalyptus marginata*
Jasmine box *Phillyrea decora*
Phyllirea vilmoriniana
Java apple *Syzygium samarangense*
Java fig *Ficus benjamina*
Java glory bean
Clerodendrum × speciosum
Java plum *Eugenia jambolana*
Syzygium cumini
Javillo *Hura crepitans*
Jeffrey's hemlock *Tsuga × jeffreyi*
Jeffrey's pine *Pinus jeffreyi*
Jelecote pine *Pinus patula*
Jelly palm *Butia capitata*
Butia yatay
Jersey elm
Ulmus minor stricta sarniensis
Ulmus × sarniensis
Ulmus stricta sarniensis
Jersey pine *Pinus virginiana*
Jerusalem pine *Pinus halepensis*
Jerusalem sage *Phlomis fruticosa*
Jerusalem thorn *Paliurus aculeatus*
Paliurus spina-christi
Parkinsonia aculeata

TREES, BUSHES, AND SHRUBS

Jesuit's bark	Cinchona calisaya
Jew's mallow	Corchorus olitorius
	Kerria japonica
Jim brush	Ceanothus sorediatus
Jim bush	Ceanothus sorediatus
Jinbul	Eucalyptus microtheca
Jobo tree	Spondias mombin
Jocote	Spondias purpurea
John Downie crab apple	
	Malus sylvestris john downie
Jointwood	Cassia nodosa
Joseph's coat	Alternant ficoidea
Joshua tree	Yucca brevifolia
Jove's fruit	Lindera melissifolia
Judas tree	Cercis siliquastrum
June berry	Amelanchier arborea
	Amelanchier laevis
	Amelanchier lamarckii
Jungle flame	Ixora coccinea
	Ixora incarnata
Jungle geranium	Ixora coccinea
	Ixora incarnata
Juniper rush	Genista raetam
Jupiter's beard	
	Anthyllis barba-jovis
Jute	Corchorus capsularis
	Corchorus olitorius
Kaffia plum	
	Acokanthera oblongifolia
Kaffir bean	Schotia afra
Kaffir fig	Ficus nekbudu
	Ficus utilis
Kaffir plum	
	Harpephyllum caffrum
Kaffir thorn	Lycium afrum
Kahika	Podocarpus dacrydioides
Kahikatea	
	Dacrycarpus dacrydioides
	Podocarpus dacrydioides
Kai apple	Aberia caffra
	Dovyalis caffra
Kaki	Diospyros chinensis
	Diospyros kaki
Kamahi tree	
	Weinmannia racemosa
Kamala tree	
	Mallotus philippinensis
Kamani	Terminalia catappa
Kamila tree	Mallotus philippinensis
Kangaroo apple	Solanum aviculare
	Solanum laciniatum
Kangaroo thorn	Acacia armata
Kanooka	Tristania laurina
Kapok bush	
	Cochlospermum frazeri
Kapok tree	Ceiba pentandra
Karaka	Corynocarpus laevigata
Karanda	Carissa carandas
Karapincha	Murraya koenigii
Karo	Pittosporum crassifolium
Karri	Eucalyptus diversicolor
Karri gum	Eucalyptus diversicolor
Karri tree	Paulownia tomentosa
Karroo thorn	Acacia karroo
Karum tree	Pongamia pinnata
Kashi holly	Ilex chinensis
	Ilex purpurea
Kashmir cypress	
	Cupressus cashmeriana
Kashmir rowan	
	Sorbus cashmiriana
Kassod tree	Cassia siamea
Katsura	
	Cercidiphyllum japonicum
Kau apple	Aberia caffra
	Dovyalis caffra
Kauri pine	Agathis australis
Kava	Piper methysticum
Kawaka	Calocedrus plumosa
Kawaka tree	Libocedrus plumosa
Kawa-kawa	Macropiper excelsum
Kaya	Torreya nucifera
Kazanlik rose	
	Rosa damascena trigintipetala
Keaki	Zelkova serrata
Keg fig	Diospyros chinensis
	Diospyros kaki
Kei apple	Aberia caffra
	Dovyalis caffra
Kellogg oak	Quercus kelloggii
Kenaf	Hibiscus cannabinus
Kenari	Canarium commune
Kentia palm	Howea forsterana
	Kentia forsterana
Kentish cob	Corylus maxima
Kentucky coffee tree	
	Gymnocladus dioica
Kermes oak	Quercus coccifera
Key lime	Citrus aurantifolia
Key palm	Thrinax morrisii
Khair	Acacia catechu
Khasya pine	Pinus insularis
	Pinus khasya
Khat	Catha edulis
Khingan fir	Abies nephrolepis
Killarney strawberry tree	
	Arbutus unedo
Kilmarnock willow	
	Salix caprea pendula
Kimberley grey box	
	Eucalyptus argillacea
	Eucalyptus leucophylla
King Boris' fir	Abies borisii-regis
Kingdon Ward's carmine cherry	Prunus cerasoides rubea
King mandarin	
	Citrus × nobilis king
King nut	Carya laciniosa
King of Siam	Citrus × nobilis king

King orange	*Citrus × nobilis king*
King protea	*Protea cynaroides*
King William pine	
	Athrotaxis selaginoides
Kinnikinick	
	Arctostaphylos uva-ursi
Kino	*Coccoloba uvifera*
Kinos	*Pterocarpus marsupium*
Kirishima azalea	*Azalea obtusa*
	Rhododendron obtusum
Kitembilla	*Aberia gardneri*
	Dovyalis hebecarpa
Kittul tree	*Caryota urens*
Klinki pine	*Araucaria hunsteinii*
Knicker tree	*Gymnocladus dioica*
Knife acacia	*Acacia cultriformis*
Knife-leaf wattle	
	Acacia cultriformis
Knobcone pine	*Pinus attenuata*
Koa	*Acacia koa*
Kohuhu	*Pittosporum tenuifolium*
Kokio	*Kokia drynarioides*
Kokoon tree	*Kokoona zeylanica*
Kola	*Cola acuminata*
	Cola nitida
Kola nut	*Cola acuminata*
Kola nut tree	*Kola vera*
Konara oak	*Quercus glandulifera*
Korean azalea	
	Rhododendron poukhanense
Korean fir	*Abies koreana*
Korean forsythia	*Forsythia ovata*
Korean hill cherry	
	Prunus leveilleana
	Prunus serrulata pubescens
Korean lilac	*Syringa meyeri palibin*
	Syringa velutina
Korean lime	*Tilia insularis*
Korean maple	
	Acer pseudosieboldianum
Korean pine	*Pinus koraiensis*
Korean thuya	*Thuya koraiensis*
Kousa	*Cornus kousa*
Kousso	*Hagenia abyssinica*
Kowhai	*Sophora tetraptera*
Koyama spruce	*Picea koyamai*
Kruse's mallee	
	Eucalyptus kruseana
Kumaon pear	*Pyrus pashia*
Kumoi	*Pyrus pyrifolia*
Kumquat	*Fortunella margarita*
Kurogane holly	*Ilex rotunda*
Kurrajong	
	Brachychiton populneus
Kusamaki tree	
	Podocarpus macrophyllus
Labrador tea plant	
	Ledum groenlandicum
	Ledum latifolium

Lacebark	*Hoheria lyallii*
	Hoheria populnea
Lacebark pine	*Pinus bungeana*
Lace-cap hydrangea	
	Hydrangea macrophylla
Lace-cap viburnum	
	Viburnum plicatum tomentosum
Lace-cup viburnum	
	Viburnum plicatum tomentosum
Lacquer tree	*Rhus verniciflua*
Lac tree	*Schleichera oleosa*
Lady banks' rose	*Rosa banksiae*
Lady-of-the-night	
	Brunfelsia americana
Lady-of-the-woods	*Betula pendula*
Lady palm	*Rhapis excelsa*
Lady's handkerchief tree	
	Davidia involucrata
Lagos ebony	
	Diospyros mespiliformis
Lambkill	*Kalmia angustifolia*
Lancashire whitebeam	
	Sorbus lancastriensis
Lancaster red rose	
	Rosa gallica officinalis
Lancaster rose	
	Rosa gallica officinalis
Lancewood	*Oxandra lanceolata*
	Pseudopanax crassifolius
Lantern tree	
	Crinodendron hookerianum
Lapland willow	*Salix lapponum*
Large-coned douglas fir	
	Pseudotsuga macrocarpa
Large gallberry	*Ilex coriacea*
	Ilex lucida
Large-leaved banyan	
	Ficus wightiana
Large-leaved cucumber tree	
	Magnolia macrophylla
Large-leaved lime	*Tilia platyphyllos*
Large-leaved magnolia	
	Magnolia macrophylla
Large-leaved podocarp	
	Podocarpus macrophyllus
Large pussy willow	*Salix discolor*
Large tupelo	*Nyssa aquatica*
Late lilac	*Syringa villosa*
Laurel	*Cordia alliodora*
	Prunus laurocerasus
Laurel magnolia	
	Magnolia grandiflora
Laurel negro	*Cordia alliodora*
Laurel oak	*Quercus imbricaria*
	Quercus laurifolia
Laurel sumac	*Rhus laurina*
Laurel tree	*Persea borbonia*
Laurel willow	*Salix pentandra*
Laurelwood	
	Calophyllum inophyllum
Laurustinus	*Viburnum tinus*

TREES, BUSHES, AND SHRUBS

Lodgepole pine

Lavender cotton
　　　　Santolina chamaecyparissus
　　　　　　　Santolina incana
Lavender tree
　　　　Heteropyxis natalensis
Lawson's cypress
　　　　Chamaecyparis lawsoniana
Lawson's holly
　　Ilex × altaclarensis lawsoniana
Lead plant　　*Amorpha canescens*
Least whitebeam　　*Sorbus minima*
Least willow　　　*Salix herbacea*
Leatherleaf
　　　　Chamaedaphne calyculata
　　　　　　Viburnum wrightii
Leather oak　　　*Quercus durata*
Leatherwood　　*Cyrilla racemiflora*
　　　　　　　Dirca palustris
　　　　　　　Eucryphia lucida
Lebanon oak　　　*Quercus libani*
Lebbek tree　　*Albizzia lebbeck*
Leechee　　　*Litchi chinensis*
Lehmann's gum
　　　　Eucalyptus lehmannii
Lemandarin　　*Citrus × limonia*
Lemon　　　　*Citrus limon*
Lemonade berry　*Rhus integrifolia*
Lemonade sumac　*Rhus integrifolia*
Lemonade tree　*Adensonia digitata*
Lemon bottlebrush
　　　　Callistemon citrinus
Lemonleaf　　*Gaultheria shallon*
Lemon plant　　*Aloysia triphylla*
　　　　　　Lippia citriodora
Lemon-scented gum
　　　　Eucalyptus citriodora
Lemon-scented ironbark
　　　　Eucalyptus staigeriana
Lemon-scented spotted gum
　　　　Eucalyptus citriodora
Lemon-scented verbena
　　　　　Aloysia triphylla
Lemon sumac　*Rhus aromatica*
Lemon verbena　*Aloysia citriodora*
　　　　　　Aloysia triphylla
　　　　　　Lippia citriodora
　　　　　　Verbena triphylla
Lemonwood
　　　　Pittosporum eugenioides
Lenga　　*Nothofagus pumilo*
Lentisco　　　*Pistacia texana*
　　　　　　Rhus virens
Lerp mallee　*Eucalyptus incrassata*
Lesser flowering quince
　　　　Chaenomeles japonica
Lettuce tree　　*Pisonia alba*
Leverwood　*Ostrya virginiana*
Leyland cypress
　　　× cupressocyparis leylandii
Liberian coffee　*Coffea liberica*

Lichfield crab apple
　　Malus sylvestris john downie
Lichi　　　*Litchi chinensis*
Licuri palm　*Syagrus coronata*
Life-of-man　*Aralia racemosa*
Lightwood　　*Acacia implexa*
　　　Ceratopetalum apetalum
Ligiri tree　　*Idesia polycarpa*
Lignum vitae　*Guaiacum officinale*
Likiang spruce　*Picea likiangensis*
Lilac broom　*Carmichaelia odorata*
Lilac　　　　*Syringa oblata*
Lillypilly　　*Acmena smithii*
　　　　　Eugenia smithii
Lily-flowered magnolia
　　　　Magnolia liliiflora
Lily-of-the-valley tree
　　　　Clethra arborea
Lily thorn　　*Catesbaea spinosa*
Lily tree　　*Magnolia denudata*
Limber pine　　*Pinus flexilis*
Limeberry　　*Triphasia trifolia*
Lime　　　*Citrus aurantifolia*
Lime-leaf maple　*Acer distylum*
Limequat
　　× Citrofortunella floridana
　　× Citrofortunella swinglei
　Citrus aurantifolia × fortunella
Linden　　　*Tilia cordata*
　　　　　Tilia × europaea
Linden viburnum
　　　　Viburnum dilatatum
Ling　　　*Calluna vulgaris*
Lion's ear　*Leonotis leonurus*
Lipstick tree　*Bixa orellana*
Litchi　　　*Litchi chinensis*
Little cokernut palm
　　　　Jubaea chilensis
　　　　Jubaea spectabilis
Little lady palm　*Rhapis excelsa*
Little-leaf fig　*Ficus australis*
　　　　　Ficus rubiginosa
Little tree willow　*Salix arbuscula*
Little walnut　*Juglans microcarpa*
　　　　　Juglans rupestris
Live oak　　*Quercus virginiana*
Lobel's maple　　*Acer lobelii*
Loblolly bay　*Gordonia lasianthus*
Loblolly magnolia
　　　　Magnolia grandiflora
Loblolly pine　　*Pinus taeda*
Lobster claw　*Clianthus puniceus*
Lobster plant
　　　　Euphorbia pulcherrima
Locust bean　*Ceratonia siliqua*
Locust tree　*Hymenaea courbaril*
　　　　Robinia pseudoacacia
Lodgepole pine　*Pinus contorta*
　　　　Pinus contorta latifolia

Logwood
Haematoxylum campeachianum
Lombardy poplar *Populus nigra*
Populus nigra italica
Lombardy poplar cherry
Prunus amanagawa
London plane *Platanus × acerifolia*
Platanus × hispanicus
Platanus hybrida
Long buchu *Agathosma crenulata*
Long-flowered marlock
Eucalyptus macrandra
Long john *Triplaris americana*
Long-leaf pine *Pinus palustris*
Long-leaved argyle apple
Eucalyptus cephalocarpa
Long-leaved Indian pine
Pinus roxburghii
Long-thatch palm
Calyptronoma occidentalis
Looking-glass bush
Coprosma baueri
Coprosma repens
Looking-glass tree
Heritiera macrophylla
Loquat *Eriobotrya japonica*
Lord's candlestick *Yucca gloriosa*
Lote tree *Celtis australis*
Lotus tree *Ziziphus lotus*
Love tree *Cercis siliquastrum*
Low-bush blueberry
Vaccinium angustifolium
Lowland fir *Abies grandis*
Low's white fir
Abies concolor lowiana
Luccombe oak *Quercus × hispanica*
Luchu pine *Pinus luchuensis*
Lucky bean tree
Erythrina lysistemon
Lucky nut *Thevetia peruviana*
Ludwig's oak
Quercus × ludoviciana
Luster-leaf holly *Ilex latifolia*
Lyall's larch *Larix lyalli*
Lychee *Litchi chinensis*
Nephelium litchi
Macadamia nut
Macadamia integrifolia
Macadamia tetraphylla
Macarthur palm
Ptychosperma macarthurii
Macartney rose *Rosa bracteata*
Macassar ebony
Diospyros ebenaster
Diospyros ebenum
Macaw-fat *Elaeis guineensis*
Macdonald oak
Quercus macdonaldii
Macedonian oak *Quercus frainetto*
Quercus macedonica
Quercus trojana

Macedonian pine *Pinus peuce*
Mackay's heath *Erica mackaiana*
McNab's cypress
Cupressus macnabiana
Madagascar nutmeg
Ravensara aromatica
Madagascar palm
Chrysalidocarpus lutescens
Madagascar plum
Flacourtia indica
Flacourtia ramontchi
Madagascar tamarind
Vangueria edulis
Madar *Calotropis gigantea*
Madden cherry
Maddenia hypoleuca
Madeira broom *Genista virgata*
Madeira holly *Ilex perado*
Madeira redwood
Swietenia mahagoni
Madeira walnut *Juglans regia*
Madeira whortleberry
Vaccinium padifolium
Madre *Gliricidia maculata*
Gliricidia sepium
Madrona *Arbutus menziesii*
Magdeburg apple
Malus × magdeburgensis
Magic flower *Cantua buxifolia*
Magnolia *Magnolia × soulangiana*
Magnolia-leaved willow
Salix magnifica
Mahala-mat *Ceanothus prostratus*
Mahaleb *Prunus mahaleb*
Mahoe *Hibiscus elatus*
Hibiscus ramiflorus
Hibiscus tiliaceus
Melicytus ramiflorus
Thespesia populnea
Mahogany *Swietenia macrophylla*
Mahogany birch *Betula lenta*
Mahogany pine *Podocarpus totara*
Ma huang *Ephedera vulgaris*
Maidenhair tree *Ginkgo biloba*
Maiden's gum *Eucalyptus maidenii*
Eucalyptus globus maidenii
Maingay's oak *Quercus maingayi*
Malabar nut *Adhatoda vasica*
Malabar plum *Syzygium jambos*
Malay apple *Eugenia malaccensis*
Syzygium malaccense
Malay banyan *Ficus retusa*
Malay ixora *Ixora chinensis*
Malay jewel vine *Derris scandens*
Malay palm *Daemonorops grandis*
Male berry *Lyonia ligustrina*
Male blueberry *Lyonia ligustrina*
Mallee *Eucalyptus dumosa*
Mallee box *Eucalyptus bakeri*
Mamey *Mammea americana*

Melon tree

Mamey colorado	*Pouteria sapota*
Mamey sapote	*Pouteria sapota*
Mammee	*Mammea americana*
Mammee apple	
	Mammea americana
Mammee sapote	*Pouteria sapota*
Mammoth tree	
	Sequoiadendron giganteum
Mamoncillo	*Melicoccus bijugatus*
Manaca	*Brunfelsia uniflora*
Manchester poplar	
	Populus nigra betulifolia
Manchineel	
	Hippomane mancinella
Manchurian alder	*Alnus hirsuta*
Manchurian apricot	
	Prunus mandshurica
Manchurian ash	
	Fraxinus mandshurica
Manchurian cherry	*Prunus maackii*
Manchurian fir	*Abies holophylla*
Manchurian lime	*Tilia mandshurica*
Manchurian walnut	
	Juglans mandshurica
Mandarin lime	*Citrus × limonia*
Mandarin orange	*Citrus reticulata*
Mandioca	*Manihot esculenta*
Mango	*Mangifera indica*
Mangosteen	*Garcinia mangostana*
Mangrove date palm	
	Phoenix paludosa
Mangrove palm	*Nypa fruticans*
Manila hemp	*Musa textilis*
Manila palm	*Veitchia merrillii*
Manila tamarind	
	Pithecellobium dulce
Manio	*Podocarpus nubigenus*
Manioc	*Manihot esculenta*
Manna ash	*Fraxinus ornus*
Manna bush	*Tamarix gallica*
Manna gum	*Eucalyptus viminalis*
Manna tree	*Alhagi maurorum*
Manuka	*Leptospermum scoparium*
Manzanita	
	Arctostaphyols manzanita
Manzanote	
	Olmediella betschlerana
Maori holly	*Olearia illicifolia*
Maple-leaved viburnum	
	Viburnum acerifolium
Maraja palm	*Bactris gasipaes*
Maranon	*Anacardium occidentale*
Maria	*Calophyllum brasiliense*
Maries fir	*Abies mariesii*
Mariposa manzanita	
	Arctostaphylos mariposa
Maritime pine	*Pinus pinaster*
Marking-nut tree	
	Semecarpus anacardium

Markry	*Rhus radicans*
Marlberry	*Ardisia escallonioides*
Marmalade box	*Genipa americana*
Marmalade plum	*Manilkara zapota*
	Pouteria sapota
Maroc fir	*Abies marocana*
Marri	*Eucalyptus calophylla*
	Eucalyptus camaldulensis
Marsh ledum	*Ledum palustre*
Marsh rosemary	
	Andromeda polifolia
Martin's maple	*Acer martinii*
Marumi kumquat	
	Fortunella japonica
Mastic tree	*Pistacia lentiscus*
	Schinus molle
Mata kuching	
	Nephelium malaiense
Matai	*Podocarpus spicatus*
	Prumnopitys taxifolia
Matasano	*Casimiroa tetrameria*
Match-me-if-you-can	
	Acalypha wilkesiana
Maté	*Ilex paraguariensis*
Matico	*Piper angustifolium*
Matrimony thorn	
	Lycium balbarum
Matrimony vine	*Lycium balbarum*
Maul oak	*Quercus chrysolepis*
Maxwell spruce	
	Picea abies maxwellii
May	*Crataegus laevigata*
	Crataegus monogyna
May flower	*Epigaea repens*
May rose	*Rosa majalis*
Mayten	*Maytenus boaria*
Mazari palm	
	Nannorrhops ritchiana
Mazzard	*Prunus avium*
Meadow fern	*Myrica gale*
Meadow rose	*Rosa blanda*
Mealberry	
	Arctostaphylos uva-ursi
Meal tree	*Viburnum lantana*
Mealy stringybark	
	Eucalyptus cinerea
Mediterranean cypress	
	Cupressus sempervirens
Mediterranean hackberry	
	Celtis australis
Mediterranean heather	
	Erica mediterranea
Mediterranean storax	
	Styrax officinalis
Medlar	*Mespilus germanica*
	Mimusops elengi
Medusa's head	
	Euphorbia caput-medusae
Meloncillo	*Passiflora suberosa*
Melon tree	*Carica papaya*

Common Name	Scientific Name
Melukhie	Corchorus olitorius
Memorial rose	Rosa wichuraina
Mercury	Rhus radicans
Merrit gum	Eucalyptus flocktoniae
Mescal bean	Sophora secundiflora
Mesquite	Prosopis glandulosa
	Prosopis juliflora
Messmate stringybark	
	Eucalyptus obliqua
Mexican apple	Casimiroa edulis
Mexican blue palm	Brahea armata
Mexican buckeye	
	Ungnadia speciosa
Mexican cherry	Prunus capuli
Mexican cypress	
	Taxodium mucronatum
Mexican cypress	
	Cupressus lusitanica
Mexican elm	Ulmus mexicana
Mexican fan palm	
	Washingtonia robusta
Mexican fire plant	
	Euphorbia cyathophora
	Euphorbia heterophylla
Mexican flameleaf	
	Euphorbia pulcherrima
Mexican hand plant	
	Chiranthodendron pentadactylon
Mexican incense bush	
	Eupatorium micranthum
	Eupatorium weinmannianum
Mexican juniper	Juniperus flaccida
Mexican lime	Citrus aurantifolia
Mexican manzanita	
	Arctostaphylos pungens
Mexican mulberry	
	Morus microphylla
Mexican nut pine	Pinus cembroides
Mexican orange blossom	
	Choisya ternata
Mexican palo verde	
	Parkinsonia aculeata
Mexican pine	Pinus patula
Mexican poppy	
	Argemone mexicana
Mexican red sage	Salvia fulgens
Mexican stone pine	
	Pinus cembroides
Mexican swamp cypress	
	Taxodium mucronatum
Mexican tassel bush	
	Garrya macrophylla
Mexican Washington palm	
	Washingtonia robusta
Mexican weeping pine	Pinus patula
Mexican white pine	
	Pinus ayacahuite
Meyer's blue juniper	
	Juniperus squamata meyeri
Mezereon	Daphne mezereum

Common Name	Scientific Name
Mickey-mouse plant	
	Ochna japonica
	Ochna serrulata
Midland hawthorn	
	Crataegus laevigata
	Crataegus oxyacanthoides
Mignonette tree	Lawsonia alba
	Lawsonia inermis
Mile tree	Casuarina equisetifolia
Milk barrel	Euphorbia cereiformis
	Euphorbia heptagona
	Euphorbia leviana
Milk bush	Euphorbia tirucalli
Milk tree	Sapium hippomane
Mimosa	Acacia dealbata
Mimosa tree	Albizzia julibrissin
Min fir	Abies recurvata
Ming aralia	Polyscias fruticosa
Miniature date palm	
	Phoenix roebelenii
Miniature fan palm	Rhapis excelsa
Miniature holly	
	Malpighia coccigera
Miraculous berry	
	Synsepalum dulcificum
Miraculous fruit	
	Synsepalum dulcificum
Mirbeck's oak	Quercus canariensis
Miro	Podocarpus ferrugineus
	Prumnopitys ferruginea
Mirror plant	Coprosma repens
Missey-mooney	Sorbus americana
Mississippi hackberry	
	Celtis laevigata
Mistletoe fig	Ficus deltoides
	Ficus diversifolia
Mistletoe rubber plant	
	Ficus deltoides
	Ficus diversifolia
Mitcham lavender	
	Lavender officinalis
	Lavender spica
Miyabe's maple	Acer miyabei
Mlanje cedar	
	Widdringtonia whytei
Mobala plum	
	Parinari curatellifolia
Mochi tree	Ilex integra
Mockernut	Carya tomentosa
Mock orange	Bumelia lycioides
	Philadelphus coronarius
	Pittosporum tobira
	Pittosporum undulatum
	Prunus caroliniana
	Styrax americanus
Modoc cypress	Cupressus bakeri
Mogadore gum	Acacia gummifera
Mole plant	Euphorbia lathyris
Molle	Schinus molle
Momi fir	Abies firma

Mountain mahoe

Monarch birch
Betula maximowicziana
Money pine   Larix kaempferi
Money tree
Eucalyptus pulverulenta
Mongolian lime   Tilia mongolica
Mongul oak   Quercus mongolica
Monkey-bread tree
Adansonia digitata
Monkey jack   Artocarpus lakoocha
Monkey nut   Lecythis zabucayo
Monkey-pistol   Hura crepitans
Monkeypod tree   Samanea saman
Monkey pot tree   Leycythis usitata
Monkey puzzle   Araucaria araucana
Monkey's dinner bell
Hura crepitans
Monk's pepper tree
Vitex agnus-castus
Monterey ceanothus
Ceanothus rigidus
Monterey cypress
Cupressus macrocarpa
Monterey pine   Pinus radiata
Montezuma pine
Pinus montezumae
Monthly rose   Rosa chinensis
Montpelier broom
Cytisus monspessulanus
Montpelier maple
Acer monspessulanum
Montpelier rock rose
Cistus monspeliensis
Moolar   Eucalyptus microtheca
Moonah   Melaleuca lanceolata
Melaleuca pubescens
Moonlight holly
Ilex aquifolium flavescens
Moon trefoil   Medicago arborea
Moorberry   Vaccinium uliginosum
Moose bark
Acer pennsylvanicum
Mooseberry   Viburnum alnifolium
Viburnum pauciflorum
Moose elm   Ulmus rubra
Moosewood   Acer pennsylvanicum
Dirca palustris
Viburnum alnifolium
Mop-head acacia
Robinia pseudoacacia inermis
Robinia pseudoacacia
umbraculifera
Mop-head hydrangea
Hydrangea hortensia
Moreton Bay chestnut
Castanospermum australe
Moreton Bay fig   Ficus macrocarpa
Ficus macrophylla
Moreton Bay pine
Araucaria cunninghamii
Morinda spruce   Picea smithiana

Morning glory bush
Ipomoea fistulosa
Morning glory tree
Ipomoea arborescens
Morning, noon and night
Brunfelsia australis
Moroccan broom
Cytisus battandieri
Moroccan fir   Abies macrocana
Morocco gum   Acacia gummifera
Morocco ironwood
Argania spinosa
Morro manzanita
Arctostaphylos morroensis
Moss rose   Rosa centifolia mucosa
Mossy cup oak   Quercus cerris
Quercus macrocarpa
Mossy locust   Robinia hispida
Motillo   Soleanea berteriana
Mottled spurge   Euphorbia lactea
Mountain agathis   Agathis alba
Mountain alder   Alnus crispa mollis
Alnus tenuifolia
Mountain ash   Eucalyptus regnans
Sorbus aucuparia
Mountain avens   Dryas octopetala
Mountain azalea
Loiseleuria procumbens
Mountain beech
Nothofagus solandri
cliffortioides
Mountain box   Arctostaphylos
uva-ursi
Mountain camellia   Stewartia ovata
Mountain cedar   Juniperus ashei
Mountain cherry   Prunus prostrata
Mountain currant   Ribes alpinum
Mountain cypress
Widdringtonia cupressoides
Mountain dogwood
Cornus nuttallii
Mountain grape
Mahonia aquifolium
Mountain guava
Psidium montanum
Mountain gum
Eucalyptus dalrympleana
Mountain hemlock
Tsuga mertensiana
Mountain hickory
Acacia penninervis
Mountain holly
Nemopanthus mucronatus
Olearia illicifolia
Prunus ilicifolia
Mountain immortelle
Erythrina poeppigiana
Mountain kiepersol
Cussonia paniculata
Mountain laurel   Kalmia latifolia
Mountain mahoe   Hibiscus elatus

Mountain mahogany	*Betula lenta*
	Cercocarpus montanus
Mountain maple	*Acer spicatum*
Mountain papaw	
	Carica cundinamarcensis
Mountain pawpaw	
	Carica cundinamarcencis
Mountain papaya	*Carica pubescens*
Mountain pepper	
	Drimys lanceolata
Mountain pine	
	Dacrydium bidwillii
	Pinus mugo
	Pinus uncinata
Mountain rimu	
	Dacrydium laxifolium
Mountain rose bay	
	Rhododendron catawbiense
Mountain silver bell	
	Halesia monticola
Mountain snowdrop tree	
	Halesia monticola
Mountain soursop	
	Annona montana
Mountain spurge	
	Pachysandra terminalis
Mountain sumac	*Rhus copallina*
Mountain-sweet	
	Ceanothus americanus
Mountain white pine	
	Pinus monticola
Mountain willow	*Salix arbuscula*
Mount Atlas mastic tree	
	Pistacia atlantica
Mount Etna broom	
	Genista aethnensis
Mount Morgan wattle	
	Acacia podalyriifolia
Mount Morrison barberry	
	Berberis morrisonensis
Mount Morrison juniper	
	Juniperus morrisonicola
Mount Morrison spruce	
	Picea morrisonicola
Mount Omei rose	*Rosa omeiensis*
	Rosa sericea
Mount wellington peppermint	
	Eucalyptus coccifera
Mourning cypress	
	Cupressus funebris
Moutan	*Paeonia suffruticosa*
Moutan paeony	*Paeonia moutan*
	Paeonia suffruticosa
Mudar	*Calotropis procera*
Mudgee wattle	*Acacia spectabilis*
Mueller's cypress pine	
	Callitris muelleri
Mugga	*Eucalyptus sideroxylon*
Muku tree	*Aphananthe aspera*
Mulberry fig	*Ficus sycomorus*
Mulga	*Acacia aneura*

Murray red gum	
	Eucalyptus camaldulensis
Murray river pine	
	Callitris columellaris
	Callitris glauca
Murtillo	*Ugni molinae*
Musk rose	*Rosa moschata*
Musk willow	*Salix aegyptiaca*
Muskwood	*Olearia argophylla*
Mu tree	*Aleurites montana*
Myallwood	*Acacia homalophylla*
Myrobalan	*Phyllanthus emblica*
	Terminalia bellirica
	Terminalia catappa
Myrobalan plum	*Prunus cerasifera*
Myrrh	*Commifera abyssinica*
	Commifera molmol
	Commifera myrrha
Myrtle	*Cyrilla racemiflora*
	Myrtus communis
	Umbellularia californica
Myrtle beech	
	Nothofagus cunninghamii
Myrtle spurge	*Euphorbia lathyris*
Mysore fig	*Ficus mysorensis*
Nagami kumquat	
	Fortunella margarita
Nagi	*Podocarpus nagi*
Naio	*Myoporum sandwicense*
Naked coral tree	
	Erythrina coralloides
Nanking cherry	*Prunus tomentosa*
Nannyberry	*Viburnum lentago*
Nanny plum	*Viburnum lentago*
Nan-shan bush	
	Cotoneaster adpressus praecox
Nanten	*Nandina domestica*
Napolean's button	
	Napoleona heudottii
Narrow-leaved ash	
	Fraxinus angustifolia
Narrow-leaved black peppermint	
	Eucalyptus nicholii
Narrow-leaved bottle tree	
	Brachychiton rupestris
Narrow-leaved ironbark	
	Eucalyptus crebra
Narrow-leaved peppermint	
	Eucalyptus radiata
Narrow-leaved pittosporum	
	Pittosporum phillyraeoides
Nashi	*Pyrus pyrifolia*
Natal fig	*Ficus natalensis*
Natal orange	*Strychnos spinosa*
Natal plum	*Carissa grandiflora*
Native frangipani	
	Hymenosporum flavum
Nazeberry	*Manilkara zapote*
Necklace poplar	*Populus deltoides*
	Populus lasiocarpa

TREES, BUSHES, AND SHRUBS

Nectarine
Prunus persica nectarina
Prunus persica nucipersica

Needle bush *Azim tetracantha*

Needle-bush wattle *Acacia rigens*

Needle fir *Abies holophylla*

Needleflower tree
Posoqueria latifolia

Needle furze *Genista anglica*

Needle juniper *Juniperus rigida*

Needle palm
Rhapidophyllum hystrix
Yucca filamentosa

Needle rose *Rosa acicularis*

Nepal barberry *Berberis aristata*

Nepalese alder *Alnus nepalensis*

Nepalese white thorn
Pyracantha crenulata

Nepal laburnum
Piptanthus laburnifolius

Nepal nut pine *Pinus gerardiana*

Nepal privet *Ligustrum lucidum*

Nero's crown
Tabernaemontana coronaria

Nest spruce *Picea abies nidiformis*

Netted willow *Salix reticulata*

Nettle tree *Celtis australis*
Celtis occidentalis

New Caledonia pine
Araucaria columnaris

New England boxwood
Cornus florida

New Jersey tea plant
Ceanothus americanus

New Zealand black pine
Podocarpus spicatus
Prumnopitys taxifolia

New Zealand christmas tree
Metrosideros excelsa
Metrosideros robusta
Metrosideros tomentosa

New Zealand flax *Phormium tenax*

New Zealand holly
Olearia macrodonta

New Zealand honeysuckle tree
Knightia excelsa

New Zealand laburnum
Sophora tetraptera

New Zealand laurel
Corynocarpus laevigata

New Zealand lilac *Hebe hulkeana*

New Zealand pittosporum
Pittosporum tenuifolium

New Zealand red beech
Nothofagus fusca

New Zealand sophora
Sophora tetraptera

New Zealand tea tree
Leptospermum scoparium

New Zealand tree fuchsia
Fuchsia excorticata

New Zealand white pine
Dacrycarpus dacrydioides

New Zealand wineberry
Aristotelia racemosa

Ngaio *Myoporum laetum*

Nibung palm
Oncosperma tigillarium

Nicaraguan cocoa-shade
Gliricidia maculata
Gliricidia sepium

Nichol's willow-leaved
peppermint
Eucalyptus nicholii

Nicker bean *Entada gigas*

Nicker tree *Gymnocladus dioica*

Nicobar breadfruit *Pandanis leram*

Niger seed *Guizotia abyssinica*

Night jasmine *Cestrum nocturnum*
Nyctanthes arbor-tristis

Night jessamine
Cestrum nocturnum

Nikau palm *Rhopalostylis sapida*

Nikko fir *Abies homolepis*

Nikko maple
Acer maximowiczianum
Acer nikoense

Nine bark *Physocarpus opulifolius*

Niobe willow *Salix × blanda*

Nipa palm *Nypa fruticans*

Nirre *Nothofagus antarctica*

Nish broom *Genista nyssana*

Nispero *Manilkara zapota*

Noah's ark juniper
Juniperus communis compressa

Noble fir *Abies procera*

Nodding pond cypress
Taxodium ascendens nutans

Noisette rose *Rosa × noisettiana*

Nootka cypress
*Chamaecyparis lawsoniana
nootkatensis*
Chamaecyparis nootkatensis

Norfolk Island hibiscus
Lagunaria patersonii

Norfolk Island pine
Araucaria excelsa
Araucaria heterophylla

North American honeysuckle
Lonicera ledebourii

North American salal
Gaultheria shallon

North American snakebark
maple
Acer pennsylvanicum

Northern bayberry
Myrica pennsylvanica

Northern bungalow palm
Archontophoenix alexandrae

Northern catalpa *Catalpa speciosa*

Northern cypress pine
Callitris intratropica

Northern downy rose
　　　　Rosa sherardii

Northern Japanese hemlock
　　　　Tsuga diversifolia

Northern Japanese magnolia
　　　　Magnolia kobus

Northern pin oak
　　　　Quercus ellipsoidalis

Northern pitch pine　Pinus rigida

Northern prickly ash
　　　　Zanthoxylum americanum

Northern red oak　Quercus rubra

Northern white cedar
　　　　Thuya occidentalis

Norway maple　Acer platanoides

Norway pine　Pinus resinosa

Norway spruce　Picea abies

Nosegay tree　Plumeria rubra

Nutgall tree　Rhus chinensis

Nutmeg　Myristica fragrans

Nutmeg hickory
　　　　Carya myristiciformis

Nut palm　Cycas media

Nut pine　Picea cembroides
　　　　Picea monophylla
　　　　Pinus cembroides
　　　　Pinus edulis
　　　　Pinus monophylla

Nuttall's dogwood　Cornus nuttallii

Nux regia　Juglans regia

Nux vomica tree
　　　　Styrchnos nux-vomica

Nyasaland mahogany
　　　　Khaya nyasica

Nyman's hybrid eucryphia
　　　　Eucryphia × nymansensis
　　　　nymansay

Nypa palm　Nypa fruticans

Oak-leaf fig　Ficus montana
　　　　Ficus quercifolia

Oak-leaf hydrangea
　　　　Hydrangea quercifolia

Obeche　Triplochiton scleroxylon

Ocean spray　Holodiscus ariifolius
　　　　Holodiscus discolor

Ocotillo　Fouquieria splendens

Octopus tree　Brassaia actinophylla

Ogechee lime　Nyssa candicans

Ohio buckeye　Aesculus glabra

Oil palm　Elaeis guineensis

Okinawa pine　Pinus leucodermis

Oklohoma plum　Prunus gracilis

Old English lavender
　　　　Lavandula angustifolia
　　　　Lavandula officinalis
　　　　Lavandula spica

Oldfield birch　Betula populifolia

Oldfield pine　Pinus taeda

Oldfield's mallee
　　　　Eucalyptus oldfieldii

Old man's beard
　　　　Chionanthus virginicus

Old red damask rose
　　　　Rosa officinalis

Oleander-leaved euphorbia
　　　　Euphorbia neriifolia

Oleander　Nerium olean

Oleaster
　　　　Elaeagnus angustifolia
　　　　Elaeagnus latifolia

Olibanus tree　Boswellia thurifera

Olive　Olea europaea

Olive bark tree　Terminalia catappa

Oliver's lime　Tilia oliveri

Omeo round-leaved gum
　　　　Eucalyptus neglecta

One-leaved nut pine
　　　　Pinus cembroides monophylla

Ontario poplar　Populus candicans

Opiuma　Pithecellobium dulce

Opopanax　Acacia farnesiana

Oppossumwood　Halesia carolina

Orange　Citrus sinensis

Orange ball tree　Buddleia globosa

Orange-bark myrtle　Myrtus luma
　　　　Luma apiculata

Orange champaca
　　　　Michelia champaca

Orange eye　Buddleia davidii

Orange jasmine
　　　　Murraya paniculata

Orange jessamine　Murraya exotica

Orange-twig willow
　　　　Salix alba chermesina

Orange wattle　Acacia cyanophylla

Orchard apple　Malus domestica

Orchid tree　Bauhinia purpurea

Oregon alder　Alnus oregona
　　　　Alnus rebra

Oregon ash　Fraxinus latifolia
　　　　Fraxinus oregona

Oregon cherry　Prunus emarginata

Oregon crab apple　Malus fusca

Oregon douglas fir
　　　　Pseudotsuga menziesii

Oregon grape
　　　　Mahonia aquifolium
　　　　Mahonia nervosa

Oregon holly　Ilex aquifolium

Oregon maple
　　　　Acer macrophyllum

Oregon myrtle
　　　　Umbellularia californica

Oregon oak　Quercus garryana

Oregon plum　Prunus subcordata

Oregon tea　Ceanothus sanguineus

Oregon white oak
　　　　Quercus garryana

Oriental alder　Alnus orientalis

Oriental arborvitae *Platycladus orientalis*
Oriental beech *Fagus orientalis*
Oriental cherry *Prunus serrulata*
Oriental cork oak *Quercus variabilis*
Oriental hornbeam *Carpinus orientalis*
Oriental pear *Pyrus pyrifolia*
Oriental plane *Platanus orientalis*
Oriental spruce *Picea orientalis*
Oriental sweet gum *Liquidambar orientalis*
Oriental thorn *Crataegus laciniata*
Crataegus orientalis
Oriental white oak *Quercus aliena*
Ornamental quince *Chaenomeles speciosa nivalis*
Osage orange *Maclura aurantiaca*
Maclura pomifera
Oshima cherry *Prunus speciosa*
Osier *Salix viminalis*
Oso-berry *Nuttallia cerasiformis*
Oemleria cerasiformis
Osmaronia cerasiformis
Otaheite apple *Spondias dulcis*
Otaheite chestnut *Inocarpus edulis*
Otaheite gooseberry *Phyllanthus acidus*
Otaheite apple *Spondias cytherea*
Otaheite orange *Citrus otaitensis*
Otaheite walnut *Aleurites moluccana*
Otay manzanita *Arctostaphylos otayensis*
Oteniqua yellowwood *Podocarpus falcatus*
Our Lord's candle *Yucca whipplei*
Ouricuri palm *Syagrus coronata*
Oval kumquat *Fortunella margarita*
Oval-leaved privet *Ligustrum ovalifolium*
Oval-leaved southern beech *Nothofagus betuloides*
Ovens' acacia *Acacia pravissima*
Ovens' wattle *Acacia pravissima*
Overcup oak *Quercus lyrata*
Overtop palm *Rhyticocos amara*
Owe cola *Cola verticilliata*
Ox-hoof tree *Bauhinia purpurea*
Oyster bay pine *Callitris rhomboides*
Ozark chestnut *Castanea ozarkensis*
Ozark white cedar *Juniperus ashei*
Ozark witch hazel *Hamamelis vernalis*
Pacaya *Chamaedorea tepejilote*

Pacific dogwood *Cornus nuttallii*
Pacific madrone *Arbutus menziesii*
Pacific plum *Prunus subcordata*
Pacific silver fir *Abies amabilis*
Pacific white fir *Abies concolor lowiana*
Pacific willow *Salix lasiandra*
Pacific yew *Taxus brevifolia*
Padang cassia *Cinnamomum burmanii*
Padauk *Pterocarpus indicus*
Paddy river box *Eucalyptus macarthurii*
Pagoda dogwood *Cornus alternifolia*
Pagoda flower *Clerodendrum paniculatum*
Clerodendrum × speciosum
Pagoda tree *Plueria rubra*
Sophora japonica
Pahautea *Calocedrus bidwillii*
Pahautea tree *Libocedrus bidwillii*
Painted leaf *Euphorbia cyathophora*
Euphorbia pulcherrima
Painted maple *Acer pictum*
Painted spurge *Euphorbia heterophylla*
Pajaro manzanita *Arctostaphylos pajaroensis*
Pale hickory *Carya pallida*
Pale laurel *Kalmia poliifolia*
Palestine oak *Quercus calliprinos*
Pali-mara *Alstonia scholaris*
Palma christi *Ricinus communis*
Palma corcho *Microcyas calocoma*
Palma pita *Yucca treculeana*
Palmella *Yucca elata*
Palmetto *Sabal palmetto*
Palmetto thatch *Thrinax parviflora*
Palm lily *Cordyline australis*
Yucca gloriosa
Palm willow *Salix caprea*
Palmyra palm *Borassus flabellifer*
Palo santo *Triplaris americana*
Palo verde *Cercidium floridum*
Palta *Persea americana*
Panama candle tree *Parmentiera cereifera*
Panama orange *× Citrofortunella mitis*
Panama rubber tree *Castilla elastica*
Pandang *Pandanus odoratissimus*
Pandanus palm *Pandanus tectorius*
Panicled dogwood *Cornus racemosa*
Papaw *Carica papaya*
Papaya *Carica papaya*
Paperbark cherry *Prunus serrula*

Paperbark maple

Paperbark maple	*Acer griseum*
Paperbark thorn	*Acacia woodii*
Paperbark tree	
	Melaleuca quinquenervia
Paper birch	*Betula papyrifera*
Paper flower	*Bougainvillea glabra*
Paper mulberry	
	Broussonetia papyrifera
Paper plant	*Aralia japonica*
	Fatsia japonica
Paradise apple	*Malus pumila*
Paradise nut	*Lecythis zabucayo*
Paradise palm	*Howea forsterana*
Paradise tree	*Melia azedarach*
	Simarouba glauca
Paraguayan trumpet tree	
	Tabebuia argentea
Paraguay jasmine	
	Brunfelsia australis
Paraguay tea	*Ilex paraguariensis*
Para nut	*Bertholleta excelsa*
Para-para	*Pisonia umbellifera*
Para rubber tree	
	Hevea brasiliensis
Parasol de Saint Julien	
	Populus tremuloides pendula
Parasol pine	
	Sciadopitys verticillata
Pareira	
	Chondrodendron tomentosum
Parlour palm	
	Chamaedorea elegans
Parrot bill	*Clianthus puniceus*
Parrot leaf	*Alternant fioidea*
Parrot's bill	*Clianthus puniceus*
Parry manzanita	
	Arctostaphylos manzanita
Parry pine	*Pinus quadrifolia*
Parsley-leaved elder	
	Sambucus nigra laciniata
Parsley-leaved thorn	
	Crataegus apiifolia
Partridge berry	
	Gaultheria procumbens
	Mitchella repens
Partridge cane	*Rhapis excelsa*
Partridge pea	*Cassia fasciculata*
Passion flower	*Passiflora caerulea*
Patagonian cypress	
	Fitzroya cupressoides
Patana palm	*Oenocarpus batava*
Paulownia	*Paulownia tomentosa*
Pawpaw	*Asimina triloba*
	Carica papaya
Peach	*Prunus persica*
Peach-leaved willow	
	Salix amygdaloides
Peach palm	*Bactris gasipaes*
	Gulielma gassipaes
Peach protea	*Protea grandiceps*

Peachwood	*Caesalpinia echinata*
	Haematoxylum campeachianum
Peacock flower	
	Caesalpinia pulcherrima
	Delonix regia
Peacock flower-fence	
	Adenanthera pavonina
Peacock thorn	
	Crataegus calpodendron
	Crataegus tomentosa
Pear-fruited mallee	
	Eucalyptus pyriformis
Pear fruit	*Margyricarpus pinnatus*
	Margyricarpus setosus
Pearl acacia	*Acacia podalyriifolia*
Pearl berry	
	Margyricarpus pinnatus
	Margyricarpus setosus
Pearl bush	*Exochorda grandiflora*
	Exochorda racemosa
Pearl fruit	*Margyricarpus pinnatus*
	Margyricarpus setosus
Pear thorn	
	Crataegus calpodendron
	Crataegus tomentosa
Pecan	*Carya illinoensis*
	Carya pecan
Peepul	*Ficus religiosa*
Pegwood	*Cornus sanguinea*
Pejibaye	*Bactris gasipaes*
Peking willow	
	Salix babylonica pekinensis
	Salix matsudana
Pencil cedar	*Juniperus virginiana*
Pencil juniper	*Juniperus virginiana*
Pencil tree	*Euphorbia tirucalli*
Pendant silver lime	*Tilia petiolaris*
Pendunculate oak	*Quercus rober*
Pennsylvania maple	
	Acer pennsylvanicum
Pepper hibiscus	
	Malaviscus arboreus
Peppermint tree	*Agonis flexuosa*
Peppermint wattle	
	Acacia terminalis
Pepperidge	*Nyssa sylvatica*
Pepper tree	*Drimys lanceolata*
	Macropiper excelsum
	Schinus molle
Pepperwood	
	Umbellularia californica
	Zanthoxylum clava-herculis
Père David's maple	*Acer davidii*
Peregrina	*Jatropha integerrima*
Perfumed cherry	*Prunus mahaleb*
Perny's holly	*Ilex pernyi*
Persian albizzia	*Albizzia julibrissin*
Persian ironwood	*Parrotia persica*
Persian lilac	*Melia azedarach*
	Syringa × persica

Persian maple	*Acer velutinum*
Persian walnut	*Juglans regia*
Persian yellow rose	
	Rosa foetida persiana
Persimmon	*Diospyros kaki*
	Diospyros virginiana
Peruvian balsam	
	Myroxylon pereirae
Peruvian bark	*Cinchona succirubra*
Peruvian fuchsia tree	
	Fuchsia boliviana
Peruvian mastic tree	*Schinus molle*
Peruvian pepper tree	*Schinus molle*
Petai	*Parkia speciosa*
Petticoat palm	
	Copernica macroglossa
	Washingtonia filifera
Petty morel	*Aralia racemosa*
Petty whin	*Genista anglica*
Pfitzer juniper	
	Juniperus × media pfitzerana
Pharoah's fig	*Ficus sycomorus*
Pheasant berry	
	Leycesteria formosa
Philippine fig	*Ficus pseudopalma*
Philippine medusa	*Acalypha hispida*
Phillyrea	*Phillyrea latifolia*
Phoenician juniper	
	Juniperus phoenicea
Phoenix tree	*Firmiana simplex*
Physic nut	*Jatropha curcus*
	Jatropha multifida
Phytolacca	*Phytolacca dioica*
Piassaba	*Attalea funifira*
	Leopoldinia piassaba
Piassava palm	*Vonitra fibrosa*
Piccabeen bungalow palm	
	Archontophoenix cunninghamiana
Piccabeen palm	*Archontophoenix cunninghamiana*
Pichi	*Fabiana imbricata*
Picrasma	*Picrasma quassioides*
Pie cherry	*Prunus cerasus*
Pigeon berry	*Duranta ellisia*
	Duranta repens
Pigeon plum	
	Coccoloba diversifolia
Pig laurel	*Kalmia angustifolia*
Pigmy juniper	
	Juniperus squamata pygmaea
Pig nut	*Carya cordiformis*
Pignut hickory	*Carya glabra*
Pignut palm	
	Hyophorbe lagenicaulis
Pillar apple	*Malus tschonoskii*
Pimbina	*Viburnum trilobum*
Pimento	*Pimenta dioica*
	Pimenta officinalis
Pinang	*Areca catechu*

Pin cherry	*Prunus pennsylvanica*
Pindo palm	*Butia capitata*
Pineapple broom	
	Cytisus battandieri
Pineapple bush	
	Dasypogon bromeliaefolius
Pineapple guava	*Feijoa sellowiana*
Pineapple sage	*Salvia rutilans*
Pineapple shrub	
	Calycanthus floridus
Pink-and-white shower	
	Cassia nodosa
Pink ball tree	*Dombeya wallichii*
Pink broom	
	Notospartium carmicheliae
Pink cassia	*Cassia javanica*
Pink cedar	*Acrocarpus fraxinifolius*
Pink dogwood	
	Cornus florida rubra
Pink horse chestnut	
	Aesculus × carnea
Pink pearl lilac	*Syringa swegiflexa*
Pink poui	*Tabebuia rosea*
	Tabebuia pentaphylla
Pink sand verbena	
	Abromia umbellata
Pink shower	*Cassia grandis*
Pink siris	*Albizzia julibrissin*
Pink snowball tree	
	Dombeya × cayeuxii
Pink tecoma	*Tabebuia pentaphylla*
Pink trumpet tree	*Tabebuia rosea*
Pink tulip tree	
	Magnolia campbellii
Pin oak	*Quercus palustris*
Pinwheel jasmine	
	Jasminum gracillimum
Pinyon pine	*Pinus cembroides*
	Pinus edulis
Pipe tree	*Sambucus nigra*
Pipperidge	*Berberis vulgaris*
Pirana pine	*Aruacaria angustifolia*
Pirul	*Schinus molle*
Pistacia nut	*Pistacia vera*
Pistachio	*Pistacia vera*
Pistol bush	
	Duvernoia adhatodioides
Pitanga	*Eugenia michelii*
	Eugenia pitanga
	Eugenia uniflora
Pitch pine	*Pinus palustris*
	Pinus rigida
Pith tree	*Herminiera elaphroxylon*
Pitomba	*Eugenia luschnathiana*
Pittosporum	
	Pittosporum tenuifolium
Pituri	*Duboisia myoporoides*
Piute cypress	*Cupressus nevadensis*
Plantain	*Musa acuminata*
	Musa × paradisiaca

Platterleaf

Platterleaf	*Coccoloba uvifera*
Plough breaker	*Erythrina zeyheri*
Plum	*Prunus domestica*
Plume albizzia	*Albizzia distachya*
	Albizzia lophantha
Plume nutmeg	
	Atherosperma moschata
Plum fir	*Podocarpus andinus*
Plum-fruited yew	
	Podocarpus andinus
Plum juniper	*Juniperus drupacea*
Plum-leaved apple	
	Malus prunifolia
Plumwood	*Eucryphia moorai*
Plum yew	*Cephalotaxus fortunii*
Plymouth crowberry	
	Corema conradii
Plymouth pear	*Pyrus cordata*
Pocket handkerchief tree	
	Davidia involucrata
Poet's jasmine	*Jasminum officinale*
Poet's laurel	*Laurus nobilis*
Pohutukawa	*Metrosideros excelsa*
Poinciana	*Delonix regia*
Poinsettia	*Euphorbia pulcherrima*
Point Reyes ceanothus	
	Ceanothus gloriosus
Poison ash	*Chionanthus virginicus*
Poison bay	*Illicium floridanum*
Poison dogwood	*Rhus vernix*
Poison elder	*Rhus vernix*
Poison haw	*Viburnum molle*
Poison ivy	*Rhus radicans*
Poison oak	*Rhus radicans*
Poison sumac	*Rhus vernix*
Polecat bush	*Rhus aromatica*
Polisandro	*Stahlia monosperma*
Polished willow	*Salix laevigata*
Pollard's almond	
	Prunus × amygdalopersica pollardii
Pomegranate	*Punica granatum*
Pomelo	*Citrus grandis*
	Citrus maxima
Pomerac jambos	
	Syzygium malaccense
Pomette bleue	
	Crataegus brachyacantha
Pompelmous	*Citrus maxima*
Pond apple	*Annona glabra*
Pond cypress	*Taxodium ascendens*
Ponderosa pine	*Pinus ponderosa*
Pontine oak	*Quercus pontica*
Pony tail	*Beaucarnea recurvata*
Poonga oil tree	*Pongamia pinnata*
Pop ash	*Fraxinus caroliniana*
Popinac	*Acacia farnesiana*
Porcupine palm	
	Rhapidophyllum hystrix

Portia tree	*Thespesia populnea*
Port Jackson fig	*Ficus australis*
	Ficus rubiginosa
Port Jackson pine	
	Callitris rhomboides
Port Jackson willow	
	Acacia cyanophylla
Port Macquarie pine	
	Callitris macleayana
Port Orford cedar	
	Chamaecyparis lawsoniana
Portugal heath	*Erica lusitanica*
Portugal laurel	*Prunus lusitanica*
Portuguese broom	*Cytisus albus*
Portuguese crowberry	
	Corema album
Portuguese cypress	
	Cupressus lusitanica
Portuguese oak	*Quercus faginea*
	Quercus lusitanica
Possum apple	
	Diospyros virginiana
Possumhaw holly	*Ilex decidua*
Possum haw	
	Viburnum acerifolium
Possum oak	*Quercus nigra*
Possumwood	
	Diospyros virginiana
Post oak	*Quercus stellata*
Posy bush	*Dais cotonifolia*
Potato tree	*Solanum crispum*
Potato vine	*Solanum jasminoides*
Potomac cherry	*Prunus yedoensis*
Pottery tree	*Moquila utilis*
Poverty pine	*Pinus virginiana*
Prairie cherry	*Prunus gracilis*
Prairie crab apple	*Malus ioensis*
Prairie mimosa	
	Desmanthus illinoensis
Prairie rose	*Rosa setigera*
Prairie senna	*Cassia fasciculata*
Prairie tea	*Croton monanthogynus*
Prairie willow	*Salix humilis*
Pretty whin	*Genista anglica*
Prickleweed	
	Desmanthus illinoensis
Prickly ash	*Aralia spinosa*
	Xanthoxylum americanum
	Zanthoxylum americanum
Prickly broom	*Ulex europaeus*
Prickly cardinal	*Erythrina zeyheri*
Prickly castor oil tree	
	Kalopanax pictus
Prickly custard apple	
	Annona muricata
Prickly cyad	
	Encephalartos altensteinii
Prickly cypress	
	Juniperus formosana
Prickly juniper	*Juniperus oxycedrus*

Prickly moses — *Acacia verticillata*
Prickly palm — *Bactris major*
Prickly pine — *Pinus pungens*
Prickly pole — *Bactris guineensis*
Prickly wattle — *Acacia juniperina*
Pride of Barbados
   Caesalpinia pulcherrima
Pride of Bolivia — *Tipuana tipu*
Pride of Burma — *Amhertsia nobilis*
Pride of China — *Melia azedarach*
Pride of India
   Koelreuteria paniculata
   Lagerstroemia speciosa
   Melia azedarach
Prim privet — *Ligustrum vulgare*
Primrose jasmine
   Jasminum mesnyi
Primrose tree
   Lagunaria patersonii
Prince Albert's yew
   Saxegothaea conspicua
Prince Rupprecht larch
   Larix gmelini
   principis-rupprechtii
Princess palm — *Dictyosperma album*
Princess tree
   Paulownia tomentosa
Prostrate broom
   Cytisus decumbens
Provence rose — *Rosa centifolia*
   Rosa gallica
Provision tree — *Pachira aquatica*
Prune — *Prunus domestica*
Puerto Rican hat palm
   Palmetto causiarum
   Sabal causiarum
Puerto Rican holly
   Olmediella betschlerana
Puerto Rican royal palm
   Roystonea borinquena
Pudding berry — *Cornus canadensis*
Pudding-pipe tree — *Cassia fistula*
Puka — *Meryta sinclairii*
Pulasan — *Nephelium lappaceum*
   Nephelium mutabile
Pumelo — *Citrus grandis*
Pummelo — *Citrus maxima*
Pumpkin ash — *Fraxinus tomentosa*
Punk tree
   Melaleuca quinquenervia
Purging buckthorn
   Rhamnus catharticus
Purging cassia — *Cassia fistula*
Purging fistula — *Cassia fistula*
Purging nut — *Jatropha curcus*
Purple anise — *Illicium floridanum*
Purple apricot — *Prunus × dasycarpa*
Purple beech
   Fagus sylvatica purpurea

Purple birch
   Betula pendula purpurea
Purple broom — *Cytisus purpurea*
Purple chokeberry
   Aronia prunifolia
   Malus floribunda
Purple crab apple
   Malus × purpurea
Purple English oak
   Quercus rober purpurescens
Purple fern-leaved beech
   Fagus sylvatica rohanii
Purple flash
   Prunus cerasifera pissardii
Purple heather — *Erica cinerea*
Purple-leaf barberry — *Berberis*
   thunbergii atropurpurea
   Berberis vulgaris atropurpurea
Purple-leaf birch
   Betula pendula purpurea
Purple-leaf bird cherry
   Prunus padus colorata
Purple-leaf sand cherry
   Prunus × cistena
Purple-leaved cob
   Corylus maxima purpurea
Purple-leaved daphne
   Daphne × houtteana
Purple-leaved filbert
   Corylus maxima purpurea
Purple-leaved plum
   Prunus cerasifera pissardii
Purple-leaved sycamore
   Acer pseudoplatanus
   altropurpureum
Purple mombin — *Spondias purpurea*
Purple orchid tree
   Bauhinia variegata
Purple osier — *Salix purpurea*
Purple plum — *Prunus cerasifera*
   atropurpurea
Purple smoke tree
   Cotinus coggygria purpureus
Purple spruce
   Picea likiangensis purpurea
Purple-twig willow — *Salix acutifolia*
Purple weigela
   Weigela florida purpurea
Pururi tree — *Vitex lucens*
Pussy willow — *Salix caprea*
   Salix discolor
Puzzle willow — *Salix × ambigua*
   Salix mutabilis
Pygmy date palm
   Phoenix roebelenii
Pygmy rowan — *Sorbus reducta*
Pyrenean oak — *Quercus pyrenaica*
Pyrenean pine
   Pinus nigra cebennensis
Pyrenean whitebeam
   Sorbus mougeotii
Qat — *Catha edulis*

Quaking aspen
  Populus tremuloides
Quandong *Fusanus acuminatus*
Queen palm
  Arecastrum romanzoffianum
Queen sago *Cycas circinalis*
Queen's cape myrtle
  Lagerstroemia speciosa
Queensland bottle tree
  Brachychiton rupestris
  Sterculia rupestris
Queensland firewheel tree
  Stenocarpus sinuatus
Queensland hog plum
  Pleiogynium cerasiferum
Queensland kauri *Agathis brownii*
Queensland lacebark
  Brachychiton discolor
Queensland nut
  Macadamia integrifolia
  Macadamia ternifolia
Queensland pittosporum
  Pittosporum rhombifolium
Queensland poplar
  Homalanthus populifolius
Queensland pyramidal tree
  Lagunaria patersonii
Queensland silver wattle
  Acacia podalyriifolia
Queensland umbrella tree
  Brassaia actinophylla
Queensland wattle
  Acacia podalyriifolia
Queensland yellowwood
  Rhodosphaera rhodanthema
Queen's umbrella tree
  Brassaia actinophylla
Quercitron *Quercus velutina*
Quick *Crataegus monogyna*
Quickbeam *Sorbus aucuparia*
Quicken tree *Sorbus aucuparia*
Quick-set thorn
  Crataegus laevigata
Quickthorn *Crataegus monogyna*
Quince *Cydonia oblonga*
Quinine *Cinchona officinalis*
Quinine bush *Garrya elliptica*
Quiverleaf
  Populus tremuloides
Rabbit-eye blueberry
  Vaccinium virgatum
Rabbit root *Aralia nidicaulis*
Raffia palm *Raphia farinifera*
  Raphia ruffia
Railway poplar *Populus regenerata*
Rainbow dogwood
  Cornus florida rainbow
Rain tree *Brunfelsia undulata*
  Samanea saman
Ramanas rose *Rosa rugosa*
Ramarama *Myrtus bullata*

Rambutan *Nephelium lappaceum*
Ramin *Gonystylus bancanus*
Ramontchi *Flacourtia indica*
  Flacourtia ramontchi
Ramsthorn *Rhamnus catharticus*
Rangpur lime *Citrus × limonia*
Rantry *Sorbus aucuparia*
Raoul beech *Nothofagus procera*
Raspberry-jam tree
  Acacia acuminata
Rata *Metrosideros robusta*
Rattan cane *Calamus rotang*
Rauli beech *Nothofagus procera*
Real yellowwood
  Podocarpus latifolius
Red alder *Alnus oregona*
  Alnus rubra
Red ash *Fraxinus pennsylvanica*
Red-barked dogwood *Cornus alba*
Red bay *Persea borbonia*
Red bearberry
  Arctostaphylos uva-ursi
Red beech *Nothofagus fusca*
Red beefwood
  Casuarina equisetifolia
Red-berried elder
  Sambucus pubens
  Sambucus racemosa
Redberry buckthorn
  Rhamnus crocea
Red-berry juniper
  Juniperus pinchotii
Red bilberry
  Vaccinium parvifolium
  Vaccinium vitis-idaea
Red birch *Betula nigra*
Red bloodwood
  Eucalyptus gummifera
Red broad-leaved lime
  Tilia platyphyllos rubra
Red buckeye *Aesculus pavia*
Redbud *Cercis canadensis*
Red-bud maple *Acer trautvetteri*
Red canella
  Cinnamodendron corticosum
Red cedar
  Acrocarpus fraxinifolius
  Juniperus virginiana
Red chokeberry
  Aronia arbutifolia
Red cinchona *Cinchona succirula*
Red cypress pine
  Callitris endlicheri
Red elder *Viburnum opulus*
Red elm *Ulmus rubra*
  Ulmus serotina
Red fir *Abies magnifica*
Red flag bush
  Mussaenda eythrophylla
Red-flowered mallee
  Eucalyptus ewartiana

River walnut

Red-flowering gum
    Eucalyptus ficifolia
Red gum   *Eucalyptus calophylla*
    Eucalyptus camaldulensis
    Ceratopetalum gummiferum
    Liquidambar styraciflua
Red haw   *Crataegus mollis*
Red hawthorn   *Crataegus laevigata*
Red heart   *Ceanothus spinosus*
Red hickory   *Carya ovalis*
Red horse-chestnut
    Aesculus × carnea
Red-hot cat-tail   *Acalypha hispida*
Red huckleberry
    Vaccinium parvifolium
Red ironbark
    Eucalyptus sideroxylon
Red jasmine   *Plumeria rubra*
Red latan   *Latania borbonica*
    Latania lontaroides
Red-leaved acacia   *Acacia rubida*
Red-leaved wattle   *Acacia rubida*
Red mahogany
    Eucalyptus resinifer
Red mallee
    Eucalyptus erythronema
Red mangrove
    Rhizophora mangle
Red manjack   *Cordia nitida*
Red maple   *Acer rubrum*
Red may   *Crataegus laevigata*
Red mombin   *Spondias purpurea*
Red moort   *Eucalyptus nutans*
Red morell   *Eucalyptus longicornis*
Red mulberry   *Morus rubra*
Red oak   *Quercus borealis*
    Quercus rubra
Red-osier dogwood   *Cornus sericea*
    Cornus stolonifera
Red-paper tree   *Albizzia rhodesica*
Red pine   *Dacrydium cupressinum*
    Pinus resinosa
    Podocarpus dacrydioides
Red pokers   *Hakea bucculenta*
Red root   *Ceanothus americanus*
Red river gum
    Eucalyptus camaldulensis
Red rose   *Rosa gallica*
Red sandalwood
    Pterocarpus santalinus
    Santalum rubrum
Red sandalwood tree
    Adenanthera pavonina
Red saunders
    Pterocarpus santalinus
Red signal heath   *Erica mammosa*
Red silk-cotton tree   *Bombax ceiba*
    Bombax malabaricum
Red silver fir   *Abies ambilis*
Red siris   *Albizzia toona*

Red snakebark maple
    Acer capillipes
Red spotted gum
    Eucalyptus mannifera
Red spruce   *Picea rubens*
    Picea rubra
Red-stemmed acacia
    Acacia rubida
Red stopper   *Eugenia confusa*
    Eugenia garberi
Red stringybark
    Eucalyptus macrorhyncha
Red titi   *Cyrilla racemiflora*
Redwater tree
    Erythrophleum guineese
    Erythrophleum suaveolens
Red willow   *Cornus amomum*
    Salix laevigata
Redwood   *Adenanthera pavonina*
    Sequoia sempervirens
Redwood rose   *Rosa gymnocarpa*
Reed palm   *Chamaedorea seifrizii*
Reed rhapis   *Rhapis humilis*
Reefwood   *Stenocarpus salignus*
Remarkable-cone pine
    Pinus radiata
Rewa rewa   *Knightia excelsa*
Rhododendron
    Rhododendron arboreum
    Rhododendron ponticum
Ribbon gum   *Eucalyptus viminalis*
Ribbon plant   *Dracaena sanderana*
Ribbonwood   *Hoheria lyallii*
    Hoheria populnea
    Hoheria sexstylosa
Ribbonwood tree
    Plagianthus regius
Rice-paper tree
    Tetrapanax papyriferus
Ridge-fruited mallee
    Eucalyptus incrassata
Rimu   *Dacrydium cupressinum*
Ring-cupped oak   *Quercus glauca*
Ringworm cassia   *Cassia alata*
Ringworm powder tree
    Andira araroba
Ringworm senna   *Cassia elata*
Rio grande cherry
    Eugenia aggregata
River birch   *Betula nigra*
River maple   *Acer saccharinum*
River oak
    Casuarina cunninghamiana
River peppermint
    Eucalyptus andreana
    Eucalyptus elata
    Eucalyptus longifolia
River tea tree
    Melaleuca leucadendron
River walnut   *Juglans microcarpa*
    Juglans rupestris

Robertson's peppermint	
	Eucalyptus robertsonii
Robinia	*Robinia pseudoacacia*
Robin redbreast bush	
	Melaleuca lateritia
Roblé beech	*Nothofagus obliqua*
Roblé blanco	*Nothofagus pumilo*
Roblé de maule	*Nothofagus glauca*
Roblé pellin	*Nothofagus obliqua*
Robusta coffee	*Coffea canephora*
Rock birch	*Betula nana*
Rock buckthorn	*Rhamnus saxitilis*
Rock cherry	*Prunus prostrata*
Rock chestnut oak	*Quercus prinus*
Rock cotoneaster	
	Cotoneaster horizontalis
Rock elm	*Ulmus thomasi*
Rock maple	*Acer glabrum*
	Acer saccharum
Rock sallow	*Salix petraea*
Rock whitebeam	*Sorbus rupicola*
Rocky mountain cherry	
	Prunus besseyi
Rocky mountain fir	
	Abies lasiocarpa
Rocky mountain maple	
	Acer glabrum
Rocky mountains bramble	
	Rubus deliciosus
Rocky mountain scrub oak	
	Quercus undulata
Rocky mountains juniper	
	Juniperus jackii
	Juniperus scopulorum
Roebelin palm	*Phoenix roebelenii*
Roman candle	*Yucca gloriosa*
Roman laurel	*Laurus nobilis*
Rooiels	*Cunonia capensis*
Ropebark	*Dirca palustris*
Rosa mundi	*Rosa gallica versicolor*
Rose acacia	*Robinia hispida*
Rose apple	*Eugenia aquea*
	Syzygium jambos
	Syzygium malaccense
Rose bay oleander	
	Nerium oleander
Rose bay	
	Rhododendron maximum
	Rhododendron ponticum
Rose box	
	Cotoneaster microphyllus
Rosebud cherry	*Prunus subhirtella*
	Prunus subhirtella ascendens
Rose gum	*Eucalyptus grandis*
Rose imperial	
	Cochlospermum vitifolium
Roselle	*Hibiscus sabdariffa*
Rose mallee	
	Eucalyptus × rhodantha
Rose mallow	*Lavatera trimestris*
Rosemary	*Rosmarinus officinalis*
Rose of sharon	*Althaea frutex*
	Hibiscus syriacus
	Hypericum calycinum
Rose of Venezuela	
	Brownea grandiceps
Rosewood	*Tipuana tipu*
Rosy trumpet tree	*Tabebuia rosea*
Rottnest Island pine	
	Callitris preissii
Rouen lilac	*Syringa × chinensis*
Rough-barked maple	
	Acer triflorum
Rough-barked Mexican pine	
	Pinus montezumae
Rough-leaved hydrangea	
	Hydrangea aspera
Rough netbush	*Calothamnus asper*
Rough-shell macadamia nut	
	Macadamia tetraphylla
Round buchu	*Agathosma betulina*
Round-eared willow	*Salix aurita*
Round kumquat	
	Fortunella japonica
Round-leaved dogwood	
	Cornus rugosa
Round-leaved mallee	
	Eucalyptus orbifolia
Round-leaved moort	
	Eucalyptus platypus
Round-leaved snow gum	
	Eucalyptus perriniana
Roundwood	*Sorbus americana*
Rowan	*Sorbus aucuparia*
Royal bay	*Laurus nobilis*
Royal fern	*Osmunda regalis*
Royal hakea	*Hakea victoriae*
Royal jasmine	
	Jasminum grandiflorum
Royal lime	*Tilia × europaea pallida*
Royal palm	*Roystonea regia*
Royal poinciana	*Delonix regia*
Royoc	*Morinda royoc*
Rubber euphorbia	
	Euphorbia tirucalli
Rubber plant	*Ficus belgica*
	Ficus elastica
Rubber tree	*Hevea brasiliensis*
Ruby saltbush	
	Enchylaena tomentosa
Rue	*Ruta graveolens*
Ruffled fan palm	*Licula grandis*
Ruffle pine	*Aiphanes caryotifolia*
Rum cherry	*Prunus serotina*
Russian almond	*Prunus tenella*
Russian cedar	*Pinus cembra*
Russian elm	*Zelkova carpinifolia*
Russian mountain ash	
	Sorbus aucuparia rossica-major

TREES, BUSHES, AND SHRUBS

Russian olive
   Elaeagnus angustifolia
Russian pea shrub *Caragana frutex*
Russian rock birch
   Betula ermanii
Russian vine
   Polygonum baldschuanicum
Rusty fig   *Ficus australis*
   Ficus rubiginosa
Rusty nannyberry
   Viburnum rufidulum
Rusty podocarp
   Podocarpus ferrugineus
Sabal   *Serenoa repens*
Sabicu *Lysiloma latisiliqua*
Sacramento rose
   Rosa stellata mirifica
Sacred bamboo
   Nandina domestica
Sacred fig *Ficus religiosa*
Sacred fir *Abies religiosa*
Sacred flower *Cantua buxifolia*
Sacred garlic pear
   Crateva religiosa
Sage-leaved pear *Pyrus salvifolia*
Sage-leaved rock rose
   Cistus salviifolius
Sage-leaved willow
   Salix salviaefolia
Sage tree *Vitex agnus-castus*
Sage willow *Salix candida*
Saghalin spruce *Picea glehnii*
Sago palm *Caryota urens*
   Cycas circinalis
   Cycas revoluta
   Metroxylon sagu
Saigon cinnamon
   Cinnamomum loureirii
Saint Daboec's heath
   Daboecia cantabrica
Saint John's bread
   Ceratonia siliqua
Saint Lucie cherry *Prunus mahaleb*
Saint Mary's wood
   Calophyllum brasiliense
Sakhalin fir *Abies sachalinensis*
Sakhalin spruce *Picea glehnii*
Sal   *Shorea robusta*
Salac *Salacea edulis*
Sallow *Salix caprea*
Sallow thorn
   Hippophae rhamnoides
Sally wattle *Acacia binervia*
Salmon berry *Rubus parviflorus*
Salmon gum
   Eucalyptus salmonophloia
Salmon white gum
   Eucalyptus lane-poolei
Salt cedar *Tamarix gallica*
Salt tree
   Halimodendron halodendron

Saman tree *Samanea saman*
Sandal tree *Sandoricum indicum*
Sandalwood *Santalum album*
Sandalwood tree
   Adenanthera pavonina
Sandbar willow *Salix interior*
Sandberry *Arctostaphylos uva-ursi*
Sandbox tree *Hura crepitans*
Sand cherry *Prunus besseyi*
   Prunus depressa
   Prunus pumila
Sanderswood
   Pterocarpus santalinus
Sandfly bush *Zieria smithii*
Sand hickory *Carya pallida*
San Diego ceanothus
   Ceanothus cyaneus
Sand jack *Quercus incana*
Sand myrtle
   Leiophyllum buxifolium
Sand pear *Pyrus pyrifolia*
   Pyrus ussuriensis
Sand pine *Pinus clausa*
Sand plum *Prunus angustifolia*
Sand willow *Salix arenaria*
San José hesper palm
   Brahea brandegeei
Santa Barbara ceanothus
   Ceanothus dentalus
   Ceanothus impressus
Santa Cruz cypress
   Cupressus abramsiana
Santa Lucia fir *Abies bracteata*
   Abies venusta
Santa Maria
   Calophyllum brasiliense
Sapele
   Entandrophragma cylindricum
Sapodilla *Manilkara zapota*
Sapodilla plum *Achras sapota*
   Manilkara zapota
Sapote *Pouteria sapota*
Sapote amarillo
   Pouteria campechiana
Sapote borracho
   Pouteria campechiana
Sappanwood *Caesalpinia sappan*
Sapphire berry
   Symplocos paniculata
Sapree wood
   Widdringtonia cupressoides
Sapucia nut *Lecythis zabucayo*
Sargent's cherry *Prunus sargentii*
Sargent's cypress
   Cupressus sargentii
Sargent spruce *Picea brachytyla*
Sargent's rowan
   Sorbus sargentiana
Sarsaparilla *Aralia nudicaulis*
Sarvis holly *Ilex amelanchier*

Sasanqua camellia

Sasanqua camellia	
	Camellia sasanqua
Sassafras	*Sassafras albidum*
Sassy bark	
	Erythrophleum guineese
Satin bush	*Podalyria sericea*
Satin hibiscus	*Hibiscus huegelii*
Satinleaf	
	Chrysophyllum oliviforme
Satinwood	*Chloroxylon swietenia*
	Fagara flava
	Liquidambar styraciflua
	Murraya paniculata
Satiny willow	*Salix pellita*
Satsuma orange	*Citrus reticulata*
Saucer magnolia	
	Magnolia × soulangiana
Sausage tree	*Kigelia africana*
	Kigelia pinnata
Savin	*Juniperus sabina*
Sawara cypress	
	Chamaecyparis pisifera
Saw briar	*Smilax glauca*
Saw cabbage palm	
	Acoelorrhaphe wrightii
Saw-leaf zelkova	*Zelkova serrata*
Saw palmetto	*Serenoa repens*
Sawtooth oak	*Quercus acutissima*
Scaly-leaved Nepal juniper	
	Juniperus squamata
Scandinavian juniper	
	Juniperus suecica
Scarab cypress	
	Chamaecyparis lawsoniana
	allumii
Scarlet bush	*Hamelia patens*
Scarlet gum	*Eucalyptus phoenicia*
Scarlet haw	*Crataegus pedicellata*
Scarlet maple	*Acer rubrum*
Scarlet oak	*Quercus coccinea*
Scarlet sumac	*Rhus glabra*
Scarlet willow	
	Salix alba chermesina
Scented paperbark	
	Melaleuca squarrosa
Scholar's tree	*Sophora japonica*
Schrenk's spruce	
	Picea schrenkiana
Scorpion senna	*Coronilla emerus*
Scotch briar	*Rosa pimpinellifolia*
Scotch broom	*Cytisus scoparius*
Scotch elm	*Ulmus glabra*
Scotch fir	*Pinus sylvestris*
Scotch heath	*Erica cinerea*
Scotch heather	*Calluna vulgaris*
Scotch laburnum	
	Laburnum alpinum
Scotch rose	*Rosa pimpinellifolia*
Scots pine	*Pinus sylvestris*
Scouler willow	*Salix scoulerana*

Screw bean	*Prosopis pubescens*
Screw pine	*Pandanus leram*
Screw-pod wattle	*Acacia implexa*
Scribbly gum	
	Eucalyptus haemastoma
Scrub bottle-tree	
	Brachychiton discolor
Scrub oak	*Quercus dumosa*
	Quercus illicifolia
Scrub palmetto	*Sabal adansonii*
	Sabal etonia
	Sabal minor
	Sabal repens
	Serenoa repens
Scrub pine	*Pinus banksiana*
	Pinus virginiana
Scrub sumac	*Rhus microphylla*
Sea apple	*Syzygium grande*
Sea ash	
	Zanthoxylum clava-herculis
	Xanthoxlyum clava-herculis
Sea buckthorn	
	Hippophae rhamnoides
Sea fig	*Ficus superba*
Sea grape	*Coccoloba uvifera*
Sealing-wax palm	
	Cyrostachys lakka
	Cyrostachys renda
Sea orach	*Atriplex halinus*
Sea purslane	
	Atriplex portulacoides
Seaside alder	*Alnus maritima*
Sea-urchin tree	*Hakea laurina*
Selu	*Cordia myxa*
Senegal date palm	
	Phoenix reclinata
Senegal gum	*Acacia senegal*
Senegal mahogany	
	Khaya senegalensis
Senegal rosewood	
	Pterocarpus erinaceus
Senna	*Cassia acutifolia*
Sentol	*Sandoricum koetjapa*
Sentry palm	*Howea forsterana*
	Kentia forsterana
September elm	*Ulmus serotina*
Serbian laurel	
	Prunus laurocerasus serbica
Serbian spruce	*Picea omorika*
Serpentine manzanita	
	Arctostaphylos obispoensis
Service tree	*Sorbus domestica*
Sessile oak	*Quercus petraea*
Seven barks	
	Hydrangea arborescens
Seven sisters rose	
	Rosa multiflora grevillei
Seville orange	*Citrus aurantium*
Shad berry	*Amelanchier laevis*
Shad blow	*Amelanchier laevis*

TREES, BUSHES, AND SHRUBS

Silver birch

Shad bush	*Amelanchier laevis*
Shaddock	*Citrus maxima*
Shagbark hickory	*Carya ovata*
Shaggy-bark manzanita	
	Arctostaphylos tomentosa
Shag-spine pea shrub	
	Carangana jubata
Shallon	*Gaultheria shallon*
Shamel ash	*Fraxinus uhdei*
Shantung maple	*Acer truncatum*
Sharp cedar	*Juniperus oxycedrus*
Shaving-brush tree	
	Pseudobombax ellipticum
Shea butter tree	
	Butyrospermum paradoxum
	Butyrospermum parkii
She balsam	*Abies fraseri*
Sheepberry	*Viburnum lentago*
	Viburnum prunifolium
Sheep laurel	*Kalmia angustifolia*
Shell-bark hickory	*Carya laciniosa*
	Carya ovata
Shensi fir	*Abies chensiensis*
She-oak	*Casuarina stricta*
She pine	*Podocarpus elatus*
Shingle oak	*Quercus imbricaria*
Shingle tree	
	Acrocarpus fraxinifolius
Shining honeysuckle	
	Lonicera nitida
Shining privet	*Ligustrum lucidum*
Shining sumach	*Rhus copallina*
Shining willow	*Salix lucida*
Shinnery oak	*Quercus havardii*
Shin oak	*Quercus gambelii*
Shipmast acacia	
	Robinia pseudoacacia
	appalachia
Shittimwood	*Acacia nilotica*
	Bumelia lanuginosa
	Bumelia lycioides
	Halesia carolina
Shore juniper	*Juniperus conferta*
Shore pine	*Pinus contorta*
Shore plum	*Prunus maritima*
Short-leaf pine	*Pinus echinata*
Shot huckleberry	
	Vaccinium ovatum
Showy crab apple	
	Malus floribunda
Shrubby dogwood	
	Cornus sanguinea
Shrubby germander	
	Teucrium fruticans
Shrubby horsetail	
	Ephedra distachya
Shrubby mallow	*Lavatera olbia*
Shrubby musk	
	Mimulus aurantiacus
Shrubby pavia	*Aesculus parviflora*

Shrubby trefoil	*Ptelea trifoliata*
Shrub tobacco	*Nicotiana glauca*
Shui-hsa	
	Metasequoia glyptostroboides
Shumard's oak	*Quercus shumardii*
Shumard's red oak	
	Quercus shumardii
Siberian apricot	*Prunus sibirica*
Siberian balsam poplar	
	Populus laurifolia
Siberian crab apple	*Malus baccata*
	Malus × robusta
Siberian dogwood	*Cornus alba*
Siberian elm	*Ulmus pumila*
Siberian fir	*Abies sibirica*
Siberian larch	*Larix russica*
	Larix sibirica
Siberian pea tree	
	Caragana arborescens
Siberian spruce	*Picea obovata*
Sibipiruna	
	Caesalpinia peltophoroides
Sicilian sumac	*Rhus coriaria*
Sickle senna	*Cassia tora*
Sicklepod	*Cassia tora*
Siebold's beech	*Fagus sieboldii*
Siebold's hemlock	*Tsuga sieboldii*
Sierra fir	*Abies concolor lowiana*
Sierra juniper	
	Juniperus occidentalis
Sierra Leone tamarind	
	Dialium guineense
Sierra plum	*Prunus subcordata*
Sierra redwood	
	Sequoiadendron giganteum
Sikkim larch	*Larix griffithiana*
	Larix griffithii
Sikkim spruce	*Picea spinulosa*
Silk-cotton tree	*Ceiba pentandra*
	Cochlospermun religiosum
Silk fruit tree	
	Seriocarpus conyzoides
Silk grass	*Yucca filamentosa*
Silk tassel bush	*Garrya elliptica*
Silk tree	*Albizzia julibrissin*
Silkworm tree	*Morus alba*
Silky camellia	
	Stuartia malacodendron
	Stewartia malacodendron
Silky dogwood	*Cornus amomum*
	Cornus purpusii
Silky oak	*Grevillea robusta*
Silky willow	*Salix sericea*
Silver beech	*Nothofagus menziesii*
Silver bell	*Halesia carolina*
	Halesia tetraptera
Silver berry	*Elaeagnus angustifolia*
	Elaeagnus argentea
	Elaeagnus commutata
Silver birch	*Betula pendula*

Silver broom palm

Silver broom palm	
	Thrinax argentea
Silver buffalo berry	
	Shepherdia argentea
Silverbush	*Sophora tomentosa*
Silver dogwood	
	Cornus alba elegantissima
Silver dollar gum	
	Eucalyptus polyanthemos
Silver dollar tree	
	Eucalyptus cinerea
Silver fir	*Abies alba*
Silver heather	
	Cassinia vauvilliersii albida
Silver hedgehog holly	
	Ilex aquifolium argentea
Silver holly	*Berberis hypokerina*
Silver-leaf manzanita	
	Arctostaphylos silvicola
Silver-leaved mountain gum	
	Eucalyptus pulverulenta
Silver-leaved poplar	*Populus alba*
Silver lime	*Tilia tomentosa*
Silver mallee scrub	
	Eucalyptus polybractea
Silver maple	*Acer saccharinum*
Silver palm	*Coccothrinax argentata*
Silver pear	*Pyrus salicifolia*
Silver peppermint	
	Eucalyptus risdonii
	Eucalyptus tenuiramis
Silver privet	*Ligustrum*
	ovalifolium argenteum
Silver saw palm	
	Acoelorrhaphe wrightii
Silver spruce	*Picea sitchensis*
Silver thatch	
	Coccothrinax argentea
Silver top	*Eucalyptus nitens*
Silver tree	
	Leucodendron argenteum
Silver trumpet tree	
	Tabebuia argentia
Silver variegated dogwood	
	Cornus alba elegantissima
Silver wattle	*Acacia dealbata*
Silver willow	*Salix alba argentea*
	Salix alba sericea
Simarouba	*Simarouba amara*
Simon's plum	*Prunus simonii*
Singapore holly	
	Malpighia coccigera
Singapore oak	*Quercus conocarpa*
Single-leaf ash	
	Fraxinus excelsior diversifolia
Single-leaf pinyon pine	
	Picea monophylla
Single-leaf pine	*Pinus monophylla*
Single-leaved ash	
	Fraxinus angustifolia veltheimii
	Fraxinus anomala

Siris tree	*Albizzia lebbeck*
Siskiyou cypress	
	Cupressus bakeri mathewsii
Siskiyou-mat	*Ceanothus pumilus*
Siskiyou spruce	*Picea brewerana*
Sissoo	*Dalbergia sissoo*
Sitka alder	*Alnus sinuata*
Sitka spruce	*Picea sitchensis*
Skewerwood	*Euonymus europaea*
Skunk bush	*Rhus trilobata*
Skyflower	*Duranta ellisia*
	Duranta repens
Slash pine	*Pinus elliotii*
Sleeping hibiscus	
	Malvaviscus arboreus
Sleepy mallow	
	Malaviscus arboreus
Slender lady palm	*Rhapis excelsa*
	Rhapis humilis
Slender smokebush	
	Conospermum huegelii
Slippery elm	*Ulmus rubra*
Sloe	*Prunus alleghaniensis*
	Prunus spinosa
Small-fruited grey gum	
	Eucalyptus propinqua
Small-fruited Queensland nut	
	Macadamia ternifolia
Small-leaved elm	*Ulmus alata*
Small-leaved gum	
	Eucalyptus parvifolia
Small-leaved lime	*Tilia cordata*
Small-leaved rubber plant	
	Ficus benjamina
Small-leaved sumac	
	Rhus microphylla
Small pussy willow	*Salix humilis*
Smoke bush	
	Conospermum huegelii
	Cotinus coggygria
Smoke tree	*Cotinus coggygria*
	Rhus cotinus
Smooth alder	*Alnus serrulata*
	Alnus rugosa
Smooth Arizona cypress	
	Cupressus glabra
Smooth-barked Arizona cypress	
	Cupressus arizonica
	Cupressus glabra
Smooth Japanese maple	
	Acer japonicum
	Acer palmatum
Smooth-leaved elm	
	Ulmus carpinifolia
Ulmus carpinifolia sarniensis	
	Ulmus minor
Smooth rambutan	
	Alectryon subcinereus
Smooth rose	*Rosa blanda*
Smooth senna	*Cassia laevigata*
Smooth sumac	*Rhus glabra*

Southern pitch pine

Smooth Tasmanian cedar
Athrotaxis cupressoides
Smooth winterberry
Ilex laevigata
Smooth withe-rod
Viburnum nudum
Smooth withy-rod
Viburnum nudum
Snailseed *Coccoloba diversifolia*
Snakebark maple *Acer capillipes*
Acer crataegifolium
Acer forrestii
Acer hersii
Acer laxiflorum
Acer pennsylvanicam
Acer rufinerve
Snake bush
Duvernoia adhatodioides
Snakewood tree *Cecropia palmata*
Snappy gum *Eucalyptus micrantha*
Eucalyptus racemosa
Snowball tree
Viburnum opulus sterile
Snowbell tree *Styrax japonica*
Snowberry *Gaultheria hispida*
Symphoricarpus albus
Symphoricarpus rivularis
Snowbush *Breynia disticha*
Ceanothus cordulatus
Snow camellia
Camellia japonica rusticana
Snowdrop tree *Halesia carolina*
Halesia tetraptera
Snowflake aralia *Trevesia palmata*
Snowflake tree *Trevesia palmata*
Snowflower
Chionanthus virginicus
Snow gum *Eucalyptus niphophila*
Snow heath *Erica herbacea*
Snow heather *Erica carnea*
Snow in summer
Helichrysum rosmarinifolium
Ozothamnus rosmarinifolius
Ozothamnus thyrsoideus
Snow pear *Pyrus nivalis*
Snowy mespil *Amelanchier laevis*
Amelanchier lamarckii
Amelanchier ovalis
Snuffbox tree *Oncoba spinosa*
Soap bark tree *Quillaia saponaria*
Soapberry *Sapindus saponaria*
Shepherdia canadensis
Soapberry tree
Sapindus drummondii
Soap bush *Noltea africana*
Soap tree *Quillaia saponaria*
Yucca elata
Soapweed *Yucca elata*
Yucca glauca
Soapwell *Yucca glauca*
Socotra cucumber tree
Dendrosicyos socotrana

Soft-leaved rose *Rosa villosa*
Soft maple *Acer rubrum*
Acer saccharinum
Soldier rose mallow
Hibiscus militaris
Soledad pine *Pinus torreyana*
Solitary palm
Ptychosperma elegans
Somali tea *Catha edulis*
Sonoma manzanita
Arctostaphylos densiflora
Sonoran palmetto *Sabal uresana*
Sorbet *Cornus mas*
Sorrel tree
Oxydendrum arboreum
Sorrowless tree *Saraca indica*
Soulard crab apple
Malus × soulardii
Sourberry *Rhus integrifolia*
Sour cherry *Prunus cerasus*
Sour gum *Nyssa sylvatica*
Sour orange *Citrus aurantium*
Soursop *Annona muricata*
Sour top *Vaccinium canadanse*
Sourwood tree
Oxydendrum arboreum
South African sagewood
Buddleia salviifolia
South American apricot
Mammea americana
South American crowberry
Empetrum rubrum
South American pine
Dacrydium fonkii
South American royal palm
Roystonea oleracea
Southern arrowwood
Viburnum dentatum
Southern balsam fir *Abies fraseri*
Southern black haw
Viburnum rufidulum
Southern blue gum
Eucalyptus globulus
Southern buckthorn
Bumelia lycioides
Southern catalpa
Catalpa bignonioides
Southern cross silver mallee
Eucalyptus crucis
Southern Japanese hemlock
Tsuga sieboldii
Southern live oak
Quercus virginiana
Southern magnolia
Magnolia grandiflora
Southern nettle tree
Celtis australis
Southern pine *Pinus palustris*
Southern pitch pine *Pinus palustris*

Southern prickly ash *Xanthoxylum clava-herculis*
Zanthoxylum clava-herculis
Southern red cedar *Juniperus silicicola*
Southern sassafras *Atherosperma moschatum*
Southern sugar maple *Acer barbatum*
Southern white cedar *Chamaecyparis thyoides*
Southern wild crab apple *Malus angustifolia*
Southern yellow pine *Pinus palustris*
Southern yew *Podocarpus macrophyllus*
South Queensland kauri *Agathis robusta*
South sea ironwood *Casuarina equisetifolia*
Spadic *Erythroxylum coca*
Spaeth's flowering ash *Fraxinus spaethiana*
Spanish bayonet *Yucca aloifolia*
Yucca baccata
Spanish broom *Genista hispanica*
Spartium junceum
Spanish buckeye *Ungnadia speciosa*
Spanish cedar *Cedrela odorata*
Toona odorata
Spanish cherry *Mimusops elengi*
Spanish chestnut *Castanea sativa*
Spanish cordia *Cordia sebestena*
Spanish dagger *Yucca aloifolia*
Yucca carnerosana
Spanish fir *Abies pinsapo*
Spanish gorse *Genista hispanica*
Spanish heath *Erica australis*
Erica carnea
Erica lusitanica
Spanish jasmine *Jasminum grandiflorum*
Spanish juniper *Juniperus thurifera*
Spanish lime *Melicoccus bijugatus*
Spanish mahogany *Swietenia mahagoni*
Spanish oak *Quercus falcata*
Quercus palustris
Spanish plum *Spondias purpurea*
Spanish red oak *Quercus falcata*
Spanish royal palm *Roystonea hispaniolana*
Spanish savin *Juniperus sabina tamariscifolia*
Spanish stopper *Eugenia buxifolia*
Eugenia foetida
Eugenia myrtoides
Speckled alder *Alnus rugosa*
Spiceberry *Ardisia crenata*
Spice bush *Benzoin aestivale*
Lindera benzoin
Spice guava *Psidium montanum*
Spicy jatropha *Jatropha integerrima*
Spikenard *Aralia nudicaulis*
Aralia racemosa
Spike winter hazel *Corylopsis spicata*
Spindle palm *Hyophorbe verschaffeltii*
Spindle tree *Euonymus europaea*
Spineless broad-leaved holly *Ilex × altaclarensis camelliifolia*
Spineless yucca *Yucca elephantipes*
Spiny pine *Aiphanes caryotifolia*
Spinning gum *Eucalyptus perriniana*
Spiral eucalyptus *Eucalyptus cinerea*
Sponge tree *Acacia farnesiana*
Spoonleaf yucca *Yucca filamentosa*
Spoon tree *Cunonia capensis*
Spoonwood *Kalmia latifolia*
Spotted dracaena *Dracaena surculosa*
Spotted emu bush *Eremophila maculata*
Spotted fig *Ficus infectoria*
Ficus lacor
Ficus virens
Spotted gum *Eucalyptus maculata*
Spotted laurel *Aucuba japonica*
Spotted mountain gum *Eucalyptus goniocalyx*
Spray bush *Holodiscus discolor*
Spread-leaved pine *Pinus patula*
Spring cherry *Prunus subhirtella*
Spring heath *Erica herbacea*
Spruce pine *Pinus glabra*
Pinus virginiana
Spurge laurel *Daphne laureola*
Spurge olive *Cneorum tricoccum*
Spur-leaf tree *Tetracentron sinense*
Square-fruited mallee *Eucalyptus tetraptera*
Squarenut *Carya tomentosa*
Squaw berry *Mitchella repens*
Squaw bush *Viburnum trilobum*
Squaw carpet *Ceanothus prostratus*
Squaw huckleberry *Vaccinium stamineum*
Squaw vine *Mitchella repens*
Stagbush *Viburnum prunifolium*
Stagger bush *Lyonia mariana*
Stag's horn sumac *Rhus hirta*
Rhus typhina
Star acacia *Acacia verticillata*

TREES, BUSHES, AND SHRUBS

Swamp immortelle

Star anise | *Illicium anisatum*
Illicium religiosum
Illicum verum
Star apple | *Chrysophyllum cainito*
Star fruit | *Damasonium alisma*
Star jasmine
Jasminum gracillimum
Jasminum multiflorum
Starleaf | *Brassaia actinophylla*
Starry magnolia | *Magnolia stellata*
Star wattle | *Acacia verticillata*
Steedman's gum
Eucalyptus steedmanii
Sticky wattle | *Acacia howittii*
Stiff dogwood | *Cornus stricta*
Stiff-leaved juniper | *Juniperus rigida*
Stinking ash | *Ptelea trifoliata*
Stinking cedar | *Torreya taxifolia*
Stinking elder | *Sambucus pubens*
Stinking juniper
Juniperus foetidissima
Stinking tutsan
Hypericum hircinum
Stinking weed | *Cassia occidentalis*
Stinkwood | *Celtis kraussiana*
Gustavia augusta
Stinking yew | *Torreya californica*
Stone pine | *Picea monophylla*
Pinus pinea
Pinus monophylla
Storax | *Liquidambar orientalis*
Styrax officinalis
Stoward's mallee
Eucalyptus stowardii
Strangler fig | *Ficus aurea*
Strawberry bush
Euonymus americana
Strawberry guava
Psidium cattleianum
Strawberry-raspberry
Rubus illecebrosus
Strawberry shrub
Calycanthus floridus
Strawberry tree | *Cornus capitata*
Euonymus americana
Strickland's gum
Eucalyptus stricklandii
Stringybark tree
Eucalyptus globulus
Striped maple
Acer pennsylvanicum
Strongback | *Bourreria ovata*
Strychnine | *Strychnos nux-vomica*
Sturt's desert pea
Clianthus formosus
Styptic weed | *Cassia occidentalis*
Subalpine fir | *Abies lasiocarpa*
Sudan gum-arabic | *Acacia senegal*
Sugar apple | *Annona squamosa*
Sugarberry | *Celtis laevigata*
Celtis occidentalis

Sugarbush | *Protea mellifera*
Protea repens
Sugar gum | *Eucalyptus cladocalyx*
Eucalyptus corynocalyx
Sugar maple | *Acer saccharum*
Sugar palm | *Arenga pinnata*
Sugar pine | *Pinus lambertiana*
Sugar tree | *Acer barbatum*
Sulfer rose | *Rosa hemisphaerica*
Rosa sulfurea
Sulphur rose | *Rosa hemisphaerica*
Rosa sulfurea
Summerberry | *Viburnum trilobum*
Summer haw | *Crataegus flava*
Summer lilac | *Buddleia davidii*
Summer sweet | *Clethra alnifolia*
Summit cedar | *Athrotaxis laxifolia*
Sun fruit | *Heliocarpus americanus*
Sunrise horsechestnut
Aesculus neglecta erythroblastos
Sunset hibiscus
Abelmoschus manihot
Sunshine wattle
Acacia botrycephala
Acacia paniculata
Suntwood | *Acacia nilotica*
Surinam cherry | *Eugenia uniflora*
Surinam quassia | *Quassia amara*
Sutchuen fir | *Abies fargesii*
Abies sutchuenensis
Swamp azalea
Rhododendron viscosum
Swamp banksia | *Banksia littoralis*
Swamp bay | *Magnolia virginiana*
Swamp bloodwood
Eucalyptus ptychocarpa
Swamp blueberry
Vaccinium corymbosum
Swamp candleberry
Myrica pennsylvanica
Swamp chestnut oak
Quercus michauxii
Quercus prinus
Swamp cottonwood
Populus heterophylla
Swamp currant | *Ribes lacustre*
Swamp cypress
Taxodium distichum
Swamp dogwood | *Ptelea trifoliata*
Swamp elder | *Viburnum aopulus*
Swamp gum | *Eucalyptus ovata*
Eucalyptus rudis
Swamp haw | *Viburnum cassinoides*
Swamp hickory | *Carya cordiformis*
Swamp holly | *Ilex amelanchier*
Swamp honeysuckle
Azalea viscosa
Rhododendron viscosum
Swamp immortelle | *Erythrina fusca*
Erythrina glauca
Erythrina ovalifolia

Swamp laurel

Swamp laurel	*Kalmia glauca*
Swamp locust	*Gleditsia aquatica*
Swamp mahogany	*Eucalyptus robustus*
Swamp mallee	*Eucalyptus spathulata*
Swamp maple	*Acer rubrum*
Swamp paperbark	*Melaleuca ericifolia*
	Melaleuca rhaphiophylla
Swamp post oak	*Quercus lyrata*
Swamp privet	*Forestiera acuminata*
Swamp red bay	*Persea borbonia*
Swamp rose mallow	*Hibiscus moscheutos*
Swamp rose	*Rosa palustris*
Swamp she oak	*Casuarina equisitifolia*
Swamp sumac	*Rhus vernix*
Swamp tea tree	*Melaleuca quinquenervia*
Swamp wattle	*Acacia elongata*
Swamp white cedar	*Chamaecyparis thyoides*
Swamp white oak	*Quercus bicolor*
Swedish birch	*Betula alba dalecarlia*
	Betula pendula dalecarlica
Swedish juniper	*Juniperus communis pyramidalis*
	Juniperus communis suecica
Swedish myrtle	*Myrtus communis*
Swedish whitebeam	*Sorbus intermedia*
	Sorbus suecica
Sweet acacia	*Acacia farnesiana*
	Acacia suaveolens
Sweet almond	*Prunus dulcis*
Sweet bay	*Laurus nobilis*
	Magnolia virginiana
	Persea borbonia
Sweet berry	*Viburnum lentago*
Sweet birch	*Betula lenta*
Sweet briar	*Rosa eglanteria*
	Rosa rubiginosa
Sweet buckeye	*Aesculus flava*
	Aesculus octandra
Sweet cassava	*Manihot dulcis*
Sweet cherry	*Prunus avium*
Sweet chestnut	*Castanea sativa*
Sweet cistin	*Halimium lasianthum formosum*
Sweet crab apple	*Malus coronaria*
Sweet elder	*Sambucus canadensis*
Sweet elm	*Ulmus fulva*
Sweet gale	*Myrica gale*
Sweet gallberry	*Ilex coriacea*
	Ilex lucida

Sweet gum	*Liquidambar styraciflua*
Sweet haw	*Viburnum prunifolium*
Sweetleaf	*Symplocos tinctoria*
Sweet lemon	*Citrus lumia*
Sweet lime	*Citrus limetta*
Sweet locust	*Gleditsia triacanthos*
Sweet olive	*Osmanthus fragrans*
Sweet orange	*Citrus sinensis*
Sweet pea bush	*Podalyrica calptrata*
Sweet pepperbush	*Clethra alnifolia*
Sweet-potato tree	*Manihot esculenta*
Sweet-scented crab apple	*Malus coronaria*
Sweet-scented sumac	*Rhus aromatica*
Sweetsop	*Annona squamosa*
Sweetspire	*Itea virginica*
Sweet sumac	*Rhus aromatica*
Sweet thorn	*Acacia karroo*
Sweet verbena tree	*Backhousia citriodora*
Sweet viburnum	*Viburnum odoratissimum*
	Viburnum prunifolium
Swiss stone pine	*Pinus cembra*
Swiss mountain pine	*Pinus mugo*
Swiss willow	*Salix helvetica*
Swollen-thorn acacia	*Acacia cornigera*
Sword bean	*Entada gigas*
Sugarbush	*Rhus ovata*
Sugar sumac	*Rhus ovata*
Sulphur rose	*Rosa hemisphaerica*
	Rosa sulphurea
Sycamore	*Acer pseudoplatanus*
Sycamore fig	*Ficus sycomorus*
Sydney blue gum	*Eucalyptus saligna*
Sydney golden wattle	*Acacia longifolia*
Sydney peppermint	*Eucalyptus piperita*
Syrian ash	*Fraxinus syriaca*
Syrian bead tree	*Melia azedarach*
Syrian juniper	*Juniperus drupacea*
Syringa	*Philadelphus coronarius*
Szechuan birch	*Betula platyphylla*
Szechwan fir	*Abies sutchuenensis*
Table dogwood	*Cornus controversa*
Table mountain pine	*Pinus pungens*
Tabletop elm	*Ulmus glabra pendula*
Tacamahak	*Populus balsamifera*
Tachibana orange	*Citrus tachibana*
Tag alder	*Alnus serrulata*

Tagasaste	Cytisus palmensis
Tagua	Phytelephas macrocarpa
Taiwan cherry	
	Prunus campanulata
Taiwan fir	Cunninghamia konishii
Taiwan spruce	Picea morrisonicola
Tala palm	Borassus flabellifer
Talipot palm	
	Corypha umbraculifera
Tall conebush	
	Isopogon anemonifolius
Tallow shrub	Myrica cerifera
Tallow tree	Detarium senegalense
	Sapium salicifolium
Tallow-wood	
	Eucalyptus microcorys
	Ximenia americana
Tall tutsan	Hypericum × inodorum
Tamarack	Larix laricina
Tamarind	Tamarindus indica
Tamarindo	Tamarindus indica
Tamarind-of-the-Indies	
	Vangueria edulis
Tamarisk	Tamarix anglica
Tanbark oak	
	Lithocarpus densiflorus
Tanekaha tree	
	Phyllocladus trichomanoides
Tangelo	Citrus × tangelo
Tangerine	Citrus reticulata
Tanglefoot	Viburnum alnifolium
Tanglefoot beech	
	Nothofagus gunnii
Tangor	Citrus × nobilis
Tanner's cassia	Cassia auriculata
Tanner's sumac	Rhus coriaria
Tanner's tree	Coriaria nepalensis
Tanoak	Lithocarpus densiflorus
Tansy-leaved thorn	
	Crataegus tanacetifolia
Tapa-cloth tree	
	Broussonetia papyrifera
Tapioca	Manihot esculenta
Tara	Caesalpinia spinosa
Tarajo	Ilex latifolia
Tarata	Pittosporum eugenioides
Tarentum myrtle	
	Myrtus communis tarentina
Tartar dogwood	Cornus alba
Tartar maple	Acer tataricum
Tartoga	Jatropha podagrica
Tasmanian beech	
	Nothofagus cunninghamii
Tasmanian blue gum	
	Eucalyptus globulus
Tasmanian brown gum	
	Eucalyptus johnstonii
Tasmanian cypress pine	
	Callitris oblonga

Tasmanian daisy bush	
	Olearia phlogopappa
Tasmanian laurel	
	Anopterus glandulosus
Tasmanian snow gum	
	Eucalyptus coccifera
Tasmanian waratah	
	Telopea truncata
Tasmanian waterbush	
	Myoporum tetrandrum
Tasmanian waxberry	
	Gaultheria hispida
Tassel cherry	Prunus litigiosa
Tassel-white	Itea virginica
Tatarian maple	Acer tataricum
Tawhiwhi	
	Pittosporum tenuifolium
Tea-berry	Gaultheria procumbens
	Viburnum cassinoides
Tea olive	Osmanthus fragrans
Tea plant	Viburnum lentago
Tea tree	
	Leptospermum scoparium
	Melaleuca quinquenervia
Tea viburnum	Viburnum setigerum
Tecate cypress	Cupressus forbesii
	Cupressus guadalupensis
Teak	Tectona grandis
Tea-leaf willow	Salix phylicifolia
Tea-oil plant	Camellia oleifera
Tea plant	Camellia sinensis
	Camellia thea
Tea rose	Rosa × odorata
Temple juniper	Juniperus rigida
Temple orange	
	Citrus × nobilis temple
Temple tree	Plumeria rubra
Tenasserim pine	Pinus kerkusii
	Pinus merkusii
Terebinth	Pistacia terebinthus
Tetterbush	Lyonia lucida
Texan buckeye	Ungnadia speciosa
Texan walnut	Juglans microcarpa
	Juglans rupestris
Texas ash	Fraxinus texensis
Texas ebony	
	Pithecellobium flexicaule
Texas mimosa	Acacia greggii
Texas mountain laurel	
	Sophora secundiflora
Texas palmetto	Sabal mexicana
Texas red oak	Quercus texana
Thatch-leaf palm	
	Howea forsterana
	Kentia forsterana
Thatch palm	Coccothrinax crinata
Thatch screw pine	
	Pandanus tectorius
Thick-leaved sallow	Salix crassifolia
Thirty thorn	Acacia seyal

Thorny elaeagnus
Elaeagnus pungens

Thread palm
Washingtonia robusta

Thurlow weeping willow
Salix elegantissima

Tibetan cherry *Prunus mugus*
Prunus serrula

Tibetan hazel *Corylus tibetica*

Ti-es *Pouteria campechiana*

Tiger-tail spruce *Picea polita*
Picea torana

Timor white gum
Eucalyptus alba
Eucalyptus platyphylla

Tinnevelly senna
Cassia angustifolia

Tingiringi gum
Eucalyptus glaucescens

Tipu tree *Tipuana tipu*

Tisswood *Persea borbonia*

Titi *Cliftonia monophylla*
Cyrilla racemiflora
Oxydendrum arboreum

Titoki *Alectryon excelsum*

Toatoa tree *Phyllocladus glaucus*

Tobacco sumac *Rhus virens*

Tobago cane *Bactris guineensis*

Tobira *Pittosporum tobira*

Toddy palm *Borassus flabellifer*
Caryota urens

Tollon *Heteromeles arbutifolia*

Tolu balsam *Myroxylon pereirae*

Tolu tree *Myroxylon balsamum*

Tonka bean *Dipteryx odorata*

Toog *Bischofia javanica*

Toon *Toona sinensis*

Toothache tree
Xanthoxylum americanum
Zanthoxylum americanum

Toothbrush tree *Salvadora persica*

Topal holly *Ilex × attenuata*

Toringo crab apple *Malus sieboldii*

Tornillo *Prosopis pubescens*

Torote *Bursera microphylla*

Torrey pine *Pinus torreyana*

Tortuguero *Polygala cowellii*

Tossa jute *Corchorus olitorius*

Totara *Podocarpus totara*

Towai tree *Weinmannia racemosa*

Toyon *Heteromeles arbitifolia*

Trailing rose *Rosa arvensis*

Trailing sallow *Salix aurita*

Tramp's spurge
Euphorbia corollata

Transcaucasian birch
Betula medwediewii

Transvaal hard pear
Olinia emarginata

Transvaal teak
Pterocarpus angolensis

Trautvetter's maple
Acer trautvetteri

Traveller's palm
Ravenala madagascariensis

Traveller's tree
Ravenala madagascariensis

Tree anemone
Carpenteria californica

Tree dracaena *Dracaena arborea*

Tree flax *Linum arboreum*

Tree fuchsia *Fuchsia arborescens*
Schotia brachypetala

Tree hazel *Corylus colurna*

Tree heath *Erica arborea*

Tree hibiscus *Hibiscus elatus*

Tree hollyhock *Althaea frutex*
Hibiscus syriacus

Tree lupin *Lupinus arboreus*

Tree mallow *Lavatera arborea*
Lavatera olbia

Tree of heaven *Ailanthus altissima*

Tree of gold *Tabebuia argentea*

Tree of kings *Cordyline fruticosa*
Cordyline terminalis
Dracaena terminalis

Tree of life *Guaiacum officinale*
Mauritia flexuosa
Mauritia setigera

Tree of sadness
Nyctanthes arbor-tristis

Tree of the sun
Chamaecyparis obtusa

Tree paeony *Paeonia delavayi*
Paeonia suffruticosa

Tree poppy *Dendromecon rigidum*

Tree purslane *Atriplex halimus*

Tree rhododendron
Rhododendron arboreum

Tree tomato
Cyphomandra betacea

Tree wisteria
Bolusanthus speciosus

Trembling aspen *Populus tremula*
Populus tremuloides

Trident maple *Acer buergeranum*

Trifoliate orange *Poncirus trifoliata*

Trinidad palm *Sabal mauritiiformis*

Trip-toe *Viburnum alnifolium*

Tropical almond
Terminalia catappa

Tropical snowflake
Trevesia palmata

Tropic laurel *Ficus benjamina*

True laurel *Laurus nobilis*

True service tree *Sorbus domestica*

Truffle oak *Quercus robur*

Trumpet tree *Cecropia peltata*

Tuart gum
Eucalyptus gomphocephalus

TREES, BUSHES, AND SHRUBS

Tuba root	Derris elliptica
Tubeflower	
	Clerodendrum indicum
Tucuma	Astrocaryum aculeatum
Tufted fishtail palm	Caryota mitis
Tufted willow	Salix nivalis
Tulipan	Spathodea campanulata
Tulip poplar	
	Liriodendron tulipifera
Tulip tree	Liriodendron tulipifera
	Spathodea campanulata
Tumbledown gum	
	Eucalyptus dealbata
Tung	Aleurites montana
Tung-oil tree	Aleurites fordii
Tung tree	Aleurites fordii
Tupelo	Nyssa sylvatica
Tupelo gum	Nyssa aquatica
Turkestan rose	Rosa rugosa
Turkey oak	Quercus cerris
	Quercus incana
	Quercus laevis
Turkish filbert	Corylus colurna
Turkish fir	Abies bornmuellerana
Turkish hazel	Corylus colurna
Turk's cap	Malaviscus arboreus
Turk's turban	
	Clerodendrum indicum
Turner's oak	Quercus × turneri
Turpentine pine	Callitris verrucosa
Turpentine tree	Coprifera mopane
	Pistacia terebinthus
	Siliphium terebinthaceum
	Syncarpia glomulifera
Turpeth	Ipomoea turpethum
Tutsan	Hypericum androsaemum
Twin flower	Linnaea borealis
Twin-flowered daphne	
	Daphne pontica
Twisted heath	Erica cinerea
Twisted-leaf pine	Pinus teocote
Twisted wattle	Acacia tortuosa
Twisted willow	
	Salix babylonica pekinensis
	tortuosa
Twistwood	Viburnum lantana
Two-leaved nut pine	
	Pinus cembroides edulis
	Pinus edulis
Two-styled hawthorn	
	Crataegus laevigata
Two-winged gimlet	
	Eucalyptus diptera
Ubame oak	Quercus phillyraeoides
Udo	Aralia cordata
Ugli fruit	
	Citrus paradisi × citrus reticulata
Ulmo	Eucryphia cordifolia

Umbrella pine	
	Hedyscepe canterburyana
	Pinus pinea
	Sciadopitys verticillata
Umbrella thorn	Acacia tortilis
Umbrella tree	Magnolia tripetala
	Musanga cecropioides
	Schefflera arboricola
Umkokolo	Aberia caffra
	Dovyalis caffra
Uni	Ugni molinae
Upas tree	Antiaris toxicaria
Upland cypress	
	Taxodium ascendens
Upland sumach	Rhus glabra
Upland tupelo	Nyssa sylvatica
Upside-down tree	
	Adansonia digitata
Urn gum	Eucalyptus urnigera
Utah ash	Fraxinus anomala
Utah juniper	
	Juniperus osteosperma
Valley oak	Quercus lobata
Valonia oak	Quercus ithaburensis
	Quercus macrolepis
Van Moltke's lime	Tilia × moltkei
Van Volxem's maple	
	Acer velutinum vanvolxemii
Variegated croton	
	Codiaeum variegatum
Variegated Japanese dogwood	
	Cornus controversa variegata
Variegated sweet chestnut	
	Castanea sativa albomarginata
	Castanea sativa aureomarginata
Varnish-leaved gum	
	Eucalyptus vernicosa
	Fraxinus xanthoxyloides
Varnish tree	Ailanthus altissima
	Aleurites moluccana
	Koelreuteria paniculata
	Rhus verniciflua
	Semecarpus anacardium
Varnish wattle	Acacia verniciflua
Vegetable mercury	
	Brunfelsia uniflora
Vegetable tallow tree	
	Sapium sebiferum
Veitch's magnolia	
	Magnolia × veitchii
Veitch's screw pine	
	Pandanus veitchii
Veitch's silver fir	Abies veitchii
Velvet ash	Fraxinus velutina
Velvet leaf	Vaccinium canadense
Velvet sumac	Rhus typhina
Velvet tamarind	Dialium guineense
Venetian sumac	Cotinus coggygria
	Rhus cotinus
Venezuelan mahogany	
	Swietenia candollea

Victoria rosemary
Westringia rosmariniformis

Victorian box
Pittosporum undulatum

Vilmorin's rowan   *Sorbus vilmorinii*

Vilmori's sorbus   *Sorbus vilmorinii*

Vine cactus   *Fouquieria splendens*

Vinegar tree   *Rhus glabra*

Vineleaf maple   *Acer cissifolium*

Vine maple   *Acer circinatum*

Violet tree   *Polygala cowellii*

Violet willow   *Salix daphnoides*

Violetwood   *Acacia homalophylla*

Virgilia   *Cladrastis lutea*

Virginia dogwood   *Cornus florida*

Virginian bird cherry
Prunus virginiana

Virginian snowflower
Chionanthus virginicus

Virginian sumac   *Rhus typhina*

Virginia sweetspire   *Itea virginica*

Virginia willow   *Itea virginica*

Virgin's palm   *Dioon edule*

Voss's laburnum   *Laburnum vossii*
Laburnum × watereri

Wadadura   *Leycythis grandiflora*

Wadalee gum tree   *Acacia catechu*

Wahoo elm
Euonymus atropurpurea
Ulmus alata

Walking-stick ebony
Diospyros monbuttensis

Walking-stick palm
Linospadix monostachya

Wallaba   *Eperua falcata*

Wallangarra   *Acacia accola*

Wall germander
Teucrium chamaedrys

Wallowa   *Acacia calamifolia*

Wallwort   *Sambucus ebulus*

Wampee   *Clausena lansium*

Wampi   *Clausena lansium*

Warminster broom
Cytisus × praecox

Warted yate
Eucalyptus megacornata

Wartleaf ceanothus
Ceanothus papillosus

Warty birch   *Betula pendula*

Washington palm
Washingtonia filifera

Washington thorn
Crataegus phaenopyrum

Water ash   *Acer negundo*
Fraxinus caroliniana
Ptelea trifoliata

Water beech   *Carpinus caroliniana*

Water birch   *Betula occidentalis*

Water blossom pea
Podalyria calyptrata

Waterbush
Myoporum tenuifolium

Water chestnut   *Pachira aquatica*

Water elder   *Viburnum opulus*

Water elm   *Planera aquatica*
Planera ulmifolia
Ulmus americana

Water-filter nut
Strychnos potatorum

Water fir
Metasequoia glyptostroboides

Water hickory   *Carya aquatica*

Water holly   *Mahonia nervosa*

Waterlily protea   *Protea aurea*

Water locust   *Gleditsia aquatica*

Water oak   *Quercus nigra*

Water rose-apple tree
Syzygium aqueum

Water sallow   *Salix aquatica*

Water tupelo   *Nyssa aquatica*

Waterwell tree
Warszewiczia coccinea

Wattle-leaved peppermint
Eucalyptus acacae formis

Waukegan juniper
Juniperus horizontalis douglasii

Wavyleaf ceanothus
Ceanothus foliosus

Wavy Saint John's wort
Hypericum undulatum

Wax-leaf privet
Ligustrum lucidum

Wax mallow   *Malvaviscus arboreus*

Wax apple
Syzygium samarangense

Waxberry   *Gaultheria hispida*
Myrica cerifera

Wax-leaf privet
Ligustrum japonicum

Wax myrtle   *Myrica carolinensis*
Myrica cerifera

Wax palm   *Ceroxylon alpinum*

Wax tree   *Rhus succedanea*

Wayfaring tree
Viburnum alnifolium
Viburnum lantana

Weaver's broom
Spartium junceum

Weddel palm
Microcoelum weddelianum

Wedding-cake tree
Cornus controversa

Weeping alder
Alnus incana pendula

Weeping ash
Fraxinus excelsior pendula

Weeping aspen
Populus tremula pendula

Weeping atlas cedar
Cedrus atlantica glauca

TREES, BUSHES, AND SHRUBS

Western tea myrtle

Weeping beech
    Fagus sylvatica pendula
Weeping birch
    Betula pendula tristis
    Betula pendula youngii
Weeping boree   *Acacia vestita*
Weeping bottlebrush
    Callistemon viminalis
Weeping cherry   *Prunus ivensii*
    Prunus subhirtella pendula
Weeping cotoneaster
    Cotoneaster hybridus pendulus
    Cotoneaster × watereri
Weeping cypress
    Cupressus funebris
Weeping elm
    Ulmus glabra camperdown
    Ulmus glabra pendula
Weeping european larch
    Larix decidua pendula
Weeping fig   *Ficus benjamina*
Weeping forsythia
    Forsythia sieboldii
    Forsythia suspensa
Weeping golden box
    Buxus aurea pendula
Weeping hawthorn
    Crataegus monogyna pendula
Weeping holly
    Ilex aquifolium pendula
Weeping larch   *Larix × pendula*
Weeping laurel   *Ficus benjamina*
Weeping mountain ash
    Sorbus aucuparia pendula
Weeping mulberry
    Morus alba pendula
Weeping myall   *Acacia pendula*
Weeping oak
    Quercus robur pendula
Weeping pear
    Pyrus salicifolia pendula
Weeping pea tree
    Caragana arborescens pendula
Weeping peking willow
    Salix matsudana pendula
Weeping podocarpus
    Podocarpus elongatus
Weeping purple osier
    Salix purpurea pendula
Weeping purple willow
    Salix purpurea pendula
Weeping rosebud cherry
    Prunus subhirtella pendula
Weeping sally
    Eucalyptus mitchelliana
    Salix caprea pendula
Weeping Scotch laburnum
    Laburnum alpinum pendulum
Weeping silver lime
    Tilia petiolaris
Weeping spring cherry
    Prunus subhirtella pendula
    rosea

Weeping spruce   *Picea brewerana*
Weeping swamp cypress
    Taxodium distichum pendens
Weeping Swedish birch
    Betula pendula dalecarlica
Weeping tea tree
    Melaleuca leucadendron
Weeping wattle   *Acacia saligna*
Weeping willow   *Salix babylonica*
    Salix babylonica pekinensis
    pendula
    Salix caprea pendula
    Salix × chrysocoma
    Salix sepulcralis chrysocoma
Weeping willow-leaved pear
    Pyrus salicifolia pendula
Weeping wych elm
    Ulmus glabra horizontalis
Weigela   *Weigela florida*
Wellingtonia
    Sequoiadendron giganteum
West African barwood
    Pterocarpus angolensis
West African ebony
    Diospyros mespiliformis
West African kino
    Pterocarpus erinaceus
West African rubber tree
    Ficus vogelii
West Asian plane
    Platanus orientalis
West Australian mahogany
    Eucalyptus marginata
Western arbor-vitae   *Thuya plicata*
Western balsam poplar
    Populus trichocarpa
Western burning bush
    Euonymus occidentalis
Western catalpa   *Catalpa speciosa*
Western choke cherry
    Prunus virginiana demissa
Western gorse   *Ulex gallii*
Western hemlock
    Tsuga heterophylla
Western Himalayan cedar
    Cedrus deodara
Western juniper
    Juniperus occidentalis
Western larch   *Larix occidentalis*
Western laurel
    Kalmia microphylla
Western lombardy poplar
    Populus nigra plantierensis
Western oak   *Quercus garryana*
Western plane
    Platanus occidentalis
Western redbud   *Cercis occidentalis*
Western red cedar   *Thuya plicata*
Western sand cherry
    Prunus besseyi
Western tea myrtle
    Melaleuca nesophylla

Western white pine

Western white pine	
	Pinus monticola
Western yellow pine	
	Pinus ponderosa
Western yew	*Taxus brevifolia*
Westfelton yew	
	Taxus baccata dovastoniana
West Himalayan fir	*Abies pindrow*
West Himalayan spruce	
	Picea smithiana
West Indian birch	
	Bursera simaruba
West Indian blackthorn	
	Acacia farnesiana
West Indian boxwood	
	Gossypiospermum praecox
West Indian cedar	
	Cedrela odorata
	Toona odorata
West Indian cherry	*Cordia nitida*
West Indian dogwood	
	Piscidia piscipula
West Indian holly	*Leea coccinea*
West Indian jasmine	
	Plumeria rubra
West Indian laurel fig	
	Ficus perforata
West Indian lime	
	Citrus aurantifolia
West Indian mahogany	
	Swietenia mahagoni
West Indian silkwood	
	Zanthoxylum flavum
West Indies walnut	
	Juglans jamaicensis
Westland pine	
	Dacrydium colensoi
Westonbirt dogwood	
	Cornus alba sibirica
Weymouth pine	*Pinus strobus*
Wheatley elm	
Ulmus carpinifolia sarniensis	
Ulmus minor stricta sarniensis	
	Ulmus × sarniensis
Wheel of fire	*Stenocarpus sinuatus*
Wheel tree	
	Trochodendron aralioides
Whin	*Ulex europaeus*
Whinberry	*Vaccinium myrtillus*
Whistlewood	
	Acer pennsylvanicum
Whistling tree	*Acacia seyal*
White alder	*Alnus incana*
	Alnus rhombifolia
	Clethra acuminata
White ash	*Eucalyptus fraxinoides*
	Fraxinus alba
	Fraxinus americana
White-barked birch	
	Betula jacquemontii
White-barked himalayan birch	
	Betula jacquemontii

White bark pine	*Pinus albicaulis*
White basswood	
	Tilia heterophylla
Whitebeam	*Sorbus aria*
White birch	*Betula papyrifera*
	Betula pendula
	Betula populifolia
	Betula pubescens
White box	*Eucalyptus albens*
White broom	*Genista raetam*
White butternut	*Juglans cinerea*
White cedar	
	Chamaecyparis thyoides
	Melia dubium
	Tabebuia pallida
	Thuya occidentalis
White cinnamon	*Canella alba*
	Canella winterana
White cypress	
	Chamaecyparis thyoides
White cypress pine	
	Callitris columellaris
	Callitris glauca
White dogwood	*Cornus florida*
White dragon tree	
	Sesbania formosa
White elm	*Ulmus americana*
White fir	*Abies amabilis*
	Abies concolor
White gum	*Eucalyptus rossii*
White-heart hickory	
	Carya tomentosa
White heather	
	Calluna vulgaris alba
White ironbark	
	Eucalyptus leucoxylon
White jasmine	
	Jasminum officinale
White jute	*Corchorus capsularis*
White-leaf manzanita	
	Arctostaphylos viscida
White-leaved marlock	
	Eucalyptus tetragona
White mahogany	
	Eucalyptus acmenioides
	Eucalyptus umbra
White maple	*Acer saccharinum*
White mountain dogwood	
	Viburnum alnifolium
White mulberry	*Morus alba*
White oak	*Quercus alba*
White peppermint	
	Eucalyptus pulchella
White pine	*Pinus strobus*
	Podocarpus elatus
	Podocarpus dacrydioides
White popinac	*Leucaena glauca*
White poplar	*Populus alba*
White Portuguese broom	
	Cytisus albus
	Cytisus multiflorus albus
White rose of York	*Rosa × alba*

Willow acacia

White sally *Eucalyptus pauciflora*
White sandalwood
Santalum album
White sapote *Casimiroa edulis*
White silk-cotton tree
Ceiba pentandra
White Spanish broom
Cytisus multiflorus
White spruce *Picea glauca*
White stinkwood *Celtis africanus*
White stopper *Eugenia axillaris*
White stringybark
Eucalyptus globoidea
White swamp azalea
Rhododendron viscosum
White tea tree
Melaleuca leucadendron
Whitethorn *Crataegus laevigata*
Crataegus monogyna
White titi *Cyrilla racemiflora*
White-top peppermint
Eucalyptus radiata
White walnut *Juglans cinerea*
White wax tree
Ligustrum lucidum
White wicky *Kalmia cuneata*
White willow *Salix alba*
White winter heather
Erica hyemalis
Whitewood
Liriodendron tulipifera
Tabebuia riparia
Tilia americana
Whiteywood
Melicytus ramiflorus
Whortleberry
Vaccinium corymbosum
Vaccinium myrtillus
Whortle-leaved willow
Salix myrsinites
Whortle willow *Salix myrsinites*
Wickson plum *Prunus × sultana*
Wicky *Kalmia angustifolia*
Wicopy *Dirca palustris*
Wig tree *Cotinus coggygria*
Wild almond *Prunus fasciculata*
Wild cherry *Prunus avium*
Prunus ilicifolia
Wild chestnut *Pachira insignis*
Wild China soapberry
Sapindus marginatus
Wild China tea
Sapindus drummondii
Wild cinnamon *Canella winterana*
Wild cocoa tree *Pachira aquatica*
Wild coffee *Polyscias guilfoylei*
Psychotria nervosa
Psychotria sulzneri
Wild cotton *Hibiscus diversifolius*
Hibiscus moscheutos

Wild crab apple
Malus angustifolia
Malus sylvestris
Wild custard-apple
Annona senegalensis
Wild date *Yucca baccata*
Wild date palm *Phoenix rupicola*
Phoenix sylvestris
Wild-goose plum
Prunus munsoniana
Wild hippo *Euphorbia corollata*
Wild holly *Ilex aquifolium*
Wild ipecac
Euphorbia ipecacuanhae
Wild irishman *Discaria toumatou*
Wild lilac *Ceanothus sanguineus*
Wild lime *Xanthoxylum fagara*
Zanthoxylum fagara
Wild olive *Elaeagnus angustifolia*
Elaeagnus latifolia
Halesia carolina
Nyssa aquatica
Olea africana
Osmanthus americanus
Wild orange *Prunus caroliniana*
Wild peach *Kigelia africana*
Prunus fasciculata
Wild pear *Pyrus communis*
Pyrus pyraster
Wild pepper tree
Vitex agnus-castus
Wild plum *Prunus domestica*
Wild poinsettia
Warszewiczia coccinea
Wild pomegranate
Burchelia bubalina
Wild pride of India
Galpinia transvaalica
Wild raisin *Viburnum cassinoides*
Viburnum lentago
Wild red cherry
Prunus pennsylvanica
Wild robusta coffee
Coffea canephora
Wild rose-apple
Syzygium pyenanthum
Wild rosemary *Croton cascarilla*
Ledum palustre
Wild sarsaparilla *Aralia nudicaulis*
Wild senna *Cassia hebecarpa*
Cassia marilandica
Wild sensitive plant
Cassia nictitans
Wild service tree *Sorbus torminalis*
Wild snowball
Ceanothus americanus
Wild soursop *Annona montana*
Wild sweet crab apple
Malus coronaria
Willimore cedar
Widdringtonia schwarzii
Willow acacia *Acacia salicina*

Willow cherry	*Prunus incana*
Willow-leaf bay	
	Laurus nobilis angustifolia
Willow-leaf magnolia	
	Magnolia salicifolia
Willow-leaved bottlebrush	
	Callistemon salignus
Willow-leaved jessamine	
	Cestrum parqui
Willow-leaved pear	
	Pyrus salicifolia
Willow-leaved poplar	
	Populus angustifolia
Willowmore cedar	
	Widdringtonia schwarzii
Willow myrtle	*Agonis flexuosa*
Willow oak	*Quercus phellos*
Willow pittosporum	
	Pittosporum phillyraeoides
Willow podocarp	
	Podocarpus chilinus
	Podocarpus salignus
Wilson's barberry	
	Berberis wilsoniae
Wilson's beauty bush	
	Kolkwitzia amabilis
Wilson's berberis	
	Berberis wilsoniae
Wilson's douglas fir	
	Pseudotsuga wilsoniana
Wilson's yellowwood	
	Cladrastis wilsonii
Wilwilli	*Erythrina monosperma*
	Erythrina tahitiensis
Windmill jasmine	
	Jasminum nitidum
Windmill palm	
	Trachycarpus fortunei
Wineberry	*Rubus phoenicolasius*
Wine palm	*Borassus flabellifer*
	Caryota urens
	Jubaea chilensis
	Jubaea spectabilis
Winged elm	*Ulmus alata*
Winged spindle tree	
	Euonymus alata
Winged wattle	*Acacia alata*
Wing-rib sumac	*Rhus copellina*
Wingseed	*Ptelea trifoliata*
Winterberry	*Ilex glabra*
	Ilex verticillata
Winter cherry	
	Prunus subhirtella autumnalis
Winter daphne	*Daphne odora*
Winter-flowering cherry	
	Prunus subhirtella autumnalis
Winter-flowering jasmine	
	Jasminum nudiflorum
Wintergreen	
	Gaultheria procumbens
Winter heath	*Erica carnea*
Winter savory	*Satureia montana*
Winter's bark	*Drimys winteri*
Wintersweet	
	Acokanthera oblongifolia
	Chimonanthus praecox
Winter thorn	*Acacia albida*
Wirilda	*Acacia retinoides*
Wiry honey myrtle	
	Melaleuca nematophylla
Wisconsin weeping willow	
	Salix × blanda
Wisteria tree	*Sesbania tripetii*
Witch alder	
	Fothergilla monticola
Witch hazel	*Corylus hamamelis*
Witch hobble	
	Viburnum alnifolium
	Viburnum lantanoides
Withe-rod	*Viburnum cassinoides*
Wi tree	*Spondias cytherea*
Wire-netting bush	
	Corokia cotoneaster
Woadwaxen	*Genista tinctoria*
Wolfberry	
	Symphoricarpus occidentalis
Wolley-dod's rose	
	Rosa villosa duplex
Wonderboom	*Ficus pretoriae*
Wonder tree	*Ricinus communis*
Wood apple	*Feronia elephantum*
	Feronia limonia
Wood rose	*Rosa gymnocarpa*
Woodward's blackbutt	
	Eucalyptus woodwardii
Woodwaxen	*Genista tinctoria*
Woolly butia palm	
	Butia eriospatha
Woollybutt	*Eucalyptus longifolia*
Woolly lavender	*Lavandula lanata*
Woolly-leaf ceanothus	
	Ceanothus tomentosus
Woolly netbush	
	Calothamnus villosus
Woolly-podded broom	
	Cytisus grandiflorus
Woolly tea tree	
	Leptospermum lanigerum
Woolly willow	*Salix lanata*
Woman's tongue tree	
	Albizzia lebbeck
Wormwood senna	
	Cassia artemisioides
Wyalong wattle	
	Acacia cardiophylla
Wych elm	*Ulmus glabra*
Yankee point ceanothus	
	Ceanothus griseus horizontalis
Yarran	*Acacia homalophylla*
Yatay palm	*Butia yatay*
Yate tree	*Eucalyptus cornuta*

Yaupon *Ilex cassine*
Ilex vomitoria

Yeddo hawthorn
Raphiolepis japonica
Raphiolepis umbellata

Yeddo spruce *Picea jezoensis*

Yellow azalea
Rhododendron luteum

Yellow banksian rose
Rosa banksiae lutea

Yellow bark *Cinchona calisaya*

Yellow-bark ash
Fraxinus excelsior jaspidea

Yellow-bark oak *Quercus velutina*

Yellow-bark thorn *Acacia woodii*

Yellow bell *Allamanda cathartica*

Yellowbells *Tecoma stans*

Yellow-berried holly
Ilex aquifolium fructuluteo

Yellow-berried mountain ash
Sorbus aucuparia xanthocarpa

Yellow-berried yew
Taxus baccata fructo-luteo

Yellow bignonia *Tecoma stans*

Yellow birch *Betula alleghaniensis*
Betula lutea

Yellow bloodwood
Eucalyptus eximia

Yellow box *Eucalyptus melliodora*

Yellow buckeye *Aesculus flava*
Aesculus octandra

Yellow butterfly palm
Chrysalidocarpus lutescens

Yellow catalpa *Catalpa ovata*

Yellow cedar *Thuya occidentalis*

Yellow chestnut oak
Quercus muehlenbergii

Yellow-cotton tree
Cochlospermum religiosum

Yellow cucumber tree
Magnolia cordata

Yellow cypress
Chamaecyparis nootkatensis

Yellow elder *Tecoma stans*

Yellow flame tree
Peltophorum pterocarpum

Yellow-flowered gum
Eucalyptus woodwardii

Yellow-fruited holly
Ilex aquifolium bacciflava

Yellow-fruited thorn
Crataegus flava

Yellow guava *Psidium guajava*

Yellow gum *Eucalyptus johnstonii*

Yellow haw *Crataegus flava*

Yellow jasmine *Jasminum mesnyi*

Yellow latan *Latania verschaffeltii*

Yellow locust tree
Robinia pseudoacacia

Yellow mombin *Spondias lutea*
Spondias mombin

Yellow oak
Quercus muehlenbergii

Yellow oleander
Thevetia peruviana

Yellow palm
Chrysalidocarpus lutescens

Yellow pine *Pinus echinata*

Yellow poplar
Liriodendron tulipifera

Yellow poui *Tabebuia serratifolia*

Yellow princess palm
Dictyosperma aureum

Yellow root
Xanthorrhiza simplicissima

Yellow silver pine
Dacrydium intermedium

Yellow-stemmed dogwood
Cornus stolonifera flaviramea

Yellow stringybark
Eucalyptus muellerana

Yellow-topped mallee ash
Eucalyptus luehmanniana

Yellow tree-lupin
Lupinus arboreus

Yellow trumpet tree *Tecoma stans*

Yellowwood *Cladrastis lutea*
Rhodosphaera rhodanthema
Zanthoxylum americanum

Yerba-de-maté
Ilex paraguariensis

Yerba mansa
Anemopsis californica

Yertchuk
Eucalyptus consideniana

Yesterday and today
Brunfelsia australis

Yew-leaved torreya
Torreya taxifolia

Yezo spruce *Picea jezoensis*

York and Lancaster rose
Rosa damascena versicolor

Yoruba ebony
Diospyros monbuttensis

Yoshino cherry *Prunus yedoensis*

Young's golden juniper
Juniperus chinensis aurea

Young's weeping birch
Betula pendula youngii

Yuca *Manihot esculenta*

Yucca *Yucca gloriosa*

Yulan *Magnolia denudata*
Magnolia heptapeta
Magnolia yulan

Yunnan lilac *Syringa yunnanensis*

Yunnan mahonia
Mahonia lomariifolia

Zamang tree *Samanea saman*

Zambak *Jasminum sambac*

Zanona palm *Socratea exorhiza*

Zanzibar coffee
Coffea zanguebariae

Zapote blanco

Zapote blanco	*Casimiroa edulis*	Zoeschen maple	
Zebra wood	*Connarus guianensis*		*Acer × zoeschense*
	Diospyros kurzii	Zombi palm	*Zombia antillarum*
Zitherwood		Zulu fig tree	*Ficus nekbudu*
	Citharexylum spinosum		*Ficus utilis*

WILD FLOWERS

It is not possible in a volume such as this to include every species of wild flower; even one limited to European or North American floras would run to a substantial number of books, therefore preference has been given to the more common and widely distributed plants.

It is now illegal to dig up wild plants in many parts of the world, and the gathering of wild flowers by collectors and amateur 'flower lovers' coupled with the widespread use of modern herbicides has resulted in the near-extinction of many species. Wild flowers should be left undisturbed to be enjoyed by all.

Common poppy –
Papaver rhoeas

Acrid lettuce

Acrid lettuce	*Lactuca virosa*
Agrimony	*Agrimonia eupatoria*
Alexanders	*Smyrnium olustratum*
Allseed	*Radiola linoides*
Alpine blue sowthistle	
	Cicerbita alpina
Alpine cinquefoil	
	Potentilla crantzii
Alpine clematis	*Clematis alpina*
Alpine enchanter's nightshade	
	Circaea alpina
Alpine fleabane	*Erigeron boreatis*
Alpine forget-me-not	
	Myosotis alpestris
Alpine lady's mantle	
	Alchemilla alpina
Alpine lettuce	*Cicerbita alpina*
Alpine meadow rue	
	Thalictrum alpinum
Alpine nightshade	*Circaea alpina*
Alpine penny cress	*Thlaspi alpestre*
Alpine rivulet saxifrage	
	Saxifraga rivularis
Alpine sawwort	*Saussurea alpina*
Alpine speedwell	*Veronica alpina*
Alpine willow herb	
	Epilobium anagallidifolium
Alpine woundwort	*Stachys alpina*
Alsike clover	*Trifolium hybridum*
Alternate-flowered water milfoil	
	Myriophyllum alterniflorum
Alternate-leaved golden saxifrage	
	Chrysosplenium alternifolium
American pondweed	
	Potamogeton epihydrus
American speedwell	
	Veronica peregrina
Amphibious bistort	
	Polygonum amphibium
Angular solomon's seal	
	Polygonatum odoratum
Annual knawel	
	Scleranthus annuus
Annual mercury	
	Mercurialis annua
Annual sea-blite	*Suaeda maritima*
Arrowhead	*Sagittaria sagittifolia*
Arrowhead orache	
	Atriplex prostrata
Asarabacca	*Asarum europaeum*
Asarina	*Asarina procumbens*
Astrantia	*Astrantia major*
Autumn felwort	
	Gentiana amarella
	Gentianella amarella
Autumn gentian	
	Gentiana amarella
	Gentianella amarella

Autumn hawkbit	
	Leontodon autumnalis
Autumn lady's tresses	
	Spiranthes autumnalis
	Spiranthes spiralis
Autumn squill	*Scilla autumnalis*
Awlwort	*Subularia aquatica*
Bachelor's buttons	
	Chrysanthemum parthenium
	Tanacetum parthenium
Balm-leaved figwort	
	Scrophularia scorodonia
Baneberry	*Actaea spicata*
Barren strawberry	
	Potentilla sterilis
Basil thyme	*Acinos arvensis*
Bath asparagus	
	Ornithogalum pyrenaicum
Beach orache	*Atriplex littoralis*
Beaked hawk's beard	
	Crepis vesicaria
Beautiful Saint John's wort	
	Hypericum pulchrum
Bee orchid	*Ophrys apifera*
Beggarticks	*Bidens frondosa*
Bell heather	*Erica cinera*
Bermuda buttercup	
	Oxalis pes-caprae
Betony	*Betonica officinalis*
	Stachys betonica
Bilberry	*Vaccinium myrtillis*
Bindweed	*Calystegia sepium*
Bird's eye primrose	
	Primula farinosa
Bird's foot trefoil	
	Lotus corniculatus
Bird's nest orchid	
	Neottia nidus-avis
Birthwort	*Aristolochia clematitis*
Birdsfoot	*Ornithopus perpusillus*
Bithynian vetch	*Vicia bithynica*
Biting stonecrop	*Sedum acre*
Bittersweet	*Solanum dulcamara*
Bitter vetch	*Lathyrus montanus*
Black bindweed	
	Fallopia convolvulus
Black bitter vetch	*Lathyrus niger*
Black bryony	*Tamus communis*
Black horehound	*Ballota nigra*
Black medick	*Medicago lupulina*
Black mullein	*Verbascum nigrum*
Black mustard	*Brassica nigra*
Black nightshade	*Solanum nigrum*
Black vetch	*Lathyrus niger*
Bladder campion	*Silene vulgaris*
Blood-drop emlets	
	Mimulus luteus
Blood-red geranium	
	Geranium sanguiuneum

Chamomile

Bloody geranium
    Geranium sanguiuneum

Blotched monkey-flower
    Mimulus luteus

Blue anemone   *Anemone apennina*

Bluebell   *Endymion non-scriptus*
    Hyacinthoides non-scripta

Blue comfrey
    Symphytum peregrinum

Blue flax   *Linum perenne*

Blue fleabane   *Erigeron acer*

Blue gromwell   *Lithospermum*
    purpurocaeruleum

Blue iris   *Iris spuria*

Blue lettuce   *Lactuca perennis*

Blue lobelia   *Lobelia urens*

Blue pimpernel *Anagallis foemina*

Blue sowthistle
    Cicerbita macrophylla
    Lactuca macrophylla

Blue water speedwell
    Veronica anagallis-aquatica

Bog arum   *Calla palustris*

Bog asphodel
    Narthecium ossifragum

Bogbean   *Menyanthes trifoliata*

Bog bilberry *Vaccinium uliginosum*

Bog dandelion
    Taraxacum spectabile

Bog pimpernel   *Anagallis tenella*

Bog pondweed
    Potamogeton oblongus
    Potamogeton polygonifolius

Bog Saint John's wort
    Hypericum elodes

Bog stitchwort   *Stellaria alsine*

Bog violet   *Viola palustris*

Bog water starwort
    Callitriche stagnalis

Bog whortleberry
    Vaccinium uliginosum

Bog willow herb
    Epilobium palustre

Branched broomrape
    Orobanche ramosa

Branched plantain
    Plantago arenaria

Breckland wormwood
    Artemisia campestris

Bristly oxtongue
    Hemintia echioides
    Picris echioides

Broad-fruited cornsalad
    Valerianella rimosa

Broad-leaved dock
    Rumex obtusifolius

Broad-leaved everlasting pea
    Lathyrus latifolius

Broad-leaved eyebright
    Euphrasia occidentalis
    Euphrasia tetraquetra

Broad-leaved helleborine
    Epipactis helleborine
    Epipactis latifolia

Broad-leaved pondweed
    Potamogeton natans

Broad-leaved ragwort
    Senecio fluviatilis

Broad-leaved spurge
    Euphorbia platyphyllos

Broad-leaved willow herb
    Epilobium montanum

Brooklime *Veronica beccabunga*

Brookweed *Samolus valerandi*

Brown knapweed
    Centaurea nemoralis

Buck's horn plantain
    Plantago coronopus

Bugle   *Ajuga reptans*

Bulbous buttercup
    Ranunculus bulbosus

Bulbous saxifrage
    Saxifraga granulata

Bur chervil *Anthriscus caucalis*

Burdock   *Arctium pubens*

Bur-marigold   *Bidens tripartita*

Bur medick   *Medicago minima*

Burnet rose   *Rosa pimpinellifolia*

Burnet saxifrage
    Pimpinella saxifraga

Burnt orchid   *Orchis ustulata*

Bush vetch   *Vicia sepium*

Butcher's broom *Ruscus aculeatus*

Butterbur   *Petasites hybridus*

Butterfly orchid
    Habenaria chlorantha
    Platanthera chlorantha

Calamint   *Calamintha sylvatica*

Canadian fleabane
    Conyza canadensis
    Erigeron canadensis

Canadian golden rod
    Solidago canadensis

Canadian waterweed
    Elodea canadensis

Canterbury bell
    Campanula medium

Caper spurge *Euphorbia lathyrus*

Carline thistle   *Carlina vulgaris*

Carrot broomrape
    Orobanche amethystea
    Orobanche maritima

Catmint   *Nepeta cataria*

Cat's ear *Hypochoeris radicata*

Celery-leaved crowsfoot
    Ranunculus sceleratus

Chaff weed   *Anagallis minima*

Chalk hill eyebright
    Euphrasia pseudokerneri

Chalk milkwort *Polygala calcarea*

Chamomile *Chamaemelum nobile*

Changing forget-me-not
Myosotis discolor

Charlock *Sinapis arvensis*

Cheddar pink
Dianthus gratianopolitanus

Chickweed *Stellaria media*

Chickweed willow herb
Epilobium alsinifolium

Chickweed wintergreen
Trientalis europaea

Chicory *Cichorum intybus*

Chinese mugwort
Artemisia verlotorum

Chives *Allium schoenoprasum*

Ciliate heath *Erica ciliaris*

Circular-leaved crowfoot
Ranunculus circinatus

Clary *Salvia horminoides*

Cleavers *Galium aparine*

Climbing corydalis
Corydalis claviculta

Cloudberry *Rubus chamaemorus*

Clove-scented broomrape
Orobanche caryophyllacea

Clustered alpine saxifrage
Saxifraga nivalis

Clustered bellflower
Campanula glomerata

Clustered dock
Rumex conglomeratus

Coastal broomrape
Orobanche amethystea
Orobanche maritima

Coastal holly *Eryngium campestre*

Coltsfoot *Tussilago farfara*

Columbine *Aquilegia vulgaris*

Comfrey *Symphytum officinale*

Common agrimony
Agrimonia eupatoria

Common bindweed
Calystegia sepium

Common bistort
Polygonum bistorta

Common bladderwort
Utricularia vulgaris

Common burdock
Arctium pubens

Common butterwort
Pinguicula vulgaris

Common calamint
Calamintha sylvatica

Common cat's ear
Hypochoeris radicata

Common centaury
Centaurium erythraea

Common chickweed
Stellaria media

Common comfrey
Symphytum officinale

Common cornsalad
Valerianella locusta

Common cow wheat
Melampyrum pratense

Common dog violet
Viola riviniana

Common duckweed *Lemna minor*

Common evening primrose
Oenothera biennis

Common eyebright
Euphrasia nemorosa

Common field speedwell
Veronica persica

Common figwort
Scrophularia nodosa

Common fleabane
Pulicaria dysenterica

Common forget-me-not
Myosotis arvensis

Common fumitory
Fumaria officinalis

Common gromwell
Lithospermum officinale

Common hawkweed
Hieracium vulgatum

Common heather
Calluna vulgaris

Common hemp nettle
Galeopsis tetrahit

Common knapweed
Centaurea nigra

Common mallow *Malva sylvestris*

Common meadow
buttercup *Ranunculus acris*

Common meadow rue
Thalictrum flavum

Common milkwort
Polygala vulgaris

Common mullein
Verbascum thapsus

Common nettle *Urtica dioica*

Common orache *Atriplex patula*

Common poppy *Papaver rhoeas*

Common ragwort
Senecio jacobaea

Common red poppy
Papaver rhoeas

Common restharrow
Ononis repens

Common rockrose
Helianthemum nummularium

Common sea lavender
Limonium vulgare

Commom slender eyebright
Euphrasia micrantha

Common sorrel *Rumex acetosa*

Common sowthistle
Sonchus oleraceus

Common spotted orchid
Dactylorhiza fuchsii

Common storksbill
Erodium cicutarium

Common teasel *Dipsacus fullonum*
Dipsacus sylvestris

Downy rose

Common toadflax   *Linaria vulgaris*

Common tormentil
　　　　Potentilla erecta

Common twayblade   *Listera ovata*

Common valerian
　　　　Valeriana officinalis

Common vetch   　　　*Vicia sativa*

Common violet   *Viola riviniana*

Common water crowfoot
　　　　Ranunculus aquatilis

Common water dropwort
　　　　Oenanthe fistulosa

Common water starwort
　　　　Callitriche stagnalis

Common whitlowgrass
　　　　Erophila verna

Common wild thyme
　　　　Thymus drucei

Common wintergreen
　　　　Pyrola minor

Coralroot orchid
　　　　Corallorhiza trifida

Corky-fruited water dropwort
　　　　Oenanthe pimpinelloides

Corn bedstraw
　　　　Galium tricornutum

Corn buttercup
　　　　Ranunculus arvensis

Corn chamomile
　　　　Anthemis arvensis

Cornflower   *Centaurea cyanus*

Corn gromwell
　　　　Lithospermum arvense

Corn marigold
　　　　Chrysanthemum segetum

Corn mignonette
　　　　Reseda phyteuma

Corn mint   *Mentha arvensis*

Corn sowthistle   *Sonchus arvensis*

Corn spurrey   *Spergula arvensis*

Cornish heath   *Erica vagans*

Corsican speedwell
　　　　Veronica repens

Cowberry   *Vaccinium vitis-idaea*

Cow parsley   *Anthriscus sylvestris*

Cow parsnip
　　　　Heracleum sphondylium

Cowslip   　　　*Primula veris*

Cranberry   *Oxycoccus palustris*
　　　　Vaccinium oxycoccus

Creamy clover
　　　　Trifolium ochroleucon

Creeping bellflower
　　　　Campanula rapunculoides

Creeping buttercup
　　　　Ranunculus repens

Creeping cinquefoil
　　　　Potentilla reptans

Creeping forget-me-not
　　　　Myosotis secunda

Creeping jenny
　　　　Lysimachia nummularia

Creeping lady's tresses
　　　　Goodyera repens

Creeping Saint John's wort
　　　　Hypericum humifusum

Creeping thistle   *Cirsium arvense*

Crimson clover
　　　　Trifolium incarnatum

Cross-leaved heath   *Erica tetralix*

Crosswort   　　*Galium cruciata*

Crowberry   *Empetrum nigrum*

Crow garlic   　　*Allium vineale*

Crown vetch   　*Coronilla varia*

Cuckoo flower
　　　　Cardamine pratensis

Cuckoo-pint   *Arum maculatum*

Curled pondweed
　　　　Potamogeton crispus

Curly dock   　　*Rumex crispus*

Cut-leaved cranesbill
　　　　Geranium dissectum

Cut-leaved dead nettle
　　　　Lamium hybridum

Cut-leaved germander
　　　　Teucrium botrys

Cut-leaved self heal
　　　　Prunella laciniata

Cyclamen   *Cyclamen hederifolium*

Cypress spurge
　　　　Euphorbia cyparissias

Daisy   　　　　*Bellis perennis*

Dame's violet   *Hesperis matronalis*

Dandelion   *Taraxacum officinale*

Dark burdock
　　　　Arctium nemorosum

Dark hair crowfoot
　　　　Ranunculus trichophyllus

Dark mullein   *Verbascum nigrum*

Dark red helleborine
　　　　Epipactis atropurpurea
　　　　Epipactis atrorubens

Deadly nightshade   *Atropa bella
　　　　donna*

Deptford pink   *Dianthus armeria*

Devil's bit scabious   *Scabiosa succisa
　　　　Succisa pratensis*

Dewberry   　　*Rubus caesius*

Dittander   *Lepidium latifolium*

Dodder   *Cuscuta epithymum*

Dog rose   　　　*Rosa canina*

Dog's mercury
　　　　Mercurialis perennis

Dog violet   　　*Viola canina*

Dove's foot cranesbill
　　　　Geranium columbinum
　　　　Geranium molle

Downy pepperwort
　　　　Lepidium heterophyllum

Downy rose   　*Rosa tomentosa*

Downy woundwort

Downy woundwort
Stachys germanica

Dragon's teeth
Tetragonolobus maritimus

Dropwort *Filipendula vulgaris*

Dune storksbill *Erodium dunense*

Dusky cranesbill
Geranium phaeum

Dusty miller *Artemisia stellerana*

Dutch clover *Trifolium repens*

Dwarf mallow *Malva neglecta*

Dwarf orchid *Orchis ustulata*

Dwarf pansy *Viola kitaibeliana*

Dwarf spurge *Euphorbia exigua*

Dwarf thistle *Cirsium acaule*

Dwarf Welsh eyebright
Euphrasia cambrica

Dyer's rocket *Reseda luteola*

Early forget-me-not
Myosotis ramosissima

Early purple orchid *Orchis mascula*

Early spider orchid
Ophrys aranifera
Ophrys sphegodes

Elecampane *Inula helenium*

Enchanter's nightshade
Circaea lutetiana

English sticky eyebright
Euphrasia anglica

English stonecrop
Sedum anglicum

Erect evening primrose
Oenothera stricta

Erect hedge parsley *Torilis japonica*

Evening catchfly *Silene noctiflora*

Evening primrose
Oenothera biennis

Everlasting *Anaphalis margaritacea*
Helichrysum arenarium

Everlasting pea *Lathyrus latifolius*

Fairy flax *Linum catharticum*

False cleavers *Galium spurium*

False thorow-wax
Bupleurum subovatum

Fat duckweed *Lemna gibba*

Fat hen *Chenopodium album*

Fen bedstraw *Galium uliginosum*

Fennel *Foeniculum vulgare*

Fennel pondweed
Potamogeton pectinatus

Fen orchid *Liparis loeselii*

Fen pondweed
Potamogeton coloratus

Fen sowthistle *Sonchus palustris*

Fenugreek
Trifolium ornithopodioides

Fen violet *Viola stagnina*

Feverfew
Chrysanthemum parthenium
Tanacetum parthenium

Field bindweed
Convolvulus arvensis

Field eryngo *Eryngium campestre*

Field felwort *Gentiana campestris*
Gentianella campestris

Field fleawort *Senecio integrifolius*

Field forget-me-not
Myosotis arvensis

Field garlic *Allium oleraceum*

Field gentian *Gentiana campestris*
Gentianella campestris

Field gromwell
Lithospermum arvense

Field pansy *Viola arvensis*

Field penny cress *Thlaspi arvense*

Field pepperwort
Lepidium campestre

Field poppy *Papaver rhoeas*

Field rose *Rosa arvensis*

Field scabious *Knautia arvensis*
Scabiosa arvensis

Field speedwell *Veronica agrestis*

Field toadflax *Linaria arvensis*

Field woundwort *Stachys arvensis*

Figwort *Scrophularia nodosa*

Fimbriate medick
Medicago polymorpha

Fine-leaved heath *Erica cinera*

Fine-leaved water dropwort
Oenanthe aquatica

Fingered speedwell
Veronica triphyllos

Flat-head clover
Trifolium glomeratum

Fleabane *Pulicaria dysenterica*

Floating pondweed
Potamogeton natans

Floating water plantain
Alisma natans
Luronium natans

Flowering nutmeg
Leycesteria formosa

Flowering rush
Butomus umbellatus

Fluellen *Kickxia elatine*

Fly honeysuckle
Lonicera xylosteum

Fly orchid *Ophrys insectifera*
Ophrys muscifera

Fool's parsley *Aethusa cynapium*

Fool's watercress
Apium nodiflorum

Forget-me-not *Myosotis arvensis*

Forked larkspur *Consolida regalis*

Fox-and-cubs
Hieracium aurantiacum

Foxglove *Digitalis purpurea*

Fragrant agrimony
Agrimonia procera

Fragrant evening primrose
Oenothera stricta

Ground thistle

Fragrant orchid
    Gymnadenia conopsea

French hawk's beard
    Crepis nicaeensis

French mint
    Mentha spicata × suaveolens

Fringed waterlily
    Nymphoides peltata

Fritillary   *Fritillaria meleagris*

Frogbit
    Hydrocharis morsus-ranae

Frog orchid   *Coeloglossum viride*

Frosted orache   *Atriplex laciniata*

Fumitory   *Fumaria officinale*

Garden chervil
    Anthriscus cerefolium

Garden cress   *Lepidium sativum*

Garlic mustard   *Alliaria petiolata*

Germander speedwell
    Veronica chamaedrys

Ghost orchid
    Epipogium aphyllum

Giant bellflower
    Campanula lactiflora
    Campanula latifolia

Giant hogweed
    Heracleum mantegazzianum

Gibbous duckweed   *Lemna gibba*

Gipsywort   *Lycopus europaeus*

Glasswort   *Salicornia europaea*

Globeflower   *Trollius europaeus*

Goat's beard *Tragopogon pratensis*

Goat's rue   *Galega officinalis*

Golden rod   *Solidago virgaurea*

Golden samphire
    Inula crithmoides

Golden saxifrage
    Chrysosplenium oppositifolium

Goldilocks   *Ranunculus auricomus*

Goldilocks buttercup
    Ranunculus auricomus

Good King Henry
    Chenopodium bonus-henricus

Goose grass   *Galium aparine*

Goutweed
    Aegopodium podagraria

Grape hyacinth
    Muscari atlanticum
    Muscari neglectum
    Muscari racemosum

Grass of parnassus
    Parnassia palustris

Grass-poly *Lythrum hyssopifolia*

Grass vetchling *Lathyrus nissolia*

Grassy orach *Atriplex littoralis*

Great bellflower
    Campanula latifolia

Great bindweed
    Calystegia silvatica

Great burdock   *Arctium lappa*

Great burnet
    Sanguisorba officinalis

Great duckweed
    Spirodela polyrhiza

Greater bird's foot trefoil
    Lotus uliginosus

Greater bladderwort
    Utricularia vulgaris

Greater broomrape
    Orobanche rapum-genistae

Greater burnet saxifrage
    Pimpinella major

Greater butterfly orchid
    Platanthera chlorantha

Greater butterwort
    Pinguicula grandiflora

Greater celandine
    Chelidonium majus

Greater chickweed
    Stellaria neglecta

Greater dodder *Cuscuta europaea*

Greater eyebright
    Euphrasia arctica

Greater hayrattle
    Rhinanthus serotinus

Greater periwinkle *Vinca major*

Greater sea spurrey
    Spergularia media

Greater stitchwort
    Stellaria holostea

Greater yellow rattle
    Rhinanthus angustifolius

Great fen ragwort
    Senecio paludodus

Great knapweed
    Centaurea scabiosa

Great lettuce   *Lactuca virosa*

Great mullein   *Verbascum thapsus*

Great pignut
    Bunium bulbocastanum

Great plantain   *Plantago major*

Great sundew   *Drosera anglica*

Great willow herb
    Epilobium hirsutum

Green field speedwell
    Veronica agrestis

Green figwort
    Scrophularia umbrosa

Green hellebore *Helleborus viridis*

Green nightshade
    Solanum sarrachoides

Green-winged orchid *Orchis morio*

Grey speedwell   *Veronica polita*

Gromwell
    Lithospermum officinale

Ground elder
    Aegopodium podagraria

Ground ivy   *Glechoma hederacea*

Groundsel   *Senecio vulgaris*

Ground thistle   *Cirsium acaute*
    Cirsium acautonauct

Hairy bindweed

Hairy bindweed   *Calystegia pulchra*
Hairy bird's foot trefoil
                    Lotus hispidus
Hairy bitter cress
                    Cardamine hirsuta
Hairy-leaved eyebright
                    Euphrasia curta
Hairy nightshade   *Solanum luteum*
Hairy rock cress   *Arabis hirsuta*
Hairy Saint John's wort
                    Hypericum hirsutum
Hairy spurge   *Euphorbia pilosa*
Hairy stonecrop   *Sedum villosum*
Hairy tare   *Vicia hirsuta*
Hairy vetchling   *Lathyrus hirsutus*
Hairy violet   *Viola hirta*
Hairy willow herb
                    Epilobium parviflorum
Hardheads   *Centaurea nigra*
Harebell   *Campanula rotundifolia*
Hare's-foot clover
                    Trifolium arvense
Harsh downy-rose   *Rosa tomentosa*
Hautbois strawberry
                    Fragaria moschata
Hawkbit   *Leontodon leysseri*
            Leontodon taraxacoides
Hawkweed
                    Hieracium umbellatum
Hawkweed ox-tongue
                    Picris hieracioides
Hayrattle   *Rhinanthus minor*
Heath bedstraw   *Galium saxatile*
Heath groundsel   *Senecio sylvaticus*
Heath milkwort
                    Polygala serpyllifolia
Heath speedwell
                    Veronica officinalis
Heath spotted orchid
                    Dactylorhiza maculata
Hedge bedstraw   *Galium album*
Hedge bindweed
                    Calystegia sepium
Hedge parsley   *Torilis japonica*
Hedgerow cranesbill
                    Geranium pyrenaicum
Hedge woundwort
                    Stachys sylvatica
Hemlock   *Conium maculatum*
Hemlock water dropwort
                    Oenanthe crocata
Hemp agrimony
                    Eupatorium cannabinum
Hemp-nettle   *Galeopsis tetrahit*
Henbane   *Hyoscyamus niger*
Henbit   *Lamium amplexicaule*
Herb bennet   *Geum urbanum*
Herb paris   *Paris quadrifolia*
Herb robert
                    Geranium robertianum

Hispid marsh mallow
                    Althaea hirsuta
Hoary cinquefoil
                    Potentilla argentea
Hoary cress   *Cardaria draba*
Hoary mullein
                    Verbascum pulverulentum
Hoary plantain   *Plantago media*
Hoary ragwort   *Senecio erucifolius*
Hoary rockrose
                    Helianthemum canum
Hogweed   *Heracleum sphondylium*
Honesty   *Lunaria annua*
Honeysuckle
                    Lonicera periclymenum
Hop   *Humulus lupulus*
Hop trefoil   *Trifolium campestre*
Horse mint   *Mentha longifolia*
Horehound   *Ballota nigra*
Horseshoe vetch
                    Hippocrepis comosa
Hyssop-leaved loosestrife
                    Lythrum hyssopifolia
Indian balsam
                    Impatiens glandulifera
Intermediate bladderwort
                    Utricularia intermedia
Intermediate dead-nettle
                    Lamium moluccellifolium
Intermediate wintergreen
                    Pyrola media
Irish eyebright
                    Euphrasia salisburgensis
Irish heath   *Erica hibernica*
Irish saxifrage   *Saxifraga rosacea*
Irish spurge   *Euphorbia hyberna*
Italian catchfly   *Silene italica*
Italian cuckoo-pint   *Arum italicum*
Italian lords-and-ladies
                    Arum italicum
Ivy broomrape   *Orobanche hederae*
Ivy duckweed   *Lemna trisulca*
Ivy   *Hedera helix*
Ivy-leaved bellflower
                    Campanula hederacea
                    Wahlenbergia hederacea
Ivy-leaved crowfoot
                    Ranunculus hederaceus
Ivy-leaved duckweed
                    Lemna trisulca
Ivy-leaved speedwell
                    Veronica hederifolia
Ivy-leaved toadflax
                    Cymbalaria muralis
Japanese knotweed
                    Reynoutria japonica
Jersey buttercup
                    Ranunculus paludosus
Jersey forget-me-not
                    Myosotis sicula
Jersey orchid   *Orchis laxiflora*

Little marsh dandelion

Jersey toadflax *Linaria pelisseriana*

Keeled-fruited cornsalad
Valerianella carinata

Kidney vetch *Anthyllis vulneraria*

Kingcup *Caltha palustris*

Knapweed *Centaurea nigra*

Knotgrass *Polygonum aviculare*

Knotted clover *Trifolium striatum*

Knotted hedge parsley
Torilis nodosa

Knotted pearlwort *Sagina nodosa*

Lady orchid *Orchis purpurea*

Lady's bedstraw *Galium verum*

Lady's slipper
Cypripedium calceolus

Lady's smock *Cardamine pratensis*

Lady's tresses
Spiranthes autumnalis
Spiranthes spiralis

Lamb's lettuce *Valerianella locusta*

Lamb's tongue *Plantago media*

Lanceolate water plantain
Alisma lanceolatum

Large bindweed
Calystegia silvatica

Large bitter cress
Cardamine amara

Large-flowered butterwort
Pinguicula grandiflora

Large-flowered evening primrose
Oenothera erythrosepala

Large-flowered hemp-nettle
Galeopsis speciosa

Large-flowered sticky eyebright
Euphrasia rostkoviana

Large hop trefoil *Trifolium aureum*

Large lizard clover
Trifolium molinerii

Larger wild thyme
Thymus pulegioides

Large thyme *Thymus pulegioides*

Large wintergreen
Pyrola rotundifolia

Large yellow foxglove
Digitalis grandiflora

Large yellow restharrow
Ononis natrix

Larkspur *Consolida ambigua*

Late spider orchid
Ophrys arachnites
Ophrys fuciflora

Leafy lousewort *Pedicularis foliosa*

Least birdsfoot
Ornithopus perpusillus

Least lettuce *Lactuca saligna*

Least waterlily *Nuphar pumila*

Least yellow trefoil
Trifolium micranthum

Leopard's bane
Doronicum pardalianches

Lesser bindweed
Convolvulus arvensis

Lesser bladderwort
Utricularia minor

Lesser broomrape
Orobanche apiculata
Orobanche minor

Lesser burdock *Arctium minus*

Lesser burnet *Sanguisorba minor*

Lesser butterfly orchid
Habenaria bifolia
Platanthera bifolia

Lesser celandine
Ranunculus ficaria

Lesser centaury
Centaurium pulchellum

Lesser dandelion
Taraxacum erythrospermum
Taraxacum laevigatum

Lesser dodder *Cuscuta epithymum*

Lesser duckweed *Lemna minor*

Lesser fleabane *Pulicaria vulgaris*

Lesser goat's beard
Tragopogon minor

Lesser herb robert
Geranium purpureum

Lesser marshwort
Apium inundatum

Lesser meadow rue
Thalictrum minus

Lesser periwinkle *Vinca minor*

Lesser sea spurrey
Spergularia marina

Lesser skullcap *Scutellaria minor*

Lesser snapdragon
Misopates orontium

Lesser solomon's seal
Polygonatum odoratum

Lesser stitchwort
Stellaria graminea

Lesser sweet briar *Rosa micrantha*

Lesser twayblade *Listera cordata*

Lesser valerian *Valeriana dioica*

Lesser water forget-me-not
Myosotis caespitosa

Lesser waterlily *Nuphar pumila*

Lesser water parsnip *Berula erecta*

Lesser water plantain
Alisma ranunculoides
Baldellia ranunculoides

Lesser wintergreen *Pyrola minor*

Lesser yellow trefoil
Trifolium dubium

Lily-of-the-valley
Convallaria majalis

Ling *Calluna vulgaris*

Little kneeling eyebright
Euphrasia confusa

Little marsh dandelion
Taraxacum palustre

Little three-lobed crowfoot

Little three-lobed crowfoot	
	Ranunculus tripartitus
Livelong	*Sedum telephium*
Lizard orchid	
	Himantoglossum hircinum
	Orchis hircina
Loddon pondweed	
	Potamogeton nodosus
Long-fruited bird's foot trefoil	
	Lotus angustissimus
Long-leaved sundew	
	Drosera intermedia
Long rough-headed poppy	
	Papaver agremone
Long smooth-headed poppy	
	Papaver dubium
Long-stalked pondweed	
	Potamogeton praelongus
Long-stemmed cranesbill	
	Geranium columbinum
Long-styled rose	*Rosa stylosa*
Lords-and-ladies	
	Arum maculatum
Lousewort	*Pedicularis sylvatica*
Lovage	*Levisticum officinale*
Lucerne	*Medicago sativa*
Lupin	*Lupinus nootkatensis*
Mackay's heath	*Erica mackaiana*
Maiden pink	*Dianthus deltoides*
Man orchid	
	Aceras anthropophorum
Mare's tail	*Hippuris vulgaris*
Marjoram	*Origanum vulgare*
Marsh bedstraw	*Galium palustre*
Marsh bird's foot trefoil	
	Lotus uliginosus
Marsh cinquefoil	
	Potentilla palustris
Marsh fleawort	*Senecio palustris*
Marsh forget-me-not	
	Myosotis secunda
Marsh gentian	
	Gentiana pneumonanthe
Marsh hawk's beard	
	Crepis paludosa
Marsh helleborine	
	Epipactis palustris
Marsh lousewort	
	Pedicularis palustris
Marsh mallow	*Althaea officinalis*
Marsh marigold	*Caltha palustris*
Marsh pea	*Lathyrus palustris*
Marsh ragwort	*Senecio aquaticus*
Marsh Saint John's wort	
	Hypericum elodes
Marsh speedwell	
	Veronica scutellata
Marsh stitchwort	*Stellaria palustris*
Marsh thistle	*Carduus palustris*
	Cirsium palustre
Marsh valerian	*Valeriana dioica*

Marsh willow herb	
	Epilobium palustre
Marsh woundwort	
	Stachys palustris
May lily	*Maianthemum bifolium*
Meadow buttercup	
	Ranunculus acris
Meadow clary	*Salvia pratensis*
Meadow cranesbill	
	Geranium pratense
Meadow rue	*Thalictrum flavum*
Meadow saffron	
	Colchicum autumnale
Meadow saxifrage	
	Saxifraga granulata
Meadowsweet	*Filipendula ulmaria*
Meadow thistle	*Carduus dissectum*
	Carduus pratensis
	Cirsium dissectum
Meadow water dropwort	
	Oenanthe silaifolia
Medium wintergreen	*Pyrola media*
Melancholy thistle	
	Carduus helenioides
	Cirsium heterophyllum
Mexican fleabane	
	Erigeron mucronatus
Milfoil	*Achillea millefolium*
Milk thistle	*Silybum marianum*
Mistletoe	*Viscum album*
Mollyblobs	*Caltha palustris*
Monkshood	*Aconitum napellus*
Monkey flower	*Mimulus guttatus*
Monkey orchid	*Orchis simia*
Moorland crowfoot	
	Ranunculus omiophyllus
Mortar pellitory	*Parietaria judaica*
Moschatel	*Adoxa moschatellina*
Moss campion	*Silene acaulis*
Mossy saxifrage	
	Saxifraga hypnoides
Moth mullein	*Verbascum blattaria*
Mountain avens	*Dryas octopetala*
Mountain campion	*Silene acaulis*
Mountain everlasting	
	Antennaria dioica
Mountain pansy	*Viola lutea*
Mountain Saint John's wort	
	Hypericum montanum
Mountain sorrel	*Oxyria digyna*
Mountain sticky eyebright	
	Euphrasia montana
Mouse-ear hawkweed	
	Hieracium pilosella
	Pilosella officinarum
Mud water starwort	
	Callitriche stagnalis
Mudwort	*Limosella aquatica*
Mugwort	*Artemisia vulgaris*
Musk	*Mimulus moschatus*

Musk mallow	*Malva moschata*
Musk orchid	
	Herminium monorchis
Musk thistle	*Carduus nutans*
Musky storksbill	
	Erodium moschatum
Naked autumn crocus	
	Crocus nudiflorus
Narrow-fruited cornsalad	
	Valerianella dentata
Narrow-leaved eyebright	
	Euphrasia salisburgensis
Narrow-leaved helleborine	
	Cephalanthera longifolia
Narrow-leaved marsh dandelion	
	Taraxacum palustre
Narrow-leaved pepperwort	
	Lepidium ruderale
Narrow-leaved Saint John's wort	
	Hypericum linarifolium
Narrow-leaved sweet briar	
	Rosa agrestis
Narrow-leaved vetch	
	Vicia angustifolia
Narrow-lipped helleborine	
	Epipactis leptochila
Nettle-cure dock	
	Rumex obtusifolius
Nettle-leaved bellflower	
	Campanula trachelium
Night-flowering catchfly	
	Silene noctiflora
Nipplewort	*Lapsana communis*
Nodding bur marigold	
	Bidens cernua
Nodding catchfly	*Silene nutans*
Nodding thistle	*Carduus nutans*
Nodding water avens	*Geum rivale*
Northern bedstraw	
	Galium boreale
Northern downy rose	
	Rosa sherardii
Norwegian mugwort	
	Artemisia norvegica
Nottingham catchfly	*Silene nutans*
Nuttall's waterweed	
	Elodea nuttallii
Oblong-leaved sundew	
	Drosera intermedia
Old man's beard	*Clematis vitalba*
One-flowered wintergreen	
	Moneses uniflora
	Pyrola uniflora
Opium poppy	
	Papaver somniferum
Orach	*Atriplex patula*
Orange balsam	*Impatiens capensis*
Orange hawkweed	
	Hieracium aurantiacum
	Pilosella aurantiaca
Orpine	*Sedum telephium*

Ox-eye daisy	
	Chrysanthemum leucanthemum
	Leucanthemum vulgare
Oxford ragwort	*Senecio squalidus*
Oxlip	*Primula elatior*
Pale butterwort	
	Pinguicula lusitanica
Pale flax	*Linum bienne*
Pale hairy buttercup	
	Ranunculus sardous
Pale heath violet	*Viola lactea*
Pale persicaria	
	Polygonum lapathifolium
Pale toadflax	*Linaria repens*
Pale willow herb	
	Epilobium Roseum
Parsley piert	*Aphanes arvensis*
Parsley water dropwort	
	Oenanthe lachenalii
Pasque flower	*Pulsatilla vernalis*
	Pulsatilla vulgaris
Pearly everlasting	
	Anaphalis margaritacea
Pedicelled willow herb	
	Epilobium roseum
Pellitory-of-the-wall	
	Parietaria judaica
Penny royal	*Mentha pulegium*
Pepper mint	*Mentha × piperita*
Pepper saxifrage	*Silaum silaus*
Perennial flax	*Linum perenne*
Perennial glasswort	
	Arthrocnemum perenne
Perennial honesty	
	Lunaria rediviva
Perennial sowthistle	
	Sonchus arvensis
Perfoliate honeysuckle	
	Lonicera caprifolium
Perfoliate penny cress	
	Thlaspi perfoliatum
Perfoliate pondweed	
	Potamogeton perfoliatus
Perforate alexanders	
	Smyrnium perfoliatum
Perforate Saint John's wort	
	Hypericum perforatum
Persian speedwell	*Veronica persica*
Petty spurge	*Euphorbia peplus*
Pheasant's eye	*Narcissus majalis*
Picris broomrape	
	Orobanche picridis
Pignut	*Conopodium majus*
Pineapple weed	
	Matricaria matricarioides
Pink butterwort	
	Pinguicula lusitanica
Pink water speedwell	
	Veronica catenata
Ploughman's spikenard	
	Inula conyza

Plymouth thistle	*Carduus pycnocephalus*
Pond bedstraw	*Galium debile*
Pond chickweed	*Myosoton aquaticum*
Portland spurge	*Euphorbia portlandica*
Prickly lettuce	*Lactuca scariola*
	Lactuca serriola
Prickly poppy	*Papaver agremone*
Prickly restharrow	*Ononis spinosa*
Prickly saltwort	*Salsola kali*
Prickly sowthistle	*Sonchus asper*
Primrose	*Primula vulgaris*
Primrose peerless	*Narcissus × bifloris*
Procumbent cinquefoil	*Potentilla anglica*
Procumbent pearlwort	*Sagina procumbens*
Procumbent yellow sorrel	*Oxalis corniculata*
Prostrate pearlwort	*Sagina procumbens*
Prostrate toadflax	*Linaria supina*
Purple broomrape	*Orobanche purpurea*
Purple corydalis	*Corydalis bulbosa*
Purple crocus	*Crocus purpureus*
	Crocus vernus
Purple dead-nettle	*Lamium purpureum*
Purple heather	*Erica cinera*
Purple loosestrife	*Lythrum salicaria*
Purple milk-vetch	*Astragalus danicus*
Purple saxifrage	*Saxifraga oppositifolia*
Purple spurge	*Euphorbia peplis*
Purple toadflax	*Linaria purpurea*
Pyramidal orchid	*Anacamptis pyramidalis*
	Orchis pyramidalis
Pyrenean cranesbill	*Geranium pyrenaicum*
Pyrenean lily	*Lilium pyrenaicum*
Pyrenean valerian	*Valeriana pyrenaica*
Radish	*Raphanus sativus*
Ragged robin	*Lychnis flos-cuculi*
Ragwort	*Senecio jacobaea*
Ramsons	*Attium ursinum*
Rape	*Brassica napus*
Raspberry	*Rubus idaeus*
Red bartsia	*Odontites verna*
Red broomrape	*Orobanche alba*
Red campion	*Lychnis dioica*
	Silene dioica
Red catchfly	*Lychnis viscaria*

Red clover	*Trifolium pratense*
Red dead-nettle	*Lamium purpureum*
Reddish pondweed	*Potamogeton alpinus*
	Potamogeton rufescens
Red hemp-nettle	*Galeopsis angustifolia*
Red pondweed	*Potamogeton alpinus*
	Potamogeton rufescens
Red rattle	*Pedicularis palustris*
Redshank	*Polygonum persicaria*
Red valerian	*Centranthus ruber*
Reflexed stonecrop	*Sedum reflexum*
Restharrow	*Ononis repens*
Reversed clover	*Trifolium resupinatum*
Ribbed melitot	*Melilotus officinalis*
Ribwort plantain	*Plantago lanceolata*
Rigid hornwort	*Ceratophyllum demersum*
River crowfoot	*Ranunculus fluitans*
River water crowfoot	*Ranunculus fluitans*
River water dropwort	*Oenanthe fluviatilis*
Rock cinquefoil	*Potentilla rupestris*
Rock samphire	*Crithmum maritimum*
Rock sea spurrey	*Spergularia rupicola*
Rock stonecrop	*Sedum forsteranum*
Rootless duckweed	*Wolffia arrhiza*
Rosebay willow herb	*Epilobium angustifolium*
Rose of sharon	*Hypericum calycinum*
Roseroot	*Rhodiola rosea*
	Sedum rosea
Rough chervil	*Chaerophyllum temulentum*
Rough clover	*Trifolium scabrum*
Rough comfrey	*Symphytum asperum*
Rough hawkbit	*Leontodon hispidus*
Rough hawk's beard	*Crepis biennis*
Round-headed leek	*Allium sphaerocephalon*
Round-headed rampion	*Phyteuma orbiculare*
	Phyteuma tenerum
Round knotweed	*Reynoutria japonica*
Round-leaved cranesbill	*Geranium rotundifolium*

Round-leaved fluellen
Kickxia spuria

Round-leaved mint
Mentha suaveolens

Round-leaved speedwell
Veronica filiformis

Round-leaved sundew
Drosera rotundifolia

Round-leaved wintergreen
Pyrola rotundifolia

Rock sea-spurrey
Spergularia rupicola

Rue-leaved saxifrage
Saxifraga tridactylites

Russian comfrey
Symphytum × uplandicum

Russian spurge
Euphorbia uralensis

Sainfoin *Onobrychis viciifolia*

Saint Patrick's cabbage
Saxifraga spathularis

Salad burnet *Sanguisorba minor*

Salsify *Tragopogon porrifolius*

Saltwort *Glaux maritima*

Samphire *Crithmum maritimum*

Sand crocus *Romulea columnae*
Romulea parviflora

Sand leek *Allium scorodoprasum*

Sand spurrey *Spergularia rubra*

Sand toadflax *Linaria arenaria*

Sandy nettle *Urtica urens*

Sandy orach *Atriplex laciniata*

Saw-wort *Serratula tinctoria*

Scarce autumn felwort
Gentiana germanica
Gentianella germanica

Scarce water figwort
Scrophularia ehrhartii
Scrophularia umbrosa

Scarlet pimpernel
Anagallis arvensis

Scented agrimony
Agrimonia procera

Scented mayweed
Matricaria recutita

Scentless chamomile
Tripleurospermum maritimum

Scentless mayweed
Tripleurospermum indorum

Scots lovage *Ligusticum scoticum*

Scottish asphodel *Tofieldia pusilla*

Scottish bluebell
Campanula rotundifolia

Scottish thistle
Onopordon acanthium

Sea aster *Aster tripolium*

Sea beet *Beta vulgaris maritima*

Sea bindweed
Calystegia soldanella

Sea-blite *Suaeda maritima*

Sea campion
Silene vulgaris maritima

Sea carrot
Daucus carota gummifer

Sea centaury *Centaurium littorale*

Sea holly *Eryngium maritimum*

Sea kale *Crambe maritima*

Sea lavender *Limonium vulgare*

Sea mayweed
Tripleurospermum maritimum

Sea milkwort *Glaux maritima*

Sea pea *Lathyrus japonicus*
Lathyrus maritimus

Sea pink *Armeria maritima*
Statice armeria

Sea plantain *Plantago maritima*

Sea purslane
Halimione portulacoides

Sea radish *Raphanus maritimus*

Sea rocket *Cakile maritima*

Seaside crowfoot
Ranunculus baudotii

Seaside pansy *Viola curtisii*

Seaside pea *Lathyrus japonicus*
Lathyrus maritimus

Sea stock *Matthiola sinuata*

Sea storksbill *Erodium maritimus*

Sea spurge *Euphorbia paralias*

Sea wormwood
Artemisia maritima

Self heal *Prunella vulgaris*

Serrated wintergreen
Orthilia secunda

Sharp-leaved fluellen
Kickxia elatine

Sheep's bit *Jasione montana*

Sheep's sorrel *Rumex acetosella*

Shepherd's cress
Teesdalia nudicaulis

Shepherd's purse
Capsella pursa-pastoris

Shining cranesbill
Geranium lucidum

Shining pondweed
Potamogeton lucens

Shoreline orache *Atriplex littoralis*

Shore weed *Littorella lacustris*
Littorella uniflora

Short-fruited willow herb
Epilobium obscurum

Short-leaved forget-me-not
Myosotis stolonifera

Short-haired eyebright
Euphrasia brevipila

Short-pedicelled rose *Rosa dumalis*

Shrubby cinquefoil
Potentilla fruticosa

Shrubby speedwell
Veronica fruticans

Sibbaldia *Sibbaldia procumbens*

Sickle-leaved hare's ear

Sickle-leaved hare's ear
Bupleurum falcatum

Sickle medick *Medicago falcata*

Silverweed *Potentilla anserina*

Single-flowered wintergreen
Moneses uniflora
Pyrola uniflora

Skullcap *Scutellaria galericulata*

Slender bedstraw
Galium pumilum

Slender-flowered thistle
Carduus tenuiflorus

Slender hare's ear
Bupleurum tenuissimum

Slender mullein
Verbascum virgatum

Slender Saint John's wort
Hypericum pulchrum

Slender scottish eyebright
Euphrasia scottica

Slender tare *Vicia tenuissima*

Slender trefoil
Trifolium micranthum

Small alpine gentian
Gentiana nivalis

Small balsam *Impatiens parviflora*

Small catchfly *Silene gallica*

Small cranberry
Oxycoccus microcarpus
Vaccinium microcarpum

Small fleabane *Pulicaria vulgaris*

Small-flowered buttercup
Ranunculus parviflorus

Small-flowered cranesbill
Geranium pusillum

Small-flowered sticky eyebright
Euphrasia hirtella

Small mallow *Malva pusilla*

Small medick *Medicago minima*

Small melilot *Melilotus indica*

Small nettle *Urtica urens*

Small restharrow *Ononis reclinata*

Small scabious
Scabiosa columbaria

Small teasel *Dipsacus pilosus*

Small toadflax
Chaenorhinum minus

Small white orchid
Habenaria albida
Leucorchis albida
Pseudorchis albida

Small yellow balsam
Impatiens parviflora

Small yellow foxglove
Digitalis lutea

Smith's pepperwort
Lepidium heterophyllum

Smooth cat's ear
Hypochoeris glabra

Smooth hawkbit
Leontodon autumnalis

Smooth hawk's beard
Crepis capillaris

Smooth sowthistle
Sonchus oleraceus

Smooth tare *Vicia tetrasperma*

Snake's head fritillary
Fritillaria meleagris

Snapdragon *Antirrhinum majus*

Sneezewort *Achillea ptarmica*

Snowdon eyebright
Euphrasia rivularis

Snowdrop *Galanthus nivalis*

Soapwort *Saponaria officinalis*

Soft clover *Trifolium striatum*

Soft cranesbill *Geranium molle*

Soft hawk's beard *Crepis mollis*

Soft-leaved rose *Rosa villosa*

Soldier orchid *Orchis militaris*

Solomon's seal
Polygonatum multiflorum

Sorrel *Rumex acetosa*

Sowthistle *Sonchus oleraceus*

Spanish catchfly *Silene otites*

Spanish daffodil
Narcissus hispanicus

Spathulate fleawort
Senecio spathulifolius

Spear-leaved orach
Atriplex prostrata

Spear-leaved willow herb
Epilobium lanceolatum

Spear mint *Mentha spicata*

Spear thistle *Cirsium vulgare*

Spiked rampion
Phyteuma spicatum

Spiked speedwell *Veronica spicata*

Spiked star of Bethlehem
Ornithogalum pyrenaicum

Spiked water milfoil
Myriophyllum spicatum

Spiny saltwort *Salsola kali*

Spotted cat's ear
Hypochoeris maculata

Spotted dead-nettle
Lamium maculatum

Spotted medick *Medicago arabica*

Spotted rockrose
Tuberaria guttata

Spreading bellflower
Campanula patula

Spreading hedge parsley
Torilis arvensis

Spring cinquefoil
Potentilla tabernaemontani

Spring crocus *Crocus purpureus*
Crocus vernus

Spring gentian *Gentiana verna*

Spring snowflake
Leucojam vernum

Spring speedwell *Veronica verna*

Spring squill	*Scilla verna*
Spring vetch	*Vicia lathyroides*
Square-stemmed Saint John's wort	
	Hypericum tetrapterum
Square-stemmed willow herb	
	Epilobium tetragonum
Star-headed clover	
	Trifolium stellata
Star of Bethlehem	
	Ornithogalum umbellatum
Starry saxifrage	*Saxifraga stellaris*
Star thistle	*Centaurea calcitrapa*
Sticky catchfly	*Lychnis viscaria*
Sticky groundsel	*Senecio viscosus*
Stinging nettle	*Urtica dioica*
Stinking bob	
	Geranium robertianum
Stinking chamomile	
	Anthemis cotula
Stinking hawk's beard	
	Crepis foetida
Stinking hellebore	
	Helleborus foetidus
Stinking iris	*Iris foetidissima*
Stinking tutsan	
	Hypericum hircinum
Stone bramble	*Rubus saxatilis*
Strawberry-headed clover	
	Trifolium fragiferum
Streaky cranesbill	
	Geranium versicolor
Striated catchfly	*Silene conica*
Subterranean clover	
	Trifolium subterraneum
Suffocated clover	
	Trifolium suffocatum
Summer lady's tresses	
	Spiranthes aestivalis
Summer snowflake	
	Leucojam aestivum
Sundew	*Drosera rotundifolia*
Sun spurge	*Euphorbia helioscopia*
Swede	*Brassica napus*
Sweet briar	*Rosa rubiginosa*
Sweet chamomile	
	Chamaemelum nobile
Sweet flag	*Acorus calamus*
Sweet lupin	*Lupinus luteus*
Sweet spurge	*Euphorbia dulcis*
Sweet violet	*Viola odorata*
Sweet william	*Dianthus barbatus*
Sweet woodruff	*Galium odoratum*
Tall broomrape	*Orobanche elatior*
	Orobanche major
Tall golden rod	*Solidago altissima*
	Solidago canadensis
Tall melilot	*Melilotus altissima*
Tansy	*Chrysanthemum vulgare*
	Tanacetum vulgare

Teasel	*Dipsacus fullonum*
	Dipsacus sylvestris
Teasel-headed clover	
	Trifolium squamosum
Teesdale violet	*Viola rupestris*
Tenby daffodil	*Narcissus obvallaris*
Thin-runner willow herb	
	Epilobium obscurum
Thistle broomrape	
	Orobanche reticulata
Thorn-apple	*Datura stramonium*
Thorow-wax	
	Bupleurum rotundifolium
Thread-leaved water crowfoot	
	Ranunculus trichophyllus
Threefold lady's tresses	
	Spiranthes romanzoffiana
Thrift	*Armeria maritima*
	Statice armeria
Thyme-leaved speedwell	
	Veronica serpyllifolia
Toothed medick	
	Medicago polymorpha
Toothwort	*Lathraea squamaria*
Tormentil	*Potentilla erecta*
Touch-me-not	
	Impatiens noli-tangere
Trailing rose	*Rosa arvensis*
Traveller's joy	*Clematis vitalba*
Tree lupin	*Lupinus arboreus*
Triangular-stemmed garlic	
	Allium triquetrum
Tricolor pansy	*Viola tricolor*
Trifid bur marigold	
	Bidens tripartita
Tuberous comfrey	
	Symphytum tuberosum
Tuberous meadow thistle	
	Cirsium tuberosum
Tuberous pea	*Lathyrus tuberosus*
Tuberous vetchling	
	Lathyrus tuberosus
Tubular water dropwort	
	Oenanthe fistulosa
Tufted centaury	
	Centaurium capitatum
Tufted loosestrife	
	Lysimachia thyrsiflora
Tufted saxifrage	*Saxifraga cespitosa*
Tufted vetch	*Vicia cracca*
Turk's cap lily	*Lilium martagon*
Turnip	*Brassica rapa*
Tutsan	*Hypericum androsaemum*
Twayblade	*Listera ovata*
Upright cinquefoil	*Potentilla erecta*
Upright clover	*Trifolium strictum*
Upright spurge	*Euphorbia stricta*
Upright hedge parsley	
	Torilis japonica

Upright yellow sorrel

Upright yellow sorrel	
	Oxalis europaea
Valerian	*Valeriana officinalis*
Various-leaved pondweed	
	Potamogeton gramineus
	Potamogeton heterophyllus
Venus's looking glass	
	Legousia hybrida
	Specularia hybrida
Vervain	*Verbena officinalis*
Violet helleborine	
	Epipactis purpurata
	Epipactis sessilifolia
Violet-horned poppy	
	Roemeria hybrida
Violet iris	*Iris spuria*
Viper's grass	*Scorzonera humilis*
Wall bedstraw	*Galium parisiense*
Wall germander	
	Teucrium chamaedrys
Wall pepper	*Sedum acre*
Wall rocket	*Diplotaxis muralis*
	Diplotaxis tenuifolia
Wall speedwell	*Veronica arvensis*
Wall whitlowgrass	*Draba muralis*
Warren crocus	
	Romulea columnae
	Romulea parviflora
Water avens	*Geum rivale*
Water chickweed	
	Myosoton aquaticum
Watercress	*Nasturtium officinale*
Water crowfoot	
	Ranunculus aquatilis
Water dock	
	Rumex hydrolapathum
Water dropwort	
	Oenanthe fistulosa
Water figwort	
	Scrophularia auriculata
Water forget-me-not	
	Myosotis scorpioides
Water germander	
	Teucrium scordium
Water lobelia	*Lobelia dortmanna*
Water mint	*Mentha aquatica*
Water pepper	
	Polygonum hydropiper
Water plantain	
	Alisma plantago-aquatica
Water purslane	*Lythrum portula*
Water soldier	*Stratiotes aloides*
Water violet	*Hottonia palustris*
Wavy bitter cress	
	Cardamine flexuosa
Wavy Saint John's wort	
	Hypericum undulatum
Weld	*Reseda luteola*
Welsh poppy	*Meconopsis cambrica*
Welted thistle	
	Carduus acanthoides

Western bladderwort	
	Utricularia major
	Utricularia neglecta
Wetland dock	
	Rumex hydrolapathum
White bryony	*Bryonia dioica*
White campion	*Silene alba*
White clover	*Trifolium repens*
White comfrey	
	Symphytum orientale
White dead-nettle	*Lamium album*
White flax	*Linum catharticum*
White helleborine	
	Cephalanthera damasonium
White horehound	
	Marrubium vulgare
White melilot	*Melilotus alba*
White mullein	*Verbascum lychnitis*
White mustard	*Sinapis alba*
White ramping fumitory	
	Fumaria capreolata
White rockrose	
	Helianthemum apenninum
White stonecrop	*Sedum album*
White waterlily	*Nymphaea alba*
Whitlowgrass	*Erophila verna*
Whorled solomon's seal	
	Polygonatum verticillatum
Whorled water milfoil	
	Myriophyllum verticillatum
Whortleberry	
	Vaccinium myrtillus
Wild angelica	*Angelica sylvestris*
Wild balsam	
	Impatiens noli-tangere
Wild basil	*Clinopodium vulgare*
Wild cabbage	*Brassica oleracea*
Wild carnation	
	Dianthus caryophyllus
Wild carrot	*Daucus carota*
Wild chamomile	
	Matricaria recutita
Wild clary	*Salvia verbenaca*
Wild daffodil	
	Narcissus pseudonarcissus
Wild leek	*Allium ampeloprasum*
Wild lentil	*Anthyllis cicer*
Wild liquorice	
	Astragalus glycyphyllos
Wild madder	*Rubia peregrina*
Wild mignonette	*Reseda lutea*
Wild onion	*Allium vineale*
Wild parsnip	*Pastinaca sativa*
Wild pea	*Lathyrus sylvestris*
Wild pink	*Dianthus plumarius*
Wild radish	
	Raphanus raphanistrum
Wild sage	*Salvia horminoides*
Wild strawberry	*Fragaria vesca*
Wild thyme	*Thymus serpyllum*

Wild tulip   *Tulipa sylvestris*
Winter aconite   *Eranthis hyemalis*
Winter heliotrope
                          Petasites fragrans
Wood anemone
                          Anemone nemorosa
Wood avens   *Geum urbanum*
Wood bitter vetch   *Vicia orobus*
Wood cranesbill
                          Geranium sylvaticum
Wood forget-me-not
                          Myosotis sylvatica
Wood garlic   *Attium ursinum*
Wood groundsel   *Senecio sylvaticus*
Woodland violet
                          Viola reichenbachiana
Wood sage   *Teucrium scorodonia*
Wood sorrel   *Oxalis acetosella*
Wood speedwell
                          Veronica montana
Wood spurge
                          Euphorbia amygdaloides
Wood stitchwort
                          Stellaria nemorum
Wood vetch   *Vicia sylvatica*
Wood woundwort
                          Stachys sylvatica
Woody nightshade
                          Solanum dulcamara
Woolly thistle   *Cirsium eriophorum*
Wormwood
                          Artemisia absinthium
Yarrow   *Achillea millefolium*
Yellow alpine milk vetch
                          Anthyllis frigidus
Yellow archangel
                          Lamiastrum galeobdolon
Yellow bartsia   *Parentucellia biscosa*
Yellow bird's nest
                          Monotropa hypopitys

Yellow bog saxifrage
                          Saxifraga hirculus
Yellow chamomile
                          Anthemis tinctoria
Yellow corydalis   *Corydalis lutea*
Yellow figwort
                          Scrophularia vernalis
Yellow flag   *Iris pseudacoris*
Yellow forget-me-not
                          Myosotis discolor
Yellow-horned poppy
                          Glaucium flavum
Yellow iris   *Iris pseudacorus*
Yellow loosestrife
                          Lysimachia vulgaris
Yellow lupin   *Lupinus luteus*
Yellow meadow vetchling
                          Lathyrus pratensis
Yellow medick   *Medicago falcata*
Yellow melilot   *Melilotus altissima*
Yellow mountain saxifrage
                          Saxifraga aizoides
Yellow pimpernel
                          Lysimachia nemorum
Yellow rattle   *Rhinanthus minor*
Yellow sorrel   *Oxalis corniculata*
Yellow star of Bethlehem
                          Gagea lutea
Yellow star thistle
                          Centaurea solstitialis
Yellow vetch   *Vicia lutea*
Yellow vetchling   *Lathyrus aphaca*
Yellow waterlily   *Nuphar lutea*
Yellow wort
                          Blackstonia perfoliata
Zigzag clover   *Trifolium medium*

BOTANICAL
NAMES

ALPINES AND ROCKERY PLANTS

Alpines are plants whose natural habitat is the mountainous area above the tree line, but in gardening circles the term includes rock-gardening plants. Very little true alpine gardening is attempted in the English-speaking parts of the world because alpine conditions are rarely encountered naturally and it is very difficult to reproduce them artificially.

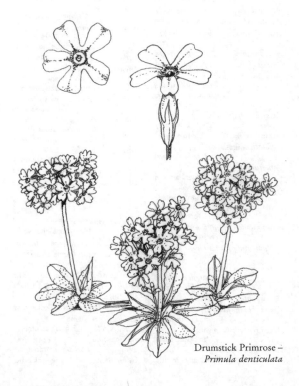

Drumstick Primrose –
Primula denticulata

Abies balsamea hudsoniana

Abies balsamea hudsoniana
    Hudson balsam fir
Abies balsamea nana
    Dwarf balsam fir
Abies cephalonica nana
    Dwarf Grecian fir
Acaena anserinifolia
    Bidgee-widgee
    Bidi-bidi
    Bididy-bid
Acaena buchananii
    New Zealand bur
Acaena inermis
    Blue Mountain bidi-bidi
Acaena microphylla
    Blue Mountain bidi-bidi
    New Zealand bur
    Scarlet bidi-bidi
Acaena novae-zealandiae
    Red bidi-bidi
Acantholimon glumaceum
    Prickly thrift
Acanthus dioscoridis
    Dwarf acanthus
Acer japonicum aconitifolium
    Japanese maple
Acer japonicum aureum
    Golden Japanese maple
Acer palmatum   Japanese maple
Achillea clavennae   Silvery milfoil
Achillea serbica   Milfoil
    Yarrow
Achillea tomentosa   Yellow milfoil
Acinos alpinus   Alpine calamint
Aconitum napellus
    Blue monkshood
    Common monkshood
    Monkshood
Actaea pachypoda
    White baneberry
Actaea rubra   Red baneberry
Acthionema saxatile
    Candy mustard
Adiantum pedatum
    Northern maidenhair fern
Adonis vernalis
    European spring adonis
    Spring adonis
    Yellow adonis
Aethionema grandiflorum
    Persian stonecress
Aethionema rotundifolium
    Candytuft
Aethionema warleyense
    Lebanon candytuft
    Store cress
Ajuga reptans   Bugle
Ajuga reptans atropurpurea
    Purple bugle
Ajuga reptans variegata
    Variegated bugle
Alchemilla alpina
    Alpine lady's mantle

Alchemilla conjuncta
    Alpine lady's mantle
Alchemilla vulgaris   Bear's foot
    Lady's mantle
    Lion's foot
Allium oreophilum
    Flowering onion
Allium moly   Golden garlic
Alyssum argenteum   Italian alyssum
Alyssum montanum
    Mountain alyson
    Mountain alyssum
Alyssum saxatile   Gold dust
    Golden alyssum
    Golden tuft
Anacyclus depressus
    Mount Atlas daisy
Anacyclus pyrethrum   Pellitory
    Spanish pellitory
Anacyclus pyrethrum depressus
    Mount Atlas daisy
Androsace carnea
    Pink rock jasmine
Androsace chamaejasme
    Bastard jasmine
Androsace helvetica
    Swiss rock jasmine
Androsace lactea
    Milkwhite rock jasmine
Androsace occidentalis
    Rock jasmine
    Rock jessamine
Anemone apennina   Anemone
Anemone narcissiflora
    Appleblossom alpine anemone
    Narcissus-flowered anemone
Anemone nemorosa
    Wood anemone
Anemone pulsatilla
    Common pasque flower
    Pasque flower
Anemone rupicola
    Rock windflower
Antennaria alpina   Alpine cat's foot
Antennaria dioica   Cat's foot
    Mountain cat's ear
    Mountain everlasting
    Pussy's toes
Anthyllis montana
    Mountain kidney vetch
Aquilegia alpina   Alpine columbine
Aquilegia atrata   Purple columbime
Aquilegia caerulea
    Rocky Mountain columbine
Aquilegia canadensis   Rock bells
Aquilegia discolor
    Dwarf Spanish columbine
Aquilegia einseleana
    Einsel's columbine
Arabis albida   Rock cress
    Snow-on-the-mountain
Arabis alpina   Alpine rock cress

ALPINES

Chamaecyparis lawsoniana minima

Arabis caucasica	Garden arabis
	White rock
Arabis ferdinandi-coburgii	
	Rock cress
Arabis hirsuta	Hairy rock cress
Arctostaphylos uva-ursi	
	Bearberry
Arenaria balearica	
	Corsican sandwort
Arenaria ciliata	Fringed sandwort
Arenaria grandiflora	
	Large-flowered sandwort
Arenaria leptoclados	
	Slender sandwort
Arenaria montana	
	Alpine sandwort
	Mountain sandwort
Arenaria norvegica	
	Arctic sandwort
Arenaria purpurascens	
	Pink sandwort
Arenaria serpyllifolia	Thyme-
	leaved sandwort
Arenaria stricta	Rock sandwort
Arenaria tetraquetra	Sandwort
Armeria alliacea	Jersey thrift
Armeria caespitosa	Thrift
Armeria juniperifolia	
	Dwarf pink thrift
Armeria maritima	Sea pink
	Thrift
Armeria maritima alba	
	White sea lavender
	White sea pink
Armeria welwitschii	Spanish thrift
Arnebia echioides	Prophet flower
Arnebia pulchra	Prophet flower
Artemisia nitida	
	Narrow-leaved wormwood
Artemisia schmidtiana nana	
	Japanese dwarf wormwood
Asarum europaeum	Asarabacca
Asperula hirta	Pyrenean woodruff
Asperula nitida	Woodruff
Asphodeline lutea	King's spear
	Yellow asphodel
Asplenium ruta-muraria	
	Wall spleenwort
Asplenium scolopendrium	
	Hart's tongue fern
Asplenium tricomanes	
	Maidenhair spleenwort
Aster alpinus	Alpine aster
	Blue alpine daisy
Aster amellus	Italian starwort
	Michaelmas daisy
Aster linosyris	Golden aster
Aubretia deltoidea	Aubretia
Bellendena montana	
	Mountain rocket
Berberis candidula	Barberry

Berteroa incana	Hoary alison
Betula nana	Dwarf birch
Blechnum spicant	Hard fern
Briza media	Quaking grass
Brunnera macrophylla	
	Siberian bugloss
Calamintha alpina	Alpine calamint
Calandrinia menziesii	Red maids
	Rock purslane
Calceolaria biflora	Slipper flower
Calceolaria plantaginea	
	Slipper flower
Calceolaria polyrrhiza	
	Patagonian slipper flower
Caltha palustris	King cup
	Marsh marigold
Campanula carpatica	
	Tussock bellflower
Campanula cochleariifolia	
	Bellflower
	Fairy's thimble
Campanula elatines	
	Starry bellflower
Campanula garganica	
	Gargano bellflower
Campanula latifolia macrantha	
	Giant bellflower
Campanula persicifolia	
	Peach-leaved bellflower
Campanula pulla	Solitary harebell
Campanula pusilla	Fairy's thimble
Campanula tridentata	
	Large bellflower
Cardamine hirsuta	
	Hairy bitter cress
Cardamine pratensis	Bitter cress
	Cuckoo flower
	Lady's smock
	Mayflower
	Meadow cress
Carex firma	Sedge
Carex montana	Mountain sedge
Carlina acanthifolia	
	Acanthus-leaved carline thistle
Carlina acaulis	Alpine thistle
Carlina acaulis simplex	
	Alpine carline thistle
Cedrus libani sargentii	
	Sargent's cedar
Centaurea montana	
	Mountain cornflower
Centaurea montana sulphurea	
	Yellow mountain cornflower
Centaurea rhapontica	
	Giant knapweed
Cerastium alpinum	
	Alpine mouse-eared chickweed
Cerastium tomentosum	
	Mouse-eared chickweed
	Snow-in-summer
Chamaecyparis lawsoniana	
minima	Dwarf lawson's cypress

*Chamaecyparis lawsoniana
minima glauca*

Chamaecyparis lawsoniana minima glauca	Dwarf blue lawson's cypress
Chamaecyparis obtusa	Hinoki cypress
Chamaecyparis obtusa nana	Dwarf hinoki cypress
Chamaecyparis pisifera filifera aurea nana	Dwarf golden sawara cypress
Chamaecyparis pisifera filifera nana	Dwarf sarawa cypress
Chelone obliqua	Turtle head
Chiastophyllum oppositifolium	Lamb's tail
Chionodoxa luciliae	Glory-of-the-snow
Chrysanthemum arcticum	Rockery daisy
Chrysogonum virginianum	Golden star
Cimicifuga racemosa	Black snakeroot
Cirsium acaule	Stemless thistle
Clematis alpina	Alpine clematis
Colchicum bornmuelleri	Autumn crocus
Convallaria majalis	Lily-of-the-valley
Convallaria majalis rosea	Pink lily-of-the-valley
Cornus canadensis	Dogwood
Corrigiola litoralis	Strapwort
Corydalis cava	Hollow fumitory
Corydalis cheilanthifolia	Fumitory
Corydalis lutea	Yellow fumitory
Corydalis solida	Fingered fumitory
Corylopsis pauciflora	Buttercup winter hazel
Cotoneaster horizontalis	Herringbone cotoneaster
Cotula coronopifolia	Brass buttons
Cyclamen hederifolium	Ivyleaf cyclamen
Cyclamen neapolitanum	Ivyleaf cyclamen
Cyclamen purpurascens	Alpine violet / Sowbread
Cymbalaria muralis	Kenilworth ivy
Cypripedium calceolus	Lady's slipper orchid
Cypripedium reginae	Queen's slipper orchid / Showy lady's slipper orchid
Cytisus decumbens	Broom
Cytisus scoparius	Common broom
Daphne cneorum	Garland flower

Daphne mezereum	Mezereon
Dianthus alpinus	Alpine pink
Dianthus caesius	Cheddar pink
Dianthus carthusianorum	Carthusian pink
Dianthus deltoides	Maiden pink
Dianthus gratianopolitanus	Cheddar pink
Dianthus pavonius	veined pink
Dianthus pinifolius	Macedonian white pink
Dianthus plumarius	Common pink / Wild pink
Dianthus superbus	Superb pink
Dicentra exima	Bleeding heart
Dictamnus albus	White burning bush
Dictamnus rubra	Red burning bush
Digitalis grandiflora	Large yellow foxglove
Digitalis purpurea	Common foxglove / Dead men's bells / Fairy thimbles / Lady's gloves / Witch's gloves
Dodecatheon meadia	Shooting star
Draba aizoides	Yellow whitlow grass
Draba sibirica	Siberian whitlow grass
Dryas octopetala	Mountain avens
Echioides longiflora	Prophet flower
Epimedium alpinum	Alpine barrenwort / Barrenwort
Eranthis hyemalis	Winter aconite
Erigeron unifloris	Fleabane
Eriophyllum lanatum	Oregon sunshine
Erodium chamaedryoides	White storksbill
Erodium cicutarium	Common storksbill
Erodium maritimum	Sea storksbill
Erodium reichardii	White storksbill
Eryngium bourgatii	Pyrenean eryngo
Erysimum alpinum	Alpine wallflower
Erythronium dens-canis	Dog's tooth violet
Euphorbia capitulata	Alpine spurge
Euphorbia myrsinites	Blue spurge / Milkwort / Spurge

Iberis sempervirens

Euphorbia palustris	Marsh spurge
Festuca cinerea	Grey fescue
Filipendula vulgaris	Dropwort
Fragaria vesca	Alpine strawberry
	Wild strawberry
Francoa ramosa	Maiden's wreath
Francoa sonchifolia	Bridal wreath
Frankenia laevis	Sea heath
Fritillaria meleagris	
	Snake's head fritillary
Galium odoratum	Sweet woodruff
Genista lydia	Broom
Gentiana acaulis	Stemless gentian
	Trumpet gentian
Gentiana alpina	Alpine gentian
Gentiana andrewsii	Bottle gentian
	Closed gentian
Gentiana asclepiadea	
	Willow gentian
Gentiana autumnalis	
	Pine-barren gentian
Gentiana brachyphylla	
	Short-leaved gentian
Gentiana catesbaei	
	Catesby's gentian
	Sampson's snakeroot
Gentiana clausa	Blind gentian
	Bottle gentian
	Closed gentian
Gentiana cruciata	Cross gentian
Gentiana dinarica	Stemless gentian
Gentiana linearis	Closed gentian
Gentiana lutea	Yellow gentian
Gentiana newberryi	Alpine gentian
Gentiana nipponica	
	Japanese gentian
Gentiana pneumonanthe	
	Calathian violet
	Marsh gentian
Gentiana punctata	Spotted gentian
Gentiana scabrae	Japanese gentian
Gentiana septemfida	
	Crested gentian
	Summer gentian
	Dragon's mouth
	Mendocino gentian
Gentiana sino-ornata	
	Autumn-flowering gentian
Gentiana tergestina	Karst gentian
Gentiana terglouensis	
	Triglav gentian
Gentiana utriculosa	
	Bladder gentian
Gentiana verna	Spring gentian
	Vernal gentian
Gentiana villosa	
	Sampson's snakeroot
Gentianopsis holopetala	
	Sierra gentian
Geranium endressii	
	Western cranesbill

Geranium macrorrhizum	
	Rock cranesbill
Geranium sanguineum	
	Bloody cranesbill
Geranium sanguineum album	
	White bloody cranesbill
Geum montanum	Alpine avens
Geum rivale	Water avens
Gillenia trifoliata	Indian physic
Globularia cordifolia	
	Matted globularia
Globularia trichosantha	
	Globe daisy
Gypsophila repens	
	Alpine gypsophila
	Baby's breath
	Chalk plant
	Creeping gypsophila
Hacquetia epipactis	Hacquetia
Hedysarum obscurum	
	Alpine sainfoin
Helianthemum chamaecistus	
	Common rockrose
Helianthemum nummularium	
	Common rockrose
	Rockrose
Helianthemum oelandicum	
	Alpine rockrose
Helleborus foetidus	
	Stinking hellebore
Helleborus niger	Christmas rose
Hemerocallis minor	
	Grass-leaved day lily
Hepatica nobilis	Liverleaf
Herniaria glabra	
	Glabrous rupturewort
Heuchera sanguinea alba	
	Coral bells
Hieracium aurantiacum	
	Orange hawkweed
Hieracium pilosella	
	Mouse-ear hawkweed
Hieracium villosum	
	Shaggy hawkweed
Horminum pyrenaicum	
	Dragon's mouth
	Pyrenean dragonmouth
Hosta fortunei aurea	
	Gold plantain lily
	Spring plantain lily
Hosta plantaginea	
	Large white plantain lily
Hutchinsia alpina	Chamois cream
Iberis amara	Candytuft
	Rocket candytuft
	Wild candytuft
Iberis gibraltarica	
	Gibraltar candytuft
Iberis saxatilis	Candytuft
Iberis sempervirens	Candytuft
	Edging candytuft
	Evergreen candytuft

Iberis umbellata

Iberis umbellata	Globe candytuft
Iris graminea	Grass-leaved iris
Iris lacustris	American dwarf iris
Iris orientalis	Yellow iris
Iris pseudacorus	Yellow flag
Iris pumila	Dwarf iris
Iris sibirica	Siberian iris
Iris tectorum	Roof iris
Jasminum nudiflorum	Winter jasmine
Jovibarba sobolifera	Hen-and-chickens houseleek
Juniperus chinensis blaauw	Blue Chinese juniper
	Dwarf Chinese juniper
Juniperus communis compressa	Dwarf common juniper
Juniperus communis depressa	Prostrate juniper
Juniperus communis hornibrookii	Creeping common juniper
Juniperus horizontalis glauca	Blue creeping juniper
Juniperus squamata glauca	Blue flaky juniper
Juniperus virginiana nana compacta	Dwarf pencil cedar
Lathyrus vernus	Spring vetchling
Leontopodium alpinum	Edelweiss
	Lion's foot
Leuzea rhapontica	Giant knapweed
Lewisia pygmaea	Pygmy lewisia
Lewisia rediviva	Bitter root
	Bitterwort
Liatris elegans	Snakeroot
Liatris spicata	Blue snakeroot
Linum flavum	Golden flax
Linum flavum compactum	Yellow flax
Linum perenne	Perennial flax
Linum suffruticosum	Shrubby white flax
Lithospermum canescens	Indian paint
	Indian warpaint
	Puccoon
Lithospermum distichum	Mexican puccoon
Lithospermum officinale	Common gromwell
	Gromwell
	Puccoon
Lobularia maritima	Sea alyssum
	Sweet alyssum
Lotus corniculatus pleniforus	Bacon and eggs
	Bird's foot trefoil
Lychnis alpina	Alpine catchfly
	Alpine lychnis
Lychnis viscaria	German catchfly
Lysimachia nummularia	Creeping jenny
Lysimachia punctata	Large yellow loosestrife
Lythrum salicaria	Purple loosestrife
Lythrum virgatum	Slender loosestrife
Maianthemum bifolium	May lily
Malva moschata	Musk mallow
Malva moschata alba	White musk mallow
Meconopsis integrifolia	Lampshade poppy
Melittis melissophyllum	Bastard balm
Mertensia virginica	Virginian cowslip
Meum athamanticum	Baldmoney
	Spignel
Minuartia graminifolia	Apennine sandwort
Minuartia hybrida	Fine-leaved sandwort
Minuartia stricta	Rock sandwort
Minuartia verna	Spring sandwort
	Vernal sandwort
Minuartia viscosa	Sticky sandwort
Moehringia muscosa	Mossy sandwort
Moehringia trinervia	Three-veined sandwort
Muscari botryoides	Grape hyacinth
Myosotis alpestris	Alpine forget-me-not
Myosotis arvensis	Field forget-me-not
Myosotis discolor	Yellow forget-me-not
Myosotis sylvatica	Wood forget-me-not
Narcissus bulbocodium	Hoop-petticoat daffodil
Nepeta × faassenii	Catmint
Oenothera missouriensis	Creeping evening primrose
Omphalodes verna	Blue-eyed mary
Opuntia engelmannii	Prickly-pear cactus
Origanum vulgare compactum	Wild marjoram
Osmunda regalis	Royal fern
Oxalis acetosella	Wood sorrel
Papaver alpinum	Alpine poppy
Papaver burseri	Alpine poppy
Papaver kerneri	Gold alpine poppy
Papaver nudicaule	Iceland poppy
Papaver rhaeticum	Rhaetian poppy

Primula forbesii

Paradisea liliastrum	Saint Bruno's lily
Parietaria diffusa	Wall pellitory
Parietaria judaica	Wall pellitory
Petasites fragrans	Sweet coltsfoot
	Winter heliotrope
Petrocallis pyrenaica	Rock beauty
Petrophila sessilis	
	Prickly conesticks
Petrorhagia saxifraga	Tunic flower
Phlox bifida	Sand phlox
Phlox borealis	Alaskan phlox
Phlox canadensis	
	Wild sweet william
Phlox divaricata	Blue phlox
	Wild sweet william
Phlox douglasii	Alpine phlox
Phlox maculata	Wild sweet william
Phlox nivalis	Trailing phlox
Phlox sibirica	Siberian phlox
Phlox subulata	Moss phlox
	Moss pink
	Mountain phlox
Phyllitis scolopendrium	
	Hart's tongue fern
Phyteuma orbiculare	
	Round-headed rampion
Phyteuma scheuchzeri	
	Horned rampion
Picea abies compressa	
	Dwarf Norway spruce
Picea abies echiniformis	
	Dwarf spruce
Picea abies pumila glauca	
	Blue dwarf spruce
Picea abies pygmaea	
	Pygmy spruce
Picea glauca	Blue spruce
Pimpinella saxifraga	
	Burnet saxifrage
Pinguicula caudata	
	Mexican butterwort
Pinguicula grandiflora	
	Great butterwort
	Large-flowered butterwort
Pinguicula montana	
	Mountain butterwort
Pinguicula vulgaris	Butterwort
	Common butterwort
Pinus aristata	Bristle-cone pine
Pinus montana	Mountain pine
Pinus mugo	Mountain pine
Pinus mugo mugo	
	Swiss mountain pine
Pinus mugo pumila	Dwarf pine
Pinus sibirica pumila	
	Dwarf Siberian pine
Pinus sibirica pumila glauca	
	Dwarf blue Siberian pine
Pinus strobus nana	
	Dwarf white pine

Pinus strobus umbraculifera	
	Dwarf weymouth pine
Pinus sylvestris beuvronensis	
	Dwarf Scots pine
Pinus sylvestris nana	
	Dwarf Scots pine
Platycodon grandiflorus	
	Balloon flower
	White bells
Podophyllum hexandrum	
	Himalayan may apple
Polygonatum commutatum	
	Giant solomon's seal
Polygonatum hookeri	
	Dwarf solomon's seal
Polygonatum × hybridum	
	Solomon's seal
Polygonum bistorta	
superbum	Bistort
	Snakeroot
Polypodium vulgare	
	Common polypody
Potentilla anserina	Goose grass
	Goose tansy
	Silverweed
Potentilla arenaria	Grey cinquefoil
Potentilla argentea	
	Hoary cinquefoil
	Silvery cinquefoil
Potentilla argentea calabra	
	Hoary cinquefoil
Potentilla aurea	Golden cinquefoil
Potentilla cinerea	Grey cinquefoil
Potentilla palustris	
	Marsh cinquefoil
	Marsh five-finger
Potentilla pyrenaica	
	Pyrenean cinquefoil
Potentilla recta warrenii	
	Sulphur cinquefoil
Potentilla rupestris	Prairie tea
	Rock cinquefoil
Potentilla simplex	
	Oldfield cinquefoil
Potentilla tridentata	
	Three-toothed cinquefoil
Potentilla verna	Spring cinquefoil
Primula auricula	Auricula
	Bear's ear
	Dusty miller
Primula denticulata	
	Drumstick primrose
Primula denticulata alba	
	White ball primrose
Primula elatior	Oxlip
Primula farinosa	
	Bird's eye primrose
Primula floribunda	
	Buttercup primrose
Primula florindae	Tibetan cowslip
Primula forbesii	Baby primrose

Primula laurentiana

Primula laurentiana	
	Bird's eye primrose
Primula malacoides	
	Baby primrose
	Fairy primrose
Primula mistassinica	
	Bird's eye primrose
Primula obconica	
	German primrose
	Poison primrose
Primula officinalis	Cowslip
Primula × polyantha	Polyanthus
Primula × pubescens	Auricula
Primula sinensis	Chinese primrose
Primula veris	Cowslip
	Fairy cups
	Herb peter
	Keyflower
	Palsywort
	Saint Peter's wort
Primula vialii	
	Red-hot poker primrose
Primula vulgaris	
	Common primrose
	English primrose
	Primrose
Prunella grandiflora	
	Large self-heal
Prunus tenella	
	Dwarf Russian almond
Pulmonaria angustifolia	
	Blue cowslip
	Lungwort
Pulmonaria angustifolia azurea	
	Narrow-leaved lungwort
Pulmonaria picta	Bethlehem sage
Pulmonaria rubra	Lungwort
Pulmonaria saccharata	
	Bethlehem sage
Pulsatilla alba	
	White pasque flower
Pulsatilla pratensis nigricans	
	Field anemone
Pulsatilla vernalis	Spring anemone
Pulsatilla vulgaris	
	Common pasque flower
	Meadow anemone
	Pasque flower
Pulsatilla vulgaris alba	
	White pasque flower
Pulsatilla vulgaris rubra	
	Red pasque flower
Ramonda myconi	
	Pyrenean primrose
	Pyrenean ramonda
Ramonda pyrenaica	
	Pyrenean primrose
Ranunculus aconitifolius	
	Fair maids of Kent
	White buttercup
Ranunculus acris multiplex	
	Meadow buttercup

Ranunculus alpestris	
	Alpine buttercup
	Mountain buttercup
Ranunculus asiaticus	
	Persian buttercup
	Persian ranunculus
Ranunculus bulbosus	
	Bulbous buttercup
	Bulbous crowfoot
Ranunculus ficaria	
	Lesser celandine
	Pilewort
	Small celandine
Ranunculus glacialis	
	Glacier crowfoot
Ranunculus gramineus	
	Grass-leaved buttercup
Ranunculus montanus	
	Mountain buttercup
Ranunculus repens	Butter daisy
	Creeping buttercup
	Creeping crowfoot
	Yellow gowan
Raoulia eximia	Vegetable sheep
Rhamnus saxitilis	Rock buckthorn
Rhododendron aperantum	
	Burmese dwarf rhododendron
Rhododendron chrysanthum	
	Prostrate rhododendron
Rhododendron ferrugineum	
	Alpenrose
	Alpine rose
Rhododendron hirsutum	
	Hairy alpine rose
Rhododendron leucaspis	
	Tibetan rhododendron
Sagina nodosa	Knotted pearlwort
Sagina pilifera	Pearlwort
Sagina procumbens	
	Common pearlwort
Sagina subulata	
	Awl-leaved pearlwort
	Heath pearlwort
Salix alpina	Mountain willow
Salix hastata wehrhahnii	
	Dwarf willow
Salix reticulata	Reticulate willow
Salvia argentea	Silver sage
Santolina chamaecyparissus	
	Lavender cotton
Saponaria caespitosa	
	Tufted soapwort
Saponaria lutea	Yellow soapwort
Saponaria ocymoides	
	Rock soapwort
	Tumbling ted
Saponaria officinalis	Bouncing bet
	Lather root
Sarothamnus scoparius	
	Common broom
Satureja montana alba	
	Winter savory

Silene caroliniana

Saxifraga aizoides
Yellow mountain saxifrage
Saxifraga aizoon major
Live-long saxifrage
Saxifraga altissima
Host's saxifrage
Saxifraga × arendsii
Mossy saxifrage
Saxifraga burserana
One-flowered cushion saxifrage
Saxifraga caesia   Blue saxifrage
Saxifraga cespitosa   Tufted saxifrage
Saxifraga cotyledon
Pyramidal saxifrage
Saxifraga granulata
Fair maids of France
Meadow saxifrage
Saxifraga hirsuta   Kidney saxifrage
Saxifraga hostii   Host's saxifrage
Saxifraga hypnoides
Dovedale moss
Mossy rockfoil
Mossy saxifrage
Saxifraga longifolia
Pyrenean saxifrage
Saxifraga moschata   Musk saxifrage
Saxifraga muscoides
Musky saxifrage
Saxifraga oppositifolia
Purple mountain saxifrage
Purple saxifrage
Saxifraga paniculata major
Live-long saxifrage
Saxifraga rivularis
Alpine brook saxifrage
Saxifraga rosacea   Irish saxifrage
Saxifraga stellata   Starry saxifrage
Saxifraga stolonifera
Beefsteak geranium
Creeping sailor
Mother-of-thousands
Strawberry begonia
Strawberry geranium
Saxifraga tennesseensis
Golden-eye saxifrage
Saxifraga umbrosa   London pride
Nancy pretty
Saxifraga × urbium
Garden London pride
None-so-pretty
Saint Patrick's cabbage
Scilla bifolia   Two-leaved scilla
Scilla hispanica   Spanish bluebell
Scutellaria alpina   Alpine scullcap
Scutellaria orientalis pinnatifida   Yellow scullcap
Sedum acre   Biting stonecrop
Golden carpet
Golden moss
Wallpepper
Yellow stonecrop
Sedum adolphi   Golden sedum

Sedum alba   Wallpepper
Whitecrop
White stonecrop
Sedum album   White stonecrop
Sedum anacampseros
Reddish stonecrop
Sedum anglicum English stonecrop
Sedum dasyphyllum suendermannii
Thick-leaved stonecrop
Sedum forsteranum
Rock stonecrop
Sedum morganianum   Beaver's tail
Burro's tail
Donkey's tail
Horse's tail
Lamb's tail
Sedum multiceps   Baby joshua tree
Dwarf joshua tree
Joshua tree
Little joshua tree
Miniature joshua tree
Sedum pachyphyllum
Jellybean plant
Jellybeans
Many fingers
Sedum reflexum
Reflexed stonecrop
Rock stonecrop
Sedum roseum   Roseroot sedum
Sedum × rubrotinctum
Christmas cheer
Pork and beans
Sedum sieboldii   October daphne
October plant
Siebold's stonecrop
Sedum spectabile   Ice plant
Sedum telephium   Livelong
Midsummer men
Orpine
Sedum live-forever
Sedum treleasii   Silver stonecrop
Sedum villosum   Hairy stonecrop
Sempervivum arachnoideum
Cobweb houseleek
Spider's web houseleek
Sempervivum calcareum
Limestone houseleek
Sempervivum montanum
Mountain houseleek
Sempervivum soboliferum
Hen-and-chickens houseleek
Sempervivum tectorum
Common houseleek
Hen-and-chickens houseleek
Houseleek
Old-man-and-woman
Sempervivum tectorum calcareum   Limestone houseleek
Silene acaulis   Cushion pink
Moss campion
Silene alpestris   Alpine catchfly
Silene caroliniana   Wild pink

Sea campion

Silene maritima	Sea campion
Silene pendula	Nodding catchfly
Silene uniflora	Sea campion
Sisyrinchium angustifolium	
	Blue-eyed grass
	Satin flower
Soldanella alpina	Alpine snowbell
Soldanella montana	
	Mountain soldanella
	Mountain tassel
Solidago virgaurea	Golden rod
Stachys byzantina	Lamb's ears
Stipa capillata	Feather grass
Tanacetum densum amani	
	Prince of Wales feathers
Taxus baccata	Common yew
	Yew
Taxus baccata compacta	
	Dwarf yew
Taxus baccata nana	Dwarf yew
Taxus cuspidata minima	
	Dwarf Japanese yew
Thalictrum aquilegifolium	
	Great meadow rue
Thlaspi alliaceum	
	Garlic pennycress
Thlaspi alpestre	Alpine pennycress
Thlaspi arvense	Fanweed
	Field pennycress
	French weed
	Mithridate mustard
	Pennycress
	Stinkweed
Thlaspi perfoliatum	
	Perfoliate pennycress
Thymus articus coccineus	
	Wild thyme
Thymus citriodorus	Lemon thyme
Thymus coccineus	Wild thyme
Thymus herba-barona	
	Caraway thyme
Thymus praecox pseudolan guinosus	Hairy thyme
Thymus serpyllum	
	Breckland thyme
	Creeping thyme
	Lemon thyme
	Wild thyme
Thymus vulgaris	Common thyme
	Garden thyme
Tiarella cordifolia	Foam flower
Tricyrtis hirta	Japanese toadlily
Trollius pumilus	Globe flower
Tsuga canadensis jeddeloh	
	Dwarf eastern hemlock
Tsuga canadensis nana	
	Dwarf hemlock
Valeriana montana	
	Mountain valerian
Valeriana supina	Valerian
Veratrum album	
	White false helleborine

Veratrum nigrum	
	Black false helleborine
Veronica alpina	Alpine speedwell
	Alpine veronica
Veronica americana	
	American brooklime
Veronica austriaca teucrium	
	Large speedwell
Veronica beccabunga	
	European brooklime
Veronica chamaedrys	Angel's eye
	Bird's eye
	Germander speedwell
Veronica filiformis	Speedwell
Veronica fruticulosa	
	Shrubby speedwell
	Shrubby-stalked speedwell
Veronica longifolia	
	Long-leaved speedwell
Veronica officinalis	
	Common speedwell
	Gypsyweed
Veronica serpyllifolia	
	Thyme-leaved speedwell
Veronica spicata incana	
	Silver speedwell
	Silver spiked speedwell
Vinca minor	Common periwinkle
	Lesser periwinkle
	Myrtle
	Running myrtle
Viola adunca	Hookspur violet
	Western dog violet
Viola beckwithii	Great basin violet
Viola biflora	Yellow wood violet
Viola blanda	Sweet white violet
Viola brittoniana	Coast violet
Viola canadensis	Canadian violet
	Tall white violet
Viola canina	Dog violet
Viola conspersa	
	American dog violet
Viola cornuta	Horned pansy
	Horned violet
Viola × emarginata	
	Triangle-leaved violet
Viola fimbriatula	
	Northern downy violet
Viola flettii	Olympic violet
	Rock violet
Viola glabella	Stream violet
Viola gracilis	Olympian violet
Viola hastata	Halberd-leaved violet
Viola hederacea	Australian violet
	Ivy-leaved violet
	Trailing violet
Viola labradorica	Labrador violet
Viola lanceolata	
	Eastern water violet
	Lance-leaved violet
Viola langsdorfii	Alaska violet
Viola lobata	Yellow wood violet

Viola macloskeyi	Western sweet white violet
Viola missouriensis	Missouri violet
Viola nephrophylla	Northern bog violet
Viola nuttallii	Yellow prairie violet
Viola ocellata	Two-eyed violet
Viola odorata	English violet
	Florist's violet
	Garden violet
	Sweet violet
Viola orbiculata	Western round-leaved violet
Viola palmata	Early blue violet
	Wild okra
Viola palustris	Alpine marsh violet
	Marsh violet
Viola pedata	Bird's foot violet
	Crowfoot violet
	Pansy violet
Viola pedatifida	Larkspur violet
	Purple prairie violet
Viola pedunculata	California golden violet
	Californian wild pansy
	Johnny-jump-up
Viola priceana	Confederate violet
Viola primulifolia	Primrose-leaved violet
Viola pubescens	Downy yellow violet
Viola rafinesquii	Field pansy
Viola renifolia	Kidney-leaved violet
	Northern white violet
Viola riviniana	Dog violet
	Wood violet
Viola rostrata	Long-spurred violet

Viola rotundifolia	Early yellow violet
	Round-leaved yellow violet
Viola sagittata	Arrow-leaved violet
Viola selkirkii	Great spurred violet
Viola sempervirens	Evergreen violet
	Redwood violet
Viola septemloba	Southern coast violet
Viola septentrionalis	Northern blue violet
Viola sororia	Woolly blue violet
Viola striata	Cream violet
	Pale violet
	Striped violet
Viola tricolor	European wild pansy
	Field pansy
	Johnny-jump-up
	Miniature pansy
Viola trinervata	Sagebrush violet
Viola viarum	Plains violet
Viola × wittrockiana	Garden pansy
	Heartsease
	Ladies' delight
	Pansy
	Stepmother's flower
Waldsteinia geoides	Barren strawberry
Yucca filamentosa	Thread agave
Yucca gloriosa	Palm lily
	Spanish dagger
Zauschneria californica	Californian fuchsia
	Humming-bird's trumpet

AQUATICS

This section applies to plants living usually in fresh water, either rooted in soil or free-floating, also to plants living in bogs, swamps, and around the edges of ponds and lakes.

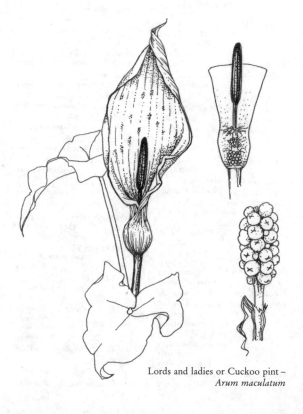

Lords and ladies or Cuckoo pint –
Arum maculatum

BOTANICAL NAMES

Acorus calamus

Acorus calamus	Sweet sedge
Aglaonema simplex	Malayan sword
Alisma plantago-aquatica	
	Mad-dog weed
	Water plantain
Anacharis canadensis	Ditch moss
	Water thyme
	Waterweed
Anacharis densa	
	Brazilian waterweed
Apium inundatum	
	Floating marshwort
Apium nodiflorum	
	Fool's watercress
Aponogeton distachyus	
	Cape asparagus
	Cape pondweed
	Water hawthorn
Aponogeton fenestralis	Laceleaf
	Latticeleaf
	Madagascar lace plant
	Water yam
Aponogeton madagascariensis	
	Laceleaf
	Latticeleaf
	Madagascar lace plant
	Water yam
Azolla caroliniana	Fairy moss
	Mosquito fern
	Mosquito plant
	Water fern
Bacopa monnieri	Baby tears
Baldellia ranunculoides	
	Lesser water plantain
Bidens cernua	
	Nodding bur marigold
Brasenia schreberi	Water shield
Cabomba caroliniana	Fanwort
	Fish grass
	Washington grass
Calla palustris	Bog arum
	Water arum
Callitriche hermaphroditum	
	Autumnal water starwort
Callitriche obtusangula	
	Blunt-fruited water starwort
Callitriche stagnalis	
	Water starwort
Caltha palustris	Kingcup
	Marsh marigold
	Molly blobs
	Water blobs
	Water cowslip
Castalia flava	Yellow water lily
Castalia odorata	Fragrant water lily
	Pond lily
	White water lily
Ceratophyllum demersum	
	American hornwort
	Hornwort
	Rigid hornwort
Ceratophyllum submersum	
	Soft hornwort

Ceratopteris pteridoides	
	Floating fern
Ceratopteris richardii	
	Triangular water fern
Ceratopteris thalictroides	
	Water fern
	Water sprite
Cicuta virosa	Water hemlock
Cryptocoryne affinis	
	Water trumpet
Cyperus alternifolius	
	Umbrella palm
	Umbrella plant
	Umbrella sedge
Cyperus esculentus	
	Nut grass
	Nut sedge
	Yellow nut grass
	Yellow nut sedge
Cyperus isocladus	Dwarf papyrus
	Miniature papyrus
Cyperus papyrus	Biblical bulrush
	Bulrush
	Paper plant
	Papyrus
Echinodorus cordifolius	
	Texas mud-baby
Echinodorus intermedius	
	Pigmy chainsword plant
Echinodorus magdalenensis	
	Dwarf amazon sword plant
Echinodorus martii	
	Pigmy chainsword plant
Echinodorus paniculatus	
	Amazon sword plant
Echinodorus radicans	
	Texas mud-baby
Echinodorus tenellus	
	Amazon sword plant
Eichhornia azurea	
	Peacock hyacinth
Eichhornia crassipes	
	Water hyacinth
Elatine hexandra	Waterwort
Eleocharis acicularis	Hair grass
	Least spike rush
	Slender spike rush
Eleocharis dulcis	
	Chinese water chestnut
	Ma-tai
Elodea callitrichoides	
	Greater water thyme
Elodea canadensis	
	Canadian pondweed
	Ditch moss
	Water thyme
	Waterweed
Elodea densa	Brazilian waterweed
Elodea nuttallii	
	Nuttall's water thyme
Eriocaulon aquaticum	Pipewort

Eupatorium maculatum
Joe-pye weed
Smokeweed

Eupatorium perfoliatum
Common boneset
Thoroughwort

Euryale ferox
Gorgon
Prickly water lily

Fontinalis antipyretica
Fountain moss
Spring moss
Water moss
Willow moss

Geum rivale
Nodding avens
Water avens

Groenlandia densa
Opposite-leaved pondweed

Heteranthera dubia
Water star grass

Heteranthera reniformis
Kidney mud plantain

Hottonia palustris   Water violet

Hydrocera angustifolia
Water balsam

Hydrocharis morsus ranae
Frog-bit

Hydrocleys nymphoides
Water poppy

Hygrophila difformis
Water wistaria

Hypericum elodes
Marsh St. John's wort

Ipomoea aquatica
Water convolvulus

Iris pseudacorus   Flag iris
Water flag
Yellow flag iris

Isnardia palustris   Water purslane

Isoetes echinospora
Spiny-spored quillwort

Isoetes engelmannii
Engelmann's quillwort

Juncus effusus   Japanese mat rush
Soft rush

Juncus effusus spiralis
Corkscrew rush
Spiral rush

Juncus lesueurii   Salt rush

Justicia americana
American water willow
Water willow

Lagerosiphon major
Curly water thyme

Lemna gibba   Fat duckweed

Lemna miniscula   Lesser duckweed

Lemna minor   Common duckweed
Duckweed
Lesser duckweed

Lemna trisulca   Ivy duckweed
Star duckweed

Lobelia dortmanna   Water lobelia

Ludwigia alternifolia   Rattlebox
Seedbox

Ludwigia palustris   Water purslane

Luronium natans
Floating water plantain

Lysichiton americanum   Bog arum
Skunk cabbage

Lysimachia clethroides
Gooseneck lysimachia

Lysimachia nummularia
Creeping charlie
Creeping jenny
Moneywort

Lysimachia punctata
Garden lysimachia

Lysimachia thyrsiflora
Tufted lysimachia

Lysimachia vulgaris
Garden lysimachia

Lythrum salicaria
Purple loosestrife
Spiked lythrum

Marsilea quadrifolia
European water clover

Mentha aquatica   Water mint

Menyanthes trifoliata   Bog bean
Brook bean
Marsh clover
Marsh trefoil
Water shamrock

Montia fontana   Water blinks

Myosotis aquaticum
Water chickweed

Myosotis scorpioides
Water forget-me-not

Myosotis secunda
Marsh forget-me-not

Myriophyllum aquaticum
Parrot's feather
Water feather

Myriophyllum hippuroides
Red water milfoil
Western milfoil

Myriophyllum spicatum
Spiked water milfoil

Myriophyllum verticillatum
Myriad leaf
Whorled water milfoil

Najas flexilis   Flexible naiad

Najas marina   Greater naiad

Narcissus jonquilla   Wild jonquil

Nelumbo lutea   American lotus
Pond nuts
Water chinquapin
Wonkapin
Yanquapin
Yellow nelumbo

Nelumbo nucifera   East Indian lotus
Sacred lotus

Nelumbo pentapetala

Nelumbo pentapetala
American lotus
Pond nuts
Water chinquapin
Wonkapin
Yanquapin
Yellow nelumbo

Nelumbo speciosa East Indian lotus
Sacred lotus

Nuphar advena
American spatterdock
Common spatterdock
Spatterdock

Nuphar luteum Brandy bottle
Yellow water lily

Nymphaea alba
European white water lily
Platterdock
White water lily

Nymphaea caerulea
Blue Egyptian lotus
Blue lotus
Egyptian lotus

Nymphaea capensis Blue water lily
Cape blue water lily

Nymphaea flava Yellow water lily

Nymphaea gigantea
Australian water lily

Nymphaea lotus Egyptian lotus
Egyptian water lily
Lotus
White Egyptian lotus

Nymphaea mexicana
Yellow water lily

Nymphaea odorata
Fragrant water lily
Pond lily
Sweet water lily
White water lily

Nymphaea pygmaea
Pygmy water lily

Nymphaea rubra
Indian red water lily

Nymphaea stellata Blue lotus
Indian blue lotus
Nile blue lotus

Nymphaea tetragona
Pygmy water lily

Nymphaea tuberosa
Magnolia water lily
Tuberous water lily

Nymphaea venusta
European white water lily
Platterdock

Oenanthe fistulosa
Common water dropwort
Water dropwort
Water lovage

Oenanthe fluviatilis
River water dropwort

Oenanthe lachenalis
Parsley water dropwort

Pistia stratiotes Shellflower
Water lettuce

Polygonium hydropiper
Smartweed
Water pepper

Pontederia cordata Pickerel weed

Potamogeton alpinus
Red pondweed
Rusty pondweed

Potamogeton coloratus
Fen pondweed

Potamogeton compressus
Grass-wrack pondweed

Potamogeton crispus
Curled pondweed

Potamogeton densus Frog's lettuce

Potamogeton epihydrus
American pondweed

Potamogeton filiformis
Slender-leaved pondweed

Potamogeton friesii
Flat-stalked pondweed

Potamogeton gramineus
Various-leaved pondweed

Potamogeton lucens
Shining pondweed

Potamogeton nathans
Floating pondweed

Potamogeton nodosus
Loddon pondweed

Potamogeton obtusifolius
Grassy pondweed

Potamogeton pectinatus
Fennel pondweed

Potamogeton perfoliatus
Perfoliate pondweed

Potamogeton polygonifolius
Bog pondweed

Potamogeton pusillus
Small pondweed

Potamogeton trichoides
Hair-like pondweed

Ranunculus aquatalis
Common water crowfoot
Water buttercup
Water crowfoot

Ranunculus fluitans
River crowfoot
River water crowfoot

Riccia fluitans Crystalwort

Rumex hydrolapathan
Great water dock
Water dock

Rumex maritimus
Golden water dock

Rumex palustris Marsh dock

Ruppia cirrhosa
Spider tassel pondweed

Ruppia maritima
Beaked tassel pondweed

Sagittaria cuneata Wapato

Sagittaria latifolia Duck potato
Wapato

Zostera noltii

Sagittaria montevidensis
Giant arrowhead
Sagittaria sagittifolia
Common arrowhead
Old world arrowhead
Swamp potato
Swan potato
Water archer
Sagittaria sagittifolia
leucopetala Japanese arrowhead
Sagittaria subulata
Awl-leaf arrowhead
Salvinia auriculata Floating fern
Salvinia rotundifolia
Floating moss
Saururus cernuus
American swamp lily
Swamp lily
Water dragon
Sparganium angustifolium
Floating bur reed
Sparganium emersum
Unbranched bur reed
Sparganium erectum
Branched bur reed
Sparganium minimum
Small bur reed
Sparganium ramosum Bur reed
Common bur reed
Spirodela polyrhiza Duckweed
Great duckweed
Greater duckweed
Water flaxseed
Stratiotes aloides Water aloe
Water soldier
Subularia aquatica Awlwort
Trapa natans Jesuit's nut
Water chestnut
Typha angustifolia Lesser bulrush
Typha latifolia Bulrush reedmace
Typha minima Least bulrush
Vallisneria americana
Water celery
Wild celery

Vallisneria spiralis Eel grass
Italian-type eel grass
Tape grass
Veronica anagallis
Water speedwell
Veronica anagallis-aquatica
Blue water speedwell
Water speedwell
Victoria amazonica
Amazon water lily
Amazon water platter
Queen Victoria water lily
Royal water lily
Victoria water lily
Water maize
Victoria cruziana
Santa Cruz water lily
Santa Cruz water platter
Victoria regia Amazon water lily
Amazon water platter
Queen Victoria water lily
Royal water lily
Victoria water lily
Water maize
Victoria trickeri
Santa Cruz water lily
Santa Crus water platter
Wolffia columbiana
Common wolffia
Wolffia
Wolffiella floridana Bogmat
Mud-midget
Zannichellia palustris
Horned pondweed
Zizania aquatica
Canadian wild rice
Water oats
Wild rice
Zostera angustifolia Eel grass
Narrow-leaved ee -grass
Narrow-leaved grass wrack
Tape grass
Zostera marina Common eel grass
Common grass wrack
Zostera noltii Dwarf eel grass
Dwarf grass wrack

BULBS

Horticulturally the term 'bulb' includes bulbs, corms, tubers, and rhizomes, but here a few stoloniferous subjects have been included (some lilies, for instance) where confusion exists in the minds of some amateur gardeners. Orchids are listed separately elsewhere in the book.

Sieber's crocus –
Crocus sieberi

Achimenes longiflora
    Hot-water plant

Agapanthus africanus   African lily
    Blue agapanthus
    Blue lily
    Lily-of-the-Nile

Agapanthus umbellatus
    African lily
    Blue agapanthus
    Lily-of-the-Nile

Allium amabile
    Chinese ornamental onion

Allium ampeloprasum   Wild leek

Allium angulosum   Mouse garlic

Allium bakeri   Rakkyo

Allium canadense   Meadow leek
    Rose leek
    Wild garlic
    Wild onion

Allium carinatum   Keeled garlic

Allium cepa   Ever-ready onion
    Multiplier onion
    Potato onion
    Shallot

Allium cernuum
    American ornamental onion
    Lady's leek
    Nodding onion
    Wild onion

Allium chinense   Rakkyo

Allium christophii   Stars-of-Persia

Allium cuthbertii   Striped garlic

Allium cyaneum   Blue onion
    Purple onion

Allium fistulosum   Ciboule
    Japanese bunching onion
    Spanish onion
    Two-bladed onion
    Welsh onion

Allium flavum   Yellow onion

Allium giganteum
    Giant ornamental onion

Allium haematochiton
    Red-skinned onion

Allium moly   Golden garlic
    Lily leek
    Yellow-star ornamental onion

Allium neapolitanum
    Daffodil garlic
    Florist's allium
    Flowering onion

Allium oleraceum   Field garlic

Allium paradoxum
    Few-flowered leek

Allium ramosum
    Fragrant-flowered garlic

Allium roseum   Rosey garlic

Allium sativum   Garlic
    Rocambole
    Serpent garlic

Allium schoenoprasum   Chive
    Cive
    Schnittlauch

Allium scorodoprasum   Giant garlic
    Rocambole
    Sand leek
    Spanish garlic

Allium senescens   German garlic

Allium sikkimense
    Pendant ornamental onion

Allium sphaerocephalum
    Round-headed garlic
    Round-headed leek

Allium stellatum   Prairie onion

Allium tanguticum
    Lavender globe lily

Allium tricoccum   Ramp
    Wild leek

Allium triquetum
    Triangular-stemmed garlic
    Triquetros leek

Allium tuberosum   Chinese chive
    Garlic chive
    Oriental garlic

Allium ursinum   Bear's garlic
    Buckrams
    Gipsy onion
    Hog's garlic
    Ramsons
    Ramsons wood garlic
    Wild garlic

Allium validum   Swamp onion

Allium vineale   Crow garlic
    Field garlic
    Stag's garlic

Alstroemeria aurantiaca
    Lily-of-the-Incas
    Peruvian lily

Alstroemeria haemantha
    Herb lily

*Alstroemeria leontochir
ovallei*   Lion's paw

Amaryllis aulica   Lily-of-the-palace

Amaryllis aurea   Golden African lily
    Golden hurricane lily
    Golden spider lily

Amaryllis belladonna
    Belladonna lily
    Cape belladonna
    Jersey lily
    March lily

Amaryllis hallii   Magic lily
    Resurrection lily

Amaryllis × johnsonii
    Saint Joseph's lily

Amaryllis phaedranassa   Queen lily

Amaryllis radiata   Red spider lily
    Spider lily

Amaryllis reticulata   Lacework lily
    Meshed lily

Amphisiphon stylosa   Cape hyacinth

Anemone appennina   Blue anemone
    Windflower

Anemone blanda
    Greek windflower
    Windflower

Anemone coronaria
De caen anemone
Poppy anemone
Saint Brigid anemone
Windflower

Anemone cylindrica
Long-headed anemone
Thimbleweed

Anemone fulgens   Scarlet anemone
Scarlet windflower

Anemone hupehensis
Japanese anemone

Anemone nemorosa
European wood anemone
Wood anemone

Anemone nuttalliana
Hartshorn plant
Lion's beard
Pasque flower
Prairie smoke
Wild crocus

Anemone patens   Pasque flower

Anemone pavonina   Windflower

Anemone pulsatilla   Pasque flower

Anemone riparia   Thimbleweed

Anemone sylvestris
Snowdrop windflower

Anemone virginiana   Thimbleweed

Aponogeton distachyos
Cape pondweed
Water hawthorn

Arisaema dracontium   Dragonroot
Green dragon

Arisaema speciosum   Cobra lily

Arisaema triphyllum   Dragonroot
Indian turnip
Jack-in-the-pulpit

Arisarum proboscideum
Mouse plant

Arum italicum   Italian arum

Arum maculatum   Adam-and-eve
Cuckoo pint
Lords and ladies

Arum palaestinum   Black calla
Solomon's lily

Arum picton   Black calla

Babiana rubrocyanea
Baboon flower
Blue-and-red baboon root
Winecups

Begonia albo-coccinea
Elephant's ear begonia

Begonia boweri   Eyelash begonia
Miniature begonia

Begonia × crestabruchii
Lettuce-leaf begonia

Begonia davisii   Davis begonia

Begonia discolor   Hardy begonia

Begonia dregei   Grape-leaf begonia
Maple-leaf begonia

Begonia × erythrophylla
Beefsteak begonia
Kidney begonia

Begonia francisii
Nasturtium-leaf begonia

Begonia goegoensis
Fire-king begonia

Begonia gracilis   Hollyhock begonia

Begonia grandis   Hardy begonia

Begonia heracleifolia   Star begonia
Star-leaf begonia

Begonia hydrocotylifolia
Miniature pond-lily begonia
Pennywort begonia

Begonia limmingheiana
Shrimp begonia

Begonia martiana
Hollyhock begonia

Begonia masoniana
Iron-cross begonia

Begonia nelumbiifolia
Lily-pad begonia
Pond-lily begonia

Begonia parvifolia
Grape-leaf begonia
Maple-leaf begonia

Begonia rex   King begonia
Painted-leaf begonia

Begonia × speculata
Grape-leaf begonia

Begonia × tuberhybrida
Hybrid tuberous begonia
Pendulous begonia

Begonia versicolor
Fairy-carpet begonia

Begonia weltoniensis
Grapevine begonia
Maple-leaf begonia

Belamcanda chinensis
Blackberry lily

Bellevalia romana   Roman hyacinth

Brimeura ida-maia
Californian firecracker

Brodiaea coronaria
Harvest brodiaea

Brodiaea elegans
Harvest brodiaea

Brodiaea uniflora   Spring starflower

Brunsvigia josephinae
Candelabra flower
Josephine's lily

Brunsvigia radulosa
Pink candelabra

Caladium bicolor   Heart-of-Jesus

Caladium × hortulanum
Fancy-leaved caladium

Calochortus albus   Fairy lantern
Globe lily

Calochortus amabilis
Golden fairy lantern
Golden globe tulip

Calochortus amoenus
Fairy lantern
Purple globe tulip

Calochortus coeruleus

Calochortus coeruleus
Beavertail grass
Cat's ear

Calochortus concolor
Golden-bowl mariposa

Calochortus kennedyi
Desert mariposa

Calochortus luteus
Yellow mariposa

Calochortus macrocarpus
Green-banded mariposa

Calochortus maweanus   Pussy ears

Calochortus nudus   Sierra star tulip

Calochortus nuttallii
Mariposa lily
Sego lily

Calochortus pulchellus
Yellow fairy lantern

Calochortus splendens
Lilac mariposa

Calochortus tolmiei   Pussy ears

Calochortus uniflorus
Pink star tulip

Calochortus venustus
White mariposa

Calochortus vestae
Goddess mariposa

Calochortus weedii
Weed's mariposa

Camassia quamash   Camass
Camosh
Common camass
Quamash

Camassia scilloides   Eastern camass
Indigo squill
Meadow hyacinth
Wild hyacinth

Canna edulis   Achira
Edible canna
Queensland arrowroot
Tous-les-mois

Canna × generalis
Common garden canna

Canna indica   Indian shot

Canna × orchiodes
Orchid-flowered canna

Cardiocrinum cathayanum
Spotted Chinese lily

Cardiocrinum cordatum
Japanese lily

Cardiocrinum giganteum
Easter lily
Giant Himalayan lily
Giant lily

Chamaescilla corymbosa
Blue star

Chionodoxa gigantea
Glory-of-the-snow

Chlidanthus fragrans
Perfumed fairy lily
Peruvian daffodil

Cleome spinosa   Giant spider plant

Clivia mineata   Bush lily
Fire lily

Colchicum × agrippinum
Meadow saffron

Colchicum autumnale
Autumn crocus
Fall crocus
Meadow saffron
Mysteria
Naked ladies
Wonder bulb

Colocasia esculenta   Dasheen
Taro

Convallaria majalis
Lily-of-the-valley

Corydalis aurea   Spring fumitory

Corydalis bulbosa   Fumewort

Corydalis sempervirens
Rock harlequin
Roman wormwood

Crinum americanum
Southern swamp crinum
Swamp lily

Crinum asiaticum
Asiatic poison bulb

Crinum lugardiae   Veldt lily

Crinum × powellii   Cape lily
Elephant lily
Indian elephant flower

Crocosmia × crocosmiiflora
Falling stars
Montbretia

Crocus angustifolius   Cloth-of-gold

Crocus biflorus   Scotch crocus

Crocus byzantinus
Iris-flowered crocus

Crocus flavus   Dutch yellow crocus

Crocus iridiflorus
Iris-flowered crocus

Crocus korolkowii
Celandine crocus

Crocus sativus   Saffron crocus

Crocus susianus   Cloth-of-gold

Crocus vernus   Dutch crocus

Curtonus paniculatus   Natal iris

Cyclamen hederifolium
Alpine violet
Baby cyclamen

Cyclamen persicum
Florist's cyclamen
Persian violet

Cyrtanthus mackennii   Fire lily
Ifafa lily

Cyrtanthus obliquus   Kynassa lily

Cyrtanthus purpureus   George lily
Scarborough lily

Dahlia imperialis   Bell tree dahlia
Candelabra dahlia
Tree dahlia

Dahlia merckii   Bedding dahlia

Dichelostemma ida-maia
Californian firecracker

Dierama pendulum
Angel's fishing rod
Grassy bell

Dierama pulcherrimum
Wandflower

Doryanthes excelsa
Australian giant lily

Dracunculus vulgaris   Black arum
Dragon arum

Endymion campanulata
Spanish bluebell

Endymion hispanicus
Bell-flowered squill
Spanish bluebell
Spanish jacinth

Endymion italicus   Italian squill

Endymion non-scriptus
English bluebell
Harebell

Endymion nutans   English bluebell

Eranthis hyemalis   Winter aconite

Eremurus robustus   Desert candle
Foxtail lily

Erythronium albidum
Blonde lilian
White dog's tooth violet

Erythronium americanum
Adder's tongue
Amberbell
Serpent's tongue
Trout lily
Yellow adder's tongue
Yellow snowdrop

Erythronium californicum
Fawn lily

Erythronium dens-canis
Dog's tooth violet

Erythronium giganteum
Avalanche lily

Erythronium grandiflorum
Avalanche lily

Erythronium montatum
Avalanche lily

Erythronium obtusatum
Avalanche lily

Erythronium revolutum
American trout lily

Eucharis amazonica   Amazon lily

Eucharis grandiflora   Amazon lily
Eucharist lily
Lily-of-the-amazon
Madonna lily

Eucomis autumnalis
Pineapple flower

Eucomis bicolor   Pineapple flower

Eucomis comosa   Pineapple flower

Eucomis pallidiflora
Giant pineapple flower
Pineapple flower

Eucomis undulata
Pineapple flower

Eucomis zambesiaca
Pineapple flower

Freesia hybrida   Outdoor freesia

Fritillaria biflora   Mission bells

Fritillaria camschatcensis
Black fritillary
Black lily
Black sarana
Kamchatka lily

Fritillaria camtschatcensis
Black fritillary
Black lily
Black sarana
Kamchatka lily

Fritillaria imperialis   Cr
imperial fritillary

Fritillaria lanceolata   Checker lily
Narrow-leaved fritillary

Fritillaria liliacea   White fritillary

Fritillaria meleagris
Checkered daffodil
Checkered lily
Guinea-hen tulip
Snake's head fritillary

Fritillaria pluriflora   Adobe lily
Pink fritillary

Fritillaria pudica   Yellow fritillary

Fritillaria pyrenaica
Pyrenean fritillary

Fritillaria recurva   Scarlet fritillary

Fritillaria uva-vulpis   Fox's grape

Galanthus elwesii   Giant snowdrop
Turkish snowdrop

Galanthus nivalis
Common snowdrop
Fair maids of February

Galanthus reginae-olgae
Autumn snowdrop

Galtonia candicans   Berg lily
Galtonia
Giant summer hyacinth
Spire lily
Summer hyacinth

Gladiolus callianthus   Acidanthera

Gladiolus dalenii
Rhodesian gladiolus

Gladiolus × hortulanus
Garden gladiolus
Sword lily

Gladiolus primulinus
Maid of the mist

Gladiolus segetum   Corn flag

Gladiolus tristis
Yellow marsh afrikander

Gloriosa rothschildiana   Flame lily
Gloriosa lily
Glory lily

Gloriosa superba   Flame lily
Gloriosa lily
Glory lily

Gloxinia perennis   Canterbury bells

Gloxinia sylvatica
Peruvian redbird

Goodyera pubescens
Rattlesnake plantain

Haemanthus katharinae

Haemanthus katharinae
Catherine-wheel

Haemanthus magnificus
Giant stove brush

Haemanthus multiflorus
African blood lily
Blood lily
Paintbrush

Haemanthus natalensis   Blood lily
Natal paintbrush
Paintbrush

Haemanthus puniceus
Royal paintbrush

Hedychium coccineum
Red ginger lily
Scarlet ginger lily

Hedychium coronarium
Butterfly ginger lily
Butterfly lily
Cinnamon jasmine
Garland flower
Ginger lily
White ginger lily

Hedychium flavescens
Yellow ginger lily

Hedychium gardneranum
Gingerwort
Kahili ginger lily
Kahli ginger

Hermodactylus tuberosus
Widow iris

Hippeastrum aulicum
Lily-of-the-palace

Hippeastrum edule   Barbados lily

Hippeastrum equestre
Barbados lily

Hippeastrum × johnsonii
Saint Joseph's lily

Hippeastrum reginae   Mexican lily

Hippeastrum reticulatum
Lacework lily
Meshed lily

Hippeastrum robustum
Lily-of-the-palace

Homoglossum merianella   Flames

Hyacinthoides campanulata
Spanish bluebell

Hyacinthoides hispanica
Giant bluebell
Spanish bluebell

Hyacinthoides non-scriptus
Culverkeys
English bluebell
Ring-of-bells
Wild hyacinth
Wood bells
Wood hyacinth

Hyacinthoides nutans
English bluebell

Hyacinthus candicans
Summer hyacinth

Hyacinthus orientalis
Common hyacinth
Dutch hyacinth
Garden hyacinth
Hyacinth
Roman hyacinth

Hyacinthus romanus
Roman hyacinth

Hymenocallis amancaes
Peruvian daffodil

Hymenocallis × festalis
Basket flower
Spider lily

Hymenocallis narcissiflora
Basket flower
Peruvian daffodil
Spider lily

Hymenocallis palmeri   Alligator lily

Ionoxalis violacea
Violet wood sorrel

Ipheion uniflorum
Spring starflower

Iris anglica   English iris

Iris basaltica   Mourning iris
Palestine iris

Iris brevicaulis   Lamance iris

Iris cristata   Crested iris
Dwarf crested iris

Iris ensata   Sword-leaved iris

Iris foetidissima   Gladwin iris
Scarlet-seeded iris
Stinking gladwin iris
Stinking iris

Iris fulva   Copper iris
Red iris

Iris × germanica   Flag
Fleur-de-lis

Iris graeberiana   Blue fall iris
Yellow fall iris

Iris hartwegii   Sierra iris

Iris kaempferi   Japanese iris

Iris latifolia   English iris

Iris missouriensis   Western blue flag

Iris ochroleuca   Butterfly iris

Iris odoratissima   Orris

Iris orchidoides   Orchid iris

Iris pallida   Orris

Iris persica   Persian iris

Iris prismatica   Slender blue flag

Iris pseudacorus   Water flag
Yellow flag
Yellow iris

Iris reticulata   Netted iris

Iris sibirica   Siberian iris

Iris spuria   Butterfly iris
Spuria iris

Iris susiana   Mourning iris
Palestine iris

Iris tectorum   Roof iris
Wall iris

Iris tingitana   Morocco iris

Lilium parryi

Iris tuberosa	Widow iris
Iris verna	Dwarf iris
	Violet iris
Iris versicolor	Blue flag
	Poison flag
	Wild iris
Iris virginica	Blue flag
	Southern blue flag
Iris xiphioides	English iris
Iris xiphium	
	Portuguese iris
	Spanish iris
Ismene calathina	Spider lily
Ixia incarnata	Clanwilliam bluebell
Ixia maculata	African corn lily
	Corn lily
	Wand flower
Ixia viridiflora	African corn lily
	Corn lily
	Green ixia
	Wand flower
Kniphofia triangularis	
	Red hot poker
	Torch lily
Lachenalia aloides	Cape cowslip
Lachenalia bulbifera	
	Cape cowslip
Lachenalia contaminata	
	Cape cowslip
	Wild hyacinth
Lachenalia glaucina	Cape cowslip
Lachenalia mutabilis	Cape cowslip
Lachenalia ribida	Cape cowslip
Lachenalia tricolor	Cape cowslip
Leucocoryne ixioides	
	Glory-of-the-snow
	Glory-of-the-sun
Leucocoryne odorata	
	Glory-of-the-sun
Leucocoryne uniflora	
	Spring starflower
Leucojum aestivum	
	Giant snowflake
	Loddon lily
	Summer snowflake
Leucojum vernum	
	Spring snowflake
Liatris aspera	Blazing star
	Gayfeather
	Prickly blazing star
Liatris spicata	Spiky gayfeather
Lilium auratum	Gold-banded lily
	Golden-banded lily
	Golden-rayed lily
	Mountain lily
Lilium bolanderi	Thimble lily
Lilium bulbiferum	Fire lily
	Orange lily
Lilium canadense	Canada lily
	Meadow lily
	Wild yellow lily
	Yellow-bell lily
	Yellow lily

Lilium candidum	Madonna lily
Lilium carolinianum	Leopard lily
	Pine lily
	Southern red lily
Lilium catesbaei	Leopard lily
	Pine lily
	Southern red lily
Lilium chalcedonicum	
	Scarlet martagon lily
	Scarlet turk's cap lily
Lilium columbianum	
	Columbia lily
	Oregon lily
Lilium concolor	Star lily
Lilium davidii	
	Orange turk's cap lily
Lilium duchartrei	
	Marble martagon lily
Lilium excelsum	Nankeen lily
Lilium formosum	
	Chinese white lily
Lilium grayi	Bell lily
	Gray's lily
	Orange-bell lily
	Roan lily
Lilium hansonii	
	Japanese turk's cap lily
Lilium × hollandicum	
	Candlestick lily
Lilium humboldtii	Humbold lily
Lilium iridollae	Pot-of-gold lily
Lilium japonicum	Japanese lily
Lilium krameri	Japanese lily
Lilium lancifolium	Japanese lily
	Showy Japanese lily
	Showy lily
	Tiger lily
Lilium leucanthum	
	Chinese white lily
Lilium longiflorum	Bermuda lily
	Easter lily
	Trumpet lily
	White trumpet lily
Lilium mackliniae	Manipur lily
Lilium makinoi	Japanese lily
Lilium maritimum	Coastal lily
Lilium martagon	Martagon lily
	Turban lily
	Turk's cap lily
Lilium medeoloides	Wheel lily
Lilium michauxii	Carolina lily
	Turk's cap lily
Lilium michiganense	Michigan lily
Lilium monadelphum	
	Caucasian lily
Lilium occidentale	Eureka lily
	Western lily
Lilium pardalinum	Leopard lily
	Panther lily
	Sunset lily
Lilium parryi	Lemon lily

Lilium parvum

Lilium parvum	Alpine lily
	Sierra lily
	Small tiger lily
Lilium philadelphicum	
	Orange-cup lily
	Wild orange-red lily
	Wood lily
Lilium pomponium	
	Lesser turk's cap lily
	Little turk's cap lily
	Minor turk's cap lily
	Turban lily
Lilium pumilum	Coral lily
Lilium pyrenaicum	
	Yellow turk's cap lily
Lilium regale	Regal lily
	Royal lily
Lilium rubescens	Chamise lily
	Chaparral lily
	Redwood lily
Lilium speciosum	Japanese lily
	Showy lily
	Showy japanese lily
Lilium superbum	
	American turk's cap lily
	Lily-royal
	Swamp lily
	Turk's cap lily
Lilium tenuifolium	Coral lily
Lilium × testaceum	Nankeen lily
Lilium tigrinum	Tiger lily
Lilium washingtonianum	
	Washington lily
Lilium × umbellatum	
	Candlestick lily
Littonia modesta	Climbing lily
Lloydia serotina	
	Mountain spiderwort
Lycoris africana	
	Golden African lily
	Golden hurricane lily
	Golden spider lily
	Spider lily
Lycoris aurea	Golden spider lily
	Spider lily
Lycoris radiata	Red spider lily
	Spider lily
Lycoris squamigera	Magic lily
	Resurrection lily
Milla biflora	Mexican star
Milla uniflora	Spring starflower
Muscari azureum	
	Turkish grape hyacinth
Muscari botryoides	
	Common grape hyacinth
	Small grape hyacinth
Muscari comosum	Cipollino
	Feather hyacinth
	Tassel hyacinth
Muscari macrocarpum	
	Yellow grape hyacinth

Muscari moschatum	
	Grape hyacinth
	Musk hyacinth
	Nutmeg hyacinth
Muscari muscarini	Musk hyacinth
Muscari neglectum	
	Grape hyacinth
Muscari racemosum	
	Grape hyacinth
	Musk hyacinth
	Nutmeg hyacinth
Muscari tubergenianum	
	Cambridge grape hyacinth
	Oxford grape hyacinth
Narcissus assoanus	Dwarf jonquil
Narcissus bulbocodium	
	Hoop-petticoat daffodil
	Petticoat daffodil
Narcissus calathinus	
	Campernelle jonquil
Narcissus canaliculatus	
	Chinese sacred lily
	Polyanthus narcissus
Narcissus hispanicus	
	Spanish daffodil
Narcissus jonquilla	Jonquil
Narcissus × medioluteus	
	Poetaz narcissus
	Primrose peerless narcissus
Narcissus obvallaris	Tenby daffodil
Narcissus × odorus	
	Campernelle jonquil
Narcissus papyraceus	
	Paperwhite narcissus
Narcissus poeticus	
	Pheasant's eye narcissus
	Poet's narcissus
Narcissus poeticus physaloides	
	Chinese lantern
Narcissus pseudonarcissus	Daffodil
	Lent lily
	Trumpet narcissus
	Wild daffodil
Narcissus requienii	Dwarf jonquil
Narcissus tazetta	
	Bunch-flowered narcissus
	Chinese sacred lily
	Polyanthus narcissus
Narcissus triandrus	Angel's tears
Narcissus watieri	
	North African narcissus
Neomarica caerulea	
	Twelve apostles
Neomarica northiana	Walking iris
Nerine bowdenii	Guernsey lily
Nerine sarniensis	Guernsey lily
Nerine undulata	Nodding nerine
Nomocharis pardanthina	
	Blotched panther-lily
Ornithogalum arabicum	
	Star-of-Bethlehem

Sinningia regina

Ornithogalum caudatum	*Ranunculus asiaticus* Crowfoot
False sea onion	Persian buttercup
German onion	Persian ranunculus
Sea onion	Turban buttercup
Ornithogalum narbonense	*Ranunculus bulbosus*
Star-of-Bethlehem	Bulbous buttercup
Ornithogalum nutans	Bulbous crowfoot
Drooping star-of-Bethlehem	*Ranunculus ficaria*
Nodding star-of-Bethlehem	Lesser celandine
Ornithogalum pyrenaicum	Pilewort
Bath asparagus	Small celandine
French asparagus	*Rhodohypoxis baurii*
Prussian asparagus	Drakensberg star
Star-of-Bethlehem	*Rhodophiala bifida* Hurricane lily
Ornithogalum saundersiae	*Richardia rehmannii* Pink calla lily
Giant chincherinchee	Red calla lily
Ornithogalum thyrsoides	*Romulea columnae* Sand crocus
African wonder flower	*Sandersonia aurantiaca*
Chincherinchee	Chinese lantern lily
Wonder flower	Christmas bells
Ornithogalum umbellatum	*Sauromatum guttatum*
Dove's dung	Lizard flower
Nap-at-noon	*Sauromatum venosum* Voodoo lily
Star-of-bethlehem	*Saururu cernuus*
Summer snowflake	American swamp lily
Ostrowskia magnifica	Swamp lily
Giant bellflower	Water dragon
Oxalis acetosella	*Scadoxus multiflorus* Blood lily
European wood sorrel	Fireball lily
Irish shamrock	*Scadoxus puniceus*
Oxalis cernua Bermuda buttercup	Royal paintbrush
Oxalis deppei Good-luck leaf	*Schizostylis coccinea* Crimson flag
Good-luck plant	Kaffir lily
Lucky clover	River lily
Oxalis enneaphylla	*Scilla amoena* Star hyacinth
Falklands scurvy grass	*Scilla autumnalis* Autumn squill
Scurvy grass	Starry hyacinth
Oxalis oregana Redwood sorrel	*Scilla bifolia* Alpine squill
Oxalis pes-caprae	Nodding squill
Bermuda buttercup	*Scilla chinensis* Chinese squill
Oxalis violacea Violet wood sorrel	Japanese jacinth
Pancratium maritimum	*Scilla hyacinthoides*
Mediterranean lily	Hyacinth squill
Sea daffodil	*Scilla monophyllos* Dwarf squill
Sea lily	*Scilla natalensis* South African squill
Paradisea liliastrum Paradise lily	*Scilla peruviana* Cuban lily
Saint Bruno's lily	Hyacinth-of-Peru
Paradisea lusitanica	Peruvian jacinth
Portuguese paradise lily	*Scilla scilloides* Chinese squill
Polianthes geminiflora	Japanese jacinth
Orange pearl	*Scilla siberica* Siberian squill
Orange tuberose	*Scilla verna* Sea onion
Polianthes tuberosa The pearl	Spring squill
Tuberose	*Simethis planifolia* Kerry lily
Pulsatilla patens Pasque flower	*Sinningia cardinalis*
Puschkinia libanotica	Cardinal flower
Lebanon squill	Helmet flower
Striped squill	*Sinningia leucotricha*
Puschkinia scilloides	Brazilian edelweiss
Lebanon squill	*Sinningia regina* Cinderella slippers
Pyrolirion tubiflorum	Violet slipper gloxinia
Peruvian mountain daffodil	
Ranunculus acris	
Bachelor's buttons	

BOTANICAL NAMES

Sinningia speciosa

Sinningia speciosa	Brazilian gloxinia
	Florist's gloxinia
	Gloxinia
	Violet slipper gloxinia
Sparaxis elegans	Harlequin flower
Sparaxis grandiflora	
	Harlequin flower
Sparaxis pendula	
	Angel's fishing rod
	Grassy bell
Sparaxis tricolor	Harlequin flower
Spigelia marilandica	Indian pink
	Maryland pink root
Sprekelia formosissima	Aztec lily
	Jacobean lily
	Maltese cross
	Orchid amaryllis
	Saint James's lily
Sternbergia lutea	Autumn daffodil
	Lily-of-the-field
	Winter daffodil
	Yellow starflower
Streptanthera elegans	
	Harlequin flower
Tecophilaea cyanocrocus	
	Chilean crocus
Tigridia pavonia	
	Mexican shell flower
	Peacock tiger flower
	Tiger flower
	Tiger lily
Trillium cernuum	
	Nodding trillium
Trillium cuneatum	
	Whippoorwill flower
Trillium erectum	Brown beth
	Purple trillium
	Squawroot
	Stinking benjamin
Trillium erectum album	
	Wax trillium
Trillium flavum	Brown beth
	Purple trillium
	Squawroot
	Stinking benjamin
Trillium grandiflorum	
	Wake robin
	White wake robin
Trillium nivale	
	Dwarf white trillium
	Snow trillium
Trillium ovatum	Coast trillium
Trillium recurvatum	
	Bloody butcher
	Purple toadshade
	Purple trillium
	Purple wake robin
Trillium sessile	Toadshade
	Wake robin
Trillium undulatum	
	Painted trillium
Trillium vaseyi	Sweet beth
Trillium viride	Wood trillium

Tulbaghia simmleri	
	Pink agapanthus
	Sweet garlic
	Wild garlic
Tulipa acuminata	Horned tulip
	Turkish tulip
Tulipa clusiana	Lady tulip
Tulipa cornuta	Turkish tulip
Tulipa kaufmanniana	
	Waterlily tulip
Tulipa occulus-solis	
	Persian sun's eye
Tulipa sylvestris	Wild tulip
Tulipa turkistanica	Turkish tulip
Urginea maritima	
	Crusader's spears
	Red squill
	Sea onion
	Sea squill
	White squill
Vallota speciosa	George lily
	Scarborough lily
Veltheimia brachteata	Forest lily
Veltheimia viridiflora	Forest lily
Zantedeschia aethiopica	Arum lily
	Calla lily
	Florist's calla lily
	Garden calla lily
	Pig lily
	Trumpet lily
Zantedeschia africana	Arum lily
	Calla lily
	Florist's calla lily
	Garden calla lily
	Pig lily
	Trumpet lily
Zantedeschia albomaculata	
	Black-throated calla lily
	Spotted calla lily
Zantedeschia elliottiana	
	Golden calla lily
	Yellow calla lily
Zantedeschia melanoleuca	
	Black-throated calla lily
	Spotted calla lily
Zantedeschia rehmannii	
	Pink arum lily
	Pink calla lily
	Red calla lily
Zephyranthes atamasco	
	Atamasco lily
	Easter lily
Zephyranthes candida	Fairy lily
	Flower of the western wind
	Flower of the wind
	Rain lily
	Storm lily
	West wind lily
	Windflower
	Zephyr lily
Zephyranthes grandiflora	
	Windflower
Zephyranthes rosea	Windflower

CACTI AND SUCCULENTS

The majority of cacti are succulent, arid- or desert-area plants with thickened stems that serve the plant both for water-storage and as photosynthetic organs, replacing the leaves which are usually miniscule or totally absent. Most are armed with vicious spines and should be handled with care. They should be kept well away from children and domestic pets.

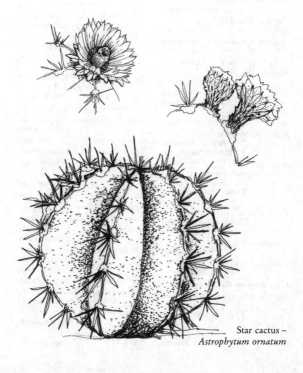

Star cactus –
Astrophytum ornatum

Adenium obesum

Adenium obesum	Desert rose
Agave americana	American aloe
	Century plant
Agave cantala	Cantala
Agave fourcroydes	Henequen
Agave lophantha	Lechuguilla
Agave palmeri	Blue century plant
Aichryson × domesticum	
	Cloud grass
	Youth-and-old-age
Aloe africana	Spiny aloe
Aloe barbadensis	Barbados aloe
	Medicinal aloe
	Unguentine cactus
Aloe ferox	Cape aloe
	Red aloe
Aloe humilis	Crocodile jaws
	Hedgehog aloe
	Spider aloe
Aloe perryi	Socotrine aloe
	Zanzibar aloe
Aloe variegata	Falcon feather
	Kanniedood
	Partridge-breasted aloe
	Pheasant's wing
	Tiger aloe
Aloe victoriae reginae	
	Queen Victoria's aloe
Ancistrocactus scheeri	
	Fish-hook cactus
Aporocactus flagelliformis	
	Rat's tail cactus
Ariocarpus fissuratus	Living rock
	Star cactus
Ariocarpus retusus	Seven stars
Astrophytum asterias	
	Sand dollar cactus
	Sea urchin cactus
	Silver dollar cactus
Astrophytum capricorne	
	Goat's horn cactus
Astrophytum myriostigma	
	Bishop's cap cactus
	Bishop's hood cactus
	Monkshood cactus
Astrophytum ornatum	
	Bishop's cap cactus
	Ornamental monkshood
	Star cactus
Borzicactus celsianus	
	Old man of the mountains
	South American old man
Borzicactus fossulatus	
	Mountain cereus
Borzicactus trollii	
	Old man of the Andes
Caralluma woodii	String of hearts
Carnegiea gigantea	Arizona giant
	Giant cactus
	Giant saguaro
	Pitahaya
	Saguaro
	Sahuaro

Cephalocereus chrysacanthus	
	Golden old man
	Golden spines
Cephalocereus fulviceps	
	Mexican giant
Cephalocereus palmeri	
	Bald old man
	Yellow old man
	Woolly torch cactus
Cephalocereus senilis	
	Old man cactus
	Old man's head
Cephalophyllum alstonii	
	Red spike
Cereus baumannii	Scarlet bugler
Cereus peruvianus	Apple cactus
	Hedge cactus
	Peruvian apple
	Peruvian apple cactus
Chamaecereus silvestrii	
	Peanut cactus
Chiastophyllum oppositifolium	
	Lamb's tail
Cleistocactus baumannii	
	Scarlet bugler
Cleistocactus smaragdifolius	
	Firecracker cactus
Cleistocactus strausii	Silver torch
Coryphantha echinus	
	Hedgehog-cory cactus
Coryphantha missouriensis	
	Missouri pincushion cactus
Coryphantha runyonii	
	Big nipple cactus
	Dumpling cactus
Coryphantha vivipara	
	Pincushion cactus
Coryphantha vivipara arizonica	Beehive cactus
Cotyledon simplicifolia	Lamb's tail
Crassula arborescens	Jade plant
	Money tree
Crassula argentea	Jade plant
Crassula barklyi	Rattlesnake tail
Crassula deltoides	Silver beads
Crassula lycopodioides	
	Rat-tail plant
Crassula ovata	Jade tree
Crassula portulacea	Jade plant
Crassula rhomboidea	Silver beads
Crassula rupestris	Bead vine
	Rosary vine
Dasylirion leiophyllum	
	Desert candle
	Spoon plant
Deamia testudo	Tortoise cactus
Dorotheanthus bellidiformis	
	Annual mesembryanthemum
Doryanthes excelsa	
	Globe spear-lily
Doryanthes palmeri	
	Palmer spear-lily

Gymnocalycium denudatum

Dracaena draco	Dragon tree
Echeveria affinis	Black echeveria
Echeveria derenbergii	Painted lady
Echeveria glauca	Blue echeveria
Echeveria leucotricha	
	Chenille plant
Echeveria multicaulis	
	Copper roses
Echeveria pulvinata	Plush plant
Echeveria rosea	Desert rose
Echeveria secunda glauca	
	Blue echeveria
Echeveria setosa	Firecracker plant
Echinocactus dasyacanthus	
	Texas rainbow cactus
Echinocactus grusonii	
	Barrel cactus
	Golden ball
	Golden barrel cactus
	Mother-in-law's armchair
Echinocactus horizonthalonius	
	Eagle-claws cactus
	Mule-crippler cactus
Echinocactus ingens	
	Blue barrel cactus
	Giant barrel cactus
	Large barrel cactus
	Mexican giant barrel
Echinocereus delaetii	
	Lesser old man cactus
Echinocereus dubius	Purple pitaya
Echinocereus enneacanthus	
	Strawberry cactus
Echinocereus horizonthalonius	
	Blue barrel cactus
Echinocereus pectinatus	
	Hedgehog cactus
Echinocereus pectinatus rigidissimus	
	Rainbow cactus
Echinocereus reichenbachii	
	Lace cactus
Echinocereus salm-dyckianus	
	Strawberry cactus
Echinocereus sarissophorus	
	Purple hedgehog cereus
Echinocereus viridiflorus	
	Green-flowered pitaya
	Green-flowered torch cactus
Echinofossulocactus zacatecasensis	Brain cactus
Echinopsis aurea	Golden lily cactus
Echinopsis eyriesii	
	Sea urchin cactus
Echinopsis multiplex	Barrel cactus
	Easter-lily cactus
	Pink easter-lily cactus
Epiphyllum ackermannii	
	Orchid cactus
Epiphyllum anguliger	
	Fishbone cactus
Epiphyllum × hybridum	
	Orchid cactus
Epiphyllum oxypetalum	
	Night-blooming cereus
	Queen of the night
Epiphyllum truncatum	
	Christmas cactus
	Crab's claw cactus
Epithelantha bokei	Button cactus
Epithelantha micromeris	
	Button cactus
Escobaria tuberculosa	Cob cactus
Espostoa lanata	Cotton-ball cactus
	Snowball cactus
Euphorbia antisyphilitica	
	Candelilla
	Wax plant
Euphorbia caput-medusae	
	Medusa's head spurge
Euphorbia gorgonis	Dragon's head
	Gorgon's head
Euphorbia mammillaris	
	Corncob cactus
Euphorbia milii	Crown of thorns
Euphorbia milii splendens	
	Crown of thorns
Euphorbia obesa	Gingham golf ball
Euphorbia pseudocactus	
	Cactus spurge
Euphorbia tirucalli	Finger tree
	Milk bush
	Rubber spurge
	Stick cactus
Faucaria tigrina	Tiger jaws
Fenestraria rhopalophylla	
	Window plant
Ferocactus corniger	Devil's tongue
Ferocactus glaucescens	
	Blue barrel cactus
Ferocactus hamatacanthus	
	Turk's head
Ferocactus histrix	Electrode cactus
Ferocactus latispinus	
	Devil's tongue
	Fish-hook cactus
Ferocactus rectispinus	
	Hatpin cactus
Ferocactus setispinus	
	Strawberry cactus
Ferocactus viridescens	
	Small barrel cactus
Ferocactus wislizenii	
	Fish-hook cactus
Fritha pulchra	Fairy-elephant's feet
Furcraea foetida	Green aloe
	Mauritius hemp
Furcraea hexapetala	Cuban hemp
Graptopetalum paraguayense	
	Ghost plant
	Mother-of-pearl plant
Graptophyllum pictum	
	Caricature plant
Gymnocalycium denudatum	
	Spider cactus

Gymnocalycium gibbosum
Chin cactus

Gymnocalycium mihanovichii
Plaid cactus
Plain cactus

Gymnocalycium schickendantzii
White chin cactus

Gymnocalycium quehlianum
Rose-plaid cactus

Hamatocactus uncinatus
Cat claw cactus

Hariota salicornioides   Bottle plant
Dancing bones
Drunkard's dream
Spice cactus

Harrisia jusbertii   Moon cactus

Harrisia martinii   Moon cactus

Hatiora salicornioides   Bottle plant
Dancing bones
Drunkard's dream
Spice cactus

Haworthia chalwinii
Aristocrat plant
Column-of-pearls

Haworthia cymbiformis
Window aloe
Window cushion
Window plant

Haworthia fasciata
Zebra haworthia

Haworthia limifolia
Fairy washboard

Haworthia margaritifera
Pearl plant

Haworthia papillosa   Pearly-dots

Haworthia pumila   Pearl plant

Haworthia setata   Lace haworthia

Haworthia tessellata
Star window plant

Hechtia scariosa   Fairy agave

Heliocereus speciosus   Sun cactus

Hylocereus undatus
Honolulu queen
Queen of the night
Night-blooming cereus

Kalanchoe tomentosa   Panda plant
Panda-bear plant
Plush plant
Pussy-ears

Lemaireocereus eruca
Creeping-devil cactus

Lemaireocereus gummosus
Dagger cactus

Lemaireocereus marginatus
Organ-pipe cactus

Lemaireocereus pruinosus
Powder-blue cereus

Lemaireocereus thurberi
Organ-pipe cactus

Lemaireocereus weberi
Candelabra cactus

Leuchtenbergia principis
Agave cactus
Prism cactus

Lithops dorotheae   Stone plant

Lithops julii   Living stones
Stone plant

Lithops lesliei   Pebble cactus

Lobivia aurea   Golden lily cactus

Lobivia bruchii
South American golden-barrel

Lobivia hertrichiana   Cob cactus

Lophocereus schottii   Senita
Totem-pole cactus
Whisker cactus

Lophophora williamsii
Devil's root cactus
Dry whisky
Dumpling cactus
Mescal button
Peyote cactus

Lothophora williamsii
Devil's root cactus
Dry whisky
Dumpling cactus
Mescal button
Peyote cactus

Machaerocereus eruca
Creeping devil cactus

Mammillaria bocasana
Fish-hook cactus
Powder-puff
Snowball cactus

Mammillaria camptotricha
Bird's nest cactus
Golden bird's nest cactus

Mammillaria candida
Snowball pincushion

Mammillaria elongata
Golden star
Gold lace
Lace cactus
Lady finger

Mammillaria fragilis
Thimble cactus
Thimble mammillaria

Mammillaria gracilis   Powder puff

Mammillaria hahniana
Old lady cactus
Old lady of Mexico
Old woman cactus

Mammillaria heyderi
Coral cactus
Cream cactus

Mammillaria karwinskiana
Royal-cross cactus

Mammillaria lanata
Old lady cactus

Mammillaria plumosa
Feather cactus

Mammillaria pringlei
Lemon-ball cactus

Mammillaria prolifera
Little candles
Silver cluster cactus

Oreocereus trollii

Mammillaria tetracantha
Ruby dumpling
Mammillaria wildii
Fish-hook pincushion cactus
Mammillaria zeilmanniana
Rose pincushion
Melocactus communis
Melon cactus
Turk's cap cactus
Turk's head cactus
Melocactus intortus
Turk's cap cactus
Melocactus maxonii
Turk's head cactus
Morangaya pensilis
Sprawling cactus
Wandering cactus
Myrtillocactus geometrizans
Blue candle
Blue flame
Blue myrtle cactus
Neobessya similis   Nipple cactus
Nopalea cochenillifera
Cochineal plant
Nopalxochia ackermannii
Orchid cactus
Red orchid cactus
Nopalxochia phyllanthoides
Empress of Germany
Pond-lily cactus
Notocactus haselbergii
Scarlet ball cactus
Notocactus leninghausii
Golden ball
Notocactus scopa   Silver ball cactus
Notocactus submammulosus
Lemon ball cactus
Nyctocereus serpentinus
Night-blooming cereus
Queen of the night
Serpent cactus
Snake cactus
Obregonia denegrii
Artichoke cactus
Opuntia arbuscula   Pencil cholla
Opuntia articulata   Paper cactus
Spruce cones
Opuntia basilaris   Beavertail cactus
Rose tuna
Opuntia bigelovii
Teddy-bear cactus
Teddy-bear cholla
Opuntia chlorotica   Flapjack cactus
Opuntia clavarioides   Black fingers
Crested opuntia
Fairy castles
Gnome's throne
Sea-coral
Opuntia cylindrica   Cane cactus
Emerald-idol
Opuntia elata   Orange tuna
Opuntia erectoclada   Dominoes

Opuntia erinacea ursina
Grizzly bear cactus
Opuntia ficus-indica
Burbank's spineless cactus
Indian fig
Prickly pear
Spineless cactus
Opuntia floccosa   Cushion cactus
Woolly sheep
Opuntia fulgida   Jumping cactus
Opuntia mamillata   Boxing glove
Club cactus
Opuntia imbricata
Chain-link cactus
Opuntia leptocaulis
Desert christmas cactus
Tasajillo
Opuntia leucotricha   Aaron's beard
Opuntia megacantha   Nopal
Opuntia microdasys   Bunny ears
Golden opuntia
Goldplush
Rabbit ears
Yellow bunny ears
Yellow rabbit ears
Opuntia microdasys albispina   Honey-bunny
Polka dots
Prickly pear
Opuntia microdasys rufida
Blind pear
Cinnamon cactus
Red bunny ears
Opuntia prolifera   Jumping cholla
Opuntia ramosissima   Pencil cactus
Opuntia rufida   Cinnamon cactus
Red bunny-ears
Opuntia santa-rita
Purple prickly pear
Opuntia schickendantzii
Lion's tongue
Mule's ears
Opuntia schottii   Devil cactus
Dog cholla
Opuntia soehrensii   Fairy needles
Opuntia sphaerica   Thimble tuna
Opuntia subulata   Eve's pin cactus
Opuntia velutina   Velvet opuntia
Opuntia versicolor   Staghorn cholla
Opuntia vestita
Cotton-pole cactus
Old man opuntia
Opuntia vilis   Little tree opuntia
Mexican dwarf tree cactus
Opuntia violacea santa-rita
Blue-blade
Dollar cactus
Opuntia vulgaris   Barbary fig
Irish mittens
Joseph's coat cactus
Prickly pear
Oreocereus trollii
Old man of the Andes

Pachycereus pecten-
  aboriginum

Pachycereus pecten-
  aboriginum   Comb cactus
                      Hairbrush cactus
                      Indian comb
                      Native's comb
Pachycereus pringlei
                      Giant Mexican cereus
                      Mexican giant cactus
Pachyphytum glutinicaule
                      Sticky moonstones
Pachyphytum oviferum
                      Moonstones
                      Sugar-almond plant
Pachypodium lamerei
                      Madagascan palm
Parodia aureispina
                      Golden tom thumb
                      Tom thumb cactus
Pedilanthus tithymaloides
                      Devil's backbone
                      Japanese poinsettia
                      Jewbush
                      Redbird cactus
                      Redbird flower
                      Ribbon cactus
                      Slipper flower
Pediocactus simpsonii
                      Snowball cactus
Pelargonium carnosum
  Fleshy-stalked pelargonium
Pelargonium ceratophyllum
  Horned-leaf pelargonium
Pelargonium cotyledonis
  Hollyhock-leaved pelargonium
  Old-father-live-forever
Pelargonium crithmifolium
  Samphire-leaved pelargonium
Pelargonium gibbosum
                      Gouty pelargonium
Pelargonium hystrix
                      Porcupine pelargonium
Pelargonium tetragonum
  Square-stemmed pelargonium
Peniocereus greggii
                      Night-blooming cereus
                      Reina-de-la-noche
Pereskia aculeata
                      Barbados gooseberry
                      Leafy cactus
                      Lemon vine
Pereskia bleo   Wax rose
Pereskia grandiflora   Rose cactus
Pilocereus celsianus
                      Old man of the mountains
Pleiospilos bolusii
                      African living rock
                      Living rock cactus
                      Mimicry plant
Pleiospilos nelii   Cleftstone
                      Mimicry plant
                      Splitrock
Plumiera acuminata
                      Frangipani tree
Portulaca grandiflora   Sun plant

Pulque agave   Agave salmiana
Rebutia grandiflora
                      Scarlet crown cactus
Rebutia kupperana
                      Red crown cactus
Rebutia minuscula
                      Mexican sunball
                      Red crown cactus
Rebutia pseudodeminuta
                      Wallflower crown
Rebutia senilis   Fire crown cactus
Rhipsalidopsis gaertneri
                      Easter cactus
Rhipsalis baccifera
                      Mistletoe cactus
Rhipsalis cassutha
                      Mistletoe cactus
Rhipsalis cereuscula   Coral cactus
                      Popcorn cactus
                      Rice cactus
Rhipsalis houlletiana
                      Snowdrop cactus
Rhipsalis paradoxa   Chain cactus
                      Chainlink cactus
                      Link plant
Rhipsalis salicornioides
                      Dancing bones
                      Drunkard's dream
                      Spice cactus
Rhipsalis warmingiana
                      Popcorn cactus
Rochea coccinea
                      Hyacinth-scented rochea
Sansevieria hahnii
                      Bird's nest sansevieria
Sansevieria trifasciata laurentii
                      Mother-in-law's tongue
Schlumbergera bridgesii
                      Christmas cactus
                      Crab's claw cactus
Schlumbergera gaertneri
                      Whitsun cactus
Schlumbergera gaertneri
  makoyana   Cat's whiskers
Schlumbergera truncata
                      Christmas cactus
                      Claw cactus
                      Crab cactus
                      Thanksgiving cactus
                      Zygocactus
Sedum anglicum   English stonecrop
                      Stonecrop
Sedum pachyphyllum
                      Jellybean plant
Sedum spectabile   Ice plant
Selenicereus grandiflorus
                      Night-blooming cereus
                      Queen of the night
Selenicereus macdonaldiae
                      Queen of the night
Selenicereus pteranthus
                      Princess of the night

CACTI

Zygocactus truncatus

Sempervivum arachnoides
Cobweb houseleek
Spider houseleek

Sempervivum arachnoideum
Cobweb houseleek

Sempervivum tectorum
Hen-and-chickens
Roof houseleek

Senecio articulatus　　Candle plant

Senecio rowleyanus　String of beads
String of pearls

Stenocereus thurberi
Organ pipe cactus

Stetsonia coryne　Toothpick cactus

Thelocactus bicolor　Glory of Texas
Texas pride

Thelocactus setispinus
Strawberry cactus

Titanopsis calcarea　　Jewel plant

Titanopsis schwantesii　White jewel

Trichocereus spachianus
Golden column
White torch cactus

Trichodiadema barbatum
Pickle plant

Trichodiadema densum
Desert rose

Wigginsia vorwerkiana
Colombian ball cactus

Wilcoxia poselgeri　　Dahlia cactus
Scented cactus

Wilcoxia schmollii
Lamb's tail cactus

Yucca brevifolia　　Joshua tree

Zygocactus truncatus
Christmas cactus
Crab's claw cactus

CARNIVOROUS PLANTS

Otherwise known as insectivorous plants, these are plants that have developed special mechanisms for trapping and digesting mainly, but not exclusively, small insects. There are several types of carnivorous plants including the pitcher plants, the sticky-leaved sundews and butterworts, and the spring-trap leaves of Venus's flytrap. The strange nature of these plants makes them popular subjects for exhibiting at horticultural shows and school study groups. They are also extensively grown indoors and in greenhouses as a natural control for flying insects.

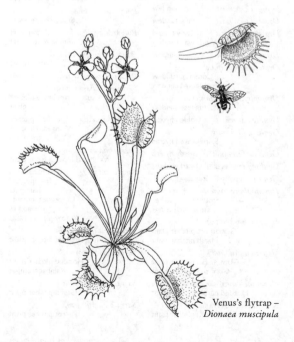

Venus's flytrap –
Dionaea muscipula

Aldrovanda vesiculosa

Aldrovanda vesiculosa
Floating pondtrap
Spikey pondtrap
Waterbug trap
Waterwheel plant

Byblis gigantea
Erect Australian sundew

Byblis liniflora
Sprawling Australian sundew

Cephalotus follicularis
Australian pitcher plant
Swamp pitcher plant

Chrysamphora californica
California pitcher plant
Cobra lily
Cobra orchid
Cobra plant
Pitcher plant

Darlingtonia californica
California pitcher plant
Cobra lily
Cobra orchid
Cobra plant
Pitcher plant

Dionaea muscipula
Flytrap sensitive
Sensitive flytrap
Tipitiwitchet
Venus's flytrap

Drosera anglica   Great sundew

Drosera auriculata   Eared sundew

Drosera brevifolia   Dwarf sundew

Drosera capensis   Sundew

Drosera capillaris   Pink sundew

Drosera filiformis   Dew thread
Thread-leaved sundew

Drosera menziesii   Pink rainbow

Drosera rotundifolia
Common sundew
Round-leaved sundew

Drosophyllum lusitanicum
Portuguese sundew

Genlisea aurea   Golden flytrap

Genlisea filiformis
Spiral-leaved flytrap

Genlisea hispidula   Bristly flytrap

Genlisea pygmaea   Dwarf genlisea

Genlisea repens   Creeping genlisea

Heliamphora minor
Small marsh pitcher
Small sun pitcher

Heliamphora nutans
Guayan sun pitcher plant
Marsh pitcher plant

Heliamphora tatei
Giant marsh pitcher plant
Giant sun pitcher plant

Nepenthes × *atrosanguinea*
Mottled purple pitcher plant

Nepenthes hookerana
Funnelform pitcher plant

Nepenthes merrilliana
Monkey pitcher
Monkey's larder
Monkey's rice pot
Mouse pitcher

Nepenthes sanguinea
Deep red pitcher plant

Nepenthes ventricosa
Pale green pitcher plant

Pinguicula alpina
Alpine butterwort

Pinguicula caerulea
Blue butterwort

Pinguicula crenatiloba
Toothed butterwort

Pinguicula grandiflora
Greater butterwort

Pinguicula ionantha
Violet butterwort

Pinguicula lilacina
Pale violet butterwort
Violet butterwort

Pinguicula lusitanica
Portuguese butterwort

Pinguicula lutea Yellow butterwort

Pinguicula pumila
Dwarf butterwort

Pinguicula ramosa
Branched butterwort

Pinguicula variegata
Variegated butterwort

Pinguicula villosa
Shaggy butterwort

Pinguicula vulgaris   Butterwort
Common butterwort

Polypompholyx multifida
Pink petticoat

Polypompholyx tenella   Pink fans

Sarracenia alabamensis
Alabama canebrake pitcher
plant

Sarracenia alata   Pale pitcher
Winged trumpets
Yellow trumpets

Sarracenia drummondii
White trumpet pitcher plant

Sarracenia flava   Huntsman's horn
Trumpet leaf
Trumpets
Umbrella trumpets
Watches
Yellow pitcher plant

Sarracenia leucophylla
White trumpet pitcher plant

Sarracenia minor
Hooded pitcher plant
Rainhat trumpet

Sarracenia oreophila
Green pitcher plant

Sarracenia psittacina
Parrot pitcher plant

Utricularia spiralis

Sarracenia purpurea
Common pitcher plant
Huntsman's cup
Indian cup
Northern pitcher plant
Pitcher plant
Purple pitcher plant
Side-saddle flower
Southern pitcher plant
Sweet pitcher plant

Sarracenia rubra
Sweet pitcher plant
Sweet trumpet

Sarracenia sledgei   Pale pitcher

Utricularia amethystina
Amethyst bladderwort

Utricularia cornuta
Horned bladderwort

Utricularia gibba
Humped bladderwort

Utricularia inflata
Floated bladderwort

Utricularia macrorhiza
Great bladderwort

Utricularia minor
Lesser bladderwort

Utricularia nova-zealandiae
New Zealand bladderwort

Utricularia pubescens
Downy bladderwort

Utricularia resupinata
Inverted bladderwort

Utricularia spiralis
Twining bladderwort

FERNS AND FERN ALLIES

These are flowerless plants bearing leaves (fronds) and reproducing by spores on the lower surface of the mature foliage. Ferns and fern allies share a similar life-cycle and are treated horticulturally in a similar manner. For example, the so-called asparagus fern *Asparagus setaceus* is not a fern but one of the *liliaceae*.

Toothed Davallia –
Davallia denticulata

Acrostichum aureum

Acrostichum aureum   Leather fern

Adiantum aethiopicum
Common maidenhair

Adiantum capillus-veneris
Maidenhair
Southern maidenhair
True maidenhair
Venus' hair

*Adiantum capillus-veneris
incisum*   Cleft maidenhair
Cleft true maidenhair

Adiantum cuneatum
Delta maidenhair

Adiantum decorum
Delta maidenhair

Adiantum diaphanum
Filmy maidenhair

Adiantum formosum
Australian maidenhair
Blackstem maidenhair
Giant maidenhair

Adiantum hispidulum
Five-fingered jack
Rosy maidenhair
Rough maidenhair

Adiantum pedatum
American maidenhair
Maidenhair
Northern maidenhair

Adiantum peruvianum
Silver dollar fern

Adiantum raddianum
Delta maidenhair

Adiantum reniforme
Kidney maidenhair

Adiantum tenerum
Brittle maidenhair

Adiantum trapeziforme
Diamond maidenhair

*Aglaomorpha goeringianum
pictum*   Japanese painted fern

Aglaomorpha pycnocarpon
Glade fern

Aglaomorpha thelypteroides
Silver glade fern

Allosorus crispus   Parsley fern

Aneimia adiantifolia   Pine fern

Angiopteris evecta   Giant fern
King fern

Anogramma leptophylla
Jersey fern

Arachniodes aristata
Prickly shield fern

Asplenium adiantum-nigrum
Black maidenhair spleenwort
Black spleenwort

*Asplenium adiantum-
nigrum ramosum*
Branched black maidenhair
spleenwort

*Asplenium adiantum-
nigrum variegatum*
Variegated black maidenhair
spleenwort
Variegated black spleenwort

Asplenium billottii
Lanceolate spleenwort

Asplenium bulbiferum
Hen-and-chickens fern
Mother fern
Mother spleenwort

Asplenium ceterach
Rusty back fern
Scaly spleenwort

Asplenium ceterach kalon
Wide-fronded scaly spleenwort

Asplenium daucifolium
Mauritius spleenwort

Asplenium flabellifolium
Necklace fern

Asplenium flaccidum
Hanging spleenwort
Weeping spleenwort

Asplenium fontanum
Rock spleenwort

*Asplenium fontanum
multifidum*
Cloven rock spleenwort

*Asplenium fontanum
refractum*
Refracted rock spleenwort

Asplenium germanicum
Alternate spleenwort

*Asplenium germanicum
acutidentatum*
Sharp-toothed alternate
spleenwort

Asplenium lanceolatum
Lanceolate spleenwort

Asplenium lanceolatum kalon
Twin-fronded lanceolate
spleenwort

Asplenium majus
Hanging spleenwort
Weeping spleenwort

Asplenium marinum
Sea spleenwort

Asplenium marinum ramosum
Branched sea spleenwort

Asplenium mayi
Hanging spleenwort
Weeping spleenwort

Asplenium nidus   Bird's nest fern
Crow's nest fern

Asplenium platyneuron
Ebony spleenwort

Asplenium ruta-muraria
Rue-leaved spleenwort
Wall rue

*Asplenium ruta-muraria
unilaterale*
One-sided rue-leaved
spleenwort

FERNS

Cystopteris fragilis furcans

Asplenium septentrionale
Forked spleenwort
Asplenium trichomanes
Maidenhair fern
Maidenhair spleenwort
Asplenium trichomanes confluens
Confluent maidenhair fern
Confluent maidenhair spleenwort
Asplenium trichomanes multifidum
Clove maidenhair fern
Cloven maidenhair spleenwort
Asplenium trichomanes ramosum
Branched maidenhair fern
Branched maidenhair spleenwort
Asplenium viride
Green spleenwort
Asplenium viride multifidum
Cloven green spleenwort
Asplenium viviparum
Mauritius spleenwort
Athyrium australe
Australian lady fern
Athyrium filix-femina Lady fern
Athyrium filix-femina corymbiferum
Tasselled lady fern
Athyrium filix-femina multifidum Cloven lady fern
Athyrium filix-femina multifidum nanum
Dwarf cloven lady fern
Athyrium filix-femina multifurcatum
Multi-forked lady fern
Athyrium filix-femina victoriae
Queen lady fern
Athyrium thelypteroides
Silvery glade fern
Silvery spleenwort
Azolla caroliniana Fairy moss
Mosquito fern
Mosquito plant
Water fern
Blechnum capense Palm-leaf fern
Blechnum cartilagineum
Australian water fern
Bristle fern
Blechnum discolor Crown fern
Blechnum nudum
Fishbone rib fern
Fishbone water fern
Blechnum occidentale
Hammock fern
Blechnum patersonii Strap rib fern
Strap water fern
Blechnum spicant Deer fern
Hard fern
Ladder fern
Blechnum spicant contractum-ramosum
Narrow-branched hard fern

Blechnum spicant duplex
Double-fronded hard fern
Blechnum spicant flabellata
Fan-like hard fern
Blechnum spicant furcans
Forked hard fern
Blechnum spicant ramosum
Branched hard fern
Blechnum watsii Hard water fern
Botrychium lunaria Moonwort
Botrychium lunaria incisum
Cleft moonwort
Botrychium multifidum
Leathery moonwort
Botrychium virginianum
Rattlesnake fern
Virginian moonwort
Camptosorus rhizophyllus
Walking fern
Ceratopteris pteridoides
Floating fern
Ceratopteris richardii
Triangular water fern
Ceratopteris thalictroides
Water fern
Ceterach officinarum
Rusty back fern
Scaly spleenwort
Cheilanthes lamosa Hairy-lip fern
Cibotium glaucum Hapu tree fern
Hawaiian tree fern
Cibotium schiedei
Mexican tree fern
Cryptogramma crispa Parsley fern
Ctenitis sloanei
American tree fern
Florida tree fern
Culcita dubia
Common ground fern
False bracken
Rainbow fern
Cyathea arborea Tree fern
West Indian tree fern
Cyathea australis Rough tree fern
Cyathea baileyana Wig tree fern
Cyathea cooperi
Australian tree fern
Cyathea dealbata Ponga
Silver king fern
Cyathea medullaris Black tree fern
Korau
Mamaku
Cyrtomium falcatum
House holly fern
Japanese holly fern
Cystopteris bulbifera
Berry bladder fern
Bulbil bladder fern
Cystopteris fragilis
Brittle bladder fern
Fragile bladder fern
Cystopteris fragilis furcans
Forked brittle bladder fern

Cystopteris montana

Cystopteris montana
　　Mountain bladder fern
Cystopteris regia
　　Alpine bladder fern
Davallia bullata　　Ball fern
　　Squirrel's foot fern
Davallia canariensis
　　Deer's foot fern
　　Rabbit's foot fern
Davallia denticulata
　　Toothed davallia
Davallia fejeensis　　Hare's foot fern
　　Rabbit's foot fern
Davallia mariesii　　Ball fern
　　Hare's foot fern
　　Squirrel's foot fern
Davallia trichomanoides
　　Squirrel's foot fern
Dennstaedia davallioides
　　Lacy ground fern
Dennstaedia punctilobula
　　Boulder fern
　　Hay-scented fern
Dicksonia antarctica
　　Soft tree fern
　　Tasmanian tree fern
　　Woolly tree fern
Dicksonia fibrosa
　　Golden tree fern
　　Wheki-ponga
　　Woolly tree fern
Dicksonia punctilobula
　　Boulder fern
　　Hay-scented fern
Dicksonia squarrosa
　　New Zealand tree fern
　　Rough dicksonia
　　Wheki
Dicksonia youngiae
　　Bristly tree fern
Diplazium acrostichoides
　　Silvery glade fern
　　Silvery spleenwort
Doodia aspera　　Hacksaw fern
　　Prickly rasp fern
　　Rasp fern
Doodia caudata　　Small rasp fern
Doodia media　　Common rasp fern
　　Hacksaw fern
Doryopteris pedata　　Hand fern
Drynaria quercifolia　　Oak-leaf fern
Dryopteris aemula
　　Hay-scented buckler fern
Dryopteris affinis　　Scaly male fern
Dryopteris austriaca
　　Broad buckler fern
Dryopteris austriaca spinulosa
　　Toothed wood fern
Dryopteris borreri
　　Golden-scaled male fern
Dryopteris carthusiana
　　Toothed wood fern

Dryopteris cristata
　　Crested buckler fern
　　Crested wood fern
Dryopteris dilatata
　　Broad buckler fern
　　Florist's fern
Dryopteris erythrosora
　　Autumn fern
　　Japanese buckler fern
　　Japanese shield fern
Dryopteris filix-mas
　　Common buckler fern
　　Male fern
Dryopteris goldiana
　　Giant wood fern
　　Goldie's fern
Dryopteris marginalis
　　Leatherwood fern
　　Marginal buckler fern
　　Marginal shield fern
Dryopteris oreades
　　Mountain male fern
Dryopteris spinulosa
　　Toothed wood fern
Dryopteris submontana
　　Rigid buckler fern
Dryopteris thelypteris　　Marsh fern
Equisetum hyemale
　　Common horsetail
　　Common scouring brush
Equisetum scirpoides
　　Dwarf horsetail
　　Dwarf scouring brush
Equisetum variegatum
　　Variegated horsetail
　　Variegated scouring brush
Gleichnia dicarpa
　　Pouched coral fern
　　Tangle fern
Gleichnia dichotoma　　Savannah fern
Gleichnia linearis　　Savannah fern
Gleichnia microphylla
　　Parasol fern
　　Scrambling coral fern
　　Umbrella fern
Grammitis australis　　Finger fern
Grammitis billardieri　　Finger fern
Gymnocarpium dryopteris
　　Common oak fern
　　Oak fern
Gymnocarpium robertianum
　　Limestone oak fern
　　Northern oak fern
Gymnogramma leptophylla
　　Annual maidenhair
Helminthostachys zeylanica
　　Malayan flowering fern
Histiopteris incisa　　Bat's wing fern
　　Oak fern
Humata tyermannii
　　Bear's foot fern
Hymenophyllum tunbridgense
　　Tunbridge filmy fern

Osmunda regalis cristata

Hymenophyllum unilaterale
One-sided filmy fern

Hypolepis punctata Bramble fern

Hypolepis millefolia
Thousand-leaved fern

Isoetes echinospora
Spiny-spored quillwort

Isoetes engelmannii
Engelmann's quillwort

Lastrea cristata
Crested buckler fern

Lastrea dilatata
Broad buckler fern

Lastrea dilatata cristata
Crested broad buckler fern

Lastrea dilatata lepidota
Scaly broad buckler fern

Lastrea filix-mas
Common buckler fern
Male fern

Lastrea filix-mas cristata
Crested male fern

Lastrea filix-mas furcans
Forked male fern

Lastrea filix-mas multi-cristata
Multi-crested male fern

Lastrea filix-mas ramosa
Branched male fern

Lastrea montana
Mountain buckler fern

Lastrea montana cristata
Crested mountain buckler fern

Lastrea montana furcans
Forked mountain buckler fern

Lastrea recurva
Hay-scented buckler fern

Lastrea rigida Rigid buckler fern

Lastrea spinulosa
Prickly buckler fern

Lastrea thelypteris
Marsh buckler fern

Lastreopsis hispida
Bristly shield fern

Lastreopsis microsora
Creeping shield fern

Leptopteris superba
Pince of Wales' feather

Lycopodium clavatum
Ground pine
Running pine

Lycopodium complanatum
Ground cedar
Ground pine

Lycopodium lucidulum
Shining club moss

Lycopodium obscurum
Ground pine
Princess pine

Lycopodium tristachyum
Ground cedar

Lygodium circinatum
Malay climbing fern

Lygodium japonicum
Japanese climbing fern

Lygodium palmatum
Climbing fern
Hartford fern

Marattia douglasii Pala

Marattia fraxinea King fern
Para fern
Potato fern

Marattia salicina King fern
Para fern
Potato fern

Marsilea crenata
Floating pepperwort

Marsilea pubescens
Stemless pepperwort

Marsilea quadrifolia
European water clover

Marsilea strigosa
Stemless pepperwort

Matteuccia struthiopteris
Ostrich-feather fern
Shuttlecock fern

Microsorium diversifolium
Kangaroo fern

Microsorium pustulatum
Fragrant fern

Microsorium scandens
Fragrant fern

Nephrolepis cordifolia
Common fishbone fern
Erect sword fern
Fishbone fern
Herringbone fern
Sword fern

Nephrolepis exaltata Boston fern
Fishbone fern
Sword fern

Onoclea sensibilis
American oak fern
Bead fern
Sensitive fern

Ophioglossum californicum
Californian adder's tongue

Ophioglossum engelmannii
Engelmann's adder's tongue

Ophioglossum lusitanicum
Little adder's tongue

Ophioglossum pendulum
Drooping adder's tongue

Ophioglossum vulgatum
Adder's tongue

Oreopteris limbosperma
Lemon-scented fern

Osmunda cinnamomea Buckhorn
Cinnamon fern
Fiddleheads

Osmunda claytoniana
Interrupted fern

Osmunda regalis Flowering fern
Royal fern

Osmunda regalis cristata
Crested royal fern

Pellaea atropurpurea

Pellaea atropurpurea
Purple cliff brake

Pellaea falcata
Australian cliff brake
Sickle fern

Pellaea rotundifolia   Button fern
New Zealand cliff brake

Pellaea viridis   Green cliff brake

Phegopteris connectilis   Beech fern
Narrow beech fern
Northern beech fern

Phlebodium aureum
Golden polypody
Hare's foot fern
Rabbit's foot fern

Phyllitis scolopendrium
Hart's tongue fern

Phymatodes quercifolia
Oak-leaf fern

Phymatodes scolopendrium
Wart fern

Pityrogramma austroamericana
Gold fern

Pityrogramma calomelanos
Silver fern

Pityrogramma chrysophylla
Gold fern

Platycerium bifurcatum   Elkhorn
Staghorn

Platycerium hillii
Northern elkhorn

Platycerium superbum   Elkhorn
Moosehorn
Staghorn

Platycerium veitchii   Silver elkhorn

Polypodium alpestre
Alpine polypody

Polypodium alpestre flexile
Flexible alpine polypody

*Polypodium alpestre
laciniatum*
Fringed alpine polypody

Polypodium angustifolium
Narrow-leaved strap fern

Polypodium aureum
Golden polypody
Hare's foot fern
Rabbit's foot fern

Polypodium calcareum
Limestone polypody

Polypodium californicum
California polypody

Polypodium dryopteris
Common oak fern
Oak fern
Triple-branched polypody

Polypodium fraxinifolium
Ash-leaf polypody

Polypodium glycyrrhiza
Licorice fern

Polypodium hesperium
Western polypody

Polypodium incanum
Resurrection fern

Polypodium integrifolium
Climbing bird's nest fern

*Polypodium integrifolium
cristatum*
Crested climbing bird's nest fern

Polypodium interjectum
Western polypody

Polypodium irioides
Climbing bird's nest fern

Polypodium phegopteris
Beech fern
Mountain polypody

*Polypodium phegopteris
multifidum*
Cloven mountain polypody

Polypodium phyllitidis
Ribbon fern
Strap fern

Polypodium phymatodes
Wart fern

Polypodium polypodioides
Resurrection fern

Polypodium punctatum
Climbing bird's nest fern

Polypodium pustulatum
Fragrant fern

Polypodium scandens
Fragrant fern

Polypodium scolopendria
Wart fern

Polypodium scouleri
Leathery polypody

Polypodium subauriculatum
Jointed pine

Polypodium virginianum
American wall fern
Rock polypody

Polypodium vulgare   Adder's fern
Common polypody
European polypody
Wall fern
Wall polypody
Wart fern

Polypodium vulgare acutum
Tapering polypody

Polypodium vulgare auritum
Ear-lobed polypody

Polypodium vulgare bifidum
Double-pinnuled polypody

Polypodium vulgare cambrican
Welsh polypody

Polypodium vulgare crenatum
Notched polypody

Polypodium vulgare cristatum
Crested polypody

Polypodium vulgare semilacerum
Irish polypody

Polystichum acrostichoides
Christmas fern
Dagger fern

FERNS

Scolopendrium vulgare multiforme

Polystichum aculeatum	Hard shield fern
	Soft shield fern
Polystichum aculeatum furcatum	
	Forked hard shield fern
Polystichum aculeatum pulchrum	
	Beautiful hard shield fern
Polystichum angulare	
	Soft prickly shield fern
Polystichum angulare cristatum	
	Crested soft prickly shield fern
Polystichum angulare depauperatum	
	Skeleton soft-prickly shield fern
Polystichum angulare grandiceps	
	Grand-tasselled shield fern
Polystichum angulare lineare	
	Narrow-lined shield fern
Polystichum angulare ramulosum	
	Branch-crested shield fern
Polystichum angulare semitripinnatum	
	Divided soft prickly shield fern
Polystichum angulare tripinnatum	
	Tri-pinnate soft prickly shield fern
Polystichum angulare truncatum	
	Truncate shield fern
Polystichum braunii	
	Braun's holly fern
Polystichum falcatum	
	Japanese holly fern
Polystichum lonchitis	Holly fern
	Mountain holly fern
Polystichum lonchitis confertum	
	Dense holly fern
	Irish holly fern
Polystichum munitum	
	Giant holly fern
	Sword fern
Polystichum proliferum	
	Mother shield fern
Polystichum setiferum	Hedge fern
	Soft shield fern
Polystichum tsus-simense	
	Dwarf leather fern
	Tsusima holly fern
Polystichum vestitum	
	Prickly shield fern
Psilotum nudum	Whisk fern
Pteridium aquilinum	Bracken
	Common bracken
Pteridium esculentum	
	Australian bracken
Pteridium latiusculum	
	Eastern bracken

Pteridium pubescens	
	Western bracken
Pteris aquilinum	Bracken
	Common bracken
Pteris aquilina bisulca	
	Split-fronded bracken
Pteris aquilina cristata	
	Crested bracken
Pteris cretica	Cretan brake
	Cretan fern
	Ribbon brake
	Ribbon fern
Pteris dentata	Fine-toothed brake
Pteris ensiformis	
	Australian slender brake
	Slender brake
	Snow brake
	Sword brake
Pteris flabellata	
	Fine-toothed brake
Pteris flaccida	Fine-toothed brake
Pteris longifolia	Chinese brake
	Ladder brake
	Rusty brake
Pteris multifida	Chinese fern
	Huguenot fern
	Spider fern
Pteris serrulata	Chinese fern
	Huguenot fern
	Spider fern
Pteris tremula	Australian brake
	Toothed brake
	Trembling brake
	Trembling fern
Pteris tripartita	Giant brake
	Trisect brake
Pteris vittata	Chinese brake
	Ladder brake
	Rusty brake
Pyrossia lingua	Japanese felt fern
	Tongue fern
Pyrossia rupestris	Rock felt fern
Rumohra adiantiformis	
	Leather fern
	Leather shield fern
	Shield hare's foot
Salvinia rotundifolia	
	Floating moss
Schizaea pusilla	Curly-grass fern
Scolopendrium vulgare crispum-latum	
	Broad curly hartstongue
Scolopendrium vulgare cristatum	
	Crested hartstongue
Scolopendrium vulgare duplex	
	Double-fronded hartstongue
Scolopendrium vulgare laceratum	
	Jagged-edge hartstongue
Scolopendrium vulgare multiforme	
	Many-shaped hartstongue

Scolopendrium vulgare
ramo-cristatum

Scolopendrium vulgare
ramo-cristatum
  Branch-crested hartstongue
Scolopendrium vulgare
ramo-palmatum
  Twin-fronded hartstongue
Scolopendrium vulgare
reniforme
  Kidney-shaped hartstongue
Scolopendrium vulgare
truncatum
  Short-fronded hartstongue
Scolopendrium vulgare
undulato-ramosum
  Wavy hartstongue

Selaginella apoda
  Basket selaginella

Selaginella braunii
  Treelet spike moss

Selaginella cuspidata   Moss fern
  Sweat plant

Selaginella densa   Basket selaginella

Selaginella douglasii
  Douglas's spike moss

Selaginella kraussiana
  Mat spike moss
  Trailing selaginella
  Trailing spike moss

Selaginella lepidophylla
  Resurrection plant
  Rose of Jericho

Selaginella pallescens   Moss fern
  Sweat plant

Selaginella rupestris
  Dwarf lycopod
  Rock selaginella

Selaginella uncinata
  Blue selaginella
  Peacock moss
  Rainbow fern
  Trailing selaginella

Selaginella willdenovii
  Peacock fern
  Willdenow's selaginella

Stenochlaena palustris
  Climbing swamp fern
Sticherus flabellatus   Shiny fan fern
  Umbrella fern
Sticherus tener   Silky fan fern
Struthiopteris germanica
  Ostrich-feather fern
  Shuttlecock fern
Tectaria cicutaria   Button fern
  Snail fern
Tectaria gemmifera   Button fern
  Snail fern
Thelypteris hexagonoptera
  Broad beech fern
  Southern beech fern
Thelypteris noveboracensis
  New York fern
Thelypteris oreopteris
  Mountain buckler fern
Thelypteris palustris   Marsh fern
Thelypteris phegopteris
  Beech fern
  Broad beech fern
  Northern beech fern
Trichomanes radicans
  European bristle fern
Trichomanes radicans furcans
  Forked bristle fern
Tricholomopsis rutilans
  Plums and custard fern
Woodsia alpina   Alpine woodsia
Woodsia ilvensis   Oblong woodsia
  Rusty woodsia
Woodsia obtusa
  Blunt-lobed woodsia
  Common woodsia
Woodwardia chamissoi
  Giant chain fern
Woodwardia fimbriata
  Giant chain fern
Woodwardia radicans
  European chain fern
Woodwardia virginica
  Virginia chain fern

FUNGI

A large group of simple plants lacking chlorophyll is covered by the word fungi. This section is concerned only with the larger edible, inedible and poisonous fungi which are visible to the naked eye. Many edible fungi are matched in appearance with inedible, or even poisonous types so it is reckless to gather wild fungi unless you are experienced and familiar with the subtle difference. In the following list, entries have been classified by the use of bracketed initions thus:

(E) – Edible, but some may be allergic to them.
(I) – Inedible for a variety of reasons.
(P) – Poisonous, but not usually fatal.
(F) – Can be fatal if eaten, sometimes within minutes.

Field mushroom – *Agaricus campestris*

Agaricus arvensis

Agaricus arvensis   Horse agaric (E)
     Horse mushroom (E)

Agaricus bisporus
     Cultivated mushroom (E)

Agaricus bitorquis
     Pavement mushroom (E)
     Urban mushroom (E)

Agaricus campestris
     Field mushroom (E)
     Pink bottom mushroom (E)

Agaricus sylvaticus
     Brown wood mushroom (E)

Agaricus silvicola
     Wood mushroom (E)

Agaricus xanthodermus
     Yellow stainer (P)

Aleuria aurantia
     Orange-peel fungus (E)

Amanita caesarea
     Caesar's mushroom (I)

Amanita citrina   False death cap (I)

Amanita fulva   Sheathed agaric (E)
     Tawny grisette (E)

Amanita mappa   False death cap (I)

Amanita muscaria   Fly agaric (P)

Amanita pantherina
     False blusher (P)
     Panther cap (P)

Amanita phalloides   Death cap (F)
     Mortician cap (F)

Amanita regalis   Royal amanita (P)

Amanita rubescens
     The blusher (E)
     Woodland pink mushroom (E)

Amanita vaginata
     Common grisette (E)

Amanita verna
     Fool's mushroom (F)
     Spring amanita (F)

Amanita virosa   Coffin filler (F)
     Destroying angel (F)

Armillaria mellea
     Bootlace fungus (E)
     Honey fungus (E)

Auricularia auricula-judae
     Judas's ear (E)

Auricularia mesenterica
     Tripe fungus (I)

Auriscalpium vulgare
     Ear-pick fungus (I)

Boleta speciosus
     Showy mushroom (E)

Boletus aereus   Bronze boletus (E)

Boletus aestivalis
     Summer boletus (E)

Boletus badius   Bay boletus (E)

Boletus calopus   Olive boletus (I)

Boletus chrysenteron
     Red cracked boletus (I)
     Crazed boletus (I)

Boletus cyanescens
     Indigo boletus (E)

Boletus edulis   Cep (E)
     Penny bun fungus (E)

Boletus erythropus
     Red-leg boletus (E)

Boletus leucophareus
     Brown birch boletus (E)
     Cow fungus (E)

Boletus luridus   Lurid boletus (E)

Boletus regius   Royal boletus (E)

Boletus reticulatus
     Summer boletus (E)

Boletus rhodoxanthus
     Purple boletus (P)

Boletus satanas   Devil's boletus (P)
     Satan's mushroom (P)

Boletus subtomentosus
     Downy boletus (E)
     Goat's lip mushroom (E)

Bulgaria inquinans
     Bachelor's buttons (E)
     Black bulgar (E)

Calocybe gambosa
     Saint George's mushroom (E)

Calvatia gigantea
     Giant puffball (E)

Calyptella capula
     Stinging-nettle fungus (I)

Cantharellus cibarius
     Chanterelle (E)

Cantharellus cornucopioides
     Horn of plenty (E)

Chlorociboria aeruginacens
     Greenstain fungus (I)
     Green wood cup (I)

Chlorosplenium aeruginosum
     Greenstain fungus (I)
     Green wood cup (I)

Chondrostereum purpureum
     Silverleaf fungus (I)

Clathrus cancellatus
     Basket fungus (E)

Clathrus ruber   Basket fungus (E)

Clavaria argillacea   Moor club (I)

Clavariadelphus pistillaris
     Giant club (E)

Claviceps purpurea   Ergot (P)
     Spurred rye (P)

Clavulina cinerea
     Grey coral fungus (P)

Clavulina coralloides
     Crested coral fungus (P)

Clavulina cristata
     Crested coral fungus (P)

Clavulina rugosa
     Wrinkled club (P)

Clitocybe clavipes   Club foot (I)

Clitocybe geotropa
     Trumpet agaric (E)

Clitocybe illudens
     Copper trumpet (P)

Helvella elastica

Clitocybe mellea
Bootlace fungus (E)
Honey fungus (E)

Clitocybe nebularis
Clouded agaric (E)
Clouded clitocybe (E)

Clitocybe odora
Aniseed toadstool (E)

Clitocybe olearia
Copper trumpet (P)

Clitopilus prunulus
Miller mushroom (E)
Plum agaric (E)
Sweetbread mushroom (E)

Collybia butyracea
Buttery collybia (E)
Butter cap (E)

Collybia confluens
Clustered tough-shank (I)

Collybia dryophila
Oaktree collybia (E)
Wood agaric (E)

Collybia fusipes   Spindle shank (E)

Collybia maculata   Foxy spot (E)
Spotted tough-shank (I)

Collybia peronata
Wood woollyfoot (I)

Collybia velutipedes
Velvet shank (E)
Winter mushroom (E)

Conocybe lactea
Milky conocybe (I)

Coprinus atramentarius
Grey inkcap (E)
Inkcap (E)

Coprinus comatus   Inkcap (E)
Lawyer's wig (E)
Shaggy cap (E)
Shaggy inkcap (E)

Coprinus disseminatus
Fairy bonnets (P)
Trooping crumble cap (P)

Coprinus micaceus
Glistening inkcap (I)
Mica inkcap (I)
Shining inkcap (I)

Coprinus niveus
Horse-dung fungus (I)

Coprinus picaceus
Magpie fungus (P)

Coprinus plicatilis
Japanese sunshade (P)
Little Japanese umbrella (P)

Cordyceps militaris
Scarlet caterpillar fungus (P)

Coricolus versicolor
Multi-zoned bracket fungus (P)

Cortinarius traganus
Goaty smell cortinarius (I)

Craterellus cornucopioides
Horn of plenty (E)

Crucibulum crucibuliforme
Bird's nest fungus (I)

Crucibulum laeve
Bird's nest fungus (I)

Cyathus striatus   Splash cup (I)

Daedalea quercina   Maze gill (P)

Daedaleopsis confragosa
Blushing bracket fungus (I)

Daldinia concentrica
King Alfred's cakes (I)
King Alfred's balls (I)
King Alfred's cramp balls (I)

Dentinum repandum
Wood hedgehog (E)

Echinodontium tinctorium
Indian paint fungus (I)

Entoloma clypeatum
Buckler agaric (I)

Entoloma lividum
Livid entoloma (P)

Entoloma sinuatum
Livid entoloma (P)

Exidia glandulosa
Witch's butter (I)

Fistulina hepatica
Beefsteak fungus (E)
Rusty oak fungus (E)

Flammulina velutipedes
Velvet shank (E)
Winter mushroom (E)

Fomes fomentarius   Hoof fungus (I)
Tinder fungus (I)

Geastrum fimbriatum   Earthstar (I)

Geastrum fornicatum   Earthstar (I)

Geastrum pectinatum   Earthstar (I)

Geastrum sessile   Earthstar (I)

Geastrum triplex   Earthstar (I)

Gomphidius glutinosus
Woodland black spot (E)

Gomphidius rutilis
Pine forest mushroom (E)

Grifola frondosa
Hen-of-the-woods (E)

Gymnosporangium clavariaeforme
Knotted fungus (I)

Gyromitra esculenta
False morel (P)

Gyromitra infula   Turban fungus (E)

Gyroporus castaneus
Bitter boletus (E)
Chestnut boletus (E)

Gyroporus cyanescens
Indigo boletus (E)

Hebeloma crustuliniforme
Fairy cake fungus (F)
Poison pie (F)

Hebeloma sacchariolens
Bitter-sweet fungus (P)

Helvella crispa
Common white helvella (P)

Helvella elastica
Distorted helvella (P)

Helvella fusca

Helvella fusca
Black-saddle helvella (P)
Helvella infula Turban fungus (E)
Helvella lacunosa
Black helvella (P)
Helvella villosa Cupped villosa (P)
Hericium erinaceum
Hedgehog fungus (E)
Heterobasidion annosum
Root fomes (I)
Hirneola auricula-judae
Jew's ear (P)
Hydnum imbricatum
Scaly hydnum (E)
Hydnum repandum
Hedgehog fungus (E)
Wood hedgehog (E)
Hydnum scabrosum
Bitter hydnum (I)
Hygrocybe conica
Conical wax cap (I)
Hygrocybe pratensis
Meadow wax cap (I)
Hygrocybe psittacina
Parrot fungus (E)
Parrot wax cap (E)
Hygrocybe virginea
Snowy wax cap (I)
Hygrophoropsis aurantiaca
False chanterelle (I)
Hygrophorus eburneus
Ivory wax cap (I)
Hygrophorus marzuolus
March mushroom (E)
Hygrophorus psittacinus
Parrot fungus (E)
Hypholoma capnoides
Smokey-gilled woodlover (I)
Hypholoma fasciculare
Sulphur tuft (P)
Hypholoma sublateritium
Brick-red agaric (I)
Inocybe fastigiata
Conical inocybe (P)
Inocybe geophylla
Common white inocybe (P)
Inocybe napipes
Skullcap inocybe (P)
Inocybe patouillardii
Red-staining inocybe (F)
Kuehneromyces mutabilis
Changeable mutabilis (E)
Rusty agaric (E)
Laccaria amethystea
Amethyst deceiver (E)
Laccaria laccata Deceiver (E)
The deceiver (E)
Lacrymaria lacrymabunda
Weeping widow (I)
Lacrymaria velutina Velvet cap (I)
Weeping widow (I)

Lactarius deliciosus Milk agaric (E)
Milk cap (E)
Saffron milk cap (E)
Lactarius glyciosmus
Coconut-scented milk cap (I)
Lactarius necator
Ugly mushroom (I)
Lactarius plumbeus
Ugly mushroom (I)
Lactarius quietus Oak milk cap (I)
Lactarius rufus Rusty milk cap (I)
Lactarius torminosus
Shaggy milk cap (I)
Woolly milk cap (I)
Lactarius turpis
Ugly mushroom (I)
Lactarius vellereus
Fleecy milk cap (I)
Laetiporus sulphureus
Sulfur polypore (E)
Sulphur polypore (E)
Langermannia gigantea
Giant puffball (E)
Lapista nuda Wood blewits (E)
Leccinum aurantiacum
Orange cap boletus (E)
Leccinum carpini
Hornbeam boletus (E)
Leccinum duriusculum
White poplar mushroom (E)
Leccinum griseum
Hornbeam boletus (E)
Leccinum holopus
White birch boletus (E)
Leccinum melaneum
Black birch boletus (E)
Leccinum quercinum
Oaktree boletus (E)
Leccinum scabrum
Brown birch boletus (E)
Cow fungus (E)
Leccinum testaceoscabrum
Orange birch boletus (E)
Leccinum versipelle
Orange birch boletus (E)
Lentinula edodes
Shiitake fungus (E)
Leota lubrica Jellybaby fungus (E)
Jellybean fungus (E)
Lepiota castanea
Tasselated toadstool (P)
Lepiota procera Fairy sunshade (E)
Parasol mushroom (E)
Lepiota rhacodes
Shaggy parasol (E)
Lepista irina Bigelow's blewit (E)
Lepista nebularis
Clouded agaric (E)
Clouded clitocybe (E)
Lepista nuda Wood blewitts (E)
Lepista saeva Blewits (E)

FUNGI

Russula claroflava

Lycoperdon echinatum
Hedgehog fungus (E)

Lycoperdon gemmatum
Common puffball (E)
Poor man's sweetbread (E)

Lycoperdon maximum
Giant puffball (E)

Lycoperdon perlatum
Common puffball (E)
Poor man's sweetbread (E)

Macrolepiota procera
Fairy sunshade (E)
Parasol mushroom (E)

Macrolepiota rhacodes
Shaggy parasol (E)

Marasmius androsaceus
Horsehair fungus (I)

Marasmius oreades
Clover windling (E)
Fairy ring mushroom (E)

Masseola crispa
Cauliflower fungus (E)

Meripilus giganteus
Giant polypore (I)

Microglossum viride
Green earth tongue (I)

Morchella conica
Conical morel (E)

Morchella elata   Morel (E)

Morchella esculenta
Common morel (E)

Mutinus caninus   Dog stinkhorn (I)

Mycena galericulata
Bonnet mycena (I)

Mycena ribula   Little nail fungus (P)

Mycena vitilis   Pixie's cap fungus (I)

Namatoloma fasciculare
Sulphur tuft (P)

Nectria cinnabarina
Coral spot fungus (I)

Neogyromitra gigas
Giant giromitra (E)

Omphalotus olearius
Copper trumpet (P)

Otidea onotica
Donkey's ear fungus (E)
Hare's ear fungus (I)

Oudemansiella mucida
Beech tuft (I)
Poached egg fungus (I)

Oudemansiella radicata
Long root mushroom (E)

Paxillus involutus
Brown roll-rim (P)
Roll-rim fungus (P)

Peziza ammophila
Brown star fungus (P)

Peziza aurantia
Orange-peel fungus (E)

Phallus hadriani
Devil's egg fungus (I)

Phallus impudicus   Stinkhorn (E)

Pholiota caperata
Gipsy mushroom (E)

Pholiota squarrosa
Shaggy pholiota (I)

Piptoporus betulinus
Birch bracket fungus (E)
Birch polypore (E)
Razor-strop fungus (E)

Pleurotus cornucopiae
Branched oyster fungus (E)

Pleurotus ostreatus
Oyster mushroom (E)

Pluteus atricapillus
Deer mushroom (E)
Fawn agaric (E)

Pluteus cervinus
Deer mushroom (E)
Fawn agaric (E)

Polyporus betulinus
Birch bracket fungus (E)
Razor-strop fungus (E)

Polyporus frondosus
Hen-of-the-woods (E)

Polyporus squamosus
Dryad's saddle (E)
Scaly polypore (E)

Polyporus versicolor
Multi-zoned bracket fungus (P)

Psalliota arvensis   Horse agaric (E)
Horse mushroom (E)

Psalliota campestris
Field mushroom (E)
Pink bottom mushroom (E)

Psalliota silvicola
Wood mushroom (E)

Psalliota sylvatica
Brown wood mushroom (E)

Pseudocoprinus disseminatus
Trooping crumble cap (P)

Pseudohydnum gelatinosum
Jello tongue (P)
Jelly tongue (P)

Psilocybe semilanceata
Liberty cap (P)

Pycnoporus cinnabarinus
Cinnabar polypore (I)

Ramaria formosa
Multi-branched fungus (P)

Rhytisma acerinum
Sycamore tarspot (I)

Rhyzina undulata
Pine fire fungus (P)

Rozites caperata
Gipsy mushroom (E)

Russula aeruginea
Grass-green russula (E)

Russula alutacea
Leathery russula (E)

Russula aurata   Golden russula (E)

Russula claroflava
Yellow swamp russula (E)

Russula cyanoxantha
Blue and yellow russula (E)
Green agaric (E)

Russula decolorans
Faded russula (E)

Russula emetica
Sickener mushroom (P)
Emetic russula (P)

Russula flava
Yellow swamp russula (E)

Russula fragilis   Fragile russula (P)

Russula mairei
Beechwood sickener (I)

Russula nigricans
Blackening russula (I)

Russula ochroleuca
Yellow russula (I)

Russula olivacea
Olive-green russula (E)

Russula undulata
Purple-black russula (P)

Russula vesca
Bare-tooth russula (E)

Russula virescens   Green agaric (E)
Green cracking russula (E)

Russula xerampelina
Dark red russula (E)

Sarcodon imbricatum
Scaly hydnum (E)

Sarcoscypha coccinea   Elf cup (E)
Pixie cup (E)
Scarlet cup (E)
Scarlet elf cap (E)

Schizophyllum commune
Split gill fungus (P)

Scleroderma citrinum
Common earthball (P)

Scutellinia scutellata
Eyelash cup fungus (I)
Eyelash fungus (I)

Sparassis crispa
Cauliflower fungus (E)
Brain fungus (E)

Sparassis ramosa
Cauliflower fungus (E)

Sphaerotheca pannosa
Rose mildew (I)

Stereum hirsutum
Hairy stereum (I)

Stropharia aeruginosa
Verdigris fungus (E)

Suillus bovinus   Cow boletus (E)
Jersey cow boletus (E)
Rainfall boletus (E)

Suillus grevillei   Larch boletus (E)

Suillus luteus   Ringed boletus (E)
Slippery jack (E)

Suillus variegatus
Variegated boletus (E)

Taphrina betulina
Witch's broom (P)

Thelephora terrestris
Carpet fungus (I)
Earth fan (I)

Trametes versicolor
Multi-zoned bracket fungus (P)
Multi-zoned polypore (P)

Tremella mesenterica
Jellybrain fungus (I)
Yellow brain fungus (I)

Tricholoma equestre
Firwood agaric (E)
Man on horseback (E)

Tricholoma flavovirens
Firwood agaric (E)
Man on horseback (E)

Tricholoma gambosa
Saint George's mushroom (E)

Tricholoma georgii
Saint George's mushroom (E)

Tricholoma nudum
Wood blewits (E)

Tricholoma pardalotum
Tiger tricholoma (P)

Tricholoma pardinum
Tiger tricholoma (P)

Tricholoma personatum
Blewits (E)

Tricholoma portentosum
Dingy agaric (E)

Tricholoma sulphureum
Yellow agaric (P)
Gas tar fungus (P)

Tricholoma terreum
Grey agaric (E)

Tricholomopsis rutilans
Plums and custard (E)

Tuber aestivum   Summer truffle (E)
Truffle (E)

Tuber magnatum   White truffle (E)
Piedmont truffle (E)

Tuber melanosporum
French truffle (E)
Perigord truffle (E)

Tylopilus felleus   Bitter bolete (I)
Bitter cep (I)

Ustilago maydis   Corn smut (P)

Volvaria speciosa
Rose-gilled grisette (E)

Volvaria volvacea
Padi-straw fungus (E)

Volvariella speciosa
Rose-gilled grisette (E)

Volvariella volvacea
Padi-straw fungus (E)

Xerocomus badius   Bay boletus (E)

Xerocomus subtomentosus
Downy boletus (E)
Goat's lip mushroom (E)

Xylaria hypoxylon
Candlesnuff fungus (I)

Xylaria polymorpha
Dead man's fingers (I)

GRASSES, REEDS, SEDGES, BAMBOOS, VETCHES, ETC.

True grasses are members of the family *Gramineae* and are found in almost every corner of the planet in one form or another, but in this section we are concerned with the ornamentals, meadow grasses, timber frasses (bamboos), soil-holding or sand-binding grasses, as well as wetland subjects such as sedges and reeds. Some grasses may also be listed under 'Aquatics'.

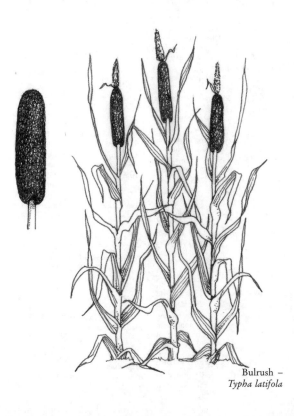

Bulrush –
Typha latifola

BOTANICAL NAMES

Agropogon littoralis
Perennial beard grass

Agropyron caninum
Bearded twitch
Bearded couch
Dog grass

Agropyron cristatum
Crested wheatgrass
Fairy crested wheatgrass

Agropyron donianum Don's twitch

Agropyron elongatum
Tall wheatgrass

Agropyron intermedium
Intermediate wheatgrass

Agropyron junceiforme
Sand couch
Sand twitch

Agropyron pungens Sea couch
Sea twitch

Agropyron repens
Creeping twitch grass
Couch grass
Quack grass
Quick grass
Quitch grass
Scutch grass
Twitch grass
Witch grass

Agropyron sibiricum
Desert wheatgrass
Siberian wheatgrass
Standard crested wheatgrass

Agropyron smithii
Western wheatgrass

Agropyron spicatum
Bluebunch wheatgrass

Agropyron trachycaulum
Slender wheatgrass

Agropyron trichophorum
Pubescent wheatgrass
Stiff hair wheatgrass

Agrostis canina Brown bent
Velvet bent

Agrostis curtisii Bristle bent

Agrostis gigantea Black bent
Red top

Agrostis nebulosa Cloud bent
Cloud grass

Agrostis perennans Autumn bent
Brown bent grass
Upland bent
Upland bent grass

Agrostis semiverticillata
Water bent

Agrostis setacea Bristly bent

Agrostis stolonifera Creeping bent

Agrostis tenuis Brown top
Colonial bent
Common bent
Fine bent
New Zealand bent
Rhode Island bent

Aira caryophyllea Silvery hair grass

Aira praecox Early hair grass

Alopecurus aequalis
Orange foxtail
Short-awn(ed) foxtail

Alopecurus alpinus Alpine foxtail

Alopecurus arundinaceus
Creeping foxtail
Reed foxtail

Alopecurus bulbosus
Bulbous foxtail
Tuberous foxtail

Alopecurus geniculatus
Floating foxtail
Marsh foxtail

Alopecurus myosuroides
Black grass
Black twitch
Slender foxtail

Alopecurus pratensis
Common foxtail
Meadow foxtail

Alopecurus pratensis 'aureus'
Golden foxtail

Ammocalamagrostis baltica
Hybrid marram grass

Ammophila arenaria
European beach grass
Marram grass

Ammophila breviligulata
American beach grass

Ampelodesmos mauritanicus
Mauritania vine reed

Andropogon gerardii
Big bluestem grass

Andropogon hallii
Sand bluestem grass

Anthoxanthum odoratum
Scented vernal grass
Sweet vernal grass

Anthoxanthum puelii
Annual vernal grass

Anthyllis montana Mountain vetch
Spanish vetch

Anthyllis vulneraria Kidney vetch
Lady's fingers
Woundwort

Apera interrupta Dense silky bent

Apera spica-venti Loose silky bent
Wind grass

Arenula pratensis
Meadow oat grass

Arrhenatherum bulbosum
Variegated oat grass

Arrhenatherum elatius
False oat grass
Oat grass
Tall oat grass
Variegated oat grass

Arundinaria amabilis
Tonkin bamboo
Tonkin cane
Tsingli cane

Arundinaria anceps
Himalayan bamboo
Ringal

Arundinaria disticha
Dwarf fern leaf bamboo

Arundinaria gigantea
Canebrake bamboo
Cane reed
Giant cane
Southern cane

Arundinaria japonica
Arrow bamboo
Metake

Arundinaria pumila
Dwarf bamboo

Arundinaria pygmaea
Pigmy bamboo

Arundinaria quadrangularis
Square-stemmed bamboo

Arundinaria simonii
Simon bamboo

Arundinaria tecta　　Small cane
Switch cane

Arundinaria variegata
Dwarf white-stripe bamboo

Arundo donax　　Carrizo
Cana brava
Giant reed

Avena barbata　　Slender wild oat

Avena fatua　　Common wild oat
Drake
Flaver
Potato oat
Spring wild oat
Tartarian oat
Wild oat

Avena ludoviciana
Winter wild oat grass
Winter wild oat

Avena pratensis
Perennial oat grass

Avena sativa　　Oats

Avena sterilis　　Animated oat grass
Animated oats
Winter wild oat

Avena strigosa　　Bristle oat
Small oat

Axonopus affinis　　Carpet grass
Common carpet grass

Bambusa arundinacea
Giant thorny bamboo

Bambusa beecheyana
Beechey bamboo

Bambusa glaucescens
Hedge bamboo
Oriental hedge bamboo

Bambusa multiplex
Hedge bamboo

Bambusa oldhamii
Oldham bamboo

Bambusa tuldoides
Punting-pole bamboo

Bambusa ventricosa
Buddha bamboo
Buddha's belly bamboo

Bambusa vulgaris
Common bamboo

Blysmus compressus
Sedge-like club rush
Flat sedge

Blysmus rufus　　Red blysmus

Boehmeria nivea　　China grass
Ramie fibre

Bothriochloa caucasica
Caucasian bluestem

Bothriochloa intermedia
Australian bluestem

Bothriochloa ischaemum
Turkestan bluestem
Yellow bluestem

Bothriochloa saccharoides
Silver beard grass

Bouteloua curtipendula
Sideoats grama

Bouteloua eriopoda　　Black grama

Bouteloua gracilis　　Blue grama
Mosquito grass

Bouteloua hirsuta　　Hairy grama

Bouteloua repens　　Slender grama

Brachiaria subquadripara
Creeping signal grass

Brachypodium pinnatum
Chalk false brome
Heath false brome
Tor grass

Brachypodium sylvaticum
False brome
Tor grass
Wood false brome

Briza maxima　　Large quaking grass
Pearl grass

Briza media
Common quaking grass
Doddering dillies
Quaking grass
Totter grass

Briza minor　　Lesser quaking grass
Little quaking grass
Small quaking grass

Bromus arvensis　　Field brome

Bromus briziformis
Rattlesnake brome
Rattlesnake chess

Bromus canadensis　　Fringed brome

Bromus carinatus
Californian brome

Bromus commutatus
Meadow brome

Bromus diandrus　　Great brome

Bromus erectus　　Erect brome
Upright brome

Bromus hordeaceus
Soft brome grass

Bromus inermis　　Awnless brome
Hungarian brome
Smooth brome

Bromus interruptus
Interrupted brome

Bromus japonicus

Bromus japonicus	Japanese brome
	Japanese chess
Bromus lanceolatus	
	Mediterranean brome
Bromus lepidus	Slender brome
Bromus madritensis	
	Compact brome
	Madrid brome
Bromus marginatus	
	Mountain brome
Bromus mollis	Soft brome grass
	Soft chess
Bromus recemosus	Smooth brome
Bromus ramosus	Hairy brome
	Woodland brome
Bromus rigidus	Stiff brome
Bromus rubens	Foxtail chess
Bromus secalinus	Rye brome
Bromus sterilis	Barren brome
Bromus tectorum	
	Drooping brome
Bromus unioloides	Prairie brome
	Rescue brome
	Rescue grass
Bromus wildenowii	Rescue brome
Buchloe dactyloides	Buffalo grass
Butomus umbellatus	
	Flowering rush
	Grassy rush
	Water gladiolus
Cabomba caroliniana	Fanwort
	Fish grass
	Washington grass
Calamagrostis canescens	
	Purple small reed
Calamagrostis epigejos	Bush grass
	Wood small reed
Calamagrostis nana	Small reed
Calamagrostis scotia	
	Scottish small reed
Calamagrostis stricta	
	Narrow small reed
Calamus rotang	Rattan
	Rattan cane
Calamus scipionum	Malacca cane
Carex acuta	Narrow-spiked sedge
	Slender-spiked sedge
Carex acutiformis	
	Lesser pond sedge
Carex appropinquata	
	Lesser tussock sedge
Carex aquatilis	
	Mountain water sedge
	Water sedge
Carex arenaria	Sand sedge
Carex atrata	Black sedge
Carex bigelowii	Stiff sedge
Carex binervis	
	Green-ribbed sedge
Carex buxbaumii	Club sedge
	Dark sedge

Carex capillaris	Hair sedge
Carex caryophyllea	Spring sedge
Carex curta	Pale sedge
	White sedge
Carex demissa	Low sedge
Carex depauperata	
	Starved wood sedge
Carex diandra	
	Double-stemmed sedge
	Lesser tussock sedge
Carex digitata	Fingered sedge
Carex dioica	Dioecious sedge
Carex distans	Distant sedge
Carex disticha	Brown sedge
	Creeping brown sedge
Carex divisa	Salt meadow sedge
Carex divulsa	Grey sedge
Carex echinata	Star sedge
Carex elata	Tufted sedge
Carex elongata	Elongated sedge
Carex ericetorum	Heath sedge
Carex extensa	Long-bracted sedge
Carex filiformis	
	Downy-fruited sedge
Carex flacca	Glaucous sedge
Carex flava	Yellow sedge
Carex grayi	Mace sedge
Carex hirta	Hairy sedge
Carex hostiana	Tawny sedge
Carex humilis	Dwarf sedge
Carex lachenalii	Hare's foot sedge
Carex laevigata	Smooth sedge
Carex lasiocarpa	
	Downy-fruited sedge
Carex limosa	Bog sedge
	Mud sedge
Carex loliacea	Darnel sedge
Carex maritima	Curved sedge
Carex montana	Mountain sedge
Carex muricata	Prickly sedge
Carex nigra	Common sedge
Carex norvegica	Alpine sedge
Carex ornithopoda	
	Bird's foot sedge
Carex otrubae	False fox sedge
Carex ovalis	Oval sedge
Carex pallescens	Pale sedge
Carex panicea	Carnation grass
	Carnation sedge
Carex paniculata	
	Greater tussock sedge
	Great tussock sedge
Carex pauciflora	
	Few-flowered sedge
Carex paupercula	
	Broad-leaved mud sedge
Carex pendula	Drooping sedge
	Pendulous sedge
	Sedge grass

Carex pilulifera	Pill sedge
Carex polyphylla	Chalk sedge
Carex pseudocyperus	Cyperus sedge
Carex punctata	Dotted sedge
Carex puticaris	Flea sedge
Carex rariflora	Few-flowered sedge
Carex recta	Caithness sedge
Carex remota	Distant-flowered sedge
Carex riparia	Great pond sedge
	Pond sedge
Carex rostrata	Beaked sedge
	Bottle sedge
Carex rupestris	Rock sedge
Carex saxatilis	Russet sedge
Carex serotina	Late-flowering sedge
Carex spicata	Spiked sedge
Carex stenolepis	Thin-glumed sedge
Carex strigosa	Loose-spiked wood sedge
	Thin-spiked wood sedge
Carex sylvatica	Wood sedge
Carex vaginata	Wide-sheathed sedge
Carex vesicaria	Bladder sedge
Carex vulpina	Fox sedge
Catabrosa aquatica	Water whorl grass
	Whorl grass
Catapodium marinum	Stiff sand grass
Catapodium rigidum	Fern grass
Chasmanthium latifolium	American wild oats
	Wild oats
Chimonobambusa falcata	Sickle bamboo
Chimonobambusa quadrangularis	Square bamboo
	Square-stem bamboo
Chionochloa conspicua	Hunangemoho
Chloris berroi	Giant finger grass
	Uruguay finger grass
Chloris gayana	Rhodes grass
Chloris truncata	Creeping windmill grass
	Star grass
Chloris ventricosa	Australian windmill grass
Chusquea culeou	Culeu
Cladium mariscus	Fenland sedge
	Great fenland sedge
Coix lacryma-jobi	Job's tears
Cortaderia argentea	Pampas grass

Cortaderia richardii	Toe-toe
Cortaderia selloana	Pampas grass
Corynephorus canescens	Grey hair grass
Cymbopogon citratus	Fevergrass
	Lemongrass
	West Indian lemongrass
Cymbopogon nardus	Citronella grass
	Nard grass
Cynodon dactylon	Bermuda grass
	Creeping dog's tooth grass
	Creeping finger grass
	Doob grass
	Kweek grass
Cynodon transvaalensis	African Bermuda grass
	Transvaal dogtooth grass
Cynosurus cristatus	Crested dogstail
Cynosurus echinatus	Rough dogstail
Cyperus alternifolius	Umbrella grass
	Umbrella palm
	Umbrella plant
	Umbrella sedge
Cyperus articulatus	Adrue
	Guinea rush
Cyperus esculentus	Chufa
	Earth almond
	Nut grass
	Nut sedge
	Rush nut
	Tiger nut
	Yellow nut grass
	Yellow nut sedge
	Zulu nut
Cyperus fuscus	Brown cyperus
Cyperus isocladus	Dwarf papyrus
	Miniature papyrus
Cyperus longus	Galingale
	Sweet galingale
Cyperus papyrus	Bulrush (biblical)
	Egyptian paper rush
	Paper plant
	Paper reed
	Papyrus
Cyperus tagetiformis	Chinese mat grass
Dactylis glomerata	Cocksfoot
	Orchard grass
Danthonia decumbens	Heath grass
Danthonia semiannularis	Australian danthonia
	Australian oat grass
Danthonia setacea	Wallaby grass
Dendrocalamus gigantea	Giant bamboo

Dendrocalamus strictus

Dendrocalamus strictus
    Calcutta bamboo
    Male bamboo
Deschampsia alpina
    Alpine hair grass
Deschampsia caespitosa
    Tufted hair grass
Deschampsia flexuosa
    Crinkled hair grass
    Wavy hair grass
Deschampsia setacea
    Bog hair grass
    Dog-hair grass
Dezmazeria rigida   Fern grass
Dezmazeria sicula   Spike grass
Dichanthium annulatum
    Brahman grass
    Diaz bluestem
    Kleberg grass
    Ringed beard grass
Dichanthium aristatum
    Angleton bluestem
    Angleton grass
Dichanthium ischaemun
    Dogstooth grass
Digitaria decumbens Pangola grass
Digitaria didactyla
    Blue couch grass
    Blue finger grass
Digitaria ischaemum
    Smooth finger grass
    Red millet
Digitaria pentzii
    Pentz finger grass
Digitaria sanguinalis   Crab grass
    Hairy crab grass
    Hairy finger grass
Digitaria serotina
    Creeping finger grass
Echinochloa crus-galli   Barn grass
    Barnyard grass
    Barnyard millet
    Cockspur grass
    Japanese millet
Ehrharta calycina
    Perennial veldt grass
Eleocharis acicularis   Hair grass
    Least spike rush
    Needle spike rush
    Slender spike rush
Eleocharis dulcis
    Chinese water chestnut
    Ma-tai
    Water chestnut
Eleocharis effusum   Saw grass
Eleocharis multicaulis
    Many-stemmed spike rush
Eleocharis palustris
    Common spike rush
Eleocharis parvula
    Dwarf spike rush
Eleocharis tuberosa
    Chinese water chestnut

Eleocharis uniglumis
    Single-glumed spike rush
    Slender spike rush
Eleusine coracana   African millet
    Finger millet
    Korakan
    Ragi
Eleusine indica   Goose grass
    Wire grass
Elymus angustus   Altai wild rye
Elymus aralensis   Aral wild rye
Elymus arenarius   Dune grass
    European dune grass
    Lyme grass
    Rancheria grass
    Sea lyme grass
Elymus canadensis
    Canadian wild rye
Elymus caninus   Bearded couch
Elymus chinensis Chinese wild rye
    False wheatgrass
Elymus condensatus
    Giant wild rye
Elymus farctus   Sand couch
Elymus glaucous   Blue wild rye
Elymus junceus Russian wild rye
Elymus pycnanthus   Sea couch
Elymus racemosus   Volga wild rye
Elymus repens   Common couch
    Couch grass
    Creeping twitch grass
    Twitch grass
    Witchgrass
Elymus sibiricus   Siberian wild rye
Elymus virginicus
    Virginian wild rye
Equisetum hyemale
    Common horsetail
    Common scouring brush
    Dutch rush
    Horsetail
    Scouring brush
Eragrostis amabilis
    Feather love grass
    Japanese love grass
Eragrostis capillaris   Lace grass
Eragrostis chloromelas
    Blue love grass
    Boer love grass
Eragrostis curvula
    Drooping love grass
    Weeping love grass
Eragrostis elegans   Love grass
Eragrostis lehmanniana
    Lehmann's love grass
Eragrostis trichodes
    Sand love grass
Eremochloa ophiuroides
    Centipede grass
    Lazy man's grass
Erianthus ravennae   Plume grass
    Ravenna grass
    Woolly beard grass

Eriochloa aristata	Branched cup grass
	Mexican everlasting grass
Eriochloa polystachya	Carib grass
	Malogilla
	Malojilla
	Malojillo
Eriochloa villosa	Hairy cup grass
Eriophorum angustifolium	
	Common cotton grass
Eriophorum gracile	
	Slender cotton grass
Eriophorum latifolium	
	Broad-leaved cotton grass
Eriophorum vaginatum	
	Hare's tail cotton grass
	Hare's tail grass
Erophila versa	Whitlow grass
Festuca altissima	Reed fescue
	Wild fescue
	Wood fescue
Festuca amethystina	Tufted fescue
Festuca arundinacea	Tall fescue
	Tall festuca
Festuca elatior	Alta fescue
	Reed fescue
	Tall fescue
Festuca gigantea	Giant fescue
Festuca glauca	Blue fescue
	Grey fescue
Festuca heterophylla	
	Various-leaved fescue
Festuca juncifolia	
	Rush-leaved fescue
Festuca longifolia	Hard fescue
Festuca ovina	Sheep's fescue
Festuca ovina glauca	Blue fescue
Festuca pratensis	English bluegrass
	Meadow fescue
Festuca rubra	Chewing's fescue
	Creeping fescue
	Red fescue
	Shade fescue
Festuca tenuifolia	
	Awnless sheep's fescue
	Fine-leaved sheep's fescue
	Hair fescue
Festulolium loliaceum	
	Hybrid fescue
Gastridium ventricosum	
	Nit grass
Glyceria declinata	
	Glaucous sweet grass
Glyceria fluitans	
	Floating sweet grass
Glyceria maxima	
	Reed sweet grass
Glyceria pedicellata	
	Hybrid sweet grass
Glyceria plicata	
	Plicate sweet grass

Gynerium sagittatum	Arrow cane
	Moa grass
	Uva grass
	Wild cane
Helictotrichon pratense	
	Meadow oat grass
Helictotrichon pubescens	
	Downy oat grass
	Hairy oat grass
Helictotrichon sempervirens	
	Oat grass
Heteranthera dubia	
	Water star grass
Heteranthera graminae	
	Water star grass
Hierochloe odorata	Holy grass
	Vanilla grass
Hilaria belangeri	Curley mesquite
Hilaria jamesii	Galleta
Hilaria mutica	Tobosa grass
Hilaria rigida	Big galleta
Holcus lanatus	Meadow soft grass
	Tufted soft grass
	Velvet grass
	Yorkshire fog
Holcus mollis	Creeping soft grass
	Soft grass
Holcus mollis variegatus	
	Variegated creeping soft grass
Holcus sorghum	Sorghum
Holcus virgatus	Tunis grass
Hordelymus europaeus	
	Wood barley
Hordeum brevisubulatum	
	Short-awned barley
Hordeum bulbosum	
	Bulbous barley
Hordeum distichon	Pearl barley
Hordeum jubatum	Foxtail barley
	Squirrel-tail barley
	Squirrel-tail grass
Hordeum marinum	Sea barley
	Squirrel-tail grass
Hordeum murinum	Wall barley
	Wild barley
Hordeum secalinum	
	Meadow barley
Hordeum vulgare	Barley
	Common barley
	Six-rowed barley
	Nepal barley
Hutchinsea alpina	Chamois grass
Juncus acutiflorus	
	Sharp-flowered rush
Juncus acutus	Sharp rush
	Sharp sea rush
Juncus alpinoarticulatus	
	Alpine rush
Juncus articulatus	Jointed rush
Juncus ballicus	Baltic rush
Juncus biglumis	Two-flowered rush
Juncus bufonius	Toad rush

BOTANICAL NAMES

Juncus bulbosus

Juncus bulbosus	Bulbous rush
Juncus capitatus	Capitate rush
	Dwarf rush
Juncus castaneus	Chestnut rush
Juncus communis	Common rush
Juncus compressus	
	Round-fruited rush
Juncus effusus	Japanese-mat rush
	Soft rush
Juncus filiformis	Thread rush
Juncus gerardii	Salt mud rush
Juncus inflexus	Hard rush
Juncus lesuerii	Salt rush
Juncus maritimus	Sea rush
Juncus mutabilis	Pigmy rush
Juncus squarrosus	Heath rush
Juncus subnodulosus	
	Blunt-flowered rush
Juncus subuliflorus	Common rush
Juncus tenuis	Slender rush
Juncus trifidus	Three-leaved rush
Juncus triglumis	
	Three-flowered rush
Kobresia simpliciuscula	
	False sedge
Koeleria cristata	Crested hair grass
Koeleria gracilis	Crested hair grass
Koeleria macrantha	
	Crested hair grass
Koeleria vallesiana	Somerset grass
Lagurus ovatus	Hare's tai
	Hare's tail grass
	Rabbit's tail grass
Lamarckia aurea	Goldentop
Lathyrus grandiflorus	
	Everlasting pea
	Two-flowered pea
Lathyrus hirsutus	Caley pea
	Rough pea
	Singletary pea
	Wild winter pea
	Winter pea
Lathyrus japonicus	Beach pea
	Heath pea
	Seaside pea
Lathyrus latifolius	Everlasting pea
	Perennial pea
Lathyrus littoralis	Beach pea
Lathyrus pratensis	
	Meadow vetchling
	Yellow vetchling
Lathyrus splendens	Pride of California
Lathyrus sylvestris	Everlasting pea
	Flat pea
	Perennial pea
Lathyrus tuberosus	Dutch mice
	Earth nut pea
	Tuberous vetch
Lathyrus vernus	Spring vetch

Leersia oryzoides	Cat grass
	Cut grass
	Rice
Lolium multiflorum	
	Australian rye grass
	Italian rye grass
Lolium perenne	English rye grass
	Lyme grass
	Perennial rye grass
	Rye grass
	Strand wheat
	Terrell grass
Lolium temulentum	Darnel
Lotus corniculatus	
	Bird's foot trefoil
Luzula arcuata	Curved wood rush
Luzula campestris	
	Common wood rush
	Field wood rush
	Wood rush
Luzula forsteri	
	Forster's wood rush
Luzula multiflora	
	Heath wood rush
	Many-flowered wood rush
Luzula nivea	Snowy wood rush
Luzula pallescens	
	Fenland wood rush
Luzula pilosa	Hairy wood rush
Luzula spicata	Spiked wood rush
Luzula sylvatica	Great wood rush
Medicago hispida	Bur clover
	Toothed bur clover
Medicago lupulina	Black medick
	Hop clover
	Nonesuch
	Trefoil
	Yellow trefoil
Medicago sativa	Alfalfa
	Lucerne
Melica altissima	
	Siberian melic grass
Melica ciliata	Eyelash pearl grass
	Silky melic grass
	Silky spike melica
Melica nutans	Mountain melick
	Nodding melick
Melica uniflora	Wood melick
Melinis minutiflora	Molasses grass
Mibora minima	Early sand grass
	Sand bent
Milium effusum	Wood millet
Milium effusum aureum	
	Bowles' golden grass
Miscanthus nepalensis	
	Himalaya fairy grass
	Nepal silver grass
Miscanthus sacchariflorus	
	Amur silver grass
Miscanthus sinensis	
	Chinese silver grass
	Eulalia

The Dictionary of Plant Names

Phylloastachys flexuosa

Miscanthus sinensis zebrinus
Tiger grass
Zebra grass

Molinia caerulea Blue bent
Flying bent
Indian grass
Moor grass
Purple moor grass

Nardus stricta Mat grass
Moor mat grass

Neyraudia reynaudiana
Burma reed

Onobrychis sativa Sainfoin

Onobrychis viciifolia Esparcet
Holy clover
Sainfoin

Oplismenus hirtellus Basket grass

Ornithopus perpusillus
Common bird's foot

Oryza sativa Rice

Oryzopsis hymenoides
Indian millet
Indian rice
Silk grass

Oryzopsis miliacea Smilo grass

Panicum antidotale
Blue panic grass
Giant panic grass

Panicum bulbosum
Bulbous panic grass

Panicum capillare Old-witch grass
Witchgrass

Panicum maximum Guinea grass

Panicum miliaceum Broomcorn
Broomcorn millet
Common millet
Hog millet
Millet
Proso

Panicum obtusum Vine mesquite

Panicum purpurascens Para grass

Panicum ramosum
Browntop millet

Panicum texanum Colorado grass

Panicum virgatum Switch grass

Parapholis incurva
Curved sea hard grass
Sickle grass

Parapholis strigosa Hard grass
Sea hard grass

Paspalum dilitatum Dallis grass

Paspalum malacophyllum
Ribbed paspalum

Paspalum notatum Bahia grass

Paspalum racemosum
Peruvian paspalum

Paspalum urvillei Vasey grass

Pennisetum alopecuroides
Chinese fountain grass
Chinese pennisetum

Pennisetum americanum
African millet
Indian millet
Pearl millet

Pennisetum ciliare Buffel grass

Pennisetum glaucum Cuscus
Pearl millet

Pennisetum latifolium
Uruguay pennisetum

Pennisetum purpureum
Elephant grass
Napier grass

Pennisetum setaceum
African fountain grass
Fountain grass

Pennisetum villosum
Abyssinian feathertop
Feathertop

Phalaris arundinacea
Reed canary grass

Phalaris arundinacea picta
Gardener's garters
Ribbon grass

Phalaris canariensis Birdseed grass
Canary grass

Phleum alpinum Alpine cat's tail
Alpine timothy

Phleum arenarium Sand cat's tail

Phleum bertolonii Lesser cat's tail

Phleum commutatum
Alpine cat's tail
Alpine timothy

Phleum nodosum Small cat's tail

Phleum phleoides
Purple-stemmed cat's tail

Phleum pratense Cat's tail grass
Common timothy
Herd's grass
Meadow cat's tail
Mountain timothy
Timothy grass

Phragmites australis Carrizo
Common reed

Phragmites communis
Common reed

Phyllostachys aurea
Fishpole bamboo
Golden bamboo

Phyllostachys aureosulcata
Forage bamboo
Golden groove bamboo
Stake bamboo
Yellow groove bamboo

Phyllostachys bambusoides
Giant timber bamboo
Hardy timber bamboo
Japanese timber bamboo
Madake
Timber bamboo

Phyllostachys dulcis
Sweetshoot bamboo

Phylloastachys flexuosa
Zigzag bamboo

Phyllostachys heterocycla
Tortoiseshell bamboo

Phyllostachys meyeri
Meyer's bamboo

Phyllostachys nigra   Black bamboo

Phyllostachys nigra henon
Henon bamboo

Phyllostachys pubescens
Moso bamboo

Poa alpina   Alpine meadow grass

Poa ampla   Big bluegrass

Poa angustifolia
Narrow-leaved meadow grass

Poa annua   Annual bluegrass
Annual meadow grass
Dwarf meadow grass
Low spear grass
Six weeks grass

Poa arachnifera   Texas bluegrass

Poa balfouri
Balfour's meadow grass

Poa bulbosa   Bulbous bluegrass
Bulbous meadow grass

Poa chaixii
Broad-leaved meadow grass

Poa compressa   Canadian bluegrass
Flat-stalked meadow grass
Wire grass

Poa flexuosa   Wavy meadow grass

Poa glauca   Glaucous meadow grass

Poa infirma   Early meadow grass
Scilly Isles meadow grass

Poa nemoralis   Wood bluegrass
Woodland meadow grass
Wood meadow grass

Poa palustris   Marsh meadow grass
Swamp meadow grass

Poa pratensis
Common meadow grass
June grass
Kentucky bluegrass
Meadow grass
Smooth meadow grass
Smooth-stalked meadow grass
Spear grass

Poa sandbergii
Sandberg's bluegrass

Poa subcaerulea
Spreading meadow grass

Poa trivialis   Rough bluegrass
Rough meadow grass
Rough-stalked bluegrass
Rough-stalked meadow grass

Polypogon monspeliensis
Annual beard grass
Rabbit-foot grass
Rabbit's foot

Polypogon viridis   Water bent

Poterium sanguisorba
Lesser burnet

Pseudosasa japonica
Arrow bamboo
Hardy bamboo
Metake

Puccinellia distans
Reflexed salt-marsh grass

Puccinellia fasciculata
Borrer's salt-marsh grass
Tufted salt-marsh grass

Puccinellia maritima
Common salt-marsh grass

Puccinellia rupestris
Stiff salt-marsh grass

Rhynchelytrum repens   Natal grass
Ruby grass

Rhynchospora alba
White beak sedge

Rhynchospora fusca
Brown beak sedge

Saccharum officinarum   Sugarcane

Saccharum sinense
Chinese sweet cane

Sasa veitchii   Kuma bamboo grass

Schizachyrium scoparium
Bluestem
Broom
Broom beard grass
Bunch grass
Little bluestem
Prairie beard grass
Wire grass

Schoenus ferrugineus
Brown bog rush

Schoenus nigricans   Black bog rush

Scirpus americanus
Jersey club rush

Scirpus cespitosus   Deer grass

Scirpus fluitans   Floating mud rush

Scirpus holoschoenus
Round-headed club rush

Scirpus lacustris   Club rush
Common bulrush

Scirpus maritimus   Sea club rush

Scirpus setaceus   Bristle club rush
Bristle scirpus

Scirpus sylvaticus   Wood club rush

Scirpus tabernaemontani
Glaucous club rush

Scirpus triquetrus
Triangular club rush

Scolochloa festucacea   Swamp grass

Secale cereale   Common rye

Semiarundinaria fastuosa
Narihira bamboo

Sesleria albicans   Blue moor grass

Sesleria caerulea   Blue moor grass

Sesleria heufleriana
Balkan bluegrass

Setaria glauca
Glaucous bristle grass
Yellow bristle grass

Trifolium pratense praecox

Setaria italica	Bengal grass
	Foxtail bristle grass
	Foxtail grass
	Foxtail millet
	Hungarian grass
	Italian millet
	Japanese millet
Setaria macrostachya	
	Plains bristle grass
Setaria palmifolia	Palm grass
Setaria poiretiana	
	Poiret's bristle grass
Setaria viridis	Bristle grass
	Green bristle grass
Sieglingia decumbens	
	Heath grass
	Mountain heath grass
Sorghastrum avenaceum	
	Indian grass
	Wood grass
Sorghum album	Johnson grass
Sorghum bicolor	Sorghum
Sorghum halepense	Aleppo grass
	Grass sorghum
	Great millet
	Egyptian millet
	Johnson grass
	Means grass
Sorghum saccharatum	
	Chinese sugar maple
Sorghum sudanese	Sudan grass
Sorghum vulgare	Broomcorn
	Sorghum
Sorghum vulgare caffrorum	
	Hegari
	Kaffir corn
Sorghum vulgare caudatum	
	Feterita
Sorghum vulgare cernuum	
	White durra
Sorghum vulgare durra	
	Brown durra
	Durra
Sorghum vulgare roxburghii	
	Shallu
Sorghum vulgare saccharatum	
	Sorgo
	Sugar sorghum
	Sweet sorghum
Sparganium angustifolium	
	Floating bur reed
Sparganium emersum	
	Unbranched bur reed
Sparganium erectum	
	Branched bur reed
Sparganium minimum	
	Small bur reed
Spartina alterniflora	
	American cord grass
	Multi-spiked cord grass
	Smooth cord grass
Spartina anglica	
	Common cord grass
Spartina maritima	Marsh grass
	Shore-line cord grass
Spartina pectinata	Cord grass
	Freshwater cord grass
	Prairie cord grass
	Slough grass
Spartina pectinata aureo-marginata	
	Variegated cord grass
Spartina townsendii	Rice grass
	Townsend's cord grass
Sporobolus cryptandrus	
	Sand dropseed
Stenotaphrum secundatum	
	Buffalo grass
	Saint Augustine's grass
	Shore grass
Stipa arundinacea	Pheasant grass
	Pheasant-tail grass
Stipa comata	Needle-and-thread
Stipa elegantissima	
	Australian feather grass
Stipa gigantea	Golden oats
Stipa leucotricha	Texas needlegrass
	Texas winter grass
Stipa pennata	
	Common feather grass
	European feather grass
	Feather grass
Stipa pulcherrima	
	Golden feather grass
Stipa splendens	Chee grass
Stipa tenacissima	Esparto grass
Stipa viridula	Feather bunchgrass
	Green needlegrass
Thamnocalamus spathaceus	
	Muriel bamboo
Tricholaena rosea	Natal grass
	Ruby grass
Trifolium agrarium	Hop clover
	Yellow clover
Trifolium alpinum	Alpine clover
Trifolium ambiguum	Kura clover
Trifolium campestre	
	Large hop clover
	Low clover
Trifolium dubium	
	Yellow suckling clover
Trifolium fragiferum	
	Strawberry clover
	Strawberry-headed clover
Trifolium hybridum	Alsike clover
Trifolium incarnatum	
	Crimson clover
	Italian clover
	Trifolium
Trifolium pannonicum	
	Hungarian clover
Trifolium pratense	Red clover
Trifolium pratense praecox	
	Broad red clover

Trifolium pratense serotinum

Trifolium pratense serotinum	
	Late-flowering red clover
	Single-cut cow grass
Trifolium pratense spontaneum	
	Wild red clover
Trifolium procumbens	
	Cow hop clover
	Irish shamrock
	Shamrock
	Small hop clover
	Yellow clover
	Yellow suckling clover
Trifolium repens	
	Dutch white clover
	Shamrock
	White clover
	White Dutch clover
Trifolium resupinatum	
	Persian clover
	Reversed clover
Trifolium subterraneum	Subclover
	Subterranean clover
Triglochia palustris	Sea arrow grass
Trisetum flavescens	
	Golden oat grass
	Yellow oat grass
Triticum aestivum	Bread wheat
	Common wheat
Triticum compactum	Club wheat
	Dwarf wheat
	Hedgehog wheat
Triticum dicoccon	
	Double grain spelt
	Double grain wheat
	Emmer
	German wheat
	Rice wheat
	Starch wheat
Triticum durum	Durum wheat
	Hard wheat
Triticum monococcum	Einkorn
	One-grained wheat
	Single grain wheat
Triticum polonicum	Giant rye
	Polish wheat
Triticum turgidum	Alaska wheat
	English wheat
	Mediterranean wheat
	Poulard wheat
	River wheat
Typha angustifolia	
	Narrow-leaved cat-tail
	Narrow-leaved reedmace
	Small bulrush
	Soft flag
Typha elephanta	Elephant grass
Typha latifolia	Bulrush
	Common cat-tail
	Cossack asparagus
	Nail-rod
	Reedmace
Uniola paniculata	Sea oats
	Spike grass

Vallisneria americana	
	Water celery
	Wild celery
Vallisneria spiralis	Eel grass
Vetiveria zizanioides	Khas-khas
	Khus-khus
	Vetiver
Vicia angustifolia	Common vetch
Vicia benghalensis	Purple vetch
Vicia cracca	Bird vetch
	Canada pea
	Cow vetch
	Tufted vetch
Vicia dasycarpa	Woolly-pod vetch
	Woolly vetch
Vicia ervilia	Bitter vetch
	Ervil
Vicia faba	Broad bean
	English bean
	European bean
	Field bean
	Horse bean
	Tick bean
	Windsor bean
Vicia gigantea	Sitka vetch
Vicia sativa	Common vetch
	Spring vetch
	Tare
Vicia villosa	Hairy vetch
	Large Russian vetch
	Winter vetch
Vulpia ambigua	Bearded fescue
Vulpia bromoides	
	Squirrel-tail fescue
Vulpia fasciculata	Dune fescue
Vulpia membranacea	Dune fescue
Vulpia myuros	Rat's tail fescue
Vulpia unilateralis	Mat grass fescue
Xerophyllum tenax	Bear grass
	Elk grass
	Fire lily
	Indian basket grass
	Squaw grass
Zea mays	Corn silk
	Corn
	Indian corn
	Maize
Zea mexicana	Teosinte
Zizania aquatica	Annual wild rice
	Indian rice
	Water oats
Zoysia japonica	Japanese lawn grass
	Korean grass
	Korean lawn grass
	Korean velvet grass
Zoysia matrella	Flawn
	Japanese carpet grass
	Manila grass
	Zoysia grass
Zoysia tenuifolia	Korean grass
	Korean lawn grass
	Korean velvet grass
	Mascarene grass

HERBS

Horticulturally, not botanically, the word 'herb' covers a range of plants used in cooking for flavouring and seasoning, as garnishes, and as domestic remedies. They are also widely used in orthodox and homeopathic medicines. The following list includes many subjects that are extremely poisonous, and drastic reactions, even occasional deaths are not unknown from the ignorant use of them. Experimentation by the general public cannot be too strongly condemned. In addition to the common and medicinal herbs, a few herbal trees have been included.

English lavender –
Lavandula angustifolia

BOTANICAL NAMES

Achillea decolorans

Achillea decolorans	English mace
Achillea millefolium	Devil's nettle
	Milfoil
	Nosebleed
	Old man's pepper
	Sneezewort
	Staunchweed
	Toothache weed
	Yarrow
Acinos arvensis	Basil thyme
Aconitum napellus	Aconite
	Blue rocket
	Friar's cap
	Helmet flower
	Monkshood
Acorus calamus	Calamus
	Sweet flag
Actaea spicata	Baneberry
	Bugbane
	Herb christopher
	Toadroot
Adonis vernalis	Adonis
Aesculus hippocastanum	
	Buckeye
	Horse chestnut
Aethusa cynapium	Dog poison
	Fool's parsley
	Lesser hemlock
Agastache anethiodora	
	Anise hyssop
	Fennel hyssop
Agastache foeniculum	
	Anise hyssop
	Fennel hyssop
Agastache rugosa	Korean mint
Agrimonia eupatoria	Agrimony
	Church steeples
	Cockleburr
	Liverwort
	Sticklewort
	Tall agrimony
Ajuga reptans	Bugle
	Bugleweed
Alchemilla vulgaris	Bear's foot
	Lady's mantle
	Lion's foot
	Nine hooks
Alchemilla xanthochlora	
	Bear's foot
	Lady's mantle
	Lion's foot
	Nine hooks
Alliaria petiolata	Garlic mustard
	Jack-by-the-hedge
Allium ampeloprasum	
	Elephant garlic
	Great-headed garlic
Allium ascalonicum	Shallot
Allium cepa aggregatum	
	Egyptian onion
Allium cepa proliferum	
	Tree onion
Allium cepa viviparum	
	Egyptian onion

Allium fistulosum	Welsh onion
Allium perutile	Everlasting onion
Allium porrum	Leek
Allium sativum	Garlic
	Poor man's treacle
Allium schoenoprasum	Chive
Allium schoenoprasum sibiricum	Giant chive
Allium tuberosum	Garlic chive
	Oriental chive
Allium ursinum	London lily
	Ramsons
	Stink bombs
	Stinking lily
	Stinking nanny
	Wild garlic
	Wood garlic
Aloe barbadensis	Aloe
	Barbados aloe
	Bitter aloe
	True aloe
Aloe vera	Aloe
	Barbados aloe
	True aloe
Aloe vulgaris	Aloe
	Barbados aloe
	True aloe
Aloysia citriodora	Lemon verbena
Aloysia triphylla	Herb louisa
	Lemon verbena
Althaea officinalis	Althea
	Marshmallow
Amaracus dictamnus	
	Crete dittany
	Hop marjoram
Anchusa officinalis	Alkanet
	Bugloss
Anchusa sempervirens	Anchusa
Anethum graveolens	Dill
Angelica archangelica	Angelica
	Garden angelica
Anisum vulgare	Anise
	Aniseed
Anthemis nobilis	Bowman
	Chamomile
	Common chamomile
	Manzanilla
	Maythen
	Roman chamomile
Anthriscus cerefolium	Chervil
Apium graveolens	Smallage
	Wild celery
Aquilegia vulgaris	Columbine
	Culverwort
	European crowfoot
	Garden columbine
	Gran's bonnet
Arctium lappa	Beggar's buttons
	Burdock
	Clot-bur
	Cockle-bur
	Fox's clote
	Gypsy's rhubarb
	Love leaves

Armoracia rusticana	Horseradish
	Mountain radish
	Red cole
Arnica montana	Arnica
	Leopard's bane
	Mountain tobacco
Artemisia abrotanum	Artemisia
	Lad's love
	Old man
	Southernwood
Artemisia absinthium	Absinthe
	Artemisia
	Common wormwood
	Green ginger
	Old woman
	Wormwood
Artemisia annua	Sweet wormwood
Artemisia arbuscula	Low sagebrush
Artemisia californica	California sagebrush
Artemisia dranunculoides	False tarragon
	Russian tarragon
Artemisia dracunculus	Artemisia
	Estragon
	False tarragon
	French tarragon
	Little dragon
	Russian tarragon
	Tarragon
Artemisia filifolia	Sand sage
Artemisia lactiflora	White mugwort
Artemisia laxa	Alpine wormwood
Artemisia ludoviciana	Cudweed
	Western mugwort
	White sage
Artemisia maritima	Wormseed
Artemisia pontica	Old warrior
Artemisia stellerana	Beach wormwood
	Dusty miller
	Old woman
Artemisia tridentata	Basin sagebrush
	Common sagebrush
	Sagebrush
Artemisia vulgaris	Felon herb
	Mugwort
	Saint John's plant
Arthrocnemum perenne	Marsh samphire
Asclepias curassavica	Blood flower
Asperula odorata	Sweet woodruff
	Woodrova
	Woodruff
	Wuderove

Atriplex hortensis	French spinach
	Orach
	Orache
	Sea purslane
Atriplex hortensis rubra	Red orache
Atropa belladonna	Belladonna
	Deadly nightshade
	Devil's cherries
Ballota nigra	Black horehound
Balsamita major	Alecost
	Mint geranium
Balsamita major tomentosum	Camphor plant
Bellis perennis	Bruisewort
	Daisy
	English daisy
Betula pendula	Silver birch
Betula verrucosa	Silver birch
Borago officinalis	Bee bread
	Borage
	Burrage
	Cool tankard
	Herb of gladness
	Star flower
	Tailwort
Brassica alba	White mustard
	Yellow mustard
Brassica hirta	White mustard
Brassica juncea	Brown mustard
Brassica nigra	Black mustard
Bryonia dioica	English mandrake
	Ladies' seal
	Tetterbury
	White bryony
	Wild vine
Buddleia salviifolia	South African wood sage
Calamintha acinos	Basil thyme
	Calamint
	Mother of thyme
	Mountain balm
Calamintha grandiflora	Calamint
Calendula officinalis	Calendula
	Golds
	Marigold
	Marygold
	Mary gowles
	Pot marigold
	Ruddes
Calluna vulgaris	Heather
Caltha palustris	Kingcup
	Marsh marigold
Calycanthus floridus	Allspice
	Carolina allspice
	Jamaica pepper
	Pineapple shrub
	Strawberry shrub
Cannabis sativa	Bhang
	Marihuana
Capsicum annuum	Pepper
Capsicum frutescens	Pimento

Cardamine pratensis

Cardamine pratensis	Bitter cress
	Cuckoo flower
	Lady's smock
Carthamus tinctorus	
	Bastard saffron
	False saffron
	Safflower
	Saffron thistle
Carum carvi	Caraway
Carum petroselinum tuberosum	Hamburg parsley
Cedronella canariensis	
	Balm of Gilead
Cedronella triphylla	
	Balm of Gilead
Centaurium minus	Centaury
	Christ's ladder
	Red centaury
Centaurium umbellatum	
	Centaury
Ceratonia siligua	Carob
Cetraria islandica	Iceland moss
Chaerophyllum temulentum	
	Chervil
Chamaemelum nobile	Chamomile
Chamomilla recutira	
	German chamomile
	Scented mayweed
Chenopodium album	Fat hen
Chenopodium bonus-henricus	
	Good King Henry
	Smearwort
Chenopodium botrys	Ambrosia
Chenopodium vulvaria	
	Stinking goosefoot
	Stinking motherwort
	Wild arrach
Chrysanthemum balsamita	
	Alecost
	Alespice
	Balsam herb
	Balsamita
	Bible leaf
	Costmary
	Mint geranium
Chrysanthemum parthenium	
	Featherfew
	Featherfoil
	Feverfew
	Flirtwort
Chrysanthemum vulgare	Alecost
	Bitter buttons
	Tansy
Cichorium intybus	Chicory
	Succory
Cinnamomum camphora	
	Camphor tree
Cinnamomum zelanicum	
	Cinnamon
Claytonia perfoliata	
	Miner's lettuce
	Winter purslane
Cnicus benedictus	Blessed thistle

Cochlearia armoracia	
	Horseradish
	Mountain radish
	Red cole
Colchicum autumnale	
	Autumn crocus
Commiphora opobalsamum	
	Balm of Gilead
Conium maculatum	
	Beaver poison
	Hemlock
	Kecksies
	Kex
	Poison hemlock
	Poison parsley
	Spotted hemlock
Convalleria majalis	
	Ladder to heaven
	Lily-of-the-valley
	May lily
	Our Lady's tears
Coriandrum sativum	
	Chinese parsley
	Coriander
Costus speciosus	Cape ginger
	Crape ginger
	Grape ginger
Crataegus oxyacantha	
	Bread-and-cheese tree
	Hawthorn
	Ladies' meat
	May
	Quickthorn
Crithmum maritimum	Samphire
	Sea fennel
Crocus sativus	Saffron
Cuminum cyminum	Cumin
Cuminum odorum	Cumin
Curcuma longa	Turmeric
Cynara cardunculus	Cardoon
	Wild artichoke
Cytisus scoparius	Broom
	Cat's peas
	Golden chair
	Lady's slipper
	Pixie's slipper
Datura stramonium	Jimson weed
	Thornapple
Delphinium ajacis	Knight's spur
	Lark's heel
	Larkspur
Dianthus caryophyllus	Gillyflower
	July flower
	Pink
Dictamnus albus	Burning bush
	False dittany
	Fraxinella
	Gas plant
	White dittany
Dictamnus fraxinella	Burning bush
	False dittany
	Fraxinella
	Gas plant
	White dittany

Humulus lupulus aureus

Digitalis lutea	Straw foxglove
Digitalis purpurea	Bloody fingers
	Dead man's bells
	Fairy thimbles
	Foxglove
	Witches' gloves
Digitalis thrapsi	
	Dwarf purple foxglove
Dipsacus fullonum	Teasel
Dipsacus sylvestris	Teasel
Dipterix odorata	Tonka bean
	Tonquin bean
Drosera rotundifolia	Sundew
Echallium elaterium	
	Squirting cucumber
Echinacea angustifolia	
	Coneflower
	Echinacea
Echium vulgare	Viper's bugloss
Eonymus europaeus	Burning bush
	Fusoria
	Indian arrowroot
	Skewerwood
	Spindle tree
	Wahoo
Equisetum arvense	Field horsetail
Eruca vesicaria	Arugula
	Salad rocket
Eryngium maritimum	Sea holly
Erythraea centaurium	Centaury
Eucalyptus globulus	Blue gum
	Tasmanian blue gum
Eucalyptus gunnii	Gum tree
Eugenia aromatica	Cloves
Eupatorium cannabinum	
	Hemp agrimony
Eupatorium purpureum	
	Gravelroot
	Trumpet weed
Euphrasia officinalis	Eyebright
Ferula communis	Giant fennel
Ferula foetida	Asafetida
Ferula gabaniflua	Galbanum
Ferula suaveolens	Sambal
Ferula sumbul	Sumbul
Filipendula hexapetala	Dropwort
	Meadowsweet
Filipendula ulmaria	Dropwort
	Meadowsweet
Filipendula vulgaris	Dropwort
	Meadowsweet
Foeniculum dulce	Finocchio
	Florence fennel
Foeniculum officinale	Fenkel
	Fennel
Foeniculum vulgare	Fenkel
	Fennel
Foeniculum vulgare azoricum	
	Anise
	Finocchio
	Florence fennel
Fragaria vesca	Alpine strawberry
	Wild strawberry
Frangula alnus	Alder buckthorn
	Black dogwood
Galega officinalis	Goat's rue
	Italian fitch
Galium odoratum	Sweet woodruff
	Woodrova
	Woodruff
	Wuderove
Galium verum	Cheese rennet
	Curdwort
	Lady's bedstraw
	Maid's hair
	Our Lady's bedstraw
	Peasant's mattress
	Yellow bedstraw
Gaultheria procumbens	
	Checkerberry
	Mountain tea
	Teaberry
	Wintergreen
Gentiana lutea	Gentian
	Yellow gentian
Glechoma hederacea	Alehoof
	Ground ivy
Glycyrrhiza glabra	Black sugar
	Licorice
	Spanish juice
Gratiola officinalis	Hedge hyssop
Hamamelis virginiana	
	Spotted alder
	Winterbloom
	Witch-hazel
Helianthus annuus	Sunflower
Helichrysum angustifolium	
	Curry plant
Helichrysum italicum	Curry plant
Heliotropium arborescens	
	Cherry pie
	Common heliotrope
Heliotropium corymbosum	
	Cherry pie
	Common heliotrope
Heliotropium peruvianum	
	Cherry pie
	Common heliotrope
Helleborus niger	Black hellebore
	Christmas rose
Herniaria glabra	
	Glabrous rupture wort
Hesperis matronalis	Dame's violet
	Rocket
	Roquette
	Sweet rocket
	Vesper flower
Heuchera richardsonii	Alum root
	Coral bells
Humulus lupulus	Hop
Humulus lupulus aureus	
	Golden hop

BOTANICAL NAMES

Hydrastis canadensis

Hydrastis canadensis	Golden seal
	Orange root
	Yellow puccoon
	Yellow root
Hyoscyamus niger	Cassilata
	Henbane
	Hog's bean
	Stinking nightshade
Hypericum perforatum	
	Saint John's wort
Hyssopus aristatus	Rock hyssop
Hyssopus officinalis	Hyssop
Ilex aquifolium	Holly
Inula helenium	Elecampane
	Horseheal
	Scabwort
	Velvet dock
	Yellow starwort
Ipomoea pes-caprae	
	Beach morning glory
Iris florentina	Orris
	Orris root
Iris germanica	Orris
	Orris root
Iris germanica florentina	Flag iris
	Florentine iris
	Orris
	Orris root
Isatis tinctoria	Dyer's weed
	Woad
Jasminum officinale	
	Common jasmine
	Jasmine
	Tea jasmine
	White jasmine
Juniperus communis	Hack matack
	Horse savin
	Juniper
Laburnum anagyroides	
	Golden chain
	Laburnum
Lamium maculatum	
	Cobbler's bench
	Dead nettle
	Spotted dead nettle
Laurus nobilis	
(Do not confuse with Kalmia latifolia (poisonous))	Bay
	Bay laurel
	Bay leaf
	Roman laurel
	Sweet bay
	True laurel
Lavandula alba	White lavender
Lavandula angustifolia	
	English lavender
	True lavender
Lavandula dentata	
	French lavender
	Fringed lavender
Lavandula officinalis	
	English lavender
	True lavender

Lavandula spica	English lavender
	True lavender
Lavandula stoechas	
	French lavender
	Spanish lavender
Lavandula vera	English lavender
	True lavender
Leonotus leonurus	Wild dagga
Leontodon taraxacum	Blowball
	Common dandelion
	Dandelion
	Peasant's clock
	Priest's crown
	Swine's snout
Leonurus cardiaca	Motherwort
Lepidium sativum	Garden cress
	Pepper cress
Levisticum officinale	Italian lovage
	Lovage
Levisticum scoticum	Scots lovage
Ligusticum paludapifolium	
	Italian lovage
	Lovage
Lilium candidum	Madonna lily
Linaria vulgaris	Buttered haycocks
	Churnstaff
	Eggs and bacon
	Flaxweed
	Fluellin
	Pattens and clogs
	Toadflax
Linum usitatissimum	Flax
Lippia citriodora	Herb louisa
	Lemon verbena
Lippia triphylla	Herb louisa
	Lemon verbena
Lonicera caprifolium	
	Perfoliate honeysuckle
Lonicera periclymenum	
	Goat's leaf
	Honeysuckle
	Woodbine
Loranthus europaeus	
	False mistletoe
Lupinus polyphyllus	Lupin
Majorana hortensis	
	Knotted marjoram
	Sweet marjoram
Malva sylvestris	Common mallow
Mandragora officinarum	
	Devil's apple
	Mandrake
	Satan's apple
Marrubium incanum	
	White horehound
Marrubium vulgare	
	Common horehound
	Hoarhound
	Horehound
	White horehound
Matricaria chamomilla	
	German chamomile
	Scented mayweed
	Wild chamomile

The Dictionary of Plant Names

Ocimum basilicum
lactucafolium

Matricaria eximia	Featherfew
	Featherfoil
	Feverfew
	Flirtwort
Matricaria recutita	
	German chamomile
Medicago sativa	Buffalo herb
Melilotus officinalis	Melilot
Melissa officinalis	Balm
	Bee balm
	Common balm
	Lemon balm
	Sweet balm
	Sweet bay
Melissa officinalis aurea	
	Golden balm
Melissa officinalis variegata	
	Variegated lemon balm
Melittis melissophyllum	
	Bastard balm
Mentha aquatica	Water mint
Mentha arvensis piperascens	
	Field mint
	Japanese mint
Mentha citrata	Bergamot mint
	Eau-de-cologne Mint
	Orange mint
Mentha crispa	Curly mint
	Spearmint
Mentha × gentilis	Bushy mint
	Ginger mint
	Red mint
	Scotch mint
Mentha longifolia	Horse mint
Mentha × piperita	Brandy mint
	Double mint
	Peppermint
Mentha × piperita citrata	
	Eau-de-cologne mint
Mentha pulegium	
	English pennyroyal
	Lurk-in-the-ditch
	Pennyroyal
	Pudding grass
	Run-by-the-ground
Mentha requienii	Corsican mint
	Crème de menthe plant
	Menthella
Mentha rotundifolia	Apple mint
	Egyptian mint
	Round-leaved mint
	Woolly mint
Mentha spicata	Common mint
	Garden mint
	Lamb mint
	Mackerel mint
	Sage of Bethlehem
	Spearmint
	Spire mint
Mentha suaveolens	Applemint
Mentha suaveolens variegata	
	Pineapple mint
	Variegated applemint

Mentha viridis	Garden mint
	Lamb mint
	Mackerel mint
	Sage of Bethlehem
	Spearmint
	Spire mint
Monarda citriodora	
	Lemon bergamot
Monarda didyma	Balm
	Bee balm
	Bergamot
	Indian plume
	Oswega tea
	Scarlet monarda
Monarda fistulosa	Wild bergamot
Monarda punctata	Horse mint
Morus alba	White mulberry
Morus nigra	Black mulberry
Muscari botryoides	Grape hyacinth
	Starch hyacinth
Myosotis arvensis	Forget-me-not
Myosotis sylvatica	Forget-me-not
Myristica fragrans	Mace
	Nutmeg
Myrrrhis odorata	Anise
	Anise fern
	British myrrh
	Great chervil
	Shepherd's needle
	Smooth cicely
	Sweet bracken
	Sweet chervil
	Sweet cicely
Myrtus communis	Myrtle
Myrtus communis tarentina	
	Myrtle
	Tarentum myrtle
Nasturtium officinale	Watercress
Nepeta cataria	Catmint
	Catnep
	Catnip
Nepeta cataria citriodorum	
	Lemon catmint
Nepeta hederacea	Alehoof
	Creeping charlie
	Field balm
	Gill-go-over-the-ground
	Ground ivy
	Haymaids
	Lizzy-run-up-the-hedge
Nepeta mussini	Border catmint
Ocimum americanum	
	Lemon balm
	Lemon basil
Ocimum basilicum	Basil
	Sweet basil
Ocimum basilicum aurauascens	
	Purple basil
Ocimum basilicum lactucafolium	
	Lettuce-leaved basil
	Monster-leaved basil

Ocimum basilicum
purpurescens

Ocimum basilicum	
purpurescens	Dark opal basil
Ocimum citriodorum	Lemon basil
Ocimum minimum	Bush basil
	Fine-leaved basil
	Greek basil
Ocimum sanctum	Holy basil
Oenothera biennis	
	Evening primrose
	King's cure-all
	Moonflower
Onobrychis viciifolia	Sainfoin
Ononis spinosa	Restharrow
Onopordon acanthium	
	Cotton thistle
Origanum dictamnus	
	Crete dittany
	Hop marjoram
Origanum heracleoticum	
	Pot marjoram
	Winter marjoram
	Wintersweet marjoram
Origanum majorana	
	Annual marjoram
	Knotted marjoram
	Sweet marjoram
Origanum onites	Pot marjoram
Origanum vulgare	Marjoram
	Organy
	Origano
	Pot marjoram
	Wild marjoram
Osmanthus fragrans	Sweet olive
Panax ginseng	Ginseng
Papaver somniferum	
	Opium poppy
Pastinaca sativa	Wild parsnip
Pelargonium × fragrans	
	Nutmeg-scented geranium
Pelargonium graveolens	
	Scented geranium
Pelargonium tomentosum	
	Peppermint-scented geranium
Pentaglottis sempervirens	
	Anchusa
Perilla frutescens crispa	
	Beefsteak plant
	Purple perilla
	Summer coleus
Petroselinum crispum	
	Curly parsley
	Parsley
	Petersylinge
Petroselinum crispum fusiformis	
	Hamburg parsley
	Turnip-rooted parsley
Petroselinum neapolitanum	
	French parsley
	Italian parsley
Petroselinum tuberosum	
	Hamburg parsley
Peucedanum graveolens	Dill

Philadelphus coronarius	
	Mock orange
Phytolacca americana	Pokeweed
Pimpinella anisum	Anise
	Aniseed
Pimpinella major	
	Greater burnet saxifrage
Pimpinella saxifraga	
	Burnet saxifrage
Polemoneum coeruleum	Charity
	Greek valerian
	Jacob's ladder
Polygonum bistorta	Bistort
Polygonum hydropiper	
	Water pepper
Populus balsamifera	
	Balsam poplar
Portulaca oleracea	Purslane
	Summer purslane
Potentilla anserina	Goose tansy
	Silver weed
Potentilla erecta	
	Common tormentil
Potentilla tormentilla	
	Common tormentil
Poterium sanguisorba	Burnet
	Salad burnet
Primula officinalis	Cowslip
Primula parthenium	Featherfew
	Featherfoil
	Feverfew
	Flirtwort
Primula veris	Cowslip
Primula vulgaris	Primrose
Prunus dulcis	Almond
Pulmonaria officinalis	
	Jerusalem cowslip
	Lungwort
Quercus petraea	Durmast oak
Quercus rober	Common oak
	Oak
Quercus sessilis	Durmast oak
Ranunculus acris	
	Bachelor's buttons
	Buttercup
	Gold knots
Reseda alba	White mignonette
Reseda lutea	Wild mignonette
Reseda odorata	Mignonette
Rhamnus catharticus	Buckthorn
	Common buckthorn
	Hartshorn
	Highway thorn
	Ram's horn
	Ram's thorn
Rheum palmatum	Rhubarb
Rheum rhabarbarum	
	Garden rhubarb
Rorippa nasturtium-aquaticum	
	Watercress
Rosa centifolia muscosa	Moss rose
Rosa eglanteria	Sweetbriar

Sesamum indicum

Rosa gallica officinalis	Apothecary's rose
Rosmarinus lavandulaceus	Compass weed
	Polar plant
	Rosemary
Rosmarinus officinalis	Compass weed
	Polar plant
	Rosemary
Rubia tinctoria	Madder root
Rubus australis	Bush lawyer
Rubus fruticosus	Bramble
Rumex acetosa	Cuckoo's meat
	Cuckoo sorrow
	Garden sorrel
	Green sauce
	Sorrel
	Sour sabs
Rumex crispus	Curled dock
Rumex obtusifolius	Broad-leaved dock
	Butter dock
	Dock
Rumex scutatus	Buckler-leaf sorrel
	French sorrel
Ruta graveolens	Herb of grace
	Rue
Sabatia angularis	American centaury
	Bitter broom
	Bitter clover
	Wild succory
Salix alba	European willow
	White willow
Salix nigra	Black American willow
	Pussy willow
	Willow
Salvia apiana	Greasewood
	White sage
Salvia argentea	Silver sage
Salvia aurea	Golden sage
Salvia azurea	Blue sage
Salvia barrelieri	Spanish sage
Salvia elegans	Pineapple sage
Salvia officinalis	Garden sage
	Sage
Salvia officinalis icterina	Golden sage
Salvia officinalis purpurescens	Red sage
Salvia officinalis tricolor	Tricolor sage
	Variegated sage
Salvia purpurescens	Purple sage
Salvia rutilans	Pineapple sage
Salvia sclarea	Clary
	Clary sage
	Clear eye
Sambucus nigra	Bore tree
	Elder
	Pipe tree
	Sweet elder
Sanguisorba minor	Burnet
	Salad burnet
Santolina chamaecyparissus	Cotton lavender
	French lavender
	Grey santolina
	Lavender cotton
	Santolina
Santolina incana	Cotton lavender
	French lavender
	Grey santolina
	Lavender cotton
	Santolina
Santolina tomentosa	Cotton lavender
	French lavender
	Grey santolina
	Lavender cotton
	Santolina
Saponaria officinalis	Bouncing bet
	Bruisewort
	Fuller's herb
	Soapwort
	Wild sweet william
Sarothamnus scoparius	Broom
	Cat's peas
	Golden chair
	Lady's slipper
	Pixie's slipper
Satureia (Satureja) hortensis	Bean herb
	Savory
	Summer savory
Satureia (Satureja) montana	Bean herb
	Savory
	Winter savory
Satureia (Satureja) repanda	Creeping savory
Scrophularia marilandica	Carpenter's square
Scutellaria galericulata	Helmet flower
	Madweed
	Scullcap
	Skullcap
	Virginian scullcap
Scutellaria laterifolia	Helmet flower
	Madweed
	Scullcap
	Skullcap
	Virginian scullcap
Selinum tenuifolium	Himalayan parsley
Sempervivum tectorum	Hen-and-chickens
	Houseleek
	St. Patrick's cabbage
	Thunder plant
Sesamum indicum	Semsem
	Sesame

Sesamum orientale	Semsem
	Sesame
Sinapis alba	White mustard
	Yellow mustard
Sinapis juncea	Brown mustard
Sinapis nigra	Black mustard
Sium sisarum	Skirret
Smyrnium olusatrum	Alexanders
Solanum dulcamara	Bittersweet
	Bittersweet nightshack
	Felonwood
	Violet bloom
	Woody nightshade
Solanum laciniatum	
	Kangaroo apple
Spiraea filipendula	Dropwort
	Meadowsweet
Stachys lanata	Donkey's ears
	Lamb's ears
	Woolly betony
Stachys officinalis	Betony
	Bishopswort
	Wood betony
	Woundwort
Stachys olympica	Donkey's ears
	Lamb's ears
	Woolly betony
Stellaria media	Chickweed
Succisa pratensis	
	Devil's bit scabious
Swertia chirata	Chiretta
Symphytum grandiflorum	
	Creeping comfrey
Symphytum officinale	Ass's ear
	Blackwort
	Boneset
	Comfrey
	Common comfrey
	Consound
	Healing herb
	Knitbone
Symphytum perigrinum	
	Russian comfrey
Symphytum uplandicum	
	Russian comfrey
Tamus communis	Black bryony
	Blackeye root
Tanacetum balsamita	Alecost
	Alespice
	Costmary
Tanacetum parthenium	
	Bachelor's buttons
	Feverfew
Tanacetum vulgare	Alecost
	Bitter buttons
	Buttons
	Golden buttons
	Tansy
Taraxacum officinale	Blowball
	Common dandelion
	Dandelion
	Peasant's clock
	Priest's crown
	Swine's snout

Taxus baccata	English yew
	Yew
Taxus brevifolia	Western yew
	Yew
Teucrium chamaedrys	Germander
	Wall germander
Teucrium scorodonia	Wood sage
Thymus alba	White thyme
Thymus × citriodorus	
	Lemon thyme
	Silver queen
Thymus × citriodorus aureus	
	Golden-edged thyme
	Golden thyme
Thymus herba-barona	
	Caraway thyme
Thymus mastichina	
	Herb masticke
Thymus mastichina × didi	Didi
Thymus pulegioides	
	Broad-leaved thyme
Thymus serphyllum	
	Creeping thyme
	Lemon thyme
	Wild thyme
Thymus vulgaris	Common thyme
	English thyme
	French thyme
	Garden thyme
	Silver posy
	Thyme
Thymus vulgaris aureus	
	Golden thyme
Tilia cordata	Small-leaved lime
Trifolium incarnatum	
	Crimson clover
	Red clover
	Trefoil
Trigonella foenum-graecum	
	Bird's foot
	Fenugreek
	Greek hayseed
Tropaeolum majus	Indian cress
	Nasturtium
Tussilago farfara	Bullsfoot
	Coltsfoot
	Coughwort
	Foalfoot
	Horsehoof
Ulmaria filipendula	Dropwort
	Meadowsweet
Ulmus fulva	Indian elm
	Moose elm
	Red elm
	Slippery elm
Urtica dioica	Nettle
	Stinging nettle
Vaccinium myrtillus	Bilberry

Zingiber officinale

Valeriana officinalis	All-heal
	Cat's valerian
	Garden heliotrope
	Heal-all
	Phew plant
	Phu
	Setwall
	Valerian
Valerianella locusta	Corn salad
	Lamb's lettuce
Valerianella olitoria	Corn salad
	Lamb's lettuce
Vanilla fragrans	Vanilla
Veratrum album	
European white hellebore	
	White hellebore
Veratrum viride	False hellebore
	Green hellebore
	White hellebore
Verbascum thapsus	Aaron's rod
	Adam's flannel
	Blanket leaf
	Great mullein
	Hag taper
	Jacob's staff
	Mullein
	Our Lady's candle
	Shepherd's club
	Torches
Verbena officinalis	
European vervain	
	Herb of grace
	Herb of the cross
	Pigeon's grass

	Simpler's joy
	Vervain
Verbena triphylla	
	Herb louisa
	Lemon verbena
Veronica officinalis	Speedwell
Vinca major	Greater periwinkle
	Periwinkle
Vinca major alba	
	White periwinkle
Viola odorata	Florist's violet
	Sweet violet
	Violet
Viola odorata alba	White violet
Viola pallida plena	Parma violet
Viola riviana	Dog violet
Viola selkirkii	
	Great spurred violet
Viola tricolor	Call-me-to-you
	Heartsease
	Herb constancy
	Kiss-her-in-the-buttery
	Kit runabout
	Love-in-idleness
	Love-lies-bleeding
	Pink-of-my-john
	Wild pansy
Viscum alba	Birdlime mistletoe
	Lignum crucis
	Mistletoe
Vitex agnus-castus	Monk's pepper
Zingiber cassumunar	Bengal root
Zingiber officinale	Ginger

HOUSE PLANTS

This section deals with those plants normally associated with hotel foyers, civic halls, restaurants, and public functions in addition to those found in private houses, sun rooms, and conservatories. Many subjects have been duplicated elsewhere in this book which, in their natural environment, would grow too large for indoor use but by regular pruning and root restriction can be controlled within acceptable limits. With a few exceptions bulbs and cacti are listed elsewhere under those headings.

Flaming katy –
Kalanchoe blossfeldiana

Acacia armata

Acacia armata	Kangaroo thorn
Acacia baileyana	
	Cootamunda wattle
Acacia cultriformis	Knife acacia
Acacia cyanophylla	
	Blue-leaved wattle
Acacia dealbata	Florist's mimosa
	Silver wattle
Acacia longifolia	
	Sydney golden wattle
Acacia lophantha	Plume albizia
Acacia melanoxylon	
	Blackwood acacia
Acacia podalyriifolia	
	Mount Morgan wattle
	Queensland silver wattle
Acacia pravissima	Oven's wattle
Acacia prominens	Golden rain
	Gosford wattle
Acacia retinodes	Wirilda
Acacia verticillata	Prickly moses
Acalypha godseffiana	
	Lance copperleaf
Acalypha hispida	Chenille plant
	Red-hot cat's tail
Acalypha wilkesiana	Copperleaf
Acca sellowiana	Pineapple guava
Acokanthera spectabilis	
	Wintersweet
Acorus gramineus	Sweet flag
Acrostichum aureum	Leather fern
Acrostichum crinitum	
	Elephant's ear fern
Adenium obesum	Desert rose
Adiantum capillus-veneris	
	Common maidenhair fern
	Maidenhair fern
Adiantum formosum	
	Australian maidenhair fern
Adiantum hispidulum	
	Rose maidenhair fern
Adiantum pubescens	
	Rose maidenhair fern
Adromischus maculatus	
	Calico hearts
Aechmea bromeliifolia	Wax torch
Aechmea fasciata	Silver vase
	Urn plant
Aechmea fulgens	Coralberry
Aerides fieldingii	Fox brush orchid
Aeschynanthus lobbianus	
	Lipstick vine
Aeschynanthus pulcher	
	Royal red bugler
Agathaea coelestis	
	Blue marguerite
Agave americana	American aloe
	Century plant
	Maguey
Agave filifera	Thread agave

Aglaonema modestum	
	Chinese evergreen
Albizia distachya	Plume albizia
Albizia julibrissin	Silk tree
Albizia lophantha	Plume albizia
Allamanda cathartica	
	Golden trumpet
Allium schoenoprasum	Chives
Allophyton mexicanum	
	Mexican foxglove
	Mexican violet
Alocasia macrorrhiza	
	Giant elephant's ear
Alocasia sanderiana	Kris plant
Aloe barbadensis	Burn plant
	Magic plant
	Medicine plant
Aloe ciliaris	Climbing aloe
Aloe striata	Coral aloe
Alonsoa warscewiczii	Mask flower
Aloysia citriodora	Lemon verbena
Alpinia calcarata	Indian ginger
Alpinia magnifica	
	Philippine wax flower
	Torch ginger
Alpinia nutans	Pink porcelain lily
	Shell ginger
Alpinia purpurata	Red ginger
Alpinia sanderae	Variegated ginger
Alpinia speciosa	Pink porcelain lily
	Shell ginger
Alpinia zerumbet	
	Pink porcelain lily
	Shell ginger
Alsophila smithii	Soft tree fern
Alsophila tricolor	Ponga
	Silver tree fern
Alstroemeria pelegrina alba	
	Lily of the incas
Alternanthera bettzickiana	
	Calico plant
Alternanthera ficoidea	Parrot leaf
Amaranthus caudatus	
	Love-lies-bleeding
Amaranthus hybridus	
	Prince's feather
Amaranthus hypochondriacus	
	Prince's feather
Amaryllis belladonna	
	Belladonna lily
Amaryllis formosissima	Aztec lily
	Jacobean lily
Amorphophallus bulbifer	
	Devil's tail
Amorphophallus rivieri	
	Devil's tongue
Ampelopsis brevipendunculata	
	Porcelain berry
Ampelopsis heterophylla	
	Porcelain berry

Babiana stricta

Ananas bracteatus	Red pineapple
	Wild pineapple
Anastatica hierochuntica	
	Resurrection plant
	Rose of Jericho
Anemia adiantifolia	Pine fern
Anemone coronaria	
	Poppy anemone
Anguloa clowesii	Tulip orchid
Anguloa uniflora	Tulip orchid
Anigozanthos flavidus	
	Tall kangaroo paw
Anigozanthos humilis	Catspaw
Anigozanthos manglesii	
	Common green kangaroo paw
	Mangle's kangaroo paw
Anigozanthos preissii	
	Albany catspaw
Anigozanthos rufus	
	Red kangaroo paw
Anigozanthos viridis	
	Green kangaroo paw
Annona cherimolia	Cherimoya
Annona reticulata	Bullock's heart
	Custard apple
Annona squamosa	Sugar apple
	Sweet sop
Anoectochilus regalis	King plant
Ansellia africana	Leopard orchid
Anthericum comosum	
	Spider plant
Anthericum elatum	Spider plant
Anthurium andreanum	Tailflower
Anthurium crystallinum	
	Crystal anthurium
Anthurium scherzerianum	
	Flamingo flower
Anthurium veitchii	
	King anthurium
Anthurium warocqueanum	
	Queen anthurium
Antigonon leptopus	Corallita
	Coral vine
Antirrhinum majus	Snapdragon
Aphelandra squarrosa	Zebra plant
Arachis hypogaea	Groundnut
	Peanut
Arachnoides aristata	
	East Indian holly fern
Aralia japonica	
	False castor-oil plant
Aralia papyrifera	Rice-paper plant
Aralia sieboldii	
	False castor-oil plant
Araucaria angustifolia	
	Candelabra tree
	Parana pine
Araucaria cunninghamii	
	Hoop pine
	Moreton Bay pine
Araucaria excelsa	
	Norfolk Island pine
Araucaria heterophylla	
	Norfolk Island pine
Araujia sericofera	Cruel plant
Arbutus unedo	Strawberry tree
Archontophoenix alexandrae	
	Alexandra palm
	Northern bungalow palm
Archontophoenix cunningh amiana	Illawarra palm
	Piccabeen bungalow palm
	Piccabeen palm
Ardisia crispa	Coralberry
	Marlberry
	Spiceberry
Aregelia marmorata	Marble plant
Arisarum proboscideum	
	Mouse plant
Aristolochia elegans	Birth wort
	Calico flower
Arum dracunculus	Dragon plant
Arundinaria amabilis	
	Tonkin bamboo
Arundo donax	Giant reed
Asclepias curassavica	Blood flower
Asparagus asparagoides	Smilax
Asparagus asparagoides myrtifolius	Baby smilax
Asparagus falcatus	Sicklethorn
Asparagus medeoloides	Smilax
Asparagus plumosus	
	Asparagus fern
Asparagus setaceus	Asparagus fern
Aspidistra elatior	Cast iron plant
Aspidistra lurida	Cast iron plant
Aspidium falcatum	Holly fern
Asplenium bulbiferum	
	Mother spleenwort
Asplenium daucifolium	
	Mother fern
Asplenium nidus	Bird's nest fern
Asplenium nidus-avis	
	Bird's nest fern
Asplenium platyneuron	
	Ebony spleenwort
Asplenium scolopendrium	
	Hart's tongue fern
Asplenium viviparum	
	Mother fern
Aster bergeriana	Kingfisher daisy
Athyrium esculentum	Paco
	Vegetable fern
Averrhoa bilimbi	Bilimbi
Averrhoa carambola	
	Carambola tree
Azalea obtusa	Japanese azalea
Azolla caroliniana	Mosquito plant
	Water fern
Babiana stricta	Baboon flower

BOTANICAL NAMES

Beaucarnea recurvata

Beaucarnea recurvata
　　　　　　Elephant foot
　　　　　　Pony tail

Begonia bowerii
　　　Miniature eyelash begonia

Begonia × cheimantha
　　　　　Christmas begonia
　　　　　Lorraine begonia

Begonia coccinea
　　　　　Angel's wing begonia

Begonia cubensis
　　　　Holly-leaved begonia

Begonia dregei
　　Miniature maple-leaf begonia

Begonia × erythrophylla
　　　　　Beefsteak begonia

Begonia × feastii
　　　　　Beefsteak begonia

Begonia foliosa　　Fernleaf begonia

Begonia fuchsioides
　　　　　　Fuchsia begonia

Begonia haageana
　　　　　Elephant's ear begonia

Begonia heracleifolia　Star begonia

Begonia leptotricha　　Woolly bear

Begonia luxurians
　　　　　Palm-leaf begonia

Begonia masoniana
　　　　　Iron cross begonia

Begonia metallica
　　　　　Metal leaf begonia

Begonia rex　　　　Fan begonia
　　　　　Painted leaf begonia

Begonia scharffii
　　　　　Elephant's ear begonia

Begonia semperflorens
　　　　　　Wax begonia

Beloperone guttata　Shrimp plant
Berberidopsis corallina　Coral plant
Bertolonia hirsuta　　Jewel plant
Bessera elegans　　Coral drops

Bignonia callistegioides
　　　　　　Trumpet vine

Bigninia capensis
　　　　　Cape honeysuckle

Bignonia purpurea　Love charm

Bignonia speciosa　Trumpet vine

Bignonia stans　　Yellow bells
　　　　　　Yellow elder

Bignonia venusta　Flame flower
　　　　　　Flame vine
　　　　　　Flaming trumpets

Billbergia nutans　Friendship plant
　　　　　Queen's tears

Biophytum sensitivum
　　　　　Sensitive plant

Blechnum patersonii
　　　　　Strap water fern

Bloomeria crocea　Golden stars

Boehmeria nivea　China grass
　　　　　　Ramie

Bougainvillea glabra　Paper flower

Bouvardia ternifolia
　　　　　Scarlet trompetilla

Bouvardia triphylla
　　　　　Scarlet trompetilla

Bowiea volubilis　Climbing onion

Brassaia actinophylla
　　　　　Octopus tree
　　　　Queensland umbrella tree

Breynia nivosa　　Snow bush

Brodiaea coccinea　Fire cracker

Brodiaea ida-maia　Fire cracker

Brodiaea laxa　　Grass nut
　　　　　Ithuriel's spear

Brodiaea volubilis　Snake lily

Browallia speciosa　Bush violet

Brunfelsia americana
　　　　　Lady of the night

Brunfelsia calycina
　　　Yesterday, today and tomorrow

Brunfelsia paucifolia calycina
　　　Yesterday, today and tomorrow

Brunfelsia undulata
　　　　　White rain tree

Brunfelsia violacea
　　　　　Lady of the night

Brunsvigia josephinae
　　　　　Josephine's lily

Caesalpinia gilliesii
　　　　　Bird of paradise flower

Caesalpinia pulcherrima
　　　　　Barbados pride

Caladium × hortulanum
　　　　　Angel's wings

Calathea insignis　Rattlesnake plant

Calathea lancifolia
　　　　　Rattlesnake plant

Calathea makoyana　Peacock plant

Calathea zebrina　　Zebra plant

Calceolaria × herbeohybrida
　　　　　Pocket book plant
　　　　　Slipper flower

Calendula officinalis
　　　　　Common marigold
　　　　　Pot marigold

Callisia elegans　Wandering jew

Callistemon citrinus
　　　　　Lemon bottlebrush

Callistemon lanceolatus
　　　　　Lemon bottlebrush

Callistemon speciosus　Bottlebrush

Calonyction bona-nox
　　　　　Moonflower

Campanula isophylla
　　　　　Italian bellflower

Campanula pyramidalis
　　　　　Chimney bellflower

Campyloneurum phyllitidis
　　　　　Ribbon fern
　　　　　Strap fern

Canna × generalis　Indian shot

Citrus limetta

Capsicum annuum	Bell pepper
	Chillies
	Green pepper
	Paprika
	Red pepper
	Sweet pepper
Cardiospermum halicacabum	
	Balloon vine
	Heart-pea
	Heart-seed
Carex morrowii	Japanese sedge
Carica papaya	Papaya
	Pawpaw
Carissa grandiflora	Natal plum
Carpobrotus acinaciformis	
	Hottentot fig
Carpobrotus chilensis	Sea fig
Carpobrotus edulis	Hottentot fig
Caryota urens	Sago palm
	Toddy palm
	Wine palm
Cassia artemisioides	
	Wormwood cassia
Catharanthus roseus	
	Madagascar periwinkle
Cattleya bowringiana	
	Cluster cattleya
Cattleya citrina	Tulip cattleya
Cattleya intermedia	
	Cocktail orchid
Cattleya labiata	Autumn cattleya
Cattleya labiata dowiana	
	Queen cattleya
Cattleya labiata mossiae	
	Easter orchid
	Spring cattleya
Cattleya labiata trianaei	
	Christmas orchid
	Winter cattleya
Cattleya mossiae	Easter orchid
	Spring cattleya
Cattleya trianaei	Christmas orchid
	Winter cattleya
Celosia argentea cristata	
	Cockscomb
Celosia argentea pyramidalis	
	Prince of Wales feathers
Celosia cristata	Cockscomb
Celosia plumosa	
	Prince of Wales feathers
Celosia pyramidalis	
	Prince of Wales feathers
Centaurea cineraria	Dusty miller
Centaurea cyanus	Cornflower
Centaurea gymnocarpa	
	Dusty miller
Centaurea moschata	Sweet sultan
Ceratonia siliqua	Algaroba
	Carob
	Locust
	Saint John's bread
Ceratopteris cornuta	Water fern
Ceratopteris pteridoides	
	Floating fern
	Water fern
Ceratopteris siliquosa	Water fern
Ceratopteris thalictroides	
	Water fern
Ceropegia caffrorum	Lamp flower
Ceropegia sandersonii	
	Fountain flower
	Parachute plant
Ceropegia woodii	
	Chinese lantern plant
	Rosary vine
	String of hearts
Chamaedorea elegans	
	Dwarf mountain palm
	Mexican dwarf palm
	Parlour palm
Chamaedorea erumpens	
	Bamboo palm
Chamaedorea metallica	
	Miniature fishtail palm
Chamaedorea seifrizii	Reed palm
Chamaelaucium uncinatum	
	Geraldton wax flower
Chamaerops humilis	
	Dwarf fan palm
Cheiranthus × allionii	
	Siberian wallflower
Cheiranthus cheiri	
	Common wallflower
	Wallflower
Chlorophytum capense	
	Spider plant
Chlorophytum comosum	
	Spider plant
Chlorophytum elatum	Spider plant
Choisya ternata	
	Mexican orangeblossom
Chrysalidocarpus lutescens	
	Areca palm
	Golden feather palm
Cineraria maritima	Dusty miller
Cissus antarctica	Kangaroo vine
Cissus capensis	Cape grape
Cissus discolor	Rex begonia vine
Cissus rhombifolia	Grape ivy
Cissus sicyoides	Princess vine
Cissus voinierianum	Chestnut vine
× Citrofortunella mitis	
	Calamondin
Citrus aurantifolia	Lime
Citrus aurantium	Seville orange
Citrus aurantium sinense	
	Sweet orange
Citrus bigarardia	Seville orange
Citrus decumanus	Pummelo
	Shaddock
Citrus grandis	Pummelo
	Shaddock
Citrus limetta	Lime

Citrus maxima

Citrus maxima	Pummelo
	Shaddock
Citrus medica	Citron
Citrus mitis	Calamondin
Citrus nobilis	Mandarin
	Satsuma
	Tangerine
Citrus paradisi	Grapefruit
Citrus reticulata	Mandarin
	Satsuma
	Tangerine
Citrus reticulata × fortunella	
	Calamondin
Citrus sinensis	Sweet orange
Clerodendrum fallax	
	Java glorybean
Clerodendrum paniculatum	
	Pagoda flower
Clerodendrum speciosissimum	
	Java glorybean
Clerodendrum thomsonae	
	Bleeding heart vine
	Glory bower
Clerodendrum ugandense	
	Blue glory bower
Clethra arborea	
	Lily-of-the-valley tree
Clianthus dampieri	Damper's pea
	Glory pea
Clianthus formosus	Damper's pea
	Glory pea
Clianthus puniceus	Kaka beak
	Lobster claw
	Parrot's bill
Clivia miniata	Kaffir lily
Clusia grandiflora	Scotch attorney
Clusia rosea	Autograph tree
	Balsam apple
	Fat pork tree
Clytostoma binatum	Love charm
Clytostoma callistegioides	
	Trumpet vine
Clytostoma purpureum	
	Love charm
Cobaea scandens	Cathedral bells
	Cup-and-saucer creeper
Coccoloba uvifera	Seaside grape
Cocos nucifera	Coconut palm
Codiaeum variegatum pictum	
	Croton
	Joseph's coat
Coffea arabica	Arabian coffee
Colchicum autumnale	
	Autumn crocus
	Meadow saffron
Coleus blumei	Flame nettle
	Painted nettle
Colocasia esculenta	Cocoyam
	Dasheen
	Elephant's ear
	Taro
Columnea gloriosa	Goldfish plant

Columnea microphylla	
	Goldfish plant
Commelina benghalensis	
	Indian day flower
Commelina coelestis	Day flower
Convallaria majalis	
	Lily-of-the-valley
Cordyline australis	Cabbage palm
	Cabbage tree
Cordyline terminalis	Ti tree
Coronilla emerus	Scorpion senna
Corynocarpus laevigatus	
	Karaka
	New Zealand laurel
Corypha elata	Gebang
	Philippines sugar plum
Corypha gembanga	Gebang
	Philippines sugar plum
Corypha umbraculifera	
	Talipot palm
Costus igneus	Spiral ginger
Costus speciosus	Crepe ginger
	Malay ginger
Cotyledon maculata	Calico-hearts
Crassula argentea	Jade plant
Crassula barklyi	Rattlesnake tail
Crassula deltoidea	Silver beads
Crassula lycopodioides	
	Rat tail plant
Crassula maculata	Calico hearts
Crassula portulacea	Jade plant
Crassula rhomboidea	Silver beads
Crassula rupestris	Bead vine
	Rosary vine
Crassula teres	Rattlesnake tail
Crinum × powellii	Swamp lily
Crossandra infundibuliformis	
	Firecracker plant
Crossandra undulifolia	
	Firecracker plant
Crotalaria agatiflora	
	Canary bird bush
Crotalaria juncea	Sunn hemp
Cryptanthus acaulis	
	Green earth star
Cryptanthus bromelioides tricolor	Rainbow star
Cunonia capensis	Red alder
Cuphea hyssopifolia	False heather
Cuphea ignea	Cigar flower
Cuphea platycentra	Cigar flower
Curculigo capitulata	Palm grass
Curculigo recurvata	Palm grass
Curcuma domestica	Turmeric
Curcuma longa	Turmeric
Cyanotis kewensis	Teddy bear vine
Cyanotis somaliensis	Pussy ears
Cyathea arborea	
	West Indian tree fern

Dryopteris pseudomas

Cyathea dealbata — Ponga / Silver tree fern

Cyathea medullaris — Black tree fern / Sago fern

Cyathea smithii — Soft tree fern

Cycas circinalis — Fern palm / Sago fern palm

Cycas revoluta — Japanese sago palm

Cycnoches ventricosum — Swan orchid

Cymbalaria muralis — Ivy-leaved toadflax / Kenilworth ivy

Cypella plumbea — Blue tiger lily

Cyperus alternifolius — Umbrella grass / Umbrella plant

Cyperus diffusus — Umbrella plant

Cyperus esculentus — Chufa nut / Tiger nut

Cyperus papyrus — Egyptian paper reed / Papyrus

Cyphomandra betacea — Tree tomato

Cyrtanthus mackenii — Ifafa lily

Cyrtomium falcatum — Holly fern

Cyrtostachys lakka — Sealing wax palm

Cytisus canariensis — Florist's genista

Daedalacanthus nervosum — Blue sage

Darlingtonia californica — Californian pitcher plant / Cobra plant

Datura × candida — Angel's trumpet

Davallia canariensis — Hare's foot fern

Davallia dissecta — Squirrel's foot fern

Davallia fijiensis — Rabbit's foot fern

Davallia mariesii — Ball fern / Squirrel's foot fern

Davallia pyxidata — Squirrel's foot fern

Davallia solida fijiensis — Rabbit's foot fern

Davallia trichomanoides — Squirrel's foot fern

Dennstaedtia davallioides — Lacy ground fern

Dianthus caryophyllus — Carnation

Dianthus chinensis — Indian pink

Dicentra spectabilis — Bleeding heart / Dutchman's breeches / Lady-in-the-bath

Dicksonia antarctica — Soft tree fern

Dieffenbachia amoena — Giant dumb cane

Dieffenbachia maculata — Common dumb cane

Dionaea muscipula — Venus flytrap

Dioon edule — Chestnut dioon / Mexican fern palm

Dioscorea batatus — Chinese yam / Cinnamon yam

Dioscorea bulbifera — Aerial yam / Air potato

Dioscorea discolor — Ornamental yam

Dioscorea opposita — Chinese yam / Cinnamon yam

Diplazium esculentum — Paco / Vegetable fern

Dischidia rafflesiana — Malayan urn vine

Dodonaea viscosa — Akeake / Hop bush

Dolichos lablab — Hyacinth bean / Indian bean / Lablab bean

Dolichos lablab lignosus — Australian pea

Dolichos lignosus — Australian pea

Dorotheanthus bellidiformis — Livingstone daisy

Doxantha unguis-cati — Cat's claw vine

Dracaena draco — Dragon's tree

Dracaena fragrans — Corn plant

Dracaena godseffiana — Gold dust dracaena

Dracaena marginata — Madagascar dragon tree

Dracaena sanderiana — Ribbon plant

Dracaena surculosa — Gold dust dracaena

Dracunculus vulgaris — Dragon plant

Drimys aromatica — Mountain pepper

Drimys colorata — Pepper tree

Drimys lanceolata — Mountain pepper

Drimys winteri — Winter's bark

Drosanthemum speciosum — Dewflower

Drosera anglica — Great sundew

Drosera menziesii — Pink rainbow

Drosera rotundifolia — Common sundew

Drynaria quercifolia — Oak fern

Dryopteris borreri — Golden male fern

Dryopteris erythrosora — Japanese buckler fern / Japanese shield fern

Dryopteris filix-mas — Male fern

Dryopteris pseudomas — Golden male fern

Duranta plumieri

Duranta plumieri	
	Golden dewdrop
	Pigeon berry
	Skyflower
Duranta repens	Golden dewdrop
	Pigeon berry
	Skyflower
Ecballium elaterium	
	Squirting cucumber
Eccremocarpus scaber	
	Chilean glory flower
Echeveria affinis	Black echeveria
Echeveria derenbergii	
	Painted lady
Echeveria glauca	Blue echeveria
Echeveria leucotricha	
	Chenille plant
Echeveria multicaulis	
	Copper roses
Echeveria paraguayense	
	Ghost plant
	Mother-of-pearl plant
Echeveria pulvinata	Plush plant
Echeveria rosea	Desert rose
Echeveria secunda glauca	
	Blue echeveria
Echeveria setosa	Firecracker plant
Echium lycopsis	
	Purple viper's bugloss
Echium plantagineum	
	Purple viper's bugloss
Eichhornia crassipes	
	Water hyacinth
Eichhornia speciosa	
	Water hyacinth
Elaphoglossum crinitum	
	Elephant's ear fern
Encephalartos altensteinii	
	Bread tree cycad
Epidendrum cochleatum	
	Cockle-shell orchid
Epipremnum aureum	Devil's ivy
	Golden pothos
	Taro vine
Episcia cupreata	Flame violet
Episcia dianthiflora	Lace flower
Eranthemum nervosum	Blue sage
Eranthemum pulchellum	
	Blue sage
Erica carnea	Winter heath
Erica herbacea	Winter heath
Eriobotrya japonica	Loquat
Ervatamia coronaria	
	Cape jasmine
	East Indian rosebay
Erythrina crista-galli	
	Cockspur coral tree
Eschscholzia californica	
	Californian poppy
Eucalyptus citriodora	
	Lemon-scented gum

Eucalyptus ficifolia	
	Red-flowering gum
Eucalyptus globulus	Blue gum
	Tasmanian blue gum
Eucalyptus macrocarpa	Mottlecah
Eucalyptus nitens	Shining gum
Eucharis amazonica	Amazon lily
Eucharis grandiflora	Amazon lily
Eucomis comosa	Pineapple flower
Eucomis pole-evansii	
	Giant pineapple flower
Eugenia australis	Brush cherry
Eugenia jambos	Malabar plum
	Rose apple
Eugenia myrtifolia	Brush cherry
Eugenia paniculata	Brush cherry
Eugenia uniflora	Pitanga
	Surinam cherry
Euphorbia caput-medusae	
	Medusa's head
Euphorbia fulgens	Scarlet plume
Euphorbia grandicornis	
	Cow's horn
Euphorbia milii	Crown of thorns
Euphorbia pseudocactus	
	Cactus spurge
Euphorbia pulcherrima	Poinsettia
Euphorbia tirucalli	Finger tree
	Milk bush
	Rubber spurge
Eustoma grandiflorum	
	Prairie gentian
Eustoma russellianum	
	Prairie gentian
Fatsia japonica	
	False castor-oil plant
Fatsia papyrifera	Rice-paper plant
Faucaria felina	Cat's jaws
Faucaria tigrina	Tiger jaws
Feijoa sellowiana	Pineapple guava
Felicia amelloides	Blue marguerite
Felicia bergeriana	Kingfisher daisy
Ficus benghalensis	Banyan
Ficus benjamina	Weeping fig
Ficus deltoidea	Mistletoe fig
Ficus diversifolia	Indoor fig
	Mistletoe fig
Ficus elastica	Rubber plant
Ficus lyrata	Fiddle-leaf fig
Ficus macrocarpa	Laurel fig
Ficus macrophylla	
	Australian banyan
	Moreton bay fig
Ficus nitida	Laurel fig
Ficus pandurata	Fiddle-leaf fig
Ficus pumila	Climbing fig
	Creeping fig
Ficus religiosa	Bo tree
	Pepul
	Sacred fig tree

Helichrysum petiolatum

Ficus repens	Climbing fig
	Creeping fig
Ficus retusa	Laurel fig
Ficus rubiginosa	Port Jackson fig
Ficus sycamorus	Mulberry fig
	Sycamore fig
Fittonia argyroneura	Silver net leaf
Fittonia verschaffeltii	Nerve plant
	Painted net leaf
Fortunella crassifolia	
	Meiwa kumquat
Fortunella hindsii	
	Hong Kong kumquat
Fortunella margarita	
	Nagami kumquat
	Oval kumquat
Francoa appendiculata	
	Bridal wreath
Fritillaria camtschatcensis	
	Black sarana
Fritillaria imperialis	
	Crown imperial
Fritillaria meleagris	
	Snake's head fritillary
Furcraea foetida	Mauritius hemp
Furcraea gigantea	Mauritius hemp
Galanthus elwesii	Giant snowdrop
Galanthus nivalis	
	Common snowdrop
	Snowdrop
Galtonia candicans	
	Summer hyacinth
Gardenia citriodora	Wild coffee
Gardenia florida	Cape jasmin
	Common gardenia
	Gardenia
Gardenia grandiflora	Cape jasmin
	Common gardenia
	Gardenia
Gardenia jasminoides	
	Cape jasmine
	Common gardenia
	Gardenia
Gasteria verrucosa	Ox tongue
Gelsemium sempervirens	
	Carolina yellow jasmine
	False yellow jasmine
Genista canariensis	
	Florist's genista
Geogenanthus undatus	Seersucker plant
Gerbera jamesonii	
	Barberton daisy
	Transvaal daisy
Gesneria cardinalis	
	Cardinal flower
Gilia capitata	Blue thimble flower
Gilia coronipifolia	Skyrocket
	Standing cypress
Gilia rubra	Skyrocket
	Standing cypress
Gilia tricolor	Bird's eyes

Gladiolus blandus	Painted lady
Gladiolus carneus	Painted lady
Gladiolus primulinus	
	Maid of the mist
Glechoma hederacea	Ground ivy
Gloriosa rothschildiana	Glory lily
Gloxinia speciosa	Gloxinia
Gomphrena globosa	
	Globe amaranth
Gossypium arboreum	Tree cotton
Gossypium herbaceum	
	Levant cotton
	Turkish cotton
Gossypium sturtianum	
	Sturt's desert rose
Gossypium sturtii	
	Sturt's desert rose
Graptopetalum paraguayense	
	Ghost plant
	Mother-of-pearl plant
Graptophyllum pictum	
	Caricature plant
Grevillea robusta	Silky oak
Guzmania berteroana	
	Flaming torch
Guzmania lingulata	Scarlet star
Guzmania picta	
	Blushing bromeliad
Gynura aurantiaca	Velvet plant
Haemanthus albiflos	Paintbrush
Haemanthus katherinae	
	Blood flower
Haemanthus multiflorus	
	Blood flower
Hardenbergia comptoniana	
	Wild sarsparilla
Haworthia fasciata	
	Zebra haworthia
Haworthia margaritifera	
	Pearl plant
Haworthia pumila	Pearl plant
Haworthia tessellata	
	Star window plant
Hedera canariensis	
	Canary Island ivy
Hedera colchica	Persian ivy
Hedera helix	Common ivy
	English ivy
Hedychium coccineum	
	Red ginger lily
	Scarlet ginger lily
Hedychium coronarium	
	Butterfly ginger lily
	Garland flower
Hedychium gardnerianum	
	Kahili ginger
Helichrysum angustifolium	
	Curry plant
Helichrysum italicum	Curry plant
Helichrysum petiolatum	
	Liquorice plant

Helichrysum serotinum

Helichrysum serotinum	Curry plant
Heliotropium arborescens	Common heliotrope
Heliotropium peruvianum	Common heliotrope
Helxine soleirolii	Baby's tears / Mind your own business
Hemigraphis alternata	Flame ivy / Red ivy
Hemigraphis colorata	Flame ivy / Red ivy
Hemitelia smithii	Soft tree fern
Hesperoyucca whipplei	Our Lord's candle
Hibbertia scandens	Guinea flower / Snake vine
Hibbertia volubilis	Guinea flower / Snake vine
Hibiscus rosa-sinensis	Rose of china
Hibiscus schizopetalus	Japanese lantern
Hippeastrum × ackermannii	Amaryllis
Hippeastrum × acramanii	Amaryllis
Hippeastrum procerum	Blue amaryllis
Homeria breyniana	Cape tulip
Homeria collina	Cape tulip
Howeia belmoreana	Curly palm / Sentry palm
Howeia forsterana	Kentia palm / Paradise palm / Sentry palm / Thatchleaf palm
Hoya bella	Miniature wax plant
Hoya carnosa	Wax plant
Huernia zebrina	Owl eyes
Humulus japonicus	Japanese hop
Humulus lupulus	Common hop
Hydrangea hortensis	Common hydrangea / French hydrangea
Hydrangea macrophylla	Common hydrangea / French hydrangea
Hylocereus undatus	Queen of the night
Hymenocallis calathina	Basket flower / Peruvian daffodil
Hymenocallis narcissiflora	Basket flower / Peruvian daffodil
Hypoestes phyllostachya	Freckle face / Polka dot plant
Imantophyllum miniatum	Kaffir lily

Impatiens balsamina	Rose balsam / Touch-me-not
Impatiens holstii	Busy lizzie / Patient lucy
Impatiens sultanii	Busy lizzie / Patient lucy
Impatiens walleriana	Busy lizzie / Patient lucy
Ipheion uniflorum	Spring star flower
Ipomoea batatas	Sweet potato
Ipomoea bona-nox	Moonflower
Ipomoea coccinea	Red morning glory / Star ipomoea
Ipomoea noctiflora	Moonflower
Ipomoea purpurea	Common morning glory / Morning glory
Ipomoea quamoclit	Cypress vine
Ipomopsis rubra	Skyrocket / Standing cypress
Iresine herbstii	Beefsteak plant
Iresine lindenii	Blood leaf
Ixora coccinea	Flame-of-the-woods
Ixora javanica	Jungle geranium
Jacobinia carnea	King's crown
Jacobinia velutina	King's crown
Jasminum mesneyi	Primrose jasmine
Jasminum nitidum	Star jasmine / Windmill jasmine
Jasminum officinale	Common white jasmine / Poet's jessamine / Summer jasmine
Jasminum polyanthum	Chinese jasmine / Pink jasmine
Jasminum primulinum	Primrose jasmine
Jasminum sambac	Arabian jasmine
Jatropha multifida	Coral plant / Physic nut
Jatropha podagrica	Gout plant / Tartogo
Jubaea chilensis	Chilean wine palm / Coquito / Honey palm
Jubaea spectabilis	Chilean wine palm / Coquito / Honey palm
Justicia carnea	King's crown
Justicia coccinea	Cardinal's guard
Kaempferia roscoana	Dwarf ginger lily / Peacock plant
Kaempferia rotunda	Tropical crocus
Kalanchoe beharensis	Velvet leaf

Maranta leuconeura
kerchoveana

Kalanchoe blossfeldiana	Flaming katy
Kalanchoe diagremontiana	Devil's backbone
Kalanchoe pilosa	Panda plant
	Pussy ears
Kalanchoe tomentosa	Panda plant
	Pussy ears
Kalanchoe tubiflora	Chandelier plant
Kennedia nigricans	Black bean
Kennedia prostrata	Running postman
Kennedia rubicunda	Dusky coral pea
Kentia belmoreana	Curly palm
	Sentry palm
Kentia forsterana	Kentia palm
	Paradise palm
	Sentry palm
	Thatchleaf palm
Kleinia articulatus	Candle plant
Kochia scoparia	Burning bush
	Summer cypress
Lachenalia aloides	Cape cowslip
Lachenalia glaucina	Opal lachenalia
Lachenalia mutabilis	Fairy lachenalia
Lachenalia tricolor	Cape cowslip
Lagenaria siceraria	Bottle gourd
	Calabash gourd
Lagenaria vulgaris	Bottle gourd
	Calabash gourd
Lagerstroemia indica	Cape myrtle
Lamium maculatum	Spotted dead nettle
Lantana camara	Yellow sage
Lapageria rosea	Chilean bell flower
Latania aurea	Yellow latan palm
Latania borbonica	Red latan palm
Latania commersonii	Red latan palm
Latania loddigesii	Silver latan palm
Latania lontaroides	Red latan palm
Latania verschaffeltii	Yellow latan palm
Laurus nobilis	Bay
	Sweet bay
Lavandula angustifolia	Common lavender
	English lavender
Lavandula stoechas	French lavender
Leptospermum nitidum	Shiny tea tree
Leptospermum scoparium	Manuka
	New Zealand tea tree
Leucadendron argenteum	Silver tree
Leucocoryne ixioides	Glory-of-the-snow
Leucospermum cordifolium	Nodding pincushion
Leucospermum nutans	Nodding pincushion
Limonia aurantifolia	Lime
Limonium sinuatum	Notch-leaf statice
	Winged statice
Limonium suworowii	Rat's tail statice
	Russian statice
Linaria cymbalaria	Ivy-leaved toadflax
	Kenilworth ivy
Linaria maroccana	Toadflax
Lippia citriodora	Lemon verbena
Lisianthus russellianus	Prairie gentian
Livistona australis	Australian fountain palm
	Gippsland fountain palm
Livistona chinensis	Chinese fountain palm
Lotus berthelotii	Coral gem
	Parrot's beak
	Winged pea
Luffa aegyptica	Loofah
	Sponge gourd
Luffa cylindrica	Loofah
	Sponge gourd
Lycopersicon esculentum	Tomato
Lycopersicon lycopersicum	Tomato
Lycopersicon lycopersicum cerasiforme	Cherry tomato
	Salad tomato
Lycopersicon pimpinellifolium	Currant tomato
Lycopodium phlegmaria	Queensland tassel fern
Malpighia coccigera	Miniature holly
Malpighia glabra	Barbados cherry
Mandevilla laxa	Chilean jasmine
Mandevilla suaveolens	Chilean jasmine
Manettia bicolor	Firecracker vine
Manettia inflata	Firecracker vine
Manettia luteo-rubra	Firecracker vine
Manihot esculenta	Cassava
	Manioc
	Tapioca
Manihot utilissima	Cassava
	Manioc
	Tapioca
Maranta arundinacea	Arrowroot
Maranta leuconeura	Prayer plant
Maranta leuconeura kerchoveana	Rabbit's foot
	Rabbit tracks

Marsilea drummondi

Marsilea drummondi	Water clover
Marsilea quadrifolia	Water clover
Matthiola incana	Stock
Medinilla magnifica	Rose grape
Melaleuca leucodendron	Cajeput
	River tea tree
Melia azederach	Bead tree
	Persian lilac
Melianthus major	Honeybush
Mesembryanthemum criniflorum	Livingstone daisy
Metrosideros collina	Lehua
Metrosideros excelsa	New Zealand christmas tree
Metrosideros tomentosa	New Zealand christmas tree
Mimosa pudica	Humble plant
	Sensitive plant
Mimulus guttatus	Monkey flower
	Monkey musk
Mimulus luteus	Monkey flower
	Monkey musk
Mimulus moschatus	Musk
Mitriostigma axillare	Wild coffee
Momordica balsamina	Balsam apple
Momordica charantia	Balsam pear
Mondo jaburan	White lily turf
Monstera deliciosa	Cerimen
	Mexican bread fruit
	Swiss cheese plant
Monstera latevaginata	Shingle plant
Monstera pertusa	Ceriman
	Mexican bread fruit
	Swiss cheese plant
Muehlenbeckia complexa	Maidenhair vine
	Wire vine
Murraya exotica	Orange jasmine
Murraya koenigii	Curry leaf
Murraya paniculata	Orange jasmine
Musa basjoo	Japanese banana
Musa coccinea	Flowering banana
	Scarlet banana
Musa × paradisiaca	Common banana
Musa × sapientum	Common banana
Myosotis sylvatica	Wood forget-me-not
Myriophyllum aquaticum	Water feather
Myriophyllum brasiliense	Water feather
Myriophyllum proserpinacoides	Water feather
Myrtus communis	Common myrtle
Nandina domestica	Heavenly bamboo
	Sacred bamboo
Neanthe elegans	Dwarf mountain palm
	Parlour palm
Nelumbium lutea	American lotus
Nelumbo lutea	American lotus
Nelumbo pentapetala	American lotus
Nemophila maculata	Five spot
Nemophila menziesii	Baby blue eyes
Neoregelia marmorata	Marble plant
Neoregelia spectabilis	Fingernail plant
Nephrolepis cordifolia	Ladder fern
	Sword fern
Nephrolepis exaltata	Sword fern
Nerine sarniensis	Guernsey lily
Nerium oleander	Oleander
	Rose bay
Nertera depressa	Coral moss
Nertera granadensis	Bead plant
Nicolaia elatior	Philippine wax flower
	Torch ginger
Nidularium fulgens	Blushing bromeliad
Nidularium innocentii	Bird's nest bromeliad
Nidularium pictum	Blushing bromeliad
Nolina recurvata	Elephant foot
	Pony tail
Nolina tuberculata	Elephant foot
	Pony tail
Nymphaea caerula	Egyptian blue lotus
Nymphaea capensis	Blue water lily
Nymphaea pygmaea	Pigmy water lily
Nymphaea stellata	Blue lotus
Nymphaea tetragona	Pigmy water lily
Ochna serrulata	Mickey mouse plant
Odontoglossum crispum	Lace orchid
Odontoglossum pulchellum	Lily-of-the-valley orchid
Olea europaea	Olive
Oncidium flexuosum	Dancing doll orchid
Oncidium ornithorhynchum	Dove orchid
Oncidium papilio	Butterfly orchid
Oncidium tigrinum	Tiger orchid
Oncidium varicosum	Golden butterfly orchid

Peperomia glabella

Ophiopogon jaburan
White lily turf
Oplismenus hirtellus   Basket grass
Ornithogalum arabicum
Star of bethlehem
Ornithogalum nutans
Drooping star of bethlehem
Ornithogalum saundersiae
Giant chincherinchee
Ornithogalum thyrsoides
Chincherinchee
Ornithogalum umbellatum
Star of bethlehem
Oxalis cernua   Bermuda buttercup
Oxalis deppei   Lucky clover
Oxalis pes-caprae
Bermuda buttercup
Pachystachys cardinalis
Cardinal's guard
Pachystachys coccinea
Cardinal's guard
Pachystachys lutea   Lollipop plant
Pancratium maritimum
Sea daffodil
Sea lily
Pandanus baptisii   Blue screw pine
Pandanus utilis
Common screw pine
Pandorea jasminoides
Bower plant
Pandorea pandorana
Wonga-wonga vine
Parochetus communis
Blue shamrock pea
Passiflora caerulea
Blue passion flower
Common passion flower
Passiflora coccinea   Red granadilla
Red passion flower
Passiflora edulis   Passion fruit
Purple granadilla
Passiflora ligularis   Sweet granadilla
Passiflora mollissima
Banana passion fruit
Curuba
Passiflora quadrangularis
Giant granadilla
Passiflora racemosa
Red passion flower
Pedilanthes tithymaloides
Redbird cactus
Slipper cactus
Pedilanthes tithymaloides
smallii   Jacob's ladder
Pelargonium capitatum
Rose-scented geranium
Rose-scented pelargonium
Pelargonium crispum
Lemon geranium
Lemon pelargonium
Prince Rupert geranium
Prince Rupert pelargonium

Pelargonium × domesticum
Fancy geranium
Fancy pelargonium
Lady Washington geraniums
Lady Washington pelargonium
Martha Washington geranium
Martha Washington pelargonium
Regal geranium
Regal pelargonium
Show geranium
Show pelargonium
Pelargonium echinatum
Cactus geranium
Cactus pelargonium
Pelargonium × fragrans
Nutmeg geranium
Nutmeg pelargonium
Pelargonium graveolens
Rose geranium
Rose pelargonium
Pelargonium × hortorum
Zonal geranium
Zonal pelargonium
Pelargonium odoratissimum
Apple-scented geranium
Apple-scented pelargonium
Pelargonium peltatum
Ivy-leaved geranium
Ivy-leaved pelargonium
Pelargonium quercifolium
Oak-leaved geranium
Oak-leaved pelargonium
Pelargonium tomentosum
Peppermint-scented geranium
Peppermint-scented pelargonium
Pelargonium zonale
Horse-shoe geranium
Horse-shoe pelargonium
Zonal geranium
Zonal pelargonium
Pellaea adiantoides
Green brake fern
Pellaea atropurpurea
Purple-stemmed cliff brake
Pellaea hastata   Green brake fern
Pellaea rotundifolia   Button fern
Pellaea viridis   Green brake fern
Pellionia daveauana
Trailing water-melon begonia
Pentas carnea   Egyptian star cluster
Star cluster
Pentas lanceolata
Egyptian star cluster
Star cluster
Peperomia argyreia
Water-melon begonia
Peperomia caperata
Emerald ripple
Peperomia clusiifolia
Baby rubber plant
Peperomia fraseri
Flowering mignonette
Peperomia glabella   Wax privet

Peperomia griseoargentea

Peperomia griseoargentea
Ivyleaf peperomia
Silverleaf peperomia

Peperomia hederifolia
Ivyleaf peperomia
Silverleaf peperomia

Peperomia maculosa
Radiator plant

Peperomia magnoliifolia
Desert privet

Peperomia marmorata Silver heart

Peperomia polybotrya Coin leaf

Peperomia prostrata
Creeping peperomia

Peperomia pulchella
Whorled peperomia

Peperomia rotundifolia pilosior
Creeping peperomia

Peperomia sandersii
Water-melon begonia

Peperomia scandens
Cupid peperomia

Peperomia verticillata
Whorled peperomia

Pereskia aculeata
Barbados gooseberry

Peristeria elata Dove orchid
Holy ghost plant

Persea americana Avocado

Persea gratissima Avocado

Petrea volubilis Purple wreath
Queen's wreath

Phaeomeria magnifica
Philippine wax flower
Torch ginger

Phaius bicolor Nun's hood orchid

Phaius blumei Nun's hood orchid

Phaius grandiflorus
Nun's hood orchid

Phaius gravesii Nun's hood orchid

Phaius tankervillae
Nun's hood orchid

Phaius wallichii Nun's hood orchid

Pharbitis purpurea
Common morning glory
Morning glory

Philodendron andreanum
Black-gold philodendron
Velour philodendron

Philodendron auritum Five fingers

Philodendron bipinnatifidum
Tree philodendron

Philodendron cordatum Heart leaf

Philodendron domesticum
Elephant's ear
Spade leaf

*Philodendron domesticum ×
erubescens*
Red-leaf philodendron

Philodendron eichleri
Tree philodendron

Philodendron erubescens
Blushing philodendron

Philodendron gloriosum Satin leaf

Philodendron hastatum
Elephant's ear
Spade leaf

Philodendron × mandaianum
Red-leaf philodendron

Philodendron melanochrysum
Black-gold philodendron
Velour philodendron

Philodendron pertusum Ceriman
Mexican bread fruit
Swiss cheese plant

Philodendron scandens Heart leaf
Sweetheart plant

Philodendron selloum
Lacy tree philodendron

Phlebodium aureum
Hare's foot fern

Phoenix canariensis
Canary Islands date palm

Phoenix dactylifera Date palm

Phoenix roebelenii
Pigmy date palm

Phormium colensoi Mountain flax

Phormium cookianum
Mountain flax

Phormium tenax
New Zealand flax

Phyllanthus nivosa Snow bush

Phyllitis scolopendrium
Hart's tongue fern

Phyllostachys aurea
Fishpole bamboo
Golden bamboo

Pilea cadierei Aluminium plant

Pilea involucrata Friendship plant
Panamiga

Pilea microphylla Artillery plant

Pilea muscosa Artillery plant

Pilea nummulariifolia
Creeping charlie

Pilea repens Black leaf panamiga

Pinguicula grandiflora
Greater butterwort

Pinguicula vulgaris Butterwort

Piper crocatum
Ornamental pepper

Piper nigrum Black pepper

Piper ornatum crocatum
Ornamental pepper

Pisonia umbellifera
Bird-catching tree
Parapara

Pistia stratiotes Water lettuce

Pittosporum crassifolium Karo

Pittosporum tenuifolium Kohuhu

Pittosporum tobira
Japanese pittosporum
Tobira

Rhaphidophora decursiva

Pittosporum undulatum
Victorian box

Platycerium alcicorne
Common stag's horn fern

Platycerium angolense
Elephant's ear fern

Platycerium biforme
Crown stag's horn

Platycerium bifurcatum
Common stag's horn fern

Platycerium coronarium
Crown stag's horn

Platycerium grande
Regal elkhorn fern

Platycerium hillii   Elkhorn fern

Plectranthus coleoides   Candle plant

Plectranthus oertendahlii
Brazilian coleus
Swedish ivy

Plumbago auriculata
Blue cape leadwort
Blue cape plumbago

Plumbago capensis
Blue cape leadwort
Blue cape plumbago

Plumbago indica   Scarlet leadwort

Plumbago rosea   Scarlet leadwort

Plumeria acuminata   Frangipani

Plumeria acutifolia   Pagoda tree

Plumeria rubra   Frangipani

Plumeria rubra acutifolia
Pagoda tree

Plumeria rubra lutea
Yellow pagoda tree

Poinciana pulcherrima
Barbados pride

Polianthes tuberosa   Tuberose

Polypodium angustifolium
Narrow-leaved ribbon fern
Narrow-leaved strap fern

Polypodium aureum
Hare's foot fern

Polypodium phyllitidis
Ribbon fern
Strap fern

Polypodium subauriculatum
Lacy pine fern

Polypodium vulgare
Common polypody

Polyscias balfouriana
Dinner-plate aralia

Polyscias filicifolia   Fern-leaf aralia

Polyscias guilfoylei   Wild coffee

Polystichum acrostichoides
Christmas fern

Polystichum aculeatum
Hard shield fern
Prickly shield fern

Polystichum aristatum
East Indian holly fern

Polystichum falcatum   Holly fern

Polystichum munitum
Giant holly fern
Western sword fern

Polystichum setiferum
Soft shield fern

Polystichum tsus-simense
Tsusina holly fern

Portulaca grandiflora   Sun plant

Pothos aureus   Devil's ivy
Golden pothos
Taro vine

Primula malacoides
Fairy primrose

Primula sinensis   Chinese primrose

Primula × tommasinii   Polyanthus

Primula vulgaris   Primrose

Pritchardia filifera
Desert fan palm
Petticoat palm

Prostanthera melissifolia
Balm mint bush

Prostanthera nivea
Snowy mint bush

Protea mellifera   Honey flower
Sugarbush

Protea repens   Honey flower
Sugarbush

Pseudowintera colorata
Pepper tree

Pteris cretica   Cretan brake
Ribbon fern
Table fern

Pteris ensiformis   Sword brake

Pteris multifida   Spider fern

Pteris serrulata   Spider fern

Pteris vittata   Ladder fern

Ptychosperma elegans
Alexander palm
Solitaire palm

Punica granatum   Pomegranate

Pyrostegia ignea   Flame flower
Flame vine
Flaming trumpets

Pyrostegia venusta   Flame flower
Flame vine
Flaming trumpets

Quisqualis indica
Rangoon creeper

Raphidophora aurea   Devil's ivy
Golden pothos
Taro vine

Ravenala madagascariensis
Traveller's tree

Reinwardtia indica   Yellow flax

Reinwardtia trigyna   Yellow flax

Rhaphidophora celatocaulis
Shingle plant

Rhaphidophora decursiva
Shingle plant

Rhapis excelsa

Rhapis excelsa	Bamboo palm
	Ground rattan
	Little lady palm
	Miniature fan palm
Rhodochiton atrosanguineum	
	Purple bell vine
Rhodochiton volubile	
	Purple bell vine
Rhoeo discolor	Boat lily
	Moses-in-a-boat
Rhoeo spathacea	Boat lily
	Moses-in-a-boat
Rhoicissus capensis	Cape grape
Ricinus communis	Castor oil plant
Rivina humilis	Rouge plant
Rivina laevis	Rouge plant
Rosmarinus lavandulaceum	
	Prostrate rosemary
Rosmarinus officinalis	Rosemary
Rosmarinus officinalis prostratus	
	Prostrate rosemary
Roystonea regia	Cuban royal palm
Ruellia mackoyana	Monkey plant
Rumohra adiantiformis	
	Leather fern
Ruscus hypoglossum	
	Butcher's broom
Russelia equisetiformis	Coral plant
	Fountain bush
Russelia juncea	Coral plant
	Fountain bush
Salpiglossis sinuata	Painted tongue
Salvia elegans	Pineapple sage
Salvia officinalis	Common sage
Salvia rutilans	Pineapple sage
Salvia splendens	Scarlet sage
Salvinia auriculata	Floating moss
Sansevieria grandicuspis	
	Star sansevieria
Sansevieria trifasciata	
	Mother-in-law's tongue
	Snake plant
Sansevieria zeylanica	
	Devil's tongue
Sarracenia flava	Huntsman's horn
	Yellow pitcher plant
Sarracenia purpurea	
	Common pitcher plant
Sauromatum guttatum	
	Monarch of the east
	Voodoo lily
Saxifraga sarmentosa	
	Mother of thousands
	Strawberry geranium
Saxifraga stolonifera	
	Mother of thousands
	Strawberry geranium
Saxifraga × urbium	London pride
Schlefflera actinophylla	
	Octopus tree
	Queensland umbrella tree

Schinus molle	Peruvian mastic tree
	Peruvian pepper tree
Schizanthus pinnatus	
	Poor man's orchid
Scilla sibirica	Siberian squill
Scindapsus aureus	Devil's ivy
	Golden pothos
	Taro vine
Seaforthia elegans	Alexander palm
	Solitaire palm
Sedum morganianum	Ass's tail
	Burro's tail
	Donkey's tail
Sedum weinbergii	Ghost plant
	Mother-of-pearl plant
Selaginella lepidophylla	
	Resurrection plant
	Rose of Jericho
Selaginella uncinata	Peacock moss
	Rainbow fern
Senecio articulatus	Candle plant
Senecio bicolor cineraria	
	Dusty miller
Senecio cineraria	Dusty miller
Senecio confusus	
	Mexican flame vine
Senecio elegans	Purple ragwort
Senecio macroglossus	Cape ivy
	Natal ivy
	Wax vine
Senecio maritimus	Dusty miller
Senecio mikanioides	German ivy
Senecio rowleyanus	String of beads
	String of pearls
Setcreasea striata	Wandering jew
Sinningia cardinalis	
	Cardinal flower
Sinningia speciosa	Gloxinia
Smilax asparagoides	Smilax
Smithiana cinnabarina	
	Temple bells
Solandra guttata	Cup of gold
Solandra hartwegii	Cup of gold
Solandra maxima	Cup of gold
Solandra nitida	Cup of gold
Solanum aviculare	Kangaroo apple
Solanum capsicastrum	
	Winter cherry
Solanum crispum	
	Chilean potato tree
Solanum jasminoides	
	Jasmine nightshade
	Potato vine
Solanum macranthum	
	Brazilian potato tree
Solanum melongena	Aubergine
	Egg-plant
Solanum pseudocapsicum	
	Jerusalem cherry
Solanum rantonnetii	
	Blue potato bush

Trachelium caeruleum

Solanum wendlandii
Giant potato vine

Soleirolia soleirolii   Baby's tears
Mind your own business

Sollya fusiformis
Australian bluebell
Australian bluebell creeper

Sollya heterophylla
Australian bluebell
Australian bluebell creeper

Sparaxis tricolor   Harlequin flower
Wand flower

Sparmannia africana
African hemp

Spathiphyllum wallisii   Peace lily
White sails

Sprekelia formosissima   Aztec lily
Jacobean lily

Stapelia hirsuta   Hairy toad plant

Stenolobium stans   Yellow bells
Yellow elder

Stenotaphrum secundatum
Saint Augustine grass

Stephanotis floribunda
Bridal flower
Madagascar jasmine
Waxy jasmine

Stigmaphyllon ciliatum
Butterfly vine
Golden creeper
Golden vine

Strelitzia reginae
Bird of paradise flower

Streptanthera cuprea
Orange kaleidoscope flower

Streptanthera elegans
White kaleidoscope flower

Streptocarpus dunnii
Red nodding bells

Streptocarpus rexii   Cape primrose

Streptocarpus saxorum
False African violet

Streptosolen jamesonii
Marmalade bush

Strobilanthes dyerianus
Persian shield

Stropholirion californicum
Snake lily

Stylidium graminifolium
Common trigger plant
Grass trigger plant
Trigger plant

Swainsona greyana
Darling river pea

Syngonium auritum   Five fingers

Syngonium podophyllum
Arrowhead vine
Goosefoot plant

Syzygium jambos   Malabar plum
Rose apple

Syzygium paniculatum
Brush cherry

Tabernaemontana coronaria
Cape jasmine
East Indian rosebay

Tabernaemontana divaricata
Cape jasmine
East Indian rosebay

Tacca chantrieri   Bat flower
Cat's whiskers

Tacca leontopetaloides
East Indian arrowroot
South sea arrowroot

Tacca pinnatifida
East Indian arrowroot
South sea arrowroot

Tacsonia mollissima
Banana passion fruit
Curuba

Tagetes erecta   African marigold
American marigold

Tagetes patula   French marigold

Tagetes signata   Signet marigold
Tagetes

Tagetes tenuifolia   Signet marigold
Tagetes

Tasmannia latifolia
Mountain pepper

Tecoma capensis   Cape honeysuckle

Tecoma stans   Yellow bells
Yellow elder

Tecomaria capensis
Cape honeysuckle

Teline canariensis   Florist's genista

Telopea speciosissima   Waratah

Tetranema mexicanum
Mexican foxglove
Mexican violet

Tetranema roseum
Mexican foxglove
Mexican violet

Tetrapanax papyriferus
Rice-paper plant

Tetrastigma voinierianum
Chestnut vine

Thevetia peruviana
Yellow oleander

Thrinax microcarpa   Key palm

Thrinax morrisii   Key palm

Thrinax parviflora
Palmetto thatch palm

Thunbergia alata
Black-eyed susan

Thunbergia grandiflora
Blue trumpet vine

Tibouchina semidecandra
Glory bush

Tibouchina urvilleana   Glory bush

Tillandsia usneioides   Spanish moss

Tolmiea menziesii   Piggyback plant

Torenia fournieri
Wishbone flower

Trachelium caeruleum
Common throatwort

Trachycarpus fortunei

Trachycarpus fortunei	
	Chusan palm
	Windmill palm
Tradescantia albiflora	
	Wandering jew
Tradescantia fluminensis	
	Wandering jew
Trevesia palmata	Snowflake aralia
Trichosanthes anguina	Snake gourd
Triteleia laxa	Grass nut
	Ithuriel's spear
Tropaeolum canariensis	
	Canary creeper
Tropaeolum majus	Nasturtium
Tropaeolum peregrinum	
	Canary creeper
Tulbaghia fragrans	Sweet garlic
Turnera trioniflora	Sage rose
Turnera ulmifolia	Sage rose
Vallota purpurea	Guernsey lily
	Scarborough lily
Vallota speciosa	Guernsey lily
	Scarborough lily
Veitchia merrillii	Christmas palm
Verbena triphylla	Lemon verbena
Viburnum tinus	Laurustinus
Vinca rosea	Madagascar periwinkle
Viola hederacea	Ivy-leaved violet
Viola × hortensis	Garden pansy
	Pansy
Viola × wittrockiana	
	Garden pansy
	Pansy
Vitis capensis	Cape grape
Vitis voinierianum	Chestnut vine
Vittaria lineata	Florida ribbon fern
Vriesea carinata	Lobster claws
Vriesea hieroglyphica	
	King of the bromeliads
Vriesea psittacina	Painted feathers
Vriesea splendens	Flaming sword

Washingtonia filifera	
	Desert fan palm
	Petticoat palm
Westringia fruticosa	
	Australian rosemary
Westringia rosmariniformis	
	Australian rosemary
Wintera aromatica	Winter's bark
Winterania latifolia	
	Mountain pepper
Worsleya rayneri	Blue amaryllis
Xanthorrhoea arborea	
	Botany bay gum
Xanthorrhoea preissii	
	Blackboy
	Common blackboy
Xanthosma lindenii	Indian kale
Xanthosma violaceum	Blue taro
	Yautia
Yucca brevifolia	Joshua tree
Yucca elata	Palmella
	Soap tree
Yucca elephantipes	Spineless yucca
Yucca gigantea	Spineless yucca
Yucca gloriosa	Spanish dagger
Yucca guatemalensis	
	Spineless yucca
Yucca whipplei	Our Lord's candle
Zamia floridana	Coontie
	Seminole bread
Zamia furfuracea	
	Florida arrowroot
Zamia pumila	Florida arrowroot
Zebrina pendula	Silvery inch plant
	Wandering jew
Zebrina purpusii	
	Bronze inch plant
Zephyranthes candida	
	Flower of the west wind
Zingiber officinale	
	Common ginger
	Ginger

ORCHIDS

Orchids are members of the very large family *Orchidaceae*. Various genera are grown by commercial specialists for the cut flower market, and by hobbyists as garden plants, in greenhouses or the home. Many artificial hybrids have been produced and are often to be found in private collections. The following list includes those most commonly offered for sale in nurseries and garden centres.

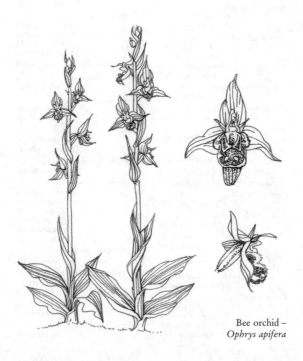

Bee orchid –
Ophrys apifera

Aceras anthropophorum

Aceras anthropophorum
Man orchid

Aceras anthropophora
Green man orchid

Aerides odorata Foxtail orchid

Amesia gigantea Chatterbox
Giant helleborine
Giant orchid
Stream orchid

Anacamptis pyramidalis
Pyramidal orchid

Anagraecum sesquipedale
Star-of-Bethlehem orchid

Anguloa clowesii Cradle orchid

Anguloa uniflora
Cradle orchid

Anoectochilus setaceus
Jewel orchid
King-of-the-forest

Aplectrum hymale Adam-and-Eve
Puttyroot

Aplectrum spicatum
Adam-and-Eve
Puttyroot

Arachnis cathcartii
Scorpion orchid

Arachnis clarkei Esmaralda

Arachnis flos-aeris Spider orchid

Arachnis moschifera Spider orchid

Arachnis × maingayi
Pink scorpion orchid
Spider orchid

Arethusa bulbosa Bog orchid
Bog rose orchid
Dragon's mouth orchid
Swamp pink orchid
Wild pink orchid

Arpophyllum giganteum
Hyacinth orchid

Arpophyllum spicatum
Hyacinth orchid

Arundina bambusifolia
Bamboo orchid

Arundina graminifolia
Bamboo orchid

Bletia alta Pine pink orchid

Bletia purpurea Pine pink orchid

Brassavola nodosa
Lady-of-the-night

Bulbophyllum refractum
Windmill orchid

Calopogon tuberosus Grass pink
Swamp pink

Calypso borealis Calypso
Cytherea
Fairy-slipper orchid
Pink-slipper orchid

Calypso bulbosa Bog orchid
Calypso
Cytherea
Fairy-slipper orchid
Pink-slipper orchid

Catasetum macrocarpum
Jumping orchid

Catasetum tridentatum
Jumping orchid

Cattleya citrina Tulip cattleya

Cattleya dowiana Queen cattleya

Cattleya gaskelliana
Summer cattleya

Cattleya labiata Autumn cattleya
Christmas cattleya
Queen cattleya

Cattleya mossiae Easter cattleya
Spring cattleya

Cattleya percivaliana
Christmas cattleya

Cattleya trianaei
Christmas orchid
Winter cattleya

Caularthron bicornutum
Virgin Mary orchid
Virgin orchid

Caularthron bilamellatum
Little virgin orchid

Cephalanthera damasonium
White helleborine

Cephalanthera rubra
Red helleborine

Chamorchis alpina
False musk orchid

Cleistes divaricata
Funnel-crest orchid
Lily-leaved pogonia
Rosebud orchid
Spreading pogonia

Coeloglossum viride Frog orchid

Coelogyne pandurata
Black orchid

Corallorhiza maculata
Large coralroot
Spotted coralroot

Corallorhiza multiflora
Large coralroot
Spotted coralroot

Corallorhiza mertensiana
Western coralroot

Corallorhiza odontorhiza
Autumn coralroot
Chicken toes
Crawley root
Dragon's claw
Late coralroot
Small coralroot

Corallorhiza trifida
Coralroot orchid

Coryanthes macrantha
Bucket orchid
Monkey orchid

Coryanthes speciosa Bat orchid
Bucket orchid

Cychnoches pentadactylon
Swan orchid

Habenaria bifolia

Cypripedium acaule
Moccasin flower
Moccasin orchid
Nerveroot
Pink lady's slipper
Two-leaved lady's slipper

Cypripedium calceolus
Lady's slipper orchid

Cypripedium pubescens
Yellow lady's slipper

Cyrtopodium punctatum
Bee-swarm orchid
Cigar orchid
Cow-horn orchid

Dactylorhiza fuchsii
Common spotted orchid

Dactylorhiza incarnata
Early marsh orchid
Meadow orchid

Dactylorhiza latifolia
Marsh orchid

Dactylorhiza maculata
Heath spotted orchid

Dactylorhiza majalis
Broad-leaved marsh orchid

Dactylorhiza praetermissa
Southern marsh orchid

Dactylorhiza purpurella
Northern marsh orchid

Dendrobium bigibbum
Cooktown orchid

Dendrobium chrysotoxum
Fried-egg orchid

Dendrobium crumenatum
Pigeon orchid

Dendrobium speciosum   Rock lily

Dendrochilum filiforme
Golden chain orchid

Dendrochilum glumaceum
Hay-scented orchid
Silver chain

Diacrium bicornutum
Virgin Mary orchid
Virgin orchid

Diacrium bilamellatum
Little virgin orchid

Epidendrum atropurpureum
Spice orchid

Epidendrum boothianum
Booth's epidendrum
Dollar orchid

Epidendrum cochleatum
Clam-shell orchid
Cockle-shell orchid

Epidendrum conopseum
Green-fly orchid

Epidendrum erythronioides
Booth's epidendrum
Dollar orchid

Epidendrum macrochilum
Spice orchid

Epidendrum × obrienianum
Baby orchid
Butterfly orchid
Scarlet orchid

Epidendrum phoeniceum
Chocolate orchid

Epidendrum prismatocarpum
Rainbow orchid

Epidendrum tampense
Butterfly orchid
Florida butterfly orchid

Epipactis atrorubans
Dark red helleborine

Epipactis dunensis
Dune helleborine

Epipactis gigantea   Chatterbox
Giant helleborine
Giant orchid
Stream orchid

Epipactis helleborine
Bastard helleborine
Broadleaved helleborine

Epipactis latifolia
Bastard helleborine
Broadleaved helleborine

Epipactis leptochila
Narrow-lipped orchid

Epipactis palustris
Marsh helleborine

Epipactis phyllanthes
Green-flowered helleborine

Epipactis purpurata
Violet helleborine

Epipogium aphyllum
Ghost orchid

Eulophia alta   Ground coco
Wild coco

Galeandra lacustris
Helmet orchid

Goodyera oblongifolia
Giant rattlesnake plantain
Menzies' rattlesnake plantain
Rattlesnake plantain

Goodyera pubescens
Downy rattlesnake orchid
Downy rattlesnake plantain
Scrofula weed

Goodyera repens
Creeping lady's tresses
Dwarf rattlesnake plantain
Lesser rattlesnake plantain
Northern rattlesnake plantain

Goodyera tesselata
Checkered rattlesnake plantain
Smooth rattlesnake plantain

Grammatophyllum sanderanum   Queen of orchids

Grammatophyllum speciosum
Queen of orchids

Gymnadenia conopsea
Fragrant orchid
Sweet-scented orchid

Habenaria bifolia
Lesser butterfly orchid

Habenaria blephariglottis

Habenaria blephariglottis
    Snowy orchid
    White fringed orchid
Habenaria ciliaris   Fringed orchis
    Orange fringe
    Orange plume
    Yellow fringed orchid
Habenaria clavellata   Frog spike
    Green rein orchid
    Green woodland orchid
    Little club-spur orchid
    Southern rein orchid
Habenaria cristata
    Crested fringed orchid
    Crested rein orchid
    Crested yellow orchid
    Golden fringed orchid
    Orange crest
Habenaria dilitata   Bog candle
    Bog orchid
    Leafy white orchid
    Scent bottle
    Tall white bog orchid
Habenaria gracilis
    Slender bog orchid
Habenaria hookeri
    Hooker's orchid
Habenaria hyperborea
    Leafy northern green orchid
    Northern green orchid
Habenaria lacera
    Green fringed orchid
    Ragged fringed orchid
    Ragged orchid
Habenaria nivea   Bog torch
    Frog spear
    Savannah orchid
    Snowy orchid
    Southern small white orchid
    White frog-arrow
    White rein orchid
Habenaria obusata   Blunt-
    leaf orchid
    Northern small bog orchid
    One-leaf rein orchid
    Single-leaf rein orchid
    Small bog orchid
Habenaria orbiculata   Heal-all
    Moon-set
    Round-leaved orchid
Habenaria peramoena
    Pride-of-the-peak
    Purple fret-lip
    Purple fringeless orchid
    Purple spire orchid
Habenaria psycodes
    Butterfly orchid
    Fairy fringe
    Lesser purple-fringed orchid
    Small purple-fringed orchid
    Soldier's plume
Habenaria saccata
    Slender bog orchid
Habenaria unalascensis
    Alaskan orchid
    Alaska piperia

Haemaria discolor
    Gold-lace orchid
Hammarbya paludosa
    Little bog orchid
Herminium monorchis
    Musk orchid
    Musk orchis
Himantoglossum hircinum
    Lizard orchid
Ipsea speciosa   Daffodil orchid
Isotria verticillata
    Green adderling
    Purple five-leaved orchid
    Whorled pogonia
Leucorchis albida
    Small white orchid
Limnorchis hyperborea
    Leafy northern green orchid
    Northern green orchid
Limodorum abortiva
    Violet bird's nest orchid
Liparis liliifolia   Large twayblade
    Mauve sleekwort
    Purple scutcheon
Liparis loeselii   Bog twayblade
    Fen orchid
    Loesel's twayblade
    Olive scutcheon
    Russet witch
    Yellow twayblade
Listeria convallarioides
    Broad-leaved twayblade
    Broad-lipped twayblade
Listeria cordata
    Heart-leaf twayblade
    Lesser twayblade
Listeria ovata   Common twayblade
Lycaste skinneri   Nun orchid
    White nun orchid
Lycaste virginalis   Nun orchid
    White nun orchid
Lysias orbiculata   Heal-all
    Moon-set
    Round-leaved orchid
Malaxis unifolia   Adder's tongue
    Green adder's mouth
    Green malaxis
    Tenderwort
    Wide adder's mouth
Miltonia candida   Pansy orchid
Miltonia flavescens   Pansy orchid
Miltonia spectabilis   Pansy orchid
Miltonia vexillaria   Pansy orchid
Neotinea maculata
    Dense-flowered orchid
Neottia nidus-avis
    Bird's nest orchid
Odontoglossum crispum
    Lace orchid
Odontoglossum grande
    Tiger orchid
Odontoglossum pulchellum
    Lily-of-the-valley orchid

Oncidium cheirophorum
Colombia buttercup

Oncidium flexuosum
Dancing-doll orchid
Dancing-lady orchid

Oncidium krameranum
Butterfly orchid

Oncidium papilio   Butterfly orchid

Ophrys apifera   Bee orchid

Ophrys fuciflora
Late spider orchid
Spider orchid

Ophrys holoserica
Late spider orchid

Ophrys insectifera   Fly orchid

Ophrys speculum   Mirror-of-venus
Mirror orchid

Ophrys sphegodes
Early spider orchid

Ophrys tenthredinifera
Sawfly orchid

Orchis coriophora   Bug orchid

Orchis latifolia   Marsh orchid

Orchis laxifolia   Jersey orchid

Orchis maderensis   Madeira orchid

Orchis mascula   Blue butcher
Dead man's fingers
Early purple orchid

Orchis militaris   Soldier orchid

Orchis morio   Gandergoose
Green-winged orchid
Salep orchid

Orchis purpurea   Lady orchid

Orchis rotundifolia   Small round-
leaved orchid
Spotted kirtle-pink orchid

Orchis simia   Monkey orchid

Orchis spectabilis
Kirtle-pink orchid
Purple-hooded orchid
Showy orchid
Woodland orchid

Orchis tridentata   Toothed orchid

Orchis ustulata   Burnt orchid
Burnt-tip orchid
Dwarf orchid

Paphiopedilum concolor
Cypripedium
Lady's slipper orchid
Slipper orchid

Paphiopedilum insigne
Cypripedium
Lady's slipper
Slipper orchid

Peristeria elata   Dove flower
Dove orchid
Holy Ghost flower

Phaius tankervilliae
Nun's hood orchid
Nun's orchid

Phalaenopsis amabilis
Moth orchid

Pholidota imbricata
Rattlesnake orchid

Phragmipedium caudatum
Lady's slipper orchid

Physosiphon tubatus   Bottle orchid

Platanthera bifolia
Lesser butterfly orchid

Platanthera chlorantha
Butterfly orchid
Greater butterfly orchid

Pleione maculata   Indian crocus

Pleurothallis macrophylla
Widow orchid

Pogonia divaricata
Funnel-crest orchid
Lily-leaved pogonia
Rosebud orchid
Spreading pogonia

Pogonia ophioglossoides
Adder's mouth orchid
Adder's tongue-leaved pogonia
Beardflower
Crested ettercap
Ettercap
Rose crest-lip
Rose pogonia
Snake's mouth orchid

Pogonia verticillata
Green adderling
Purple five-leaved orchid
Whorled pogonia

Polyradicion lindenii
Palm-polly
White butterfly orchid

Polyrrhiza lindenii   Palm-polly
White butterfly orchid

Rodriguezia secunda   Coral orchid

Spiranthes aestivalis
Summer lady's tresses

Spiranthes cernua
Common lady's tresses
Lady's tresses
Nodding lady's tresses
Screw-augur

Spiranthes gracilis
Green pearl-twist
Long tresses
Slender lady's tresses
Southern lady's tresses

Spiranthes grayi
Little lady's tresses
Little pearl-twist

Spiranthes praecox
Giant lady's tresses
Grass-leaved lady's tresses
Water tresses

Spiranthes romanzoffiana
Hooded lady's tresses
Irish lady's tresses
Romanzoff's lady's tresses

Spiranthes spiralis
Autumn lady's tresses

Tipularia discolor	Cranefly orchid
	Crippled cranefly
	Elfin-spur
	Mottled cranefly orchid
Tipularia unifolia	Cranefly orchid
	Crippled cranefly
	Elfin-spur
	Mottled cranefly orchid
Traunsteinera globosa	
	Round-headed orchid
Vanda coerulea	Blue orchid

Vanilla articulata	Link vine
	Worm vine
	Wormwood
Vanilla barbellata	Link vine
	Worm vine
	Wormwood
Vanilla grandiflora	
	Pompona vanilla
	West Indian vanilla
Vanilla planifolia	Vanilla
Vanilla pompona	Pompona vanilla
	West Indian vanilla

POPULAR GARDEN PLANTS

Annuals, biennials, and perennials that are not usually listed under specific sections elsewhere. Popular flowering plants grown in many gardens as bedding plants, container plants, or climbers are covered.

Marguerite –
Argyranthemum frutescens

BOTANICAL NAMES

Abronia latifolia

Abronia latifolia	Sand verbena
Abronia umbellata	
	Pink sand verbena
Acaena anserinifolia	
	Bidgee-widgee
Acaena inermis	
	Blue mountains bidi-bidi
Acaena microphylla	
	Blue mountains bidi-bidi
	New Zealand burr
	Scarlet bidi-bidi
Achillea ageratum	Sweet nancy
Achillea eupatorium	
	Fernleaf yarrow
Achillea filipendulina	
	Fernleaf yarrow
Achillea millefolium	
	Common yarrow
	Milfoil
	Nosebleed
	Thousand weed
	Yarrow
Achillea ptarmica	Goosewort
	Sneezeweed
	Sneezewort
Achillea tomentosa	Alpine yarrow
Achlys triphylla	Vanilla leaf
Aciphylla aurea	Golden spaniard
Aciphylla colensoi	Spaniard
	Wild spaniard
Aciphylla scott-thomsonii	
	Giant spaniard
Aconitum anthora	
	Yellow monkshood
Aconitum lycoctonum	Wolfsbane
Aconitum lycoctonum lycotonum	Northern wolfsbane
Aconitum lycoctonum vulgaria	Wolfsbane
Aconitum lycoctonum vulparia	Foxbane
Aconitum napellus	
	Common monkshood
	Friar's cap
	Monkshood
Aconitum napellus lycoctonum	
	Yellow aconite
Aconitum orientale	
	Russian aconite
Aconitum vulparia	Wolfsbane
Actaea alba	White baneberry
	White cohosh
Actaea erythocarpa	Red baneberry
Actaea pachypoda	
	White baneberry
Actaea rubra	Red baneberry
Actaea spicata	Black baneberry
Actaea spicata alba	
	White baneberry
Actaea spicata rubra	
	Red baneberry

Actinea grandiflora	
	Pigmy sunflower
Actinotus helianthi	Flannel flower
Adenophora lilifolia	
	Common ladybell
	Grand bellflower
	Ladybell
Adonis aestivalis	Summer adonis
	Summer pheasant's eye
Adonis annua	Pheasant's eye
Adonis vernalis	Spring adonis
	Yellow pheasant's eye
Adoxa moschatellina	
	Five-faced bishop
	Moschatel
	Town hall clock
Aethusa cynapium	Dog poison
	Fool's parsley
Agathaea coelestis	Blue daisy
	Blue marguerite
Ageratum houstonianum	
	Floss flower
Ageratum mexicanum	
	Floss flower
Agrimonia eupatoria	Agrimony
	Church steeples
	Common agrimony
	Sticklewort
Agrostemma coronaria	
	Mullein pink
	Rose campion
Agrostemma flos-jovis	
	Flower of Jove
Agrostemma githago	
	Corn campion
	Corn cockle
	Corn pink
Ajuga chamaepitys	Ground pine
	Yellow bugle
Ajuga genevensis	Blue bugle
Ajuga pyramidalis	Pyramidal bugle
Ajuga reptans	Bugle
	Carpenter's herb
	Common bugle
Alcea chinensis	Garden hollyhock
	Hollyhock
Alcea ficifolia	Antwerp hollyhock
	Figleaf hollyhock
Alcea rosea	Garden hollyhock
	Hollyhock
Alchemilla alpina	
	Alpine lady's mantle
Alchemilla mollis	
	Common lady's mantle
	Lady's mantle
Alchemilla vulgaris	Bear's foot
	Common lady's mantle
	Lady's mantle
	Lion's foot
Aletris farinosa	Ague root
	Blazing star
	Colic root
	Starwort

POPULAR GARDEN PLANTS

Arnebia echioides

Alliaria petiolata
Jack-by-the-hedge
Alonsoa warscewiczii Mask flower
Aloysia triphylla Lemon verbena
Althaea chinensis
Garden hollyhock
Hollyhock
Althaea ficifolia
Antwerp hollyhock
Figleaf hollyhock
Althaea rosea Garden hollyhock
Hollyhock
Alyssum argenteum Yellow tuft
Alyssum maritimum
Sweet alyssum
Alyssum murale Yellow tuft
Alyssum saxatile
Common yellow alyssum
Gold dust
Alyssum spinosum Spiny alyssum
Amaracus dictamnus
Cretan dittany
Amaranthus albus White amaranth
Amaranthus caudatus
Love-lies-bleeding
Tassel flower
Amaranthus graecizans
Tumbleweed
Amaranthus hybridus
Green amaranthus
Amaranthus hypochondriacus
Prince's feather
Amaranthus retroflexus
Amaranth
Common amaranth
Amaranthus tricolor Joseph's coat
Ammi majus Bishop's flower
False bishop's weed
Ammobium alatum Sand flower
Winged everlasting
Amsonia roseus
Madagascar periwinkle
Rose periwinkle
Anacyclus depressus
Mount Atlas daisy
Anacyclus pyrethrum Pellitory
Pellitory of Spain
Spanish pellitory
Anagallis arvensis
Poor man's weather glass
Scarlet pimpernel
Shepherd's barometer
Anagallis foemina Blue pimpernel
Anagallis linifolia Blue pimpernel
Anagallis minima Chaff weed
Anagallis monelli linifolia
Blue pimpernel
Anagallis tenella Bog pimpernel
Anchusa arvensis Bugloss
Anchusa azurea Italian bugloss
Large blue alkanet
Anchusa caespitosa Tufted alkanet

Anchusa capensis Annual anchusa
Cape forget-me-not
Summer forget-me-not
Anchusa italica Italian bugloss
Anchusa officinalis Alkanet
Androsace carnea
Pink rock jasmine
Androsace chamaejasme
Bastard jasmine
Androsace lactea
Milkwhite rock jasmine
Milky rock jasmine
Anemone vernalis Spring anemone
Anemonopsis californica
Apache beads
Yerba mansa
Anemonopsis macrophylla
False anemone
Anthemis arabicus
Palm Springs daisy
Anthemis nobilis
Common chamomile
Garden chamomile
Green chamomile
Roman chamomile
Russian chamomile
Anthemis sancti-johannis
Saint John's chamomile
Anthemis tinctoria
Golden marguerite
Ox-eye chamomile
Antirrhinum majus Snapdragon
Weasel's snout
Aquilegia canadensis
American wild columbine
Aquilegia vulgaris
European wild columbine
Granny's bonnet
True columbine
Arctotis breviscapa African daisy
Arctotis grandis African daisy
Argemone grandiflora
Prickly poppy
Argemone mexicana Devil's fig
Mexican poppy
Argemone platyceras
Crested poppy
Argyranthemum frutescens
Marguerite
Paris daisy
Aristolochia durior
Dutchman's pipe
Aristolochia elegans Calico plant
Aristolochia macrophylla
Dutchman's pipe
Aristolochia sipho
Dutchman's pipe
Armeria maritima Common thrift
Sea pink
Armeria plantaginea Border thrift
Armeria pseudarmeria
Border thrift
Arnebia echioides Prophet flower

Artemisia abrotanum

Artemisia abrotanum	Lad's love
	Old man
	Southernwood
Artemisia absinthium	Absinthe
	Wormwood
Artemisia gnaphalodes	Cudweed
	Western mugwort
	White sage
Artemisia lactiflora	
	White mugwort
Artemisia ludoviciana	Cudweed
	Western mugwort
	White sage
Artemisia purshiana	Cudweed
	Western mugwort
	White mugwort
	White sage
Artemisia stellerana	
	Beach wormwood
	Dusty miller
	Old woman
Artemisia tridentata	Sage brush
Aruncus dioicus	Goat's beard
Aruncus sylvester	Goat's beard
Aruncus vulgaris	Goat's beard
Aster amellus	Italian aster
Aster ericoides	Heath aster
Aster linosyris	Goldilocks
Aster novae-angliae	
	Michaelmas daisy
	New England aster
Aster novi-belgii	New York aster
	True michaelmas daisy
Aster tenacetifolius	Tahoka daisy
Atriplex hortensis rubra	
	Red mountain spinach
	Red orach
Atriplex lociniata	Frosted orach
Atriplex patula	Common orach
Aubretia deltoides	
	Common aubretia
Aurinia saxatilis	
	Common yellow alyssum
	Gold dust
Baptisia tinctoria	Horsefly
	Wild indigo
Bartonia aurea	Blazing star
Begonia semperflorens	
	Bedding begonia
	Fibrous-rooted begonia
Bellis perennis	Common daisy
	English daisy
	Meadow daisy
Betonica grandiflora	Betony
	Woundwort
Betonica macrantha	Betony
	Woundwort
Betonica officinalis	Bishop's wort
	Wood betony
Bilderdykia aubertii	
	China fleece flower
	Silver lace vine

Bilderdykia baldschuanicum	
	Bokhara fleece flower
	Russian vine
Bocconia cordata	Plume poppy
Bocconia microcarpa	
	Lesser plume poppy
Brachycome iberidifolia	
	Swan river daisy
Brassica oleracea acephala	
	Ornamental cabbage
Brunnera macrophylla	
	Siberian bugloss
Buphthalum salicifolium	
	Willow-leaf ox-eye
	Yellow ox-eye
Bupleurum fruticosum	Bupleurum
Calamintha grandiflora	Calamint
Calamintha nepeta nepeta	
	Calamint
Calandrinia menziesii	Red maids
Calandrinia umbellata	
	Rock purslane
Calendula officinalis	Golds
	Pot marigold
	Scotch marigold
Calendula officinalis prolifera	
	Hen and chickens marigold
Callistephus chinensis	
	Annual aster
	China aster
Calluna vulgaris	Heather
	Ling
Caltha palustris	Kingcup
	Marsh marigold
	Water cowslip
Caltha polypetala	Giant kingcup
Campanula alliariifolia	
	Spurred bellflower
Campanula allionii	
	Alpine campanula
Campanula alpestris	
	Alpine campanula
Campanula barbata	
	Bearded bellflower
Campanula carpatica	
	Carpathian bellflower
	Carpathian harebell
	Tussock bellflower
Campanula cochleariifolia	
	Fairy's thimbles
Campanula elatines garganica	
	Adriatic bellflower
Campanula garganica	
	Adriatic bellflower
Campanula glomerata	
	Clustered bellflower
Campanula grandiflora	
	Canterbury bell
Campanula grandis	
	Peach-leaved bellflower
	Willow bellflower

POPULAR GARDEN PLANTS

Chrysanthemum carinatum

Campanula isophylla
Italian bellflower
Star of Bethlehem
Campanula lactiflora
Milky bellflower
Campanula latifolia
Giant bellflower
Campanula latiloba
Peach-leaved bellflower
Willow bellflower
Campanula medium
Canterbury bell
Campanula medium calycanthema
Cup-and-saucer Canterbury bell
Campanula patula
Spreading bellflower
Campanula persicifolia
Peach-leaved bellflower
Willow bellflower
Campanula portenschlagiana
Wall harebell
Campanula poscharskyana
Serbian bellflower
Campanula pusilla
Fairy's thimbles
Campanula pyramidalis
Chimney bellflower
Steeple bellflower
Campanula rapunculus   Rampion
Rampion bellflower
Campanula rotundifolia   Bluebell
English harebell
Harebell
Harebell bellflower
Scottish bluebell
Campanula thyrsoides
Yellow bellflower
Campanula trachelium
Bats-in-the-belfry
Coventry bells
Nettle-leaved bellflower
Campanula urticifolia
Bats-in-the-belfry
Coventry bells
Nettle-leaved bellflower
Campsis chinensis
Chinese trumpet creeper
Campsis grandiflora
Chinese trumpet creeper
Campsis radicans
American trumpet creeper
Trumpet vine
Capsicum annuum   Red pepper
Catananche coerulea
Blue cupidone
Blue succory
Cupid's dart
Catharanthus roseus
Madagascar periwinkle
Rose periwinkle
Celosia argentea cristata
Cockscomb

Celosia cristata childsii
Cockscomb
Celosia cristata plumosa
Prince of Wales' feathers
Celosia plumosa   Plume flower
Celsia arcturus   Cretan bear's tail
Cretan mullein
Cenia barbata   Pincushion plant
Centaurea americana
Basket flower
Centaurea calcitrapa
Red star thistle
Star thistle
Centaurea candidissima
Dusty miller
Centaurea cineraria   Dusty miller
Centaurea cyanus
Blue cornflower
Bluebottle
Cornflower
Centaurea dealbata
Perennial cornflower
Centaurea gymnocarpa
Dusty miller
Centaurea imperialis   Sweet sultan
Centaurea macrocephala
Globe centaurea
Great golden knapweed
Centaurea montana
Mountain bluet
Mountain knapweed
Perennial cornflower
Centaurea moschata   Sweet sultan
Centaurea nigra   Black knapweed
Hardheads
Knapweed
Lesser knapweed
Centaurea phrygia   Wig knapweed
Centaurea ragusina   Dusty miller
Centaurea rhapontium
Giant knapweed
Centaurea scabiosa
Great knapweed
Centaurea solstitalis
Saint Barnaby's thistle
Yellow star thistle
Centranthus ruber   Bouncing bess
Drunken sailor
Jupiter's beard
Pretty betsy
Red valerian
Cephalaria gigantea
Giant scabious
Cephalaria tatarica   Giant scabious
Cheiranthus × allionii
Siberian wallflower
Cheiranthus cheiri
Common wallflower
English wallflower
Cheiranthus maritimus
Virginian stock
Chrysanthemum carinatum
Painted daisy

Chrysanthemum coccineum
Painted daisy
Pyrethrum

Chrysanthemum coronarium　Crown daisy

Chrysanthemum leucanthemum　Moon daisy
Ox-eye daisy

Chrysanthemum maximum
Shasta daisy

Chrysanthemum parthenium
Feverfew

Chrysanthemum rubellum
Korean chrysanthemum

Chrysanthemum segetum
Corn marigold

Chrysanthemum serotinum
Giant daisy
Hungarian daisy

Chrysanthemum × superbum
Shasta daisy

Chrysanthemum uliginosum
Giant daisy
Hungarian daisy

Cicendia filiformis　Yellow centaury

Cimicifuga americanum
American bugbane

Cimicifuga racemosa
Black snakeroot

Cissus antarctica　Kangaroo vine

Clarkia amoena
Farewell-to-spring
Satin flower

Clarkia concinna　Red ribbons

Clarkia elegans　Flore pleno

Clarkia unguiculata　Clarkia
Mountain garland

Cleome spinosa　Spider flower

Cleretum bellidiforme
Livingstone daisy

Clianthus dampieri　Glory pea

Clianthus formosus　Glory pea

Clianthus puniceus　Lobster claw
Parrot's bill

Clianthus speciosus　Glory pea
Sturt's desert pea

Cnicus benedictus　Blessed thistle
Holy thistle
Saint Benedict's thistle

Cobaea scandens　Cathedral bells
Cup-and-saucer vine
Mexican ivy
Monastery bells
Steeple bells

Collinsia bicolor　Chinese houses
Innocence

Collinsia grandiflora
Blue-eyed mary
Blue lips

Collinsia heterophylla
Chinese houses

Consolida ambigua　Larkspur
Rocket larkspur

Consolida regalis
Branched larkspur
Forking larkspur

Convolvulus cneorum
Bush morning glory

Convolvulus minor
Dwarf morning glory

Convulvulus tricolor
Dwarf morning glory

Coreopsis grandiflora　Tickseed

Cortaderia argentea　Pampas grass

Cortaderia selloana　Pampas grass

Cosmos atrosanguineus
Black cosmos
Chocolate cosmos

Cosmos bipinnatus　Mexican aster

Cotula barbata　Pincushion plant

Cotula cenia　Pincushion plant

Cotula coronopifolia
Brass buttons

Crepis biennis
Greater hawk's beard
Rough hawk's beard

Crepis capillaris
Smooth hawk's beard

Crepis foetida
Stinking hawk's beard

Crepis incana　Pink dandelion

Crepis mollis
Northern hawk's beard

Crepis nicaeensis
French hawk's beard

Crepis paludosa
Marsh hawk's beard

Crepis pygmaea
Pigmy hawk's beard

Crepis rubra　Hawk's beard

Crepis vesicaria
Beaked hawk's beard

Cryophytum crystallinum
Ice plant
Sea fig

Cuphea ignea　Cigar flower
Firecracker plant

Cyananthus lobatus
Trailing bellflower

Cynoglossum amabile
Chinese forget-me-not
Hound's tongue

Dahlia juarezii　Cactus dahlia

Dahlia merckii　Bedding dahlia

Daubentonia tripetii
Scarlet wisteria

Delphinium ajacis　Rocket larkspur

Delphinium cardinale
Scarlet larkspur

Delphinium consolida　Larkspur

Delphinium nudicaule
Christmas horns

Delphinium staphisagria
Stavesacre

Echinops ritro

Desmodium gyrans
    Telegraph plant
Dianthus × allwoodii Garden pinks
Dianthus alpinus   Alpine pink
Dianthus arenarius   Sand pink
Dianthus armeria   Deptford pink
Dianthus × arvernensis
    Auvergne pink
Dianthus barbatus   Sweet william
Dianthus caesius   Cheddar pink
Dianthus caryophyllus
    Border carnation
    Carnation
    Clove pink
    Cottage pink
    Gilliflower
    Picotee
    Wild carnation
Dianthus chinensis   Annual pink
    Chinese pink
    Indian pink
    Rainbow pink
Dianthus deltoides   Maiden pink
Dianthus glacialis   Glacier pink
Dianthus gratianopolitanus
    Cheddar pink
Dianthus × heddewigii
    Japanese pink
Dianthus inodorus   Wood pink
Dianthus × latifolius   Button pink
Dianthus neglectus   Glacier pink
Dianthus pavonius   Glacier pink
Dianthus plumarius   Border pink
    Common pink
    Cottage pink
    Grass pink
    Wild pink
Dianthus sinensis   Chinese pink
Dianthus superbus   Fringed pink
    Large pink
    Lilac pink
Dianthus sylvestris   Wood pink
Diascia barberae   Twinspur
Dicentra canadensis   Squirrel corn
    Staggerweed
    Turkey corn
    Turkey pea
Dicentra chrysantha
    Golden eardrops
Dicentra eximia
    Fringed bleeding heart
Dicentra formosa
    Western bleeding heart
Dicentra spectabilis
    Bleeding heart
    Chinaman's breeches
    Common bleeding heart
    Dutchman's breeches
    Lady's locket
    Lyre flower
Dictamnus albus   Burning bush
    Dittany
    Gas plant

Dictamnus fraxinella
    Burning bush
    Dittany
    Gas plant
Didiscus caerulea   Blue lace flower
Digitalis ferruginea   Rusty foxglove
Digitalis grandiflora
    Large yellow foxglove
Digitalis lanata   Woolly foxglove
Digitalis lutea
    Small yellow foxglove
Digitalis purpurea
    Common foxglove
    Dead men's bells
    Fairy thimbles
    Foxglove
    Lady's gloves
    Witch's gloves
Dimorphotheca annua
    Annual cape marigold
    Cape marigold
Dimorphotheca aurantiaca
    Star of the veldt
Dimorphotheca barberae
    Dwarf cape marigold
Dimorphotheca osteospermum   African daisy
Dimorphotheca pluvialis
    Namaqualand daisy
    Rain daisy
Dimorphotheca sinuata
    Namaqualand daisy
    Star of the veldt
Diplacus glutinosus
    Bush monkey flower
Diplarrhena moraea   Butterfly flag
Diplotaxis erucoides   White rocket
Diplotaxis muralis
    Annual wall rocket
Diplotaxis tenuifolia
    Perennial wall rocket
    Wall mustard
    Wall rocket
Dodecatheon alpinum
    Shooting star
Dodecatheon jeffreyi
    Sierra shooting star
Dodecatheon meadia
    Common shooting star
    Shooting star
Doronicum caucasicum
    Leopard's bane
Doronicum pardalianches
    Great leopard's bane
Dorotheanthus bellidiflorus
    Livingstone daisy
Dregea sinensis
    Chinese wax flower
Echinacea angustiflora
    Kansas niggerhead
Echinacea purpurea   Black samson
    Purple coneflower
Echinops ritro   Globe thistle

Echites andrewsii

Echites andrewsii	Savannah flower
Echium lycopsis	Viper's bugloss
Echium plantagineum	
	Purple bugloss
	Viper's bugloss
Echium vulgare	Blueweed
	Viper's bugloss
Emmenanthe penduliflora	
	Californian golden bells
	Californian whispering bells
Eomecon chionanthe	Snow poppy
Epilobium alsinifolium	
	Chickweed willowherb
Epilobium angustifolium	
	Fireweed
	Rosebay willowherb
Epilobium brunnescens	
	New Zealand willowherb
Epilobium ciliatum	
	American willowherb
Epilobium hirsutum	
	Codlins and cream
	Great willowherb
Epilobium lanceolatum	
	Spear-leaved willowherb
Epilobium montanum	
	Broad-leaved willowherb
Epilobium obcordatum	
	Rock fringe willowherb
Epilobium palustra	
	March willowherb
Epilobium parviflorum	
	Hairy willowherb
	Hoary willowherb
Epilobium roseum	
	Pale willowherb
	Pink willowherb
Epilobium tetragonum	
	Square-stalked willowherb
Episcia cupreata	Flame violet
Episcia dianthiflora	Lace flower
Erechtites hieracifolia	Fireweed
	Pilewort
Erica vulgaris	Heather
	Ling
Erigeron acre	Blue fleabane
Erigeron annuus	Sweet scabious
Erigeron aurantiacus	
	Double orange daisy
	Orange daisy
Erigeron borealis	Alpine fleabane
Erigeron karkinskianus	
	Australian fleabane
	Mexican fleabane
	Wall daisy
Erinus alpinus	Fairy foxglove
	Summer starwort
Eritrichium nanum	
	Herald of heaven
	King of the alps
Eryngium maritimum	Sea holly

Erysimum alpinum	
	Alpine wallflower
Erysimum asperum	
	Siberian wallflower
Erysimum cheiranthoides	
	Treacle mustard
Erysimum perofskianum	
	Siberian wallflower
Eschscholzia california	
	Californian poppy
Eucharidium concinna	
	Red ribbons
Eupatorium ageratoides	
	White sanicle
	White snakeroot
Eupatorium cannabinum	
	Dutch agrimony
	Hemp agrimony
	Holy rope
Eupatorium coelestinum	
	Blue boneset
	Hardy ageratum
	Mistflower
Eupatorium maculatum	
	Joe-pye weed
Eupatorium perfoliatum	
	Thoroughwort
Eupatorium purpureum	
	Gravel root
	Gravel weed
	Joe-pye weed
	Purple boneset
	Queen of the meadow
Eupatorium rugosum	Hardy age
	Mist flower
	White sanicle
	White snakeroot
Eupatorium teucrifolium	
	Wild horehound
	Wild horsehound
Euphorbia angydaloides	
	Wood spurge
Euphorbia arctica	Great eyebright
Euphorbia caput-medusae	
	Medusa's head
Euphorbia corollata	
	Flowering spurge
	White purslane
Euphorbia cyparissias	
	Cypress spurge
Euphorbia dulcis	Sweet spurge
Euphorbia epithymoides	
	Cushion spurge
Euphorbia esula	Leafy spurge
Euphorbia exigua	Dwarf spurge
Euphorbia fulgens	Scarlet plume
Euphorbia helioscopia	Sun spurge
Euphorbia heterophylla	
	Annual poinsettia
	Fire on the mountain
	Mexican fire plant
	Painted spurge

POPULAR GARDEN PLANTS

Geranium phaeum

Euphorbia hirta   Asthma weed
Pill-bearing spurge
Euphorbia hyberna   Irish spurge
Euphorbia lathyris   Caper spurge
Mole plant
Euphorbia maculata   Milk purslane
Euphorbia marginata
Mountain snow
Snow on the mountain
Euphorbia myrsinites   Blue spurge
Euphorbia palustris   Bog spurge
Fen spurge
Euphorbia paralias   Sea spurge
Euphorbia peplis   Petty spurge
Purple spurge
Euphorbia peplus   Petty spurge
Purple spurge
Euphorbia pilulifera   Cat's hair
Euphorbia platyphyllos
Broad-leaved spurge
Euphorbia polychroma
Cushion spurge
Euphorbia pulcherrima
Christmas star
Fire plant
Lobster plant
Poinsettia
Euphorbia robbiae   Robb's bonnet
Euphorbia stricta   Upright spurge
Euphorbia villosa   Hairy spurge
Eutoca viscida   Sticky phacelia
Exacum affine   Arabian violet
German violet
Persian violet
Felicia amelloides   Blue daisy
Blue marguerite
Felicia bergerana   Kingfisher daisy
Festuca glauca   Blue fescue
Festuca ovina   Sheep's fescue
Festuca ovina glauca   Blue fescue
Filipendula hexapetala   Dropwort
Filipendula rubra
Queen of the prairie
Filipendula ulmaria
Common meadowsweet
Meadowsweet
Queen of the meadow
Filipendula vulgaris   Dropwort
Francoa ramosa   Maiden's wreath
Francoa sonchifolia   Bridal wreath
Fumaria capreolata
Ramping fumitory
White fumitory
Fumaria indica   American fumitory
Fumaria muralis
Common ramping fumitory
Wall fumitory
Fumaria officinalis
Common fumitory
Earth smoke
Fumitory

Fumaria vesicaria
Bladder fumitory
Gaillardia aristata   Blanket flower
Gaillardia pulchella
Annual gaillardia
Blanket flower
Galega officinalis   French lilac
Goat's rue
Galeobdolon luteum
Golden dead nettle
Yellow archangel
Gazania × hybrids
Treasure flowers
Gazania leucolaena
Trailing gazania
Gazania rigens leucolaena
Trailing gazania
Gazania uniflora   Trailing gazania
Gentiana acaulis   Stemless gentian
Trumpet gentian
Gentiana asclepiadea
Willow gentian
Gentiana brachyphylla
Short-leaved gentian
Gentiana cruciata   Cross gentian
Gentiana kochiana
Trumpet gentian
Gentiana lutea   Yellow gentian
Gentiana pneumonanthe
Calathian violet
Marsh gentian
Gentiana punctata   Spotted gentian
Gentiana scabrae   Japanese gentian
Gentiana septemfida
Crested gentian
Gentiana utriculosa
Bladder gentian
Gentiana verna   Spring gentian
Vernal gentian
Gentiana verna angulosa
Spring gentian
Geranium columbinum
Dove's foot cranesbill
Geranium dissectum
Cut-leaved cranesbill
Geranium endressii
French cranesbill
Geranium ibericum
Iberian cranesbill
Geranium lucidum
Shining cranesbill
Geranium macrorrhizum
Balkan cranesbill
Rock cranesbill
Geranium maculatum
American cranesbill
Wild cranesbill
Wild geranium
Geranium molle   Soft cranesbill
Geranium phaeum
Dusky cranesbill
Mourning widow

Geranium pratense	Meadow cranesbill
	Meadow geranium
Geranium purpurea	Lesser herb robert
Geranium pyrenaicum	Hedgerow cranesbill
	Mountain cranesbill
Geranium robertianum	Herb robert
	Stinking bob
Geranium sanguineum	Blood-red geranium
	Bloody cranesbill
Geranium sylvaticum	Crow flower
	Wood cranesbill
Gerbera jamesonii	Barberton daisy
	Transvaal daisy
Geum chiloense	Chilean avens
Geum coccineum	Chilean avens
Geum montanum	Alpine avens
Geum quellyon	Chilean avens
Geum reptans	Creeping avens
Geum rivale	Indian chocolate
	Nodding avens
	Purple avens
	Water avens
Geum urbanum	Avens
	Cloveroot
	Herb bennet
	Indian chocolate
	Water flower
	Wood avens
Gilia californica	Prickly phlox
Gilia capitata	Blue thimble flower
	Queen Anne's thimbles
Gilia coronopifolia	Skyrocket
	Standing cypress
Gilia hybrida	Stardust
Gilia lutea	Stardust
Gilia rubra	Skyrocket
	Standing cypress
Gilia tricolor	Bird's eyes
Glaucium corniculatum	Red horned poppy
	Sea poppy
Glaucium flavum	Horned poppy
	Yellow horned poppy
Glaucium grandiflorum	Red horned poppy
	Sea poppy
Glaucium luteum	Yellow horned poppy
Godetia amoena	Farewell to spring
Godetia grandiflora	Godetia
	Satin flower
Gomphrena globosa	Globe amaranth
Gypsophila elegans	Baby's breath

Gypsophila muralis	Annual gypsophila
Gypsophila paniculata	Baby's breath
	Chalk plant
Gypsophila repens	Alpine gypsophila
Hebe hulkeana	New Zealand lilac
Hedyotis caerulea	Bluets
	Innocence
Helenium autumnale	Helenium
	Sneezeweed
Helianthus annuus	Annual sunflower
	Common sunflower
	Giant marigold
	Marigold of Peru
	Peruvian marigold
	Sunflower
Helichrysum angustifolium	Curry plant
	White-leaved everlasting
Helichrysum bellidiodes	Everlasting daisy
Helichrysum bracteatum	Strawflower
Helichrysum ledifolium	Kerosene bush
Helichrysum petiolatum	Liquorice plant
Helichrysum seotinum	Curry plant
Helichrysum stoechas	Goldilocks
Helichrysum thyrsoideum	Snow in summer
Heliophila longifolia	Cape stock
Heliopsis helianthoides scabra	Heliopsis
Heliopsis scabra	Heliopsis
Heliotropium arborescens	Cherry pie
Heliotropium corymbosum	Cherry pie
Heliotropium hybridum	Cherry pie
Heliotropium peruvianum	Cherry pie
Helipterum manglesii	Sunray
	Swan river everlasting
Helleborus argutifolius	Corsican hellebore
Helleborus corsicus	Corsican hellebore
Helleborus foetidus	Setterwort
	Stinking hellebore
Helleborus lividus	Corsican hellebore
Helleborus niger	Black hellebore
	Christmas rose
Helleborus orientalis	Lenten rose
Helleborus viridus	Green hellebore

Ipomoea quamoclit

Hesperis matronalis   Damask violet
Dame's rocket
Dame's violet
Rocket
Sweet rocket

Heuchera hispida   Satin leaf

Heuchera sanguinea   Coral bells
Coral flower

Hieracium aurantiacum
Devil's paintbrush
Grim collier
Orange hawkweed

Hieracium brunneocroceum
Orange hawkweed

Hieracium lanatum
Woolly hawkweed

Hieracium maculatum
Spotted hawkweed

Hieracium umbellatum
Leafy hawkweed

Hieracium villosum
Shaggy hawkweed

Hieracium vulgatum
Common hawkweed

Homogyne alpina   Alpine coltsfoot

Horminum pyranaicum
Dragon mouth

Hypericum hirsutum
Hairy Saint John's wort

Hypericum humifusum
Creeping Saint John's wort

Hypericum lanuginosum
Downy Saint John's wort

Hypericum linarifolium
Flax-leaved Saint John's wort

Hypericum perforatum
Perforate Saint John's wort

Hypericum tetrapterum
Square-stemmed Saint John's
wort

Hyssopus aristatus   Hyssop

Iberis amara   Candytuft
Rocket candytuft
Wild candytuft

Iberis coronaria   Rocket candytuft

Iberis umbellata   Annual candytuft
Candytuft
Common candytuft
Globe candytuft

Iliamna rivularis
Mountain hollyhock

Impatiens aurea   Balsam weed
Jewel weed

Impatiens balsamina   Balsam
Rose balsam
Touch-me-not

Impatiens biflora   Jewel weed
Spotted touch-me-not

Impatiens capensis   Jewel weed
Orange balsam
Spotted touch-me-not

Impatiens glandulifera
Himalayan balsam
Himalayan touch-me-not
Indian balsam
Jumping jack
Policeman's helmet

Impatiens noli-tangere
Touch-me-not
Wild balsam

Impatiens parviflora   Small balsam

Impatiens roylei
Himalayan touch-me-not

Impatiens sultanii   Busy lizzie
Patience
Patient lucy

Impatiens wallerana   Busy lizzie
Patience
Patient lucy

Incarvillea delavayi
Chinese trumpet flower

Incarvillea grandiflora
Chinese trumpet flower

Inula conyza
Ploughman's spikenard

Inula crithmoides   Golden samphire

Inula ensifolia
Narrow-leaved inula

Inula helenium   Elecampane
Scabwort
Wild sunflower

Inula magnifica   Giant inula

Inula royleana
Himalayan elecampane

Ionopsidium acaule   Carpet plant
Diamond flower
Violet cress

Ipomoea acuminata
Blue dawn flower
Morning glory
Perennial morning glory

Ipomoea alba   Moonflower
Moonvine

Ipomoea bona-nox   Moonflower
Moonvine

Ipomoea cardinalis
Cardinal climber

Ipomoea coccinea
Red morning glory
Star ipomoea

Ipomoea lobata
Crimson star glory

Ipomoea × multifida
Cardinal climber

Ipomoea nil
Japanese morning glory

Ipomoea noctiflora   Moonflower
Moonvine
Queen of the night
Moonvine

Ipomoea purpurea
Common morning glory
Morning glory

Ipomoea quamoclit   Cypress vine

Ipomoea roxburghii

Ipomoea roxburghii
  Moonflower
Jasminum mesnyi
  Japanese jasmine
  Primrose jasmine
Jasminum nudiflorum
  Winter jasmine
Jasminum officinale
  Common white jasmine
  Poet's jessamine
  Summer jasmine
  White jasmine
Jasminum parkeri   Dwarf jasmine
Jasminum polyanthum
  Chinese jasmine
Jasminum primulinum
  Japanese jasmine
  Primrose jasmine
Jovibarba soboliferum
  Hen-and-chickens houseleek
Kalistroemia grandiflora
  Arizona poppy
Kentranthus ruber   Red valerian
Kirengeshoma palmata   Waxbells
Knautia arvensis   Field scabious
Kochia scoparia trichophylla
  Belvedere
  Broom cypress
  Burning bush
  Fire bush
  Mock cypress
  Summer cypress
Kochia trichophylla   Burning bush
Lamiastrum galeobdolon
  Golden deadnettle
  Yellow archangel
Lamium album   Archangel
  Bee nettle
  Blind nettle
  Weasel's snout
  White deadnettle
Lamium amplexicaule
  Henbit
  Henbit deadnettle
Lamium galeobdolon
  Golden deadnettle
  Weasel's snout
  Yellow archangel
Lamium maculatum   Dead nettle
  Spotted deadnettle
Lamium orvala   Giant deadnettle
Lamium purpureum
  Purple archangel
  Purple deadnettle
  Red deadnettle
Lathyrus aphaca   Yellow vetchling
Lathyrus hirsutus   Hairy vetchling
Lathyrus japonicus   Sea pea
Lathyrus latifolius   Everlasting pea
  Perennial pea
  Perennial sweet pea
Lathyrus littoralis   Beach pea

Lathyrus maritimus
  Beach pea
  Sea pea
Lathyrus montanus   Bitter vetch
Lathyrus nervosus
  Lord Anson's pea
Lathyrus nissolia   Grass vetchling
Lathyrus odoratus   Sweet pea
Lathyrus palustris   Marsh pea
Lathyrus rotundifolius
  Persian everlasting pea
Lathyrus sativus   Chickling pea
  Grass pea
Lathyrus splendens
  Californian pea
  Pride of California
Lathyrus sylvestris   Wild pea
Lathyrus tingitanus   Tangier pea
  Tangier scarlet pea
Lathyrus tuberosus   Tuberous pea
Lathyrus vernuus   Spring vetch
Lavatera trimestris   Annual mallow
  Rose mallow
Layia platyglossa   Tidy tips
Layia elegans   Tidy tips
Legousia speculum-veneris
  Venus's looking glass
Leontopodium alpinum
  Common edelweiss
  Edelweiss
  Lion's foot
Leptosiphon hybridus   Stardust
Leucanthemella serotina
  Hungarian daisy
  Moon daisy
Leucanthemopsis alpina
  Alpine moon daisy
Leucanthemum vulgare   Dog daisy
  Dun daisy
  Field daisy
  Horse daisy
  Marguerite
  Moon daisy
  Ox-eye daisy
  White weed
Leucanthemum × superbum
  Shasta daisy
Lewisia rediviva   Bitter root
Liatris callilepis   Kansas gayfeather
Liatris odoratissima   Deer's tongue
  Vanilla leaf
  Wild vanilla
Liatris pycnostachya
  Cat-tail gayfeather
  Kansas gayfeather
  Prairie blazing star
Liatris scariosa   Tall gayfeather
Liatris spicata   Blazing star
  Button snakeroot
  Gayfeather
  Spike gayfeather
Liatris squarrosa
  Rattlesnake master

Lupinus pubescens

Ligularia japonica	Giant ragwort
Limnanthes douglasii	
	Marsh flower
	Meadow foam
	Poached egg flower
	Poached egg plant
Limonium bellidifolium	
	Matted sea lavender
Limonium binervosum	
	Rock sea lavender
Limonium bonduellii	
	Algerian statice
Limonium carolinianum	
	American sea lavender
Limonium latifolium	
	Border sea lavender
	Broad-leaved sea lavender
	Statice
Limonium sinuatum	
	Notch-leaf statice
	Statice
	Winged statice
Limonium suworowii	
	Pink pokers
	Rat's-tail statice
	Russian statice
Linanthus grandiflorus	
	Mountain phlox
Linaria alpina	Alpine toadflax
Linaria arenaria	Sand toadflax
Linaria maroccana	Bunny rabbits
	Toadflax
Linaria purpurea	Purple toadflax
Linaria repens	Pale toadflax
Linaria vulgaris	Brideweed
	Butter and eggs
	Calve's snout
	Common toadflax
	Eggs and bacon
	Flaxweed
	Pedlar's basket
	Yellow toadflax
Lindheimera texana	Star daisy
Linum bienne	Pale flax
Linum catharticum	Fairy flax
	White flax
Linum flavum	Golden flax
	Yellow flax
Linum grandiflorum	Red flax
	Scarlet flax
Linum lewisii	Prairie flax
Linum monogynum	
	New Zealand flax
Linum perenne	Blue flax
Linum rubrum	Red flax
	Scarlet flax
Linum usitatissimum	
	Annual blue flax
	Common blue flax
	Flax
	Linseed
Lippia citriodora	Lemon verbena

Lobelia cardinalis	Cardinal flower
	Scarlet lobelia
Lobelia erinus	Bedding lobelia
	Edging lobelia
Lobelia erinus pendula	
	Trailing lobelia
Lobelia fulgens	Cardinal flower
Lobelia inflata	Asthma weed
	Indian tobacco
Lobelia siphililea	Great lobelia
Lobelia siphilitica	Blue lobelia
Lobelia urens	Blue lobelia
	Heath lobelia
Lobularia maritima	Sea alyssum
	Sweet alison
	Sweet alyssum
Lonicera × brownii	
	Scarlet trumpet honeysuckle
Lonicera caprifolium	
	Goat-leaf honeysuckle
Lonicera hildebrandiana	
	Giant honeysuckle
Lonicera involucrata	Twinberry
Lonicera japonica	
	Japanese honeysuckle
Lonicera nitida	Box honeysuckle
Lonicera periclymenum	
	Common honeysuckle
	European honeysuckle
	Honeysuckle
	Wild woodbine
	Woodbine
Lonicera pileata	
	Privet honeysuckle
Lonicera sempervirens	
	Trumpet honeysuckle
Lonicera tatarica	
	Tartarian honeysuckle
Lonicera tragophylla	
	Chinese woodbine
Lonicera xylosteum	
	Fly honeysuckle
Lotus berthelotii	Parrot's beak
	Winged pea
Lotus corniculatus	Bacon and eggs
	Bird's foot trefoil
Lotus scoparius	Deer weed
Lunaria annua	Honesty
	Money plant
	Moonwort
	Satin flower
Lunaria biennis	Honesty
	Money plant
	Moonwort
	Satin flower
Lunaria rediviva	Honesty
	Perennial honesty
Lupinus albus	White lupin
Lupinus lepidus	Prairie lupin
Lupinus luteus	Yellow lupin
Lupinus polyphyllus	Garden lupin
Lupinus pubescens	Downy lupin

BOTANICAL NAMES

Lupinus subcarnosus

Lupinus subcarnosus
Texas blue bonnet
Lupinus texensis Texas blue bonnet
Lupinus vallicola Valley lupin
Lychnis alpina Alpine campion
Lychnis chalcedonica
Jerusalem cross
Maltese cross
Lychnis coeli-rosa Rose of heaven
Lychnis coronaria Mullein pink
Rose campion
Lychnis dioica Red campion
Lychnis flos-cuculi Ragged robin
Lychnis flos-jovis Flower of Jove
Lychnis silene Catchfly
Lychnis viscaria Catchfly
German catchfly
Red catchfly
Sticky catchfly
Lychnis vulgaris Catchfly
German catchfly
Lycopsis arvensis Lesser bugloss
Lycopus europaeus Gipsywort
Lycopus virginicus Bugleweed
Gipsyweed
Sweet bugle
Water bugle
Lynosyris vulgaris Goldilocks
Lysimachia clethroides
Chinese loosestrife
Shepherd's crook
Lysimachia nemorum
Wood pimpernell
Yellow pimpernell
Lysimachia nummularia
Creeping jenny
Moneywort
String of sovereigns
Wandering jenny
Lysimachia punctata
Circle flower
Dotted loosestrife
Garden loosestrife
Spotted loosestrife
Yellow loosestrife
Lysimachia vulgaris
Wood pimpernel
Yellow loosestrife
Yellow willowherb
Lythrum salicaria
Purple loosestrife
Purple willowherb
Spiked loosestrife
Macleaya cordata Plume poppy
Macleaya microcarpa
Lesser plume poppy
Malcolmia maritima
Virginian stock
Malope trifolia Mallow wort
Malva alcea Cut-leaved mallow
Hollyhock mallow
Malva crispa Curled mallow
Curly mallow

Malva moschata Musk mallow
Malva neglecta Dwarf mallow
Malva pusilla Small mallow
Malva sylvestris Common mallow
Maranta leuconeura Prayer plant
Martynia louisiana Unicorn plant
Matricaria eximia Feverfew
Matthiola bicornis Evening stock
Night-scented stock
Matthiola incana Brompton stock
Gillyflower
Stock
Matthiola incana annua
Ten-week stock
Meconopsis baileyi
Himalayan blue poppy
Meconopsis betonicifolia
Blue poppy
Himalayan blue poppy
Meconopsis cambrica Welsh poppy
Meconopsis integrifolia
Lampshade poppy
Yellow chinese poppy
Meconopsis napaulensis
Satin poppy
Meconopsis quintuplinerva
Harebell poppy
Medicago arabica Spotted medick
Medicago echinus Calvary clover
Medicago falcata Yellow medick
Medicago lupulina Black medick
Nonsuch
Shamrock
Medicago minima Bur medick
Melandrium diurnum
Red campion
Mentzelia lindleyi Blazing star
Mertensia ciliata American bluebell
Mertensia maritima
Northern shore wort
Oyster plant
Mertensia pulmonarioides
Virginian cowslip
Mertensia virginica
Virginia bluebell
Virginia cowslip
*Mesembryanthemum
criniflorum* Livingstone daisy
*Mesembryanthemum
crystallinum* Ice plant
Sea fig
Mimulus aurantiacus
Bush monkey flower
Shrubby musk
Mimulus cardinalis
Scarlet monkey flower
Mimulus glutinosus
Bush monkey flower
Mimulus guttatus
American monkey flower
Mimulus luteus Monkey flower
Monkey musk

POPULAR GARDEN PLANTS

Mimulus moschatus	Musk
Mimulus ringens	
	Allegheny monkey flower
Mina lobata	Crimson star glory
Minuartia rubella	
	Mountain sandwort
Minuartia sedoides	Cyphel
	Mossy cyphel
Minuartia verna	Spring sandwort
	Vernal sandwort
Minuartia viscosa	Sticky sandwort
Mirabilis jalapa	Four o'clock plant
	Marvel of Peru
Mirabilis longiflora	
	Sweet four o'clock
Moluccella laevis	Bells of Ireland
	Molucca balm
	Shell flower
Monarda didyma	Bee balm
	Bergamot
	Oswego tea
	Sweet bergamot
Monotropa hypophega	
	Yellow bird's nest
Monotropa uniflora	Ghost flower
	Indian pipe
Montia perfoliata	Spring beauty
Montia sibirica	Pink purslane
Morina longifolia	
	Himalayan whorlflower
	Whorlflower
Mutisia decurrens	
	Climbing gazania
Myosotidium hortensia	
	Antarctic forget-me-not
	Chatham Island lily
	Giant forget-me-not
Myosotidium nobile	
	Antarctic forget-me-not
	Chatham island lily
	Giant forget-me-not
Myosotis alpestris	
	Alpine forget-me-not
	Forget-me-not
Myosotis arvensis	
	Field forget-me-not
Myosotis discolor	Yellow forget-me-not
Myosotis oblongata	
	Forget-me-not
Myosotis palustris	
	Water forget-me-not
Myosotis sylvatica	Forget-me-not
	Wood forget-me-not
Nemophila maculata	Five-spot
	Five-spot nemophila
Nemophila insignis	
	Baby blue-eyes
Nemophila menziesii	
	Baby blue-eyes
Nemophila phacelia	
	Californian bluebell

Nepeta cataria	Catmint
	Catnep
	Catnip
Nepeta × *faassenii*	Catmint
Nepeta mussinii	Catmint
Nicandra physalodes	
	Apple of Peru
	Shoo-fly
Nicotiana affinis	Tobacco plant
Nicotiana alata	Tobacco plant
Nicotiana glauca	
	Yellow bush tobacco
Nicotiana sylvestris	
	Flowering tobacco
Nicotiana rustica	Turkish tobacco
Nicotiana tabacum	
	Common tobacco
	Tobacco
Nierembergia caerulea	
	Lavender cup
Nierembergia hippomanica	
	Lavender cup
Nierembergia repens	White cup
Nigella damascena	Love-in-a-mist
Nolana acuminata	
	Chilean bellflower
Nolana rupicola	Chilean bellflower
Oenothera biennis	
	Evening primrose
	Field primrose
Oenothera fruticosa	
	American sundrops
	Sundrops
Oenothera glazioviana	
	Large-leaved evening primrose
Oenothera linearis	
	American sundrops
	Sundrops
Oenothera macrocarpa	
	Ozark sundrops
Oenothera missouriensis	
	Ozark sundrops
	Prairie evening primrose
Oenothera perennis	
	Dwarf sundrops
Oenothera pumila	
	Dwarf sundrops
Oenothera rosea	
	Pink evening primrose
Oenothera stricta	
	Fragrant evening primrose
Omphalodes cappadocica	
	Navelwort
Omphalodes linifolia	
	Venus's navelwort
Omphalodes umbilicus	Navelwort
Omphalodes verna	
	Blue-eyed mary
	Creeping forget-me-not
Ononis natrix	Goat root
	Yellow rest harrow
Ononis repens	Rest harrow

Onopordum acanthium

Onopordum acanthium	
	Cotton thistle
	Downy thistle
	Scotch thistle
	Woolly thistle
Onopordum arabicum	
	Arabian thistle
	Heraldic thistle
	Silver thistle
Onopordum nervosum	
	Arabian thistle
	Heraldic thistle
	Silver thistle
Onosma pyramidale	Donkey plant
	Himalayan comfrey
Onosma tauricum	Golden drop
Origanum dictamnus	
	Cretan dittany
Origanum vulgare	
	Common marjoram
	Marjoram
	Oregano
	Wild marjoram
Osteospermum barberae	
	Dwarf cape marigold
Ourisia macrophylla	
	Mountain foxglove
Oxalis acetosella	Shamrock
	Wood sorrel
Oxalis articulata	Pink oxalis
Oxalis corniculata	Yellow sorrel
Oxalis deppei	Good-luck plant
Oxyria dignya	Mountain sorrel
Ozothamnus ledifolium	
	Kerosene bush
Ozothamnus thyrsoideum	
	Snow-in-summer
Pachysandra procumbens	
	Allegheny spurge
Pachysandra terminalis	
	Japanese spurge
Paeonia albiflora	Chinese paeony
Paeonia arborea	Moutan paeony
	Tree paeony
Paeonia lactiflora	Chinese paeony
Paeonia moutan	Moutan paeony
	Tree paeony
Paeonia officinalis	
	European wild paeony
	Wild paeony
Paeonia suffruticosa	
	Moutan paeony
	Tree paeony
Paeonia tenuifolia	
	Fern-leaved paeony
Papaver alpinum	Alpine poppy
Papaver burseri	Alpine poppy
Papaver commutatum	
	Ladybird poppy
Papaver dubium	
	Long-headed poppy
Papaver glaucum	Tulip poppy

Papaver nudicaule	Arctic poppy
	Iceland poppy
Papaver orientale	Oriental poppy
Papaver pavonium	
	Peacock poppy
Papaver radicatum	Arctic poppy
Papaver rhoeas	
	Common red poppy
	Corn poppy
	Field poppy
	Flanders poppy
Papaver rupifragum	
	Spanish poppy
Papaver somniferum	
	Opium poppy
	White poppy
Passiflora caerulea	
	Blue passionflower
	Common blue passionflower
Passiflora edulis	Purple granadilla
Passiflora laurifolia	
	Jamaica honeysuckle
Passiflora mollissima	
	Banana passionfruit
	Curuba
Passiflora racemosa	
	Red passion flower
Pedicularis palustris	Red rattle
Pedicularis sylvatica	Lousewort
Pelargonium capitatum	
	Rose-scented geranium
	Rose-scented pelargonium
Pelargonium citriodorum	
	Lemon-scented geranium
	Lemon-scented pelargonium
Pelargonium crispum	
	Lemon-scented geranium
	Lemon-scented pelargonium
Pelargonium × domesticum	
	Lady Washington geraniums
	Lady Washington pelargoniums
	Martha Washington geraniums
	Martha Washington pelargoniums
	Regal geraniums
	Regal pelargoniums
	Show geraniums
	Show pelargoniums
Pelargonium × hortorum	
	Zonal geraniums
	Zonal pelargoniums
Pelargonium peltatum	
	Ivy-leaved geraniums
	Ivy-leaved pelargoniums
Peltiphyllum peltatum	
	Umbrella plant
Penstemon alpinus	
	Alpine penstemon
Penstemon cordifolius	
	Shrubby penstemon
Phacelia campanularia	
	California bluebell
Phacelia tanacetifolia	
	Tansy phacelia

POPULAR GARDEN PLANTS

Potentilla verna

Phacelia viscida	Sticky phacelia
Phacelia whitlavia	
	Californian bluebell
Phlox bifida	Sand phlox
Phlox canadensis	Blue phlox
Phlox decussata	Garden phlox
Phlox divaricata	Blue phlox
Phlox douglasii	Alpine phlox
Phlox drummondii	Annual phlox
Phlox paniculata	Garden phlox
Phlox reptans	Creeping phlox
Phlox setacea	Moss phlox
	Moss pink
Phlox stolonifera	Creeping phlox
Phlox subulata	Moss phlox
	Moss pink
Physalis alkekengi	Bladder cherry
	Chinese lantern
Physostegia virginiana	
	False dragonhead
	Lion's heart
	Obedient plant
Phyteuma comosum	
	Horned rampion
Phyteuma nigrum	Black rampion
Phyteuma spicatum	
	Spiked rampion
Pinguicula grandiflora	
	Greater butterwort
	Large-flowered butterwort
Pinguicula vulgaris	Butterwort
	Common butterwort
Platycodon grandiflorum	
	Balloon flower
	Chinese bellflower
Platystemon californicus	
	Cream cups
Podophyllum emodii	
	Himalayan mayflower
Podophyllum peltatum	May apple
Polemonium caeruleum	
	Greek valerian
	Jacob's ladder
Polemonium reptans	Abcess root
	American Greek valerian
	Blue bells
	Creeping jacob's ladder
	Sweat root
Polygala calcarea	Chalk milkwort
	Milkwort
Polygala chamaebuxus	
	Bastard box
	Ground box
Polygala senega	Rattlesnake root
	Senega
	Snakeroot
Polygala serpyllifolia	
	Heath milkwort
Polygala vulgaris	
	Common milkwort
Polygonum amplexicaule	
	Mountain fleece

Polygonum ariculare	Armstrong
Polygonum aubertii	
	China fleece flower
	Silver lace vine
Polygonum aviculare	
	Bird's tongue
	Common knotgrass
	Knotgrass
	Nine-joints
Polygonum baldschuanicum	
	Bokhara fleece flower
	Russian vine
Polygonum bistorta	Snakeweed
Polygonum campanulatum	
	Himalayan knotweed
Polygonum capitatum	
	Pink-head knotweed
Polygonum erectum	
	Russian knotgrass
Polygonum lapathifolium	
	Pale persicaria
Polygonum persicaria	
	Common persicaria
	Red legs
	Red shank
Polygonum viviporum	
	Alpine bistort
Portulaca grandiflora	Rose moss
	Sun plant
Potentilla alba	White cinquefoil
Potentilla anglica	
	Procumbent cinquefoil
Potentilla anserina	Silver weed
	Silvery cinquefoil
Potentilla argentea	
	Hoary cinquefoil
Potentilla cinerea	Grey cinquefoil
Potentilla crantzii	
	Alpine cinquefoil
Potentilla erecta	Bloodroot
	Ewe daisy
	Red root
	Tormentil
Potentilla palustris	
	Marsh cinquefoil
Potentilla recta	
	Sulfer cinquefoil
	Sulphur cinquefoil
	Upright cinquefoil
Potentilla reptans	
	Creeping cinquefoil
	Five fingers
	Five-leaved grass
Potentilla rupestris	
	Rock cinquefoil
Potentilla sterilis	
	Barren strawberry
Potentilla tabernaemontani	
	Spring cinquefoil
Potentilla tormentilla	
	Shepherd's knot
Potentilla verna	Spring cinquefoil

Poterium canadensis

Poterium canadensis	
	American burnet
	Canadian burnet
Primula acaulis	English primrose
	Primrose
Primula alpicola	
	Moonlight primula
Primula auricula	Alpine auricula
	Auricula
	Bear's breeches
	Bear's ear
	Dusty miller
Primula denticulata	
	Drumstick primula
Primula elatior	Oxlip
	Paigles
Primula farinosa	
	Bird's eye primrose
Primula florindae	Giant cowslip
	Himalayan cowslip
Primula helodoxa	
	Glory-of-the-marsh
Primula japonica	
	Japanese primrose
Primula malacoides	
	Fairy primrose
Primula microdonta alpicola	
	Moonlight primula
Primula obconica	
	German primrose
Primula officinalis	Cowslip
Primula polyantha	Polyanthus
Primula sikkimensis	
	Himalayan cowslip
Primula veris	Cowslip
	Fairy cups
	Herb peter
	Keyflower
	Palsywort
	Saint Peter's wort
Primula vulgaris	English primrose
	Primrose
Proboscidea jussieui	Unicorn plant
Psylliostachys suworowii	
	Rat's-tail statice
	Russian statice
Pulmonaria angustifolia	
	Blue cowslip
Pulmonaria officinalis	
	Jerusalem cowslip
	Jerusalem sage
	Soldiers and sailors
	Spotted dog
Pulmonaria saccharata	
	Bethlehem sage
Pulsatilla alba	
	White pasque flower
Pulsatilla alpina	Alpine anemone
Pulsatilla vernalis	Spring anemone
Pulsatilla vulgaris	
	Meadow anemone
	Pasque flower
Puya alpestris	Puya

Puya berteroniana	Puya
Pyrethrum hybridum	
	Painted daisy
	Pyrethrum
Pyrethrum roseum	Painted daisy
	Pyrethrum
Quamoclit lobata	
	Crimson star glory
Ranunculus aconitifolius	
	Aconite-leaved buttercup
	Fair maids of Kent
	White bachelor's buttons
Ranunculus acris	
	Bachelor's buttons
	Gold cup
	Meadow bloom
	Meadow buttercup
	Yellow bachelor's buttons
Ranunculus alpestris	
	Alpine buttercup
Ranunculus amplexicaulis	
	White buttercup
Ranunculus arvensis	
	Corn buttercup
	Corn crowfoot
Ranunculus asiaticus	
	Persian buttercup
	Turban buttercup
Ranunculus auricumus	Goldilocks
Ranunculus bulbosus	
	Bulbous buttercup
Ranunculus ficaria	
	Lesser celandine
	Pilewort
Ranunculus flammula	
	Lesser spearwort
Ranunculus glacialis	
	Glacier crowfoot
Ranunculus hederaceus	
	Ivy-leaved crowfoot
Ranunculus lingua	
	Great spearwort
Ranunculus lyalli	Rockwood lily
Ranunculus repens	
	Creeping buttercup
Ranunculus sceleratus	
	Celery-leaved crowfoot
Rehmannia angulata	
	Chinese foxglove
Reseda alba	White mignonette
Reseda lutea	Wild mignonette
Reseda luteola	Dyer's rocket
	Weld
Reseda odorata	Mignonette
Reseda phyteuma	
	Corn mignonette
Rhazya orientalis	
	Oriental periwinkle
Rhodanthe manglesii	Sunray
	Swan river everlasting
Rhodiola rosea	Roseroot
Ricinus communis	Castor bean
	Castor-oil plant

Rodgersia pinnata	Feathered bronze leaf
Rudbeckia fulgida	Cone flower
Rudbeckia hirta	Annual rudbeckia
	Black-eyed susan
	Yellow daisy
Rudbeckia triloba	Brown-eyed susan
Ruta graveolens	Herb of grace
	Rue
Sagina maritima	Sea pearlwort
Sagina nodosa	Knotted pearlwort
Sagina procumbens	Common pearlwort
Sagina subulata	Heath pearlwort
Saintpaulia ionantha	African violet
Salpiglossis sinuata	Painted tongue
	Salpiglossis
	Velvet flower
Salvia argentea	Silver sage
Salvia azurea	Blue sage
Salvia farinacea	Mealy-cup sage
Salvia fulgens	Cardinal sage
	Cardinal salvia
	Mexican red sage
Salvia glutinosa	Jupiter's distaff
	Sticky sage
Salvia horminoides	Wild sage
Salvia horminum	Annual clary
	Bluebeard
Salvia nemorosa	Wild sage
Salvia officinalis	Common sage
	Sage
Salvia officinalis purpurascens	Purple sage
Salvia patens	Blue sage
	Gentian sage
Salvia pratensis	Meadow clary
Salvia rutilans	Pineapple sage
Salvia sclarea	Clary
	Clear eye
	True clary
Salvia splendens	Scarlet sage
Salvia superba	Perennial sage
Salvia uliginosa	Bog sage
Salvia verbenacea	Wild clary
Salvia viridis	False clary
Sanguinaria canadensis	Bloodroot
Sanguisorba canadensis	American burnet
	Canadian burnet
Sanvitalia procumbens	Creeping zinnia
Saponaria ocymoides	Rock soapwort
	Tumbling ted
Saponaria officinalis	Bouncing bet
	Soapwort
Saponaria vaccaria	Cow herb
	Dairy pink

Satureia montana	Winter savory
Saxifraga aizoides	Yellow mountain saxifrage
Saxifraga caesia	Blue saxifrage
Saxifraga cespitosa	Tufted saxifrage
Saxifraga cotyledon	Pyramidal saxifrage
Saxifraga granulata	Fair maids of France
	Meadow saxifrage
Saxifraga hieracifolia	Hawkweed saxifrage
Saxifraga hirsuta	Hairy saxifrage
	Kidney saxifrage
Saxifraga hypnoides	Dovedale moss
	Mossy rockfoil
	Mossy saxifrage
Saxifraga moschata	Musky saxifrage
Saxifraga oppositifolia	Purple saxifrage
Saxifraga peltata	Umbrella plant
Saxifraga rosacea	Irish saxifrage
Saxifraga sarmentosa	Mother of thousands
	Strawberry geranium
Saxifraga stellaris	Starry saxifrage
Saxifraga stellata	Starry saxifrage
Saxifraga stolonifera	Mother of thousands
	Strawberry geranium
Saxifraga tridactylotes	Rue-leaved saxifrage
Saxifraga umbrosa	London pride
	Saint Patrick's cabbage
Saxifraga × urbium	London pride
	Nancy pretty
	None-so-pretty
	Saint Patrick's cabbage
Scabiosa atropurpurea	Mournful widow
	Pincushion flower
	Sweet scabious
Scabiosa caucasica	Florist's scabious
	Pincushion flower
Scabiosa columbaria	Small scabious
Scabiosa columbaria ochraleuca	Yellow scabious
Scabiosa lucida	Brilliant scabious
	Shining scabious
Schizocodon soldanelloides	Fringebell
Sedum acre	Biting stonecrop
	Golden moss
	Wall pepper
Sedum adolphi	Golden sedum
Sedum album	White stonecrop
Sedum anglicum	English stonecrop

Sedum dasyphyllum	Thick-leaved stonecrop
Sedum forsteranum	Rock stonecrop
Sedum maximum	Ice plant
Sedum morganianum	Ass's tail
	Beaver tail
	Burro's tail
	Donkey's tail
	Horse's tail
	Lamb's tail
Sedum pachyphyllum	Jelly-bean plant
Sedum reflexum	Reflexed stonecrop
	Stone orpine
Sedum rhodiola	Roseroot
Sedum rosea	Roseroot
	Roseroot sedum
Sedum × rubrotinctum	Pork and beans
Sedum spectabile	Ice plant
Sedum telephium	Live forever
	Livelong
	Midsummer men
	Orpine
Sedum villosum	Hairy stonecrop
Sempervivum arachnoideum	Cobweb houseleek
	Spider houseleek
Sempervivum montanum	Mountain houseleek
Sempervivum soboliferum	Hen-and-chickens houseleek
Sempervivum tectorum	Bullock's eye
	Common houseleek
	Roof houseleek
Senecio aquaticus	Marsh ragwort
Senecio aureus	Golden groundsel
Senecio bicolor	Silver ragwort
Senecio confusus	Mexican flame vine
Senecio erucifolius	Hoary ragwort
Senecio fluviatilis	Broad-leaved ragwort
Senecio integrifolius	Field fleawort
Senecio jacobaea	Jacobea
	Ragwort
	Saint James' wort
	Staggerwort
Senecio nemorensis	Wood ragwort
Senecio palustris	Marsh fleawort
Senecio petasites	Velvet groundsel
Senecio rowleyanus	String of beads
	String of pearls
Senecio squalidus	Oxford ragwort
Senecio sylvaticus	Wood groundsel
Senecio viscosus	Sticky groundsel
Senecio vulgaris	Groundsel

Serratula shawii	Sawwort
Sesbania tripetii	Scarlet wisteria
Shortia soldanelloides	Fringebell
Silaum silaus	Pepper saxifrage
Silene acaulis	Cushion pink
	Moss campion
Silene alba	White campion
Silene alpestris	Alpine campion
Silene armeria	Sweet william catchfly
Silene coeli-rosa	Rose of heaven
Silene conica	Sand catchfly
	Striated catchfly
Silene dichotoma	Forked catchfly
Silene dioica	Red campion
Silene gallica	Small catchfly
Silene italica	Italian catchfly
Silene latifolia	White campion
Silene maritima	Sea campion
Silene noctiflora	Night-flowering catchfly
Silene nutans	Nottingham catchfly
Silene oculata	Rose of heaven
Silene otites	Spanish catchfly
Silene pendula	Nodding catchfly
Silene quadrifida	Alpine campion
Silene rupestris	Rock campion
Silene vulgaris	Bladder campion
Silene vulgaris maritima	Sea campion
Silybum marianum	Blessed thistle
	Holy thistle
	Milk thistle
	Our Lady's milk thistle
	Saint Mary's milk thistle
	Saint Mary's thistle
Sisymbrium altissimum	Tall rocket
Sisymbrium irio	London rocket
Sisymbrium loeselii	False London rocket
Sisymbrium officinale	Hedge mustard
Sisymbrium orientale	Eastern rocket
	Oriental rocket
Sisyrinchium angustifolium	Blue-eyed grass
Sisyrinchium bellum	California blue-eyed grass
Sisyrinchium californicum	Golden-eyed grass
Sisyrinchium douglasii	Grass widow
	Purple-eyed grass
	Spring bell
Sisyrinchium stratiatum	Satin flower
Solanum capsicastrum	Winter cherry

POPULAR GARDEN PLANTS

Tacsonia mollissima

Solanum carolinense
Apple of sodom
Bull nettle
Horse nettle
Poison potato

Solanum crispum
Chilean potato tree

Solanum dulcamara Bittersweet
Woody nightshade

Solanum jasminoides
Jasmine nightshade
Potato vine

Solanum laciniatum
Kangaroo apple
Poroporo

Solanum nigrum Black nightshade

Solanum rantonnetii Potato bush

Solanum sosomeum
Apple of sodom

Solanum wendlandii
Giant potato vine

Soldanella alpina Alpine snowbell

Soldanella montana
Mountain snowbell
Mountain tassel

Soldanella pusilla Dwarf snowbell

Solidago canadensis
Canadian golden rod
Golden rod

Solidago odora Sweet golden rod

Solidago virgaurea
Golden rod
Woundwort

Spathiphyllum wallisii White sails

Specularia speculum
Venus's looking glass

Specularia speculum-veneris
Venus's looking glass

Spiraea aruncus Goat's beard

Spiraea lobata
Queen of the prairie

Stachys affinis Chinese artichoke
Chorogi
Japanese artichoke
Knotroot

Stachys arvensis Corn woundwort
Field woundwort

Stachys betonica Betony
Bishop's wort
Wood betony

Stachys byzantina Lamb's ear
Lamb's lugs
Lamb's tongue
Sow's ear
Woolly betony
Woolly woundwort

Stachys germanica
Downy woundwort

Stachys grandiflora Woundwort

Stachys lanata Lamb's ear
Lamb's tongue
Woolly betony

Stachys macrantha Woundwort

Stachys officinalis Betony
Bishop's-wort
Wood betony

Stachys olympica Lamb's ear
Lamb's tongue
Woolly betony

Stachys palustris
Marsh woundwort

Stachys recta Yellow woundwort

Stachys sylvatica
Hedge woundwort
Wood woundwort

Stapelia gigantea Giant stapelia
Giant starfish
Giant toad plant
Zulu giant

Stapelia variegata Starfish plant
Toad cactus
Toad plant

Stapelia hirsuta
Hairy starfish flower
Hairy toad plant
Shaggy starfish

Statice bonduellii Algerian statice

Statice latifolium
Border sea lavender
Broad-leaved sea lavender
Statice

Statice sinuatum
Notch-leaf statice
Winged statice

Statice suworowii Rat's-tail statice
Russian statice

Stokesia cyanea Cornflower aster
Stokes's aster

Stokesia laevis Cornflower aster
Stokes's aster

Streptocarpus hybridus
Cape primrose

Streptocarpus saxorum
False African violet

Stylomecon heterophylla
Blood drop
Flaming poppy
Wind poppy

Stylophorum diphyllum
Celandine poppy
Wood poppy

Symphytum officinale Boneset
Bruisewort
Comfrey
Common comfrey
Knitbone

Symphytum orientale
White comfrey

Symphytum peregrinum
Russian comfrey

Symphytum × uplandicum
Russian comfrey

Tacsonia mollissima
Banana passionfruit
Curuba

Tagetes erecta

Tagetes erecta	African marigold
	American marigold
	Aztec marigold
	Big marigold
Tagetes filifolia	Irish lace
Tagetes lucida	Sweet mace
	Sweet-scented marigold
Tagetes minuta	Muster-john-henry
Tagetes patula	French marigold
Tagetes signata	Signet marigold
	Tagetes
Tagetes tenuifolia	Signet marigold
	Tagetes
Tanacetum cinerariifolium	
	Dalmatian pellitory
	Dalmatian pyrethrum
	Pyrethrum
Tanacetum coccineum	Feverfew
	Painted daisy
	Pyrethrum
Tanacetum densum amani	
	Prince of Wales' feathers
Tanacetum parthenium	
	Bachelor's buttons
	Feverfew
Tanacetum vulgare	Buttons
	Tansy
Taraxacum erythrospermum	
	Lesser dandelion
Taraxacum laevicatum	
	Lesser dandelion
Taraxacum officinale	Dandelion
	Fairy clock
	Lion's teeth
	Pee the bed
	Piss the bed
	Swine's snout
Telekia speciosa	
	Large yellow ox-eye
Tetranema mexicana	
	Mexican foxglove
Tetranema roseum	
	Mexican foxglove
	Mexican violet
Thalictrum alpinum	
	Alpine meadow rue
Thalictrum aquilegiifolium	
	Meadow rue
Thalictrum clavatum	Lady rue
Thalictrum coreanum	
	Dwarf meadow rue
Thalictrum dioicum	
	Early meadow rue
	Quicksilver weed
Thalictrum flavum	
	Common meadow rue
	Yellow meadow rue
Thalictrum minus	Lesser meadow rue
Thalictrum polygamum	
	King-of-the-meadow
	Muskrat weed
	Tall meadow rue

Thermopsis caroliniana	
	Carolina lupin
Thlaspi alliaceum	
	Garlic pennycress
Thlaspi alpestre	Alpine pennycress
Thlaspi arvense	Fanweed
	Field pennycress
	Frenchweed
	Mithridate mustard
	Pennycress
	Stinkweed
Thlaspi perfoliatum	
	Perfoliate pennycress
Thunbergia alata	
	Black-eyed susan
Thunbergia grandiflora	
	Clock vine
Thymus × citriodorus	
	Lemon-scented thyme
Thymus drucei	
	European wild thyme
	Wild thyme
Thymus herba-barona	
	Caraway thyme
Thymus nitidus	Sicily thyme
Thymus praecox	Hairy thyme
Thymus pulegioides	Large thyme
Thymus richardii nitidus	
	Sicily thyme
Thymus serpyllum	
	Breckland thyme
	Creeping thyme
	European wild thyme
	Wild thyme
Thymus vulgaris	Common thyme
	Garden thyme
Tiarella cordifolia	Coolwort
	Foam flower
Tiarella polyphylla	Foam flower
Tiarella unifoliata	Sugar scoop
Tithonia rotundifolia	
	Mexican sunflower
Tithonia speciosa	
	Mexican sunflower
Torenia fournieri	Blue wings
	Wishbone flower
Trachelium caeruleum	
	Blue throatwort
	Common throatwort
Trachymene caerulea	
	Blue lace flower
Tradescantia albiflora	
	Wandering jew
Tradescantia × andersoniana	
	Spiderworts
	Trinity flowers
Tradescantia fluminensis	
	Wandering jew
Tradescantia virginiana	
	Spiderworts
	Trinity flowers
Tradescantia zebrina	Inch plant

POPULAR GARDEN PLANTS

Verbena tenera

Trollius × *cultorum*
    Garden globe flowers
Trollius europaeus   Boule d'or
    Common globe flower
    Globe flower
Trollius × *hybridus*
    Garden globeflowers
Trollius laxus
    Spreading globe flower
Trollius pumilis
    Dwarf globe flower
Tropaeolum canariensis
    Canary creeper
Tropaeolum lobbianum
    Shield nasturtium
Tropaeolum majus
    Garden nasturtium
    Indian cress
    Tall nasturtium
Tropaeolum minus
    Dwarf nasturtium
Tropaeolum peltophorum
    Shield nasturtium
Tropaeolum peregrinum
    Canary-bird flower
    Canary-bird vine
    Canary creeper
Tropaeolum polyphyllum
    Tropaeolum
Tropaeolum speciosum
    Flame creeper
    Flame nasturtium
    Scotch creeper
    Scottish flame flower
Umbilicus rupestris   Kidneywort
    Navelwort
    Pennywort
    Wall pennywort
Uvularia grandiflora   Bellwort
    Cowbells
    Haybells
    Merry bells
Uvularia perfoliata   Strawbells
Vaccaria pyramidata   Cockle
    Cow herb
    Dairy pink
    Saponaria
Valeriana dioica   Marsh valerian
Valeriana montana
    Mountain valerian
Valeriana officinalis   Cat's valerian
    Common valerian
    Garden heliotrope
    Phu
Valeriana pyrenaica
    Heart-leaved valerian
    Pyrenean valerian
Valeriana saxatilis   Dwarf valerian
Valeriana walichii   Indian valerian
Vancouveria hexandra
    American barrenwort
Vancouveria planipetala
    Inside-out flower
    Redwood ivy

Venidium fastuosum   Cape daisy
    Monarch of the veldt
    Namaqualand daisy
Veratrum album
    White false hellebore
    White helleborine
Veratrum californicum   Corn lily
Veratrum nigrum
    Black false hellebore
    Black helleborine
Veratrum viride
    American white hellebore
    Indian poke
    Itchweed
    White helleborine
Verbascum blattaria   Moth mullein
Verbascum lychnitis
    White mullein
Verbascum nigrum   Dark mullein
Verbascum phlomoides
    Orange mullein
Verbascum phoeniceum
    Purple mullein
Verbascum pulverulentum
    Hoary mullein
Verbascum thapsus   Aaron's rod
    Adam's flannel
    Candlewick
    Common mullein
    Flannel mullein
    Hag's taper
    Jacob's staff
    Jupiter's staff
    Lady's foxglove
    Rag paper
    Shepherd's club
    Velvet mullein
    White mullein
    Woolly mullein
Verbascum virgatum
    Twiggy mullein
Verbena aubletia   Creeping vervain
    Rose verbena
Verbena bipinnatifida
    Dakota vervain
Verbena bracteata
    Prostrate vervain
Verbena canadensis   Clump vervain
    Creeping vervain
    Rose vervain
Verbena hastata   Blue vervain
    Simpler's joy
Verbena × *hortensis*
    Garden verbenas
Verbena × *hybrida*
    Garden verbenas
Verbena jamaicensis
    Jamaica vervain
Verbena lasiostachys   Vervain
Verbena officinalis   Vervain
Verbena rigida   Vervain
Verbena stricta   Hoary vervain
Verbena tenera   Italian verbena

Verbena tenuisecta

Verbena tenuisecta	Moss verbena
Verbena urticifolia	White vervain
Verbesina encelioides	Butter daisy
	Golden crown beard
Veronica agrestis	Field speedwell
Veronica alpina	Alpine speedwell
Veronica americana	
	American brooklime
Veronica arvensis	Wall speedwell
Veronica austriaca	
	Austrian speedwell
	Large speedwell
Veronica beccabunga	Brooklime
	Cow cress
	European brooklime
	Water pimpernel
Veronica candida	
	Woolly speedwell
Veronica chamaedrys	Angel's eye
	Bird's eye
	Germander speedwell
Veronica filiformis	
	Round-leaved speedwell
Veronica fruticans	Rock speedwell
Veronica hederifolia	
	Ivy-leaved speedwell
Veronica hulkeana	
	New Zealand lilac
Veronica incana	Woolly speedwell
Veronica montana	
	Mountain speedwell
	Wood speedwell
Veronica officinalis	
	Common speedwell
	Gipsyweed
	Heath speedwell
	Speedwell
Veronica peregrina	
	American speedwell
Veronica perfoliata	
	Digger's speedwell
Veronica persica	
	Buxbaum's speedwell
	Persian speedwell
Veronica prostrata	
	Rockery speedwell
Veronica repens	
	Corsican speedwell
Veronica scutellata	
	Marsh speedwell
Veronica serpyllifolia	
	Thyme-leaved speedwell
Veronica spicata	Spiked speedwell

Veronica verna	Spring speedwell
Veronica virginica	Black root
	Culver's root
Veronicastrum virginicum	
	Black root
	Culver's root
Vinca major	Band plant
	Blue buttons
	Greater periwinkle
	Larger periwinkle
Vinca minor	Common periwinkle
	Lesser periwinkle
	Running myrtle
	Trailing myrtle
Vinca rosea	Madagascar periwinkle
	Rose periwinkle
Viola cornuta	Horned violet
	Tufted pansy
Viola cucullata	Marsh violet
Viola hederacea	Australian violet
	Trailing violet
Viola lutea	Mountain pansy
Viola odorata	Sweet violet
Viola saxatilis	Yellow violet
Viola tricolor	Heartsease pansy
	Wild pansy
Viscaria alpina	Alpine campion
Viscaria elegans	Rose of heaven
Viscaria vulgaris	Catchfly
	German catchfly
Wahlenbergia albomarginata	
	Bellflower
	Tufted harebell
Wahlenbergia hederacea	
	Ivy-leaved bellflower
	Ivy-leaved harebell
Wattakaka chinensis	
	Chinese wax flower
Wattakaka sinensis	
	Chinese wax flower
Xeranthemum anuum	
	Common immortelle
	Immortelle
Zauschneria californica	
	Californian fuchsia
	Humming bird's trumpet
Zinnia angustifolia	
	Narrow-leaved zinnia
Zinnia elegans	Common zinnia
	Youth and old age
Zinnia haageana	Mexican zinnia
	Narrow-leaved zinnia

TREES, BUSHES, AND SHRUBS

It is often said that the difference between trees and shrubs is simple; trees have a single woody stem from which branches grow to form a crown whereas a shrub has several woody stems rising from ground level, forming a crown. But this is over-simplification. The exact shape of a tree can be completely altered by wind action, by a difference in spacing or even by artificial pruning.

A bush is generally defined as a woody plant that is between a shrub and a tree in size.

Silver maple –
Acer saccharinum

Abelmoschus manihot	
	Sunset hibiscus
Aberia caffra	Kai apple
	Kau apple
	Kei apple
	Umkokolo
Aberia gardneri	
	Ceylon gooseberry
	Kitembilla
Abies alba	Common silver fir
	European silver fir
	Silver fir
Abies amabilis	Alpine fir
	Beautiful fir
	Cascade fir
	Pacific silver fir
	Red silver fir
	White fir
Abies balsamea	Balm of gilead
	Balsam fir
Abies borisii-regis	Bulgarian fir
	King Boris's fir
Abies bornmuellerana	
	Bornmüller's fir
	Turkish fir
Abies bracteata	Bristle-cone fir
	Santa Lucia fir
Abies cephalonica	Grecian fir
	Greek fir
Abies chensiensis	Shensi fir
Abies cilicica	Cilician fir
Abies concolor	Colorado white fir
	White fir
Abies concolor lowiana	
	Low's white fir
	Pacific white fir
	Sierra fir
Abies delavayi	Delavay's silver fir
Abies delavayi forrestii	Forrest's fir
	Forrest's silver fir
Abies fargesii	Farge's fir
	Sutchuen fir
Abies firma	Japanese fir
	Momi fir
Abies fraseri	Fraser's balsam fir
	She balsam
	Southern balsam fir
Abies grandis	Giant fir
	Grand fir
	Lowland fir
Abies holophylla	Manchurian fir
	Needle fir
Abies homolepis	Nikko fir
Abies koreana	Korean fir
Abies lasiocarpa	Alpine fir
	Rocky mountain fir
	Subalpine fir
Abies lasiocarpa arizonica	
	Arizona cork fir
	Cork fir
Abies macrocana	Moroccan fir

Abies magnifica	Californian red fir
	Red fir
Abies mariesii	Maries' fir
Abies marocana	Maroc fir
Abies nephrolepis	East Siberian fir
	Khingan fir
Abies nordmanniana	Caucasian fir
Abies numidica	Algerian fir
Abies pindrow	West Himalayan fir
Abies pinsapo	Hedgehog fir
	Spanish fir
Abies pinsapo glauca	
	Blue Spanish fir
Abies procera	Bracted fir
	Feather-cone fir
	Noble fir
Abies recurvata	Min fir
Abies religiosa	Sacred fir
Abies sachalinensis	Sakhalin fir
Abies siberica	Siberian fir
Abies spectabilis	East Himalayan fir
	Himalayan fir
Abies squamata	Flaky fir
Abies sutchuenensis	Farges fir
	Sutchuen fir
	Szechwan fir
Abies veitchii	Veitch's silver fir
Abies venusta	Bristle-cone fir
	Santa Lucia fir
Abies webbiana	East Himalayan fir
	Himalayan fir
Abronia umbellata	
	Pink sand verbena
Acacia abyssinica	Ethiopean acacia
Acacia accola	Wallangarra
Acacia acinacea	Gold dust
Acacia acuminata	
	Raspberry-jam tree
Acacia alata	Cedar wattle
	Winged wattle
Acacia albida	
	Ana tree
	Apple-ring acacia
	Winter thorn
Acacia aneura	Mulga
Acacia arabica	Indian gum
Acacia armata	Hedge wattle
	Kangaroo thorn
Acacia baileyana	
	Cootamundra wattle
	Golden mimosa
Acacia berteriana	Bastard logwood
Acacia binervia	Coastal myall
	Sally wattle
Acacia botrycephala	
	Sunshine wattle
Acacia brachybotrya	Grey mulga
Acacia bynoeana	Dwarf nealie
Acacia calamifolia	Broom wattle
	Wallowa

TREES, BUSHES, AND SHRUBS

Acacia woodii

Acacia cardiophylla	
	Wyalong wattle
Acacia catechu	Black cutch tree
	Catechu
	Cutch
	Khair
	Wadalee gum tree
Acacia cornigera	Bull-horn acacia
	Swollen-thorn acacia
Acacia cultriformis	Knife acacia
	Knife-leaf acacia
Acacia cyanophylla	Blue-leaf wattle
	Blue wattle
	Golden willow
	Orange wattle
	Port Jackson willow
Acacia dealbata	Mimosa
	Silver wattle
Acacia decora	Graceful wattle
Acacia decurrens	Green wattle
Acacia dunnii	Elephant's-ear wattle
Acacia elongata	Swamp wattle
Acacia farnesiana	Cassie
	Green wattle
	Huisache
	Opopanax
	Popinac
	Sponge tree
	Sweet acacia
	West Indian blackthorn
Acacia galpinii	Apiesdoring
Acacia giraffae	Camel thorn
Acacia greggii	Catclaw acacia
	Texas mimosa
Acacia gummifera	Barbary gum
	Mogadore gum
	Morocco gum
Acacia homalophylla	
	Fragrant myall
	Gidgee myall
	Myallwood
	Violetwood
	Yarran
Acacia horrida	Cape gum
Acacia howittii	Sticky wattle
Acacia implexa	Lightwood
	Screw-pod wattle
Acacia juniperina	Prickly wattle
Acacia karroo	Karroo thorn
	Sweet thorn
Acacia kettlewelliae	Buffalo wattle
Acacia koa	Koa
Acacia leprosa	Cinnamon wattle
Acacia longifolia	
	Sydney golden wattle
Acacia mearnsii	Black wattle
Acacia melanoxylon	
	Australian blackwood
	Blackwood
	Blackwood acacia

Acacia nilotica	Babul
	Gum acacia
	Gum-arabic tree
	Shittimwood
	Suntwood
Acacia nudicaulis	Bamboo briar
Acacia paniculata	Sunshine wattle
Acacia pendula	Weeping myall
Acacia penninervis	Blackwood
	Mountain hickory
Acacia podalyriifolia	
	Mount Morgan wattle
	Pearl acacia
	Queensland silver wattle
	Queensland wattle
Acacia pravissima	Oven's acacia
	Oven's wattle
Acacia prominens	
	Golden-rain wattle
Acacia pruinosa	Frosty wattle
Acacia pubescens	Hairy wattle
Acacia pycnantha	Golden wattle
Acacia retinodes	Wirilda
Acacia rigens	Needle-bush wattle
Acacia rubida	Red-leaved wattle
	Red-stemmed acacia
Acacia saileyana	
	Cootamundra wattle
Acacia salicina	Cooba
	Willow acacia
Acacia saligna	Golden wreath
	Weeping wattle
Acacia senegal	Cape gum
	Cape jasmine
	Egyptian thorn
	Gum acacia
	Gum-arabic tree
	Senegal gum
	Sudan gum-arabic
Acacia seyal	Gum-arabic tree
	Thirty thorn
	Whistling tree
Acacia spadicigera	
	Bull's horn acacia
Acacia spectabilis	Glory wattle
	Mudgee wattle
Acacia suaveolens	Sweet acacia
Acacia terminalis	Cedar wattle
	Peppermint wattle
Acacia tortilis	Umbrella thorn
Acacia tortuosa	Corkscrew wattle
	Twisted wattle
Acacia verniciflua	Varnish wattle
Acacia verticillata	Prickly moses
	Star acacia
	Star wattle
Acacia vestita	Weeping boree
Acacia victoriae	Bramble acacia
	Bramble wattle
Acacia woodii	Paper bark thorn
	Yellow bark thorn

Acacia xanthophloea

Acacia xanthophloea	
	Fever tree
Acalypha hispida	Chenille plant
	Foxtail
	Phillipine medusa
	Red-hot cat-tail
Acalypha wilkesiana	
	Beefsteak plant
	Copper-leaf
	Fire-dragon
	Jacob's coat
	Match-me-if-you-can
Acer argutum	Deep-veined maple
Acer barbatum	Florida maple
	Southern sugar maple
	Sugar tree
Acer buergeranum	Trident maple
Acer campestre	Common maple
	Field maple
	Hedge maple
Acer capillipes	
	Japanese snakebark maple
	Red snakebark maple
	Snakebark maple
Acer cappadocicum	
	Cappadocian maple
	Caucasian maple
Acer carpinifolium	Hornbeam-leaved maple
	Hornbeam maple
Acer circinatum	Vine maple
Acer cissifolium	Vineleaf maple
Acer crataegifolium	Hawthorn-leaved maple
	Snakebark maple
Acer davidii	
	Chinese snakebark maple
	Pére David's maple
Acer diabolicum	Devil's maple
	Horned maple
Acer distylum	Lime-leaf maple
Acer forrestii	Forrest's maple
	Snakebark maple
Acer ginnala	Amur maple
Acer glabrum	Rock maple
	Rocky mountain maple
Acer glabrum douglasii	
	Douglas maple
Acer griseum	Paper bark maple
Acer heldreichii	Balkan maple
	Heldreich's maple
Acer hersii	Hers's maple
	Snakebark maple
Acer hyrcanum	Balkan maple
Acer japonicum	
	Downy Japanese maple
	Full-moon maple
	Japanese maple
	Smooth Japanese maple
Acer japonicum aconitifolium	
	Coral bark maple
Acer japonicum aureum	
	Golden moon maple

Acer laxiflorum	Snakebark maple
Acer leucoderme	Chalk maple
Acer lobelii	Lobel's maple
Acer macrophyllum	
	Big-leaved maple
	Canyon maple
	Oregon maple
Acer martinii	Martin's maple
Acer maximowiczianum	
	Nikko maple
Acer miyabei	Miyabe's maple
Acer monspessulanum	
	Montpelier maple
Acer negundo	Ashleaf maple
	Box elder
	Water ash
Acer negundo auratum	
	Golden ashleaf maple
Acer nigrum	Black maple
Acer nikoense	Nikko maple
Acer opalus	Italian maple
Acer palmatum	Japanese maple
	Smooth Japanese maple
Acer palmatum atropurpureum	
	Blood-leaf Japanese maple
Acer palmatum senkaki	
	Coral bark maple
Acer pennsylvanicum	Moose bark
	Moosewood
	North American snakebark maple
	Pennsylvania maple
	Snakebark maple
	Striped maple
	Whistlewood
Acer pictum	Painted maple
Acer platanoides	Norway maple
Acer platanoides laciniatum	
	Eagle's claw maple
Acer pseudoilatanus worlei	
	Golden sycamore
Acer pseudoplatanus	Sycamore
Acer pseudoplatanus altropurpureum	
	Purple-leaved sycamore
Acer pseudoplatanus costorphinense	
	Costorphine plane
Acer pseudosieboldianum	
	Korean maple
Acer rubrum	Canadian maple
	Red maple
	Scarlet maple
	Soft maple
	Swamp maple
Acer rufinerve	
	Grey-budded snakebark maple
	Snakebark maple
Acer saccharinum	Bird's eye maple
	River maple
	Silver maple
	Soft maple
	White maple

Acer saccharum	Hard maple
	Rock maple
	Sugar maple
Acer sempervirens	Cretan maple
Acer shirasawanum aureum	
	Golden-leaved Japanese maple
Acer spicatum	Mountain maple
Acer tataricum	Tartar maple
	Tatarian maple
Acer tataricum ginnala	
	Amur maple
Acer tetramerum	Birch-leaf maple
Acer trautvetteri	Red-bud maple
	Trautvetter's maple
Acer triflorum	
	Rough-barked maple
Acer truncatum	Shantung maple
Acer velutinum	Persian maple
Acer velutinum vanvolxemii	
	Van Volxem's maple
Acer × zoeschense	Zoeschen maple
Achras sapota	Chicle
	Sapodilla plum
Acmena smithii	Lillypilly
Acoelorrhaphe wrightii	
	Everglades palm
	Saw cabbage palm
	Silver saw palm
Acokanthera oblongifolia	
	Kaffia plum
	Wintersweet
Acrocarpus fraxinifolius	
	Pink cedar
	Red cedar
	Shingle tree
Acrocomia mexicana	Coyoli palm
Actinorhytis calapparia	
	Calappa palm
Adansonia digitata	Baobab
	Dead-rat tree
	Monkey-bread tree
	Upside-down tree
Adansonia gregori	Bottle tree
Adenanthera pavonina	
	Barbados pride
	Coral pea
	Coralwood
	Peacock flower fence
	Red sandalwood tree
	Redwood
	Sandalwood tree
Adenium obesum	Desert rose
Adensonia digitata	Lemonade tree
Adhatoda vasica	Malabar nut
Aegle marmelos	Bael tree
	Ball tree
	Bela tree
	Bengal quince
	Golden apple
	Indian bael
Aesculus californica	
	Californian buckeye chestnut
	Californian horse chestnut

Aesculus × carnea	
	Pink horse chestnut
	Red horse chestnut
Aesculus flava	Sweet buckeye
	Yellow buckeye
Aesculus glabra	Ohio buckeye
Aesculus hippocastanum	
	Common horse chestnut
	Horse chestnut
Aesculus × hybrida	
	Hybrid buckeye
Aesculus indica	
	Indian horse chestnut
Aesculus neglecta	
erythroblastos	
	Sunrise horse chestnut
Aesculus octandra	Sweet buckeye
	Yellow buckeye
Aesculus parviflora	
	Bottlebrush buckeye
	Dwarf buckeye
	Dwarf horse chestnut
	Shrubby pavia
Aesculus pavia	
	American red buckeye
	Red buckeye
Aesculus turbinata	
	Japanese horse chestnut
Agathis alba	Amboina pitch tree
	Mountain agathis
Agathis australis	Kauri pine
Agathis brownii	Queensland kauri
Agathis dammara	Amboina pine
	Dammar
Agathis microstachys	
	Black kauri pine
Agathis robusta	
	South Queensland kauri
Agathis vitiensis	Fijian kauri pine
Agathosma betulina	Round buchu
Agathosma crenulata	Long buchu
Agonis flexuosa	
	Australian willow myrtle
	Peppermint tree
	Willow myrtle
Ailanthus altissima	Copal tree
	Tree of heaven
	Varnish tree
Ailanthus glandulosa	Ailanto
Ailanthus vilmoriniana	
	Downy tree of heaven
Aiphanes caryotifolia	Ruffle pine
	Spiny pine
Albizzia distachya	Plume albizzia
Albizzia julibrissin	Mimosa tree
	Persian albizzia
	Pink siris
	Silk tree
Albizzia lebbeck	
	East Indian walnut
	Lebbek tree
	Siris tree
	Woman's tongue tree

BOTANICAL NAMES

Albizzia lophantha   Plume albizzia
Albizzia odoratissima
                       Ceylon rosewood
Albizzia rhodesica   Red-paper tree
Albizzia toona   Red siris
Alectryon excelsum   Titoki
Alectryon subcinereus
                       Smooth rambutan
Aleurites cordata
                Japanese wood oil tree
Aleurites fordii
                Chinese wood oil tree
                         Tung oil tree
                             Tung tree
Aleurites moluccana
                     Candleberry tree
                        Candlenut tree
                        Country walnut
                         Indian walnut
                       Otaheite walnut
                          Varnish tree
Aleurites montana   Mu tree
                                  Tung
Alhagi camelorum   Camel thorn
Alhagi maurorum   Manna tree
Allamanda cathartica   Allamanda
                      Buttercup flower
                      Golden trumpet
                          Yellow bell
Alnus cordata   Italian alder
Alnus crispa mollis
                 American green alder
                          Green alder
                       Mountain alder
Alnus glutinosa   Black alder
                        Common alder
Alnus glutinosa imperialis
                      Cut-leaved alder
Alnus hirsuta   Japanese hairy alder
                     Manchurian alder
Alnus incana   European alder
                           Grey alder
                          White alder
Alnus incana pendula
                        Weeping alder
Alnus japonica   Japanese alder
Alnus maritima   Seaside alder
Alnus nepalensis   Nepalese alder
Alnus nitida   Himalayan alder
Alnus oregano   Oregon alder
                            Red alder
Alnus orientalis   Oriental alder
Alnus rhombifolia   White alder
Alnus rubra   Oregon alder
                            Red alder
Alnus rugosa   Hazel alder
                        Smooth alder
                        Speckled alder
Alnus serrulata   Smooth alder
                             Tag alder
Alnus sinuata   Sitka alder
Alnus subcordata   Caucasian alder

Alnus tenuifolia   Mountain alder
Alnus viridis
                 European green alder
                          Green alder
Aloysia citriodora   Lemon verbena
Aloysia triphylla   Lemon plant
               Lemon-scented verbena
                       Lemon verbena
Alstonia scholaris
                 Australian fever bush
                          Bitter bark
                          Devil's bit
                           Devil tree
                            Dita bark
                           Pali-mara
Alternant ficoidea   Joseph's coat
                          Parrot leaf
Althaea frutex   Althaea
                      Bush hollyhock
                        Bush mallow
                            Hibiscus
                      Rose of sharon
                       Tree hollyhock
Amelanchier arborea   June berry
Amelanchier laevis
             Allegheny service berry
                          June berry
                          Shad berry
                          Shad blow
                          Shad bush
                       Snowy mespil
Amelanchier lamarckii   June berry
                       Snowy mespil
Amelanchier ovalis   Snowy mespil
Amhertsia nobilis   Burmese pride
                      Pride of Burma
Amorpha canescens   Lead plant
Amorpha fruticosa   Bastard indigo
                         False indigo
Anacardium occidentale   Cashew
                            Maranon
Andira araroba   Araroba
                        Cabbage tree
               Ringworm powder tree
Andromeda polifolia
                        Bog rosemary
                      Marsh rosemary
Anemopsis californica
                        Yerba mansa
Annona cherimola   Cherimalla
                          Cherimoya
                       Custard apple
Annona diversifolia   Anona blanca
                               Ilama
Annona glabra   Alligator apple
                          Pond apple
Annona montana
                    Mountain soursop
                        Wild soursop
Annona muricata   Guanabana
                Prickly custard apple
                            Soursop
Annona palustris   Alligator apple

Arctostaphylos tomentosa

Annona reticulata	Bullock's heart
	Custard apple
Annona senegalensis	
	Wild custard apple
Annona squamosa	Custard apple
	Sugar apple
	Sweetsop
Anopterus glandulosus	
	Tasmanian laurel
Anthockistazam besiaca	
	Forest fever tree
Anthyllis barba-jovis	
	Jupiter's beard
Antiaris toxicaria	Upas tree
Antidesma bunius	Bignay
	Chinese laurel
Aphananthe aspera	Muku tree
Aralia chinensis	
	Chinese angelica tree
Aralia cordata	Udo
Aralia elata	Angelica tree
	Japanese angelica tree
Aralia hispida	Bristly sarsaparilla
Aralia japonica	Castor oil plant
	Fig-leaf palm
	Formosa rice tree
	Japanese fatsia
	Paper plant
Aralia nudicaulis	
	American sarsaparilla
	Rabbit root
	Sarsaparilla
	Spikenard
	Wild sarsaparilla
Aralia racemosa	
	American spikenard
	Life-of-man
	Petty morel
	Spikenard
Aralia sieboldii	Fig-leaf palm
Aralia spinosa	Angelica tree
	Devil's walking-stick
	Hercules' club
	Prickly ash
Araucaria angustifolium	
	Brazilian araucaria
	Brazilian pine
	Candelabra tree
	Pirana pine
Araucaria araucana	Chile pine
	Monkey-puzzle
Araucaria bidwillii	Bunya-bunya
	Bunya pine
Araucaria columnaris	
	New caledonia pine
Araucaria cunninghamii	
	Hoop pine
	Moreton Bay pine
Araucaria excelsa	
	Norfolk Island pine

Araucaria heterophylla	
	Australian pine
	House pine
	Norfolk Island pine
Araucaria hunsteinii	Klinki pine
Arbutus andrachne	
	Cyprus strawberry tree
	Eastern strawberry tree
	Grecian strawberry tree
Arbutus × andrachnoides	
	Hybrid strawberry tree
Arbutus menziesii	Madrona
	Pacific madrone
Arbutus unedo	Cane apple
	Killarney strawberry tree
Archontophoenix alexandrae	
	Alexandra palm
	Northern bungalow palm
Archontophoenix cunninghamiana	
	Piccabeen bungalow palm
	Piccabeen palm
Arctostaphylos andersonii	
	Heart-leaf manzanita
Arctostaphylos canescens	
	Hoary manzanita
Arctostaphylos cinerea	
	Del norte manzanita
Arctostaphylos columbiana	
	Hairy manzanita
Arctostaphylos crustacea	
	Brittle-leaf manzanita
Arctostaphylos densiflora	
	Sonoma manzanita
Arctostaphylos glandulosa	
	Eastwood manzanita
Arctostaphylos glauca	
	Big-berry manzanita
Arctostaphylos insularis	
	Island manzanita
Arctostaphylos manzanita	
	Bearberry
	Manzanita
	Parry manzanita
Arctostaphylos mariposa	
	Mariposa manzanita
Arctostaphylos morroensis	
	Morro manzanita
Arctostaphylos obispoensis	
	Serpentine manzanita
Arctostaphylos otayensis	
	Otay manzanita
Arctostaphylos pajaroensis	
	Pajaro manzanita
Arctostaphylos patula	
	Greenleaf manzanita
	Green manzanita
Arctostaphylos pungens	
	Mexican manzanita
Arctostaphylos silvicola	
	Silver-leaf manzanita
Arctostaphylos tomentosa	
	Shaggy-bark manzanita

Arctostaphylos uva-ursi	
	Bear's grape
	Common bearberry
	Hog cranberry
	Kinnikinick
	Mealberry
	Mountain box
	Red bearberry
	Sandberry
Arctostaphylos viscida	
	White-leaf manzanita
Arctous alpinus	Black bearberry
Ardisia crenata	Coralberry
	Spiceberry
Ardisia escallonioides	Marlberry
Areca aleracea	Betel-nut palm
	Cabbage palm
Areca catechu	Areca-nut palm
	Betel-nut palm
	Betel palm
	Catechu
	Pinang
Areca lutescens	Butterfly palm
Arecastrum romanzoffianum	
	Queen palm
Arenga pinnata	Areng palm
	Black fibre palm
	Gomuti palm
	Sugar palm
Argania spinosa	Argan tree
	Morocco ironwood
Argemone mexicana	Devil's fig
	Mexican poppy
Aristotelia racemosa	
	New Zealand wineberry
Aronia arbutifolia	Chokeberry
	Red chokeberry
Aronia melanocarpa	
	Black chokeberry
Aronia prunifolia	
	Purple chokeberry
Artocarpus altilis	Breadfruit
Artocarpus heterophyllus	Jack fruit
Artocarpus incisus	Breadfruit
Artocarpus lakoocha	Monkey jack
Asimina triloba	Pawpaw
Astragalus gummifer	
	Gum tragacanth
Astrocaryum aculeatum	Tucuma
Atherosperma moschata	
	Plume nutmeg
Atherosperma moschatum	
	Black sassafras
	Southern sassafras
Athrotaxis cupressoides	
	Smooth Tasmanian cedar
Athrotaxis laxifolia	Summit cedar
Athrotaxis selaginoides	
	King William pine
Atriplex canescens	Grey sage brush
Atriplex halimus	Sea orach
	Tree purslane

Atriplex portulacoides	Sea purslane
Attalea funifira	Piassaba
Aucomea klainiana	Gaboon
Aucuba japonica	Japanese laurel
	Spotted laurel
Austrocedrus chilensis	
	Chilean cedar
	Chilean incense cedar
Averrhoa bilimbi	Bilimbi
Avicennia nitida	Black mangrove
Azalea obtusa	Kirishima azalea
Azalea oldhamii	Formosan azalea
Azalea procumbens	Alpine azalea
Azalea viscosa	Swamp honeysuckle
Azara integrifolia	Goldspire
Azim tetracantha	Needle bush
Backhousia citriodora	
	Sweet verbena tree
Bactris gasipaes	Maraja palm
	Peach palm
	Pejibaye
Bactris guineensis	Prickly pole
	Tobago cane
Bactris major	Prickly palm
Banksia grandis	
	Australian honeysuckle
	Bull banksia
Banksia integrifolia	Coast banksia
Banksia littoralis	Swamp banksia
Baphia nitida	
	Barwood
	Camwood
Barringtonia acutangula	
	Indian oak
Bauhinia purpurea	Bull-hoof tree
	Butterfly tree
	Camel's foot
	Orchid tree
	Ox-hoof tree
Bauhinia variegata	Ebonywood
	Purple orchid tree
Beaucarnea recurvata	
	Elephant's foot
	Ponytail
Benzoin aestivale	Spice bush
Berberis aristata	Nepal barberry
Berberis hypokerina	Silver holly
Berberis ilicifolia	
	Holly-leaved barberry
Berberis morrisonensis	
	Mount Morrison barberry
Berberis thunbergii	
	Japanese barberry
Berberis thunbergii atropurpurea	
	Purple-leaf barberry
Berberis thunbergii aurea	
	Golden-leaved barberry
Berberis vulgaris	Barberry
	Common barberry
	Pipperidge

Berberis vulgaris atropurpurea
Purple-leaf barberry

Berberis wilsoniae
Wilson's barberry
Wilson's berberis

Bertholletia excelsa Brazil nut
Cream nut
Para nut

Betula alba dalecarlica
Swedish birch

Betula albosinensis
Chinese red-barked birch

Betula alleghaniensis Grey birch
Yellow birch

Betula coerulea-grandis
Blue birch

Betula ermanii Erman's birch
Russian rock birch

Betula glandulosa Dwarf birch

Betula grossa
Japanese cherry birch

Betula jacquemontii
Himalayan birch
Jacquemont's birch
White-barked birch
White-barked Himalayan birch

Betula japonica
Japanese white birch

Betula lenta Black birch
Cherry birch
Mahogany birch
Mountain mahogany
Sweet birch

Betula lutea Yellow birch

Betula mandschurica
Japanese white birch

Betula maximowicziana
Japanese large-leaved birch
Japanese red birch
Monarch birch

Betula medwediewii
Transcaucasian birch

Betula nana Dwarf birch
Rock birch

Betula nigra Black birch
Red birch
River birch

Betula occidentalis Water birch

Betula papyrifera Canoe birch
Paper birch
White birch

Betula pendula
Common silver birch
European white birch
Lady-of-the-woods
Silver birch
Warty birch
White birch

Betula pendula dalecarlica Cut-
leaf birch
Swedish birch
Weeping Swedish birch

Betula pendula purpurea
Purple birch

Purple-leaf birch

Betula pendula tristis
Weeping birch

Betula pendula youngii
Weeping birch
Young's weeping birch

Betula platyphylla Szechuan birch

Betula platyphylla japonica
Japanese white birch

Betula populifolia Fire birch
Grey birch
Oldfield birch
White birch

Betula pubescens
Common white birch
Downy birch
Hairy birch
White birch

Betula utilis Himalayan birch

Bischofia javanica Toog

Bixia orellana Achiote
Annatto
Lipstick tree

Blighia sapida Akee

Bolusanthus speciosus Tree wisteria

Bombax buonopozense
Gold coast bombax

Bombax ceiba
Red silk-cotton tree

Bombax malabaricum Cotton tree
Indian silk-cotton tree
Red silk-cotton tree

Borassus flabellifer Doub palm
Palmyra palm
Tala palm
Toddy palm
Wine palm

Boswellia thurifera Frankincense
Olibanus tree

Bougainvillea glabra Paper flower

Bourreria ovata Strongback

Brachychiton acerifolius
Flame bottle tree
Flame tree
Illawarra flame tree

Brachychiton australis
Broad-leaved bottle tree
Flame tree

Brachychiton discolor Hat tree
Queensland lace bark
Scrub bottle tree

Brachychiton gregorii
Desert kurrajong

Brachychiton populneus Kurrajong

Brachychiton rupestris
Narrow-leaved bottle tree
Queensland bottle tree

Brahea armata Blue fan palm
Blue hesper palm
Grey goddess
Mexican blue palm

Brahea brandegeei
San José hesper palm

Brahea edulis

Brahea edulis	Guadalupe palm
Brahea elegans	Franceschi palm
Brassaia actinophylla	
	Australian ivy palm
	Australian umbrella tree
	Octopus tree
	Queensland umbrella tree
	Queen's umbrella tree
	Starleaf
Breynia disticha	Foliage flower
	Snowbush
Brosimum alicastrum	Breadnut
	Cow tree
Broussonetia papyrifera	
	Paper mulberry
	Tapa-cloth tree
Brownea grandiceps	
	Rose of Venezuela
Brunfelsia americana	
	Lady-of-the-night
Brunfelsia australis	
	Morning-noon-and-night
	Paraguay jasmine
	Yesterday-and-today
Brunfelsia undulata	Rain tree
Brunfelsia uniflora	Manaca
	Vegetable mercury
Bucida buceras	Black olive
Buddleia alternifolia	
	Butterfly bush
	Fountain buddleia
Buddleia davidii	Buddleia
	Butterfly bush
	Orange eye
	Summer lilac
Buddleia globosa	Orange ball tree
Buddleia salviifolia	
	South African sagewood
Bumelia lanuginosa	Black haw
	Chattamwood
	False buckthorn
	Gum elastic
	Shittimwood
Bumelia lycioides	Buckthorn
	Ironwood
	Mock orange
	Shittimwood
	Southern buckthorn
Burchelia bubalina	
	Wild pomegranate
Bursaria spinosa	Box thorn
Bursera microphylla	Elephant tree
	Torote
Bursera simaruba	Gumbo-limbo
	Gum-elemi
	West Indian birch
Butia capitata	Jelly palm
	Pindo palm
Butia eriospatha	Woolly butia palm
Butia yatay	Jelly palm
	Yatay palm
Butyrospermum paradoxum	
	Shea butter tree

Butyrospermum parkii	
	Shea butter tree
Buxus aurea pendula	
	Weeping golden box
Buxus balearica	Balearic box
Buxus macowani	Cape box
Buxus prostrata	Horizontal box
Buxus sempervirens	Boxwood
	Common box
	Dudgeon
Buxus suffruticosa	Edging box
Byrsonima crassifolia	
	Charcoal tree
Caesalpinia braziliensis	
	Brazilwood
Caesalpinia coriaria	Divi-divi
Caesalpinia echinata	Brazilwood
	Peachwood
Caesalpinia ferrea	
	Brazilian ironwood
Caesalpinia gilliesii	
	Bird of paradise
Caesalpinia peltophoroides	
	False brazilwood
	Sibipiruna
Caesalpinia pulcherrima	
	Barbados pride
	Dwarf poinciana
	Flower fence
	Peacock flower
	Pride of Barbados
Caesalpinia sappan	Brazilwood
	Sappanwood
Caesalpinia spinosa	Tara
Caesalpinia vesicaria	Brasiletto
Calamus rotang	Rattan cane
Callicarpa americana	
	Beautyberry
	French mulberry
Callistemon citrinus	Bottlebrush
	Crimson bottlebrush
	Lemon bottlebrush
Callistemon salignus	
	Willow-leaved bottlebrush
Callistemon speciosus	
	Albany bottlebrush
Callistemon viminalis	
	Weeping bottlebrush
Callitris calcarata	
	Black cypress pine
Callitris columellaris	
	Murray river pine
	White cypress pine
Callitris endlicheri	
	Black cypress pine
	Red cypress pine
Callitris glauca	Murray river pine
	White cypress pine
Callitris intratropica	
	Northern cypress pine
Callitris macleayana	
	Port Macquarie pine

TREES, BUSHES, AND SHRUBS

Carpenteria californica

Callitris muelleri
    Mueller's cypress pine
Callitris oblonga
    Tasmanian cypress pine
Callitris preissii
    Common cypress pine
    Rottnest island pine
Callitris rhomboides
    Oyster-bay pine
    Port Jackson pine
Callitris robusta
    Common cypress pine
Callitris verrucosa   Turpentine pine
Calluna erica   Heather
Calluna vulgaris   Ling
    Scotch heather
Calluna vulgaris alba
    White heather
Calocedrus bidwillii   Pahautea
Calocedrus chilensis
    Chilean incense cedar
Calocedrus decurrens
    California incense cedar
    Incense cedar
Calocedrus formosana
    Formosa incense cedar
Calocedrus macrolepis
    Chinese incense cedar
Calocedrus plumosa   Kawaka
Calodendrum capense
    Cape chestnut
Calophyllum brasiliense
    Calaba tree
    Jacareuba
    Maria
    Saint Mary's wood
    Santa Maria
Calophyllum inophyllum
    Alexandrian laurel
    Indian laurel
    Laurelwood
Calothamnus asper
    Rough netbush
Calothamnus gilesii Giles' netbush
Calothamnua validus
    Barren's clawflower
Calothamnus villosus
    Woolly netbush
Calotropis gigantea
    Bowstring hemp
    Crown plant
    Madar
Calotropis procera   Calotropis
    Mudar
Calycanthus fertilis
    Carolina allspice
Calycanthus floridus
    Carolina allspice
    Pineapple shrub
    Strawberry shrub
Calycanthus occidentalis
    Californian allspice

Calycophyllum candissimum
    Degame
Calyptronoma dulcis
    Cuban manac
Calyptronoma occidentalis
    Long-thatch palm
    Jamaican manac
Camellia japonica
    Common camellia
Camellia japonica rusticana
    Snow camellia
Camellia oleifera   Tea oil plant
Camellia sasanqua
    Sasanqua camellia
Camellia sinensis   Tea plant
Camellia sinensis assamensis
    Assam tea
Camellia thea   Tea plant
Camellia × williamsii
  c.f.coates   Fishtail camellia
Cananga odorata   Ilang-ilang
Canarium commune   Kenari
Canella alba   White cinnamon
Canella winterana
    White cinnamon
    Wild cinnamon
Cantua buxifolia   Magic flower
    Sacred flower
Capparis cynophallophora
    Jamaica caper tree
Capparis spinosa   Caper bush
Caragana arborescens
    Siberian pea tree
Caragana arborescens pendula
    Weeping pea tree
Caragana frutex
    Russian pea shrub
Caragana jubata
    Shag-pine pea shrub
Caragana pygmaea
    Dwarf pea tree
Carica cundinamarcensis
    Mountain papaw
    Mountain pawpaw
Carica papaya   Common papaw
    Common pawpaw
    Melon tree
    Papaw
    Papaya
    Pawpaw
Carica pubescens Mountain papaya
Carissa bispinosa   Hedge thorn
Carissa carandas   Karanda
Carissa grandiflora   Amatungulu
    Natal plum
Carissa macrocarpa   Amatungulu
Carmichaelia odorata Lilac broom
Carpenteria californica
    Californian anemone bush
    Californian mock orange
    Tree anemone

Carpinus betulus
Common hornbeam
European hornbeam
Hornbeam

Carpinus caroliniana
American hornbeam
Blue beech
Water beech

Carpinus japonica
Japanese hornbeam

Carpinus orientalis
Eastern hornbeam
Oriental hornbeam

Carya aquatica Bitter pecan
Water hickory

Carya cathayensis Chinese hickory

Carya cordiformis Bitter nut
Pig nut
Swamp hickory

Carya glabra Broom hickory
Hog nut
Pignut hickory

Carya illinoensis Pecan

Carya laciniosa King nut
Shellbark hickory

Carya myristiciformis
Nutmeg hickory

Carya ovalis Red hickory

Carya ovata Shagbark hickory
Shellbark hickory

Carya pallida Pale hickory
Sand hickory

Carya pecan Pecan

Carya tomentosa Bigbud hickory
Mockernut
Squarenut
White-heart hickory

Caryota mitis
Burmese fishtail palm
Clustered fishtail palm
Tufted fishtail palm

Caryota urens Jaggery palm
Kittul tree
Sago palm
Toddy palm
Wine palm

Casimiroa edulis Mexican apple
White sapote
Zapote blanco

Casimiroa tetrameria Matasano

Cassia acutifolia Alexandrian senna
Senna

Cassia alata Candlestick senna
Christmas candle
Empress candle plant
Ringworm cassia
Ringworm senna

Cassia angustifolia Indian senna
Tinnevelly senna

Cassia artemisioides
Feathery cassia
Wormwood senna

Cassia auriculata Avaram
Tanner's cassia

Cassia chamaecrista Ground senna

Cassia corymbosa Buttercup bush

Cassia covesii Desert cassia

Cassia didymobotrya Candle bush
Golden wonder

Cassia elata Ringworm senna

Cassia eremophila Desert cassia

Cassia fasciculata Golden cassia
Partridge pea
Prairie senna

Cassia fistula Golden rain
Golden shower
Indian laburnum
Pudding-pipe tree
Purging cassia
Purging fistula

Cassia grandis Horse cassia
Pink shower

Cassia hebecarpa Wild senna

Cassia javanica
Appleblossom cassia
Appleblossom senna
Pink cassia

Cassia laevigata Smooth senna

Cassia marilandica Wild senna

Cassia moschata Bronze shower

Cassia nictitans
Wild sensitive plant

Cassia nodosa Jointwood
Pink-and-white shower

Cassia occidentalis Coffee senna
Stinking weed
Styptic weed

Cassia senna Alexandrian senna

Cassia siamea Kassod tree

Cassia splendida Golden wonder

Cassia tora Sicklepod
Sickle senna

Cassine glauca Ceylon tea

Cassine laneana
Bermuda olivewood bark

Cassine orientalis False olive

Cassinia fulvida Golden bush
Golden heather

Cassinia vauvilliersii albida
Silver heather

Castanea alnifolia
Bush chinquapin
Downy chestnut

Castanea crenata
Japanese chestnut

Castanea dentata
American chestnut

Castanea mollissima
Chinese chestnut

Castanea ozarkensis
Ozark chestnut

Castanea pumila
Chinquapin chestnut

Castanea sativa European chestnut
Spanish chestnut
Sweet chestnut

Castanea sativa albomarginata
  Variegated sweet chestnut
Castanea sativa
  aureomarginata
  Variegated sweet chestnut
Castanea sempervirens
  Bush chinquapin
Castanopsis chrysophylla
  Giant chinquapin
Castanopsis cuspidata
  Japanese chinquapin
Castanopsis megacarpa
  Great Malayan chestnut
Castanopsis sempervirens
  Bush chinquapin
Castanospermum australe
  Black bean tree
  Moreton bay chestnut
Castilla elastica
  Castilla rubber tree
  Panama rubber tree
Casuarina cunninghamiana
  Australian river oak
  River oak
Casuarina equisetifolia
  Australian beefwood
  Australian pine
  Beechwood
  Horsetail she-oak
  Horsetail tree
  Mile tree
  Red beefwood
  South sea ironwood
  Swamp she-oak
Casuarina nana   Dwarf she-oak
Casuarina stricta
  Drooping she-oak
  She-oak
Casuarina torulosa
  Australian forest oak
Catalpa bignonioides   Catalpa
  Indian bean tree
  Southern catalpa
Catalpa bignonioides aurea
  Golden-leaved catalpa
Catalpa × *erubescens*
  Hybrid catalpa
Catalpa fargesii   Farges catalpa
Catalpa × *hybrida*   Hybrid catalpa
Catalpa ovata   Chinese catalpa
  Yellow catalpa
Catalpa speciosa   Catawba
  Cigar tree
  Indian bean
  Northern catalpa
  Western catalpa
Catesbaea spinosa   Lily thorn
Catha edulis   Abyssinian tea
  Arabian tea
  Cafta
  Chat
  Khat
  Qat
  Somali tea

Cavanillesia plantanifolia   Cuipo
Ceanothus americanus
  Mountain-sweet
  New Jersey tea plant
  Red root
  Wild snowball
Ceanothus arboreus
  Catalina ceanothus
  Catalina mountain lilac
  Felt-leaf ceanothus
Ceanothus caeruleus
  Azure ceanothus
Ceanothus cordulatus   Snowbush
Ceanothus crassifolius
  Hoaryleaf ceanothus
Ceanothus cuneatus   Buckbrush
Ceanothus cyaneus
  San Diego ceanothus
Ceanothus dentatus
  Santa Barbara ceanothus
Ceanothus foliosus
  Wavyleaf ceanothus
Ceanothus gloriosus
  Point Reyes ceanothus
Ceanothus griseus
  Carmel ceanothus
Ceanothus griseus horizontalis
  Carmel creeper
  Yankee point ceanothus
Ceanothus impressus
  Santa Barbara ceanothus
Ceanothus integerrimus
  Deerbrush
  Deerbush
Ceanothus masonii
  Bolinas ridge ceanothus
Ceanothus papillosus
  Wart leaf ceanothus
Ceanothus prostratus
  Mahala-mat
  Squaw carpet
Ceanothus pumilus   Siskiyou-mat
Ceanothus purpureus
  Holly leaf ceanothus
Ceanothus ramulosis
  Coast ceanothus
Ceanothus rigidus
  Monterey ceanothus
Ceanothus sanguineus   Oregon tea
  Wild lilac
Ceanothus sorediatus   Jim brush
  Jim bush
Ceanothus spinosus
  Green-bark ceanothus
  Red-heart
Ceanothus thyrsiflorus
  Blueblossom
  Californian lilac
Ceanothus thyrsiflorus repens
  Creeping blueblossom
Ceanothus tomentosus
  Woolly-leaf ceanothus
Cecropia palmata   Snakewood tree

Cecropia peltata

Cecropia peltata	Trumpet tree
Cedrela odorata	Barbados cedar
	Cigar-box cedar
	Spanish cedar
	West Indian cedar
Cedrela sinensis	Chinese cedar
Cedronella canariensis	
	Balm of gilead
	Canary balm
Cedrus atlantica	Atlas cedar
Cedrus atlantica glauca	
	Blue atlas cedar
	Blue cedar
Cedrus atlantica pendula	
	Weeping atlas cedar
Cedrus brevifolia	Cyprian cedar
	Cyprus cedar
Cedrus deodara	Deodar
	Himalayan cedar
	Indian cedar
Cedrus deodara aurea	
	Golden deodar cedar
	Western Himalayan cedar
Cedrus libani	Cedar of Lebanon
Ceiba pentandra	Kapok tree
	Silk-cotton tree
	White silk-cotton tree
Celtis africanus	White stinkwood
Celtis australis	Honeyberry
	Lote tree
	Mediterranean hackberry
	Nettle tree
	Southern nettle tree
Celtis caucasica	
	Caucasian nettle tree
Celtis iguanaea	Granjeno
Celtis japonica	Chinese hackberry
	Japanese hackberry
Celtis kraussiana	Stinkwood
Celtis laevigata	
	Mississippi hackberry
	Sugarberry
Celtis occidentalis	Hackberry
	Nettle tree
	Sugarberry
Celtis sinensis	Chinese hackberry
	Japanese hackberry
Cephaelis ipecacuanha	
	Ipecacuanha
Cephalanthus occidentalis	
	Button bush
Cephalotaxus fortunii	
	Chinese plum yew
	Cowtail pine
	Plum yew
Cephalotaxus harringtonia	
	Cowtail pine
	Harrington plum yew
	Japanese cowtail pine
	Japanese plum-fruited yew
Cephalotaxus harringtonia drupacea	Drooping cowtail pine
	Japanese plum yew

Cephalotaxus sinensis	
	Chinese cowtail pine
Ceratonia siliqua	Algarroba bean
	Carob
	Locust bean
	Saint John's bread
Ceratopetalum apetalum	
	Lightwood
Ceratopetalum gummiferum	
	Red gum
Cercidiphyllum japonicum	
	Katsura
Cercidium floridum	Palo verde
Cercis canadensis	
	American judas tree
	American redbud
	Redbud
Cercis chinensis	Chinese redbud
Cercis occidentalis	
	Western redbud
Cercis racemosa	Chinese redbud
Cercis siliquastrum	Judas tree
	Love tree
Cercocarpus montanus	
	Mountain mahogany
Ceroxylon alpinum	Wax palm
Cestrum diurnum	Day cestrum
	Day jessamine
Cestrum nocturnum	
	Night jasmine
	Night jessamine
Cestrum parqui	
	Willow-leaved jessamine
Chaenomeles japonica	
	Dwarf quince
	Lesser flowering quince
Chaenomeles speciosa	
	Flowering quince
	Japanese quince
Chaenomeles speciosa nivalis	
	Ornamental quince
Chamaecistus procumbens	
	Alpine azalea
Chamaecyparis formosensis	
	Formosan cedar
	Formosan cypress
Chamaecyparis lawsoniana	
	Lawson's cypress
	Port Orford cedar
Chamaecyparis lawsoniana allumii	Scarab cypress
Chamaecyparis lawsonia nootkatensis	Nootka cypress
Chamaecyparis lawsoniana stewartii	
	Golden lawson's cypress
Chamaecyparis nootkatensis	
	Alaska cedar
	Alaska yellow cedar
	Canoe cedar
	Nootka cypress
	Yellow cypress

Citrullus colocynthis

Chamaecyparis obtusa
Hinoki cypress
Japanese false cypress
Tree of the sun

Chamaecyparis obtusa crippsii
Golden hinoki cypress

Chamaecyparis pisifera
Sawara cypress

Chamaecyparis thyoides
Atlantic white cedar
Southern white cedar
Swamp white cedar
White cedar
White cypress

Chamaedaphne calyculata
Cassandra
Leather leaf

Chamaedorea elegans
Good-luck palm
Parlour palm

Chamaedorea erumpens
Bamboo palm

Chamaedorea seifrizii   Reed palm

Chamaedorea tepejilote   Pacaya

Chamaelaucium uncinatum
Geraldton wax

Chamaerops humilis
Dwarf fan palm
European fan palm

Chilopsis linearis   Desert willow
Flowering willow

Chimonanthus praecox
Wintersweet

Chionanthus retusa
Chinese fringe tree

Chionanthus virginicus
American fringe tree
Fringe tree
Old man's beard
Poison ash
Snowflower
Virginian snowflower

Chiranthodendron pentadactylon
Handflower tree
Mexican hand plant

Chlorophora excelsa   Iroko

Chlorophora tinctoria   Fustic

Chloroxylon swietenia
East Indian satinwood
Satinwood

Choisya ternata
Mexican orange blossom

Chondrodendron tomentosum
Curare
Pareira

Chorisia speciosa   Floss silk tree

Chrysalidocarpus lutescens
Areca palm
Butterfly palm
Golden-feather palm
Madagascar palm
Yellow butterfly palm
Yellow palm

Chrysobalanus icaco   Coco palm
Coco plum
Icaco

Chrysolepis chrysophylla
Golden chestnut

Chrysolepis cuspidata
Japanese chestnut

Chrysolepis megacarpa
Greater Malayan chestnut

Chrysolepis sempervirens
Bush chinquapin

Chrysophyllum cainito   Caimita
Star apple

Chrysophyllum oliviforme
Jamaican damson plum
Satinleaf

Cinchona calisaya   Calisaya
Jesuit's bark
Yellow bark

Cinchona cordifolia
Cartagena bark

Cinchona micrantha   Huanuco

Cinchona officinalis   Quinine

Cinchona succirubra
Peruvian bark

Cinchona succirula   Red cinchona

Cinnamodendron corticosum
False winter's bark
Red canella

Cinnamomum burmanii
Padang cassia

Cinnamomum camphora
Camphor tree

Cinnamomum cassia   Cassia
Cassia bark tree
Chinese cinnamon

Cinnamomum loureirii
Cassia-flower tree
Saigon cinnamon

Cinnamomum zeylanicum
Ceylon cinnamon
Cinnamon
Cinnamon tree

Cistus ladanifer   Gum cistus

Cistus monspeliensis
Montpelier rock rose

Cistus salviifolius
Sage-leaved rock rose

Citharexylum fruticosum
Fiddlewood

Citharexylum spinosum
Fiddlewood
Zitherwood

× *Citrofortunella floridana*
Limequat

× *Citrofortunella mitis*
Calamondin
Panama orange

× *Citrofortunella swinglei*
Limequat

× *Citroncirus webberi*   Citrange

Citrullus colocynthis   Bitter apple

Citrus aurantifolia	Key lime
	Lime
	Mexican lime
	West Indian lime
Citrus aurantifolia × fortunella	Limequat
Citrus aurantium	Bigarade
	Bitter orange
	Seville orange
	Sour orange
Citrus aurantium bergamia	Bergamot
	Bergamot orange
Citrus bergamia	Bergamot orange
Citrus grandis	Pomelo
	Pumelo
Citrus ichangensis	Ichang lemon
Citrus limetta	Sweet lime
Citrus limon	Lemon
Citrus × limonia	Lemandarin
	Mandarin lime
	Rangpur lime
Citrus lumia	Sweet lemon
Citrus otaitensis	Otaheite orange
Citrus maxima	Pomelo
	Pompelmous
	Pummelo
	Shaddock
Citrus medica	Citron
Citrus medica cedra	Cedrat lemon
Citrus × nobilis	Tangor
Citrus × nobilis king	King mandarin
	King of Siam
	King orange
Citrus × nobilis temple	Temple orange
Citrus × paradisi	Grapefruit
Citrus paradisi × citrus reticulata	Ugli fruit
Citrus reticulata	Clementine
	Mandarin orange
	Satsuma orange
	Tangerine
Citrus sinensis	Orange
	Sweet orange
Citrus tachibana	Tachibana orange
Citrus × tangelo	Tangelo
Citrus trifoliata	Hardy orange
Cladrastis chinensis	Chinese yellow-wood
Cladrastis lutea	American yellowwood
	Virgilia
	Yellowwood
Cladrastis platycarpa	Japanese yellowwood
Cladrastis sinensis	Chinese yellowwood
Cladrastis tinctoria	American yellowwood

Cladrastis wilsonii	Wilson's yellowwood
Clausena lansium	Wampee
	Wampi
Clerodendrum fargesii	Glory bower
	Glory tree
Clerodendrum indicum	Tube flower
	Turk's turban
Clerodendrum paniculatum	Pagoda flower
Clerodendrum × speciosum	Java glory bean
	Pagoda flower
Clerodendrum thomsoniae	Bag flower
	Bleeding glory-bower
	Bleeding-heart vine
	Glory tree
Clerodendrum trichotomum	Glory tree
Clethra acuminata	White alder
Clethra alnifolia	Sweet pepperbush
	Summer-sweet
Clethra arborea	Folhado
	Lily-of-the-valley tree
Clethra tomentosa	Downy clethra
Clianthus formosus	Glory pea
	Sturt's desert pea
Clianthus puniceus	Lobster claw
	Parrot bill
	Parrot's bill
Cliftonia monophylla	Black titi
	Buckwheat brush
	Buckwheat tree
	Ironwood
	Titi
Clitoria ternatea	Butterfly pea
Cneorum tricoccum	Spurge olive
Coccoloba diversifolia	Pigeon plum
	Snailseed
Coccoloba uvifera	Kino
	Platterleaf
	Sea grape
Coccothrinax argentata	Florida silver palm
	Silver palm
Coccothrinax argentea	Broom palm
	Silver thatch
Coccothrinax crinata	Thatch palm
Cochlospermum frazeri	Kapok bush
Cochlospermum religiosum	Buttercup tree
	Silk-cotton tree
	Yellow-cotton tree
Cochlospermum vitifolium	Buttercup tree
	Rose imperial

TREES, BUSHES, AND SHRUBS

Cocos nucifera   Coconut palm
Codiaeum variegatum   Croton
    Variegated croton
Codonocarpus cotinifolius
    Bell-fruit tree
Coffea arabica   Arabian coffee
    Coffee
Coffea canephora   Robusta coffee
    Wild robusta coffee
Coffea liberica   Liberian coffee
Coffea zanguebariae
    Zanzibar coffee
Cola acuminata   Abata cola
    Cola tree
    Goora nut
    Kola
    Kola nut
Cola anomala   Bamenda cola
Cola nitida   Cola
    Gbanja cola
    Kola
Cola verticilliata   Owe cola
Coleonema pulchrum
    Confetti bush
Colpothrinax wrightii   Barrel palm
    Bottle palm
    Cuban belly palm
Combretum erythrophyllum
    Bush willow
Combretum microphyllum
    Burning bush
    Flame creeper
Commifera abyssinica   Myrrh
Commifera molmol   Myrrh
Commifera myrrha   Myrrh
Conium maculatum   Hemlock
Connarus guianensis   Zebra wood
Conocarpus erectus   Buttonwood
Conospermum huegelii
    Slender smoke bush
    Smoke bush
Conospermum stoechadis
    Australian smoke bush
Copernica cerifera   Carnanba palm
    Carnauba palm
Copernica macroglossa
    Petticoat palm
Coprifera mopane   Turpentine tree
Copernica prunifera
    Carnauba wax palm
Coprosma baueri
    Looking-glass bush
Coprosma repens
    Looking-glass bush
    Mirror plant
Corchorus capsularis   Jute
    White jute
Corchorus olitorius   Jew's mallow
    Jute
    Melukhie
    Tossa jute

Cordia alliodora   Ecuador laurel
    Laurel
    Laurel negro
Cordia boissieri   Anacahuita
Cordia dentata   Jackwood
Cordia myxa   Assyrian plum
    Selu
Cordia nitida   Red manjack
    West Indian cherry
Cordia sebestena   Anaconoa
    Cordia
    Geiger tree
    Geranium tree
    Spanish cordia
Cordyline australis   Cabbage tree
    Fountain dracaena
    Giant dracaena
    Grass palm
    Palm lily
Cordyline fruticosa
    Good-luck plant
    Tree of kings
Cordyline indivisa   Blue dracaena
Cordyline terminalis
    Good-luck plant
    Hawaiian good-luck plant
    Tree of kings
Corema album
    Portuguese crowberry
Corema conradii
    Plymouth crowberry
Coriaria nepalensis   Tanner's tree
Coriaria ruscifolia   Deu
Cornus alba   Red-barked dogwood
    Siberian dogwood
    Tartar dogwood
Cornus alba aurea
    Golden dogwood
Cornus alba elegantissima
    Silver dogwood
    Silver variegated dogwood
Cornus alba sibirica
    Westonbirt dogwood
Cornus alba spaethii
    Golden variegated dogwood
Cornus alternifolia   Green osier
    Pagoda dogwood
Cornus amomum   Red willow
    Silky dogwood
Cornus canadensis   Bunchberry
    Crackerberry
    Creeping dogwood
    Dwarf cornel
    Puddingberry
Cornus capitata   Bentham's cornel
    Strawberry tree
Cornus capitata florida
    Flowering dogwood
Cornus capitata mas
    Cordelian cherry

Cornus controversa
Giant dogwood
Japanese dogwood
Table dogwood
Wedding-cake tree

Cornus controversa variegata
Variegated Japanese dogwood

Cornus florida
American boxwood
Flowering dogwood
New England boxwood
Virginia dogwood
White dogwood

Cornus florida rainbow
Rainbow dogwood

Cornus florida rubra
Pink dogwood

Cornus glabrata Brown dogwood

Cornus kousa Japanese dogwood
Kousa

Cornus kousa chinensis
Chinese dogwood

Cornus mas Cornel
Cornelian cherry
Sorbet

Cornus nuttallii
Mountain dogwood
Nuttall's dogwood
Pacific dogwood

Cornus officinalis
Japanese cornel
Japanese cornelian cherry

Cornus purpusii Silky dogwood

Cornus racemosa Grey dogwood
Panicled dogwood

Cornus rugosa
Round-leaved dogwood

Cornus sanguinea
Blood-twig dogwood
Common dogwood
Dogberry
Dogwood
Pegwood
Shrubby dogwood

Cornus sericea American dogwood
Red osier dogwood

Cornus stolonifera
Red osier dogwood

Cornus stolonifera flaviramea
Yellow-stemmed dogwood

Cornus stricta Stiff dogwood

Cornus suecica Dwarf cornel

Corokia cotoneaster
Wire-netting bush

Coronilla emerus Scorpion senna

Corpinus betulus
European hornbeam

Correa alba Botany bay tea tree

Corylopsis paucifolia
Buttercup winter hazel

Corylopsis spicata Corylopsis
Spike winter hazel

Corylus americana
American filbert
American hazel

Corylus avellana Cobnut
Common hazel
Filbert

Corylus avellana aurea
Golden hazel

Corylus avellana contorta
Contorted hazel
Corkscrew hazel
Harry Lauder's walking stick

Corylus avellana heterophylla Cut-leaved hazel

Corylus chinensis Chinese filbert
Chinese hazel

Corylus colurna Tree hazel
Turkish filbert
Turkish hazel

Corylus cornuta Beaked filbert
Beaked hazel

Corylus hamamelis Witch hazel

Corylus maxima Filbert
Giant filbert
Kentish cob

Corylus maxima purpurea
Purple-leaved cob
Purple-leaved filbert

Corylus sieboldiana
Japanese hazel

Corylus tibetica Tibetan hazel

Corynocarpus laevigata
Karaka
New Zealand laurel

Corypha australis
Australian cabbage palm
Australian fan palm
Cabbage palm
Gippsland palm

Corypha elata Gebang palm

Corypha umbraculifera
Talipot palm

Cotinus americanus
American smoke tree
Chittamwood

Cotinus coggygria Smoke bush
Smoke tree
Venetian sumach
Wig tree

Cotinus coggygria purpureus
Burning bush
Purple smoke tree

Cotinus obovatus
American smoke tree
Chittamwood

Cotoneaster adpressus praecox Nan-shan bush

Cotoneaster apiculatus
Cranberry cotoneaster

Cotoneaster frigidus Cotoneaster
Himalayan tree cotoneaster

Cotoneaster horizontalis
Rock cotoneaster

Cotoneaster hybridus pendulus
Weeping cotoneaster

Cotoneaster microphyllus
Rose box

Cotoneaster simonsii
Himalayan cotoneaster

Cotoneaster × watereri
Weeping cotoneaster

Coula edulis   African walnut

Couroupita guianensis
Cannonball tree
Carrion tree

Crataegomespilus dardari
Bronvaux medlar

Crataegus altaica
Altai mountain thorn

Crataegus apiifolia
Parsley-leaved thorn

Crataegus azarolus   Azarole

Crataegus brachyacantha
Pomette bleue

Crataegus calpodendron
Blackthorn
Peacock thorn
Pear thorn

Crataegus crus-galli
Cockspur thorn

Crataegus douglasii
Black hawthorn

Crataegus flava   Summer haw
Yellow-fruited thorn
Yellow haw

Crataegus laciniata   Oriental thorn

Crataegus laevigata
Double crimson thorn
Double pink thorn
Double white thorn
English hawthorn
May
Midland hawthorn
Quick-set thorn
Red hawthorn
Red may
Two-styled hawthorn
White thorn

Crataegus × lavallei
Hybrid cockspur thorn

Crataegus mollis   Downy hawthorn
Red haw

Crataegus monogyna
Bread and cheese
Common hawthorn
Hawthorn
May
Quick
Quickthorn
Whitethorn

Crataegus monogyna biflora
Glastonbury thorn

Crataegus monogyna compacta
Dwarf hawthorn

Crataegus monogyna pendula
Weeping hawthorn

Crataegus monogyna praecox
Glastonbury thorn

Crataegus nigra
Hungarian hawthorn
Hungarian thorn

Crataegus orientalis
Oriental thorn

Crataegus oxyacanthoides
Midland hawthorn

Crataegus pedicellata   Scarlet haw

Crataegus pentagyna
Five-seeded hawthorn

Crataegus phaenopyrum
Washington thorn

Crataegus pinnatifida
Chinese hawthorn

Crataegus praecox
Glastonbury thorn

Crataegus × prunifolia
Broadleaf cockspur thorn
Frosted thorn

Crataegus submollis
Emmerson's thorn

Crataegus tanacetifolia
Tansy-leaved thorn

Crataegus tomentosa
Peacock thorn
Pear thorn

+ *Crataegomespilus dardarii*
Bronvaux medlar

Crataera gynandra   Garlic pear

Crateva religiosa
Sacred garlic pear

Crescentia cujete   Calabash tree

Crinodendron hookeriana
Lantern tree

Croton cascarilla   Cascarilla
Wild rosemary

Croton monanthogynus
Prairie tea

Cryptomeria japonica
Japanese cedar
Japanese red cedar

Cudrania tricuspidata
Chinese silkworm thorn

Cunninghamia konishii   Taiwan fir

Cunninghamia lanceolata
Chinese fir

Cunonia capensis   African red alder
Rooiels
Spoon tree

× *Cupressocyparis leylandii*
Leyland cypress

Cupressus abramsiana
Santa Cruz cypress

Cupressus arizonica
Arizona cypress
Smooth-barked Arizona cypress

Cupressus bakeri   Modoc cypress

Cupressus bakeri mathewsii
Siskiyou cypress

Cupressus cashmeriana
Kashmir cypress

Cupressus duclouxiana
Bhutan cypress

Cupressus forbesii   Tecate cypress

Cupressus funebris
Chinese weeping cypress
Mourning cypress
Weeping cypress

Cupressus glabra
Smooth Arizona cypress
Smooth-barked Arizona cypress

Cupressus goveniana
Californian cypress
Gowen's cypress

Cupressus guadalupensis
Guadalupe cypress
Tecate cypress

Cupressus lusitanica   Cedar of Goa
Mexican cypress
Portuguese cypress

Cupressus macnabiana
Macnab's cypress

Cupressus macrocarpa
Monterey cypress

Cupressus nevadensis
Piute cypress

Cupressus sargentii
Sargent's cypress

Cupressus sempervirens
Italian cypress
Mediterranean cypress

Cupressus stephensonii
Californian cypress
Cuyamaca cypress

Cupressus torulosa   Bhutan cypress
Himalayan cypress

Cussonia paniculata   Cabbage tree
Mountain kiepersol

Cussonia spicata   Cabbage tree

Cycas circinalis   Fern palm
Queen sago
Sago palm

Cycas media   Nut palm

Cycas revolta   Japanese fern palm
Japanese sago palm
Sago palm

Cyclanthera pedata   Achocha

Cydonia oblonga   Common quince
Quince

Cyphomandra betacea
Tree tomato

Cyrilla racemiflora   Black titi
Huckleberry
Ironwood
Leatherwood
Myrtle
Red titi
Titi
White titi

Cyrostachys lakka
Sealing-wax palm

Cyrostachys renda
Sealing-wax palm

Cytisus albus   Portuguese broom
White Portuguese broom

Cytisus battandieri
Moroccan broom
Pineapple broom

Cytisus canariensis   Genista

Cytisus decumbens
Prostrate broom

Cytisus demissus   Dwarf broom

Cytisus genista   Common broom

Cytisus grandiflorus
Woolly-podded broom

Cytisus monspessulanus
Montpelier broom

Cytisus multiflorus
White Spanish broom

Cytisus multiflorus albus
White Portuguese broom

Cystus palmensis   Tagasaste

Cytisus × praecox
Warminster broom

Cystus proliferus   Escabon

Cytisus purpureus   Purple broom

Cytisus scoparius   Common broom
Scotch broom

Daboecia cantabrica
Connemara heath
Irish heath
Saint Daboec's heath

Dacrycarpus dacrydioides
Kahikatea
New Zealand white pine

Dacrydium bidwillii
Mountain pine

Dacrydium colensoi   Westland pine

Dacrydium cupressinum   Imou pine
Red pine
Rimu

Dacrydium fonkii
South American pine

Dacrydium franklinii   Huon pine

Dacrydium intermedium
Yellow silver pine

Dacrydium laxifolium
Mountain rimu

Daemonorops draco
Dragon's blood

Daemonorops grandis   Malay palm

Dais cotonifolia   Posy bush

Dalbergia latifolia   Black wood

Dalbergia sissoo   Sissoo

Damasonium alisma   Star fruit

Danae racemosa
Alexandrian laurel

Daphne aurantiaca
Golden-flowered daphne

Daphne cneorum
Garland flower bush

Dracaena sanderana

Daphne × houtteana	
	Purple-leaved daphne
Daphne laureola	Spurge laurel
Daphne mezereum	
	Cottage mezereon
	February daphne
	Mezereon
Daphne odora	Winter daphne
Daphne pontica	
	Twin-flowered daphne
Dasypogon bromeliaefolius	
	Pineapple bush
Datura suaveolens	
	Angel's trumpet
Davidia involucrata	Dove tree
	Ghost tree
	Handkerchief tree
	Lady's handkerchief tree
	Pocket handkerchief tree
Delonix regia	Fancy annie
	Flamboyant tree
	Flame of the forest
	Flame tree
	Gulmohur
	Peacock flower
	Poinciana
	Royal poinciana
Dendromecon rigidum	
	Tree poppy
Dendrosicyos socotrana	
	Socotra cucumber tree
Derris elliptica	Derris
	Tuba root
Derris scandens	Malay jewel vine
Desmanthus illinoensis	
	Prairie mimosa
	Prickleweed
Detarium senegalense	
	Dattock tree
	Tallow tree
Deutzia gracilis	Deutzia
	Japanese snow flower
Dialium guineense	
	Sierra Leone tamarind
	Velvet tamarind
Dictyosperma album	
	Princess palm
Dictyosperma aureum	
	Yellow princess palm
Dillenia indica	Elephant apple tree
	Hondapara
Dioon edule	Chestnut dioon
	Virgin's palm
Diospyros chinensis	
	Chinese persimmon
	Date palm
	Japanese persimmon
	Kaki
	Keg fig
Diospyros digyna	Black sapote
Diospyros ebenaster	Ceylon ebony
	East Indian ebony
	Ebony
	Macassar ebony

Diospyros ebenum	Ceylon ebony
	East Indian ebony
	Ebony
	Macassar ebony
Diospyros kaki	
	Chinese persimmon
	Date plum
	Japanese persimmon
	Kaki
	Keg fig
	Persimmon
Diospyros kurzii	Andaman marble
	Zebra wood
Diospyros lotus	Date plum
	Godsberry
Diospyros melanoxylon	
	Coromandel ebony
Diospyros mespiliformis	
	Lagos ebony
	West African ebony
Diospyros monbuttensis	
	Walking-stick ebony
	Yoruba ebony
Diospyros nigra	Black persimmon
	Black sapote
Diospyros texana	
	Black persimmon
Diospyros virginiana	
	American persimmon
	Common persimmon
	Date plum
	Persimmon
	Possum apple
	Possumwood
Diospyros whyteana	Black bark
	Bladder nut
Dipteryx odorata	Tonka bean
Dirca palustris	Leatherwood
	Moosewood
	Ropebark
	Wicopy
Discaria toumatou	Wild irishman
Distylium racemosum	Isu tree
Dombeya × cayeuxii	
	Pink snowball tree
Dombeya wallichii	Pink ball tree
Dorema ammoniacum	
	Ammoniacum
	Gum ammoniac
Doryalis - see *Dovyalis*	
Dovyalis caffra	Kai apple
	Kau apple
	Kei apple
	Umkokolo
Dovyalis hebecarpa	
	Ceylon gooseberry
	Kitembilla
Dracaena arborea	Tree dracaena
Dracaena draco	Dragon tree
Dracaena indivisa	Blue dracaena
Dracaena sanderana	
	Belgian evergreen
	Ribbon plant

Dracaena surculosa
Gold-dust dracaena
Spotted dracaena

Dracaena terminalis
Good-luck plant
Hawaiian good-luck plant
Tree of kings

Drimys lanceolata
Mountain pepper
Pepper tree

Drimys winteri Winter's bark

Dryas octopetala Mountain avens

Duboisia myoporoides
Corkwood tree
Pituri

Duranta ellisia Brazilian skyflower
Golden dewdrop
Pigeon berry
Skyflower

Duranta repens
Brazilian skyflower
Golden dewdrop
Pigeon berry
Skyflower

Durio zibethinus Durian

Duvernoia adhatodioides
Pistol bush
Snake bush

Elaeagnus angustifolia Oleaster
Russian olive
Silver berry
Wild olive

Elaeagnus argentea
American silverberry
Silver berry

Elaeagnus commutata
American silver berry
Silver berry

Elaeagnus edulis Cherry elaeagnus
Gumi

Elaeagnus latifolia Oleaster
Wild olive

Elaeagnus multiflora
Cherry elaeagnus
Gumi

Elaeagnus pungens
Thorny elaeagnus

Elaeagnus umbellata
Autumn olive

Elaeis guineensis African oil palm
Macaw-fat
Oil palm

Elaeis melanococca
American oil palm

Elaeis oleifera American oil palm

Elaeocarpus reticulatus
Blueberry ash

Elaeocarpus serratus Ceylon olive

Elaeocarpus stauntonii
Chinese mint bush

Embothrium coccineum
Chilean fire bush
Chilean fire tree

Empetrum nigrum Crowberry

Empetrum rubrum
South American crowberry

Enallagma latifolia Black calabash

Encephalartos altensteinii
Bread tree
Prickly cyad

Enchylaena tomentosa
Ruby saltbush

Entada gigas Nicker bean
Sword bean

Entandrophragma cylindricum Sapele

Enterolobium cyclocarpum
Elephant's ear

Epacris impressa Australian heath

Eperua falcata Wallaba

Ephedera distachya
Shrubby horsetail

Ephedera vulgaris Desert tea
Ma huang

Epigaea repens Mayflower

Eremophila maculata Emu bush
Spotted emu bush

Eretia tinifolia Bastard cherry

Erica arborea Briar
Tree heath

Erica australis Spanish heath

Erica baccans Berry heath

Erica canaliculata
Christmas heather

Erica carnea Snow heather
Spring heath
Winter heath

Erica ciliaris Ciliate heath
Dorset heath
Fringed heath

Erica cinerea Bellflower heather
Bell heather
Grey heath
Purple heather
Scotch heath
Twisted heath

Erica doliiformis
Everblooming French heather

Erica erigena Irish heath

Erica herbacea Snow heath
Spring heath

Erica hyemalis Cape heath
French heather
White winter heather

Erica lusitanica Portugal heath
Spanish heath

Erica mackaiana Mackay's heath

Erica mammosa Red signal heath

Erica mediterranea
Irish heath
Mediterranean heather

Erica scoparia Besom heath

Erica terminalis Corsican heath

Erica tetralix Bog heather
Cross-leaved heath

Erica vagans — Cornish heath

Erinacea anthyllis — Blue broom
Branch thorn
Hedgehog broom

Eriobotrya japonica
Japanese loquat
Japanese medlar
Japanese plum
Loquat

Erythea armata — Blue fan palm
Blue hesper palm
Blue palm

Erythrina arborea — Cardinal spear
Cherokee bean
Coral bean

Erythrina corallodendron
Common coral bean
Coral tree

Erythrina coralloides
Naked coral tree

Erythrina crista-galli — Cock's comb
Cockspur coral tree
Coral tree
Cry-baby tree

Erythrina fusca
Swamp immortelle

Erythrina glauca
Swamp immortelle

Erythrina herbacea — Cardinal spear
Cherokee bean
Coral bean

Erythrina lysistemon
Lucky bean tree

Erythrina monosperma — Wilwilli

Erythrina ovalifolia
Swamp immortelle

Erythrina poeppigiana
Mountain immortelle

Erythrina tahitiensis — Wilwilli

Erythrina vespertilio
Grey corkwood

Erythrina zeyheri — Plough breaker
Prickly cardinal

Erythrophleum guineese
Redwater tree
Sassy bark

Erythrophleum suaveolens
Redwater tree

Erythroxylum coca — Coca
Cocaine plant
Spadic

Escallonia macrantha — Escallonia

Eucalyptus acacae formis
Wattle-leaved peppermint

Eucalyptus acmenioides
White mahogany

Eucalyptus agglomerata
Blue-leaved stringybark

Eucalyptus aggregata — Black gum

Eucalyptus alba — Timor white gum

Eucalyptus albens — White box

Eucalyptus alpina
Grampian stringybark

Eucalyptus amplifolia
Cabbage gum

Eucalyptus amygdalina
Black peppermint

Eucalyptus andreana
River peppermint

Eucalyptus archeri — Alpine gum

Eucalyptus argillacea
Kimberley grey box

Eucalyptus astringens
Brown mallee

Eucalyptus bakeri — Malee box

Eucalyptus baxteri
Brown stringybark

Eucalyptus blakelyi
Blakely's red gum

Eucalyptus blaxlandii
Blaxland's stringybark

Eucalyptus bosistoana
Bosisto's box

Eucalyptus botryoides — Bungalay

Eucalyptus bridgesiana
Apple box

Eucalyptus burracoppinensis
Burracoppin mallee

Eucalyptus caesia — Gungurru

Eucalyptus calophylla — Marri
Red gum

Eucalyptus camaldulensis — Marri
Murray red gum
Red gum
Red river gum

Eucalyptus camphora
Broad-leaved sally

Eucalyptus capitallata
Brown stringybark

Eucalyptus cephalocarpa
Long-leaved argyle apple

Eucalyptus cinerea — Argyle apple
Mealy stringybark
Silver dollar tree
Spiral eucalyptus

Eucalyptus citriodora
Lemon-scented gum
Lemon-scented spotted gum

Eucalyptus cladocalyx — Sugar gum

Eucalyptus clavigera — Apple gum
Cabbage gum

Eucalyptus coccifera
Mount Wellington peppermint
Tasmanian snow gum

Eucalyptus consideniana — Yertchuk

Eucalyptus cordata
Heart-leaved silver gum

Eucalyptus cornuta — Yate tree

Eucalyptus corynocalyx
Sugar plum

Eucalyptus cosmophylla — Cup gum

Eucalyptus crebra
Narrow-leaved ironbark

Eucalyptus crucis
Southern cross silver mallee

Eucalyptus dalrympleana
Broad-leaved kindling bark
Mountain gum

Eucalyptus dealbata
Tumbledown gum

Eucalyptus deanei   Deane's gum

Eucalyptus delegatensis   Alpine ash
Gum-top stringybark

Eucalyptus desmondensis
Desmond mallee

Eucalyptus diptera   Bastard gimlet
Two-winged gimlet

Eucalyptus diversicolor   Karri
Karri gum

Eucalyptus dives
Broad-leaved peppermint

Eucalyptus dumosa   Congo mallee
Mallee

Eucalyptus elaeophora   Bundy

Eucalyptus elata   River peppermint

Eucalyptus eremophila
Horned mallee

Eucalyptus erythrocorys   Illyarie
Illyarri

Eucalyptus erythronema
Red mallee

Eucalyptus ewartiana
Ewart's mallee
Red-flowered mallee

Eucalyptus eximia
Yellow bloodwood

Eucalyptus fastigiata
Brown barrel
Cut-tail

Eucalyptus fibrosa
Broad-leaved ironbark

Eucalyptus ficifolia
Red-flowering gum

Eucalyptus flocktoniae   Merrit gum

Eucalyptus forrestiana
Forrest's marlock
Fuchsia gum

Eucalyptus fraxinoides   White ash

Eucalyptus gigantea   Alpine ash

Eucalyptus glaucescens
Tingiringi gum

Eucalyptus globoidea
White stringybark

Eucalyptus globulus   Blue gum
Southern blue gum
Stringybark tree
Tasmanian blue gum

Eucalyptus globulus maidenii
Maiden's gum

Eucalyptus gomphocephalus
Tuart gum

Eucalyptus goniocalyx   Bundy
Spotted mountain gum

Eucalyptus grandis   Flooded gum
Rose gum

Eucalyptus grossa
Coarse-leaved mallee

Eucalyptus gummifera
Red bloodwood

Eucalyptus gunnii   Cider gum

Eucalyptus haemastoma
Scribbly gum

Eucalyptus incrassata   Lerp mallee
Ridge-fruited mallee

Eucalyptus johnstonii
Tasmanian brown gum
Yellow gum

Eucalyptus kruseana
Kruse's mallee

Eucalyptus lane-poolei
Salmon white gum

Eucalyptus lansdowneana
Crimson mallee box

Eucalyptus largiflorens   Black box

Eucalyptus lehmannii   Bushy yate
Lehmann's gum

Eucalyptus leucophylla
Kimberley grey box

Eucalyptus leucoxylon
White ironbark

Eucalyptus longicornis   Red morell

Eucalyptus longifolia
River peppermint
Woollybutt

Eucalyptus luehmanniana
Yellow-topped mallee ash

Eucalyptus macarthurii
Camden woollybutt
Paddy river box

Eucalyptus macrandra
Long-flowered marlock

Eucalyptus macrocarpa   Bluebush

Eucalyptus macrorhyncha
Red stringybark

Eucalyptus maculata   Spotted gum

Eucalyptus maidenii   Maiden's gum

Eucalyptus mannifera
Red-spotted gum

Eucalyptus marginata
Jarrah
West Australian mahogany

Eucalyptus megacarpa   Bullick

Eucalyptus megacornata
Warted yate

Eucalyptus melliodora   Yellow box

Eucalyptus micrantha   Snappy gum

Eucalyptus microcorys
Tallow-wood

Eucalyptus microtheca   Coolibah
Flooded box
Jinbul
Moolar

Eucalyptus miniata
Darwin woollybutt

Eucalyptus mitchelliana
Weeping sally

Eucalyptus moluccana   Grey box

Eucalyptus muellerana
Yellow stringybark

Eucalyptus neglecta
    Omeo round-leaved gum

Eucalyptus nicholii
    Narrow-leaved black peppermint
    Nichol's willow-leaved peppermint

Eucalyptus niphophila   Snow gum

Eucalyptus nitens   Silver top

Eucalyptus nutans   Red moort

Eucalyptus obliqua
    Messmate stringybark

Eucalyptus occidentalis
    Flat-topped yate

Eucalyptus oldfieldii
    Oldfield's mallee

Eucalyptus orbifolia
    Round-leaved mallee

Eucalyptus ovata   Swamp gum

Eucalyptus paniculata
    Grey ironbark

Eucalyptus papuana   Ghost gum

Eucalyptus parvifolia
    Small-leaved gum

Eucalyptus pauciflora
    Cabbage gum
    White sally

Eucalyptus perriniana
    Round-leaved snow gum
    Spinning gum

Eucalyptus phoenicia   Scarlet gum

Eucalyptus pilularis   Blackbutt

Eucalyptus piperita
    Sydney peppermint

Eucalyptus platyphilla
    Timor white gum

Eucalyptus platypus
    Round-leaved moort

Eucalyptus polyanthemos
    Australian beech
    Silver dollar gum

Eucalyptus polybractea
    Silver mallee scrub

Eucalyptus populifolia   Bimble box

Eucalyptus populnea   Bimble box

Eucalyptus preissiana
    Bell-fruited mallee

Eucalyptus propinqua
    Small-fruited grey gum

Eucalyptus ptychocarpa
    Swamp bloodwood

Eucalyptus pulchella
    White peppermint

Eucalyptus pulverulenta
    Money tree
    Silver-leaved mountain gum

Eucalyptus punctata   Grey gum

Eucalyptus pyriformis
    Pear-fruited mallee

Eucalyptus racemosa   Snappy gum

Eucalyptus radiata
    Grey peppermint
    Narrow-leaved peppermint
    White-top peppermint

Eucalyptus × rariflora   Black box

Eucalyptus regnans
    Australian mountain ash
    Giant gum
    Mountain ash

Eucalyptus resinifer
    Red mahogany

Eucalyptus × rhodantha
    Rose mallee

Eucalyptus risdonii
    Silver peppermint

Eucalyptus robertsonii
    Robertson's peppermint

Eucalyptus robusta
    Swamp mahogany

Eucalyptus rossii   White gum

Eucalyptus rubida
    Candle-bark gum

Eucalyptus rudis   Desert gum
    Swamp gum

Eucalyptus salicifolia
    Black peppermint

Eucalyptus saligna
    Sydney blue gum

Eucalyptus salmonophloia
    Salmon gum

Eucalyptus salubris   Gimlet gum

Eucalyptus sepalcralis
    Blue weeping gum

Eucalyptus sideroxylon   Mugga
    Red ironbark

Eucalyptus sieberi
    Black mountain ash

Eucalyptus smithii
    Blackbutt peppermint
    Gully ash
    Gully gum

Eucalyptus spathulata
    Swamp mallee

Eucalyptus staigeriana
    Lemon-scented ironbark

Eucalyptus steedmanii
    Steedman's gum

Eucalyptus stellulata   Black sally

Eucalyptus stowardii
    Stoward's mallee

Eucalyptus stricklandii
    Strickland's gum

Eucalyptus stricta
    Blue mountain mallee

Eucalyptus tenuiramis
    Silver peppermint

Eucalyptus tereticornis
    Forest red gum
    Grey gum

Eucalyptus tetradonta
    Darwin stringybark

Eucalyptus tetragona
    White-leaved marlock

Eucalyptus tetraptera

Eucalyptus tetraptera
  Four-winged mallee
  Square-fruited mallee
Eucalyptus torquata   Coral gum
Eucalyptus umbra
  White mahogany
Eucalyptus urnigera   Urn gum
Eucalyptus vernicosa
  Varnish-leaved gum
Eucalyptus viminalis   Manna gum
  Ribbon gum
Eucalyptus woodwardii
  Woodward's blackbutt
  Yellow-flowered gum
Eucommia ulmoides
  Chinese rubber tree
  Chinese silk thread tree
  Gutta-percha tree
Eucryphia cordifolia   Ulmo
Eucryphia glutinosa   Eucryphia
Eucryphia lucida   Leatherwood
Eucryphia moorai   Plumwood
Eucryphia × nymansensis
  nymansay
  Nyman's hybrid eucryphia
Eucryphia pinnatifolia   Eucryphia
Eugenia aggregata
  Rio Grande cherry
Eugenia aquea   Rose apple
Eugenia axillaris   White stopper
Eugenia brasiliensis   Brazil cherry
  Grumichama
  Grumixameira
Eugenia buxifolia   Spanish stopper
Eugenia caryophyllus   Clove tree
Eugenia cheken   Cheken
Eugenia confusa   Ironwood tree
  Red stopper
Eugenia dombeyi   Brazil cherry
  Grumichama
  Grumixameira
Eugenia foetida   Spanish stopper
Eugenia garberi   Ironwood tree
  Red stopper
Eugenia jambolana   Jambolan
  Jambul
  Java plum
Eugenia luschnathiana   Pitomba
Eugenia malaccensis   Malay apple
Eugenia michelii   Barbados cherry
  Brazil cherry
  Cayenne cherry
  Pitanga
Eugenia myrtifolia
  Australian brush cherry
Eugenia myrtoides
  Spanish stopper
Eugenia pitanga   Pitanga
Eugenia smithii   Lilly-pilly
Eugenia ugni   Chilean guava

Eugenia uniflora   Barbados cherry
  Brazil cherry
  Cayenne cherry
  Pitanga
  Surinam cherry
Euodia daniellii   Daniell's euodia
Euodia hupehensis   Euodia
Euonymus alata
  Winged spindle tree
Euonymus americana
  Bursting heart
  Strawberry bush
  Strawberry tree
Euonymus atropurpurea
  Burning bush
  Wahoo elm
Euonymus europaea
  Common spindle tree
  European spindle tree
  Skewerwood
  Spindle tree
Euonymus hamiltonianus
  yedoensis   Japanese spindle tree
Euonymus japonica
  Evergreen spindle tree
  Japanese euonymus
  Japanese spindle tree
Euonymus latifolius
  Broad-leaved spindle
Euonymus occidentalis
  Western burning bush
Eupatorium micranthrum
  Mexican incense bush
Eupatorium weinmannianum
  Mexican incense bush
Euphorbia antisyphilitica
  Candelilla
Euphorbia candelabrum
  Candelabra tree
Euphorbia caput-medusae
  Medusa's head
Euphorbia cereiformis   Milk-barrel
Euphorbia corollata
  Flowering spurge
  Tramp's spurge
  Wild hippo
Euphorbia cyathophora
  Fiddler's spurge
  Fire-on-the-mountain
  Mexican fire plant
  Painted leaf
Euphorbia cyparissias
  Cypress spurge
Euphorbia grandidens
  Big-tooth euphorbia
Euphorbia heptagona   Milk-barrel
Euphorbia heterophylla
  Annual poinsettia
  Fire-on-the-mountain
  Mexican fire plant
  Painted spurge
Euphorbia horrida
  African milk-barrel
Euphorbia ingens   Candelabra tree

TREES, BUSHES, AND SHRUBS

Ficus glomerata

Euphorbia ipecacuanhae
Carolina ipecac
Carolina spurge
Ipecac spurge
Wild ipecac

Euphorbia lactea
Candelabra cactus
Dragon bones
False cactus
Hat-rack cactus
Mottled spurge

Euphorbia lathyris   Caper spurge
Mole plant
Myrtle spurge

Euphorbia leviana   Milk-barrel

Euphorbia marginata   Ghostweed
Snow-on-the-mountain

Euphorbia neriifolia
Hedge euphorbia
Oleander-leaved euphorbia

Euphorbia pulcherrima
Christmas star
Lobster plant
Mexican flameleaf
Painted leaf
Poinsettia

Euphorbia tirucalli   Finger tree
Indian tree spurge
Milk bush
Pencil tree
Rubber euphorbia

Euphorbia trigona
Abyssinian euphorbia
African milk tree

Euptelea polyandra
Japanese euptelea

Euterpe edulis   Assai palm

Euterpe oleracea   Assai palm

Exocarpus cupressiformis
Australian cherry

Exochorda grandiflora   Pearl bush

Exochorda racemosa   Pearl bush

Fabiana imbricata   False heath
Pichi

Fagara flava   Satinwood

Fagus americana   American beech

Fagus crenata   Japanese beech

Fagus englerana   Chinese beech
Engler's beech

Fagus grandifolia   American beech

Fagus japonica   Japanese beech

Fagus longipetiolata
Chinese beech

Fagus orientalis   Oriental beech

Fagus sieboldii   Japanese beech
Siebold's beech

Fagus sylvatica   Common beech

Fagus sylvatica asplenifolia
Fernleaf beech

Fagus sylvatica cristata
Cockscomb beech

Fagus sylvatica dawyck
Dawick beech

Fagus sylvatica fastigiata
Fastigiate beech

Fagus sylvatica heterophylla
Cut-leaved beech
Fern-leaved beech

Fagus sylvatica pendula
Weeping beech

Fagus sylvatica purpurea
Copper beech
Purple beech

Fagus sylvatica rohanii
Cut-leaf purple beech
Purple fern-leaved beech

Fagus sylvatica zlatia
Golden beech

Fallugia paradoxa   Apache plume

Fatsia japonica   Castor oil palm
False castor oil plant
Figleaf palm
Formosa rice tree
Japanese fatsia
Japanese figleaf palm
Paper plant

Feijoa sellowiana   Feijoa
Pineapple guava

Feronia elephantum
Elephant apple
Wood apple

Feronia limonia   Elephant apple
Wood apple

Ficus altissima   Council tree

Ficus aspera   Clown fig

Ficus aurea   Florida strangler fig
Golden fig
Strangler fig

Ficus australis   Little-leaf fig
Port Jackson fig
Rusty fig

Ficus belgica   Assam rubber tree
India rubber tree
Rubber plant

Ficus benghalensis   Banyan
East Indian fig
Indian banyan

Ficus benjamina   Benjamin tree
Java fig
Small-leaved rubber plant
Tropic laurel
Weeping fig
Weeping laurel

Ficus capensis   Bush fig
Cape fig

Ficus carica   Common fig

Ficus deltoides   Mistletoe fig
Mistletoe rubber plant

Ficus diversifolia   Mistletoe fig
Mistletoe rubber plant

Ficus dryepondtiana   Congo fig

Ficus elastica   Assam rubber
India rubber tree
Rubber plant

Ficus glomerata   Cluster fig

Ficus indica	Banyan
	East Indian fig tree
	Indian banyan
Ficus infectoria	Spotted fig
Ficus lacor	Spotted fig
Ficus lyrata	Fiddle-leaf fig
Ficus macrocarpa	
	Australian banyan
	Moreton Bay fig
Ficus macrophylla	
	Australian banyan
	Moreton bay fig
Ficus montana	Oak-leaf fig
Ficus mysorensis	Mysore fig
Ficus natalensis	Natal fig
Ficus nekbudu	Kaffir fig
	Zulu fig tree
Ficus pandurata	Fiddle-leaf fig
Ficus perforata	
	West Indian laurel fig
Ficus pretoriae	Wonderboom
Ficus pseudopalma	Dracaena fig
	Philippine fig
Ficus pumila	Climbing fig
	Creeping fig
	Creeping rubber plant
Ficus quercifolia	Oak-leaf fig
Ficus racemosa	Cluster fig
Ficus religiosa	Bo tree
	Peepul
	Sacred fig
Ficus repens	Climbing fig
	Creeping fig
	Creeping rubber plant
Ficus retusa	Chinese banyan
	Glossy-leaf fig
	Indian laurel
	Malay banyan
Ficus rubiginosa	Little-leaf fig
	Port Jackson fig
	Rusty fig
Ficus stipulata	Climbing fig
	Creeping fig
	Creeping rubber plant
Ficus superba	Sea fig
Ficus sycomorus	Bible fig
	Egyptian sycamore
	Mulberry fig
	Pharoah's fig
	Sycamore fig
Ficus utilis	Kaffir fig
	Zulu fig tree
Ficus virens	Spotted fig
Ficus vogelii	
	West African rubber tree
Ficus wightiana	
	Large-leaved banyan
Firmiana simplex	
	Chinese bottle tree
	Chinese parasol tree
	Japanese varnish tree
	Phoenix tree

Fitzroya cupressoides	Alerce
	Patagonian cypress
Flacourtia indica	Batoko plum
	Governor's plum
	Madagascar plum
	Ramontchi
Flacourtia ramontchi	Batoko plum
	Governor's plum
	Madagascar plum
	Ramontchi
Forestiera acuminata	Swamp privet
Forestiera neomexicana	
	Desert olive
Forsythia europaea	
	European golden ball
Forsythia × intermedia	Forsythia
Forsythia ovata	Korean forsythia
Forsythia sieboldii	
	Weeping forsythia
Forsythia suspensa	Golden bell
	Weeping forsythia
Forsythia suspensa fortunei	
	Arching forsythia
Fortunella japonica	
	Marumi kumquat
	Round kumquat
Fortunella margarita	Kumquat
	Nagami kumquat
	Oval kumquat
Fothergilla monticola	Witch alder
Fouquieria splendens	Coach-whip
	Jacob's staff
	Ocotillo
	Vine cactus
Frangula alnus	Alder buckthorn
Franklinia alatamaha	
	Franklin tree
Frasera carolinensis	
	American colombo
Fraxinus alba	American white ash
	White ash
Fraxinus americana	American ash
	American white ash
	White ash
Fraxinus angustifolia	
	Narrow-leaved ash
Fraxinus angustifolia *veltheimii*	Single-leaved ash
Fraxinus anomala	Single-leaved ash
	Utah ash
Fraxinus caroliniana	Carolina ash
	Pop ash
	Water ash
Fraxinus chinensis	Chinese ash
Fraxinus dipetala	Flowering ash
Fraxinus excelsior	Common ash
	European ash
Fraxinus excelsior aurea pendula	
	Golden weeping ash
Fraxinus excelsior diversifolia	
	Single-leaf ash

Fraxinus excelsior jaspidea	
	Golden ash
	Golden-bark ash
	Yellow-bark ash
Fraxinus excelsior pendula	
	Weeping ash
Fraxinus latifolia	Oregon ash
Fraxinus mandshurica	
	Manchurian ash
Fraxinus mariesii	
	Chinese flowering ash
Fraxinus nigra	Black ash
Fraxinus oregona	Oregon ash
Fraxinus ornus	Flowering ash
	Manna ash
Fraxinus oxycarpa	Caucasian ash
Fraxinus oxycarpa raywood	Claret ash
Fraxinus pennsylvanica	Green ash
	Red ash
Fraxinus quadrangulata	Blue ash
Fraxinus spaethiana	
	Spaeth's flowering ash
Fraxinus syriaca	Syrian ash
Fraxinus texensis	Texas ash
Fraxinus tomentosa	Pumpkin ash
Fraxinus uhdei	Evergreen ash
	Shamel ash
Fraxinus velutina	Arizona ash
	Velvet ash
Fraxinus xanthoxyloides	
	Afghan ash
	Varnish-leaved gum
Fraxinus xanthoxyloides dimorpha	Algerian ash
Fuchsia arborescens	Tree fuchsia
Fuchsia boliviana	
	Peruvian fuchsia tree
Fuchsia conica	Hardy fuchsia
Fuchsia excorticata	
	New Zealand tree fuchsia
Fuchsia magellanica	Hardy fuchsia
Fusanus acuminatus	Quandong
Galpinia transvaalica	
	Wild pride of India
Garcinia mangostana	Mangosteen
Gardenia florida	Cape jasmine
	Common gardenia
Gardenia grandiflora	
	Cape jasmine
	Common gardenia
Gardenia jasminoides	
	Cape jasmine
	Common gardenia
Garrya elliptica	Quinine bush
	Silk tassel bush
Garrya fremontii	Fever bush
Garrya macrophylla	
	Mexican tassel bush

Gaultheria hispida	Snowberry
	Tasmanian waxberry
	Waxberry
Gaultheria procumbens	Boxberry
	Canadian tea
	Checkerberry
	Creeping winterberry
	Partridge berry
	Tea berry
	Wintergreen
Gaultheria shallon	Lemonleaf
	North American salal
	Shallon
Gaylussacia baccata	
	Black huckleberry
Gaylussacia brachycera	
	Box huckleberry
Gaylussacia dumosa	
	Dwarf huckleberry
Gaylussacia frondosa	Blue tangle
	Dangleberry
	Dwarf huckleberry
Gaylussacia resinosa	
	Black huckleberry
Gaylussacia ursina	
	Bear huckleberry
	Buckberry
Genipa americana	Genipap
	Marmalade box
Genista aethnensis	
	Mount Etna broom
Genista anglica	Needle furze
	Petty whin
	Pretty whin
Genista canariensis	Florist's genista
Genista dalmatica	
	Dalmatian broom
Genista germanica	
	German greenweed
Genista hispanica	Spanish broom
	Spanish gorse
Genista januensis	Genoa broom
Genista lydia	Balkan gorse
Genista nyssana	Nish broom
Genista pilosa	Hairy greenweed
	Hairy greenwood
Genista raetam	Juniper rush
	White broom
Genista sagittalis	Arrow broom
Genista sylvestris pungens	
	Dalmatian broom
Genista tinctoria	Dyer's broom
	Dyer's greenweed
	Greenweed
	Woadwaxen
	Woodwaxen
Genista virgata	Madeira broom
Gevuina avellana	Chilean hazel
	Chilean nut
Ginkgo biloba	Duck's foot tree
	Maidenhair tree
Gleditsia aquatica	Swamp locust
	Water locust

Gleditsia caspica

Gleditsia caspica   Caspian locust
Gleditsia chinensis
    Chinese honey locust
Gleditsia japonica
    Japanese honey locust
Gleditsia sinensis
    Chinese honey locust
Gleditsia triacanthos   Honey locust
    Honeyshuck
    Sweet locust
Gliricidia maculata   Madre
    Nicaraguan cocoa-shade
Gliricidia sepium   Madre
    Nicaraguan cocoa-shade
Glycosmis pentaphylla
    Jamaica mandarin orange
Glyptostrobus lineatus
    Chinese swamp cypress
    Chinese water pine
Gonystylus bancanus   Ramin
Gordonia lasianthus   Black laurel
    Loblolly bay
Gossypiospermum praecox
    West Indian boxwood
Graptophyllum hortense
    Caricature plant
Graptophyllum pictum
    Caricature plant
Grevillea aquifolium
    Holly-leaved grevillea
Grevillea robusta   Silky oak
Grevillea wilsonii   Firewheel
Guaiacum officinale   Lignum vitae
    Tree of life
Guazuma ulmifolia   Bastard cedar
Guizotia abyssinica   Niger seed
Gulielma gassipaes   Peach palm
Gustavia augusta   Stinkwood
Gymnocladus chinensis
    Chinese coffee tree
Gymnocladus dioica   Chicot
    Kentucky coffee tree
    Knicker tree
    Nicker tree
Haematoxylum
  campeachianum   Bloodwood
    Campeachy-wood
    Logwood
    Peachwood
Hagenia abyssinica   Kousso
Hakea bucculenta   Red pokers
Hakea laurina   Sea-urchin tree
Hakea victoriae   Royal hakea
Halesia carolina   Carolina silverbell
    Oppossumwood
    Shittimwood
    Silver bell
    Snowdrop tree
    Wild olive
Halesia monticola
    Mountain silver bell
    Mountain snowdrop tree

Halesia tetraptera   Silver bell
    Snowdrop tree
Halimium lasianthum
  formosum   Sweet cistin
Halimodendron halodendron
    Salt tree
Hamamelis japonica
    Japanese witch hazel
Hamamelis mollis
    Chinese witch hazel
Hamamelis vernalis
    Ozark witch hazel
Hamamelis virginiana
    Common witch hazel
Hamelia patens   Firebush
    Scarlet bush
Hardenbergia monophylla
    Australian lilac
Hardenbergia violacea
    Australian sarsaparilla
Harpephyllum caffrum
    Kaffir plum
Hebe cupressoides   Cypress hebe
Hebe hulkeana   New Zealand lilac
Hedyscepe canterburyana
    Umbrella palm
Helichrysum rosmarinifolium
    Snow in summer
Helichrysum serotinum
    Curry plant
Helichrysum stoechas   Goldilocks
Heliocarpus americanus   Sun fruit
Hemidesmus indica
    Indian sarsaparilla
Heritiera macrophylla
    Looking-glass tree
Herminiera elaphroxylon   Ambash
    Pith tree
Heteromeles arbitifolia
    Christmas berry
    Tollon
    Toyon
Heteropyxis natalensis
    Lavender tree
Hevea brasiliensis   Caoutchouc
    Para rubber tree
    Rubber tree
Hibiscus cannabinus   Bastard jute

    Bimli jute
    Bimlipatum
    Deccan hemp
    Deckaner hemp
    Indian hemp
    Kenaf
Hibiscus diversifolius
    Cape hibiscus
    Wild cotton
Hibiscus elatus   Cuban bast
    Mahoe
    Mountain mahoe
    Tree hibiscus

Ilex aquifolium

Hibiscus farragei
    Desert rose mallow

Hibiscus grandiflorus
    Great rose mallow

Hibiscus huegelii   Satin hibiscus

Hibiscus militaris
    Soldier rose mallow

Hibiscus moscheutos
    Common rose mallow
    Swamp rose mallow
    Wild cotton

Hibiscus mutabilis
    Confederate rose
    Cotton rose

Hibiscus rosa-sinensis
    Chinese hibiscus

Hibiscus sabdariffa   Indian sorrell
    Jamaica sorrell
    Roselle

Hibiscus schizopetalus
    Coral hibiscus
    Fringed hibiscus
    Japanese hibiscus
    Japanese lantern

Hibiscus sinensis   Blacking plant
    China rose
    Chinese hibiscus
    Hawaiian hibiscus

Hibiscus syriacus   Althaea
    Bush hollyhock
    Bush mallow
    Hibiscus
    Rose of sharon
    Tree hollyhock

Hibiscus tiliaceus   Mahoe

Hibiscus trionum   Bladder ketmia
    Flower-of-an-hour

Hippomane mancinella
    Manchineel

Hippophae rhamnoides
    Sallow thorn
    Sea buckthorn

Hoheria lyallii   Lacebark
    Ribbonwood

Hoheria populnea   Lacebark
    Ribbonwood

Hoheria sexstylosa   Ribbonwood

Holacantha emoryi
    Crucifixion thorn

Holodiscus ariifolius   Cream bush
    Ocean spray

Holodiscus discolor   Cream bush
    Ocean spray
    Spray brush

Homalanthus populifolius
    Queensland poplar

Houmiria floribunda
    Bastard bullet tree

Hovenia dulcis   Japanese raisin tree

Howea belmoreana
    Belmor sentry palm
    Curly palm
    Curly sentry palm

Howea forsterana
    Forster's sentry palm
    Kentia palm
    Paradise palm
    Sentry palm
    Thatch-leaf palm

Hura crepitans   Javillo
    Monkey-pistol
    Monkey's dinner bell
    Sandbox tree

Hydrangea arborescens
    Seven barks

Hydrangea aspera
    Rough-leaved hydrangea

Hydrangea hortensia
    Mop-head hydrangea

Hydrangea macrophylla
    Lace-cap hydrangea

Hydrangea quercifolia
    Oak-leaf hydrangea

Hymenaea courbaril   Anime resin
    Locust tree

Hymenosporum flavum
    Native frangipani

Hyophorbe lagenicaulis
    Bottle palm
    Pignut palm

Hyophorbe verschaffeltii
    Spindle palm

Hypericum androsaemum
    Bible leaf
    Tutsan

Hypericum calycinum
    Aaron's beard
    Rose of sharon

Hypericum hircinum
    Stinking tutsan

Hypericum undulatum
    Wavy Saint John's wort

Hypericum × inodorum
    Tall tutsan

Hyphaene thebaica   Doom palm
    Doum palm
    Egyptian
    doom palm
    Gingerbread palm

Idesia polycarpa   Idesia
    Igiri tree
    Ligiri tree

Idria columnaris   Boojum tree

*Ilex × altaclarensis
camelliifolia*
    Spineless broadleaved holly

*Ilex × altaclarensis golden
king*
    Highclere holly

Ilex × altaclarensis lawsoniana
    Lawson's holly

Ilex amelanchier   Sarvis holly
    Swamp holly

Ilex aquifolium   Common holly
    English holly
    Hulver bush
    Oregon holly
    Wild holly

Ilex aquifolium argentea
Silver hedgehog holly

Ilex aquifolium aurea
Golden holly

Ilex aquifolium aurea pendula
Golden weeping holly

Ilex aquifolium bacciflava
Yellow-fruited holly

Ilex aquifolium ferox
Hedgehog holly

Ilex aquifolium ferox aurea
Golden-blotched hedgehog holly

Ilex aquifolium flavescens
Moonlight holly

Ilex aquifolium fructuluteo
Yellow-berried holly

Ilex aquifolium pendula
Weeping holly

Ilex × attenuata Topal holly

Ilex cassine Cassina
Dahoon holly
Yaupon

Ilex chinensis Kashi holly

Ilex coriacea Bay gall bush
Large gallberry
Sweet gallberry

Ilex cornuta Chinese holly
Horned holly

Ilex crenata Box-leaved holly
Japanese holly

Ilex decidua Possumhaw holly

Ilex dipyrena Himalayan holly

Ilex geniculata Furin holly

Ilex glabra Appalachian tea
Bitter gallberry
Gallberry
Inkberry
Winterberry

Ilex integra Japanese holly
Mochi tree

Ilex laevigata Smooth winterberry

Ilex latifolia Lustre-leaf holly
Tarajo

Ilex lucida Bay gall bush
Large gallberry
Sweet gallberry

Ilex × meservae Blue holly

Ilex opaca American holly

Ilex paraguariensis Maté
Paraguay tea
Yerba-de-maté

Ilex perado Azorean holly
Canary holly
Madeira holly

Ilex pernyi Perny's holly

Ilex platyphylla
Canary Islands holly

Ilex purpurea Kashi holly

Ilex rotunda Kurogane holly

Ilex serrata Japanese winterberry

Ilex verticillata Black alder
Winterberry

Ilex vomitoria Cassina
Yaupon

Illicium anisatum
Aniseed tree
Chinese anise
Japanese anise
Star anise

Illicium floridanum Aniseed tree
Poison bay
Purple anise

Illicium religiosum Star anise

Illicium verum Chinese star anise
Star anise

Inocarpus edulis
Otaheite chestnut

Ipomoea arborescens
Morning glory tree

Ipomoea fistulosa
Morning glory bush

Ipomoea purga Jalap

Ipomoea turpethum Indian jalap
Turpeth

Isopogon anemonifolius
Tall conebush

Itea illicifolia Hollyleaf sweetspire

Itea japonica Japanese sweetspire

Itea virginica Sweetspire
Tassel-white
Virginia sweetspire
Virginia willow

Ixora chinensis Chinese ixora
Malaya ixora

Ixora coccinea
Flame-of-the-woods
Jungle flame
Jungle geranium

Ixora incarnata
Flame-of-the-woods
Jungle flame
Jungle geranium

Jacaranda acutifolia Fearn tree
Jacaranda

Jacaranda mimosifolia Jacaranda

Jacaranda procera Carob tree

Jacquinia armillaris Barbasco
Bracelet wood

Jacquinia barbasco Barbasco

Jasminum gracillimum
Pinwheel jasmine
Star jasmine

Jasminum grandiflorum
Catalonian jasmine
Royal jasmine
Spanish jasmine

Jasminum humile
Himalayan jasmine
Italian jasmine

Jasminum mesnyi
Japanese jasmine
Primrose jasmine
Yellow jasmine

Jasminum multiflorum
Star jasmine

TREES, BUSHES, AND SHRUBS

Jasminum nitidum
Angelwing jasmine
Confederate jasmine
Windmill jasmine

Jasminum nudiflorum
Winter-flowering jasmine

Jasminum officinale
Common white jasmine
Poet's jasmine
White jasmine

Jasminum sambac Arabian jasmine
Zambak

Jateorhiza calumba Calumba

Jatropha curcus Barbados nut
French physic nut
Physic nut
Purging nut

Jatropha integerrima
Guatemalan rhubarb
Peregrina
Spicy jatropha

Jatropha multifida Coral plant
Physic nut

Jatropha podagrica
Australian bottle plant
Tartoga

Jubaea chilensis Chilean wine palm
Coquito palm
Honey palm
Little cokernut palm
Wine palm

Jubaea spectabilis
Chilean wine palm
Coquito palm
Honey palm
Little cokernut palm
Wine palm

Juglans ailantifolia Heartnut
Japanese walnut

Juglans californica
California walnut

Juglans cathayensis
Chinese butternut
Chinese walnut

Juglans cinerea Butternut
White butternut
White walnut

Juglans hindsii
Californian black walnut

Juglans jamaicensis
West Indies walnut

Juglans major Arizona walnut

Juglans mandshurica
Manchurian walnut

Juglans microcarpa Little walnut
River walnut
Texan walnut

Juglans nigra Black walnut

Juglans regia Common walnut
English walnut
Madeira walnut
Nux regia
Persian walnut

Juglans regia laciniata
Cut-leaf walnut

Juglans rupestris Little walnut
River walnut
Texan walnut

Juniperus ashei Ashe juniper
Mountain cedar
Ozark white cedar

Juniperus bermudiana
Bermuda cedar

Juniperus californica
Californian juniper

Juniperus cedrus
Canary Islands juniper

Juniperus chinensis
Chinese juniper

Juniperus chinensis aurea
Golden Chinese juniper
Young's golden juniper

*Juniperus chinensis
columnaris glauca*
Blue Chinese juniper

Juniperus chinensis kaizuka
Hollywood juniper

Juniperus communis
Common juniper

*Juniperus communis
compressa* Noah's ark juniper

Juniperus communis depressa
Canadian juniper

Juniperus communis hibernica
Irish juniper

*Juniperus communis
pyramidalis* Swedish juniper

Juniperus communis stricta
Columnar juniper
Irish juniper

Juniperus communis suecica
Swedish juniper

Juniperus conferta Shore juniper

*Juniperus deppeana
pachyphlaea* Alligator juniper
Chequered juniper

Juniperus depressa
Canadian dwarf juniper

Juniperus drupacea Habbel
Plum juniper
Syrian juniper

Juniperus excelsa Grecian juniper

Juniperus flaccida Mexican juniper

Juniperus foetidissima
Stinking juniper

Juniperus formosana
Prickly cypress

Juniperus horizontalis
Creeping cedar
Creeping juniper
Creeping savin juniper

*Juniperus horizontalis
douglasii* Waukegan juniper

Juniperus jackii
Rocky mountains juniper

Juniperus × media pfitzerana	Pfitzer juniper
Juniperus monosperma	Cherrystone juniper
Juniperus morrisonicola	Mount Morrison juniper
Juniperus occidentalis	California juniper
	Sierra juniper
	Western juniper
Juniperus osteosperma	Utah juniper
Juniperus oxycedrus	Cade
	Prickly juniper
	Sharp cedar
Juniperus pachyphloea	Alligator juniper
Juniperus phoenicea	Phoenician juniper
Juniperus pinchotii	Red-berry juniper
Juniperus procera	African juniper
	East African juniper
Juniperus procumbens	Creeping juniper
Juniperus recurva	Drooping juniper
	Himalayan juniper
Juniperus recurva coxii	Coffin juniper
	Cox's juniper
Juniperus rigida	Needle juniper
	Stiff-leaved juniper
	Temple juniper
Juniperus sabina	Savin
Juniperus sabina tamariscifolia	Spanish savin
Juniperus scopulorum	Colorada red cedar
	Rocky Mountains juniper
Juniperus silicicola	Southern red cedar
Juniperus squamata	Scaly-leaved Nepal juniper
Juniperus squamata meyeri	Meyer's blue juniper
Juniperus squamata pygmaea	Pigmy juniper
Juniperus suecica	Scandinavian juniper
Juniperus thurifera	Incense juniper
	Spanish juniper
Juniperus utahensis	Desert juniper
Juniperus virginiana	Eastern red cedar
	Pencil cedar
	Pencil juniper
	Red cedar
Juniperus wallichiana	Black juniper
Kallstroemia platyptera	Cork hopbush

Kalmia angustifolia	Dwarf laurel
	Lambkill
	Pig laurel
	Sheep laurel
	Wicky
Kalmia cuneata	White wicky
Kalmia glauca	American swamp laurel
	Swamp laurel
Kalmia latifolia	American laurel
	Calico bush
	Ivybush
	Mountain laurel
	Spoonwood
Kalmia microphylla	Alpine laurel
	Western laurel
Kalmia poliifolia	Bog kalmia
	Bog laurel
	Pale laurel
Kalopanax pictus	Castor aralia
	Prickly castor oil tree
Kentia belmoreana	Belmore sentry palm
	Curly palm
Kentia forsterana	Forster's sentry palm
	Kentia palm
	Sentry palm
	Thatch-leaf palm
Kerria japonica	Jew's mallow
Kerria japonica plena	Bachelor's buttons
Keteleeria davidiana	Chinese pine
Khaya nyasica	African mahogany
	Nyasaland mahogany
Khaya senegalensis	African mahogany
	Senegal mahogany
Kigelia africana	Sausage tree
	Wild peach
Kigelia pinnata	Sausage tree
Knightia excelsa	New Zealand honeysuckle tree
	Rewa rewa
Koelreuteria elegans	Flamegold
Koelreuteria paniculata	China tree
	Golden rain tree
	Pride of India
	Varnish tree
Kokia drynarioides	Kokio
Kokoona zeylanica	Kokoon tree
Kola vera	Kola nut tree
Kolkwitzia amabilis	American beautybush
	Beautybush
	Wilson's beautybush
+ *Laburnocytisus adamii*	Adam's laburnum
Laburnum alpinum	Alpine laburnum
	Scotch laburnum
Laburnum alpinum pendulum	Weeping scotch laburnum

TREES, BUSHES, AND SHRUBS

Leopoldinia piassaba

Laburnum anagyroides
    Common laburnum

*Laburnum anagyroides
aureum*   Golden chain
    Golden-leaved laburnum
    Golden rain

Laburnum vossii   Voss's laburnum

Laburnum vulgare
    Common laburnum
    Golden chain
    Golden rain

Laburnum × watereri
    Golden chain tree
    Voss's laburnum

Lagarostrobus franklinii
    Huon pine

Lagerstroemia indica   Cape myrtle
    Cranesbill myrtle

Lagerstroemia speciosa
    Pride of India
    Queen's cape myrtle

Lagunaria patersonii
    Cow itch tree
    Norfolk Island hibiscus
    Primrose tree
    Queensland pyramidal tree

Larix decidua   Common larch
    European larch

Larix decidua pendula
    Weeping european larch

Larix × eurolepis   Dunkeld larch
    Hybrid larch

Larix gmelinii   Dahurian larch

*Larix gmelinii principis-
rupprechtii*
    Prince Rupprecht larch

Larix griffithiana   Sikkim larch

Larix griffithii   Himalayan larch
    Sikkim larch

Larix kaempferi   Japanese larch
    Money pine

Larix laricina   American larch
    Black larch
    Eastern larch
    Hackmatack
    Tamarack

Larix lyalli   Alpine larch
    Lyall's larch

Larix occidentalis   Western larch

Larix × pendula   Weeping larch

Larix potaninii   Chinese larch

Larix russica   Siberian larch

Larix sibirica   Siberian larch

Larrea divaricata   Creosote bush

Larrea tridentata   Creosote bush

Latania borbonica   Bourbon palm
    Red latan

Latania loddigesii   Blue latan

Latania lontaroides   Red latan

Latania verschaffeltii   Yellow latan

Laurus azorica   Canary Island laurel

Laurus canariensis
    Canary Island laurel

Laurus maderensis
    Canary Island laurel

Laurus nobilis   Bay laurel
    Poet's laurel
    Roman laurel
    Royal bay
    Sweet bay
    True laurel

Laurus nobilis angustifolia
    Willow-leaf bay

Laurus nobilis aureus   Golden bay

Lavandula angustifolia
    Common lavender
    Old English lavender

Lavandula angustifolia vera
    Dutch lavender

Lavandula dentata
    Fringed lavender

Lavandula lanata   Woolly lavender

Lavandula officinalis
    Old English lavender
    Mitcham lavender

Lavandula spica
    Old English lavender
    Mitcham lavender

Lavandula stoechas
    Butterfly lavender
    French lavender

Lavandula vera   Dutch lavender

Lavatera arborea   Tree mallow

Lavatera assurgentiflora
    Californian tree mallow

Lavatera olbia   Bush mallow
    Shrubby mallow
    Tree mallow

Lavatera trimestris   Annual mallow
    Rose mallow

Lawsonia alba   Henna
    Mignonette tree

Lawsonia inermis   Egyptian privet
    Henna
    Mignonette tree

Ledum groenlandicum
    Labrador tea plant

Ledum latifolium
    Labrador tea plant

Ledum palustre
    Marsh ledum
    Wild rosemary

Lecythis zabucayo   Monkey nut
    Paradise nut
    Sapucia nut

Leea coccinea   West Indian holly

Leiophyllum buxifolium
    Box sand myrtle
    Sand myrtle

Leitneria floridana   Corkwood
    Florida corkwood

Leonotis leonorus   Lion's ear

Leopoldinia piassaba   Piassaba

Leptospermum laevigatum
Australian tea tree
Leptospermum lanigerum
Woolly tea tree
Leptospermum scoparium
Manuka
New Zealand tea tree
Tea tree
Leucaena glauca   White popinac
Leucodendron argenteum
Silver tree
Leucothoe fontanesiana
Fetterbush
Leycesteria formosa
Flowering nutmeg
Himalayan honeysuckle
Pheasant berry
Leycythis grandiflora   Wadadura
Leycythis usitata   Monkey pot tree
Libocedrus bidwillii   Pahautea tree
Libocedrus decurrens
Incense cedar
Libocedrus plumosa   Kawaka tree
Licula grandis   Ruffled fan palm
Ligustrum amurense   Amur privet
Ligustrum japonicum
Japanese privet
Wax-leaf privet
Ligustrum lucidum   Chinese privet
Glossy privet
Nepal privet
Shining privet
Wax-leaf privet
White wax tree
Ligustrum ovalifolium
Californian privet
Japanese privet
Oval-leaved privet
Ligustrum ovalifolium argenteum   Silver privet
Ligustrum ovalifolium aureum   Golden privet
Ligustrum sinense   Chinese privet
Ligustrum vulgare
Common privet
Prim privet
Lindera benzoin   Benjamin bush
Benzoin
Fever bush
Spice bush
Lindera melissifolia   Jove's fruit
Linnaea borealis   Twin flower
Linospadix monostachya
Walking-stick palm
Lippia citriodora   Lemon plant
Lemon verbena
Liquidambar formosana
Chinese sweet gum
Formosan gum
Liquidambar orientalis
Oriental sweet gum
Storax

Liquidambar styraciflua
American sweet gum
Bilsted gum
Red gum
Satinwood
Sweet gum
Liriodendron chinense
Chinese tulip tree
Liriodendron tulipifera
Tulip poplar
Tulip tree
Whitewood
Yellow poplar
Litchi chinensis   Leechee
Lichi
Litchi
Lychee
Lithocarpus densiflorus
Tanbark oak
Tanoak
Livistona australis
Australian cabbage palm
Australian fan palm
Cabbage palm
Gippsland fountain palm
Gippsland palm
Livistona chinensis
Chinese fan palm
Chinese fountain palm
Lodoicea maldavica   Coco-de-mer
Double coconut
Loiseleuria procumbens
Alpine azalea
Mountain azalea
Lonicera ledebourii
North American honeysuckle
Lonicera nitida
Shining honeysuckle
Bush honeysuckle
Lonicera xylosteum
Fly honeysuckle
Luma apiculata
Orange-bark myrtle
Luma chequen   Cheken
Lupinus arboreus   Tree lupin
Yellow tree lupin
Lycium afrum   Kaffir thorn
Lycium balbarum
Matrimony thorn
Matrimony vine
Lycium barbarum
Chinese box thorn
Duke of Argyll's tea tree
Lycium chinense
China tea
Duke of Argyll's tea tree
Chilean tea tree
Lycium gracillianum
Chilean tea tree
Lycium pallidum
Fremont's box thorn
Lyonia ligustrina   Male berry
Male blueberry

Malus ioensis plena

Lyonia lucida   Fetterbush
Tetterbush
Lyonia mariana   Stagger bush
Lyonothamnus floribundus
Catalina ironwood
Lysiloma latisiliqua   Sabicu
Macadamia integrifolia
Australian nut
Macadamia nut
Queensland nut
Macadamia ternifolia
Queensland nut
Small-fruited Queensland nut
Macadamia tetraphylla
Macadamia nut
Rough-shell macadamia nut
Macaranga grandifolia   Coral tree
Maclura aurantiaca   Osage orange
Maclura pomifera   Bow-wood tree
Osage orange
Macropiper excelsum   Kawa-kawa
Pepper tree
Maddenia hypoleuca
Madden cherry
Magnolia acuminata
Blue magnolia
Cucumber tree
Magnolia ashei   Ashe magnolia
Magnolia campbellii
Campbell's magnolia
Pink tulip tree
Magnolia cordata
Yellow cucumber tree
Magnolia delavayi
Chinese evergreen magnolia
Magnolia denudata   Lily tree
Yulan
Magnolia fraseri
Ear-leaved umbrella tree
Magnolia grandiflora   Bull bay
Evergreen magnolia
Laurel magnolia
Loblolly magnolia
Southern magnolia
Magnolia heptapeta   Yulan
Magnolia hypoleuca
Japanese bigleaf magnolia
Japanese cucumber tree
Magnolia kobus
Northern Japanese magnolia
Magnolia lilliflora
Lily-flowered magnolia
Magnolia macrophylla
Large-leaved cucumber tree
Large-leaved magnolia
Magnolia obovata
Japanese magnolia
Magnolia salicifolia
Willow-leaf magnolia
Magnolia sinensis
Chinese magnolia

Magnolia × soulangiana
Hybrid magnolia
Magnolia
Saucer magnolia
Magnolia sprengeri deva
Goddess magnolia
Magnolia stellata   Starry magnolia
Magnolia tripetala   Umbrella tree
Magnolia × veitchii
Veitch's magnolia
Magnolia virginiana   Swamp bay
Sweet bay
Magnolia yulan   Yulan
Mahonia aquifolium   Blue barberry
Holly barberry
Holly mahonia
Mountain grape
Oregon grape
Mahonia japonica
Japanese mahonia
Mahonia lomariifolia
Yunnan mahonia
Mahonia nervosa   Oregon grape
Water holly
Mahonia repens   Creeping barberry
Malaviscus arboreus
Pepper hibiscus
Sleepy mallow
Turk's cap
Mallotus philippinensis
Kamala tree
Kamila tree
Malpighia coccigera   Dwarf holly
Miniature holly
Singapore holly
Malpighia glabra   Barbados cherry
Malpighia urens   Cow-itch cherry
Malus angustifolia
American crab apple
Southern wild crab apple
Wild crab apple
Malus baccata   Siberian crab apple
Malus coronaria
Garland crab apple
Sweet crab apple
Sweet-scented crab
Wild sweet crab
Malus domestica   Cultivated apple
Orchard apple
Malus florentina
Hawthorn-leaf crab apple
Malus floribunda
Japanese crab apple
Purple chokeberry
Showy crab apple
Malus fusca   Oregon crab apple
Malus halliana   Hall's crab apple
Malus hupehensis
Chinese crab apple
Hupeh crab apple
Malus ioensis   Prairie crab apple
Malus ioensis plena
Bechtel crab apple

Malus × magdeburgensis	Magdeburg apple
Malus prunifolia	Plum-leaved apple
Malus pumila	Commercial apple
	Paradise apple
Malus × purpurea	Purple crab apple
Malus × robusta	Siberian crab apple
Malus sieboldii	Toringo crab
Malus × soulardii	Soulard crab
Malus spectabilis	Chinese crab apple
	Chinese flowering apple
	Hai-tung crab apple
Malus sylvestris	Common crab apple
	John Downie crab apple
	Lichfield crab apple
	Wild crab apple
Malus tschonoskii	Pillar apple
Malvaviscus arboreus	Sleeping hibiscus
	Sleepy mallow
	Wax mallow
Mammea americana	Mamey
	Mammee
	Mammee apple
	South American apricot
Mandevilla suaveolens	Chilean jasmine
Mangifera indica	Mango
Manihot dulcis	Sweet cassava
Manihot esculenta	Bitter cassava
	Cassava
	Mandioca
	Manioc
	Sweet-potato tree
	Tapioca
	Yuca
Manihot glaziovii	Ceara rubber
Manihot utilissima	Bitter cassava
Manilkara bidentata	Balata
Manilkara zapota	Chicozapote
	Marmalade plum
	Nazeberry
	Nispero
	Sapodilla
	Sapodilla plum
Margyricarpus pinnatus	Pear fruit
	Pearl berry
	Pearl fruit
Margyricarpus setosus	Pear fruit
	Pearl berry
	Pearl fruit
Mauritia flexuosa	Ita palm
	Tree-of-life
Mauritia setigera	Ita palm
	Tree-of-life
Maximiliana caribaea	Cucurite palm
	Inaja palm

Maximiliana maripa	Cucurite palm
	Inaja palm
Maximiliana regia	Cucurite palm
	Inaja palm
Maytenus boaria	Mayten
Medicago arborea	Moon trefoil
Melaleuca armillaris	Bracelet honey myrtle
Melaleuca elliptica	Granite bottlebrush
Melaleuca ericifolia	Swamp paperbark
Melaleuca huegelii	Honey myrtle
Melaleuca lanceolata	Moonah
Melaleuca lateritia	Robin redbreast bush
Melaleuca leucadendron	Cajaput
	River tea tree
	Weeping tea tree
	White tea tree
Melaleuca nematophylla	Wiry honey myrtle
Melaleuca nesophylla	Western tea myrtle
Melaleuca pubescens	Moonah
Melaleuca quinquenervia	Paperbark tree
	Punk tree
	Swamp tea tree
	Tea tree
Melaleuca rhaphiophylla	Swamp paperbark
Melaleuca squarrosa	Scented paperbark
Melastoma malabathricum	Indian rhododendron
Melia azedarach	Azediracta
	Bead tree
	Chinaberry
	China tree
	Indian lilac
	Japanese bead tree
	Paradise tree
	Persian lilac
	Pride of China
	Pride of India
	Syrian bead tree
Melia dubium	Ceylon mahogany
	White cedar
Melia indica	Indian neem tree
Melianthus major	Honey bush
Melicoccus bijugatus	Genipe
	Honeyberry
	Mamoncillo
	Spanish lime
Melicytus ramiflorus	Mahoe
	Whiteywood
Meryta sinclairii	Puka
Mespilus germanica	Medlar
Mesurea ferrea	Ironwood

Myrtus chequen

Metasequoia glyptostroboides
    Dawn redwood
    Shui-hsa
    Water fir

Metrosideros excelsa
    New Zealand christmas tree
    Pohutukawa

Metrosideros robusta   Iron tree
    New Zealand christmas tree
    Rata

Metrosideros tomentosa
    New Zealand christmas tree

Metroxylum sagu   Sago palm

Michelia champaca   Champaca
    Fragrant champaca
    Orange champaca

Michelia figo   Banana shrub

Microcitrus australasica
    Australian finger lime

Microcitrus australis
    Australian round lime

Microcoelum weddellianum
    Weddel palm

Microcycas calocoma   Palma corcho

Mimulus aurantiacus
    Shrubby musk

Mimusops balata   Beefwood

Mimusops elengi   Medlar
    Spanish cherry

Mitchella repens   Checkerberry
    Partridge berry
    Squaw berry
    Squaw vine

Monodora myristica
    African nutmeg
    Calabash nutmeg
    Jamaica nutmeg

Moquila utilis   Pottery tree

Morinda citrifolia   Awl tree
    Indian mulberry

Morinda royoc   Royoc

Moringa oleifera   Ben oil tree
    Horseradish tree

Moringa pterygosperma
    Horseradish tree

Morus alba   Silkworm tree
    White mulberry

Morus alba pendula
    Weeping mulberry

Morus australis   Aino mulberry

Morus microphylla
    Mexican mulberry

Morus nigra   Black mulberry
    Common mulberry

Morus rubra   American mulberry
    Red mulberry

Muntingia calabura   Calabur

Murraya exotica   Orange jessamine

Murraya koenigii   Curry-leaf tree
    Karapincha

Murraya paniculata   Chinese box
    Cosmetic bark tree
    Curry-leaf tree
    Orange jasmine
    Satinwood

Musa acuminata   Banana
    Edible banana
    Plantain

Musa fehi   Fehi banana

Musa nana   Dwarf banana

Musa ornata   Flowering banana

Musa × paradisiaca   Edible banana
    Plantain

Musa textilis   Abaca
    Manila hemp

Musa troglodytarum   Fehi banana

Musanga cecropioides
    Umbrella tree

Mussaenda eythrophylla
    Red flag bush

Myoporum insulare   Boobyalla

Myoporum laetum   Ngaio

Myoporum sandwicense
    Bastard sandalwood
    Naio

Myoporum tenuifolium
    Waterbush

Myoporum tetrandrum
    Tasmanian waterbush

Myrciaria cauliflora   Jaboticaba

Myrica californica
    California bayberry
    California wax myrtle

Myrica carolinensis
    Candleberry myrtle
    Wax myrtle

Myrica cerifera
    Candleberry myrtle
    Tallow shrub
    Waxberry
    Wax myrtle

Myrica faya   Candleberry myrtle

Myrica gale   Bog myrtle
    Gale
    Meadow fern
    Sweet gale

Myrica pennsylvanica   Bayberry
    Candleberry
    Northern bayberry
    Swamp candleberry

Myristica fragrans   Nutmeg

Myroxylon balsamum   Tolu tree

Myroxylon pereirae
    Balsam of Peru
    Peruvian balsam
    Tolu balsam

Myrsine africana
    African boxwood
    Cape myrtle

Myrtus bullata   Ramarama

Myrtus chequen   Chilean myrtle

Myrtus communis

Myrtus communis	Common myrtle
	Greek myrtle
	Myrtle
	Swedish myrtle
Myrtus communis tarentina	
	Tarentum myrtle
Myrtus luma	Orange-bark myrtle
Myrtus ugni	Chilean guava
Mysporum parvifolium	
	Creeping boobialla
Nandina domestica	
	Chinese sacred bamboo
	Heavenly bamboo
	Nanteen
	Sacred bamboo
Nannorrhops ritchiana	
	Mazari palm
Napoleona heudottii	
	Napolean's button
Nauclea latifolia	African peach
Nectandra rodiaei	Greenheart
Nemopanthus mucronatus	
	Catberry
	Mountain holly
Neopanax arboreus	
	Five fingers tree
Nephelium lappaceum	Pulasan
	Rambutan
Nephelium litchi	Lychee
Nephelium malaiense	
	Mata kuching
Nephelium mutabile	Pulasan
Nerium oleander	
	Common oleander
	Oleander
	Rose bay oleander
Neviusia alabamensis	
	Alabama snow wreath
Nicotiana glauca	Shrub tobacco
Noltea africana	Soap bush
Normanbya normanbyi	
	Black palm
Nothofagus antarctica	
	Antarctic beech
	Guindo
	Nirre
Nothofagus betuloides	
	Coigue de magellanes
Oval-leaved southern beech	
Nothofagus cliffortioides	
	Mountain beech
Nothofagus cunninghamii	
	Myrtle beech
	Tasmanian beech
Nothofagus dombeyi	Coigue
	Dombey's southern beech
Nothofagus fusca	
New Zealand red beech	
	Red beech
Nothofagus glauca	Hualo
	Roblé de maule
Nothofagus gunnii	
	Tanglefoot beech

Nothofagus menziesii	Silver beech
Nothofagus moorei	
	Australian beech
Nothofagus obliqua	Roblé beech
	Roblé pellin
Nothofagus procera	Raoul beech
	Rauli beech
Nothofagus pumilo	Lenga
	Roblé blanco
Nothofagus solandri	Black beech
Nothofagus solandri cliffortioides	Mountain beech
Nothofagus truncata	Hard beech
Notospartium carmicheliae	
	Pink broom
Nuttallia cerasiformis	Oso-berry
Nuytsia floribunda	Christmas tree
	Fire tree
Nyctanthes arbor-tristis	
	Indian night jasmine
	Night jasmine
	Tree-of-sadness
Nypa fruticans	Mangrove palm
	Nipa palm
	Nypa palm
Nyssa aquatica	Cotton gum
	Large tupelo
	Tupelo gum
	Water tupelo
	Wild olive
Nyssa candicans	Ogechee lime
Nyssa sylvatica	Black gum
	Black tupelo
	Pepperidge
	Sour gum
	Tupelo
	Upland tupelo
Ochna japonica	Bird's eye bush
	Mickey-mouse plant
Ochna serrulata	Bird's eye bush
	Mickey-mouse plant
Ochroma pyramidale	Balsa wood
	Corkwood
Ocotea bullata	Black stinkwood
	Greenheart
Ocotea radiaei	Greenheart
Oemleria cerasiformis	Indian plum
	Oso-berry
Oenocarpus batava	Patana palm
Olea africana	Wild olive
Olea europaea	Common olive
	Olive
Olea ferruninea	Indian olive
Olea laurifolia	Black ironwood
Olearia argophylla	Muskwood
Olearia illicifolia	Maori holly
	Mountain holly
Olearia macrodonta	
	New Zealand holly
Olearia nummularifolia	
	Daisy bush

Passiflora suberosa

Olearia phlogopappa
Daisy bush
Tasmanian daisy bush

Olinia emarginata
Transvaal hard pear

Olmediella betschlerana
Costa Rican holly
Manzanote
Puerto Rican holly

Olneya tesota Desert ironwood

Oncoba spinosa Snuffbox tree

Oncosperma tigillarium
Nibung palm

Oplopanax horridus Devil's club

Orbignya barbosiana Babassu

Orbignya cohune Cohune palm

Orbignya speciosa Babassu palm

Osmanthus americanus
American olive
Devil wood
Wild olive

Osmanthus fragrans Fragrant olive
Sweet olive
Tea olive

Osmanthus heterophyllus
Chinese holly
False holly
Holly-leaved olive

Osmaronia cerasiformis
Oso-berry

Osmunda regalis Royal fern

Ostrya carpinifolia
European hop-hornbeam
Hop hornbeam

Ostrya japonica
Japanese hop-hornbeam

Ostrya virginiana
American hop-hornbeam
Eastern hop-hornbeam
Ironwood
Leverwood

Oxandra lanceolata Lancewood

Oxycoccus macrocarpus
American cranberry

Oxycoccus oxycoccus
European wild cranberry

Oxycoccus palustris
European wild cranberry

Oxydendrum arboreum
Sorrel tree
Sourwood tree
Titi

Ozothamnus rosmarinifolius
Snow in summer

Ozothamnus thyrsoidens
Snow in summer

Pachira aquatica Guiana chestnut
Provision tree
Water chestnut
Wild cocoa tree

Pachira insignis Wild chestnut

Pachysandra procumbens
Alleghany spurge

Pachysandra terminalis
Mountain spurge

Paeonia delavayi Tree peony

Paeonia suffruticosa Moutan
Moutan paeony
Tree peony

Palaquium gutta Gutta percha

Paliurus aculeatus Christ's thorn
Jerusalem thorn

Paliurus australis Christ's thorn

Paliurus spina-christi
Christ's thorn
Crown of thorns
Jerusalem thorn

Paliurus virgatus Christ's thorn

Palmae hyphaene Doum palm
Gingerbread palm

Palmetto causiarum
Puerto Rican hat palm

Pandanus leram
Nicobar breadfruit
Screwpine

Pandanus odoratissimus
Breadfruit
Pandang

Pandanus tectorius Pandanus palm
Thatch screw palm

Pandanus utilis
Common screw palm

Pandanus veitchii
Veitch's screw pine

Pandorea jasminiodes
Australian bower plant
Bower plant

Parinari curatellifolia
Mobala plum

Parinari excelsa Guinea plum

Parinari macrophylla
Gingerbread plum
Gingerbread tree

Parkia biglobosa African locust

Parkia filicoidea
African locust bean

Parkia speciosa Petai

Parkinsonia aculeata
Jerusalem thorn
Mexican palo verde

Parmentiera cereifera
Candle tree
Panama candle tree

Parmentiera edulis Cuachilote
Guajilote

Parrotia persica Iron tree
Persian ironwood

Passiflora caerulea
Blue passion flower
Brazilian passion flower
Passion flower

Passiflora suberosa Meloncillo

Paulownia tomentosa
 Empress tree
 Foxglove tree
 Karri tree
 Paulownia
 Princess tree

Peltophorum pterocarpum
 Copper-pod tree
 Yellow flame tree

Persea americana
 Aguacate
 Alligator pear
 Avocado pear
 Palta

Persea borbonia Florida mahogany
 Laurel tree
 Red bay
 Swamp red bay
 Sweet bay
 Tisswood

Persea indica Indian laurel

Peumus boldus Boldo
 Chilean boldo tree

Phellodendron amurense
 Amur cork tree

Phellodendron chinensis
 Chinese cork tree

Phellodendron japonicum
 Japanese cork tree

Philadelphus coronarius
 Mock orange
 Syringa

Phillyrea decora Jasmine box

Phillyrea latifolia Phillyrea

Phillyrea vilmoriniana
 Jasmine box

Phoenix abyssinica
 Ethiopian date palm

Phoenix canariensis Canary palm
 Canary date palm
 Canary Island date

Phoenix dactylifera Date palm

Phoenix paludosa
 Mangrove date palm

Phoenix reclinata
 Senegal date palm

Phoenix roebelenii
 Miniature date palm
 Pygmy date palm
 Roebelin palm

Phoenix rupicola Cliff date palm
 East Indian wine palm
 India date palm
 Wild date palm

Phoenix sylvestris India date palm
 Wild date palm

Phoenix zeylanica
 Ceylon date palm

Phorium tenax New Zealand flax

Photinia glabra Japanese photinia

Photinia serrulata
 Chinese hawthorn

Phygelius capensis Cape figwort

Phyllanthus acidus
 Gooseberry tree
 Indian gooseberry
 Otaheite gooseberry

Phyllanthus emblica Emblic
 Myrobalan

Phyllirea vilmoriniana
 Jasmine box

Phyllocladus alpinus
 Alpine celery-topped pine
 Celery pine

Phyllocladus asplenifolius
 Adventure bay pine
 Celery pine
 Celery-topped pine

Phyllocladus glaucus Toatoa tree

Phyllocladus rhomboidalis
 Celery-top pine

Phyllocladus trichomanoides
 Celery pine
 Tanekaha tree

Physocarpus opulifolius Ninebark

Phytelephas macrocarpa
 Ivory-nut palm
 Ivory palm
 Tagua

Phytolacca dioica Phytolacca

Picea abies Christmas tree
 Common spruce
 Norway spruce

Picea abies carpathica
 Carpathian spruce

Picea abies maxwellii
 Maxwell spruce

Picea abies nidiformis Nest spruce

Picea alcoquiana Alcock's spruce

Picea asperata Chinese spruce
 Dragon spruce

Picea bicolor Alcock's spruce

Picea brachytyla Sargent's spruce

Picea brewerana
 Brewer's weeping spruce
 Siskiyou spruce
 Weeping spruce

Picea cembroides Nut pine

Picea engelmannii
 Engelmann's spruce

Picea glauca Cat spruce
 White spruce

Picea glauca albertiana
 Alberta white spruce

Picea glauca albertiana nana
 Dwarf alberta spruce

Picea glehnii Saghalin spruce
 Sakhalin spruce

Picea jezoensis Yeddo spruce
 Yezo spruce

Picea jezoensis hondoensis
 Hondo spruce

Picea koyamai Koyama spruce

Picea likiangensis Likiang spruce

TREES, BUSHES, AND SHRUBS

Pinus jeffreyi

Picea likiangensis purpurea	
	Purple spruce
Picea mariana	Black spruce
	Bog spruce
	Double spruce
Picea maximowiczii	
	Japanese spruce
Picea montigena	
	Candelabra spruce
Picea monophylla	Nut pine
	Single-leaf pinyon pine
	Stone pine
Picea morrisonicola	
	Mount Morrison spruce
	Taiwan spruce
Picea nigra	Black spruce
	Bog spruce
	Double spruce
Picea obovata	Siberian spruce
Picea omorika	Serbian spruce
Picea orientalis	Oriental spruce
Picea polita	Japanese spruce
	Tiger-tail spruce
Picea pungens	Blue spruce
	Colorado spruce
Picea pungens glauca	Blue spruce
	Colorado blue spruce
Picea rubens	American red spruce
	Red spruce
Picea rubra	Red spruce
Picea schrenkiana	Schrenk's spruce
Picea sitchensis	Silver spruce
	Sitka spruce
Picea smithiana	Himalayan spruce
	Indian spruce
	Morinda spruce
	West Himalayan spruce
Picea spinulosa	
	East Himalayan spruce
	Sikkim spruce
Picea torana	Tiger-tail spruce
Picraena excelsa	Bitter ash
	Jamaica quassia
Picramnia antidesma	Cascara
Picramnia pentandra	Bitterbush
Picrasma quassioides	Picrasma
Pilocarpus jaborandi	Jaborand
	Jaborandi
Pilostegia viburnoides	
	Climbing hydrangea
Pimenta dioica	Allspice
	Pimento
Pimenta officinalis	Allspice
	Jamaica pepper
	Pimento
Pimenta racemosa	Bay tree
	Bay-
	rum tree
Pinckneya pubens	Bitter bark
	Fever tree
	Georgia bark tree
Pinus albicaulis	White-bark pine

Pinus aristata	Bristle-cone pine
	Hickory pine
Pinus armandii	Armand's pine
	Chinese white pine
	David's pine
Pinus attenuata	Knobcone pine
Pinus ayacahuite	
	Mexican white pine
Pinus balfouriana	Foxtail pine
Pinus banksiana	Grey pine
	Jack pine
	Scrub pine
Pinus brutia	Calabrian pine
Pinus bungeana	Lacebark pine
Pinus canariensis	
	Canary Island pine
Pinus caribaea	Caribbean pine
	Cuban pine
Pinus cembra	Arolla pine
	Russian cedar
	Swiss stone pine
Pinus cembroides	Mexican nut pine
	Mexican stone pine
	Nut pine
	Pinyon pine
Pinus cembroides monophylla	
	One-leaved nut pine
Pinus cembroides edulis	
	Two-leaved nut pine
Pinus clausa	Sand pine
Pinus contorta	Beach pine
	Lodgepole pine
	Shore pine
Pinus contorta latifolia	
	Inland lodgepole pine
	Lodgepole pine
Pinus coulteri	Big-cone pine
Pinus densiflora	Japanese red pine
Pinus densiflora oculus-draconis	
	Dragon-eye pine
Pinus echinata	Short-leaf pine
	Yellow pine
Pinus edulis	Nut pine
	Pinyon pine
	Two-leaved nut pine
Pinus elliottii	Elliott's pine
	Slash pine
Pinus engelmannii	Apache pine
Pinus excelsa	Bhutan pine
Pinus flexilis	Limber pine
Pinus gerardiana	Chilghoza pine
	Gerard's pine
	Nepal nut pine
Pinus glabra	Cedar pine
	Spruce pine
Pinus greggii	Gregg's pine
Pinus halepensis	Aleppo pine
	Jerusalem pine
Pinus × holfordiana	Holford pine
Pinus insularis	Benguet pine
	Khasya pine
Pinus jeffreyi	Jeffrey's pine

Pinus kerkusii

Pinus kerkusii	Tenasserim pine
Pinus khasya	Khasya pine
Pinus koraiensis	Korean pine
Pinus lambertiana	Giant pine
	Sugar pine
Pinus leucodermis	Bosnian pine
	Okinawa pine
Pinus luchuensis	Luchu pine
Pinus merkusii	Tenasserim pine
Pinus monophylla	Nut pine
	Single-leaf pine
	Stone pine
Pinus montezumae	
	Montezuma pine
	Rough-barked Mexican pine
Pinus monticola	
	Californian mountain pine
	Mountain white pine
	Western white pine
Pinus mugo	Dwarf mountain pine
	Mountain pine
	Swiss mountain pine
Pinus mugo pumilo	
	European scrub pine
Pinus muricata	Bishop pine
Pinus nigra	Austrian pine
Pinus nigra caramanica	
	Austrian pine
	Crimean pine
Pinus nigra cebennensis	
	Cevennes pine
	Pyrenean pine
Pinus nigra maritima	
	Corsican pine
Pinus nigra nigra	Austrian pine
Pinus occidentalis	Cuban pine
Pinus palustris	Georgia pine
	Long-leaf pine
	Pitch pine
	Southern pine
	Southern pitch pine
	Southern yellow pine
Pinus parviflora	
	Japanese white pine
Pinus patula	Jelecote pine
	Mexican pine
	Mexican weeping pine
	Spread-leaved pine
Pinus peuce	Macedonian pine
Pinus pinaster	Bournemouth pine
	Cluster pine
	Maritime pine
Pinus pinea	Italian stone pine
	Stone pine
	Umbrella pine
Pinus ponderosa	Ponderosa pine
	Western yellow pine
Pinus ponderosa arizonica	
	Arizona pine
Pinus pumila	Dwarf Siberian pine
	Dwarf stone pine
	Japanese pine

Pinus pungens	Hickory pine
	Prickly pine
	Table mountain pine
Pinus quadrifolia	Parry pine
Pinus radiata	Monterey pine
	Remarkable cone pine
Pinus resinosa	American red pine
	Canadian red pine
	Norway pine
	Red pine
Pinus rigida	Northern pitch pine
	Pitch pine
Pinus roxburghii	Indian cher pine
	Long-leaved Indian pine
Pinus sabiniana	Digger pine
Pinus strobus	Deal pine
	Eastern white pine
	Weymouth pine
	White pine
Pinus sylvestris	Scotch fir
	Scot's pine
Pinus rubra	Highland pine
Pinus tabuliformis	Chinese pine
Pinus taeda	Frankincense pine
	Loblolly pine
	Oldfield pine
Pinus teocote	Twisted-leaf pine
Pinus thunbergii	Black pine
	Japanese black pine
Pinus toeda	Frankincense pine
Pinus torreyana	Soledad pine
	Torrey pine
Pinus uncinata	Mountain pine
Pinus virginiana	Jersey pine
	Poverty pine
	Scrub pine
	Spruce pine
Pinus wallichiana	Bhutan pine
	Blue pine
	Himalayan pine
	Himalayan white pine
Piper angustifolium	Matico
Piper betel	Betel
	Betel pepper
Piper betle	Betel
	Betel pepper
Piper methysticum	Kava
Piptanthus laburnifolius	
	Evergreen laburnum
	Nepal laburnum
Piptanthus nepalensis	
	Evergreen laburnum
Piscidia erythrina	Fish-poison tree
	Jamaica dogwood
Piscidia piscipula	
	Jamaican dogwood
	West Indian dogwood
Pisonia alba	Lettuce tree
Pisonia grandis	
	Brown cabbage tree
Pisonia umbellifera	
	Bird-catcher tree
	Para-para

Podocarpus spicatus

Pistacia atlantica
Mount Atlas mastic tree
Pistacia chinensis Chinese pistachio
Pistacia lentiscus Chios mastic tree
Mastic tree
Pistacia terebinthus
Chian turpentine tree
Cyprus turpentine tree
Terebinth
Turpentine tree
Pistacia texana American pistachio
Lentisco
Pistacia vera Green almond
Pistachio
Pistacia nut
Pithecellobium dulce Huamuchii
Manila tamarind
Opiuma
Pithecellobium flexicaule
Texas ebony
Pithecellobium guadalupense
Blackbead
Pithecellobium unguis-cati
Blackbead
Cat's claw
Pittosporum crassifolium Karo
Pittosporum eugenioides
Lemonwood
Tarata
Pittosporum phillyraeoides
Narrow-leaved pittosporum
Willow pittosporum
Pittosporum rhombifolium
Queensland pittosporum
Pittosporum tenuifolium Kohuhu
New Zealand pittosporum
Pittosporum
Tawhiwhi
Pittosporum tobira
Australian laurel
Japanese pittosporum
Mock orange
Tobira
Pittosporum undulatum
Mock orange
Victorian box
Pittosporum viridiflorum
Cape pittosporum
Plagianthus regius
Ribbonwood tree
Planera aquatica Water elm
Planera ulmifolia Water elm
Platanus × acerifolia
London plane
Platanus × hispanicus
London plane
Platanus hybrida London plane
Platanus occidentalis
American plane
American sycamore
Buttonball
Buttonwood
Eastern sycamore
Western plane

Platanus orientalis Chennar tree
Oriental plane
West Asian plane
Platanus orientalis insularis
Cyprian plane
Platycladus orientalis
Oriental arborvitae
Pleiogynium cerasiferum
Burdekin plum
Queensland hog plum
Plueria rubra Pagoda tree
Plumeria acuminata Frangipani
Plumeria rubra Frangipani tree
Nosegay tree
Red jasmine
Temple tree
West Indian jasmine
Podalyria calyptrata
Sweet pea bush
Water blossom pea
Podalyria sericea Satin bush
Podocarpus amarus Black pine
Podocarpus andinus Chilean yew
Plum fir
Plum-fruited yew
Podocarpus chilinus
Willow podocarp
Podocarpus dacrydioides Kahika
Kahikatea
Red pine
White pine
Podocarpus elatus Brown pine
She pine
White pine
Podocarpus elongatus
African yellowwood
Fern podocarpus
Weeping podocarpus
Podocarpus falcatus
Common yellowwood
Oteniqua yellowwood
Podocarpus ferrugineus Miro
Rusty podocarp
Podocarpus gracilior
African fern pine
Podocarpus latifolius
Real yellowwood
Podocarpus macrophyllus
Buddhist pine
Japanese yew
Kusamaki tree
Large-leaved podocarp
Southern yew
Podocarpus nagi
Broadleaf podocarpus
Nagi
Podocarpus nivalis Alpine totara
Podocarpus nubigenus
Chilean totara
Manio
Podocarpus salignus
Willow podocarp
Podocarpus spicatus Matai
New Zealand black pine

Podocarpus totara	Mahogany pine
	Totara
Poinciana gilliesii	Bird of paradise
Polygala cowellii	Tortuguero
	Violet tree
Polygonum baldschuanicum	
	Russian vine
Polyscias balfouriana	
	Balfour's aralia
Polyscias filicifolia	Fern-leaf aralia
Polyscias fruticosa	Ming aralia
Polyscias guilfoylei	Coffee tree
	Geranium-leaf aralia
	Wild coffee
Poncirus trifoliata	Hardy orange
	Japanese bitter orange
	Trifoliate orange
Pongamia pinnata	Karum tree
	Poonga oil tree
Populus adenopoda	Chinese aspen
Populus alba	Abele
	Silver-leaved poplar
	White poplar
Populus angulata	Carolina poplar
Populus angustifolia	
	Willow-leaved poplar
Populus balsamifera	
	Balsam poplar
	Hackmatack
	Tacamahak
Populus × berolinensis	
	Berlin poplar
Populus × canadensis	
	Carolina poplar
	Hybrid black poplar
Populus candicans	Balm of gilead
	Ontario poplar
Populus canescens	Grey poplar
Populus deltoides	Cottonwood
	Eastern cottonwood
	Necklace poplar
Populus eugenei	Carolina poplar
Populus fremontii	Fremont poplar
Populus gileadensis	Balm of gilead
Populus grandidentata	
	Big-toothed aspen
Populus heterophylla	
	Black cottonwood
	Downy poplar
	Swamp cottonwood
Populus lasiocarpa	
	Chinese necklace poplar
	Chinese poplar
	Necklace poplar
Populus laurifolia	
	Siberian balsam poplar
Populus maximowiczii	
	Japanese poplar
Populus nigra	Black poplar
	Lombardy poplar
Populus nigra betulifolia	
	Downy black poplar
	Manchester poplar

Populus nigra italica	Italian poplar
	Lombardy poplar
Populus nigra italica foemina	
	Female lombardy poplar
Populus nigra plantierensis	
	Western lombardy poplar
Populus regenerata	Railway poplar
Populus robusta	
	False lombardy poplar
Populus sargentii	
	Great plains cottonwood
Populus serotina	
	Black italian poplar
Populus serotina aurea	
	Golden poplar
Populus sieboldii	Japanese aspen
Populus tacamahaca	
	Balsam poplar
Populus tremula	Aspen
	European aspen
	Trembling aspen
Populus tremula pendula	
	Weeping aspen
Populus tremuloides	
	American aspen
	Quaking aspen
	Quiverleaf
	Trembling aspen
Populus tremuloides pendula	
	Parasol de Saint. Julien
Populus trichocarpa	
	Black cottonwood
	Western balsam poplar
Portulacaria afra	Elephant bush
Posoqueria latifolia	
	Needleflower tree
Pouteria campechiana	Canistel
	Eggfruit
	Sapote amarillo
	Sapote borracho
	Ti-es
Pouteria sapota	Mamey colorado
	Mamey sapote
	Mammee sapote
	Marmalade plum
	Sapote
Pritchardia pacifica	Fiji fan palm
Prosopsis chilensis	Algarrobo
Prosopsis glandulosa	Mesquite
Prosopsis juliflora	Algarrobo
	Mesquite
Prosopsis pubescens	Screw bean
	Tornillo
Protea aurea	Waterlily protea
Protea barbigera	
	Giant woolly protea
Protea cynaroides	Giant protea
	King protea
Protea grandiceps	Peach protea
Protea mellifera	Honey flower
	Honey protea
	Sugarbush
Protea repens	Sugarbush

TREES, BUSHES, AND SHRUBS

Prunus ivensii

Prumnopitys ferruginea	Miro
Prumnopitys taxifolia	Matai
New Zealand black pine	
Prunus alleghaniensis	
Alleghany plum	
American sloe	
Sloe	
Prunus amanagawa	
Erect Japanese cherry	
Lombardy poplar cherry	
Prunus americana	
American red plum	
American wild plum	
August plum	
Goose plum	
Hog plum	
Prunus × amygdalopersica	
pollardii	Pollard's almond
Prunus amygdalus	
Common almond	
Prunus andersonii	Desert peach
Prunus angustifolia	
Chickasaw plum	
Sand plum	
Prunus armeniaca	Apricot
Common apricot	
Prunus avium	Bird cherry
Gean	
Mazzard	
Sweet cherry	
Wild cherry	
Prunus avium plena	Double gean
Double white cherry	
Prunus avium sylvestris	Gean
Prunus besseyi	
Rocky mountain cherry	
Sand cherry	
Western sand cherry	
Prunus (blireana	
Double cherry-plum	
Prunus brigantina	
Briançon apricot	
Prunus campanulata	
Bell-flowered cherry	
Formosan cherry	
Taiwan cherry	
Prunus canescens	Greyleaf cherry
Prunus capuli	Mexican cherry
Prunus caroliniana	
American mock orange	
Cherry laurel	
Mock orange	
Wild orange	
Prunus cerasifera	Cherry plum
Flowering plum	
Greenglow plum	
Myrobalan plum	
Prunus cerasifera	
atropurpurea	Purple plum
Prunus cerasifera nigra	
Black-leaved plum	
Blaze	

Prunus cerasifera pissardii	
Purple flash	
Purple-leaved plum	
Prunus cerasoides rubea	
Kingdon Ward's carmine cherry	
Prunus cerasus	Pie cherry
Sour cherry	
Prunus cerasus semperflorens	
All saints cherry	
Prunus × cistena	
Crimson dwarf cherry	
Purple-leaf sand cherry	
Prunus communis	
Common almond	
Prunus conradinae	Chinese cherry
Prunus cornuta	
Himalayan bird cherry	
Prunus × dasycarpa	Black apricot
Purple apricot	
Prunus davidiana	Chinese peach
Prunus depressa	Sand cherry
Prunus domestica	Damson
Plum	
Prune	
Wild plum	
Prunus domestica institia	Bullace
Damson	
Prunus domestica italica	
Greengage	
Prunus dulcis	Almond
Common almond	
Sweet almond	
Prunus dulcis amara	
Bitter almond	
Prunus dulcis roseoplena	
Double almond	
Prunus × effusus	Duke cherry
Prunus emarginata	Bitter cherry
Oregon cherry	
Prunus fasciculata	Desert almond
Wild almond	
Wild peach	
Prunus fremontii	Desert apricot
Prunus fruticosa	Dwarf cherry
Ground cherry	
Prunus glandulosa	
Chinese bush cherry	
Flowering almond	
Prunus gracilis	Oklahoma plum
Prairie cherry	
Prunus × gondouinii	Duke cherry
Prunus ilicifolia	Evergreen cherry
Holly-leaved cherry	
Islay plum	
Mountain holly	
Wild cherry	
Prunus incana	Willow cherry
Prunus incisa	Fuji cherry
Prunus insititia	Bullace
Damson	
Prunus ivensii	Weeping cherry

BOTANICAL NAMES

Prunus jacquemontii

Prunus jacquemontii	
	Afghan cherry
	Flowering almond
Prunus japonica	Flowering almond
	Japanese bush cherry
	Japanese plum
Prunus laurocerasus	Cherry laurel
	Common laurel
	English laurel
	Laurel
Prunus laurocerasus serbica	
	Serbian laurel
Prunus leveilleana	
	Korean hill cherry
Prunus litigiosa	Tassel cherry
Prunus lusitanica	Portugal laurel
Prunus lyonii	Catalina cherry
Prunus maackii	Manchurian cherry
Prunus mahaleb	Mahaleb
	Perfumed cherry
	Saint lucie cherry
Prunus mandshurica	
	Manchurian apricot
Prunus maritima	Beach plum
	Shore plum
Prunus mugus	Tibetan cherry
Prunus mume	Japanese apricot
Prunus munsoniana	
	Wild-goose plum
Prunus mutabilis stricta	
	Chinese hill cherry
Prunus nigra	Canada plum
Prunus nipponica	
	Japanese alpine cherry
Prunus padus	Bird cherry
	European bird cherry
	Hagberry
Prunus padus colorata	
	Purple-leaved bird cherry
Prunus pennsylvanica	Bird cherry
	Fire cherry
	Pin cherry
	Wild red cherry
Prunus persica	Common peach
	Peach
Prunus persica nectarina	
	Nectarine
Prunus persica nucipersica	
	Nectarine
Prunus prostrata	Mountain cherry
	Rock cherry
Prunus pumila	
	Dwarf American cherry
	Dwarf cherry
	Sand cherry
Prunus reverchonii	Hog plum
Prunus rufa	Himalayan cherry
Prunus salicifolia	Capulin cherry
Prunus salicina	Japanese plum
Prunus sargentii	
	Japanese hill cherry
	Sargent's cherry

Prunus serotina	
	American black cherry
	Black cherry
	Rum cherry
Prunus serrula	Birchbark cherry
	Paperbark cherry
	Tibetan cherry
Prunus serrulata	Hill cherry
	Japanese cherry
	Oriental cherry
Prunus serrulata hupehensis	
	Chinese hill cherry
	Hupeh cherry
Prunus serrulata kanzan	
	Japanese double pink cherry
Prunus serrulata pubescens	
	Korean hill cherry
Prunus serrulata spontanea	
	Hill cherry
Prunus sibirica	Siberian apricot
Prunus simonii	Apricot plum
	Simon's plum
Prunus speciosa	Oshima cherry
Prunus spinosa	Blackthorn
	Sloe
Prunus subcordata	Oregon plum
	Pacific plum
	Sierra plum
Prunus subhirtella	Higan cherry
	Rosebud cherry
	Spring cherry
Prunus subhirtella ascendens	
	Rosebud cherry
Prunus subhirtella autumnalis	
	Autumn cherry
	Higan cherry
	Winter cherry
	Winter-flowering cherry
Prunus subhirtella pendula	
	Weeping cherry
	Weeping rosebud cherry
Prunus subhirtella pendula rosea	
	Weeping spring cherry
Prunus × sultana	Wickson plum
Prunus tai-haku	
	Great white cherry
Prunus tenella	
	Dwarf Russian almond
	Russian almond
Prunus tomentosa	
	Chinese bush cherry
	Downy cherry
	Hansen's cherry
	Nanking cherry
Prunus triflora	Japanese plum
Prunus triloba	Flowering almond
Prunus virginiana	Choke cherry
	Virginian bird cherry
Prunus virginiana demissa	
	Western choke cherry

TREES, BUSHES, AND SHRUBS

Prunus yedoensis
Japanese flowering cherry
Potomac cherry
Yoshino cherry

Pseudobombax ellipticum
Shaving-brush tree

Pseudocydonia sinensis
Chinese quince

Pseudolarix amabilis   Golden larch

Pseudolarix kaempferi
Golden larch

Pseudopanax crassifolius
Lancewood

Pseudotsuga japonica
Japanese douglas fir

Pseudotsuga macrocarpa
Big-cone spruce
Large-coned douglas fir

Pseudotsuga menziesii   Douglas fir
Oregon douglas fir

Pseudotsuga menziesii caesia
Frazer river douglas fir
Grey douglas fir

Pseudotsuga menziesii glauca
Blue douglas fir

Pseudotsuga sinensis
Chinese douglas fir

Pseudotsuga wilsoniana
Wilson's douglas fir

Psidium cattleianum
Strawberry guava

Psidium friedrichsthalianum
Costa Rican guava

Psidium guajava   Apple guava
Common guava
Guava
Yellow guava

Psidium guineense   Guava

Psidium montanum
Mountain guava
Spice guava

Psychotria emetica   False ipecac

Psychotria nervosa   Wild coffee

Psychotria sulzneri   Wild coffee

Ptelea trifoliata   Hop tree
Shrubby trefoil
Stinking ash
Swamp dogwood
Water ash
Wingseed

Pterocarpus angolensis
Transvaal teak
West African barwood

Pterocarpus erinaceus   Barwood
Senegal rosewood
West African kino

Pterocarpus indicus
Burmese rosewood
Padauk

Pterocarpus marsupium
Bastard teak
Kinos

Pterocarpus santalinus
Red sandalwood
Red saunders
Sanderswood

Pterocarya fraxinifolia
Caucasian wing nut

Pterocarya × rehderana
Hybrid wing nut

Pterocarya rhoifolia
Japanese wing nut

Pterocarya stenoptera
Chinese wing nut

Pterostyrax hispida   Asgara
Epaulette tree

Ptychosperma elegans
Alexander palm
Solitary palm

Ptychosperma macarthurii
Hurricane palm
Macarthur palm

Punica granatum   Pomegranate

Punica granatum nana
Dwarf pomegranate

Pyracantha atalantoides
Gibb's firethorn

Pyracantha coccinea
Buisson ardent
Firethorn

Pyracantha crenulata
Nepalese white thorn

Pyrus amygdaliformis
Almond-leaved pear

Pyrus austriaca   Austrian pear

Pyrus caucasica   Caucasian pear

Pyrus communis   Common pear
Wild pear

Pyrus cordata   Plymouth pear

Pyrus kawakamii   Evergreen pear

Pyrus nivalis   Snow pear

Pyrus pashia   Kumaon pear

Pyrus pyraster   Wild pear

Pyrus pyrifolia   Asian pear
Chinese sand pear
Japanese pear
Kumoi
Nashi
Oriental pear
Sand pear

Pyrus salicifolia   Silver pear
Willow-leaved pear

Pyrus salicifolia pendula
Weeping pear
Weeping willow-leaved pear

Pyrus salvifolia   Sage-leaved pear

Pyrus ussuriensis   Chinese pear
Sand pear

Quassia amara   Bitterwood
Surinam quassia

Quercus acuta
Japanese evergreen oak
Japanese red oak

Quercus acutissima

Quercus acutissima	Chestnut oak
	Japanese chestnut oak
	Sawtooth oak
Quercus agrifolia	Californian field oak
	Californian live oak
	Encina
Quercus alba	White oak
Quercus aliena	Oriental white oak
Quercus alnifolia	
	Cyprus golden oak
	Golden oak
Quercus bicolor	
	American white oak
	Swamp white oak
Quercus borealis	Red oak
Quercus calliprinos	Palestine oak
Quercus canariensis	Algerian oak
	Mirbeck's oak
Quercus castaneifolia	Chestnut-leaved oak
Quercus cerris	Bitter oak
	Mossy cup oak
	Turkey oak
Quercus chrysolepis	
	Californian live oak
	Canyon live oak
	Golden-cup oak
	Maul oak
Quercus coccifera	Kermes oak
Quercus coccinea	Scarlet oak
Quercus conferta	Hungarian oak
Quercus conocarpa	Singapore oak
Quercus dentata	Daimyo oak
Quercus douglasii	Blue oak
Quercus dumosa	
	Californian scrub oak
	Scrub oak
Quercus durata	Leather oak
Quercus ellipsoidalis	Jack oak
	Northern pin oak
Quercus emoryi	Emory oak
Quercus engelmannii	
	Engelmann's oak
Quercus faginea	Portuguese oak
Quercus falcata	Spanish oak
	Spanish red oak
Quercus frainetto	Hungarian oak
	Italian oak
	Macedonian oak
Quercus gambelii	Gambel's oak
	Shin oak
Quercus × *ganderi*	Gander's oak
Quercus garryana	Oregon oak
	Oregon white oak
	Western oak
Quercus glandulifera	Konara oak
Quercus glauca	Ring-cupped oak
Quercus havardii	Havard oak
	Shinnery oak
Quercus × *heterophylla*	
	Bartram oak

Quercus × *hispanica*	
	Luccombe oak
Quercus × *hispanica lucombeana*	
	Exeter oak
Quercus ilex	Evergreen oak
	Holly oak
	Holm oak
Quercus ilicifolia	Bear oak
	Scrub oak
Quercus imbricaria	Laurel oak
	Shingle oak
Quercus incana	Bluejack oak
	High-ground willow oak
	Sand jack
	Turkey oak
Quercus ithaburensis	Valonia oak
Quercus kelloggii	
	Californian black oak
	Kellogg oak
Quercus laevis	Catesby oak
	Turkey oak
Quercus laurifolia	Darlington oak
	Laurel oak
Quercus libani	Lebanon oak
Quercus lobata	
	Californian white oak
	Valley oak
Quercus lusitanica	
	Portuguese oak
Quercus × *ludoviciana*	
	Ludwig's oak
Quercus lyrata	Overcup oak
	Swamp post oak
Quercus macdonaldii	
	Macdonald oak
Quercus macedonica	
	Macedonian oak
Quercus macranthera	
	Caucasian oak
Quercus macrocarpa	Burr oak
	Mossy cup oak
Quercus macrolepis	Valonia oak
Quercus maingayi	Maingay's oak
Quercus marilandica	
	Blackjack oak
	Blackthorn oak
	Jack oak
Quercus michauxii	
	Swamp chestnut oak
Quercus mirbeckii	Algerian oak
Quercus mongolica	Mongul oak
Quercus muehlenbergii	
	Chestnut oak
	Yellow chestnut oak
	Yellow oak
Quercus myrsinaefolia	
	Bamboo-leaved oak
Quercus nigra	Possum oak
	Water oak
Quercus palustris	Pin oak
	Spanish oak
Quercus petraea	Durmast oak
	Sessile oak

TREES, BUSHES, AND SHRUBS

Rhododendron catawbiense

Quercus phellos	Willow oak
Quercus phillyraeoides	
	Ubame oak
Quercus pontica	Armenian oak
	Pontine oak
Quercus prinoides	Chinquapin oak
	Dwarf chestnut oak
Quercus prinus	
	Bamboo-leaved oak
	Basket oak
	Chestnut oak
	Rock chestnut oak
	Swamp chestnut oak
Quercus pubescens	Downy oak
	Green oak
Quercus pyrenaica	Pyrenean oak
Quercus rober	Common oak
	English oak
	Pendunculate oak
	Truffle oak
Quercus rober concordia	
	Golden oak
Quercus rober pendula	
	Weeping oak
Quercus rober purpurescens	
	Purple English oak
Quercus robur asplenifolia	
	Fern-leaved oak
Quercus robur fastigiata	
	Cypress oak
Quercus robur filicifolia	
	Cut-leaf oak
Quercus rubra	American red oak
	Northern red oak
	Red oak
Quercus sadlerana	Deer oak
Quercus shumardii	Shumard's oak
	Shumard's red oak
Quercus stellata	Post oak
Quercus suber	Cork oak
Quercus texana	Texas red oak
Quercus tomentella	Island oak
Quercus trojana	Macedonian oak
Quercus (turneri	Turner's oak
Quercus undulata	
	Rocky mountain scrub oak
Quercus vaccinifolia	
	Huckleberry oak
Quercus variabilis	
	Chinese cork oak
	Oriental cork oak
Quercus velutina	Black oak
	Quercitron
	Yellow-bark oak
Quercus velutina rubrifolia	
	Champion's oak
Quercus virginiana	Live oak
	Southern live oak
Quercus warburgii	Cambridge oak
Quercus wislizenii	
	Interior live oak

Quillaia saponaria	Soap bark tree
	Soap tree
Raphi farinifera	Raffia palm
Raphia ruffia	Raffia palm
Raphiolepis indica	Indian hawthorn
Raphiolepis japonica	
	Yeddo hawthorn
Raphiolepis umbellata	
	Indian hawthorn
	Yeddo hawthorn
Ravenala madagascariensis	
	Traveller's palm
	Traveller's tree
Ravensara aromatica	
	Madagascar nutmeg
Rhamnus alaternus	
	Italian buckthorn
Rhamnus alpina	Alpine buckthorn
Rhamnus californica	Coffee berry
Rhamnus caroliniana	
	Carolina buckthorn
	Indian cherry
Rhamnus catharticus	
	Common buckthorn
	Purging blackthorn
	Ramsthorn
Rhamnus crocea	
	Redberry buckthorn
Rhamnus davurica	
	Dahurian buckthorn
Rhamnus frangula	
	Alder buckthorn
	Black dogwood
Rhamnus infectoria	Avignon berry
Rhamnus pumila	
	Dwarf buckthorn
Rhamnus purshiana	Bearberry
	Californian buckthorn
	Cascara sagrada
Rhamnus saxitilis	Rock buckthorn
Rhapidophyllum hystrix	
	Blue palmetto
	Needle palm
	Porcupine palm
Rhapis excelsa	Bamboo palm
	China cane
	Fern rhapis
	Ground rattan cane
	Lady palm
	Little lady palm
	Miniature fan palm
	Partridge cane
	Slender lady palm
Rhapis humilis	Reed rhapis
	Slender lady palm
Rhizophora mangle	
	American mangrove
	Red mangrove
Rhododendron arboreum	
	Rhododendron
	Tree rhododendron
Rhododendron catawbiense	
	Mountain rose bay

Rhododendron ferrugineum

Rhododendron ferrugineum
Alpen rose

Rhododendron hirsutum
Hairy alpen rose

Rhododendron luteum
Common yellow azalea
Yellow azalea

Rhododendron maximum
Great laurel
Rose bay

Rhododendron obtusum
Kirishima azalea

Rhododendron oldhamii
Formosan azalea

Rhododendron ponticum
Great laurel
Rhododendron
Rose bay

Rhododendron poukhanense
Korean azalea

Rhododendron simsii
Indian azalea

Rhododendron viscosum
Clammy azalea
Swamp azalea
Swamp honeysuckle
White swamp azalea

Rhodomyrtus tomentosa
Downy myrtle
Hill gooseberry
Hill guava

Rhodosphaera rhodanthema
Queensland yellowwood
Yellowwood

Rhopalostylis sapida
Feather-duster palm
Nikau palm

Rhus aromatica
Fragrant sumac
Lemon sumac
Polecat bush
Sweet-scented sumac
Sweet sumac

Rhus chinensis
Nutgall tree

Rhus copallina
Dwarf sumac
Mountain sumac
Shining sumach
Wing-rib sumac

Rhus coriaria
Elm-leaved sumac
Sicilian sumac
Tanner's sumac

Rhus cotinus
Smoke tree
Venetian sumac

Rhus glabra
Scarlet sumac
Smooth sumac
Upland sumac
Vinegar tree

Rhus hirta
Stag's horn sumac

Rhus integrifolia
Lemonade berry
Lemonade sumac
Sourberry

Rhus laurina
Laurel sumac

Rhus microphylla
Correosa
Desert sumac
Scrub sumac
Small-leaved sumac

Rhus ovata
Sugarbush
Sugar sumac

Rhus potaninii
Chinese varnish tree

Rhus radicans
Cow-itch
Markry
Mercury
Poison ivy
Poison oak

Rhus succedanea
Wax tree

Rhus trilobata
Skunk bush

Rhus typhina
Stag's horn sumac
Velvet sumac
Virginian sumac

Rhus verniciflua
Japanese lacquer tree
Japanese varnish tree
Lacquer tree
Varnish tree

Rhus vernix
Poison dogwood
Poison elder
Poison sumac
Swamp sumac

Rhus virens
Evergreen sumac
Lentisco
Tabacco sumac

Rhyticocos amara
Overtop palm

Ribes alpinum
Alpine currant
Mountain currant

Ribes americanum
American blackcurrant

Ribes aureum
Buffalo currant
Golden currant

Ribes bracteosum
Californian blackcurrant

Ribes lacustre
Swamp currant

Ribes nigrum
Blackcurrant

Ribes odoratum
Buffalo currant
Golden currant

Ribes sanguineum
Flowering currant

Ribes speciosum
Flowered gooseberry

Ribes uva-crispa
Common gooseberry
Gooseberry
Goosegog

Ribes viburnumifolium
Evergreen currant

Ricinus communis
Castor bean
Castor oil plant
Palma christi
Wonder tree

Robinia hispida
Bristly locust
Mossy locust
Rose acacia

Robinia pseudoacacia
    Black locust tree
    Common acacia
    False acacia
    Locust tree
    Robinia
    Yellow locust tree

Robinia pseudoacacia appalachia   Shipmast acacia

Robinia pseudoacacia frisia
    Golden acacia
    Golden locust

Robinia pseudoacacia inermis   Mop-head acacia

Robinia pseudoacacia umbraculifera   Mop-head acacia

Robinia viscosa   Clammy locust

Robus fructicosus   Blackberry

Rosa acicularis   Needle rose

Rosa agrestis   Field briar

Rosa × alba   Jacobite rose
    White rose of York

Rosa alpina   Alpine rose

Rosa arkansana   Arkansas rose

Rosa arvensis   Ayrshire rose
    Field rose
    Trailing rose

Rosa banksiae   Banksian rose
    Lady Banks's rose

Rosa banksiae lutea   Yellow banksian rose

Rosa blanda   Meadow rose
    Smooth rose

Rosa × borboniana   Bourbon rose

Rosa bracteata   Macartney rose

Rosa brunonii   Himalayan musk rose

Rosa canina   Briar rose
    Common briar
    Dog briar
    Dog rose

Rosa centifolia   Cabbage rose
    Provence rose

Rosa centifolia cristata   Crested moss rose

Rosa centifolia mucosa   Moss rose

Rosa chinensis   China rose
    Monthly rose

Rosa chinensis minima   Fairy rose

Rosa chinensis viridiflora   Green rose

Rosa damascena   Damask rose

Rosa damascena trigintipetala   Kazanlik rose

Rosa damascena versicolor   York and Lancaster rose

Rosa eglanteria   Eglantine rose
    Sweet briar

Rosa foetida   Austrian briar
    Austrian yellow rose

Rosa foetida bicolor   Austrian copper rose

Rosa foetida persiana   Persian yellow rose

Rosa gallica   French rose
    Provence rose
    Red rose

Rosa gallica officinalis   Apothecary's rose
    Lancaster red rose
    Lancaster rose

Rosa gallica versicolor   Rosa mundi

Rosa gymnocarpa   Baldhip rose
    Redwood rose
    Wood rose

Rosa hemisphaerica   Sulfer rose
    Sulphur rose

Rosa laevigata   Cherokee rose

Rosa lutea hoggii   Hog's double yellow rose

Rosa majalis   Cinnamon rose
    May rose

Rosa moschata   Musk rose

Rosa multiflora grevillei   Seven sisters rose

Rosa × noisettiana   Champney rose
    Noisette rose

Rosa × odorata   Tea rose

Rosa officinalis   Apothecary's rose
    Old red damask rose

Rosa omeiensis   Mount Omei rose

Rosa palustris   Swamp rose

Rosa pimpinellifolia   Burnet rose
    Scotch briar
    Scotch rose

Rosa primula   Incense rose

Rosa roxburghii   Burr rose
    Chestnut rose
    Chinquapin rose

Rosa rubiginosa   Eglantine rose
    Sweet briar

Rosa rugosa   Hedgehog rose
    Japanese rose
    Ramanas rose
    Turkestan rose

Rosa sempervirens   Evergreen rose

Rosa sericea   Mount Omei rose

Rosa setigera   Prairie rose

Rosa sherardii   Northern downy rose

Rosa stellata mirifica   Sacramento rose

Rosa sulphurea   Sulfer rose
    Sulphur rose

Rosa tomentosa   Downy rose

Rosa villosa   Apple rose
    Soft-leaved rose

Rosa villosa duplex   Wolley-dod's rose

Rosa wichuraiana   Memorial rose

Rosmarinus officinalis   Rosemary

Roystonea borinquena   Puerto Rican royal palm

Roystonea elata	Florida royal palm
Roystonea hispaniolana	
	Spanish royal palm
Roystonea oleracea	Cabbage palm
	Caribbean royal palm
	South American royal palm
Roystonea regia	Cuban royal palm
	Royal palm
Rubus cockburnianus	
	Chinese bramble
Rubus deliciocus	
	Rocky Mountains bramble
Rubus fructicosus	Bramble
Rubus illecebrosus	
	Strawberry-raspberry
Rubus laciniatus	
	Fern-leaved bramble
Rubus parviflorus	Salmon berry
Rubus phoenicolasius	Wineberry
Ruprechtia coriacea	Biscochito
Ruscus aculeantus	
	Butcher's broom
Russelia equisetiformis	
	Coral plant
	Fountain bush
Russelia juncea	Coral plant
	Firecracker
	Fountain bush
Ruta graveolens	Rue
Sabal adansonii	Bush palmetto
	Dwarf palmetto
	Scrub palmetto
Sabal bermudana	
	Bermuda palmetto
Sabal causiarum	
	Puerto Rican hat palm
Sabal etonia	Scrub palmetto
Sabal jamaicensis	Bull thatch
	Jamaica palmetto
Sabal mauritiiformis	Trinidad palm
Sabal mexicana	Texas palmetto
Sabal minor	Bush palmetto
	Dwarf palmetto
	Scrub palmetto
Sabal palmetto	Blue palmetto
	Cabbage palmetto
	Cabbage tree
	Palmetto
Sabal repens	Scrub palmetto
Sabal uresana	Sonoran palmetto
Sabinea carinalis	Carib wood
Salacea edulis	Salac
Salix acutifolia	Caspian willow
	Purple-twig willow
Salix adenophylla	Furry willow
Salix aegyptiaca	
	Calif of Persia willow
	Musk willow
Salix alba	White willow
Salix alba argentea	Silver willow

Salix alba britzensis	
	Coralbark willow
Salix alba caerulea	
	Blue willow
	Cricket-bat willow
Salix alba chermesina	
	Coral-bark willow
	Orange-twig willow
	Scarlet willow
Salix alba coerulea	Bat willow
Salix alba sericea	Silver willow
Salix alba vitellina	Egg-yolk willow
	Golden willow
Salix × ambigua	Puzzle willow
Salix amygdaloides	
	Almond willow
	Peach-leaved willow
Salix andersoniana	
	Green mountain sallow
Salix aquatica	Water sallow
Salix arbuscula	Little tree willow
	Mountain willow
Salix arctica	Arctic willow
Salix arenaria	Sand willow
Salix aurita	Eared willow
	Round-eared willow
	Trailing sallow
Salix babylonica	Weeping willow
Salix babylonica pekinensis	
	Peking willow
Salix babylonica pekinensis	
pendula	Weeping willow
Salix babylonica pekinensis	
tortuosa	Contorted willow
	Corkscrew willow
	Dragon's claw willow
	Twisted willow
Salix babylonica pekinensis	
tortuosa aurea	Golden curls tree
Salix basfordiana	Basford willow
Salix bebbiana	Beak willow
Salix × blanda	Niobe willow
	Wisconsin weeping willow
Salix caesia	Blue willow
Salix candida	Sage willow
Salix caprea	Florist's willow
	Goat willow
	Great sallow
	Palm willow
	Pussy willow
	Sallow
Salix caprea chermesina	
	Coralbark willow
Salix caprea pendula	
	Kilmarnock willow
	Weeping sally
	Weeping willow
Salix × chrysocoma	
	Weeping willow
Salix cinerea	Common sallow
	Grey sallow
	Grey willow

Sambucus pubens

Salix cinerea atrocinerea	Grey sallow
Salix cinerea oleifolia	Common sallow
Salix cordata	Furry willow
	Heart-leaved willow
Salix crassifolia	Thick-leaved sallow
Salix daphnoides	Violet willow
Salix discolor	Large pussy willow
	Pussy willow
Salix elaeagnos	Hoary willow
Salix elegantissima	Thurlow weeping willow
Salix exigua	Coyote willow
Salix fragilis	Brittle willow
	Crack willow
Salix fragilis decipiens	Cardinal willow
Salix gracilistyla	Japanese pussy willow
Salix hastata	Halberd-leaved willow
Salix helvetica	Swiss willow
Salix herbacea	Dwarf willow
	Least willow
Salix humilis	Grey willow
	Prairie willow
	Small pussy willow
Salix interior	Sandbar willow
Salix laevigata	Polished willow
	Red willow
Salix lanata	Woolly willow
Salix lapponum	Downy willow
	Lapland willow
Salix lasiandra	Pacific willow
Salix lasiolepis	Arroyo willow
Salix lucida	Shining willow
Salix magnifica	Magnolia-leaved willow
Salix matsudana	Peking willow
Salix matsudana pendula	Weeping Peking willow
Salix matsudana tortuosa	Contorted willow
	Corkscrew willow
	Dragon's claw willow
Salix melanostachys	Black pussy willow
Salix mutabilis	Puzzle willow
Salix myrsinifolia	Dark-leaved willow
Salix myrsinites	Whortle-leaved willow
	Wortle willow
Salix nigra	Black willow
Salix nigricans	Dark-leaved willow
Salix nivalis	Tufted willow
Salix pellita	Satiny willow
Salix pentandra	Bay willow
	Laurel willow
Salix petraea	Rock sallow
Salix phylicifolia	Tea-leaf willow
Salix purpurea	Basket willow
	Purple osier
Salix purpurea pendula	Weeping purple osier
	Weeping purple willow
Salix pyrifolia	Balsam willow
Salix repens	Creeping willow
Salix reticulata	Netted willow
Salix × rubens basfordiana	Basford willow
Salix salviaefolia	Sage-leaved willow
Salix scoulerana	Scouler willow
Salix sepulcralis chrysocoma	Golden weeping willow
	Weeping willow
Salix sericea	Silky willow
Salix triandra	Almond willow
	French willow
Salix urbaniana	Japanese willow
Salix uva-ursi	Bearberry willow
Salix viminalis	Basket willow
	Common osier
	Osier
Salix xerythroflexuosa	Golden curls willow
Salvadora persica	Toothbrush tree
Salvia fulgens	Mexican red sage
Salvia officinalis	Common sage
Salvia rutilans	Pineapple sage
Samanea saman	Monkeypod tree
	Rain tree
	Saman tree
	Zamang tree
Sambucus caerulea	Blue elder
Sambucus canadensis	American elder
	Sweet elder
Sambucus canadensis aurea	Golden American elder
Sambucus ebulus	Dane's elder
	Danewort
	Dwarf elder
	Wallwort
Sambucus nigra	Black elder
	Bourtree
	Common elder
	European elder
	Pipe tree
Sambucus nigra aurea	Golden elder
Sambucus nigra laciniata	Cut-leaved elder
	Fern-leaved elder
	Parsley-leaved elder
Sambucus pubens	American red elder
	Red-berried elder
	Stinking elder

Sambucus racemosa

Sambucus racemosa	Alpine elder
	European red elder
	Red-berried elder
Sandoricum indicum	Sandal tree
Sandoricum koetjapa	Sentol
Santalum album	Sandalwood
	White sandalwood
Santalum rubrum	
	Red sandalwood
Santolina chamaecyparissus	
	Lavender cotton
Santolina incana	Lavender cotton
Santolina rosmarinifolia	Holy flax
Sapindus drummondii	
	Soapberry tree
	Wild China tea
Sapindus marginatus	
	Wild China soapberry
Sapindus mukorossi	
	Chinese soapberry
Sapindus saponaria	
	False dogwood
	Jaboncillo
	Soapberry
Sapium hippomane	Milk tree
Sapium salicifolium	Tallow tree
Sapium sebiferum	
	Chinese tallow tree
	Vegetable tallow tree
Saraca indica	Asoka tree
	Sorrowless tree
Sarcococca buxacaea	
	Christmas box
Sassafras albidum	Ague tree
	Sassafras
Satureia montana	Winter savory
Saxegothaea conspicua	
	Prince Albert's yew
Schefflera arboricola	
	Umbrella tree
Schinus molle	
	American mastic tree
	Australian pepper tree
	Californian pepper tree
	Mastic tree
	Molle
	Pepper tree
	Peruvian mastic tree
	Peruvian pepper tree
	Pirul
Schinus terebinthifolia	
	Brazilian pepper tree
	Christmas berry tree
Schizophragma viburnoides	
	Climbing hydrangea
Schleichera oleosa	Ceylon oak
	Gum-lac
	Lac tree
Schotia afra	Hottentot's bean
	Kaffir bean
Schotia brachypetala	Tree fuchsia
Schotia latifolia	
	Elephant hedge bean tree

Sciadophyllum brownii	
	Galapee tree
Sciadopitys verticillata	
	Japanese umbrella pine
	Parasol pine
	Umbrella pine
Semecarpus anacardium	
	Dhobi's nut
	Marking-nut tree
	Varnish tree
Sequoia sempervirens	
	Californian coast redwood
	Californian redwood
	Coast redwood
	Redwood
Sequoiadendron giganteum	
	Californian big tree
	Giant sequoia
	Mammoth tree
	Sierra redwood
	Wellingtonia
Serenoa repens	Sabal
	Saw palmetto
	Scrub palmetto
Seriocarpus conyzoides	
	Silk fruit tree
Sesbania formosa	
	White dragon tree
Sesbania tripetii	Wisteria tree
Severinia buxifolia	
	Chinese box orange
Shepherdia argentea	Buffalo berry
	Silver buffalo berry
Shepherdia canadensis	
	Buffalo berry
	Soapberry
Shorea robusta	Sal
Sicana odorifera	Cassa-banana
Siliphium terebinthaceum	
	Turpentine tree
Simaba cedron	Cedron
Simarouba amara	Bitter damson
	Dysentery bark
	Simarouba
Simarouba glauca	Aceituno
	Bitterwood
	Paradise tree
Smilax glauca	Saw briar
Smilax hispida	Hag briar
Smilax ornata	Jamaica sarsaparilla
Smilax rotundifolia	Green briar
	Horse briar
Socratea exorhiza	Zanona palm
Solanum aviculare	Kangaroo apple
Solanum crispum	Potato tree
Solanum jasminoides	Potato vine
Solanum laciniatum	
	Kangaroo apple
Solanum topiro	Cocona
Soleanea berteriana	Motillo

TREES, BUSHES, AND SHRUBS

Staphylea pinnata

Sophora japonica
  Chinese scholar tree
  Japanese pagoda tree
  Pagoda tree
  Scholar's tree
Sophora japonica + pendula
  Contorted pagoda tree
Sophora secundiflora   Mescal bean
  Texas mountain laurel
Sophora tetraptera   Kowhai
  New Zealand laburnum
  New Zealand sophora
Sophora tomentosa   Silverbush
Sorbus alnifolia
  Alder-leaved rowan
Sorbus americana
  American mountain ash
  Dogberry
  Missey-mooney
  Roundwood
Sorbus anglica   Cheddar whitebeam
Sorbus aria   Chess apple
  Whitebeam
Sorbus aria wilfred fox
  European whitebeam
Sorbus aucuparia
  Common mountain ash
  Common rowan
  European mountain ash
  Mountain ash
  Quickbeam
  Quicken tree
  Rantry
  Rowan
Sorbus aucuparia asplenifolia
  Cut-leaved mountain ash
Sorbus aucuparia pendula
  Weeping mountain ash
Sorbus aucuparia rossica-major
  Russian mountain ash
Sorbus aucuparia xanthocarpa
  Yellow-berried mountain ash
Sorbus austriacus
  Austrian whitebeam
Sorbus cashmiriana
  Kashmir rowan
Sorbus chamaemespilus
  Alpine whitebeam
  False medlar
Sorbus commixta   Japanese rowan
Sorbus commixta embleyi
  Chinese scarlet rowan
Sorbus cuspidata
  Himalayan whitebeam
Sorbus devoniensis   French hales
Sorbus discolor
  Chinese scarlet rowan
Sorbus domestica   Service tree
  True service tree
Sorbus fennica   Finnish whitebeam
Sorbus folgneri   Chinese whitebeam
  Folgner's whitebeam
Sorbus graeca   Greek whitebeam

Sorbus hupehensis
  Chinese mountain ash
  Chinese rowan
  Hupeh rowan
Sorbus × hybrida
  Finnish whitebeam
Sorbus intermedia
  Swedish whitebeam
Sorbus lancastriensis
  Lancashire whitebeam
Sorbus latifolia
  Broad-leaved whitebeam
Sorbus × latifolia
  Fontainebleau service tree
Sorbus minima   Least whitebeam
Sorbus mougeotii
  Pyrenean whitebeam
Sorbus reducta
  Creeping mountain ash
  Pygmy rowan
Sorbus rupicola   Cliff whitebeam
  Rock whitebeam
Sorbus sargentiana   Sargent's rowan
Sorbus suecica   Swedish whitebeam
Sorbus × thuringiaca
  Bastard service tree
  Hybrid rowan
Sorbus torminalis   Chequer tree
  Wild service tree
Sorbus vilmorinii   Vilmorin's rowan
  Vilmorin's sorbus
Sparmannia africana
  African hemp
  House lime
Spartium junceum   Spanish broom
  Weaver's broom
Spathodea campanulata
  African tulip tree
  Flame of the forest
  Fountain tree
  Tulipan
  Tulip tree
Spiraea salicifolia   Bridgewort
Spondias cytherea   Ambarella
  Golden apple
  Otaheite apple
  Wi tree
Spondias dulcis   Otaheite apple
Spondias lutea   Golden apple
  Jamaica plum
  Yellow mombin
Spondias mombin   Hog plum
  Jobo tree
  Yellow mombin
Spondias purpurea   Jocote
  Purple mombin
  Red mombin
  Spanish plum
Stahlia monosperma   Cobana
  Polisandro
Staphylea holocarpa   Bladdernut
Staphylea pinnata   Anthony nut
  European bladdernut

Staphylea trifolia

Staphylea trifolia
American bladdernut

Stenocarpus salignus Reefwood

Stenocarpus sinuatus
Firewheel tree
Queensland firewheel tree
Wheel of fire

Sterculia acerfolia Flame tree

Sterculia foetida Indian almond

Sterculia rupestris
Queensland bottle tree

Stewartia malacodendron
Silky camellia

Stewartia ovata Mountain camellia

Stewartia pseudocamellia
Deciduous camellia
Japanese stewartia

Stewartia sinensis
Chinese stewartia
Chinese stuartia

Strychnos ignatii Ignatius bean

Strychnos nux-vomica
Nux-vomica tree
Strychnine

Strychnos potatorum Clearing nut
Water-filter nut

Strychnos spinosa Natal orange

Strychnos toxifera Curare

Styrax americanus
American storax
Mock orange

Styrax benzoin Benzoin

Styrax hemsleyana
Hemsley's storax

Styrax japonica Japanese snowbell
Snowbell tree

Styrax obassia Big-leaved storax
Fragrant snowbell

Styrax officinalis
Mediterranean storax
Storax

Swietenia candollea
Venezuelan mahogany

Swietenia macrophylla
Broad-leaved mahogany
Honduras mahogany
Mahogany

Swietenia mahogoni
Madeira redwood
Spanish mahogany
West Indian mahogany

Syagrus coronata Licuri palm
Ouricuri palm

Symphoricarpos albus Snowberry

Symphoricarpos occidentalis
Wolfberry

Symphoricarpos orbiculatus
Coralberry
Indian currant

Symphoricarpos rivularis
Snowberry

Symphoricarpos rubra vulgaris Coralberry
Indian currant

Symphoricarpos vulgaris
Coralberry
Indian currant

Symplocos paniculata
Asiatic sweetleaf
Sapphire berry

Symplocos tinctoria Horse sugar
Sweetleaf

Synadenium grantii
African milkbush

Syncarpia glomulifera
Turpentine tree

Synsepalum dulcificum
Miraculous berry
Miraculous fruit

Syringa amurensis Amur lilac

Syringa × chinensis Chinese lilac
Rouen lilac

Syringa emodi Himalayan lilac

Syringa josikaea Hungarian lilac

Syringa laciniata Cut-leaf lilac

Syringa meyeri palibin
Korean lilac

Syringa microphylla superba
Daphne lilac

Syringa oblata Lilac

Syringa × persica Persian lilac

Syringa reticulata
Japanese tree lilac

Syringa swegiflexa Pink pearl lilac

Syringa velutina Korean lilac

Syringa villosa Late lilac

Syringa vulgaris Common lilac

Syringa yunnanensis Yunnan lilac

Syzygium aqueum
Water rose apple tree

Syzygium aromaticum Clove tree

Syzygium coolminianum
Blue lilly-pilly

Syzygium cumini Black plum
Jambolan plum
Jambool
Jambu
Java plum

Syzygium grande Sea apple

Syzygium jambos Malabar plum
Rose apple

Syzygium malaccense Malay apple
Pomerac jambos
Rose apple

Syzygium paniculatum
Australian brush cherry
Brush cherry

Syzygium pyenanthum
Wild rose-apple

Syzygium samarangense Jamboil
Jambosa
Java apple
Wax apple

Tabebuia argentea
Paraguayan trumpet tree
Silver trumpet tree
Tree of gold

Tabebuia chrysantha
Golden trumpet tree

Tabebuia flavescens Green ebony

Tabebuia pallida
Cuban pink trumpet tree
White cedar

Tabebuia pentaphylla Pink poui
Pink tecoma

Tabebuia riparia
Jamaican trumpet tree
Whitewood

Tabebuia rosea Pink poui
Pink trumpet tree
Rosy trumpet tree

Tabebuia serratifolia Apamata
Yellow poui

Tabernaemontana coronaria
Adam's apple
Cape jasmine
Nero's crown

Tabernaemontana divaricata
Adam's apple
Cape gardenia
Cape jasmine
Flower-of-love

Taiwania flousiana Coffin tree

Tamarindus indica Tamarind
Tamarindo

Tamarix anglica Tamarisk

Tamarix aphylla Athel

Tamarix gallica French tamarisk
Manna bush
Salt cedar

Taxodium ascendens Pond cypress
Upland cypress

Taxodium ascendens nutans
Nodding pond cypress

Taxodium distichum Bald cypress
Deciduous cypress
Swamp cypress

Taxodium distichum pendens
Weeping swamp cypress

Taxodium mucronatum
Ahuehuete
Mexican cypress
Mexican swamp cypress

Taxus baccata Common yew
English yew

Taxus baccata aurea Golden yew

Taxus baccata aureovariegata
Golden Irish yew

Taxus baccata dovastoniana
Westfelton yew

Taxus baccata fastigiata Irish yew

Taxus baccata fastigiata aurea
Golden Irish yew

Taxus baccata fructo-luteo
Yellow-berried yew

Taxus brevifolia American yew
Californian yew
Pacific yew
Western yew

Taxus canadensis American yew
Canadian yew

Taxus celebica Chinese yew

Taxus chinensis Chinese yew

Taxus cuspidata Japanese yew

Taxus floridana Florida yew

Taxus media Anglo-Japanese yew

Taxus media hicksii Hicks' yew

Taxus wallichiana Himalayan yew

Tecoma stans Yellowbells
Yellow bignonia
Yellow elder
Yellow trumpet tree

Tectona grandis Teak

Telopea oreades
Gippsland waratah

Telopea truncata
Tasmanian waratah

Terminalia alata Indian laurel

Terminalia bellirica Myrobalan

Terminalia catappa Indian almond
Kamani
Myrobalan
Olive bark tree
Tropical almond

Terminalia ivorensis Indigbo

Terminalia superba Afara

Tetracentron sinense Spur-leaf tree

Tetraclinis articulata Alerce
Arar tree

Tetrapanax papyriferus
Rice-paper tree

Teucrium chamaedrys
Wall germander

Teucrium fructicans
Shrubby germander

Teucrium marum Cat thyme

Theobroma cacao Cacao
Chocolate tree
Cocoa

Thespesia populnea Bhendi tree
Mahoe
Portia tree

Thevetia peruviana Be-still tree
Lucky nut
Yellow oleander

Thrinax argentea Broom palm
Silver broom palm

Thrinax morrisii Key palm

Thrinax parviflora
Florida thatch palm
Palmetto thatch

Thujopsis dolabrata Hiba
Hiba arbor-vitae

Thuya koraiensis Korean thuya

Thuya occidentalis
American arbor-vitae
Arbor-vitae
Northern white cedar
White cedar
Yellow cedar

Thuya orientalis
Chinese arbor-vitae
Chinese thuya
Chinese white cedar

Thuya plicata Giant cedar
Western arbor-vitae
Western red cedar

Thuya standishii
Japanese arbor-vitae
Japanese thuya

Thuyopsis dolabrata Hiba
Hiba arbor-vitae

Tilia americana
American basswood
American lime
Basswood
Whitewood

Tilia amurensis Amur lime

Tilia cordata Linden
Small-leaved lime

Tilia × *euchlora* Caucasian lime
Crimean lime

Tilia × *europaea* Common lime
Linden

Tilia × *europaea pallida*
Royal lime

Tilia heterophylla
White basswood

Tilia insularis Korean lime

Tilia japonica Japanese lime
Japanese linden

Tilia mandshurica
Manchurian lime

Tilia × *moltkei* Von Moltke's lime

Tilia mongolica Mongolian lime

Tilia oliveri Chinese lime
Oliver's lime

Tilia petiolaris Pendant silver lime
Weeping silver lime

Tilia platyphyllos
Broad-leaved lime
Large-leaved lime

Tilia platyphyllos rubra
Red broad-leaved lime

Tilia tomentosa Silver lime

Tilia × *vulgaris* Common lime

Tipuana tipu Pride of Bolivia
Rosewood
Tipu tree

Toona odorata Spanish cedar
West Indian cedar

Toona sinensis Chinese cedar
Toon

Torreya californica
Californian nutmeg
Stinking yew

Torreya nucifera Japanese nutmeg
Japanese torreya
Kaya

Torreya taxifolia Foetid yew
Stinking cedar
Yew-leaved torreya

Trachycarpus fortunei
Chusan palm
Hemp palm
Windmill palm

Treculia africana
African bread tree

Trevesia palmata Snowflake aralia
Snowflake tree
Tropical snowflake

Triphasia trifolia Limeberry

Triplaris americana Ant tree
Long john
Palo santo

Triplaris surinamensis
Guayabo hormiguero

Triplochiton scleroxylon Obeche

Tristania conferta Brisbane box
Brush box

Tristania laurina Kanooka

Trochodendron aralioides
Wheel tree

Tsuga canadensis
Canadian hemlock
Canada pitch
Eastern hemlock

Tsuga caroliniana
Carolina hemlock

Tsuga chinensis Chinese hemlock

Tsuga diversifolia
Northern Japanese hemlock

Tsuga dumosa Himalayan hemlock

Tsuga formosana
Formosan hemlock

Tsuga heterophylla
Western hemlock

Tsuga × *jeffreyi* Jeffrey's hemlock

Tsuga mertensiana
Mountain hemlock

Tsuga sieboldii Japanese hemlock
Siebold's hemlock
Southern Japanese hemlock

Turpinia occidentalis
Cassada wood
Cassava wood

Ugni molinae Chilean guava
Murtillo
Uni

Ulex europaeus Common gorse
Furze
Gorse
Prickly broom
Whin

Ulex europaeus plenus
Double flowered gorse

Ulex europaeus strictus Irish gorse

Ulex gallii Western gorse

Vaccinium parvifolium

Ulex minor	Dwarf furze
	Dwarf gorse
Ulmus alata	Small-leaved elm
	Wahoo elm
	Winged elm
Ulmus americana	American elm
	Water elm
	White elm
Ulmus angustifolia	Cornish elm
	Goodyer elm
Ulmus angustifolia cornubiensis	Cornish elm
Ulmus carpinifolia	
	European field elm
	Smooth-leaved elm
Ulmus carpinifolia cornubiensis	Cornish elm
Ulmus carpinifolia sarniensis	
	Guernsey elm
	Smooth-leaved elm
	Wheatley elm
Ulmus crassifolia	Cedar elm
Ulmus davidiana japonica	
	Japanese elm
Ulmus fulva	Sweet elm
Ulmus glabra	Scotch elm
	Wych elm
Ulmus glabra camperdown	
	Camperdown elm
	Weeping elm
Ulmus glabra horizontalis	
	Weeping wych elm
Ulmus glabra pendula	
	Tabletop elm
	Weeping elm
Ulmus × hollandica	Dutch elm
Ulmus × hollandica smithii	
	Downton elm
Ulmus × hollandica vegata	
	Huntingdon elm
Ulmus japonica	Japanese elm
Ulmus laevis	European white elm
Ulmus major	Dutch elm
Ulmus mexicana	Mexican elm
Ulmus minor	Smooth-leaved elm
Ulmus minor stricta cornubiensis	Cornish elm
Ulmus minor stricta sarniensis	
	Guernsey elm
	Jersey elm
	Wheatley elm
Ulmus parvifolia	Chinese elm
Ulmus procera	Common elm
	English elm
Ulmus pumila	Dwarf elm
	Siberian elm
Ulmus rubra	Indian elm
	Moose elm
	Red elm
	Slippery elm
Ulmus × sarniensis	Jersey elm
	Wheatley elm

Ulmus serotina	Red elm
	September elm
Ulmus stricta	Cornish elm
Ulmus stricta sarniensis	Jersey elm
Ulmus thomasii	Cork elm
	Rock elm
Ulmus × vegata	Chichester elm
	Huntingdon elm
Umbellularia californica	
	Californian bay
	Californian laurel
	Californian olive
	Californian sassafras
	Myrtle
	Oregon myrtle
	Pepperwood
Ungnadia speciosa	False buckeye
	Mexican buckeye
	Spanish buckeye
	Texan buckeye
Uragoga ipecacuanha	
	Ipecacuanha
Vaccinium angustifolium	
	Lowbush blueberry
Vaccinium arboreum	Farkleberry
Vaccinium arctostaphylos	
	Caucasian whortleberry
Vaccinium atrococcum	
	Black highbush blueberry
Vaccinium caespitosum	
	Dwarf bilberry
Vaccinium canadense	Sour top
	Velvet leaf
Vaccinium corymbosum	
	Blueberry
	Highbush blueberry
	Swamp blueberry
	Whortleberry
Vaccinium elliottii	
	Elliott's blueberry
Vaccinium hirsutum	
	Hairy huckleberry
Vaccinium macrocarpon	
	American cranberry
	Cranberry
Vaccinium myrsinites	
	Evergreen blueberry
Vaccinium myrtillus	Bilberry
	Blaeberry
	Huckleberry
	Whinberry
	Whortleberry
Vaccinium ovatum	
	Box blueberry
	California huckleberry
	Shot huckleberry
Vaccinium oxycoccus	Cranberry
	European wild cranberry
Vaccinium padifolium	
	Madeira whortleberry
Vaccinium parvifolium	
	Red bilberry
	Red huckleberry

Vaccinium stamineum

Vaccinium stamineum	Deerberry
	Squaw huckleberry
Vaccinium uliginosum	
	Bog bilberry
	Bog whortleberry
	Moorberry
Vaccinium virgatum	
	Rabbit-eye blueberry
Vaccinium vitis-idaea	Cowberry
	Cranberry
	Foxberry
	Red bilberry
Vangueria edulis	
	Madagascar tamarind
	Tamarind-of-the-Indies
Vangueria esculenta	
	Forest wild medlar
Veitchia merrillii	Christmas palm
	Manila palm
Verbena triphylla	Lemon verbena
Viburnum acerifolium	
	Arrowwood
	Dockmackie
	Maple-leaved viburnum
	Possum haw
Viburnum alnifolium	
	Devil's shoestrings
	Dogberry
	Dog hobble
	Hobblebush
	Hobble marsh
	Mooseberry
	Moosewood
	Tanglefoot
	Trip-toe
	Wayfaring tree
White mountain dogwood	
	Witch hobble
Viburnum cassinoides	Swamp haw
	Teaberry
	Wild raisin
	Withe-rod
Viburnum dentatum	Arrowwood
	Southern arrowwood
Vibernum dilatatum	
	Linden vibernum
Viburnum japonicum	
	Japanese viburnum
Viburnum lantana	Hoarwithy
	Meal tree
	Twistwood
	Wayfaring tree
Viburnum lantanoides	
American wayfaring tree	
	Hobble bush
	Witch hobble
Viburnum lentago	Black haw
	Cowberry
	Nannyberry
	Nanny plum
	Sheepberry
	Sweetberry
	Tea plant
	Wild raisin

Viburnum macrocephalum	
	Chinese snowball
Viburnum molle	Black alder
	Poison haw
Viburnum nudum	
	Smooth withe-rod
	Smooth withy-rod
Viburnum odoratissimum	
	Sweet viburnum
Viburnum opulus	Crampback
	Cranberry bush
European cranberry bush	
	Guelder rose
	Red elder
	Swamp elder
	Water elder
Viburnum opulus sterile	
	Snowball tree
Viburnum pauciflorum	
	Mooseberry
Viburnum plicatum	
	Japanese snowball
Viburnum plicatum tomentosum	
	Lace-cap viburnum
	Lace-cup viburnum
Viburnum prunifolium	Black haw
	Sheepberry
	Stag bush
	Sweet haw
	Sweet viburnum
Viburnum rufidulum	Blue haw
	Rusty nannyberry
	Southern black haw
Viburnum setigerum	
	Tea viburnum
Viburnum tinus	Laurustinus
Viburnum trilobum	Crampbark
	Cranberry bush
	Cranberry tree
	Grouseberry
	Highbush cranberry
	Pimbina
	Squawbush
	Summerberry
Viburnum wrightii	Leatherleaf
Vitex agnus-castus	Chaste tree
	Hemp tree
	Indian spice tree
	Monk's pepper tree
	Sage tree
	Wild pepper tree
Vitex lucens	Pururi tree
Vonitra fibrosa	Piassava palm
Warszewiczia coccinea	Chaconia
	Waterwell tree
	Wild poinsettia
Washingtonia filifera	
	Californian fan palm
	Desert fan palm
	Petticoat palm
	Washington palm

Zombia antillarum

Washingtonia robusta
Mexican fan palm
Mexican Washington palm
Thread palm

Weigela florida Weigela
Weigela florida purpurea
Purple weigela

Weinmannia racemosa
Kamahi tree
Towai tree

Westringia fruticosa
Australian rosemary

Westringia rosmariniformis
Victoria rosemary

Widdringtonia cupressoides
African cypress
Berg cypress
Mountain cypress
Sapree wood

Widdringtonia juniperoides
Clanwilliam cedar

Widdringtonia schwarzii
Willimore cedar
Willowmore cedar

Widdringtonia whytei
Mlanje cedar

Wisteria sinensis
Chinese kidney bean

Xanthorrhiza simplicissima
Yellow root

Xanthorrhoea arborea
Botany Bay gum

Xanthorrhoea australis
Grass tree

Xanthorrhoea preissii Black boy

Xanthoxylum americanum
Prickly ash
Toothache tree

Xanthoxylum clava-herculis
Southern prickly ash

Xanthoxylum fagara Wild lime

Ximenia americana Hog plum
Tallowwood

Xylopia aethiopica Guinea pepper

Yucca aloifolia Dagger plant
Spanish bayonet
Spanish dagger

Yucca baccata Banana yucca
Blue yucca
Datil
Spanish bayonet
Wild date

Yucca brevifolia Joshua tree
Yucca carnerosana Spanish dagger
Yucca elata Palmella
Soap tree
Soapweed

Yucca elephantipes Spineless yucca

Yucca filamentosa Adam's needle
Needle palm
Silk grass
Spoonleaf yucca

Yucca glauca Soapweed
Soapwell

Yucca gloriosa Adam's needle
Lord's candlestick
Palm lily
Roman candle
Yucca

Yucca recurvifolia Century plant

Yucca treculeana Palma pita

Yucca whipplei Our lord's candle

Zanthoxylum americanum
Northern prickly ash
Prickly ash
Toothache tree
Yellowwood

Zanthoxylum clava-herculis
Hercules' club
Pepperwood
Sea ash
Southern prickly ash

Zanthoxylum fagara Wild lime

Zanthoxylum flavum
West Indian silkwood

Zanthoxylum piperitum
Japan pepper

Zelkova abelicea Abelitzia
Cretan zelkova

Zelkova carpinifolia
Caucasian elm
Russian elm

Zelkova crenata Caucasian elm

Zelkova serrata Japanese zelkova
Keaki
Sawleaf zelkova

Zelkova sinica Chinese zelkova

Zelkova sinica verschaffeltii
Cutleaf zelcova

Zieria smithii Sandfly bush

Ziziphus jujuba Chinese date
Chinese jujube tree
Common jujube tree

Ziziphus lotus Lotus tree

Ziziphus mucronata Buffalo thorn

Ziziphus mauritania
Cottony jujube
Indian jujube

Zombia antillarum Zombi palm

WILD FLOWERS

It is not possible in a volume such as this to include every species of wild flower; even one limited to European or North American floras would run to a substantial number of books, therefore preference has been given to the more common and widely distributed plants.

It is now illegal to dig up wild plants in many parts of the world, and the gathering of wild flowers by collectors and amateur 'flower lovers' coupled with the widespread use of modern herbicides has resulted in the near-extinction of many species. Wild flowers should be left undisturbed to be enjoyed by all.

Common poppy –
Papaver rhoeas

Aceras anthropophorum
Man orchid

Achillea millefolium
Milfoil
Yarrow

Achillea ptarmica Sneezewort

Acinos arvensis Basil thyme

Aconitum napellus Monkshood

Acorus calamus Sweet flag

Actaea spicata Baneberry

Adoxa moschatellina Moschatel

Aegopodium podagraria
Goutweed
Ground elder

Aethusa cynapium Fool's parsley

Agrimonia eupatoria Agrimony
Common agrimony

Agrimonia procera
Fragrant agrimony
Scented agrimony

Ajuga reptans Bugle

Alchemilla alpina
Alpine lady's mantle

Alisma lanceolatum
Lanceolate water plantain

Alisma natans
Floating water plantain

Alisma plantago-aquatica
Water plantain

Alisma ranunculoides
Lesser water plantain

Alliaria petiolata Garlic mustard

Allium ampeloprasum Wild leek

Allium oleraceum Field garlic

Allium schoenoprasum Chives

Allium scorodoprasm Sand leek

Allium sphaerocephalon
Round-headed leek

Allium triquetrum
Triangular-stemmed garlic

Allium vineale Crow garlic
Wild onion

Althaea hirsuta
Hispid marsh mallow

Althaea officinalis Marsh mallow

Anacamptis pyramidalis
Pyramidal orchid

Anagallis arvensis
Scarlet pimpernel

Anagallis foemina Blue pimpernel

Anagallis minima Chaff weed

Anagallis tenella Bog pimpernel

Anaphalis margaritacea
Everlasting
Pearly everlasting

Anemone apennina Blue anemone

Anemone nemorosa
Wood anemone

Angelica sylvestris Wild angelica

Antennaria dioica
Mountain everlasting

Anthemis arvensis
Corn chamomile

Anthemis cotula
Stinking chamomile

Anthemis tinctoria
Yellow chamomile

Anthriscus caucalis Bur chervil

Anthriscus cerefolium
Garden chervil

Anthriscus sylvestris Cow parsley

Anthyllis cicer Wild lentil

Anthyllis frigidus
Yellow alpine milk vetch

Anthyllis vulneraria Kidney vetch

Antirrhinum majus Snapdragon

Aphanes arvensis Parsley piert

Apium inundatum
Lesser marshwort

Apium nodiflorum
Fool's watercress

Aquilegia vulgaris Columbine

Arabis hirsuta Hairy rock cress

Arctium lappa Great burdock

Arctium minus Lesser burdock

Arctium nemorosum
Dark burdock

Arctium pubens Burdock
Common burdock

Aristolochia clematitis Birthwort

Armeria maritima Sea pink
Thrift

Artemisia absinthium Wormwood

Artemisia campestris
Breckland wormwood

Artemisia maritima
Sea wormwood

Artemisia norvegica
Norwegian mugwort

Artemisia stellerana Dusty miller

Artemisia verlotorum
Chinese mugwort

Artemisia vulgaris Mugwort

Arthrocnemum
Perennial glasswort

Arum italicum Italian cuckoo-pint
Italian lords-and-ladies

Arum maculatum Cuckoo-pint
Lords-and-ladies

Asarina procumbens Asarina

Asarum europaeum Asarabacca

Aster tripolium Sea aster

Astragalus danicus
Purple milk vetch

Astragalus glycyphyllos
Wild liquorice

Astrantia major Astrantia

Atriplex laciniata Frosted orach
Sandy orach

Atriplex littoralis Beach orach
Grassy orach
Shoreline orach

Centaurea solstitialis

Atriplex patula	Common orach
	Orach
Atriplex prostrata	
	Arrowhead orach
	Spear-leaved orach
Atropa bella-donna	
	Deadly nightshade
Attium ursinum	Ramsons
	Wood garlic
Baldellia ranunculoides	
	Lesser water plantain
Ballota nigra	Black horehound
	Horehound
Bellis perennis	Daisy
Berula erecta	Lesser water parsnip
Beta vulgaris maritima	Sea beet
Betonica officinalis	Betony
Bidens cernua	
	Nodding bur marigold
Bidens frondosa	Beggarticks
Bidens tripartita	Bur marigold
	Trifid bur marigold
Blackstonia perfoliata	Yellowwort
Brassica napus	Rape
	Swede
Brassica nigra	Black mustard
Brassica oleracea	Wild cabbage
Brassica rapa	Turnip
Bryonia dioica	White bryony
Bunium bulbocastanum	
	Great pignut
Bupleurum falcatum	
	Sickle-leaved hare's ear
Bupleurum rotundifolium	
	Thorow-wax
Bupleurum subovatum	
	False thorow-wax
Bupleurum tenuissimum	
	Slender hare's ear
Butomus umbellatus	
	Flowering rush
Cakile maritima	Sea rocket
Calamintha sylvatica	Calamint
	Common calamint
Calla palustris	Bog arum
Callitriche stagnalis	
	Bog water starwort
	Common water starwort
	Mud water starwort
Calluna vulgaris	Common heather
	Ling
Caltha palustris	Kingcup
	Marsh marigold
	Mollyblobs
Calystegia pulchra	
	Hairy bindweed
Calystegia sepium	Bindweed
	Common bindweed
	Hedge bindweed
Calystegia silvatica	
	Great bindweed
	Large bindweed

Calystegia soldanella	
	Sea bindweed
Campanula glomerata	
	Clustered bellflower
Campanula hederacea	
	Ivy-leaved bellflower
Campanula lactiflora	
	Giant bellflower
Campanula latifolia	
	Giant bellflower
	Great bellflower
Campanula medium	
	Canterbury bell
Campanula patula	
	Spreading bellflower
Campanula rapunculoides	
	Creeping bellflower
Campanula rotundifolia	Harebell
	Scottish bluebell
Campanula trachelium	
	Nettle-leaved bellflower
Canvallaria majalis	
	Lily-of-the-valley
Capsella bursa-pastoris	
	Shepherd's purse
Cardamine amara	
	Large bitter cress
Cardamine flexuosa	
	Wavy bitter cress
Cardamine hirsuta	
	Hairy bitter cress
Cardamine pratensis	
	Cuckoo flower
	Lady's smock
Cardaria draba	Hoary cress
Carduus acanthoides	
	Welted thistle
Carduus dissectum	Meadow thistle
Carduus helenioides	
	Melancholy thistle
Carduus nutans	Musk thistle
	Nodding thistle
Carduus palustris	Marsh thistle
Carduus pratensis	Meadow thistle
Carduus pycnocephalus	
	Plymouth thistle
Carduus tenuiflorus	
	Slender-flowered thistle
Carlina vulgaris	Carline thistle
Centaurea calcitrapa	Star thistle
Centaurea cyanus	Cornflower
Centaurea nemoralis	
	Brown knapweed
Centaurea nigra	
	Common knapweed
	Hardheads
	Knapweed
Centaurea scabiosa	
	Great knapweed
Centaurea solstitialis	
	Yellow star thistle

Centaurium capitatum

Centaurium capitatum
    Tufted centaury
Centaurium erythraea
    Common centaury
Centaurium littorale   Sea centaury
Centaurium pulchellum
    Lesser centaury
Centranthus ruber   Red valerian
Cephalanthera damasonium
    White helleborine
Cephalanthera longifolia
    Narrow-leaved helleborine
Ceratophyllum demersum
    Rigid hornwort
Chaenorhinum minus
    Small toadflax
Chaerophyllum temulentum
    Rough chervil
Chamaemelum nobile   Chamomile
    Sweet chamomile
Chelidonium majus
    Greater celandine
Chenopodium album   Fat hen
Chenopodium bonus-
  henricus   Good King Henry
Chrysanthemum
  leucanthemum   Ox-eye daisy
Chrysanthemum parthenium
    Bachelor's buttons
    Feverfew
Chrysanthemum segetum
    Corn marigold
Chrysanthemum vulgare   Tansy
Chrysosplenium alternifolium
   Alternate-leaved golden saxifrage
Chrysosplenium oppositifolium
    Golden saxifrage
Cicerbita alpina
    Alpine blue sowthistle
    Alpine lettuce
Cicerbita macrophylla
    Blue sowthistle
Cichorium intybus   Chicory
Circaea alpina
   Alpine enchanter's nightshade
    Alpine nightshade
Circaea lutetiana
    Enchanter's nightshade
Cirsium acaule   Dwarf thistle
Cirsium acaute   Ground thistle
Cirsium acautonauct
    Ground thistle
Cirsium arvense   Creeping thistle
Cirsium dissectum   Meadow thistle
Cirsium eriophorum   Woolly thistle
Cirsium heterophyllum
    Melancholy thistle
Cirsium palustre   Marsh thistle
Cirsium tuberosum
    Tuberous meadow thistle
Cirsium vulgare   Spear thistle

Clematis alpina   Alpine clematis
Clematis vitalba   Old man's beard
    Traveller's joy
Clinopodium vulgare   Wild basil
Coeloglossum viride   Frog orchid
Colchicum autumnale
    Meadow saffron
Conium maculatum   Hemlock
Conopodium majus   Pignut
Consolida ambigua   Larkspur
Consolida regale   Forked larkspur
Convolvulus arvensis
    Field bindweed
    Lesser bindweed
Conyza canadensis
    Canadian fleabane
Corallorhiza trifida
    Coralroot orchid
Coronilla varia   Crown vetch
Corydalis bulbosa
    Purple corydalis
Corydalis claviculta
    Climbing corydalis
Corydalis lutea   Yellow corydalis
Cramble maritima   Sea kale
Crepis biennis   Rough hawk's beard
Crepis capillaris
    Smooth hawk's beard
Crepis foetida
    Stinking hawk's beard
Crepis mollis   Soft hawk's beard
Crepis nicaeensis
    French hawk's beard
Crepis paludosa
    Marsh hawk's beard
Crepis vesicaria
    Beaked hawk's beard
Crithmum maritimum
    Rock samphire
    Samphire
Crocus nudiflorus
    Naked autumn crocus
Crocus purpureus   Purple crocus
    Spring crocus
Crocus vernus   Purple crocus
    Spring crocus
Cuscuta epithymum   Dodder
    Lesser dodder
Cuscuta europaea   Greater dodder
Cyclamen hederifolium   Cyclamen
Cymbalaria muralis
    Ivy-leaved toadflax
Cypripedium calceolus
    Lady's slipper
Dactylorhiza fuchsii
    Common spotted orchid
Dactylorhiza maculata
    Heath spotted orchid
Datura stramonium   Thorn apple
Daucus carota   Wild carrot

Euphorbia lathyrus

Daucus carota gummifer	Sea carrot
Dianthus armeria	Deptford pink
Dianthus barbatus	Sweet william
Dianthus caryophyllus	Wild carnation
Dianthus deltoides	Maiden pink
Dianthus gratianopolitanus	Cheddar pink
Dianthus plumarius	Wild pink
Digitalis grandiflora	Large yellow foxglove
Digitalis lutea	Small yellow foxglove
Digitalis purpurea	Foxglove
Diplotaxis muralis	Wall rocket
Diplotaxis tenuifolia	Wall rocket
Dipsacus fullonum	Common teasel / Teasel
Dipsacus pilosus	Small teasel
Dipsacus sylvestris	Common teasel / Teasel
Doronicum pardalianches	Leopard's bane
Draba muralis	Wall whitlowgrass
Drosera anglica	Great sundew
Drosera intermedia	Long-leaved sundew / Oblong-leaved sundew
Drosera rotundifolia	Round-leaved sundew / Sundew
Dryas octopetala	Mountain avens
Elodea canadensis	Canadian waterweed
Elodea nuttallii	Nuttall's waterweed
Empetrum nigrum	Crowberry
Endymion non-scriptus	Bluebell
Epilobium alsinifolium	Chickweed willow herb
Epilobium anagallidifolium	Alpine willow herb
Epilobium angustifolium	Rosebay willow herb
Epilobium hirsutum	Great willow herb
Epilobium lanceolatum	Spear-leaved willow herb
Epilobium montanum	Broad-leaved willow herb
Epilobium obscurum	Short-fruited willow herb / Thin-runner willow herb
Epilobium palustre	Bog willow herb / Marsh willow herb
Epilobium parviflorum	Hairy willow herb
Epilobium roseum	Pale willow herb / Pedicelled willow herb
Epilobium tetragonum	Square-stemmed willow herb
Epipactis atropurpurea	Dark red helleborine
Epipactis atrorubens	Dark red helleborine
Epipactis helleborine	Broad-leaved helleborine
Epipactis latifolia	Broad-leaved helleborine
Epipactis leptochila	Narrow-lipped helleborine
Epipactis palustris	Marsh helleborine
Epipactis purpurata	Violet helleborine
Epipactis sessilifolia	Violet helleborine
Epipogium aphyllum	Ghost orchid
Eranthis hyemalis	Winter aconite
Erica ciliaris	Ciliate heather
Erica cinera	Bell heather / Fine-leaved heath / Purple heather
Erica hibernica	Irish heath
Erica mackaiana	Mackay's heath
Erica tetralix	Cross-leaved heath
Erica vagans	Cornish heath
Erigeron acer	Blue fleabane
Erigeron boreatis	Alpine fleabane
Erigeron canadensis	Canadian fleabane
Erigeron mucronatus	Mexican fleabane
Erodium cicutarium	Common storksbill
Erodium dunense	Dune storksbill
Erodium maritimus	Sea storksbill
Erodium moschatum	Musky storksbill
Erophila verna	Common whitlowgrass / Whitlowgrass
Eryngium campestre	Coastal holly / Field eryngo
Eryngium maritimum	Sea holly
Eupatorium cannabinum	Hemp agrimony
Euphorbia amygdaloides	Wood spurge
Euphorbia cyparissias	Cypress spurge
Euphorbia dulcis	Sweet spurge
Euphorbia exigua	Dwarf spurge
Euphorbia helioscopia	Sun spurge
Euphorbia hyberna	Irish spurge
Euphorbia lathyrus	Caper spurge

Euphorbia paralias

Euphorbia paralias	Sea spurge
Euphorbia peplis	Purple spurge
Euphorbia peplus	Petty spurge
Euphorbia pilosa	Hairy spurge
Euphorbia platyphyllos	Broad-leaved spurge
Euphorbia portlandica	Portland spurge
Euphorbia stricta	Upright spurge
Euphorbia uralensis	Russian spurge
Euphrasia anglica	English sticky eyebright
Euphrasia arctica	Greater eyebright
Euphrasia brevipila	Short-haired eyebright
Euphrasia cambrica	Dwarf Welsh eyebright
Euphrasia confusa	Little kneeling eyebright
Euphrasia curta	Hairy-leaved eyebright
Euphrasia hirtella	Small-flowered sticky eyebright
Euphrasia micrantha	Common slender eyebright
Euphrasia montana	Mountain sticky eyebright
Euphrasia nemorosa	Common eyebright
Euphrasia occidentalis	Broad-leaved eyebright
Euphrasia pseudokerneri	Chalk hill eyebright
Euphrasia rivularis	Snowdon eyebright
Euphrasia rostkoviana	Large-flowered sticky eyebright
Euphrasia salisburgensis	Irish eyebright / Narrow-leaved eyebright
Euphrasia scottica	Slender Scottish eyebright
Euphrasia tetraquetra	Broad-leaved eyebright
Fallopia convolvulus	Black bindweed
Filipendula ulmaria	Meadowsweet
Filipendula vulgaris	Dropwort
Foeniculum vulgare	Fennel
Fragaria moschata	Hautbois strawberry
Fragaria vesca	Wild strawberry
Fritillaria meleagris	Fritillary / Snake's head fritillary
Fumaria capreolata	White ramping fumitory
Fumaria officinale	Common fumitory / Fumitory

Gagea lutea	Yellow star of Bethlehem
Galanthus nivalis	Snowdrop
Galega officinalis	Goat's rue
Galeopsis angustifolia	Red hemp-nettle
Galeopsis speciosa	Large-flowered hemp-nettle
Galeopsis tetrahit	Common hemp-nettle / Hemp-nettle
Galium album	Hedge bedstraw
Galium aparine	Cleavers / Goose grass
Galium boreale	Northern bedstraw
Galium cruciata	Crosswort
Galium debile	Pond bedstraw
Galium odoratum	Sweet woodruff
Galium palustre	Marsh bedstraw
Galium parisiense	Wall bedstraw
Galium pumilum	Slender bedstraw
Galium saxatile	Heath bedstraw
Galium spurium	False cleavers
Galium tricornutum	Corn bedstraw
Galium uliginosum	Fen bedstraw
Galium verum	Lady's bedstraw
Gentiana amarella	Autumn felwort / Autumn gentian
Gentiana campestris	Field felwort / Field gentian
Gentiana germanica	Scarce autumn felwort
Gentiana nivalis	Small alpine gentian
Gentiana pneumonanthe	Marsh gentian
Gentiana verna	Spring gentian
Gentianella campestris	Field felwort / Field gentian
Gentianella germanica	Scarce autumn felwort
Geranium columbinum	Dove's foot cranesbill / Long-stemmed cranesbill
Geranium dissectum	Cut-leaved cranesbill
Geranium lucidum	Shining cranesbill
Geranium molle	Dove's foot cranesbill / Soft cranesbill
Geranium phaeum	Dusky cranesbill
Geranium pratense	Meadow cranesbill

Inula conyza

Geranium purpureum
Lesser herb robert

Geranium pusillum
Small-flowered cranesbill

Geranium pyrenaicum
Hedgerow cranesbill
Pyrenean cranesbill

Geranium robertianum
Herb robert
Stinking bob

Geranium rotundifolium
Round-leaved cranesbill

Geranium sanguineum
Blood-red geranium
Bloody geranium

Geranium sylvaticum
Wood cranesbill

Geranium versicolor
Streaky cranesbill

Geum rivale Nodding water avens
Water avens

Geum urbanum Herb bennet
Wood avens

Glaucium flavum
Yellow horned poppy

Glaux maritima Saltwort
Sea milkwort

Glechoma hederacea Ground ivy

Goodyera repens
Creeping lady's tresses

Gymnadenia conopsea
Fragrant orchid

Habenaria albida
Small white orchid

Habenaria bifolia
Lesser butterfly orchid

Habenaria chlorantha
Butterfly orchid

Halimione portulacoides
Sea purslane

Hedera helix Ivy

Helianthemum apenninum
White rockrose

Helianthemum canum
Hoary rockrose

Helianthemum nummularium
Common rockrose

Helichrysum arenarium
Everlasting

Helleborus foetidus
Stinking hellebore

Helleborus viridis
Green hellebore

Hemintia echioides
Bristly oxtongue

Heracleum mantegazzianum
Giant hogweed

Heracleum sphondylium
Cow parsnip
Hogweed

Herminium monorchis
Musk orchid

Hesperis matronalis Dame's violet

Hieracium aurantiacum
Fox-and-cubs
Orange hawkweed

Hieracium pilosella
Mouse-ear hawkweed

Hieracium umbellatum
Hawkweed

Hieracium vulgatum
Common hawkweed

Himantoglossum hircinum
Lizard orchid

Hippocrepis comosa
Horseshoe vetch

Hippuris vulgaris Mare's tail

Hottonia palustris Water violet

Humulus lupulus Hop

Hyacinthoides non-scriptus
Bluebell

Hydrocharis morsus-ranae
Frogbit

Hyoscyamus niger Henbane

Hypericum androsaemum Tutsan

Hypericum calycinum
Rose of sharon

Hypericum elodes
Bog Saint John's wort
Marsh Saint John's wort

Hypericum hircinum
Stinking tutsan

Hypericum hirsutum
Hairy Saint John's wort

Hypericum humifusum
Creeping Saint John's wort

Hypericum linarifolium
Narrow-leaved Saint John's wort

Hypericum montanum
Mountain Saint John's wort

Hypericum perforatum
Perforate Saint John's wort

Hypericum pulchrum
Beautiful Saint John's wort

Hypericum tetrapterum
Square-stemmed Saint John's wort

Hypericum undulatum
Wavy Saint John's wort

Hypochoeris glabra
Smooth cat's ear

Hypochoeris maculata
Spotted cat's ear

Hypochoeris radicata Cat's ear
Common cat's ear

Impatiens capensis Orange balsam

Impatiens glandulifera
Indian balsam

Impatiens noli-tangere
Touch-me-not
Wild balsam

Impatiens parviflora Small balsam
Small yellow balsam

Inula conyza
Ploughman's spikenard

Inula crithmoides	Golden samphire
Inula helenium	Elecampane
Iris foetidissima	Stinking iris
Iris pseudacorus	Yellow flag
	Yellow iris
Iris spuria	Blue iris
	Violet iris
Jasione montana	Sheep's bit
Kickxia elatine	Fluellen
	Sharp-leaved fluellen
Kickxia spuria	Round-leaved fluellen
Knautia arvensis	Field scabious
Lactuca macrophylla	Blue sowthistle
Lactuca perennis	Blue lettuce
Lactuca saligna	Least lettuce
Lactuca scariola	Prickly lettuce
Lactuca serriola	Prickly lettuce
Lactuca virosa	Acrid lettuce
	Great lettuce
Lamiastrum galeobdolon	Yellow archangel
Lamium album	White dead-nettle
Lamium amplexicaule	Henbit
Lamium hybridum	Cut-leaved dead-nettle
Lamium maculatum	Spotted dead-nettle
Lamium moluccellifolium	Intermediate dead-nettle
Lamium purpureum	Purple dead-nettle
	Red dead-nettle
Lapsana communis	Nipplewort
Lathraea squamaria	Toothwort
Lathyrus aphaca	Yellow vetchling
Lathyrus hirsutus	Hairy vetchling
Lathyrus japonicus	Sea pea
	Seaside pea
Lathyrus latifolius	Broad-leaved everlasting pea
	Everlasting pea
Lathyrus maritimus	Sea pea
	Seaside pea
Lathyrus montanus	Bitter vetch
Lathyrus niger	Black bitter vetch
	Black vetch
Lathyrus nissolia	Grass vetchling
Lathyrus palustris	Marsh pea
Lathyrus pratensis	Yellow meadow vetchling
Lathyrus sylvestris	Wild pea
Lathyrus tuberosus	Tuberous pea
	Tuberous vetchling
Legousia hybrida	Venus's looking glass
Lemna gibba	Fat duckweed
	Gibbous duckweed
Lemna minor	Common duckweed
	Lesser duckweed
Lemna trisulca	Ivy duckweed
	Ivy-leaved duckweed
Leontodon autumnalis	Autumn hawkbit
	Smooth hawkbit
Leontodon hispidus	Rough hawkbit
Leontodon leysseri	Hawkbit
Leontodon taraxacoides	Hawkbit
Lepidium campestre	Field pepperwort
Lepidium heterophyllum	Downy pepperwort
	Smith's pepperwort
Lepidium latifolium	Dittander
Lepidium ruderale	Narrow-leaved pepperwort
Lepidium sativum	Garden cress
Leucanthemum vulgare	Ox-eye daisy
Leucojum aestivum	Summer snowflake
Leucojum vernum	Spring snowflake
Leucorchis albida	Small white orchid
Levisticum officinale	Lovage
Leycesteria formosa	Flowering nutmeg
Ligusticum scoticum	Scots lovage
Lilium martagon	Turk's cap lily
Lilium pyrenaicum	Pyrenean lily
Limonium vulgare	Comon sea lavender
	Sea lavender
Limosella aquatica	Mudwort
Linaria arenaria	Sand toadflax
Linaria arvensis	Field toadflax
Linaria pelisseriana	Jersey toadflax
Linaria purpurea	Purple toadflax
Linaria repens	Pale toadflax
Linaria supina	Prostrate toadflax
Linaria vulgaris	Common toadflax
Linum bienne	Pale flax
Linum catharticum	Fairy flax
	White flax
Linum perenne	Blue flax
	Perennial flax
Liparis loeselii	Fen orchid
Listera cordata	Lesser twayblade
Listera ovata	Common twayblade
	Twayblade
Lithospermum arvense	Corn gromwell
	Field gromwell
Lithospermum officinale	Common gromwell
	Gromwell

Myosotis ramosissima

Lithospermum purpurocaeruleum	Blue gromwell
Littorella lacustris	Shore weed
Littorella uniflora	Shore weed
Lobelia dortmanna	Water lobelia
Lobelia urens	Blue lobelia
Lonicera caprifolium	Perfoliate honeysuckle
Lonicera periclymenum	Honeysuckle
Lonicera xylosteum	Fly honeysuckle
Lotus angustissimus	Long-fruited bird's foot trefoil
Lotus corniculatus	Bird's foot trefoil
Lotus hispidus	Hairy bird's foot trefoil
Lotus uliginosus	Greater bird's foot trefoil
	Marsh bird's foot trefoil
Lunaria annua	Honesty
Lunaria rediviva	Perennial honesty
Lupinus arboreus	Tree lupin
Lupinus luteus	Yellow lupin
Lupinus nootkatensis	Lupin
Luronium natans	Floating water plantain
Lychnis dioica	Red campion
Lychnis flos-cuculi	Ragged robin
Lychnis viscaria	Red catchfly
	Sticky catchfly
Lycopus europaeus	Gipsywort
Lysimachia nemorum	Yellow pimpernel
Lysimachia nummularia	Creeping jenny
Lysimachia thyrsiflora	Tufted loosestrife
Lysimachia vulgaris	Yellow loosestrife
Lythrum hyssopifolia	Grass-poly
	Hyssop-leaved loosestrife
Lythrum portula	Water purslane
Lythrum salicaria	Purple loosestrife
Maianthemum bifolium	May lily
Malva moschata	Musk mallow
Malva neglecta	Dwarf mallow
Malva pusilla	Small mallow
Malva sylvestris	Common mallow
Marrubium vulgare	White horehound
Matricaria matricarioides	Pineapple weed
Matricaria recutita	Scented mayweed
	Wild chamomile
Matthiola sinuata	Sea stock
Meconopsis cambrica	Welsh poppy

Medicago arabica	Spotted medick
Medicago falcata	Sickle medick
	Yellow medick
Medicago lupulina	Black medick
Medicago minima	Bur medick
	Small medick
Medicago polymorpha	Fimbriate medick
	Toothed medick
Medicago sativa	Lucerne
Melampyrum pratense	Common cow wheat
Melilotus alba	White melilot
Melilotus altissima	Tall melilot
	Yellow melilot
Melilotus indica	Small melilot
Melilotus officinalis	Ribbed melilot
Mentha aquatica	Water mint
Mentha arvensis	Corn mint
Mentha longifolia	Horse mint
Mentha × piperita	Pepper mint
Mentha pulegium	Penny royal
Mentha spicata	Spear mint
Mentha spicata × suaveolens	French mint
Mentha suaveolens	Round-leaved mint
Menyanthes trifoliata	Bogbean
Mercurialis annua	Annual mercury
Mercurialis perennis	Dog's mercury
Mimulus guttatus	Monkey flower
Mimulus luteus	Blood-drop emlets
	Blotched monkey flower
Mimulus moschatus	Musk
Misopates orontium	Lesser snapdragon
Moneses uniflora	One-flowered wintergreen
	Single-flowered wintergreen
Monotropa hypopitys	Yellow bird's nest
Muscari atlanticum	Grape hyacinth
Muscari neglectum	Grape hyacinth
Muscari racemosum	Grape hyacinth
Myosotis alpestris	Alpine forget-me-not
Myosotis arvensis	Common forget-me-not
	Field forget-me-not
	Forget-me-not
Myosotis caespitosa	Lesser water forget-me-not
Myosotis discolor	Changing forget-me-not
	Yellow forget-me-not
Myosotis ramosissima	Early forget-me-not

Myosotis scorpioides

Myosotis scorpioides
Water forget-me-not
Myosotis secunda
Creeping forget-me-not
Marsh forget-me-not
Myosotis sicula
Jersey forget-me-not
Myosotis stolonifera
Short-leaved forget-me-not
Myosotis sylvatica
Wood forget-me-not
Myosoton aquaticum
Pond chickweed
Water chickweed
Myriophyllum alterniflorum
Alternate-flowered water milfoil
Myriophyllum spicatum
Spiked water milfoil
Myriophyllum verticillatum
Whorled water milfoil
Narcissus × bifloris
Primrose peerless
Narcissus hispanicus
Spanish daffodil
Narcissus majalis Pheasant's eye
Narcissus obvallaris Tenby daffodil
Narcissus pseudonarcissus
Wild daffodil
Narthecium ossifragum
Bog asphodel
Nasturtium officinale Watercress
Neottia nidus-avis
Bird's nest orchid
Nepeta cataria Catmint
Nuphar lutea Yellow waterlily
Nuphar pumila Least waterlily
Lesser waterlily
Nymphaea alba White waterlily
Nymphoides peltata
Fringed waterlily
Odontites verna Red bartsia
Oenanthe aquatica
Fine-leaved water dropwort
Oenanthe crocata
Hemlock water dropwort
Oenanthe fistulosa
Common water dropwort
Tubular water dropwort
Water dropwort
Oenanthe fluviatilis
River water dropwort
Oenanthe lachenalii
Parsley water dropwort
Oenanthe pimpinelloides
Corky-fruited water dropwort
Oenanthe silaifolia
Meadow water dropwort
Oenothera biennis
Common evening primrose
Evening primrose
Oenothera erythrosepala
Large-flowered evening primrose

Oenothera stricta
Erect evening primrose
Fragrant evening primrose
Onobrychis viciifolia Sainfoin
Ononis natrix
Large yellow restharrow
Ononis reclinata Small restharrow
Ononis repens
Common restharrow
Restharrow
Ononis spinosa Prickly restharrow
Onopordon acanthium
Scottish thistle
Ophrys apifera Bee orchid
Ophrys arachnites
Late spider orchid
Ophrys aranifera
Early spider orchid
Ophrys fuciflora
Late spider orchid
Ophrys insectifera Fly orchid
Ophrys muscifera Fly orchid
Ophrys sphegodes
Early spider orchid
Orchis hircina Lizard orchid
Orchis laxiflora Jersey orchid
Orchis mascula Early purple orchid
Orchis militaris Soldier orchid
Orchis morio
Green-winged orchid
Orchis purpurea Lady orchid
Orchis pyramidalis
Pyramidal orchid
Orchis simia Monkey orchid
Orchis ustulata Burnt orchid
Dwarf orchid
Origanum vulgare Marjoram
Ornithogalum pyrenaicum
Bath asparagus
Spiked star of Bethlehem
Ornithogalum umbellatum
Star of Bethlehem
Ornithopus perpusillus Birdsfoot
Least birdsfoot
Orobanche alba Red broomrape
Orobanche amethystea
Carrot broomrape
Coastal broomrape
Orobanche apiculata
Lesser broomrape
Orobanche caryophyllacea
Clove-scented broomrape
Orobanche elatior Tall broomrape
Orobanche hederae Ivy broomrape
Orobanche major Tall broomrape
Orobanche maritima
Carrot broomrape
Coastal broomrape
Orobanche minor
Lesser broomrape

Potamogeton gramineus

Orobanche picridis
Picris broomrape

Orobanche purpurea
Purple broomrape

Orobanche ramosa
Branched broomrape

Orobanche rapum-genistae
Greater broomrape

Orobanche reticulata
Thistle broomrape

Orthilia secunda
Serrated wintergreen

Oxalis acetosella   Wood sorrel

Oxalis corniculata
Procumbent yellow sorrel
Yellow sorrel

Oxalis europaea
Upright yellow sorrel

Oxalis pes-caprae
Bermuda buttercup

Oxycoccus microcarpus
Small cranberry

Oxycoccus palustris   Cranberry

Oxyria digyna   Mountain sorrel

Papaver agremone
Long rough-headed poppy
Prickly poppy

Papaver dubium
Long smooth-headed poppy

Papaver rhoeas   Common poppy
Common red poppy
Field poppy

Papaver somniferum
Opium poppy

Parentucellia viscosa
Yellow bartsia

Parietaria judaica
Mortar pellitory
Pellitory-of-the-wall

Paris quadrifolia   Herb paris

Parnassia palustris
Grass of parnassus

Pastinaca sativa   Wild parsnip

Pedicularis foliosa   Leafy lousewort

Pedicularis palustris
Marsh lousewort
Red rattle

Pedicularis sylvatica   Lousewort

Petasites fragrans
Winter heliotrope

Petasites hybridus   Butterbur

Phyteuma orbiculare
Round-headed rampion

Phyteuma spicatum
Spiked rampion

Phyteuma tenerum
Round-headed rampion

Picris echioides   Bristly oxtongue

Picris hieracioides
Hawkweed oxtongue

Pilosella aurantiaca
Orange hawkweed

Pilosella officinarum
Mouse-ear hawkweed

Pimpinella major
Greater burnet saxifrage

Pimpinella saxifraga
Burnet saxifrage

Pinguicula grandiflora
Greater butterwort
Large-flowered butterwort

Pinguicula lusitanica
Pale butterwort
Pink butterwort

Pinguicula vulgaris
Common butterwort

Plantago arenaria
Branched plantain

Plantago coronopus
Buck's horn plantain

Plantago lanceolata
Ribwort plantain

Plantago major   Great plantain

Plantago maritima   Sea plantain

Plantago media   Hoary plantain
Lamb's tongue

Platanthera bifolia
Lesser butterfly orchid

Platanthera chlorantha
Butterfly orchid
Greater butterfly orchid

Polygala calcarea   Chalk milkwort

Polygala serpyllifolia
Heath milkwort

Polygala vulgaris
Common milkwort

Polygonatum multiflorum
Solomon's seal

Polygonatum odoratum
Angular solomon's seal
Lesser solomon's seal

Polygonatum verticillatum
Whorled solomon's seal

Polygonum amphibium
Amphibious bistort

Polygonum aviculare   Knotgrass

Polygonum bistorta
Common bistort

Polygonum hydropiper
Water pepper

Polygonum lapathifolium
Pale persicaria

Polygonum persicaria   Redshank

Potamogeton alpinus
Reddish pondweed
Red pondweed

Potamogeton coloratus
Fen pondweed

Potamogeton crispus
Curled pondweed

Potamogeton epihydros
American pondweed

Potamogeton gramineus
Various-leaved pondweed

Potamogeton heterophyllus

Potamogeton heterophyllus
Various-leaved pondweed
Potamogeton lucens
Shining pondweed
Potamogeton natans
Broad-leaved pondweed
Floating pondweed
Potamogeton nodosus
Loddon pondweed
Potamogeton oblongus
Bog pondweed
Potamogeton pectinatus
Fennel pondweed
Potamogeton perfoliatus
Perfoliate pondweed
Potamogeton polygonifolius
Bog pondweed
Potamogeton praelongus
Long-stalked pondweed
Potamogeton rufescens
Reddish pondweed
Red pondweed
Potentilla anglica
Procumbent cinquefoil
Potentilla anserina   Silverweed
Potentilla argentea
Hoary cinquefoil
Potentilla crantzii   Alpine cinquefoil
Potentilla erecta
Common tormentil
Tormentil
Upright cinquefoil
Potentilla fruticosa
Shrubby cinquefoil
Potentilla palustris
Marsh cinquefoil
Potentilla reptans
Creeping cinquefoil
Potentilla rupestris
Rock cinquefoil
Potentilla sterilis
Barren strawberry
Potentilla tabernaemontani
Spring cinquefoil
Primula elatior   Oxlip
Primula farinosa
Bird's eye primrose
Primula veris   Cowslip
Primula vulgaris   Primrose
Prunella laciniata
Cut-leaved self heal
Prunella vulgaris   Self heal
Pseudorchis albida
Small white orchid
Pulicaria dysenterica
Common fleabane
Fleabane
Pulicaria vulgaris   Lesser fleabane
Small fleabane
Pulsatilla vernalis   Pasque flower
Pulsatilla vulgaris   Pasque flower

Pyrola media
Intermediate wintergreen
Medium wintergreen
Pyrola minor
Common wintergreen
Lesser wintergreen
Pyrola rotundifolia
Large wintergreen
Round-leaved wintergreen
Pyrola uniflora
One-flowered wintergreen
Single-flowered wintergreen
Radiola linoides   Allseed
Ranunculus acris
Common meadow buttercup
Meadow buttercup
Ranunculus aquatilis
Common water crowfoot
Water crowfoot
Ranunculus arvensis
Corn buttercup
Ranunculus auricomus
Goldilocks
Goldilocks buttercup
Ranunculus baudotii
Seaside crowfoot
Ranunculus bulbosus
Bulbous buttercup
Ranunculus circinatus   Circul
leaved crowfoot
Ranunculus ficaria
Lesser celandine
Ranunculus fluitans
River crowfoot
River water crowfoot
Ranunculus hederaceus
Ivy-leaved crowfoot
Ranunculus omiophyllus
Moorland crowfoot
Ranunculus paladosus
Jersey buttercup
Ranunculus parviflorus
Small-flowered buttercup
Ranunculus repens
Creeping buttercup
Ranunculus sardous
Pale hairy buttercup
Ranunculus sceleratus
Celery-leaved crowfoot
Ranunculus trichophyllus
Dark-hair crowfoot
Thread-leaved water crowfoot
Ranunculus tripartitus
Little three-lobed crowfoot
Raphanus maritimus   Sea radish
Raphanus raphanistrum
Wild radish
Raphanus sativus   Radish
Reseda lutea   Wild mignonette
Reseda luteola   Dyer's rocket
Weld
Reseda phyteuma
Corn mignonette

Sedum forsteranum

Reynoutria japonica	
	Japanese knotweed
	Round knotweed
Rhinanthus angustifolius	
	Greater yellow rattle
Rhinanthus minor	Hayrattle
	Yellow rattle
Rhinanthus serotinus	
	Greater hayrattle
Rhodiola rosea	Roseroot
Roemeria hybrida	
	Violet horned poppy
Romulea columnae	Sand crocus
	Warren crocus
Romulea parviflora	Sand crocus
	Warren crocus
Rosa agrestis	
	Narrow-leaved sweet briar
Rosa arvensis	Field rose
	Trailing rose
Rosa canina	Dog rose
Rosa dumalis	
	Short-pedicelled rose
Rosa micrantha	Lesser sweet briar
Rosa pimpinellifolia	Burnet rose
Rosa rubiginosa	Sweet briar
Rosa sherardii	
	Northern downy rose
Rosa stylosa	Long-styled rose
Rosa tomentosa	Downy rose
	Harsh downy rose
Rosa villosa	Soft-leaved rose
Rubia peregrina	Wild madder
Rubus caesius	Dewberry
Rubus chamaemorus	Cloudberry
Rubus idaeus	Raspberry
Rubus saxatilis	Stone bramble
Rumex acetosa	Common sorrel
	Sorrel
Rumex acetosella	Sheep's sorrel
Rumex conglomeratus	
	Clustered dock
Rumex crispus	Curly dock
Rumex hydrolapathum	
	Water dock
	Wetland dock
Rumex obtusifolius	
	Broad-leaved dock
	Nettle-cure dock
Ruscus aculeatus	Butcher's broom
Sagina nodosa	Knotted pearlwort
Sagina procumbens	
	Procumbent pearlwort
	Prostrate pearlwort
Sagittaria sagittifolia	Arrowhead
Salicornia europaea	Glasswort
Salsola kali	Prickly saltwort
	Spiny saltwort
Salvia horminoides	Clary
	Wild sage
Salvia pratensis	Meadow clary
Salvia verbenaca	Wild clary
Samolus valerandi	Brookweed
Sanguisorba minor	Lesser burnet
	Salad burnet
Sanguisorba officinalis	
	Great burnet
Saponaria officinalis	Soapwort
Saussurea alpina	Alpine sawwort
Saxifraga aizoides	
	Yellow mountain saxifrage
Saxifraga cespitosa	Tufted saxifrage
Saxifraga granulata	
	Bulbous saxifrage
	Meadow saxifrage
Saxifraga hirculus	
	Yellow bog saxifrage
Saxifraga hypnoides	
	Mossy saxifrage
Saxifraga nivalis	
	Clustered alpine saxifrage
Saxifraga oppositifolia	
	Purple saxifrage
Saxifraga rivularis	
	Alpine rivulet saxifrage
Saxifraga rosacea	Irish saxifrage
Saxifraga spathularis	
	Saint Patrick's saxifrage
Saxifraga stellaris	Starry saxifrage
Saxifraga tridactylites	
	Rue-leaved saxifrage
Scabiosa arvensis	Field scabious
Scabiosa columbaria	
	Small scabious
Scabiosa succisa	
	Devil's bit scabious
Scilla autumnalis	Autumn squill
Scilla verna	Spring squill
Scleranthus annuus	Annual knawel
Scorzonera humilis	Viper's grass
Scrophularia auriculata	
	Water figwort
Scrophularia ehrhartii	
	Scarce water figwort
Scrophularia nodosa	
	Common figwort
	Figwort
Scrophularia scorodonia	
	Balm-leaved figwort
Scrophularia umbrosa	
	Green figwort
	Scarce water figwort
Scrophularia vernalis	
	Yellow figwort
Scutellaria galericulata	Skullcap
Scutellaria minor	Lesser skullcap
Sedum acre	Biting stonecrop
	Wall pepper
Sedum album	White stonecrop
Sedum anglicum	English stonecrop
Sedum forsteranum	
	Rock stonecrop

Sedum reflexum

Sedum reflexum	Reflexed stonecrop
Sedum rosea	Roseroot
Sedum telephium	Livelong
	Orpine
Sedum villosum	Hairy stonecrop
Senecio aquaticus	Marsh ragwort
Senecio erucifolius	Hoary ragwort
Senecio fluviatilis	Broad-leaved ragwort
Senecio intergrifolius	Field fleawort
Senecio jacobaea	Common ragwort
	Ragwort
Senecio paludosus	Great fen ragwort
Senecio palustris	Marsh fleawort
Senecio spathulifolius	Spathulate fleawort
Senecio squalidus	Oxford ragwort
Senecio sylvaticus	Heath groundsel
	Wood groundsel
Senecio viscosus	Sticky groundsel
Senecio vulgaris	Groundsel
Serratula tinctoria	Sawwort
Sibbaldia procumbens	Sibbaldia
Silaum silaus	Pepper saxifrage
Silene acaulis	Moss campion
	Mountain campion
Silene alba	White campion
Silene conica	Striated catchfly
Silene dioica	Red campion
Silene gallica	Small catchfly
Silene italica	Italian catchfly
Silene noctiflora	Evening catchfly
	Night-flowering catchfly
Silene nutans	Nodding catchfly
	Nottingham catchfly
Silene otites	Spanish catchfly
Silene vulgaris	Bladder campion
Silene vulgaris maritima	Sea campion
Silybum marianum	Milk thistle
Sinapsis alba	White mustard
Sinapsis arvensis	Charlock
Smyrnium olustratum	Alexanders
Smyrnium perfoliatum	Perforate alexanders
Solanum dulcamara	Bittersweet
	Woody nightshade
Solanum luteum	Hairy nightshade
Solanum nigrum	Black nightshade
Solanum sarrachoides	Green nightshade
Solidago altissima	Tall golden rod
Solidago canadensis	Canadian golden rod
	Tall golden rod
Solidaga virgaurea	Golden rod
Sonchus arvensis	Corn sowthistle
	Perennial sowthistle
Sonchus asper	Prickly sowthistle
Sonchus oleraceus	Common sowthistle
	Smooth sowthistle
	Sowthistle
Sonchus palustris	Fen sowthistle
Specularia hybrida	Venus's looking glass
Spergula arvensis	Corn spurrey
Spergularia marina	Lesser sea spurrey
Spergularia media	Greater sea spurrey
Spergularia rubra	Sand spurrey
Spergularia rupicola	Rock sea spurrey
Spiranthes aestivalis	Summer lady's tresses
Spiranthes autumnalis	Autumn lady's tresses
	Lady's tresses
Spiranthes romanzoffiana	Threefold lady's tresses
Spiranthes spiralis	Autumn lady's tresses
	Lady's tresses
Spirodela polyrhiza	Great duckweed
Stachys alpina	Alpine woundwort
Stachys arvensis	Field woundwort
Stachys betonica	Betony
Stachys germanica	Downy woundwort
Stachys palustris	Marsh woundwort
Stachys sylvatica	Hedge woundwort
	Wood woundwort
Statice armeria	Sea pink
	Thrift
Stellaria alsine	Bog stitchwort
Stellaria graminea	Lesser stitchwort
Stellaria holostea	Greater stitchwort
Stellaria media	Chickweed
	Common chickweed
Stellaria neglecta	Greater chickweed
Stellaria nemorum	Wood stitchwort
Stellaria palustris	Marsh stitchwort
Stratiotes aloides	Water soldier
Suaeda maritima	Annual sea-blite
	Sea-blite
Subularia aquatica	Awlwort
Succisa pratensis	Devil's bit scabious